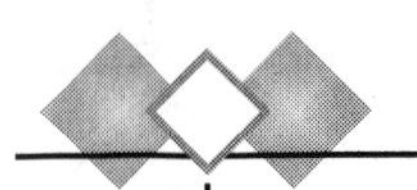

St[rategy]
in action

Strategy in action

Strategic thinking, understanding and practice

Gordon Pearson

An imprint of Pearson Education

Harlow, England · London · New York · Reading, Massachusetts · San Francisco
Toronto · Don Mills, Ontario · Sydney · Tokyo · Singapore · Hong Kong · Seoul
Taipei · Cape Town · Madrid · Mexico City · Amsterdam · Munich · Paris · Milan

First published 1999
Pearson Education Limited
Edinburgh Gate
Harlow
Essex CM20 2JE
England

and Associated Companies throughout the world

Visit us on the World Wide Web at:
http://www.pearsoneduc.com

Typeset in Plantin Light 10/12 pt by 3

Printed and bound in Great Britain by Biddles Ltd, www.biddles.co.uk

Library of Congress Cataloging-in-Publication Data

Pearson, Gordon J., 1939–
Strategy in action: strategic thinking, understanding & practice / Gordon Pearson.
p. cm.
Includes bibliographical references and index.
ISBN 0–13–453580–4 (alk paper)
1. Strategic planning. 2. Industrial management. 3. Business planning. I. Title.
HDB0.28.P3474 1999
658.4'012—dc21 99–17235
CIP

British Library Cataloguing in Publication Data

A catalogue record for this book is available from the British Library

ISBN... 0-13-453580-4

10 9 8 7 6 5 4 3
04 03 02 01 00

Contents

	Preface	*page* x
	Acknowledgements	xiv
Part One	**Strategy basics**	1
1	**Organisations in context**	3
	1.1 Introduction	3
	1.2 Historical perspective	5
	1.3 Financial pressures	9
	1.4 Technological progress	11
	1.5 The global market	14
	1.6 The ethical perspective	16
	1.7 A future perspective	19
	Summary	22
2	**The strategic idea**	24
	2.1 Introduction	24
	2.2 The purposive nature of strategy	25
	2.3 The inputs and outputs of strategy	29
	2.4 Purpose of strategy	36
	2.5 Levels of strategy	41
	2.6 Analytical and transformational perspectives	47
	Summary	48
3	**Strategy and objectives**	50
	3.1 Introduction	50
	3.2 Multiple objectives	51
	3.3 Hierarchy of objectives	53
	3.4 Pleasing customers	58
	3.5 Strategic objectives	63
	3.6 Strategic milestones	64

	3.7 Measures of strategic health	66
	Summary	67
4	**Corporate strategy**	69
	4.1 Introduction	69
	4.2 Objectives and organisational types	69
	4.3 Diversification	73
	4.4 Acquisition	77
	Summary	79
Part Two	**Strategy frameworks**	81
5	**Planning frameworks**	85
	5.1 Introduction	85
	5.2 Accounts-based budget planning	86
	5.3 Forecast-based budget planning	89
	5.4 Development-based budget planning	92
	5.5 The bureaucratic tendency	95
	Summary	97
6	**Evolutionary frameworks**	99
	6.1 Introduction	99
	6.2 Basic systems model	100
	6.3 Evolution and system goals	101
	6.4 Life cycles	105
	6.5 Using life cycles	109
	6.6 Experience curves	112
	6.7 Using experience curves	116
	Summary	117
7	**Portfolio frameworks**	119
	7.1 Introduction	119
	7.2 Boston's original portfolio	120
	7.3 Derivative portfolios	124
	7.4 Using portfolios	129
	Summary	134
8	**Competitive strategy**	135
	8.1 Introduction	135
	8.2 Industry analysis	136
	8.3 Competitor analysis	139
	8.4 Generic strategies	141
	8.5 The value chain and competitive strategy	146
	8.6 Strategic marketing	151
	8.7 Competitive strategy revisited	158
	Summary	159

9	**Transformational frameworks**	161
	9.1 Introduction	161
	9.2 Statements of mission	163
	9.3 Core competence framework	170
	9.4 Entrepreneurial framework	177
	Summary	183
10	**The contingency approach**	185
	10.1 Introduction	185
	10.2 Framework characteristics	186
	10.3 Generic strategy framework	190
	10.4 Contingency principles	194
	10.5 Customised frameworks	197
	10.6 Change and dynamic strategy	200
	Summary	201
Part Three	**Strategic change and action**	203
11	**Innovation and change**	205
	11.1 Introduction	205
	11.2 The shape of technological progress	206
	11.3 Forecasting technological change	209
	11.4 Innovation as a competitive weapon	211
	11.5 The innovation process	212
	Summary	221
12	**Structure, culture and symbolism**	223
	12.1 Introduction	223
	12.2 Organisational structure	225
	12.3 Alliances, networks and teams	230
	12.4 Organisational culture	237
	12.5 Organisational symbolism	244
	12.6 Manageable characteristics	246
	Summary	248
13	**Creating innovative teams**	250
	13.1 Introduction	250
	13.2 The strategy dimension	253
	13.3 The culture dimension	254
	13.4 The matrix	256
	13.5 Repositioning	263
	Summary	269
14	**Implanting strategy**	271
	14.1 Introduction	271
	14.2 Planning and formality	272

14.3 The strategic portfolio 273
14.4 Strategy processes 275
14.5 Repositioning actions 278
Conclusions 280

Part Four **Reading reviews** 283

1. T. Levitt, 'The dangers of social responsibility', *Harvard Business Review*, September/October 1958 285
2. T. Levitt, 'Marketing myopia', *Harvard Business Review*, July/August 1960 287
3. P.F. Drucker, 'Business realities', *Managing for Results*, Harper & Row, 1964(rev. edn, Heinemann, 1989) 289
4. Boston Consulting Group, *Perspectives on Experience*, BCG, 1968 291
5. Boston Consulting Group, *The Product Portfolio*, BCG, 1968 294
6. M.E. Porter, 'How competitive forces shape strategy', *Harvard Business Review*, March/April 1979 296
7. Porter's Generic competitive strategies, various sources 298
8. R.H. Hayes and W.J. Abernathy, 'Managing our way to economic decline', *Harvard Business Review*, July/August 1980 300
9. W.K. Hall, 'Survival strategies in a hostile environment', *Harvard Business Review*, September/October 1980 302
10. R.H. Hayes and D. Garvin, 'Managing as if tomorrow mattered', *Harvard Business Review*, May/June 1982 304
11. G.J. Pearson, 'Impacts of investment appraisal methods: a comparison of US and Japanese practices', *The Strategic Discount*, Wiley, 1985 307
12. W. Skinner, 'The productivity paradox', *Harvard Business Review*, July/August 1986 309
13. H. Mintzberg, 'The strategy concept I: Five Ps for strategy', *California Management Review*, Fall 1987 311
14. H. Mintzberg, 'The strategy concept II: Another look at why organizations need strategies', *California Management Review*, Fall 1987 313

15. G. Hamel and C.K. Prahalad, 'Strategic intent', *Harvard Business Review*, May/June 1989 315
16. M.E. Porter, 'Competitive advantage of nations', *Harvard Business Review*, March/April 1990 318
...Hamel, 'The core ...poration', *Harvard* ...une 1990 321
...ahalad, 'Corporate ...itionary marketing', ...*ew*, July/August 1991 324
...cum Jr and D. Lei, ...s in learning ...*zational Dynamics*, 327
...gy of change: some ...*gy of Change*, Routledge, 330
...rahalad, 'Strategy as ... *Harvard Business Review*, 332
...*apitalist Society*, ...mann, 1993 335
...tegic termites', *Imaginization: The art of creative management*, Sage, 1993 343
24. D.A. Garvin, 'Building a learning organization', *Harvard Business Review*, July/August 1993 345
25. T. Grundy, 'Putting value on strategy' *Long Range Planning*, Vol. 26, No. 3, 1993 347
26. M. Goold, A. Campbell and M. Alexander, *Corporate level strategy: Creating value in the multibusiness company*, Wiley, 1994 349
27. L.T. Hosmer, 'Strategic planning as if ethics mattered', *Strategic Management Journal*, Vol. 15: 17–34, 1994 351
28. S. Jönnson, 'Decoupling hierarchy and accountability: an examination of trust and reputation', *International Thomson Business Press*, 1996 353
29. M.E. Porter, 'What is strategy?', *Harvard Business Review*, November/December 1996 356
30. R. Whittington, 'Strategy as practice', *Long Range Planning*, Vol. 29, No. 5, 1996 358

Part Five Case studies 361
Hesketh Design Partnership 365

Grand Prix racing 369
Bird's the Confectioners Ltd 376
Harry Ramsden's Plc 385
Mills Office Equipment Ltd 396
Après Shower 403
Autoliv AB 410
Guy Tobin Plc 418
British Industrial Adhesives Ltd 426
Baxters of Speyside Ltd 434
H & R Johnson Tiles Ltd 442

References 451
Index 459

Preface

My overriding aim for this book is for it to be of practical use to the reader, who is envisaged as either a part-time MBA student armed with intelligence, experience and assertiveness, or a final-year undergraduate making up for lack of experience with a lively mixture of IQ, energy and boldness. The practical use I intend is not simply with the grisly process of passing exams but also with the much more interesting exercise of managing the strategy of a business; non-student practitioners are extremely welcome.

The aim to be practically useful is not the universal intention of academic texts. A higher priority is sometimes given to providing students with an intellectual challenge which, it is more-or-less universally agreed, should be a component of any degree course. However, the theory of strategy is not always intellectually challenging. The real problems with it are more to do with its practical implementation.

Business strategy, or strategic management, stands or falls as an academic field of study on the quality of research done in it, on the body of knowledge developed, and on its success as a liberal arts subject. Its legitimacy is not dependent on it being effective in changing the practice of business. *Business strategy* is therefore to be distinguished from *strategy in business*, or indeed from *strategy for business. Strategy in business* is typified by the work of Mintzberg and others who study what actually happens in business organisations. Mintzberg, for example, notes that strategy often *emerges* without much deliberate management intervention. *Strategy in business* identifies the different strands of theory and practice such as the *emergent* strand, sometimes identifying them as 'schools', but it shrinks from prescribing one rather than another. *Strategy for business*, on the other hand, has no such scruples. It seeks to identify action that would be likely to be managerially effective. This is dangerous ground. At its worst, it can degenerate into crude checklists of dos and don'ts, supported by no more than polemic. But at its best, *strategy for business* can be both academically sound and practically useful, and is a significant part of the established and dominant functionalist management literature.

Emergent strategy is not the only 'school' of strategy management that academics have invented. There is also held to be a design school, a resource-based school and another school, dominated by Michael Porter, which focuses on competition in product markets. Whether they are schools, paradigms, perspectives or merely strands of theory, their difference has drawn the attention of many academics. Writers on strategy management argue the merits of the different schools as though one could be right and the others wrong. A typical debate was included in De Wit and Meyer (1994) with Mintzberg scorning the bureaucratic detail and assumed linearity of Ansoff's design school thinking and Ansoff emphasising that Mintzberg's emergent strategy as the product of non-strategists could hardly be theorised.

In this text the different schools are not treated as incommensurable but merely as approaches to strategy management which give emphasis to different aspects, whether it is internal aspects of the business, the externalities of its product–market–technology situation or the way these two are related to each other through the strategy process. The focus here is not on different schools of thinking, but on different strategy frameworks which businesses have found useful in practice. Practical usefulness is what matters.

In recent years the resource-based school has achieved considerable prominence in the academic study of business strategy (as opposed to *strategy in business* or *strategy for business*). This has been led by theoretical economists who have recognised the possibility of a way forward from their classical microeconomics model of general equilibrium which has effectively locked them into the nineteenth century. Although they may trace their resource-based origins back to mainstream contributions such as Selznick (1957) and Chandler (1962), the real backbone of the approach is in work of quite a different kind by Penrose (1959), Demsetz (1973), Wernerfelt (1984) and others. This is the world of managerial services, property rights, transaction costs, artificial scarcity, economies of scope, competitive imperfections and so on, bound together with a mixture of differential equations and linear programmes. An overview of the approach is provided in Foss (1997). It is largely excluded here on the grounds that, like classical economics itself (see Ormerod, 1994), it has only limited relevance to *strategy in business* and *strategy for business*.

Certainly the resource-based approach contains much that could fulfil the requirement of being intellectually challenging, but its shortcomings in terms of usefulness for the practitioner has led to its being excluded here. The contributions of Hamel and Prahalad are the only exceptions, although, experience undoubtedly being a valuable resource, Boston's early frameworks should also carry the resource-based designation. Hamel and Prahalad's work is different in kind from the body of resource-based contributions. Theirs is not the work of theoretical economists but of mainstream management researchers concerned both for theory development and the problems of practice. This is the approach I have tried to follow here. Theory is important – there is nothing so practical as a good theory – but it is not included for its own sake. Where the theory of business strategy appears not to lead to a practical result, it is excluded.

The aim for practical usefulness is not satisfied by quick-fix checklists, but rather by an attempt to increase understanding. The focus is on organisations, their environments and the various simplifying strategy frameworks that may be used to relate the two. The strategy frameworks are themselves simplifications of the relationship between the organisation and its environments and they serve to assist the process of understanding in order that managements can take better informed decisions. It is important to understand all three – organisations, environments and frameworks – in order to be able to use the most relevant strategy framework for the organisation's greatest strategic benefit.

The plan of the book is as follows. *Part One* describes the fundamental concepts of strategy – strategy basics – which seem to pertain whichever approach to strategy is adopted. *Part Two* describes the various approaches or frameworks and is intended to provide an understanding of the possibilities and limitations of each. *Part Three* focuses on aspects of strategic change and action, identifying how change occurs and affects organisations and how organisations can respond to it and exploit it. Part Three ends with a brief chapter on implanting strategy in an organisation. This final chapter of the main text is based on practical experience rather more than the rest of the text, and I have tried to make this clear in the style of writing. It may not be of much use to undergraduate students, but I hope it is of interest to practitioners.

Part Four includes brief reviews of a number of significant contributions to the field, some articles, others extracts from or synopses of books. These are referred to in the main text but are provided in this part without interpretation or comment. Read in chronological order they show how the ideas of strategy management have developed over the past few decades. The reviews are intended to provide some understanding of the work of these contributors and also to whet the reader's appetite for the original material.

The final part, *Part Five,* includes a number of case studies. These are included as vehicles for the simulated application of understanding. They are a proxy for real organisations and real situations and as such are only a poor substitute for the real thing. They do, however, offer two advantages. First, a case study provides a common focus for groups of readers to consider and discuss. This is rarely the case otherwise. Secondly, they can be chosen to illustrate particular aspects of organisation or environment or the application of a particular strategy framework.

Only a small selection of case studies is included here because there is no shortage already published – more than four hundred are available in the English language strategic management texts currently in print and many more in various 'clearing houses'. The cases included here are rather more concise than many strategic management cases and do not include a great deal of unnecessary information. This enables them to be read, understood and used in rather less time than longer cases. They also give rather more focus to small and medium-sized enterprises (SMEs) for the following main reasons:

1. There is a paucity of interesting cases on SMEs, probably because information is easier to obtain for strategy case studies relating to the large, international corporations.
2. Only a small proportion of students will be quickly in a position to participate in managing strategy in large corporations, but many may influence strategy in SMEs.
3. The SME situation is intrinsically less complicated than that of the large corporation and this simplicity means that extraneous data do not needlessly get in the way of learning.

Guidance on the use of case studies is provided in the introduction to Part Five.

Gordon Pearson

Acknowledgements

I am indebted to all those writers, theorists and practitioners to whose work I have referred in the following pages and particularly to those whose work is reviewed in Part Four. I am also grateful to all those companies whose situation is featured in the case studies of Part Five and also to Ian Wilson for Après Shower and Tom Hartman for Autoliv.

part 1

Strategy basics

As the title suggests this first part is concerned with fundamental ideas about strategy. These basics are pertinent no matter which approach to strategy is adopted. Part Two considers the various strategy frameworks or approaches which are each based on different assumptions about what is really important in a particular situation and may produce radically different outcomes. But the different frameworks all share a common foundation and it is this foundation which is identified in Part One.

Chapter 1 provides an overview of some issues which are important as context for the formation of strategy. This is necessarily a selective view of the issues involved and their relative importance to strategy, and readers are encouraged to think critically both about this content and the priority given to the different issues.

Chapter 2 identifies aspects of management which are peculiarly strategic. These fundamental concepts together identify the strategy idea. They are from the mainstream of strategic management theory and attention is focused both on simple, basic ideas, for example, the paradox of strategic control, the top-down/bottom-up dichotomy, and the possible conflict between analytical and transformational aspects of strategy.

Chapter 3 focuses on objectives, perhaps the most crucial of all strategic issues. The subject of objectives is neither revolutionary nor mysterious, but in a strategic context relatively little that is coherent has been written. This chapter's treatment of objectives not only provides a practical structure and a way of combining strategic, financial and operational objectives, it also embeds ethical thinking in the strategic management process right from this fundamental level.

Chapter 4 looks briefly at corporate issues. This book is about business strategy as a model for all forms of organisation, business and non-business alike. The business model focuses on the strategy of achieving the purpose of the business, i.e. the purpose for which the business organisation was created. It is about wealth creation rather than ownership. Chapter 4 provides a brief overview of corporate ownership concepts.

Chapter 1

Organisations in context

Organisations are mediated and shaped by many different factors. This chapter provides a perspective on some important influences and pressures in the business context.

The shape of business organisations has changed radically from pre-industrial days, through the factory era and the development of professional management, to the present, post-industrial, post-capitalist, innovative period. As well as this evolutionary development there are four specific forces currently having a particular influence on the shape and practice of contemporary organisations. They are the pressures of finance, the demands of technology, increasingly global competition and the complication of ethical imperatives.

This thumbnail sketch of the business context, how it has developed and is currently being influenced, is intended to provide some background for judging how different approaches to strategy might be valid in particular situations.

1.1 Introduction

It is over one hundred years since the first tentative steps in defining a modern theory of management were taken. These early contributions were based more on experience than economic or sociological theory and the experience was gained mainly in large-scale industries, some of which were maturing even in the nineteenth century. Fayol (1916), heading up the French mining industry, or later Taylor in American steel and Ford in the motor industry and their many contemporaries shared a common managerial problem:

> *how to get large numbers of relatively unskilled and uneducated people to do unpleasant work and do it efficiently in return for wages set low enough to make a satisfactory profit.* (Pearson, 1990)

From the beginning simple *rules* of organisation were spelled out relating to centralisation, 'unity of command', the 'flow of communications', specialisation, hierarchical organisation and such like. This didactic checklist approach to management – a practical restatement of the bureaucratic principles Weber found so depressing – now has less relevance. The world has changed and become significantly more variable, interesting and challenging. The managerial problem is now focused on highly skilled and educated people, working in smaller numbers with a high degree of autonomy and with their rates of pay no longer the main cost drivers.

Nevertheless, some things remain the same. The organisation exists only to achieve some purpose – it is the existence of a joint purpose which turns a group of people into an organisation. The structuring of the organisation according to managerial rules was intended simply to facilitate the achievement of the organisation's purpose, i.e. its strategy.

But strategy itself does not take place in a vacuum. There is a context of time and place which shapes the strategy process, and this chapter outlines some of the more significant aspects of that context in which organisations now have to fulfil their aims.

The word 'organisation' is used in preference to 'business' because organisations from the public, not-for-profit and voluntary sectors share the same problem. The distinction between business and non-business is today less pronounced since organisations of all kinds are adopting the business model as the most efficient and effective way of organising. In the UK, local government services, for example, are provided on the basis of competitive tendering; medical practitioners compete in a market of health services and buy resources in similarly businesslike fashion; throughout the United States, the EU and most Pacific Rim countries, hospitals increasingly specialise in their distinctive competences and outsource the rest; and even some college lecturers look on students as customers, and courses as products.

These developments are not entirely progressive. The brand of management which is being widely introduced in the public sector is based largely on an outdated model. The widespread preoccupation with accounting's 'bottom line' springs directly from nineteenth century ideas about economic man operationalised by Taylor's work study (1947) and Ford's mass production of the 1920s. Adoption of these norms ignores current business realities and seems just as likely to fail in the public sector as it has in the private.

A progressive business model – one which takes current realities into account – nevertheless remains appropriate for purposive organisations. In this way, their purpose can be defined, efforts focused, resources created, multiplied and allocated effectively, and outcomes measured and assessed.

The following section takes a brief look at the development of business organisations and how they have sought to exploit their opportunities. This is followed by an overview of the main pressures and influences currently impacting on organisations and some of the organisation designs to cope with and exploit these pressures and influences.

This overview moves from the apparent certainties and stability of the past to the volatility, riskiness and unknowns of the present and future. With hindsight, the past looks easy to manage; the future looks problematic. It was always this way in management: accounting for the past is easy; strategy for the future is altogether more exciting.

1.2 Historical perspective

The earliest large-scale organisations were military, and a lot of management theory was developed from the experience of controlling large armies. The earliest large-scale non-military organisation is usually held to be the Church in which it is also possible to detect many of the traditional rules of management structure. Today both the military and church organisations are rejecting their former rules of organisation and are adopting a more flexible, contemporary approach.

Modern business organisations and the problem of managing them started to get interesting in the eighteenth century textile industry. Prior to the Industrial Revolution it was the role of the entrepreneur/capitalist to buy raw wool fibre, take it to the spinners who spun it into yarn and then take the yarn to the weavers who wove it into fabric. The spinners and weavers used domestic-scale equipment, usually in their own homes, and were paid by the piece. The material remained the property of the entrepreneur/capitalist who was responsible for its delivery and collection, but in most cases the spinning wheels and looms were owned by the spinners and weavers. This early form of organisation was extremely flexible. The entrepreneur/capitalist had no responsibilities for employing people or keeping them in work. He could expand his business, so long as he could sell the finished fabric, simply by buying more raw fibre and distributing it to more spinners and weavers. There was no need for large central premises and overhead costs of any kind.

The entrepreneur's basic task was to be an effective buyer and seller of materials so that a reasonable margin could be earned between the two transactions. But this early form of organisation required in addition that the entrepreneur focus on two issues which are today still of great concern. First, it was vital to manage logistics efficiently so as to eliminate any cash being tied up unnecessarily in work in progress: *just-in-time* delivery to and collection from his spinners and weavers would have played an extremely significant part in the entrepreneur's controllable costs. Secondly, it was also vital for the entrepreneur to create and maintain an effective relationship with the independent spinners and weavers. They largely controlled the quality, cost and availability of finished product. If they did not perform effectively, the entrepreneur would fail. So the entrepreneur's relationship with these highly skilled and ultimately autonomous workers, was in reality the foundation of business.

The Industrial Revolution changed all this. Water power, quickly followed by steam power, made it feasible to use large-scale machinery rather than simple, manually operated equipment, and technological developments revolutionised the productivity and output of machines. The entrepreneur/capitalist had progressively accumulated surplus profits to invest in this capital equipment. With water power it was as cheap to drive a bank of large-scale machines as to drive a single machine and so factories were built in which large numbers of people were employed. In a few short years the scale and nature of business organisation had been changed for ever. Labour, no matter how skilled, lost its autonomy and became dependent on the employing factories.

With the factories came the necessity for rules and regulations. The machinery would necessarily all start and finish working at the same time, so times were set each day and workers became subservient to machines. Moreover, there had to be rules which achieved consistency in the quality of work produced; there had to be rules related to the safety of work; and there had to be people responsible for seeing the rules were obeyed.

In addition, with the creation of the factories, the nature of the work itself changed. The specialisation of labour resulted in new skilled, semi-skilled and, particularly, unskilled work, with different jobs each being paid differently. Each generation of new machinery removed the requirement for some element of personal skill by the operator and progressively even craft work became de-skilled. Unskilled labour, often concerned predominantly with moving material from one workplace to the next, involved large numbers of people. As the factory system developed over the next 150 years, the complexities of work and working arrangements multiplied and new tasks and roles were developed to manage this complexity. Thus, various systems of management were developed (classical, scientific, human relations, and so on), each approach growing out of the factory era when the management problem was how to manage large numbers of semi-skilled and unskilled people, doing work which was largely boring and repetitive and ultimately alienating. These problems are quite different from those faced prior to the factory era and also quite different from the era we are now entering.

The essence of the factory era was standardisation. Machinery and factories themselves were designed to achieve a specific purpose in the most efficient way. Just as the water wheel driving the factories' rotary power could only go one way, so the factory processes were themselves designed to do one thing efficiently with no need for flexibility or variation. This standardisation of process was the key to economic results. Long production runs, over which the fixed costs of setting up machines could be absorbed, were seen by Drucker as late as the 1960s as being the basis of profitability. Ford's famous dictum, 'any colour so long as it's black', expresses the same principle.

Most of management theory, until quite recently, was based on an analysis of these factory-era conditions and circumstances. Burns and Stalker (1994) were among early researchers of the new ways of managing. They studied attempts to adapt old, inflexible factory-era cultures to the imperatives of new technologies. They developed the much quoted distinction between mechanistic and organic systems of management. 'Mechanistic' was the term Burns and Stalker applied to the old-style bureaucracies they studied which were almost entirely incapable of innovation. They were adapted to stable conditions. Their management tasks were broken down into precisely defined specialisms. They had a clear hierarchy of control, vertical communications, overall knowledge and co-ordination only at the top of the hierarchy and an insistence on loyalty and obedience.

The organic organisation was more difficult to define. It was the organisation form which Burns and Stalker found to be effective at innovating, adapted to dealing with unstable conditions, continually confronting new and unfamiliar problems, to which specialists contributed as and when needed. Organic organisations enjoyed open communications, leadership by expertise and a much higher degree of commitment to organisational goals. Formal organisation in the shape of charts, job descriptions and so on just did not exist in the organic firms.

The two types of organisation were distinguished also in terms of their age, the mechanistic form typically being mature while the organic forms were invariably young, rapidly developing organisations. It appeared, therefore, that there might be a natural ageing process which inexorably led to older organisations becoming mechanistic or bureaucratic. Using this biological analogy such a process has been widely recognised.

When a business is first formed, its structure is simple. There are few co-ordination problems that are not handled by direct supervision. There is little opportunity, let alone need, for job specialisation. There is initially no need for formalisation of behaviour in operating instructions, job descriptions, company rules and so forth. The small entrepreneurial business has none of the big company problems of extended lines of communication and command. The dilemma of how far to decentralise control does not arise. In short, most of the structural problems which have puzzled practitioners over the years simply do not exist. This was the situation of the original entrepreneur/capitalists. However, as the organisation grows, all these problems closely associated with the factory era inevitably emerge and become the focus of research interest.

Rigid and naive-sounding rules were prescribed governing such matters as the maximum number of levels in a management hierarchy, the maximum span of control of an individual manager, the distinction between line and staff and so forth (for example, Urwick, 1947; Breck, 1957).

Firms tend to progress through various evolutionary phases as they grow and adopt different structural arrangements depending on the firm's phase of development and its size. However, there are other factors which exert influence. Researchers found that production technology was a key determinant of structure (Woodward, 1958), that the most appropriate structure depends on the firm's environment (Lawrence and Lorsch, 1967), or that structure results mainly from changing pressures in the marketplace (Chandler, 1962).

From all this one might conclude that the firm's organisation structure is an almost involuntary reaction to its circumstances rather than the result of overt senior management decision. But structure is not a natural phenomenon. It results from specific decisions, although in many cases these are reactive, with changes in the formal organisation merely reflecting changes that have already occurred in the real organisation.

Mintzberg (1983) traced this development of organisation from the simple structure to various forms of bureaucracy. Machine bureaucracy, fundamentally unsuited to innovation, was the creation of the factory era and stems directly from the process of industrialisation. It is increasingly inappropriate to contemporary needs for flexibility and speed of response. Its dominance by large-scale business has, until quite recently, been more-or-less complete, not only within the older industries but also in the new industries which large-scale business has bought into. There is a natural tendency to seek out stability and set up an organisational form that would prosper in such conditions. Bureaucratisation is, therefore, for all its faults, an almost inevitable process which will only be avoided or reversed as a result of great and deliberate effort.

The tendency to bureaucratise allows large parts of an organisation to be put into 'auto-pilot'. If the auto-pilot system worked well enough to cope with the volatility and uncertainty of the real world then this would be an effective solution; but this is clearly not the case. Nevertheless, the auto-pilot system – bureaucracy – is easier for managers to handle if they ignore its shortcomings.

The pressures on divisional managers to conform to bureaucratic norms are immense. The rules, the customs, practice and culture of the firm all lead to the conclusion that conformity is the most rational form of behaviour. Non-conformity is in essence high-risk behaviour which places salary, career and pension very much on the line. Despite the many stories of the exceptions (for example, Pinchot, 1985), most managers do conform, thus further reinforcing the predominance of the bureaucratic form. The predominance of bureaucracy at divisional level creates severe problems for divisional managers working at the business face. They need to innovate to achieve business success, but the bureaucratic organisation inhibits them. They have three options: they can become bureaucrats themselves; they can try to change the organisation as a whole; or they can set up a small sub-organisation, within the main business, where different rules apply and where individuals can be given the freedom to innovate.

The domination of management by the accounting language has added to the pressures of bureaucratic conformity. Conservatism, risk avoidance, strict budgetary control and the principle that time is money are the dominant rules.

This philosophy which frustrates creativity and innovation, is enshrined in the belief that success comes simply from 'hard work and achieving budget' (Norburn and Schurz, 1984). It can lead to a repressive, cost-oriented style of management and a professional negligence of technology and markets. Dominance of this approach to management coincided with industrial decline in both Britain and America (see Hayes and Abernathy, 1980; Hayes and Garvin, 1982; Skinner, 1986; and others in Reading Reviews 8–12 in Part Four). It led to a buy-and-sell philosophy of business. Rather than solving business problems, such managements dispose of problem businesses. Rather than investing in innovations and physical assets to exploit business opportunities, such managements focus on investing in quickly realisable stocks and shares. Rather than make long-term commitments which involve risk, such managements prefer to borrow long and lend short. Such a philosophy is well suited to managing a unit trust, but not a business.

The tendency to bureaucratise and the increasing dominance of the accounting philosophy are complementary and together led managements almost inevitably to adopt a planning-oriented approach to strategy. Planning is itself a bureaucratic activity. Financial planning satisfies the requirements of both bureaucracy and accounting. Long-range financial planning therefore emerged as the natural format for the expression of business strategy in many large-scale businesses and, through the requirements of the banking system, in small businesses also.

This brief and necessarily selective review has highlighted some of the historical influences on organisations. History is an important part of the context and important to understanding the present predicament of organisations and what managers can do to improve them. The present is dominated by rapid change. One of the few changes that management writers such as Drucker have needed to make in their prescriptive approach to management over the past half-century is in the emphasis they give to standardisation. It used to be the source of profitability, but it has become a source of inflexibility. Burns and Stalker's organic organisation has become the archetypal model of contemporary organisation.

The following sections look in rather more detail at the main pressures and changes affecting organisations arising from the financial and technological environments, from global competition and from the pressure for businesses to behave unethically. Although these issues are discussed separately, they are in reality all intimately intertwined and interdependent.

1.3 Financial pressures

Today's financial environment was created largely to provide for the needs of industry. The earliest financial institutions were created to raise finance for projects which were beyond the means of single or small groups of investors. Financial markets were initiated to fund commercial expeditions on the high seas; they grew to finance the great eighteenth century trading companies and they matured in the experience of financing the railways and the rest of the nineteenth century's great industrialisations.

Long-term finance is still needed. New technologies place ever-increasing financing burdens on organisations. The financing requirements of new technology often increase exponentially from generation to generation. This is not new. The development costs of aero engines, exploding each generation, led inexorably to the bankruptcy of Rolls Royce in 1971. In addition to the financing requirements of developing technology, there is the everyday need to finance the growth of fixed and working capital of every expanding business.

The financial markets, however, no longer exist primarily to serve these needs. They have developed their own purposes, to provide a range of opportunities and returns to savers, investors and speculators. Thus industry is subject to almost irresistible short-term financial pressure from the financial sector. The roles appear to have reversed, with industry now in danger of becoming significant only as a pretext for the transactions of the financial sector.

The dominance of the financial world which is necessarily shaped to provide quick returns acts as a sometimes decisive constraint on strategy management. In the short term, shareholder wealth can more easily be increased by opportunistic acquisitions than by persevering in the development of manufacturing. Innovations may therefore be unavailable to managements who are pressured to milk their 'cash cow' to the last. Long-term organic growth may be beyond the reach of such firms; the long term is discounted to insignificance.

The more efficiently that financial markets work, the more it pays to take a short-term view. As Wall Street and London have become more efficient, so they have become less able to support the manufacturer of products who wants to invest in developing the next generation of technology. It may be difficult to persuade shareholders whose concerns are with weeks, days and sometimes even hours, to remain patient for five or ten years while the development is completed and brought into profit. A neutral shareholder would be unlikely to turn down a deal that his broker advised would generate, say, 30 per cent return overnight. For a professional manager, looking after a portfolio of investments on behalf of, say, a pension fund, to do so might be regarded as a dereliction of duty.

The efficiency of the financial markets is based on more information, available faster and cheaper. Dealing is easier, faster and cheaper. Big investors use short-term performance criteria to make fast returns and would be widely regarded as eccentric and irrational if they based their investment decisions on sentiment. Most will take the corporate raider's money as soon as anyone else's. The innovative business must expend great effort informing investors of its unique needs and expectations. Otherwise it should expect scant long-term support from the financial world.

This tension between industry and the financial world is pervasive. Box 1.1 provides an illustration of how satisfying the continuing short-term needs of financial institutions can erode the brand strength of even the greatest.

BOX 1.1

Brand values

Heinz and its '57 Varieties', one of the world's great brand names, seems to be running out of steam. Earnings growth in 1996 was around 6 per cent on sales up around 11 per cent, and even that was achieved, according to City analysts, largely through asset disposals and other one-off gains. John McMillin at Prudential Securities said, 'O'Reilly was the best chief executive during the high growth period of 1980s, but in this age of lower selling prices and sharper competition I think Bill Johnson [O'Reilly's chosen successor] is the best man for the job.' The City needs to see more urgency from Heinz in real improvements in earnings.

Under a $650m restructuring plan Heinz has identified six core businesses and earmarked $500m annual business disposals along with closure of 25 of its 111 manufacturing plants. Despite several earlier restructuring efforts, Johnson is expected to find areas where he can still cut costs and boost earnings. 'They will always find ways to cut costs,' says Bob Cummins, analyst with Wertheim Schroders.

According to William Leach of brokers Donaldson, Lufkin & Jenrette, 'Heinz brands have turned into commodities. Almost everything they produce is produced by other companies and there is so much competition.' The quality of most own-brand products is now competitive with Heinz.

In 1996, Heinz spent considerably less on advertising than it had ten years previously. O'Reilly's plan for 1997 was to improve earnings by increasing prices, but analysts recognised that you cannot do that and at the same time cut down on advertising. The plan did not work: where prices were raised business was lost, particularly in Weight Watchers and tuna, two of the businesses identified as core. In an attempt to increase efficiency, Heinz, unlike Kellogg, has entered a number of own-label production arrangements which, some argue, further devalues the Heinz brand name.

DISCUSSION POINT

Consider the broad cost and price options open to Heinz. Compare the financial and business implications of each.

During the 1990s, the pressure to provide short-term financial results has been an important consideration for strategy management where the focus is on long-term performance. Perhaps the extreme pressures of the 1980s (see Skinner in Reading Review 12) have been moderated somewhat by a wider recognition of the 'productivity paradox' and the importance of long-term strategic business. At the time of writing, stock prices across the globe look vulnerable and already many otherwise sound companies are worth more than the value of their shares. If a bear market develops, the attractions of short-term returns will inevitably become dominant once more. Strategy management cannot assume loyalty on the part of their shareholders.

1.4 Technological progress

The Industrial Revolution has had a most profound effect on mankind. At the beginning of the nineteenth century no country in Europe had yet re-attained the living standard of Imperial Rome. But over the past one hundred years or so, real income per head rose by 700 per cent on average, labour productivity by 1,200 per cent and median exports by over 6,000 per cent (Maddison, 1982).

The real per-capita income in the United States in 1870 was about the same as it is in the Philippines today, and slightly below that of Egypt. Growth rates in this period have exploded by comparison with anything achieved before. The explanation is simply, technological innovation. Otherwise, as Baumol put it, 'the economic history of the period, and its contrast with the world's economic performance in the previous, say, fifteen centuries, is difficult to account for' (Baumol, 1986). From the past it is easy to see how dramatic technological progress has been and how, once started, it seems to go forward with an ever-quickening momentum.

Technological innovation, whether it is in the product itself or the process of its production, is the engine which drives economic, social and organisational change. In the past, war has also been a stimulus and some such changes may also have resulted from the effects of plague. Today, however, technological innovation is the key. The connection between innovation and economic growth has been widely accepted since the original work of Kondratiev which was developed by Schumpeter (1939). Economists may disagree in detail, but most analysts associate the great expansions with periods when there were major innovations. Piatier (1984), for example, in his study for the European Commission, identified three such 'revolutions' illustrated in Figure 1.1.

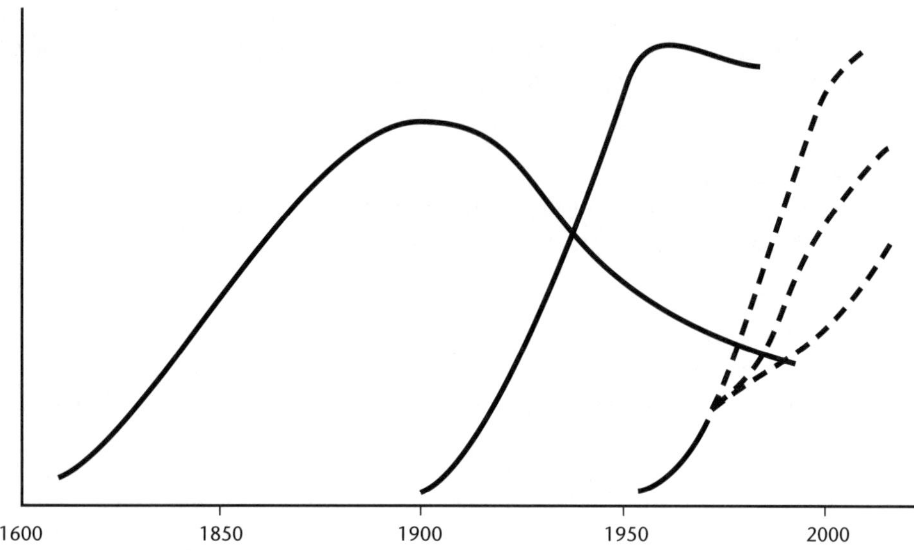

Figure 1.1 The three industrial revolutions (based on Piatier, 1984)

The first, the eighteenth century industrial revolution, already referred to in section 1.2, was based on innovations in the physical power extracted from coal and the steam engine which gave rise to the mechanisation of textiles and other manufacturing industry, plus the development of steel and railway transport on a massive scale and the launching of inorganic chemistry. The ingredients of this revolution and its results in terms of economic growth are readily identifiable and dramatic. According to Piatier's analysis, coal, steel, railways, textiles and inorganic chemistry grew up and grew old together: the 1930s depression was neither a short-term economic crisis nor a crisis of capitalism, but signalled the end of a great wave of major innovations (Piatier, 1984).

The second industrial revolution had its embryonic phase in the 1930s and was based on oil, motor vehicles, aircraft, sheet steel, organic chemistry and synthetic materials. The growth from this revolution was interrupted by the Second World War, but was realised in the period of post-war reconstruction in the 1950s and 1960s, slowing down in the 1970s, perhaps being brought to an early maturity by the oil price crises of the mid-1970s, but definitely in decline by the 1980s.

The current revolution, Piatier's third, is based primarily on electronics, information technology, new forms of energy and energy substitutes, biotechnology, molecular engineering, genetic engineering, ocean development and possibly new forms of transport or transport substitutes.

We have become so used to rapid technological development that it is difficult to imagine the process ever coming to an end, although it seems that the economic potential of technology is finite. As yet, biotechnology and genetic engineering have hardly started but already their impact on agriculture is emphatic. If only 2 per cent productivity gain is maintained, then around one-third of today's farmland will be surplus to agricultural requirements in ten years' time, and already farmers in the United States and the EU can earn more for doing nothing through such schemes as set aside than by farming their land.

Molecular engineering will in due course make no less an impact with, for example, new synthetic materials surpassing the performance characteristics of steel at an inherently lower cost. The technology of melting metal could in due course be consigned to museums and small craft units.

The electronics and information technology (IT) strands of the revolution have reached an advanced stage of commercial exploitation, but appear still to be full of further potential. Commercial exploitation is rippling out from a core which is still bubbling with primary innovations.

The result is that products and services are becoming cheaper, more reliable, more flexible, more sophisticated and 'intelligent'. Flexibility and variety in these industries is instantly available. One-offs are often as cheap as standard products. Labour costs have become largely irrelevant. The implications will be revolutionary for all firms, large or small and whether at the forefront of technology or languishing in the maturest of mature industries.

This third revolution is changing the nature of work as well as eliminating jobs on a massive scale. The jobs that remain are either highly skilled manufacturing jobs, highly skilled professional services associated with production, or in distribution and personal services. Up to the present, governments have been reluctant to acknowledge and legislate for this process, but in due course it is inevitable that shorter hours, shorter working lives and more part-time work, work sharing and working from home will result. Many of these effects are already being experienced across manufacturing as a whole, not simply the new, high technology industries. It remains to be seen how much pain and social unrest will occur before governments act.

Thus changes in technology are causing other organisational and social changes, which will themselves feed back into industry, generating needs for further new products and services. The revolution is all-pervasive, though perhaps not everlasting. The various interpretations of the data on innovation at least agree that we are currently enjoying an era of technological change that is affecting pretty well every aspect of our world, and that it will not go on for ever.

Major changes in the structure of markets have in the past usually resulted from the efforts of one or more participants to improve their position by aggressive pricing strategies. Such improvements are generally only available at substantial cost that only the biggest firms can afford. Thus there is a natural tendency for the big to get bigger and the smaller firms to be driven into small niches of the market. Thus the market structure is set firm. However, during the course of a technological revolution, when all manner of new products and new processes are becoming available, competitive positions become less rigid, the market structure becomes fluid and individual firms can achieve major changes in their position at a relatively low cost.

The present technological revolution is presenting just such opportunities. However, at some stage in every market, the competitive jelly will reset and major inroads to new markets will then again be achieved only at great cost. As commercial applications of the current wave of new technologies become available, so opportunities will multiply. Each of the strands of new technology – electronics, information technology, biotechnology, genetic engineering, molecular engineering, ocean development – will offer opportunities for changing the competitive rules and structures, both in its own industry and the industries it supplies.

1.5 The global market

The market environment is also experiencing some interesting tensions. While technology enables flexibility and short production runs, the markets themselves are becoming increasingly global and thus increasingly able to sustain ever longer production runs, albeit within ever shorter timespans as new technology replaces old.

The most distinctive feature of the contemporary market environment is global *competition.* This has long been apparent in many mature industries. Although Britain started the machine tool industry, by the 1980s it had less than 3 per cent of the world market. It once had 100 per cent of the textile machinery market, but now has less than 10 per cent. Thirty years ago Britain was number three in world steel production, now it is tenth. Britain used to export motorcycles to a hundred foreign markets, but then the British motorcycle industry was more-or-less wiped out within a generation. The pattern was repeated in shipbuilding, textiles, cars, trucks and many other markets. Global competition is not new.

The United States has been similarly affected. There is a long list of industries in which it used to be dominant, if not in world markets at least on the domestic scene, but in which it lost ground to competitors from the other side of the Pacific Ocean who now own plants which form an important part of American manufacturing. The position remains unstable, particularly during this period of readjustment in South East Asian markets.

There is a virtuous cycle of technological development requiring a scale of investment which needs rapid exploitation in order to be financially justified. Rapid exploitation requires quick introduction on a global scale, which itself is dependent on a global convergence of consumer tastes which is aided by global marketing initiatives. Ohmae (1989) has described this process and it has clearly been a major development over the past two decades. Twenty years ago it would have been most unlikely that a consumer in London or Stockholm would have been targeted using the same promotion of the same product as consumers in New York, Paris and Tokyo. Now it is commonplace. Tastes have converged; we now not only watch the same films, we also drive the same cars, eat the same food, wear the same clothes and use the same cosmetics.

So far has convergence of markets gone that the reaction is already discernible with a new emphasis on 'localisation' from the newly dominant global producers, who find it economically worthwhile to customise their offerings to fit local tastes. The first generation of world cars has been produced by flexible manufacturing plant in multiple factories across the world: fundamentally standardised products from plant capable of non-standard production. Global competitiveness is raised further by the emergence of several major groupings on the international scene. Initially, the highly competitive economies of the Far East – Hong Kong, Taiwan, South Korea and Singapore – trod the Japanese trail. Major companies from the little tiger economies made huge investments in new technology production facilities in the UK, USA and elsewhere. Their strength had long been recognised. In their wake there was a further group of emerging economies (for example Malaysia, Thailand, Indonesia and Vietnam) which despite periodic currency upheavals and crises, remain capable of increasing their attack on global markets with ever decreasing costs.

Moreover, both China and India are raising their sights on international competitiveness in selected markets. China not only has the earth's largest human population, but has also experienced the fastest rate of economic growth, and with its new front access through Hong Kong its potential seems limitless, though not without risk while political stability is preserved by 'the barrel of a gun'.

Finally, there is a huge new energy on the global stage emerging from the former communist countries of the Soviet bloc. When these countries emerged their industries were backward, producing products which, though cheap, were not of acceptable quality to the West. Under the current, more liberal economic regimes they are attracting inward investment to exploit their unique combination of educated people and low salary and wage costs, resulting in the migration of much manufacturing from the more advanced economies. Within the global markets there are also regional groupings resulting from the same political will behind the process of free trade and globalisation, expressed through the GATT agreements and through such organisations as the EU, ASEAN in Asia and the American Common Market.

Technology, product markets and finance are all global. The world is in effect a smaller place. The technology is in place for a customer in, say, Buffalo, USA, to connect directly to a knitting machine in a Taiwanese factory and instruct it in detail about the number, pattern and colour of garments to be produced. Long production runs, high value work in progress and finished goods stocks are things of the past: global just-in-time is available now.

The economic case for the unrestrained exploitation of technology is substantial and mounting. Low cost telecommunications have eliminated distance as a significant cost in many situations. Airlines use a telephone overflow system. If you ring British Airways at night from the UK your call will be answered in America; if you call in America at night you will be answered in the UK. Doctors in Washington dictate memos by phone to Bangalore and receive the typed version on computer seconds later. The Philippines has become the leader in 'remote data entry' because their typists earn less than 10 per cent of the American wage. Hewlett Packard's European technical support is centralised in Amsterdam because so many Dutch are multilingual. Some London boroughs have outsourced their parking fine work to the Scottish Highlands.

The Internet itself has so far achieved only a fraction of its potential, but it already offers a cheap, quick communications and information medium and is smashing political, economic and language barriers in ways which were unimaginable only a few years ago. It provides new opportunities for small firms to compete with multinational giants. Instant, comprehensive, universal and interactive information exchange is almost with us and its full consequences cannot truly be predicted, except to say it will lead to a world that is different from before in ways that will affect all our lives.

The global market presents many tensions. Some fear that it will damage the old economies and press for the imposition of protectionist tariffs and trade barriers. Others believe in the fundamental power of international trade to increase the overall wealth and they press for completely unrestricted global markets that would maximise the world's welfare. Others fear that totally free trade will disadvantage the weak and benefit the strong, thus producing an ever more inequitable distribution of the world's resources leading inevitably to social trauma.

Whatever the validity of these different views, it is clear that the globalisation of technology, finance, markets and competition has arrived and managements must understand the implications for their business in their particular industry.

1.6 The ethical perspective

Increasing global competition and rapidly developing technology have increased the financial pressures on business. Some managements have responded to this by operating in unethical or even illegal ways in order to make a profit or survive. There has always been a natural tension between behaviour which is broadly accepted as being ethical and the imperatives of a successful business. The 1980s, often characterised as a decade of unbridled greed by the few at the expense of the many, certainly raised concerns among some that business was not being run according to acceptable ethical standards. Inequity and inequality seemed to rule the day.

Employees were weakened by high rates of unemployment, their union representatives derecognised and their employment contracts unilaterally 'renegotiated'. High street customers, in Gerald Ratner's words, were being sold 'total crap' and, should they get into financial difficulties, were exploited by high street banks. At a time of punitively high interest rates, suppliers with little bargaining power were exploited by dominant customers systematically delaying payments. Exploitative pricing was exercised wherever monopoly power permitted, most notably in the case of the newly privatised utilities. And while all this was going on, company directors appeared to be paying themselves extraordinary remuneration for far from extraordinary performance and if their incompetence became a matter for termination their severance payments were the envy of the working population.

Nor was this a purely British phenomenon. Similar processes were visible in the United States, continental Europe and even Japan. Nor was it uniquely impacting on business. Every walk of life, notably including politics and the media, seemed to have become infected.

It may always have been so – the evidence of moral decline is inconclusive. Many statistics suggest that the world is becoming more violent and more criminal, but on the other hand, the average law-abiding citizen is more aware, more caring and more generous than ever before. There is, no doubt, more violence on television now than previously, but television audiences give more generously to charity than was ever before dreamed possible.

In business, there may be more outrageous stories of fraud and crime than ever before, but, on the other hand, many of the acts, particularly in the financial sector, which are now rightly treated as criminal, were previously just custom and common practice among 'the great and the good'. There will always be crooks and a few of them will always get into powerful positions in industry, as in other sectors, but this does not mean that the majority of businesspeople are any less virtuous than in other eras or other walks of life.

Over the past two decades there has been a rising tide of anxiety and indignation among the media, seeking to influence the population at large, as to the rights and wrongs of business, particularly big, multinational business. This concern caught the attention of politicians and, even among businesspeople themselves, it became a subject of much debate. As a result a number of steps were taken. Specific initiatives such as the Cadbury report on corporate governance (Cadbury, 1987) and the adoption of codes of practice by the CBI and several of the professional bodies are symptomatic of the times, despite Levitt's early warnings about the dangers of being distracted from business concerns (Levitt, 1958, and Reading Review 1). In addition, there have been some more general moves, such as the adoption of business ethics as a core topic by most MBA teaching programmes. Worldwide, business schools now offer hundreds of courses in business ethics and literally scores of professorships have been established in the subject as well as many centres of academic research.

Society seems to be maintained, more-or-less, in a state of equilibrium through such checks and balances. The excesses of one era produce periods of reaction. However, permanent changes *do* take place. In our own time, for example, new technological developments have provided fresh opportunities for both unethical excesses and for improvement. From these there is no going back. Nor, one must suppose, will there be any going back to church on Sundays and consequent adoption of some exogenous value system which will mediate the behaviour of the mass of people. To this extent we are therefore in new territory.

Business ethics is certainly a fashionable idea, but it is unclear that any of the initiatives with which it is associated has had, or will have, any significant effect. It is not even clear whether that is the intention. A cynic might argue, for example, that so long as business is *seen* to be concerned, that will be sufficient: a well publicised code of ethical practice may have greater public relations impact than any actual improvement in ethical behaviour. Box 1.2 illustrates one kind of ethical dilemma as an opportunity for reflection on the principles involved.

BOX 1.2

Morris Retail Group

Morris Retail Group (MRG) is a large company which enjoys an excellent reputation for quality at reasonable prices. It has a large number of suppliers, many of whom are small private companies which are very dependent on MRG for their economic survival. So long as they can supply MRG, the owners and employees of these companies do fairly well out of the relationship. However, MRG often drives a hard bargain and a few top executives control decision-making about suppliers. MRG buyers are also important in negotiating the products to be supplied, but if a supplier is looked on favourably by a senior executive then difficulties and obstacles which might otherwise have been insuperable are eased and amicable solutions found. MRG prefers to remain loyal to its existing suppliers rather than using a system of open competitive tendering.

In these circumstances some practices have become common between MRG and its suppliers. At Christmas suppliers give presents to buyers and to key executives. For example, assistant buyers are often given a bottle of whisky, a buyer might be given a CD player or tape recorder or equivalent, a junior executive might be given a Harrod's hamper worth anything up to £1,000 while top executives had been offered holidays in the Canaries.

Smaller suppliers, though they felt obliged to give gifts were unable to compete with their bigger rivals. Some companies maintained a no-gifts policy but accepted that it put them at a disadvantage with MRG. It was not clear if any buying decisions were taken as a direct result of these practices, but the possibility, and intention, of having such an impact is clearly present.

DISCUSSION POINTS

1. Are these practices in themselves unethical? If so, what is it that makes them so?
2. What should be done to ensure that all stakeholders to the situation behave ethically?

Businesspeople operate in an area which explicitly and deliberately butts up against ethical boundaries. It is extremely easy for them to step over the boundary and in so doing enjoy substantial personal gains. Whether or not direct personal gain is involved, crossing the ethical boundaries may sometimes be obvious and overt, sometimes covert, sometimes not obvious, and sometimes even done unwittingly. Being innocently unethical, or even unethical but well intentioned, may be concepts which the media and the non-business public regard with some cynicism. However, the whole area is distinguished by shades of grey – the blacks and whites of fraud on the one hand and altruism on the other certainly exist, but it is the murky greys of normal business life which make this whole subject so problematic. Moreover, the greatest difficulty is in deciding between alternatives which contain both ethical and unethical aspects, and this distinguishes very many business decisions.

The *spirit of capitalism* was, according to Weber (1947), 'a peculiar ethic' based on the simple idea that it is a person's duty to ensure the increase of his or her capital. This ethos seems to impose on an individual the *duty* of profit maximisation. The tension between ethical behaviour and business was then apparent from the beginnings of the modern capitalist system.

'Greed works' was the 1980s expression of this same ethos. While at the micro level of the individual, avarice and selfishness are surely reprehensible, the spirit of capitalism holds that through the workings of the market, they serve to optimise the allocation of resources to the benefit of all at the macro level. In theory, a perfect market of profit maximisers results in maximised social welfare.

Even though the theory required underlying assumptions which were wholly unrealistic in order to make the calculus work, the idea of profit maximisation remains extremely powerful. The profit maximisation approach suggests that a finance director who pays a penny more to the tax authorities than is strictly necessary, or a buyer who fails to achieve the greatest benefit from his suppliers, a salesperson who gives his customers more value than they are prepared to pay for, a manager who pays his staff more than they require to work effectively, are all examples of waste which dissipate the company's resources and would progressively reduce its capacity to build a sustainable competitive advantage.

Yet, it is clear that profit maximisation does not work. At the macro level, social welfare is not maximised for the simple reason that society does not comprise individuals of equal strength. The weak suffer and the strong prosper in such an unregulated system. At the micro level also it fails. The problem is that the spirit of capitalism and the idea of profit maximisation are concepts which take no account of timescale. Profit maximisation is a mathematical concept which works for individual transactions but does not necessarily hold good for streams of transactions. We might accept that a travelling salesperson, if he was only coming that way once, might use confidence tricks to make a sale at an outrageous price and thereby maximise profits on the individual transaction. However, if this were to be part of a permanent territory, then he would need to be trusted by his customers. Acting in this way he would not maximise profits on the individual transaction, but would be likely to do better in the long run. Long-run profit maximisation may be an ideal but it is impossible to make operational because its meaning is so imprecise.

The notion of a stream of transactions, even a partnership between a business and its customers, gets very close to the idea of strategy. Strategy is concerned with such partnerships between the business and all its stakeholders, not just its customers, but its employees, shareholders, suppliers, creditors, its local community and the environment which stands proxy for future generations. Strategy is only concerned with profit maximisation *in the long run*, but it has to be recognised that this is a non-quantifiable concept; and even if it could be quantified it could only be achieved by a business that was trusted by all its stakeholders. This link between interdependence with stakeholders and their perception of the organisation's integrity is made in several sections of this text and is widely proclaimed by the business ethics movement, for example Hosmer (1994 and Reading Review 27). Jönnson (1996 and Reading Review 28) provides a social-theoretical examination of the role of ethics in enabling looser and less hierarchical organisation forms to work through a form of lateral control whose foundation is trust.

1.7 A future perspective

It is relatively simple to extrapolate from current trends, but extremely difficult to predict discontinuities and changes in direction. Several of the currently most significant trends have been referred to in the preceding sections and one can assume a continuation of financial pressure, technological change and globalisation, all moderated by some unevenly applied ethical constraint. But what are the structural changes or discontinuities?

One structural change which is widely documented, but which as yet remains futuristic is the demise of the factory system. Terms like post-industrialisation refer to this phenomenon but are perhaps too broad for a specialist text like this. Post-industrial society is one where the old smokestack industries have given way to shopping malls and green space, where consideration is focused on the problems of unemployment, of leisure and of non-industrial enterprise. However, the demise of the factory system with its large numbers of low-skilled people and its encyclopaedic organisational rulebooks poses a more specific problem which is of interest here. What will replace it? A shopping mall seems a rather flimsy replacement for a steel works.

Globally, the costs of manufacturing have been attacked through a series of initiatives such as just-in-time, total quality management (TQM), benchmarking, business process re-engineering as well as technology-enabled automation. In most mature economies, manufacturing has died a thousand deaths, whole industries have died or migrated to the developing economies and been replaced, at least in terms of employment, by service industries where the capacity to produce wealth may be rather less convincing.

An alternative replacement of the old machine bureaucracies would be a huge number of small, flexible, responsive organisations of highly skilled people which compete effectively as wealth creators in this new high-tech world.

For a small number of firms the old management style and organisational structure framed for the factory era may still be appropriate – they continue to employ large numbers of unskilled and semi-skilled workers and operate as though their markets and technologies were stable and unchanging. But in the end, the change will surely be forced on them too.

The technological revolution and its requirements for flexibility and speed of response have encouraged many attempts to circumvent the bureaucracy and tight accounting control of existing businesses. There has been a great deal of interest in setting up an organisation within the organisation, specifically charged with the task of 'entrepreneuring'. The main organisation continues to be managed on a more-or-less bureaucratic basis because this is still believed to be the most efficient mode for stable conditions, the implicit assumption being made that conditions will continue to be stable. But the new, the changing, innovative activity is set up quite separately in a new venture group or department or even a separate company.

The case for separate organisations for innovation rests on three main assumptions:

1. It is essential to separate the new from the ongoing business to ensure it gets sufficient attention.
2. It is necessary to provide the appropriate climate and structure which is radically different from the climate and structure of ongoing business.
3. It is necessary to insulate the new business from the dominant values and norms of the existing business.

Under these rather negative assumptions, innovation and change are seen as disruptive of the ongoing activities of the firm. Production systems may have to be altered to accommodate new products; selling skills may have to be augmented to promote new products. Sometimes a firm may be so locked into manufacturing and marketing its existing products that there is little or no expertise for product innovation. In essence, the separate organisations are attempts to get round the existing organisation. Some such efforts are even made underground:

> *small independent groups of imaginative action takers working to circumvent, or even sabotage, the formal systems that supposedly manage innovation. These courageous souls form underground teams that routinely bootleg company resources or 'steal' company time to work on their own missions. They make things happen while those trying to innovate by the official route are still waiting for permission to begin.*
> (Peters and Austin, 1985)

Clearly some organisations are so incapable of change that such 'intrapreneuring' has become a corporate necessity. However, getting round bureaucracy is an inadequate response to the problems it poses. The current instability of more-or-less all technological and product market environments appears to make a flexible, organic form of organisation universally more desirable, and the particular requirements for innovation underwrite this desirability. In this era of change, there is no longer a role for bureaucratic organisation. Getting round bureaucracy is therefore an insufficient answer; the organisations must be made organic. The only possible exceptions are some service industries, for example fast-food operations such as McDonald's who, it is sometimes argued, can still make good use of mechanistic organisation.

Changing an organisation from mechanistic to organic may not be easy, but it is possible. Few managers, apparently, desire to change the structure of the *whole* organisation, or if they do, few are in a position to achieve it. Moreover, those that do, in the main change their organisations by imposing structure and control, for example Alfred Sloan at General Motors, thus acting as agents of the process to bureaucracy. Deliberate change of the whole organisation in the opposite, liberating, direction is much less common and more difficult. Strategy management must achieve this change if it is to exploit the technological opportunities being presented.

The machine was a suitable metaphor for the old system of management but, true to its type, there is no single dominant metaphor for the new. Different writers have suggested a spider's web, a jazz 'combo' (Peters, 1994), a spider plant or a termite heap (Morgan, 1993, and Reading Review 23), a surgeon's team, a film production unit, the Desert Storm force in the Gulf War (Bowen, 1994) and endless others. Drucker's essay on post-capitalist society (Drucker, 1993 and Reading Review 22) provides a typically elegant *gestalten* understanding (albeit studded with detail inaccuracies) and proposes various organisational metaphors for the future: a baseball team, football team, tennis doubles partnership and a symphony orchestra. The essential aspect of all these metaphors is that they are not bound by rigid structure and hierarchy but focus on the growing autonomy and interdependence of both organisations and individuals in the organisations. They are organisations of networks and alliances, of collaborations, teams and partnerships where being perceived as trustworthy is prerequisite of such autonomy and interdependence.

Summary

- Prior to the factory era, business was based largely on the entrepreneur's relationship with highly skilled, semi-autonomous workers on the one hand and autonomous suppliers and buyers on the other.
- The factory system brought together large numbers of unskilled and uneducated people doing fundamentally boring and unpleasant work.
- Most of management theory emerged from studying the problem of how to manage such 'factories'. Classical management resulted in the mechanistic structures and bureaucratic systems while the scientific approach further de-skilled work and contributed to the alienation of people at work.
- Today, the more pressing management problem is how to provide interest and excitement for highly skilled people to compete with the world's best. Old structures are being torn down and replaced by what Burns and Stalker referred to as organic systems of management.
- Financial institutions were created to fund large-scale capital projects. Their success has created an industry which has its own *raison d'être* quite separate from, and even opposed to, the continuing financing needs of manufacturing industry. This can result in a requirement for returns which in the short term are not achievable from industrial investment.
- The efficiency of the financial sector, particularly in the Anglo-Saxon world, has led progressively to a dominance of industry by the language of accounting and a focus on rationalistic, short-term analysis.
- We are currently experiencing a technological revolution – Piatier's third industrial revolution – based on electronics, information technology, new forms of energy and energy substitutes, biotechnology, molecular engineering, genetic engineering, ocean development and new forms of transport or transport substitutes.
- This revolution is changing the nature of work, eliminating jobs on a massive scale, breaking down the old monolithic organisations and providing great flexibility in ways of working. It is affecting all industries, not just the new technologies, and is resulting in the migration of work to the emerging economies.
- Technologies are now truly global and markets are rapidly becoming so. Consequently, all organisations are having to operate in a global context, facing global competition even if their served market is restricted to national or regional boundaries.
- Globalisation appears set to continue and to present many opportunities for new products, new technologies and new markets. However, it also creates many tensions and especially in the mature economies there are likely to be sporadic outbreaks of protectionism. Global free trade is not assured.
- Competition in the global market is beyond the scope of most individual

organisations in isolation and millions of new technological and market collaborative partnerships are now being formed. Moreover, the technological revolution is requiring new forms of organisation based on teams, networks and (semi-)autonomous workgroups. Thus partnership and interdependence have become the organisational norm.

- Untrustworthy, exploitative and dishonest organisations will be excluded from these strategic partnerships, both locally in terms of recruitment and retention of high calibre people and globally in terms of strategic interorganisational collaborations. Establishment of trust is therefore a cornerstone of the new organisation.
- This brief and selective examination of the context of organisations highlights a number of specific concerns which must occupy strategy management and are the main subject matter of this book. These include:
  - Efficient and flexible organisation.
  - Liberation from short-termist financial constraints.
  - Exploitation of new technologies.
  - Success against global competitors.
  - Partnerships of integrity as well as technological, operational and market strength.

Further reading

This chapter is a generalist introduction and the recommended further reading is intended also to give generalist but different, intelligent and challenging perspectives rather than any particular content.

Drucker, P.F., *Post-capitalist Society*, Butterworth/Heinemann, 1993.

Kay, J., *The Business of Economics*, Oxford University Press, 1996.

Ridley, M., *The Origins of Virtue*, Viking Books, 1996.

Reading Reviews 1 and 2.

Chapter 2

The strategy idea

Social groups become organisations when they have some common purpose which binds them together. This purpose is what underlies the idea of strategic direction.

The defining ingredients which strategy brings to management can be described in extremely simple terms. They are the definition of direction, the consistent concentration on pursuit of that direction, and the retention of flexibility to change should the direction become inappropriate.

In order to define direction there must be a starting point and an end point, i.e. 'Where are we now?' and 'Where do we want to get to?' To make it operational there must be a route between the two, i.e. 'How do we get there?'

Sometimes the answers to these questions are not formally addressed but simply emerge. But whether planned or emergent, the strategy process embodies actions and behaviour that would not otherwise have taken place.

The job of strategy management is to assist this process.

2.1 Introduction

The strategy idea is confused by the lack of consensus over definitions of quite simple terms. Even the word 'strategy' means many different things. For some, strategy is simply a 'corporate plan'; for others it may be a plant replacement programme, a long-term market projection, or even a five-year cash forecast. Most conceptions of strategy would subsume a long timescale, a broad significance, or a recognisable, structural change of some kind. More-or-less all conceptions would include the idea that strategy is, in some way or another, important: if it's unimportant it's not strategic. In certain circumstances, and at certain times, almost anything can be strategic. Moreover, one person's strategy is another person's tactics; what seems tactical today may be strategic tomorrow.

The strategy business is also messy because, although planning seems logical and the likelihood of it being effective entirely plausible, its techniques are not as clinical as they often appear. Even numbers may be psychologically loaded. Simple accounting calculations can depend substantially on value judgements, and profit itself (depending as it does on, among other things, the valuation of stocks) can be largely a matter of opinion. Techniques and quantifications can contribute to strategic decision making, but they are not the solid foundations of sound strategy that they at first appear.

Despite many attempts to identify a direct causal link, formal planning has not been found to have any decisive correlation with corporate success. Leontiades and Tezel (1980) found no relationship between formal planning and orthodox financial measures; Kudla (1980) found there was no relationship between formal planning and common stock returns; Robinson and Pearce (1983) found no relationship between formal planning and profit measures; Fredrickson and Mitchell (1984) found a negative relationship between comprehensive planning and profitability; Greenley (1986) reviewed the literature and found no conclusive relationship in manufacturing industry between strategic planning and company performance; similarly Prescott *et al.* (1986) and Miller (1990). As Miller put it: 'strategies must be matched with complementary environments and structures to promote success'.

Perhaps strategic planning is itself a paradox. Planning is in essence a bureaucratic process – to do it well requires excellence in the administrative virtues. Strategy, on the other hand, depends at least in part on entrepreneurial capabilities in spotting and taking advantage of opportunities; an entrepreneurial business is unlikely to focus its energies on bureaucratic processes.

Strategy is not about planning, but about thinking and doing. It is not a technique, but a way of understanding and managing the business according to a strategic perspective or framework. Only with understanding are strategies likely to be matched with complementary environments and structures, no matter how thorough the planning.

This chapter seeks to clarify the most basic concepts of strategic thinking, what it is and what it can do. The ideas examined seem to apply whatever strategy framework is used. However, there is no definitive explanation of strategy: this is necessarily only a partial explanation, a selective view of the whole reality. The reader should therefore be critical and accept what is written only after the most careful consideration.

2.2 The purposive nature of strategy

There have been various attempts at imposing categories on the different approaches to strategy. Some have been referred to as schools (for example, Mintzberg, 1994a; Whittington, 1993). There is said to be the 'design school of strategic management' whose adherents are thought to believe that everything occurs logically, in linear fashion, in response to deliberate management initiatives. Ansoff (1965) is now identified as a founding father of this school, but in reality Ansoff never professed a belief in the linearity and coherence of strategy, seeking merely to propose a rational approach to its formulation.

A radically different approach has been identified as the 'emergent school' whose adherents are said to believe that strategy emerges from a serendipitous process of trial and error. Mintzberg was an early describer of emergent strategy and clearly recognises its potency (Mintzberg, 1987a, and Reading Review 13).

Those that focus attention on the internal resources or assets of a business, its core competences and capabilities, are said to belong to the 'resource-based school'. This approach has been adopted by theoretical economists whose interests are not focused on practical realities, and though currently fashionable in academic circles it is of limited interest to the practitioner.

There is also a school which focuses interest on the competitive situation, particularly in the product market. These various categories are simply labels which divide the subject of strategy management into manageable-sized chunks. They have no practical reality and no implications for practice. The idea, for example, of an emergent *approach* to strategy is patently ludicrous. Strategy management is nothing if it has no purpose. The purposive nature of strategy is its unique contribution to the field of management as Mintzberg himself acknowledges (Mintzberg, 1987b, and Reading Review 14).

Drucker also focused on the purposive issue when he asked the three fundamental questions at the start of any general management consultancy assignment:

1. What business are you in?
2. Who are your customers?
3. What do they value?

Simple though Drucker's questions are, they are perceptive, and answering them is by no means problem-free. The first question demands some ability to think strategically about the business and what it does.

The question about customers is equally searching. Is the question about existing, potential, all or best customers? Are we looking backwards or forwards? How do we describe the customer – geographically or in demographic, psychographic or lifestyle terms?

How can you begin to answer the final question: 'What does the customer value?' We may think we know what the customer values: 'We deliver it and the customer keeps coming back for more'. But what do they *really* value? How could you increase the value to the customer of your product by more than an increase in its cost? How does the customer value your offering in comparison to competitive products? Why do they not buy more of your product and less of competitors'?

Clearly, comprehensive answers to all three of Drucker's questions will involve a deep understanding of the business and its purpose and competitive strengths. These are basic considerations for the strategy manager.

A truism about strategy management is illustrated by the above discussion: the theory of strategy management is simple, even trivial; its application is problematic. Implementing strategic decisions, on the basis of imperfect knowledge, is often extremely difficult, both to do and to justify.

Even not-for-profit organisations still have a purpose and serve 'customers' who will still value the product or service provided. Do they really know what business their organisation is in? According to Drucker, if everyone in the organisation understands the answers to these three questions, they have no need of his assistance. But few organisations are really satisfied they do know enough about those three questions.

To see how searching Drucker's three questions are consider the case of Cooper Soft Drinks (see Box 2.1). This is a fairly typical multi-business company situation. Clearly the information provided is far from comprehensive. There may be some lack of clarity in the way Cooper conceives of itself and there may be confusion, even conflict, between the parent company and its subsidiary. Consider the questions raised as discussion points at the end of Box 2.1.

BOX 2.1

Cooper Soft Drinks Ltd

Cooper Soft Drinks Ltd was, until recently, under family ownership but is now a separate division of Hudson Holdings Plc, a large, financially oriented conglomerate. Cooper has a strong market position in the UK Midlands, being much the largest 'independent' with sales through general retail outlets and supermarkets, public houses and off-licences. It sells under the Cooper brand and also under various own-labels for supermarket chains. However, it does not have any bottling and distribution arrangements with major national or international brands such as Coca-Cola or Pepsi-Cola. Over the past few years it has expanded by achieving national distribution through the major supermarket chains. There is little scope for further growth through this channel.

Each April, Cooper is required by the parent company, Hudson Holdings, to submit a five-year business plan. This document extends to around seventy pages and includes numerous five-year financial projections. These are intended to indicate the extent to which Cooper contributes to the parent company's stated objectives of 17 per cent return on capital employed (ROCE) and 9 per cent growth per annum in earnings per share.

In addition, Cooper has annual cash generation targets imposed by the parent company which are invariably difficult to achieve.

Within these constraints imposed by Hudson Holdings, Cooper expresses its own business objectives in what it refers to as its 'mission statement'. These objectives include:

1. Being the lowest-cost producer in the region.
2. Achieving national coverage through all existing outlets.
3. Providing 'excellent' customer service in terms of delivery, quality and manufacturing flexibility.

In the past year Cooper has opened the world's most advanced automated soft drinks bottling plant which permits it to respond flexibly to changes in demand. In the press release announcing the opening of this new facility, chairman Tony Marchment said:

> *In this industry, flexibility means tripling production because of a heat wave. It means a special promotion for a single retail store wanting, say, pink bottles with*

a special label. It means producing ten lines of 1,000 bottles as cheaply and quickly as one line of 10,000 bottles. It means delivering the same high Cooper quality to the customer no matter what the product.

DISCUSSION POINTS

1. Put yourself in the shoes of a senior executive at Cooper Soft Drinks Ltd currently involved in preparing the next business plan. As part of this process you have to consider what business Cooper is really in. It could be in soft drinks, bottling, distribution, transportation or all four. It is clearly difficult to give a definitive answer to this question on the limited information provided. Nevertheless, on the information provided in the case, what business do you think Cooper is in?
2. Does it matter what business Cooper is in?
3. What would be the implications of your answer for Cooper's business strategy?

Drucker's three questions have introduced some of the key issues of strategy management, but they have not offered any definition of strategy. Perhaps there is no satisfactory definition. Some writers spend more time identifying what strategy is not than offering a succinct definition. Strategy is certainly concerned with long-term prosperity and long-term asset growth, rather than short-term profit. Focusing on short-term profitability, to the exclusion of strategic considerations, leads organisations to make short-term financial decisions which, whilst in accounting terms may be perfectly rational, may lack any coherence or consistency and lead to the business becoming widely diversified, highly complex and in the end unmanageable.

Strategy management is often seen in terms of corporate navigation using the strategy as the means by which direction is set and progress measured. This is perhaps the most commonly used analogy. The idea of direction is basic to all strategic considerations. The answer to Drucker's 'What business are you in?' requires an examination of strategic direction. Thus, the familiar and very simple idea underlying the cyclical strategy process shown in Figure 2.1 emerges.

The ways of addressing each question in Figure 2.1 are many and various according to the strategy approach or framework being used. Each of the frameworks dis-

- Where are we now?
- Where do we want to get to?
- How shall we bet there?
  Start moving
- How are we doing?

Figure 2.1 The idea behind strategy

cussed in Part Two prescribes analysis of a particular kind and generates its own particular outputs.

In general, however, each question raises basic considerations, aspects of which are common to all frameworks. 'Where are we now?' requires an analysis of products, technologies, customers, markets and competitors, i.e. an analysis of both internal and external factors. The analysis needs to take account of both the existing realities and potential futures – it is vital, if obvious, that the analysis be focused forwards and does not simply reflect the status quo, i.e. the fruits of the past.

'Where do we want to get to?' requires some definition of the ultimate aim of the business, what would be its ultimate measure of success, the basic purpose for which it exists. For the moment we shall refer to this strategic objective as 'mission'.

'How shall we get there?' demands the definition of the milestones (specific, measurable, quantified if possible and dated), stages along the way to achieving the mission. The answer will very probably comprise non-routine, change-based programmes and projects, and the allocation of discretionary resources: people (i.e. knowledge, skills and enthusiasm), money and equipment, to those programmes and projects.

'Start moving' refers to the resultant action – the new programmes and projects, the reorganisations, as well as the concentration by way of stopping doing certain things.

'How are we doing?' refers to the monitoring of performance by review of achievement against milestones.

The process is repeated in a continuous cycle over a timescale which is appropriate to the particular organisation (or business) and environment (or industry). This is the generic process which underlies every approach to strategy formation.

The last few paragraphs have introduced many ideas which have not yet been defined or discussed in any depth. In the main they are simple, but they are the basis of all strategy management. The problem, as in the case of Cooper Soft Drinks, is that the application of these simple ideas is not necessarily so simple. A more rounded account of the various concepts will emerge over the next few chapters as they are applied to a variety of situations.

2.3 The inputs and outputs of strategy

2.3.1 Inputs

While strategy is most often thought of as being deliberately planned, usually written down with the intention of being implemented, Mintzberg was right to suggest (1987a, 1994b) that strategy can also emerge progressively over time with no explicit attempt to manage the process. As it emerges it can become a well recognised, though unplanned, pattern or recipe, an ultimately agreed way of doing things, that may or may not be written down. It may be a pattern peculiar to a particular organisation or it may be a recipe that is widely used throughout an industry. This is the 'emergent strategy' referred to previously.

The inputs to strategy therefore include these two broad categories: deliberate inputs and almost accidental inputs.

The rationale for deliberate inputs – formal strategic plans of some description –

seems compelling. Formal planning appears, first of all, to provide managers with a means of understanding their organisation, which becomes more and more important since most organisations get hugely more complex as they mature. This is because firms have to adapt continually to their rapidly changing environments, and while some firms adapt incrementally to change, many take the temptingly easier looking route of diversification, in search of 'greener grass'. Diversification has become so frequent for many firms that they lose sight of their original aims so that there is no longer any single unifying purpose relevant to the different parts of the business. In this situation, managers feel the need for an effective planning system which will reduce the complexity of the business and bring back the feeling of coherence that it has lost and the sense of direction and focus it so badly needs.

Moreover, in a world that is subject to increasingly rapid change, exploding with new technology and financed by a form of international roulette, it seems intuitively important to have a clear idea about where you are now, where you want to get to and what there is likely to be along the way. It also surely seems important to know how far you have progressed and how much further there is to go. It seems on the face of it that sales, marketing, market share, manufacturing, technology, profit, cash, earnings per share and a score of other factors need to be planned and monitored in such an unstable and basically hostile environment. But it is uncertain whether such detailed planning achieves anything of value.

Planning helps a company to recognise problems while there is still time to deal with them. If, for example, there is likely to be a weak point in a company's future cash flow profile, or if a company's production technology is likely to become obsolete, the fact must be understood and necessary action identified. It must be decided whether to raise the finance to replace the plant, to withdraw from the market or to buy into some entirely new business. Drifting planless into such situations is clearly a prescription for disaster.

The search for a satisfactory strategic planning system has progressed through several phases. Early approaches tended to be simply extensions of one-year financial budgets. Mostly they projected forwards five, or in some cases, even ten years.

In the early 1960s, strategic planning was fashionable. Planning departments, employing specialist planners and often reporting direct to the chief executive, developed sophisticated systems based on exhaustive analyses of the strengths and weaknesses of the firm and the threats and opportunities in its environments, and the development of formal plans for every function, timescale and purpose. Figure 2.2 shows a typical outline of such a system. All the possible actions that could be taken were identified and, typically, senior managers were presented with explicit alternatives to choose from.

But as has already been indicated, although much research has been carried out to establish the effectiveness of these approaches to strategy, it remains uncertain whether they have made any significant impact. Some have argued that the *process* of strategic planning was what really mattered, rather than the development of any specific strategy, the process being seen as a means of communication and motivation. However, this seems a weak justification for such an expensive and time-consuming activity, which would be doubly counterproductive if the outcomes were seen as not worthwhile.

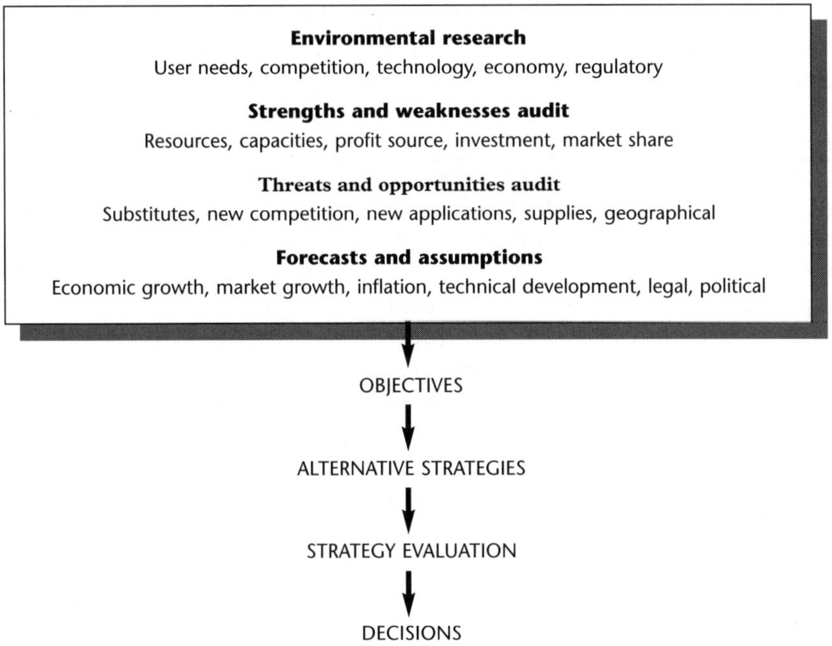

Environmental research
User needs, competition, technology, economy, regulatory

Strengths and weaknesses audit
Resources, capacities, profit source, investment, market share

Threats and opportunities audit
Substitutes, new competition, new applications, supplies, geographical

Forecasts and assumptions
Economic growth, market growth, inflation, technical development, legal, political

↓

OBJECTIVES

↓

ALTERNATIVE STRATEGIES

↓

STRATEGY EVALUATION

↓

DECISIONS

Figure 2.2 Typical linear planning system

Why these planning approaches should have achieved so little is unclear. Two explanations have been offered. First, planning tends to degenerate into bureaucratic systems for producing huge amounts of paperwork which managers barely have time to read let alone action. Secondly, planning flouted the basic rule of concentration. 'Concentration is the key to real economic results', according to Drucker (1964, and Reading Review 3), but strategic planning systems often generated exhaustive lists of actions to exploit strengths, rectify weaknesses, grasp opportunities and avoid threats. The almost inevitable result of such systems was a thin spread of resources across a very wide front, with consequently very little being achieved.

Moreover, the idea of forecasting the future and meeting budget on which many strategic plans were based (Norburn and Schurz, 1984), is clearly no longer an adequate response. If a business is to grasp the opportunities of new technology, rather than being defeated by others who do, its management must go well beyond meeting budget. They must think strategically and be prepared to take risks which in orthodox accounting terms may seem irrational in order to create the future.

While planning does not necessarily succeed, many firms which appear to have clear strategies, apparent and understood by company members and the outside world alike, may have never made any attempt to develop a formal strategic plan of any kind. The strategy emerged naturally from the normal process of management. Competent managers will continually seek out better ways of doing things and so will achieve incremental improvements in performance. Thus, by a process of what Quinn (1978) called logical incrementalism, strategy, in the form of recognised patterns or recipes, could emerge.

A study of any industry is likely to reveal that the strategy of many organisations does in fact emerge in this way. Such businesses may have clear and focused strategies without ever having given strategy management any deliberate attention. Such firms may not only have survived without any explicit knowledge of strategy issues, but they may well be highly prosperous, their prosperity resulting wholly from a process of competent management. A study of any industry is likely also to reveal that many, if not the majority, of organisations competing for a share of the industry's business, go bankrupt in the attempt. These failures may or may not have had clear strategies or competent managers, but it would be rash to assume that logical incrementalism, or reliance on an emergent strategy, was sufficient for success.

The logical increments of unplanned strategy may arise in any number of ways, often in response to customer needs or the imperatives of cost reduction. This can happen either overtly when, for example, a customer specifically demands some new product attribute which may become the cornerstone of future business, or more typically through a process of prolonged trial and error during which the firm progressively identifies what is most profitable or what it is best at producing or selling. Such strategy emerges slowly as the successful approaches gradually merge into a pattern of action that becomes the strategy. For example, Henry Ford's cost oriented 'any colour so long as it's black' became that company's strategy, symbolising an attitude to standardisation and an attitude to the customer, even to the operator on the shopfloor, which was for a long time the source of Ford's great strength.

Unplanned strategy that is realised in this way is likely, by its very nature, to be robust; those that are not robust are not realised. A firm with such a realised strategy will have established a pattern of behaviour, or recipe, which ensures concentration, consistently over time, even though it is not formally planned.

Such unplanned strategies are often inferred by outsiders, notably journalists or academics, who seek to identify a pattern in corporate behaviour. Identification of the pattern offers a means of making sense of corporate behaviour and thus predicting future behaviour. The pattern may be real or it may be a rationalised myth, willed into existence by the need to explain 'strategy'. Managers may infer strategies about a competitor. They may go further and impute intention where none exists, or is rationalised only subsequently.

So the inputs to strategy may comprise highly analytical plans and completely unplanned patterns or recipes as well as combinations of both plans and unplanned opportunities.

2.3.2 Outputs

Whether planned or unplanned, strategy affects the way individual decisions are taken, and in the aggregate has two overwhelmingly important outcomes: position and culture.

By position is meant the position of the organisation with regard to its external environment. A firm might be the technological leader, the lowest-cost producer or dominant in some particular product market niche. This position, whatever it is, might be a perfectly adequate expression of the firm's strategy.

Alternatively, strategy might take the form of a dominant culture. By culture is meant the corporate personality, or ideology, as perceived collectively by organisation members and other stakeholders.

Strategy achieves these position and culture outputs as a result of people's activity largely determined by strategic decisions, both large and small, implicit and explicit. Individual strategic decisions are usually thought of as the big, one-off investments, diversifications, divestments or acquisitions. These are the decisions which, because of their scale or structural impact, are clearly of strategic significance and warrant the most careful scrutiny. In most businesses they would be treated as strategic whether or not any system of strategic planning was actually in place. With an effective system that has identified the strategic direction of the business, such decisions can be taken in a concentrated and consistent way so that the strategy is progressed.

In addition, there are other less obvious decisions that can be guided by a clear strategic direction. For example, when a new product is introduced, arrangements may be made for the salesforce to give it special attention. In some cases additional sales personnel may be recruited dedicated to the new line. During the introductory phase this may be appropriate, but it may not remain so. Unless overt decisions are taken to reallocate the time of the salesforce to the whole product range, it is probable that the new product will continue to consume a disproportionate amount of resource, not just in selling, but in marketing, production and even administration. Thus resources will tend to become misallocated unless explicit management decisions are taken to avoid this happening. With a clear direction such decisions can readily be taken; without it such decisions are improbable and the end result of such processes would be for resources of all kinds not to be concentrated on the few products, customers or technologies of greatest strategic importance.

Influencing individual decisions is one important result of effective strategy. From this emerges a clear and understandable position, recognised by all who interact with the business. One obvious example of position is the market sector or niche that the organisation occupies. A niche is a position that is occupied in order to avoid mainstream competition. Product market niches may be defined in terms of the existing and potential customers, geographically determined, or fixed by demographics, psychographics or lifestyle. Alternatively, product market niches might be defined in terms of product attributes such as price, quality or design.

Not all organisations are focused on product markets. Some may be driven by technology, others by financial markets. A firm's ability to develop new products quickly may be the vital ingredient that sets it apart from potential competitors; for another, technical sophistication in the product itself may be the unique selling point.

Achieving the lowest costs is also a position strategy, although the niche in this case may be defined as industry-wide. The strategy of Bic, for example, whether planned or unplanned, is clearly imprinted on the public imagination as a producer of high-utility, low-cost disposable plastic products, whether it be ballpoint pens, razors or cigarette lighters. Bic's strategy, in terms of position, is perfectly clear. Its position would only be confused by an attempt to compete with names like Cross or Mont Blanc. Bic's position is as a cost leader and it should seek out head-to-head price competition in order to beat its competitors.

Competition through quality is another potent positional strategy. The aim here is to earn a premium price through some aspect of quality which will not be eroded by head-on price competition. This is the positional strategy of Cross and Mont Blanc referred to above and the aim is precisely to avoid price competition.

Positional strategies have long been acknowledged as a prime concern of top management. Throughout the past two hundred years, one of the most important strategic functions of large company top management was the setting up of competition avoidance arrangements, through the auspices of trade associations, international technology exchange organisations, joint ventures, interlocking directorships, long-standing customs and practices as to who competed in which markets, and, where all else failed, by the formation of covert constraints on competition. The globalisation of markets over the past twenty years probably results more from the collapse of these international cartels than from the market and technological pressures more widely acknowledged.

Currently the limits on international competition are again being painstakingly rebuilt through international strategic alliances, based on overt agreements covering the exchange of technology and often involving an exchange of shares. Global competition avoidance is again assuming great strategic importance. Box 2.2 gives one

BOX 2.2

Collaborating competitors: the case of Kodak and Canon

Kodak and Canon both started out in photography and subsequently entered the photocopier business. In both fields they are fierce competitors but have nevertheless established a powerful strategic alliance. It is just one example of collaborating competitors; such relationships are rife in the motor and computer industries.

The reason is that nobody has all the answers when technology continues to develop so rapidly. No one company can afford to bear all the costs of research and development and marketing and sales, and still deliver an ever-more sophisticated product at a competitive price. Consequently, businesses are identifying their own core strengths and buying in the rest from their competitors through these long-lasting alliances.

Mike Mansell, Kodak's manager for the UK office-imaging business, was recently quoted as saying: 'There is little sense in investing huge amounts of capital in areas outside your core expertise if a good complementary fit with a business partner can be identified' (Trapp, 1993).

Such a fit allows partners to achieve both a strong business position and a better financial return. Kodak has a number of arrangements with such companies as IBM, Lotus, Olivetti and Unisys.

Kodak has identified its core strengths as design and development allied to customer service and support, while Canon's are manufacturing and distribution. Both partners are strong on marketing, but they use different distribution channels, with Kodak selling direct and Canon through dealerships. Moreover, their products are also complementary, with Canon serving the low to medium volume end of the market and Kodak focusing on the very high volume user.

example from many of collaboration between otherwise fierce competitors. The situation described is not a cartel, it is not monopolistic and it is certainly not illegal. But the huge costs of new technology are themselves imposing limitations on the extent of competition.

The other output of strategy is culture. Whereas position defines the organisation externally, culture defines what the organisation is internally. Culture explains how people in the organisation perceive the organisation, and consequently determines how they behave. Organisational culture has been defined in many different ways, but 'those writers who treat culture not as a metaphor but as an actual phenomenon generally agree that culture comprises shared values, beliefs and ways of behaving and thinking that are unique to a particular organisation' (Child and Faulkner, 1998, p. 230).

However, culture is not simply homogeneous, as is often assumed in such concepts as 'strong culture'. It is the sum of many subcultures, each of which contributes its own nuances of meaning and its own rituals and images. Although there is a view that culture is 'the glue that binds organisation together' (Deal and Kennedy, 1982), it is clear that culture can in fact be divisive, just as easily as cohesive. In the absence of any dominant superculture, the various subcultures may well be in conflict with each other. On occasion this conflict may become overt and sometimes highly dysfunctional, but more usually the conflict will be bubbling below the surface. Culture has thus been described as a 'melange of cross-cutting subcultures', continually reacting against each other in some more or less cohesive, or divisive, not necessarily stable, equilibrium (Gregory, 1983).

Peters and Waterman recounted how 'stories, myths and legends appear to be very important, because they convey the organisation's shared values, or culture. Without exception, the *dominance* and *coherence* of culture proved to be an essential quality of the excellent companies' (Peters and Waterman, 1982). The implication is that culture can in some way be controlled to make management's desired culture both coherent in itself and dominant over other subcultures.

In management literature there are many stories, even legends or myths about the great and good, or not so good, originators of such organisations as IBM, Hewlett Packard, NCR, ITT and McDonald's. These businesses all share 'strong', deliberately established and maintained, coherent, dominant 'cultures'. They have gained the active participation of all their members, the consistent concentration of effort on pushing their organisation further in its intended direction.

The distinctive feature of strategy as culture is that it is shared by organisation members. The shared assumptions about the organisation and the way to behave in the organisation represent a powerful means of getting strategy implemented via the 'hearts and minds' of all organisation members. Thus, potentially, culture offers a way for people in the organisation to concentrate their efforts, consistently to achieve the strategic aims of the business. It contributes to the sense of direction and climate of success, far beyond what could be achieved through more orthodox management approaches. The meaning that these phrases convey is in essence subjective. To one manager they may seem to get to the core of what management is all about. To another, they may seem meaningless. To many, the divisions between management, manipulation and brainwashing are becoming too fragile (see Chapter 12). The con-

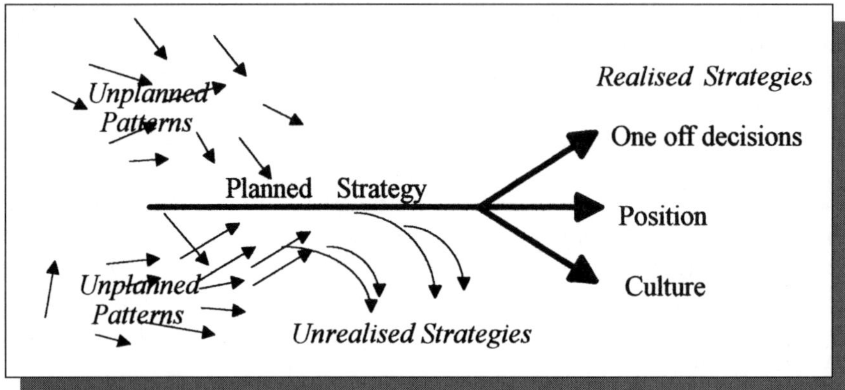

Figure 2.3 The inputs and outputs of strategy

cept of culture is still riddled with such ambiguities, but there is nevertheless a substantial strategic benefit in the cultural output as people internalise the direction of the business.

2.3.3 Interrelating the inputs and outputs

The inputs and outputs of strategy are indicated in Figure 2.3. The inputs, i.e. planned and unplanned strategy, are independent of each other. Plans may go unrealised, patterns not be preconceived. Similarly, the outputs of realised strategy, which may comprise simply a few operational commitments or individual decisions, but may more potently also include the cumulative definition of thousands of mini-decisions which contribute to both position and culture, may all be independent of each other. However, for the most potent strategy, the outputs must all be consistent.

Plans and patterns can be altered, but positions and cultures are much less easy to change. Plans and patterns must therefore be made compatible with position and culture. Mintzberg examples the McDonald's Egg McMuffin as a strategically consistent new product introduction, and contrasts this nicely with a tantalising inconsistency: the McDuckling à l'Orange by candlelight (Mintzberg, 1987a, 1994b).

Strategic planning will not work if it is inconsistent with the unplanned patterns and recipes which emerge over time. Nor will it work if the plans are inconsistent with the position and culture of the organisation. All four aspects of strategy – plans, patterns, position and culture – are needed, and they need to be made compatible with each other.

2.4 Purpose of strategy

Having discussed the purposive nature of strategy and looked briefly at its inputs and outputs we should now be in a position to say exactly what its purpose is. It clearly has a purpose which goes beyond the normal responsibilities of day-to-day management. Day-to-day management is concerned with the efficiency and effectiveness with which operations are carried out; it is concerned with the use of resources, including especially people; it is concerned with the organisation's interrelations with its various stakeholders, both internal and external; and it is concerned with the survival and prosperity of the organisation. So what else is there for strategy to contribute?

Intuitively it might appear obvious that strategy is worthwhile only in as much as it contributes to the profitability of a business. At the same time it is equally obvious that strategy is to do with the longer term and is unlikely to contribute much to the current year's profit and loss.

Herein lies a problem. Orthodox financial measures, with an impeccable logic, accord the greatest value to the quickest gain. A pound now is worth more than a pound in a year's time. Yet strategy is very often concerned with a five- or ten-year horizon or even longer. Strategic considerations frequently result in very different evaluations from those produced using orthodox accounting criteria. For example, when Blue Circle Industries put its sand and gravel business up for sale, the business had a balance sheet total net asset value of around £9m. A professional revaluation of the land and minerals in the business produced a surplus over book value of almost £10m, implying an asset value of £19m. An alternative valuation was made by estimating the maintainable level of earnings multiplied by the then current sector price/earnings ratio plus a 50 per cent premium to reflect the price increase that would inevitably occur as soon as the bid was announced. This produced a valuation of almost £20m. A third valuation was based on an estimate of all future cash flows from the business discounted at 15 per cent to a present value of £16.8m. These three different methods of valuing the business showed an average valuation of £18.6m. The business was actually sold for around £30m.

The justification for the premium was strategic. It was not possible to justify the price in any rational accounting terms. The Blue Circle Aggregates business included huge deposits of minerals in the West Midlands. Many of these were not currently being exploited – some appeared unlikely to be used for as long as forty years – because of their location. The value now of £1 in forty years' time, discounted at 15 per cent, is a mere 0.373 pence, but the strategic value of having a secure business for the next twenty years could be immense, equivalent in Blue Circle's case to a 50 per cent premium over non-strategic valuations. Strategic value, whether it is invested in minerals under the ground, long-term research and development or a structural or positioning change in the business, is not measurable in orthodox financial language. This is the source of the great irreconcilable dichotomy between accounting and strategy, which is referred to elsewhere in this text. Orthodox accounting does not measure strategy; it speaks a different language. Using accounting concepts to measure strategy is like trying to analyse a graphical image using an amplifier and loudspeaker.

Strategy is to do with long-term prosperity. It is to ensure that the business is still around in ten or twenty years' time. It is concerned with long-term asset growth, not short-term profit. Focusing on short-term profitability, to the exclusion of explicit strategic considerations, leads organisations to make short-term opportunistic decisions which, whilst financially rational in themselves, may lack any coherence or consistency and thus lead to the business becoming widely diversified, highly complex and in the end unmanageable.

2.4.1 Direction

The purpose of strategy is therefore not best conceived in terms of its impact on the bottom line. Instead it can be identified in more operational terms as setting the direction of a business as in the familiar underlying strategic idea Where are we now?, Where do we want to get to?

This directional idea is far from being the whole story, but it is nevertheless surely crucial. Once the direction is set, it becomes possible to take decisions in a consistent manner with regard to strategy. Only when direction is set is it possible for all members of the business to know which way they are headed, and only then can they shape their own efforts accordingly. With no direction, members may well allocate their efforts and enthusiasm in random and conflicting directions and investments be made similarly with no prospect of building a coherent position and culture.

2.4.2 Concentration

Drucker and others have continuously highlighted the power of concentration. 'Concentration is the key to real economic results' (Drucker, 1964, and Reading Review 3) is one of the many of his assertions that seems likely to stand the test of time. Managers must concentrate their efforts on the smallest number of products, product lines, services, customers, markets and so on. Such statements have continuously highlighted the power of concentration and the need for strategic focus.

Concentration applies to the large-scale capital investments, of course, but more importantly to the million and one mini-decisions about apparently unimportant jobs and work priorities, that are taken every day by people at every level in an organisation. The cumulative weight of the mini-decisions is what makes concentration so important. In most firms they are ignored unless catastrophe threatens.

Concentration seems to be one of those concepts about which there is a high degree of consensus, but with only few exceptions, businesses continually fail to put it into practice. The 80:20 rule is a monument to the failure to concentrate. Resources tend to be misallocated and spread thinly across all activities, products and customers. No other principle of effectiveness is violated as constantly as the basic principle of concentration.

The reasons for lack of concentration are various. The most difficult aspect of concentration is the management decision not to do things. If there is a known market, which a business could satisfy using existing competences and which looks profitable, then why not go for it? Very few managers would be able to mount a persuasive argument and even fewer would be prepared to stand by it and insist the opportunity is passed up, in order just to stay concentrated. This is one of the most difficult of all managerial decisions taking considerable courage to advocate and implement, especially in the face of apparently attractive shorter-term alternatives.

Porter (1988) interviewed John Rollwagon, CEO of Cray Research, the world leaders in supercomputers. Cray had identified the then looming market for mini-supercomputers, worth many millions of dollars. Cray itself had a prior position technologically and also in marketing terms. Cray's customers wanted the company to enter the market. It developed a detailed plan and the whole thing looked highly profitable. But in the end Cray decided to turn down the opportunity, in order just to stay focused on manufacturing the world's most powerful computer. Rollwagon pointed to this decision as the key to Cray's success.

Concentrating was difficult for Cray. It was a decision not to start doing something that looked in itself highly profitable and made a lot of sense. But if it was difficult for Cray not to start, how much more difficult is it to take a decision to stop doing something solely in order to focus. This is the situation for most businesses. In these cases, stopping doing something means accepting a reduction in sales volume and most often a reduction in profit, at least a reduction in contribution to overheads in the short term. How can such a decision be justified?

Porter's account of Skil Corporation (Porter, 1988) again showed that such decisions to concentrate can be extremely effective. Power tool producer Skil had been acquired by Emerson Electric after years of inadequate performance with a huge product range sold into many markets with no clear product position. The decision was taken to give up 40 per cent of sales volume in order to trim the product range and concentrate on just a few distribution channels. The executives concerned in the decision to concentrate were not burdened by having been associated with the old Skil business. They had no longstanding psychological investments to be jettisoned when the decision was taken to concentrate. Nevertheless, the decision was difficult and required considerable courage. The first problem was simply being believed by their own people.

Skil and Cray had both developed a clear strategic direction. Without clear direction there can be no concentration simply because there will be no agreement as to what to concentrate on. Most organisations do not have simply stated, unifying strategic objectives such as 'the most powerful computer in the world'. Few businesses really understand what their particular specialism is. Most formally stated strategies are not simple, but reflect the complex world in which the business operates. As a consequence, strategy statements often appear to convey conflicting messages and strategic managements seem reluctant to acknowledge the simplicity of effective strategic concepts.

Peters and Waterman found concentration was a prime requirement of 'excellent' business performance (Peters and Waterman, 1982). Operate with a simple structure and a lean staff so that efforts can be concentrated on 'the knitting' i.e. the core business. Concentration remains one of the key determinants of business success; but with no direction there can be no concentration.

2.4.3 Consistency

A third main purpose of strategy is to provide consistency. All that has been said of concentration applies to consistency. Consistency is simply concentration over time. Like concentration it applies to the big, one-off investment decisions and it applies to the myriad mini-decisions which determine how an individual's time, effort and enthusiasm will be allocated.

Without consistency the organisation will continually change direction, flitting like a butterfly from one project to another, developing no critical mass of expertise or even proficiency let alone any form of position or culture.

Direction, concentration and consistency, extremely simple ideas in themselves, are the unique contributions made by strategy management. They represent the only reasons why investing in the strategy process can ever be justified. An appropriate direction on which resources are consistently concentrated is the key to long-term prosperity. It can lead to the establishment of a leadership position, based on a continually developing body of knowledge, skill and expertise which generates real economic results.

2.4.4 Flexibility

The successful behaviour patterns which are regularly reinforced, the successfully established position and effective culture of the organisation gradually become more deeply imprinted on organisation members and their behaviour gradually becomes more rigid and automatic. Individual members become expert and make heavy personal and psychological investments in their expertise and the organisation as a whole accumulates substantial investment in, and commitment to, the existing and successful technology, customers, competitive positions and ways of doing things. The successful strategy, pursued consistently, will tend gradually to blinker the organisation and render it less capable of noticing, let alone creating, change. Success has obsolescence built in.

As Drucker pointed out, 'any leadership position is transitory and likely to be short-lived' and 'what exists is getting old' (Drucker, 1964). If it was true in 1964, it is far more true at the turn of the millennium, and the need to be flexible and responsive to these changes is more vital than ever before. In fact Drucker's advice for the 1990s was that 'every organisation has to prepare for the abandonment of everything it does' (Drucker, 1993).

Strategy needs to set direction, concentrate effort and provide consistency, but at the same time, it needs to ensure organisational flexibility. The concepts of direction, concentration and consistency are simple, but flexibility is rather more complex. A flexible strategy may be almost a contradiction in terms, yet this is the other main purpose of strategy management.

Direction, concentration and consistency do not arise from any natural process but require determined management action for their achievement. And when achieved, they militate against flexibility. Thus the purpose of strategy, summarised in Figure 2.4, is rather subtle: a balance between commitment to a successful direction and the ability to change direction when required.

These ideas are all simple in theory, but rather more difficult to put into practice. Consider any well known organisation and whether it has a clearly defined strategic direction that its stakeholders (employees, customers, suppliers, shareholders and so on) understand. If it does, then to what extent does it concentrate its resources on pursuit of direction? And for how long has it maintained that direction consistently? Finally, what are the fundamental issues on which that direction is based, what are the main external and internal changes which may make that direction inappropriate,

The purpose of strategy is to achieve the following four elements:

1. Setting direction
Defining a clear and simple long-term goal which is capable of motivating effort.

2. Concentrating resources
Focusing all investment (large and small, capital and revenue), efforts and enthusiasm of people in the agreed direction.

3. Maintaining consistency
Progressing in the same direction, with the same focus over long periods of time, deviating only when necessary.

4. Retaining flexibility
As a successful strategy becomes more embedded in the organisation's culture it tends to become set and increasingly resistant to change. It is therefore vital to maintain a continuous assessment of the various environments and key variables on which the strategy depends and continually review the necessity for revising the agreed strategy.

Figure 2.4 The purpose of strategy

and how capable would the organisation be of responding to those changes if they occur? The theory is simple; the practice problematic.

Finally, in relation to the purpose of strategy, consider the Cooper Soft Drink situation again (Box 2.3).

2.5 Levels of strategy

The Cooper Soft Drinks case serves to highlight one further issue which is fundamental to a consideration of strategy management. Strategy works at various levels in an

BOX 2.3

Cooper Soft Drinks Ltd (2)

The UK soft drinks market is mature and growing only very slowly, if at all. Cooper has now achieved national coverage with the existing product range through the existing types of outlet, but still needs to satisfy the parent company's growth objectives of 9 per cent per annum.

How can Cooper continue to achieve growth at this rate? Consider possible ways forward against the need to achieve or maintain a clear strategic direction, concentration and consistency.

organisation. In business organisations, strategy operates on at least three levels: corporate, business and functional, and it is important to distinguish the different levels.

2.5.1 Corporate strategy

Corporate strategy refers to the strategy of the company as a legal entity, whether it is a multibusiness, multinational conglomerate, or a single-site, single-product business. It is concerned with the development of the company in relation to the criteria of its owners: for quoted companies this means such measures as market capitalisation, assets per share, price/earnings performance, earnings per share growth, return on equity and so forth.

Corporate strategy is not simply the summation of the strategies of the different businesses in the company – it is different in kind from business strategy. Nor is corporate strategy concerned directly with the details of any particular business strategy, but it may be concerned with maintaining a portfolio of businesses, balanced in terms of such concepts as growth, cash flow and profit.

The decisions of corporate strategy are therefore mainly concerned with the following:

1. The acquisition of individual businesses.
2. Levels of new investment in those businesses and the returns obtained.
3. The liquidation and/or disposal of individual businesses.
4. The maintenance of a balanced portfolio of businesses.

The corporate strategist adopts the perspective of the shareholder, or potential shareholder with respect to the subsidiary business. Responsibilities for corporate strategy are more like those of unit trust management than they are those of business management.

If a subsidiary business does not perform, the corporate strategist has a relatively limited array of options which should be considered:

1. The top management of the business can be changed.
2. New investment can be increased or curtailed.
3. The business can be sold or closed down.
4. The results of the business can be more closely monitored.

However, corporate managers are not normally sufficiently knowledgeable of the individual business to take responsibility for its management. The way the subsidiary business operates, the technologies it uses and the way it serves its customers are the specific responsibility of the subsidiary business management.

In practice, however, it often happens as a result of simple hierarchical pecking orders, that the corporate strategist has the power to interfere in the day-to-day running of subsidiary businesses and the temptation for such interference is often not resisted. It is often done simply by directing how the subsidiary business should be run, or by dictating the strategic direction of future capital investments. Very often it is achieved through the simple means of requiring unrealistic cash and profit targets to be met by the subsidiary business. This necessarily prevents the subsidiary business managers taking a truly strategic view of their business, having instead to concentrate on short-term targets. This is the opposite effect of that intended by the 'balanced portfolio' concept which provides a benign setting in which the troughs of one subsidiary might be offset by the peaks of a sister business.

Sometimes the inhibition of focus on business strategy is mitigated by the existence of a common thread between separate subsidiary businesses which allows the corporate element to provide business support in terms of shared resources such as R&D. This reduces costs to the subsidiary or provides facilities which would not otherwise be affordable. However, the resulting confusion of strategy usually results in simple conglomeration where the common thread is random. Although benign corporate parenting is feasible, as Goold *et al.* have pointed out (1994, and Reading Review 26), it remains problematic and there are few examples of prolonged successful conglomeration.

ABB of Zurich is a widely quoted example of a successful organisation which appears to operate in this way. ABB employs around 225,000 people in more than 1,200 subsidiary companies and over 5,000 profit centres with no more than 100 people at corporate headquarters. There are strands of commonality connecting various of the subsidiaries who contribute in groups to shared resource centres which open up possibilities not available to them individually. However, the key to ABB's success is generally ascribed to the degree of autonomy granted to the subsidiary businesses which certainly control their own business strategy: it is not dictated, or even second guessed, by ABB corporate management.

Whether overt and deliberate or implicit and unintended, the result of corporate management dictating subsidiary business strategy is to undercut and constrain the effectiveness of subsidiary business management, as indicated in the work of Hayes, Abernathy, Garvin, Skinner and others (see Reading Reviews 8, 10 and 12). As Goold *et al.* suggest,

> *while a few multibusiness companies have corporate strategies that create substantial value, the large majority do not; they are value destroyers.*
>
> (Goold *et al.*, 1994 p. 3)

2.5.2 Business strategy

Business strategy is concerned with how to make an individual business survive and grow and to be profitable in the long term. The main considerations are:

1. The creation of customers.
2. The identification of appropriate market niches where a leadership position can be achieved.
3. The identification of customer needs and how best they can be satisfied.
4. The application of technology and its future development or substitution.
5. The understanding of competitors and how direct competition may be avoided.
6. The motivation of people to put their efforts and enthusiasm behind the strategic aims of the business.

These are matters of considerable complexity and detail. If they were to be fully managed by the corporate centre of a company of any significant size, they would require a huge and costly headquarters staff which in the end would be self-defeating. On the other hand, such things are the essence of business management, in constant contact with their customers, expert in their technology and intimately knowledgeable about their competitors.

This separation of corporate and business strategies is relatively simple as stated above, but the dichotomy raises a fundamental question. Which is the more important in running a company: corporate strategy or the multiple business strategies of its component parts? This question gets to the core of an individual's business philosophy. For people such as Sir James Goldsmith, Jim Slater and Lord Hanson, for example, corporate strategy was all important. Their companies were deliberately and overtly in the business of buying and selling assets, being concerned primarily with matters of wealth ownership. The individual businesses matter only as contributors to the corporate balance sheet. Each plays a transient role in the ever-changing portfolio of businesses making up the corporate whole, but their individual business strategies are largely irrelevant. The existence of such financially oriented companies arises mainly because of the increasing failure of financial markets to provide secure long-term finance for industry. Proactive corporate strategy of this kind is, however, not the present concern; this book is concerned with wealth creation rather than ownership.

For wealth-creating companies, the individual businesses matter most and such companies are in the vast majority in the UK. For them, corporate prosperity is the summation of the prosperity of the individual businesses, and corporate management's role is to give subsidiary businesses maximum autonomy, support and long-term commitment in order to assist the wealth-creation process.

2.5.3 Functional strategy: marketing

A basic tenet of marketing theory is that marketing management is concerned with the controllable variables of product, price, promotion and distribution, i.e. the marketing mix. Consequently, marketing strategy should logically be concerned with the long-term development of these four important issues. If this is so, then marketing strategy appears to have a considerable overlap with business strategy as outlined above.

However, in practice, most businesses operate along rather different lines. It is almost universally the general manager of a business who has the final responsibility for profit, and one of the key determinants of profit is product price. Thus, although marketing management may recommend price levels and changes, it is usually general management that holds price responsibility and takes the final decision. Moreover, there are usually considerable constraints over marketing management's discretion with regard to product decisions. They may recommend product changes, or product developments, but again it is most often general management that has the ultimate decision responsibility.

Thus there seems to be a substantial divide between the theory and practice of marketing. Theoretical literature seems to suggest that marketing management has more-or-less total responsibility at the business level. In practice, marketing strategy is very much concerned with promotion and distribution strategies and with the initiation and introduction of new products. Thus defined, marketing strategy is a subset of business strategy, though in many situations a most important subset.

The problem arises because marketing can be a set of techniques, a function or department, or even a philosophy, and it is often not clear which definition is being used. The marketing strategy, which is the direct responsibility of the marketing function, is much more limited than the strategy arising from the marketing philosophy.

2.5.4 Functional strategy: operations

Operations strategy might seem at first to be almost a contradiction in terms – an issue can be operational or strategic. However, direction, concentration and consistency are likely to be achieved through the implementation of operations, be they the production of a product or delivery of a service. Moreover, during this period of rapidly developing technology, operations and the maintenance of their competitive edge may be the most costly and organisationally traumatic of all aspects of strategy.

Technological developments have over the past ten years been so fundamental that they have allowed competitive structures which have been set rigid for decades suddenly to be dissolved. They have eliminated huge tranches of unskilled labour and their associated costs, and they have permitted the economic production of entirely new products and services designed specifically to satisfy specialised customer needs.

While these possibilities are available, operations strategy is a vital source of competitive strength. A survey of manufacturing strategy in Europe, America and the Far East suggests, further, that the most fierce global competitive battle is over the issue of manufacturing strategy (Meyer *et al.*, 1989). Many businesses still focus their operations efforts on traditional cost reduction programmes through standardisation, especially of quality standards, and particularly through long production runs. However, the leaders are concentrating on achieving cost efficiency based on flexible manufacturing and so are better equipped to handle the ever shorter product life cycles and more volatile product demand that now seem inevitable.

Operations strategy is concerned with service decisions just as much as production and the investment in new technology, systems and structures to improve the level or efficiency of customer service are becoming progressively more important issues.

Thus operations strategy, like a tightly defined marketing strategy, is a subset of business strategy identifying a set of management actions required to achieve the overall business strategy.

2.5.5 The integration of strategy

All these different aspects of strategy can be considered separately. Corporate strategy relates to the company's interface with the providers of its capital, while business strategy and its two main substrategies in marketing and operations are concerned with what makes the business prosper in relation to its customers, competitors and technologies.

Although separate, if strategy as a whole is to be effective, the separate elements must be consistent with each other and reinforce each other, rather than be incompatible or even competitive. If corporate strategy and business strategy conflict, as they not infrequently do, it often tends to be the business which is prevented from achieving its potential as a result of corporate constraints. This problem is almost inevitable in a large multibusiness company.

The hierarchical structure of strategy has implications for the way organisations are structured. It is now widely seen as desirable to take decisions as near to the front line as possible. Local managers are inevitably more in touch with the pertinent realities, so better decisions are taken locally. Decisions can also be taken faster the closer they are to the action. Moreover, the devolution of responsibility and authority has a powerful motivational effect.

However, the 'simple form and lean staff' which are the aims of most large companies today, have served mainly to preserve the bureaucratic form. Typically, the lean staff at headquarters impose control on subsidiary or divisional businesses, first by retaining responsibility for strategy and, secondly, through a small number of financial performance measures, usually set at levels which include some 'stretch'. The practical result of this is that the divisional-level business operates as the most rigid form of machine bureaucracy (Mintzberg, 1983). There are immense pressures on divisional managers to conform to the performance rules, customs and practice, and culture of the parent organisation. Their salaries, careers and pensions depend on conformity. The attempt to give divisions the benefits of autonomy together with the muscle of financial security has in the main failed because the autonomy is not compatible with control, and control is extremely difficult to devolve.

The business unit is the wealth producer on which the rest of the company depends. The problems of balancing a portfolio of business units are of secondary importance compared with the prime business function of wealth creation. Thus although business unit management may report to corporate management and although business strategy is in essence a subset of corporate strategy, it is important to recognise that it is the business unit that really matters and getting *business* strategy right is the key to long-term financial results. Now consider Cooper Soft Drinks again (see Box 2.4).

BOX 2.4

Cooper Soft Drinks Ltd (3)

Over the years, Cooper has tried many times to introduce distinctive new products in an attempt to replicate, even in a small way, the Coca-Cola story. In this quest it has recently unearthed the recipe for a soft drink which had been highly successful in the Midlands region between the wars but had been discontinued when its producer was taken over and closed down as part of an industry rationalisation process in 1953. This product was previously called 'Spa Tona Iron Brew'. It contained a reduced amount of sugar, was rich in iron and had a distinctive 'dry' flavour. It had been popular both as a normal soft drink and as a component of beer shandy. Cooper had seen old advertisements for the product emphasising its health-giving properties. Having recreated Spa Tona strictly according to the old recipe, Cooper conducted very careful test markets in the Midlands and in the South East. These had been very encouraging in terms of consumer acceptance of the product. It was recognised as a valid health drink, particularly amongst adults.

Cooper propose to produce Spa Tona and promote it as a health product, distributed nationally through chemists and health food specialists, and priced with a substantial premium. Once established in this market niche, Cooper envisaged exploiting its premium image by wider promotion through all the main existing outlets.

DISCUSSION POINTS

Put yourself in the place of a director of Hudson Holdings, Cooper's parent company. You have been shown a dossier on the proposed new product Spa Tona and the plan for its promotion initially as a specialist product and subsequently to the mass market. The Spa Tona proposal includes an interesting but, for Cooper's, a very costly promotion campaign including a level of advertising many times higher than any previous product.

1. What are your immediate views for the prospects of success for the new product?
2. What information would you require Cooper to provide before you could reach any decision about the validity of the proposal?
3. How do you feel the proposal lines up with Cooper's stated strategy?

2.6 Analytical and transformational perspectives

Orthodox strategic planning of the sort outlined in Figure 2.2 is clearly dependent on extensive analysis. For example, an analysis of the firm's internal capabilities is made to assess its potential for exploiting opportunities presented by the market. Its weaknesses and limitations are analysed to see how critical they are in the light of the threats posed by technological, financial and product environments. Analysis is extensive, in practice often too extensive, giving rise to the adage 'paralysis by analysis'. The uncertain outcome of such formal planning systems clearly indicates that analysis alone is an insufficient guarantor of success.

Analysis may contribute to the definition of direction, but it may not much assist the process of concentration. To achieve this the direction must be communicated to the people in the organisation in a way which is memorable and capable of gaining widespread support and commitment. Only if it is communicated and supported will it in any way transform what people in the organisation actually do; and unless it has this transformational effect it will clearly not achieve the purpose of strategy.

Most approaches to strategy are analytical and not transformational, some are neither. Most strategy frameworks are based on analytical tools and lack any intrinsic transformational impact. Financial planning, life cycle analysis, experience curves, business portfolios, economic analysis, scenario-based planning and many more are all analytically based and lack transformational power. A few approaches are driven by missionary zeal with little requirement for sound analysis. These can be self-defeating if they are completely unrealistic. To be effective, strategy must be both analytical and transformational.

Strategy itself is transformational. Competent management achieves increments in performance through the application of ordinary management disciplines. This is the context in which various fashionable initiatives prosper such as business process re-engineering, downsizing, de-layering, just-in-time, total quality management, kaisen, kanban, quality circles, management by objectives, and so on. These are legitimate management tools based on a common rationale and their application should lead to continuous improvement. But they do not lead to transformational step changes in performance or direction. Only strategy achieves the transformational changes.

But strategy is unlikely to achieve the step changes if it is not itself to some degree inspirational. An exploitative, manipulative strategy is unlikely to gain the support and wholehearted commitment of people (Reynolds, 1986). To achieve this, a strategy must be ethical – an unethical strategy is unlikely to inspire many and will therefore fail to transform the organisation.

This brief section may have been largely prescriptive and rather didactic and the reader is encouraged to be critical. The analytical and transformational theme will be returned to when considering each of the strategy frameworks in Part Two. For the moment, the dual requirement for strategy has been stated, if not yet fully justified, and the reader is encouraged to consider the stated requirement in relation to the strategies of either case study organisations or real businesses they know. These two questions need to be asked of any approach to strategy:

1. Is it analytically sound?
2. Is it transformational?

Summary

- Strategy is concerned with thinking and doing, not about planning. It is not a technique but a way of understanding and managing an organisation according to a strategic perspective.
- Strategy management is essentially purposive – the idea of an 'emergent school' of strategy management is empty.
- Drucker's initial enquiry of an organisation focuses on key strategic issues:
  - What business are you in?
  - Who are your customers?

  - What do they value?
- The idea behind strategy is extremely simple:
  - Where are we now?
  - Where do we want to get to?
  - How shall we get there?
    Start moving.
  - How are we doing?
- The inputs to strategy include analysis, plans, unplanned patterns, trial and error and simple good luck.
- The outputs from strategy include individual decisions (including millions of mini-decisions about the allocation of effort and enthusiasm as well as major one-off investment decisions), patterns of decisions, position, culture and failure (i.e. unrealised strategy).
- The purpose of strategy which goes beyond the aims of day-to-day management is:
  - Setting direction
  - Achieving concentration
  - Maintaining consistency
  - Retaining flexibility
- Strategy works at various levels in an organisation:
  - Corporate strategy
  - Business strategy
  - Functional strategy: marketing and operations
- The different levels of strategy should be complementary and compatible, not conflicting.
- Strategy of the business unit is the main focus of attention here since that is the strategy of wealth creation, whereas corporate strategy is the strategy of wealth ownership.
- To be effective, strategy needs to be based on sound analysis and also to be capable of motivating people in the organisation, i.e. to be transformational.

Further reading

Mintzberg, H., 'Crafting strategy', *Harvard Business Review*, July/August, 1987.
Reading Reviews 13 and 14.

Chapter 3

Strategy and objectives

If an organisation is a purposive group, albeit shaped and influenced by various external factors; and the distinctive characteristic that strategy gives to an organisation is a direction on which to concentrate, then objectives are the means of making these ideas operational.

There have been various theoretical approaches to objectives derived from economics, finance, the social science of management itself and from managerialists. But there has been no general model of business and corporate objectives.

This chapter proposes a general model which incorporates the aims of business organisations which takes account of their economic, financial and strategic aims and also provides a way of incorporating the social/moral responsibilities of business.

3.1 Introduction

Objectives are the cornerstone of any management activity. They are the means of expressing the purpose of organisation. They may describe a desired end state or the processes in which the organisation will engage; an intended level of performance or minimum levels of achievement for survival. They can refer to immediate activities or long-term aims, activities of an individual or to the whole organisation, qualitative or quantitative. The concept is so general as to be almost meaningless and it is tempting therefore to engage in definitions which, for example, ascribe precise meaning to terms like strategic objectives, strategic intent, mission and vision. The problem with this is that there is no general consensus over the meanings, so any precision would be lost outside this particular text. The alternative approach is not to worry about definitions; understanding will not be inhibited so long as the particular meaning is clear as the terms are being used.

The following sections trace the development of ideas about business objectives, from classical economists through to more recent practitioners. This suggests the logic for a hierarchical ordering of all objectives which incorporates corporate, business strategic and operational objectives in a comprehensive and integrated model, the description of which occupies the major part of this chapter.

One of the key strategic issues of any organisation, acknowledged time after time by top practitioners, is the question of ethical performance. It is clear from the rapid growth of interest in business ethics that integrity is a characteristic which lies deep in the culture of organisations. It is not simply an additional factor which organisations may or may not adopt as the occasion suits. It is clearly seen as an important factor in strategy management. Yet there is no recognised way of building integrity into the strategy process. In its academic treatment it tends to be taught as a separate subject, though recognised as all-pervasive.

For a short-term profit maximiser, integrity would be seen simply as a constraint which they might well choose to ignore. But for strategy managers, integrity demands their attention as both an input and output of the strategy process. The point is laboured here because some considerable part of the hierarchical model of objectives is devoted to an explanation of how integrity can be built into the fabric of an organisation's strategy.

3.2 Multiple objectives

Classical economics was based on the mathematically convenient concept of profit maximisation. The entrepreneur was held to equate marginal revenue with marginal cost, at which point his level of profit would be maximised. The beauty of this was its mathematical simplicity – for economists, basic calculus solves the problem of management – but the theory only works if all the underpinnings of perfect competition are assumed. This is quite unrealistic and not useful to practitioners.

Slightly more realistic ideas were developed, such as sales revenue maximisation (Baumol, 1959), management utility maximisation (Williamson, 1963) and the behavioural model of Cyert and March (1963). This latter model indicated that major decisions tended to be made by compromise between coalitions of managers aiming to satisfy at least the minimum requirements of all interested parties. Whilst realistic, the Cyert and March model defied any attempt to make it mathematically tractable so it lost much of its theoretical attraction.

Accountancy has had a major impact on the theory, as well as the practice, of business objectives. Accounting considerations lead to multiple financial objectives which may have an internal focus such as return on assets, asset turnover, margins on sales, and so on, or an external focus such as share performance targets (price/earnings ratios, dividend yields). Whilst these are frequently adopted as corporate objectives, they have limited strategic value.

Almost half a century ago Drucker (1955) cited the necessity for objectives in the areas of market standing, innovation, productivity, physical and financial resources, profitability, manager performance and development, worker performance and attitude, and, finally, public responsibility. Some of these ideas have dated somewhat – the distinction between manager development and worker attitude now seems inappropriate – but the general picture is still applicable. It is a complex picture where objectives will often be in opposition to each other. Maximising one would inevitably lead to failure with another. A balance has to be achieved, but it is not clear how this should best be done. Drucker's idea was an unstructured checklist. Management's job was to achieve the optimum balance between conflicting objectives, and how this should be done was left up to the individual manager and individual organisation.

The systems approach (Emery and Trist, 1965) presented the firm as a complex open system having a constantly changing relationship with its various environments. These are the firm's product markets, its suppliers, technological, financial and labour environments, government and society. Management's job was to control the boundary conditions of the firm, i.e. its relationship with these various environments.

The idea of boundary management and of constantly changing relationships cast some new light on the subject. The idea of managing the firm's relationship with, for example, its financial environment, implies managing the firm's share price. This would not simply be a matter of maximising the shareholders' wealth, but managing the share so that its performance was sufficient to permit adequate performance in other boundary areas. Increasing the shareholders' wealth by more than necessary would be just as wasteful as over-designing a product, i.e. giving the customer something they neither wanted nor were prepared to pay for. The idea of managing the firm's relations with its various, and often competing environments, still implies management's role is basically a balancing act. There is no intrinsic direction, no suggestion of a dominant, overarching objective.

The objectives set by the parent company of Cooper Soft Drinks are typical of those many firms use and it would be useful at this stage to give some consideration to the questions raised in Box 3.1.

Norton and Kaplan (1997) took up the issue of objectives in developing the concept of the 'balanced scorecard', which addresses both operational and strategic performance. They found that most companies still measure their performance in terms of financial ratios plus some process measures such as quality, productivity and unit costs. These were measures of past performance not future potential. When Norton and Kaplan looked at the factors which determined the company's success they

BOX 3.1
Cooper's objectives

Review the material in Box 2.1.

1. Are Hudson's objectives (17 per cent return on capital employed and 9 per cent annual growth in earnings per share) strategic? Explain your answer.
2. Do the objectives have strategic implications for its subsidiary businesses like Cooper? If so, what are they?

found that success was largely dependent on things that went unmeasured, such as customer satisfaction and loyalty, employee commitment and speed of organisational learning. There was thus a measurement gap. Norton and Kaplan also identified what they referred to as a strategy gap, i.e. the avowed strategy was rarely expressed in measurable terms. The 'balanced scorecard' is a way of overcoming these two gaps by adopting appropriate operational measures. As with strategy itself, the concept is simple but the practice rather more difficult. It requires a detailed analysis of the particular situation, decisions as to what really matters to the organisation and development of measures of those really important factors for inclusion on the scorecard.

Norton and Kaplan have reduced the confusion which arises from unstructured multiple objectives which require trading off against each other. The aim of the hierarchical model described in the next section is to prioritise the different objectives so that they can be used to focus effort and guide the firm towards a unified strategic approach.

3.3 Hierarchy of objectives

The systems approach to boundary management implies that the firm ought to set financial objectives, for instance, which would ensure the share price performed well enough to safeguard the firm's continued independence, together with its ability to raise such finance as would be required to perform on other objectives, such as market standing and innovation. Thus the financial objectives would be required to be achieved, in order that other objectives could be aimed for.

This seems to imply a hierarchical ordering of objectives, as shown in Figure 3.1, which may be regarded as a hierarchy of intrinsic business needs. At the lowest level,

Top level – business strategy objectives
Exploiting the distinctive competence of the business

Third level – satisfaction of stakeholders
Satisfaction of customers, employers, shareholders, suppliers, directors and bankers, etc.

Second level – business survival
Cash flow and liquidity, profitability, stock market, suppliers, directors and bankers

First level – business existence
Customers, people with skills and knowledge, money, equipment, raw materials and indirect supplies

Figure 3.1 Hierarchy of objectives

the business needs basic resources of customers, people, money, machines and raw materials. Without these it could not exist. Above these are the needs for survival against both insolvency and being taken over. Above these are the needs to satisfy the stakeholders in the firm, including its customers, employees, shareholders and suppliers. The top level need, analogous to Maslow's self-actualisation, is the fulfilment of the purpose of the business, doing what it is uniquely good at, exploiting what Selznick referred to as its 'distinctive competence' (Selznick, 1957).

When a low-level need has been satisfied, the business moves up to the next level. When liquidity and profitability are sufficient to ensure survival, and when this reality is being reflected in the price level of the company's shares, then the business is able to turn its attention to satisfying its stakeholders.

Integrity has an important role to play in these objectives. One of the foundations of stakeholder satisfaction is trustworthiness. It would not matter how well paid employees were, for example; if they did not trust their employers they would only regard their relationship as economic and opportunistic. The same applies to all stakeholders. If potential customers regarded a supplier as untrustworthy they would be reluctant to buy the product, fearing its integrity in terms of reliability, quality, longevity, or even the supplier's aftersales service. Real satisfaction has to be based on a perception of integrity. In fact, integrity goes deeper than merely satisfaction. If a firm is seen as being untrustworthy it will, all other things being equal, be excluded from all manner of mutually beneficial partnerships and alliances which form the basis of most contemporary organisations. Gauthier's two farmers described in Box 3.2 highlight the importance of trust. This model is really a simple version of the prisoner's dilemma games theory model which serves to generalise the relationships of the two farmers.

The prisoner's dilemma involves two individuals both accused of the same crime being kept separate from each other during interrogation. If they both plead guilty they get one year each. If one prisoner pleads not guilty and turns evidence on the other he gets off and the other gets ten years. If they both plead not guilty and blame each other they both get five years. How should each plead? Obviously the best out-

BOX 3.2

Co-operating/competing farmers

Gauthier (1991) describes two neighbouring farmers, we will call them Milosevic and Mandela. They share a fairly simple primitive philosophy. They are both essentially rational human beings who act as profit maximisers in their business decisions and are unconstrained by any particular views of morality.

They discuss their arable crops. Milosevic's crop is ready for harvesting immediately, while Mandela's will not be ready for two weeks. If they work alone to harvest their crops it will take 200 hours each. If they work together on each other's crops it will take 25 per cent less time.

How do you think each farmer would and should proceed?

come for either individual is to blame the other so long as the other prisoner pleads guilty. If the game is played just once, some players might adopt this strategy though it clearly has a risk – if they both adopt it then they both get five years.

Axelrod studied prisoner's dilemma tournaments and noted that the tendency for players to co-operate (i.e. both plead guilty) increased dramatically whenever a player was paired repeatedly with the same partner (Axelrod, 1984). In this situation a strategy emerged as follows: co-operate on the first move, then follow suit on all subsequent moves, i.e. co-operate when your partner co-operates, cheat if they cheat, at least until the end of the game is in sight. This was referred to as a tit-for-tat strategy.

Tit-for-tat is a strategy of co-operation in the first period and from then on mimics the rival's action from the previous period.

> *Tit-for-tat embodies four principles that should be evident in any effective strategy: clarity, niceness, provocability, and forgivingness. Tit-for-tat is as clear and simple as you can get. It is nice in that it never initiates cheating. It is provocable, that is, it never lets cheating go unpunished. And it is forgiving, because it does not hold a grudge for too long and is willing to restore co-operation.*
>
> (Dixit and Nalebuff, 1991, pp. 106–7)

Axelrod showed that players adopting the tit-for-tat strategy would seek each other out and go on to accumulate higher scores than other players who adopted more short-term strategies of defection. This conclusion was repeated again and again both in computer tournament results and from computer simulations as well as being paralleled in biological systems. This suggests that the specific example of Gauthier's farmers (Box 3.2) has a more general validity.

Ridley goes further, suggesting even the success of species is not simply a matter of survival of the fittest made operational through selfish genes, but is dependent on social behaviour based on well founded mutual trust (Ridley, 1996), which in organisational terms can replace the necessity of hierarchy by enabling trust-based lateral control (Jönnson, 1996, and Reading Review 28). Clearly, as Hosmer suggests, it will be important to build this into the strategy process (Hosmer, 1994, and Reading Review 27).

Integrity can be made operational in many different ways which will be considered later, though it should be stressed from the outset that business at least is not purely altruistic; ethical considerations are important but they are not the purpose of business. As Levitt put it so long ago, the business of business is making profits not 'sweet music' (Levitt, 1958, see also Reading Review 1).

The hierarchy of objectives makes a similar point. Where management is involved in making trade-off decisions, the priority accorded to the satisfaction of its stakeholders is at level 3. That is, it is not in itself the object of the business, but it represents a higher level of aspiration then mere survival.

If at any time the business is threatened by shortage of cash, or any basic resource, this threat immediately becomes operative and is likely to dominate the whole business activity, even to the exclusion of ethical considerations. When the threat has been overcome and survival is no longer a problem, then the business can resume aiming to satisfy the higher-level needs which embody considerations of trust and integrity.

All objectives have their place in the hierarchy, and the way they are defined will depend on what they are. Financial objectives will be expressed quantitatively and they will be set at a level where their satisfaction ensures the independent survival of the business. The whole hierarchy is ever present, although the levels which are operational at any one time will change.

None of the objectives below the top level is a maximisation objective. They only require some minimum level of achievement in order that the business may then seek to satisfy the next higher level in the hierarchy.

The business is focused on achieving its top level, strategy objectives. Anything more than satisfaction of needs at lower levels merely serves to inhibit the firm in its attempts to satisfy its strategic objective. From time to time the lower-level needs become operative and then the firm has to shift its attention away from, say, the long-term strategy towards short-term survival. This is common enough experience when managements may find it prudent to ration capital, postpone long-term developments, slash R&D expenditure, and so on. In a cost-driven culture, such actions can take on an almost heroic aspect, as though the sole aim of the business is to cut costs and operate efficiently, rather than these being merely means to the strategic end.

The hierarchical view of objectives provides a systematic way in which a firm may balance the conflicting priorities of various opposing interests. In particular, it helps management to balance the long-term interests of the business itself against the short-term interests of the firm's financial environment and to give the ethical concerns of a business – its need to be perceived as trustworthy – their appropriate priority.

Businesses really do co-operate in many different ways with all the different agencies with which they transact, whether they are internal or external stakeholders. For example, businesses extend each other reciprocal credit so long as their relationship is expected to continue. However, if liquidation of one party looms, then co-operation would be terminated, no matter how long the history of previous co-operation. The assumed continuity of the relationship is crucial to its viability.

Figure 3.2 shows a refined version of the hierarchy in which the existence level objectives have been omitted as they are relevant only in a start-up situation. The rules of prepotency still hold, but the picture has been complicated by the inclusion of social responsibility objectives relating to the local community and to the environment. In addition, the nature of the strategic objectives has been identified in rather more detail and the treatment of customers separated from other stakeholders. Pleasing customers is prerequisite to concentrating on the strategic objective, but is not itself the ultimate focus of the business. This version of the hierarchy also formalises the inclusion of the organisation's need to be recognised as trustworthy by all stakeholders.

It is crucial for managers always to be aware of the level in the hierarchy on which the business is focused. A business whose survival is threatened may be expected to behave in a quite different fashion from a business which is securely focused on achieving its strategic aim, whatever that is. In this a business is no different from any other biological or social system. Constraints which are fully operative under normal stable conditions, including the treatment of all stakeholders and consideration given to ethical constraints, are completely broken when survival is threatened.

Strategic objective or mission

BEATING COMPETITORS through:
a LEADERSHIP position, or,
a UNIQUE characteristic, or
a SUPERLATIVE in some aspect of performance
that is PERCEIVED and VALUED by the customer

Pleasing customers

By conformance to all expectations on all product (or service) attributes and exceeding expectations on at least one attribute which customers regard as important

Satisfying stakeholders

By equitable and acceptable performance in all transactions with employees, suppliers, shareholders, directors, bankers, the local community and the environment

Survival

Performance in terms of liquidity and transactions with creditors

Figure 3.2 Hierarchy of business objectives

The suggested level of performance at the intermediate levels of the objectives hierarchy is that which will enhance the organisation's reputation for integrity rather than diminish it. Clearly this is not a simple mechanistic calculation but a matter for management judgement in the individual case.

At the top strategic level, different rules apply. The focus at this level is in essence to be better than competitors; to provide the customer with better value than competitors in ways that the customer thinks important. This is the normal meaning of beating competitors. Where competitors try to provide value by exactly the same means there is head-to-head competition and then the intention to beat competitors may lead ultimately to their destruction. Indeed, in these circumstances, their destruction may be the deliberate intention of an effective strategy.

The objectives hierarchy provides a rational explanation of how financial and strategic objectives relate to each other. Any rationale for this is generally lacking otherwise. Many writers acknowledge the difference, even the incommensurability of the two. For example, Porter (1988) highlights the fact that financial and strategic measures are often diametrically opposed and contradictory, as discussed in section 3.7 below. Grundy (1993 and Reading Review 25) investigates how the two can be linked in practice, but is in the end forced to acknowledge the difficulty.

The following sections look in rather more detail at the top two levels of objectives.

3.4 Pleasing customers

Pleasing customers is not the ultimate strategic aim of the business, but a means to that end. Therefore the resources devoted to it are calculated, rather than lavished sentimentally or passionately as some writers suggest. Having a passion for the customer will lead to waste and to inhibiting the achievement of strategic objectives.

Some businesses do stick at this level and never identify or pursue a higher-level strategic aim. The distinction between pleasing customers and beating competitors may not always be clear, but this is largely because many firms fall so far short of pleasing their customers.

The customer/supplier relationship is generally managed through the set of variables which are said to be controllable by marketing managers and include promotion, product, price and distribution – the 4 Ps or marketing mix.

The first contact with the customer is through promotion. This is likely to set the tone of the whole relationship whether it is in the form of advertising, personal selling, public relations or sales promotion. The aims of promotion may be to inform, to persuade, or to alter the underlying affections and perceptions of the audience. Whatever the promotional activity and whatever its aims, it will always be vital to create and maintain an image of trustworthiness and credibility. If the audience disbelieves the message, its communication will be counterproductive.

Advertising, public relations and personal selling have the power to create whatever image the promoter desires. There are notoriously deceptive examples of each: the advertisement claiming for its product magical powers to reduce the weight of the purchaser; the public relations 'story' being a thinly veiled advertisement; the secondhand car salesman claiming one careful owner and extremely low mileage. Some may be deceived, but not many. The implicit message of such promotional initiatives is that the promoter is not to be trusted. While the reality and the image are in conflict the resulting perception is likely to be exactly the opposite of what was intended.

Advertising, public relations and personal selling are the means of creating first impressions. The initial expectations of trustworthiness and credibility are established, to be reinforced or reversed by the product or service itself and the subsequent relationship.

The most important transaction with the customer is through the product itself. The degree to which it satisfies customer expectations will be the most powerful and lasting communication of all. So, what is a product? It is clearly more than just the physical object. An expensive bottle of wine is not usually purchased simply to satisfy a thirst; a car is not bought solely as a means of transportation. Products are loaded, both physically and psychologically, with many extras that may be important determinants of sales success. Marketing literature is replete with descriptions of the many and various components that comprise the modern conception of a product.

One widely held view sees the product as having several layers: the core benefit or service, the formal or expected product and the outer, augmented product layer which includes such things as warranty, service support and so on (for example Kotler, 1984). This onion-like model implies that the product can be unpeeled to reveal hidden depths (see Figure 3.3). The analogy only partially stands up to scrutiny.

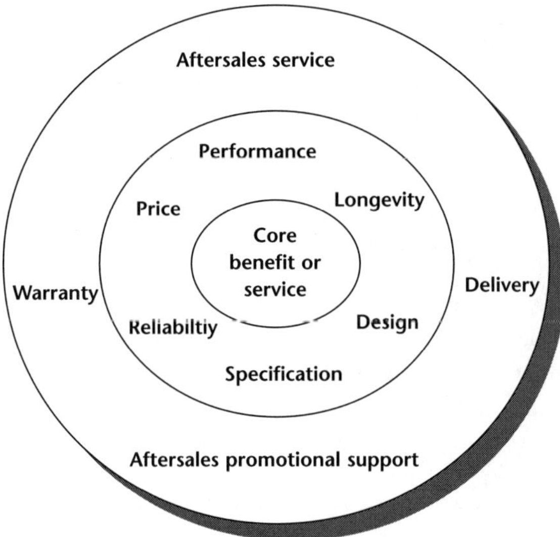

Figure 3.3 Multi-attribute product

There are many and various product attributes that could be categorised for convenience as physical, implied and psychological, but they are not necessarily related in any predictable fashion, onion-like or otherwise.

What matters about this complex product is the customers' perceptions of its various attributes. Producing the best mousetrap is of no avail if it is not perceived as such by potential customers. The customers' perception of the product is an amalgam of their perception of the various product attributes, *any* of which may be critical in adding up to a concept of value which is a combination of price and quality. Moreover, the concept of quality is not simply one-dimensional, but complex. Its definition clearly depends on the type of product or service being delivered. For example, in the case of food products, distribution is clearly critical, whereas in the case of memory chips for computers, failure rates and reliability may be more important to the customer.

Garvin suggested eight characteristics of quality, any of which might be crucial in particular circumstances (Garvin, 1987). The eight characteristics were:

1. Primary performance
2. Secondary features
3. Reliability
4. Conformance
5. Durability
6. Serviceability
7. Aesthetics
8. Perceived quality

Primary performance refers to the product or service's primary operating characteristics, and Garvin noted that these were usually capable of objective measurement. In the case of cars, for example, performance would include such measures as speed, acceleration and noise levels. In the case of fast-food, or airlines, performance may be mainly a matter of prompt service.

Secondary features are also usually amenable to objective measurement. They are the extras which may differentiate an otherwise standard product. The following are examples of secondary features:

- Customer selection of detailed product specification, for example General Motors dealers provide computer terminals which allow customers to select the features they want and the specified car is delivered within seven days.
- Free drinks on an aeroplane.
- 'Clever' remote controls for a hi-fi.
- Flexibility and a wide variety of options in personal investment plans.

Reliability refers to the probability of a product breaking down in use. Clearly this is the key characteristic of many industrial and consumer durable products. Improved standards of reliability achieved in one sector, notably in electronics, appears to have a knock-on effect in other sectors. Customers are now generally less tolerant of poor product reliability than previously.

Conformance refers to the achievement of product specifications, for example dimensions within agreed tolerances. Again this is usually critical in industrial products, particularly where products are to be assembled with other products of similarly defined specifications.

Durability is the expected product life and may be determined either by technical or economic factors. Durability is a characteristic which differs widely between brands – Garvin cites as examples washing machines which have expected lives of from 5.8 to 18 years, and tumble dryers of 6 to 17 years, for makes of differing quality.

Serviceability refers to the ease, speed, competence and courtesy with which service is provided (i.e. products delivered, queries answered, repairs achieved and so on). Clearly this characteristic is in some respects less amenable to objective measurement. Actual machine downtimes resulting from breakdown may be open to accurate measurement, but the competence and courtesy of the service engineer are subjective measures likely to be influenced by individual circumstances. Subjectivity highlights the importance of customer complaints handling and, in particular, obtaining the maximum amount of information about customer perceptions as a result of these transactions.

Aesthetics – the look, feel, sound, taste or smell of a product – are clearly a subjective measure, which again means deliberate and calculated steps need to be taken to achieve any measure of consumer perceptions.

Perceived quality refers to consumers' perceptions of quality which may or may not be the same as reality. A firm may have established a reputation for quality which naturally attaches to any product the company offers. The corporate or brand image affects the way that potential customers will perceive the product even before its introduction. Clearly this is a powerful factor which may make the difference between success and failure with the introduction of a new product.

These eight dimensions of quality are largely in accord with the product attributes of Figure 3.3. The main omission is the price attribute. However, Garvin's dimensions of quality strike much deeper into the organisation than do the marketer's product attributes, affecting the way each individual in the organisation does his or her job. The marketer's product attributes may, in organisational terms, be quite superficial even though they may be important aspects of the product or service itself. For example, packaging may contribute substantially to the customer's perception of the product, but the impact of packaging on individuals in the organisation may be minimal.

A ten-characteristic product (see Figure 3.4), based on Garvin's dimensions of quality and including also the essential characteristics of price and a tenth one labelled 'attribute X' is proposed here as the vehicle for pleasing the customers. Attribute X is not simply a selling proposition (unique or otherwise), or a marketing gimmick of some kind, but an additional characteristic which arises directly from the core competences of the producer and which is intended to provide customer satisfaction above expectations. As such, attribute X may be the means of beating competitors, i.e. of achieving the strategic objective.

Canon's infinitely scaleable fonts on its low-cost laser printer was an added ingredient which gave it an extra competitive advantage over its main rivals when it was first offered. In the case of service sector businesses, attribute X may well relate to special elements of superior service which differentiate the business from its competitors. Attribute X is not simply a marginal factor in differentiation, it is a remarkable added attribute which takes the customer by surprise. It is a fundamental characteristic, stemming directly from the firm's core competences and is therefore

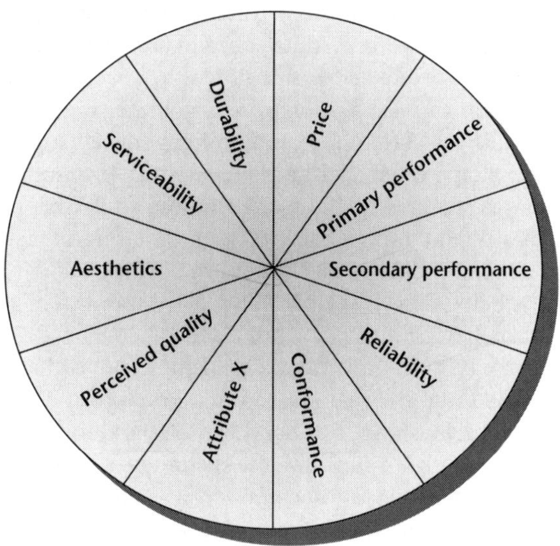

Figure 3.4 The ten-characteristic product

not easy for competitors to replicate. Clearly it will not be possible for every business to develop a product or service with a real attribute X, but for those that do, it may be the most important characteristic of all.

These ten characteristics are the components of value which the firm delivers to please its customer. Few firms could successfully pursue all ten; being leader simultaneously in all ten would be hardly possible. Being the price leader may well preclude leadership on any other attribute, and several of the others may well conflict. Management's aim must be to provide a balance of characteristics which accords with the requirements of customers. This is the business of pleasing customers and is clearly a far more demanding task than simply satisfying them. The integrity of the ten-characteristic product is crucial.

Delivery and distribution channels can play an important part in confirming the image that has been created by promotion and by the product itself. An inappropriate distribution channel might severely dent the impact of the image so far created, and standard marketing texts are comprehensive in addressing this issue. However, there is an aspect of distribution which is particularly important to the current examination.

In Porter's competitive strategy video (Porter, 1988) a fairly detailed case study was provided on Skil Corporation, the American power tool manufacturer. Skil had around 7 per cent of the US market against Black & Decker's 44 per cent, had no particular competitive strengths against Black & Decker and no very strong strategic focus. After extremely moderate financial performance Skil was taken over by Emerson Electric in 1979.

Emerson standardised and improved Skil's product range, cut back and re-equipped its manufacturing facilities and introduced total quality management (TQM), just-in-time (JIT), kaizen and a whole raft of modern management approaches to improve Skil's performance. However, the key to Skil's subsequent strategic success was its distribution strategy. It stopped selling to mass merchandisers and discounters and promised its specialist retailers that it would no longer have to compete with Skil products for sale down the road at cut prices. Black & Decker, which depended on the discounters for its volume, was unable to follow suit. As a consequence, Skil was able to demand and get special support from its chosen distributors, in the shape of special displays, in-store promotion and product support. The strategy was successful. The distributors and Skil had formally reached a relationship of strategic importance to both. Their agreement to collaborate was of great mutual benefit. Skil chose its distributors with great care, the credibility of their trustworthiness being a prime factor. The distributors were also careful. At first they were frankly disbelieving that Skil would refuse to deal with the mass merchandisers. Only as the strategy was implemented and they found that Skil kept its word were they finally hooked into the relationship. It worked for both parties.

Distribution is always important and can be paramount. So too can the aftersales relationship that a business has with its customers. This may vary according to the product. A fast-moving consumer good will require detailed control of the often repeated transactions, order processing, delivery and payment. Reliability and predictability in these various parts of the transaction can be vital, especially with more firms requiring just-in-time service. One-off major purchases need attention to quite different characteristics. For example, the advertising of Porsche cars has had to focus on past purchasers, not simply to maintain customer loyalty but also to eliminate the phenomenon marketers refer to as *cognitive dissonance* – the uncomfortable feeling that spending around £70,000 on a means of getting from A to B was not smart.

Pleasing customers is not just an ill-defined sentimental intention. It involves all of the customer transactions outlined above in a detailed calculation of how the greatest pleasure can be created for the least cost. If each aspect is effectively managed they will all serve to reinforce the customer's initial perceptions. If any particular aspect is not focused effectively on pleasing the customer, it will tend to undercut the intended image and customer perceptions and severely reduce the level of trust that the business is able to establish.

3.5 Strategic objectives

The strategic objective was identified in Figure 3.2 as 'beating competitors, through a leadership position, a unique characteristic or a superlative in some aspect of performance that is perceived and valued by the customer'. This is the objective on which every business should be focused. Making profits, creating shareholder wealth and pleasing customers, are only means to the end of being better than competitors at something the customer values.

Kim and Henderson (1997) warn against using competitors as the focus of strategic objectives. Benchmarking competitor offerings leads to logical increments and to continuous improvement, but it does not lead to strategic innovations and leadership. This is an area of continuing debate. Focusing on competitors can clearly lead to a 'me too' strategy, rather than a strategy which 'dares to be different'. Kim and Henderson asked not what it would take to be better than competitors but what it would take to win the mass of buyers even without marketing. The exclusion of marketing is simply to emphasise their findings that a radical approach to strategy appears to be more successful than incrementalism.

Every viable business has some 'distinctive competence', something at which it is peculiarly effective. It may not be absolutely unique and the firm may not be the best in the world, but at least, in some respect, it must be better than the competitors which also serve its markets. If it were not so, the firm would go out of business.

For the distinctive competence to be of any strategic value it must be embodied in the product or service the customer buys. For example, a firm may be peculiarly effective in R&D, but if the fruits of its research are not incorporated in the firm's product this competence will avail it nothing. Similarly, the distinctive competence might relate to some aspect of cost, but if that strength is not embodied in the product in the form of either reduced price or increased quality it will have no strategic impact.

If the distinctive competence accords with the customer need and is embodied in the product, it creates a leadership position. The idea that profitability is only earned by leadership has been a central Drucker concept over the years (Drucker, 1964 and Reading Review 3). His idea of leadership is, however, not simply a question of market share. For him, leadership has to relate to 'something of value to the customer'. It might be in service, or distribution, or some quite narrow aspect of the product, it might even relate to the firm's 'ability to convert ideas into saleable products'.

A leadership position can potentially attach to any product attribute. So long as it is valued by the customer it can provide the business with economic results. With no leadership position, even if the firm has the major share of the market, the business will at best be 'marginal'. Porter suggested there were just two ways in which leadership could be achieved: by having the lowest costs or the highest prices. Although this approach has been regularly criticised since it was first published in 1979, it has established a prominence in strategy management literature and so far, despite the contributions of Hamel, Prahalad, Quinn, Mintzberg, Porter himself and others, Porter's original model has not been substantially improved. Moreover, it has the great virtue of simplicity.

The aim of competitive strategy is quite simply to achieve a leadership position or competitive advantage so that the firm can beat its competitors. It may do this directly if it achieves the lowest costs and therefore seeks to compete head-on in the knowledge that in any price war it will be the winner. Alternatively, a firm can achieve the highest prices by differentiating its product in some way that customers value. If a leadership position is successfully achieved, by whichever means, it will inevitably attract new competition. Thus, even with a differentiation strategy, it will not prove possible to avoid competitors for ever. In the end, every successful business, whether or not it competes head-on from the outset as the lowest cost producer would, will find itself in direct competition. No matter how reluctant, it will have to deal with the problem of competition and its aim must simply be to beat competitors.

Beating competitors sounds like a rather unethical project, and it is true that some firms adopt dubious tactics to achieve it. But no matter how fierce the competition, whether or not a competitor is driven out of business, the key issue remains one of how to compete in such a way that stakeholder perceptions of the firm's trustworthiness are not diminished and preferably even enhanced. It is by no means clear that tolerating a weak competitor is the strategy most likely to achieve this aim. If a firm cannot be trusted to operate as an effective competitor, could it be trusted in a crucially important strategic alliance?

3.6 Strategic milestones

In this hierarchical model, the lower-level objectives are clearly not milestones along the way to achieving the strategic objective. They may inhibit a focus on trying to attain the top-level objective, but they are not stages along the route. They are simply different in kind, expressed mostly in different language to achieve quite different, though compatible, aims.

Objectives are used in order to focus efforts on achievement and it is usual then to measure achievement against the objectives in order to answer questions like 'How are we doing?' This is simple to answer in financial terms. For example, 15 per cent return on capital employed and 9 per cent per annum growth in earnings per share. But how do these measures relate to the strategic well-being of the business?

Strategic milestones are quite different from the lower-level objectives. Strategic milestones are the measurable steps towards achievement of the top-level, competitor beating, objective. They may be quantified; they will almost certainly be dated; and they will most probably refer to some critical stage along the route. Without exception they will be measurable in the sense that it will be clear when they have been achieved.

One widely quoted example of a strategic objective is Canon's 'Beat Xerox'. This remarkable example was first enunciated at a time when Canon had no position in the photocopier market and ended when it had effectively overtaken and substantially changed the long dominant Xerox Corporation. Had Canon run out of cash along the way it would have had to interrupt its concentration on 'beating Xerox'. But so long as none of the lower-level objectives became prepotent then concentration on the stated direction would be consistently maintained. The milestones along the way to its achievement are summarised in Box 3.3.

Clearly Canon's milestones refer to critical events or stages in the process, which had to be achieved in order to fulfil the overall strategic intent. They are spread over a very long timescale, but it would presumably not be difficult to identify a subset of shorter-term milestones on the achievement of which these major events would be dependent.

Thus, strategic progress is assessed by achievement against strategic milestones, rather than by achievement against lower-level objectives or any orthodox financial assessment.

BOX 3.3

Canon's milestones to beating Xerox

Canon's strategic objective or intent was 'Beat Xerox'. The milestones along the way to its achievement included the following:

Identify existing core competences.

Understand Xerox technology including patents.

Identify the necessary core competences.

Obtain Xerox technology under licence to gain market experience.

Begin to acquire the core competences not already owned.

Invest in R&D to improve on the existing technology.

Progressively acquire necessary core competences.

License out own technology to fund further R&D.

Start by attacking markets where Xerox weakest.

Subsequently make innovative attack on markets where Xerox is strongest (e.g. selling rather than leasing, through channels rather than direct, etc.)

(Based on Hamel and Pralahad, 1989)

 Measures of strategic health

Each successful business has, implicitly or explicitly, a unique strategic objective. In addition, each business may, again implicitly or explicitly, adopt different lower-level objectives. The question arises as to how it is possible to measure how well a business is doing strategically.

The hierarchy of objectives provides some insights; clearly, orthodox financial measures will not do. Accounting methods measure only past performance. Reported profitability is not even a measure of short-term health and performance. Accounting, with impeccable logic, accords the greatest value to the quickest gain – a pound now is worth more than a pound in a year's time, and the quickest pound will be earned from past actions. But strategy is concerned with the future of probably a five or ten year horizon or even longer and it is crucial to have an adequate measure of strategic health and success.

Porter (1988) examined this issue with the CEO of Skil Corporation, the power tool business taken over by Emerson Electric in 1979. Five years after the acquisition Skil was still not very profitable and had lost market share over the period. However, during that five years a lot of action had been taken. The product range had been rationalised to standardise on far fewer components. The number of components in each product had been slashed. Three-quarters of the production factories had been closed. Production facilities had been radically upgraded or replaced with modern flexible plant. Stocks and work in progress had been largely eliminated. The distribution channels had been radically reorganised and Skil had taken the brave decision to stop supplying mass merchandisers who represented around 40 per cent of the total market. The company had been given a new, highly focused strategy, and management had put much effort into communicating this strategy both inside and outside the company so everyone knew what Skil was about. Nevertheless, after five years' hard work, Skil was still not very profitable and had lost market share. From an accountant's perspective the situation would have looked desperate. But from the strategic perspective things looked good. The company had a clear strategic aim. It had concentrated all its efforts on its core technologies and was buying in components where it had no advantage; it had improved its quality and at the same time slashed its costs; it had developed an excellent relationship with its key distributors which were the fastest growing in the industry. It was on target in passing the various milestone objectives towards achievement of its strategy. It was poised for great things, but, as Porter suggested, 'if you had come in from Mars you would have thought Skil was not doing very well'.

Clearly, strategic health and strategic performance were far more important to Skil than its short-term financial performance – it was focused on its high-level objectives. In that particular case, the development of close relationships with specialist distributors was the key to Skil's subsequent success. Skil had around 7 per cent of the US market against Black & Decker's 44 per cent. Skil's wholesale prices to its specialist outlets were higher than its products' retail prices in the mass merchandisers. The same applied of course to Black & Decker, but because of its scale of operation Black & Decker was unable to adopt Skil's strategy, which was in essence the decision to stop supplying mass merchandisers and to create a position of mutual dependence and loyalty between itself and its specialist distributors. The establishment of this interdependent relationship was the basis of Skil's strategy and the source of its success which ultimately, after several years, showed through in enviable profitability.

The measurement of Skil's strategic health could only be achieved by analysing the viability of its strategy, and measurement of its strategic performance in terms of its progress in passing milestones to achieving its strategic objectives. Skil's strategy and strategic objectives were clearly unique to itself. There are no universal measures of strategic health and performance: they are always unique to the individual business and its particular situation. Thus the assessment of strategic health and performance must be made by understanding two particular issues which are unique to the individual business:

1. The strategic aims of the business as expressed in a hierarchy of objectives, and focusing particularly on the practical milestones derived from the statement of strategic aim or mission.
2. The level of objectives on the hierarchy which are operative at any particular time. For example, it is vital to understand whether the business is able to attack its strategic objective or if it is forced to be concerned with survival.

Finally, the links between strategy and finance, though extremely problematic as Grundy (1993) demonstrates, can be made through the objectives hierarchy.

Summary

- The theory of objectives goes back to nineteenth century classical economics with the notion of economic man and the associated idea of profit maximisation which, although interesting mathematically, was recognised as unrealistic.
- In a search for greater realism, economists proposed sales revenue maximisation and subsequently management utility maximisation.
- The behavioural theory of the firm broke away from maximisation and recognised the reality that managements work as coalitions and that organisational objectives result from a trading process which achieves each manager's minimum requirements but no one's maximum.
- Accountants have developed various proxies for maximising shareholder wealth through various stock market ratios, for example dividend yields or price/earnings ratios.
- Drucker proposed that management's responsibility should be to achieve a balance between eight competing responsibilities.
- System's theorists suggested management's job was to control the boundary conditions of the firm, that is, to control the organisation's relationship with its various environments.
- These ideas suggest that management must control the organisation among various competing demands, maximising any one would result in others being unsatisfied and therefore starting to dominate.

- This suggests a model along the lines of Maslow's hierarchy of personal needs and such a model was identified:
  - Top level – mission/strategic intent = beating competitors
  - Third level – pleasing customers
  - Second level – satisfying stakeholders
  - Lowest level – survival
- Contemporary organisations depend on a multitude of partnerships, the existence and success of which depend on the partners being able to trust each other. This applies to internal partnerships between the organisation and its members who are increasingly highly skilled, semi-autonomous individuals or teams. It also applies to external alliances with suppliers, technological collaborators and possibly even co-operating competitors.
- The intermediate-level objectives need to be achieved in a way which enhances, rather than diminishes, the perceived integrity of the business, so that it is as a result the more attractive as a potential partner both internally and externally.
- A relationship of trust or integrity can be conducted by adopting a tit-for-tat strategy. This embodies four principals: clarity, niceness, provocability and forgivingness.
- Stakeholders to be satisfied include employees, suppliers, shareholders, directors, the local community and the environment which is a proxy for future generations.
- Pleasing customers is achieved through all the interactions involved in promotion, the product, its distribution and aftersales interactions.
- The integrity of the product must be perceived in all its primary performance, secondary features, reliability, conformance, durability, serviceability, aesthetics, perceived quality, price and 'attribute X'.
- Beating competitors is the top-level, strategic objective. Its achievement can be planned and monitored by the definition of key milestones.
- Milestones should be tangible, measurable, dated target events.
- Achievement of objectives at lower levels on the hierarchy do not indicate achievement on the way to fulfilling strategic aims. However, their non-achievement will detract from a focus on the strategic objective and inhibit its fulfilment.
- Strategic health is measured by an assessment of how well the organisation is doing against its strategic objective, not by orthodox financial measures.

Further reading

Dixit, A. and Nalebuff, B., *Thinking Strategically: The competitive edge in business, politics and everyday life*, W.W. Norton, 1991.

Drucker, P.F., *Managing for Results*, Harper and Row, 1964 (rev. edn Heinemann, 1989).

Norton, D. and Kaplan, R., *The Balanced Scorecard*, Harvard Business School Press, 1997.

Chapter 4

Corporate strategy

Although this book is concerned almost exclusively with business organisations, under some circumstances diversification and acquisition can be valid ways of progressing business strategy. Moreover, proactive corporate ownership strategies do exist and acquisitive, asset-stripping conglomerates are a fact of life even though they may contribute little to wealth creation.

This chapter briefly reviews this area of business concern, relates it to the hierarchy of objectives identified in the previous chapter, proposes certain categories to clarify corporate strategy and suggests business circumstances where corporate initiatives might be appropriate.

4.1 Introduction

This book is about the strategy of wealth creation, that is, the strategy of an organisation which deals with suppliers and customers and which uses technologies to make and deliver products and services. It is the wealth-creation process that pays for education, health and the other social services which contribute so much to the quality of life of the mass of people. The subject of this chapter, corporate strategy, is concerned with matters of wealth ownership and its reward.

In order to achieve its strategic aim a firm must first satisfy the needs of ownership. The two occupy different positions on the objectives hierarchy. Some firms are driven by considerations of ownership and it is important to examine the distinction between those and firms which are driven by wealth creation. The following section identifies three different organisational types with different strategic orientations.

4.2 Objectives and organisational types

Figure 4.1 shows objectives in the hierarchy introduced in Chapter 3 and identifies them as business or corporate. For most organisations the top two objectives are related to business issues, being concerned with competitors and customers.

Mission/strategic intent
A business objective

Pleasing customers
A business objective

Satisfying stakeholders
By equitable and acceptable performance in all transactions with suppliers, employees, directors, local community and the environment

Business objectives

By equitable and acceptable performance in all transactions with shareholders, bankers, and the financial community

Corporate objectives

Survival
A corporate objective

Figure 4.1 Hierarchy of objectives

Satisfying stakeholders such as suppliers is a business issue while satisfying shareholders is a matter for corporate strategy. Survival is an issue for corporate strategy. Thus corporate strategy is concerned solely with survival and the satisfaction of some of the stakeholders, but not with the higher-level objectives which help to define the organisation's direction and facilitate concentration on that direction consistently over time.

This division between business and corporate objectives is appropriate in most business organisations but not all. In some organisations the business *is* corporate and all the usual definitions are turned on their head. It is important, therefore, to distinguish between different sorts of corporate organisation and to recognise which is the focus of concern, because the rules which apply for one organisational type may be quite inappropriate for another.

For the present purpose it is sufficient to distinguish between three different organisational types:

1. Single business company (SBC)
2. Multibusiness company (MBC)
3. Acquisitive financial conglomerate (AFC)

There have been many AFCs which have been highly successful for certain periods. British examples include Hanson, Tomkins, Trafalgar House, BTR, Williams Holdings, Wassall and, going back to an earlier era, Slater Walker, Jessel Securities and Barclay Securities. A continued slump in share prices would no doubt see another generation of AFCs emerging across the globe.

These acquisitive, financially oriented conglomerates are balance-sheet driven. They buy companies and sell assets. The companies they acquire are the equivalent of their raw materials. The assets they strip out and sell could be regarded as their finished goods. Their focus is on increasing the value of their balance sheet by maximising the value added between acquisition and asset disposal. For such organisations, customers are the shareholders and the aim is to please customers by the company's share performance. There is no strategic objective beyond a continuation of achievement of the lower-level objectives, i.e. the simple aim to maximise shareholder wealth.

The lack of strategic objective for AFCs is clearly apparent when they are viewed over the longer term. Slater Walker and Jessel Securities, two of the most successful of the 1970s, long ago ceased to exist. Trafalgar House tried to establish itself with an industrial logic but failed, and its remnants were taken over. Hanson, which originated around the same time, survived longest, but could not outlive its founding entrepreneurs, Lords Whyte and Hanson and was broken up. Lonrho, similarly the creation of an individual, could not survive the departure of that individual, and was disposed of piecemeal by his successor. In each of these cases, the demise of the founding entrepreneur led inevitably to the company's break-up, sometimes following a vain attempt to impose a business logic on the company.

Sir James Goldsmith, himself a considerable AFC operator in his time, suggested the fate of all AFCs would be to die with their founders, although many founding entrepreneurs who became successful by the AFC route try to metamorphose their creations into MBCs. The change is extremely difficult. The rules for achieving success are entirely different. Whilst business success requires huge commitment to an industry, its technologies, its customers and suppliers and to achieving leadership within that setting, AFC success is dependent on having no such commitments but a willingness to move in and out of industries without hesitation if the immediate balance sheet impact is advantageous.

The rules which are used by AFCs have often been confusingly adopted by SBC and MBC managements and a populist macho-language has developed which emphasises the short-term financial imperatives rather than the longer-term strategic.

For the MBC, corporate strategy can play a *facilitative* role, balancing the peaks and troughs in cash flow, for example, between the different businesses, ensuring support is provided where and when it is needed most or appears likely to create the greatest benefit, this being accomplished within a regime which satisfies, but does not maximise, the various intermediate-level objectives.

For the SBC, corporate issues are the mirror-image of business issues. The success achieved within business strategy will be translated directly into corporate performance and, if it is not reflected in dividend payments, it will eventually be in the capital gains of share price movements.

In practice, most companies fall into the MBC category. Few could be truly described as single businesses except when they are in their start-up phase. Even a company like Marks & Spencer defines itself as many different businesses – food, clothing, furnishings – defined in as much detail as required – purchasing, retailing and distribution, UK, Europe, America and so on. Yet these many businesses are bound together by a single strategic focus which has been maintained consistently over many years. Marks & Spencer, almost uniquely for a major company, may be treated as an SBC from a strategy viewpoint.

Similarly, though to a lesser extent, companies like General Motors are focused around a single strategic concept, and are, to almost all intents and purposes, SBCs. From within, such a company is seen as many different businesses: the different brands, the different locations, the different activities. The distinction between SBC and MBC is sometimes unclear and will depend on the purpose for which the distinction is being made.

When General Motors (GM) was attacked by the Japanese motor industry it tried to reinvent itself as an AFC and simply ran away from the competition. It bought into information technology, management consulting, white goods, artificial intelligence, insurance, airlines and many other industries more-or-less unrelated to its core business. Moreover, when the attractions of these unrelated businesses started to pall, as for example when Frigidaire started to report losses, GM, like any self-respecting AFC, simply sold the businesses off. In 1980, GM reported its first loss since 1921 and it was not until it had returned to a focused motor industry strategy that its future was secured. GM was an SBC, or for some purposes an MBC, but it was never an AFC and its attempt to become one was doomed to failure from the outset.

In contrast, Williams Holdings was clearly an AFC, built from an orthodox series of asset-stripping acquisitions. As an AFC it then struggled to become an MBC by defining an industrial logic behind its diverse activities and organising itself into a limited number of core activities on which future developments would be focused. Hardly had this industrial logic been enunciated when it received an offer for its most successful core activity, the paints division. The offer was too good for an AFC to refuse and the division was sold. Williams Holdings remains an AFC, although having espoused an industrial logic it has cut itself off from the many AFC opportunities that do not fit. It has therefore become relatively dormant, its earlier opportunistic acquisition activity being replaced by the occasional deal with a credible industrial logic, such as the 1997 acquisition of Chubb for which a heavy price premium had to be paid. The future for Williams looks bleak compared with its exciting past, and presumably will remain so until some AFC opportunity presents itself which is so tempting as to persuade Williams to give up its attempt to become a genuine MBC. BTR is another former AFC which is attempting to follow the MBC logic and is producing disappointing results as a consequence.

The distinctions between AFCs, MBCs and SBCs are thus made up of shades of grey, but they are nevertheless crucial. An AFC which adopts an MBC strategy is no more likely to succeed than an MBC which tries to drive forward on the basis of a pure AFC strategy. The distinction can best be made by simply identifying which strategy is dominant: wealth creation or wealth ownership. From the macro perspective it is clear that wealth creation is of greater importance. Provision for health, education, defence and social services are all financed by the proceeds of wealth creation and strategies for wealth creation. By comparison, wealth ownership provides few wider benefits. Indeed, it is likely that the financial focus of firms driven by wealth-ownership objectives is likely to reduce wider benefits. This arises not only from the short-term cost-cutting focus which leads ultimately to disinvestment, but also from direct focus on tax avoidance as a major aspect of corporate strategy. For example, the shape of Trafalgar House was determined largely by tax avoidance considerations, from the time it acquired Cunard for its accumulated tax losses and so moved into shipping as one of its major activities, to the time of its demise.

Corporate objectives are typically measured by ratios such as:

- Net assets per share
- Earnings per share
- Price per share
- Dividend per share

These ratios are more revealing when related to each other (for example price/earnings, dividend yield, assets/price) and compared with the performance of reference companies or sectors. These then become the focus of activity, rather than merely the by-product of business activities focused on competitors, customers, technologies and suppliers and so on. The difference is fundamental. The corporate-objectives focus leads to a more-or-less random spread of business activities as companies are acquired because their assets are undervalued, or because their earnings or dividend payments are not fully reflected in their current share price, or because of their peculiar tax position. The relatedeness or otherwise of the acquired company's business to any of the acquirer's is not significant to the AFC; diversification is not perceived as a problem. For an MBC, however, driven by business strategy, diversification can be highly problematic, as it proved for General Motors.

Diversification

Most companies start out as single businesses. As they grow they become more complex. Chandler (1962) highlighted three kinds of growth. The simplest and most obvious was geographical expansion, i.e. the simple extension of customer territory or the replication of the business in new territory. Vertical integration was Chandler's second form of growth. This might also be an obvious growth route for a business to take, but clearly added considerable complexity to the company's activities by introducing new suppliers, new technologies and, possibly, new customers. Finally, Chandler indicated diversification as the growth route which introduced the greatest complexity.

Ansoff also identified diversification as a legitimate business growth strategy. He emphasised the importance of maintaining a common thread. The least risky way of achieving growth was to increase market penetration with existing products. Growth might also be achieved through development of either the market or the product or by developing new products for new markets (i.e. diversification). This breaks the common thread and multiplies risk from the new (Ansoff, 1965/1987). New risk also arises from technologies; pursuing the new on all three maximises risk (see Figure 4.2). Many researchers have found that risk-maximising diversification tends not to work financially, and the less related the diversification the worse the financial result (see Thompson, 1993).

For an AFC, the notion of diversification has little meaning. Any acquisition

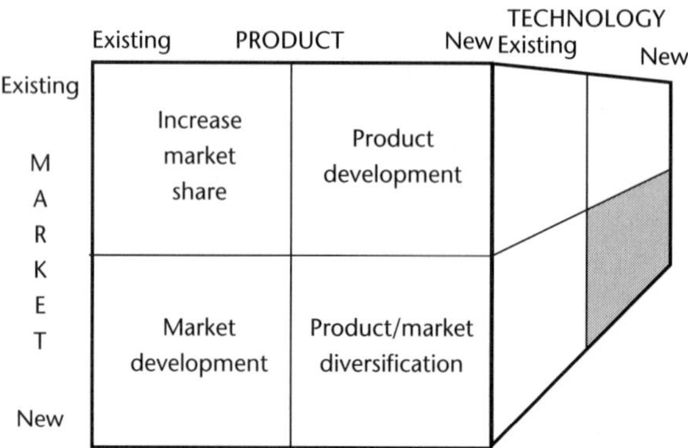

Figure 4.2 Alternative growth routes

which did not involve diversification would be purely coincidental since an AFC's intentions have nothing to do with business logic or a 'common thread'. The risks are therefore limited since the short-term balance sheet impacts are not only fairly predictable, but can to some extent be *fixed.* The long-term position is very different and can be seen at the end of the AFC's life. Two 1996 demergers illustrate the long-term weakness of AFC operations.

Thorn–EMI, an MBC, recognised the lack of 'common thread' between its Thorn TV rental business and its EMI music activities and decided to split them off in separate quoted companies. Both businesses were regarded as attractive in their own right and the Thorn–EMI share price responded positively to the proposed demerger, at least initially. In contrast, Hanson's proposal to split into four was recognised as confirmation that the company had run out of steam as an AFC. The four separate Hanson businesses were described in the press as 'under-invested, cash squeezed companies' (Warner, 1996). More than this,

> *Hanson may never have been what it seemed. Its success may always have been as much a result of acquisition accounting and tax avoidance as anything else. Now that it is breaking itself up into four distinct companies, each individually making some kind of sense, comes the final reckoning. And it is not pleasant. It may be that the four collectively cannot afford the dividend the whole has been blithely paying out to shareholders all these years. Even the greatest illusionists cannot keep it up for ever.*
> (Warner, 1996)

The Hanson dividends resulted from its AFC activity. As soon as it was proposed to replace its core competence in buying shares and selling assets with making and selling *things*, confidence collapsed.

The risks associated with diversification are more those associated with managing a new business based on unfamiliar technology, producing unfamiliar products or services for unfamiliar customers. If business strategy is about defining a strategic direction and concentrating on it consistently over time, diversification seems to be a failure of business strategy. Creating or acquiring a new business, which would, by definition, require its own strategy, goes beyond the scope of business strategy.

Nevertheless, most companies do at some stage diversify and become MBCs. In so doing they add greatly to the complexity of management and often, as a consequence, they lose sight of their original purpose and strategic focus. Diversification may arise because the existing business lacks a coherent strategy and simply drifts into diversification. This is, therefore, symbolic of strategic failure, walking away from the present situation to start afresh on what is all too often vainly hoped to be 'greener grass on the other side of the hill'. This is how businesses get what Porter called 'stuck in the middle' (Porter, 1980).

Leaving aside the AFC motivation for diversification through acquisition and leaving aside the the non-strategic drift, there are two further and rather more challenging situations where diversification may seem attractive:

1. Where the industry is in decline.
2. Where the business is generating surplus funds.

Being trapped in a declining industry presents four options:

1. Do nothing, i.e. stay with the industry and decline with it.
2. Liquidate the business and return it to the stakeholders.
3. Determine to become the industry survivor and achieve a new lease of life.
4. Diversify into a new industry.

Doing nothing is clearly unattractive since nobody wins from this strategy.

Liquidating the business is difficult to achieve in an equitable way. Disposing of a failing business and passing the proceeds back to the shareholders is a feasible option, but the other stakeholders, in particular the employees, are more difficult to recompense. Paying redundancy bonuses out of the asset disposals would be unlikely to compensate for loss of employment.

The third option, though apparently risky, would clearly have merit so long as the industry was not in terminal decline and there remains sufficient volume to allow the business to prosper.

Against these possible strategies the option of diversification appears to have considerable attractions. Diversification can be implemented ahead of the existing business decline. It can be achieved progressively, growing the new business as the existing declines. It presents management with many choices and the feeling of being in strategic control.

It is not surprising, therefore, that diversification has been a widely used strategy. Even more is this the case where businesses generate funds which cannot be used effectively for their own future development. Such situations are not common, even among so-called cash cows there are usually multiple opportunities for further investment. Most businesses exist on the basis of limited investment and could achieve further growth or more sustainable leadership through investment in volume, in product development, in process technology, in systems or in marketing. Nevertheless, where sustainable leadership is already achieved and prices are maintained at a level that generates surplus funds, the question remains as to how that surplus should best be invested. There are limited options available:

1. Return them to the stakeholders.
2. Invest in managerial slack.
3. Accumulate them.
4. Diversify.

Returning surplus funds to stakeholders is again not completely straightforward. The shareholders could fairly easily be compensated through additional dividends, share issues or share buybacks (which would increase the price of those shares still in issue). Employees could be compensated through the payment of bonuses, customers by price reductions, and so forth. However, such initiatives would have an unpredictable effect on stakeholder expectations which might not be easy to control.

Investments in managerial slack are easy to make and a frequently used way of disposing of surplus funds. These may range from simple increases in salary or bonuses, the provision of perks or status symbols of various descriptions, and the availability of enhanced facilities. These are still widely used although they may be increasingly difficult to justify.

Accumulating the surplus is merely delaying a decision. Ultimately, either the funds will be invested by the present management, or alternatively their continued accumulation would render the company vulnerable to being acquired simply in order to free the accumulated funds for others to take the decision.

Diversification again seems a relatively attractive option presenting management with choices for exercising 'strategic control'. It is clearly the most obvious and plausibly defensible of management decisions. Moreover, under a cost-cutting and accounting-oriented regime many businesses are arbitrarily starved of investment in order to make funds available for diversification.

From a strategy perspective, diversification is seen to increase risk by increasing the unknown and to reduce performance by increasing complexity and reducing concentration. Thus diversification tends to destroy value.

Goold *et al.* looked at this problem from the point of view of the MBC itself and investigated how parent company MBCs might influence and relate to their subsidiary businesses. They had found that 'while a few multi-business companies have corporate strategies that create substantial value, the large majority do not; they are value destroyers' (Goold *et al.*, 1994, and see also Reading Review 26). Value creation can be achieved, according to Goold *et al.*, by permitting the subsidiary business to replicate the advantages of independence, by providing beneficial linkages with other subsidiary businesses, by providing central services and functions, and by providing corporate development (for example through linkages with other newly acquired subsidiaries).

Goold *et al.*'s contribution to the role of MBCs as corporate parents is original and valuable. However, they fail to make the MBC/AFC distinction and treat AFCs such as Hanson as though they were wealth creators rather than simply wealth accumulators. In assessing AFCs, Goold *et al.* focus simply on the the AFC's own balance sheet whereas other researchers have sought to assess the overall impact of acquisitions and found it destructive (Porter, 1987) or have distinguished between financial and strategic takeovers and found that the financially motivated deals are unprofitable (Healy *et al.*, 1997).

4.4 Acquisition

For the AFC, acquisition is the fundamental transaction, motivated simply by the opportunity to buy balance sheet value at a discount. AFCs are uninhibited by considerations of 'parenting' or how to make the acquisition work once acquired and are not concerned with behavioural and cultural problems of fitting the new business into the existing organisation. However, for other organisational types, acquisition is a means of achieving strategy, whether it is business strategy or diversification.

Acquisition offers a number of potential benefits over other means of achieving strategy:

1. Crucial components of an acquisition might include people, technology, brands, physical assets such as land, buildings and equipment, order books, customers, market share, patents, contracts, image, and so on.
2. Speed of achieving position compared with developing that position organically.
3. Increasing market share without adding capacity.
4. Possibility of achieving a leadership position.
5. Possibility of synergy.

These are all desirable benefits that may be achieved through acquisition, any of which may be crucial components of strategy. As such, their value may be extremely high but difficult to assess in normal accounting terms. By contrast, assessing the financial value of an acquisition is relatively simple and it is usually this which forms the basis of any negotiation or bid battle.

There are three rational ways of estimating the financial value of any quoted company.

1. The book value of its net assets employed, adjusted as far as possible for any known revaluations not incorporated in the balance sheet.
2. The pre-acquisition market capitalisation, to which should be added a premium to reflect the inevitable rise in share price following the bid.
3. The net present value (NPV) of projected net cash flows.

These appear to be simple enough ways of calculating a financial value of a business, but they are not without problems as indicated in the case of Blue Circle Aggregates (see section 2.4). One of the most surprising aspects of acquisitions is the degree of imprecision in valuation. Bid prices differ hugely and there is no agreed formula, but if this is true of financial valuation it is even more so in relation to strategic valuation. How should the strategic value of an acquisition be assessed? There is no agreed way. In practice, companies are prepared to pay more than the financial valuation for acquisitions which they believe provide a strategic benefit, i.e. they are prepared to pay a strategic premium.

The orthodox wisdom is that the premium should be justified by the planned achievement of some synergy, some joint benefit or advantage not available to the two companies separately. But, it is now also the orthodox wisdom that synergies are never achieved in practice, beyond the cost savings, largely realised through making people redundant. The achievement of any greater synergy tends to be frustrated by the unexpected costs incurred by amalgamating two cultures.

Thus, estimation of the financial value of a company is only available approximately and the strategic premium over and above that financial value is not truly measurable at all. Nevertheless, acquisitions of a strategic and non-strategic nature are happening all the time, because the people making the deals are prepared to act on the basis of this imperfect information. Pearson (see Box 4.1) illustrates the problem of establishing and maintaining a strategic premium for a conglomerate company.

An unequivocal way of assessing the value of a business would be useful. Various models have been devised, such as the capital asset pricing model, but they all use information about the past to generate assumptions about the future and they all assume aspects of rationality in relation to stock market performance. These are flimsy foundations and a practical success seems unlikely ever to be achieved.

BOX 4.1

Whither Pearson?

In early 1997, the financial press were exercised about which way Pearson's new chief executive, Marjorie Scardino, would take the diverse media and leisure conglomerate.

The company had five main product areas with leading brands in each: books (Penguin), television (Thames Television with an enviable library of TV classics, shares in BSkyB and Channel 5), financial information (Extel, Financial Times and the Economist), theme parks (Madame Tussaud's and Alton Towers) and banking (Lazard's).

They should be a potent combination, but the company had achieved only moderate financial results, with earnings per share stagnating at less than 35p over the five years to 1996 with an undistinguished return on capital.

What Pearson lacked, according to investors and analysts, was direction. The company began deciding what it wanted to be under Scardino's predecessor, Frank Barlow. He oversaw the disposal of Westminster Press and the Royal Doulton china business. But the City was looking for more. Investors wanted better news from Mindscape, the loss-making software division, and Channel 5 which had had a difficult prenatal period. But more than this they wanted to see the Scardino plan. When she took over the helm she had quoted General MacArthur: 'Have a plan, execute it violently and do it today.'

Almost any strategy, including the break-up of Pearson, was possible. The problem with all the disposal programmes would be that Pearson would saddle itself with huge capital gains tax liabilities. But yet if she kept the company together, only concentrating on doing it better, this could well open the door to takeover. If the market was not impressed and analysts got their calculators out they would have found the company was one of the cheapest buys in media.

DISCUSSION POINTS

1. If possible, look at Pearson's latest report. Is the company an MBC or an AFC? Should it be driven by corporate strategy or by the strategies of its businesses?
2. Outline two alternative plans for Scardino to consider.
3. What could Pearson do to ensure that its corporate parenting might create value?

Acquisition, as practised by the AFC, is a fairly straightforward means to short-term gains. However, as a means to achieving strategic ends, acquisition is more problematic. The first guiding principle is to be absolutely clear in defining the strategic end that is being sought through the acquisition and to be as specific as possible about the ways in which the particular acquisition will contribute. Only then will it be possible to assess whether the particular acquisition justifies the payment of any strategic premium over and above the financial value.

Summary

- Business strategy is concerned with wealth creation, but corporate strategy is concerned only with the much less important matter of wealth ownership and its reward.
- Corporate objectives are concerned with survival and the satisfaction of some stakeholders. It is not usually concerned with strategic objectives, i.e. with pleasing customers or beating competitors.
- For some organisations, however, the business is corporate. An acquisitive financial conglomerate (AFC) buys companies and sells assets to create an immediate balance sheet surplus. These companies define themselves quite differently from multi- or single-business companies (MBCs and SBCs respectively).
- AFCs generally do not survive their founding entrepreneurs.
- It is extremely difficult for an AFC to transform itself into an MBC – most do not survive the attempt.
- It is difficult for an MBC to become an AFC.
- Most SBCs transform naturally into MBCs and in so doing lose their clear strategic focus and direction.
- Diversification is a move beyond business strategy.
- For an MBC or SBC, diversification can be justified as a strategy only where the industry is in decline or where the business is generating surplus funds.
- Acquisition, a special case of diversification, has a number of potential benefits over non-acquisition:
  - acquisition of key business attributes or strengths

  - speed
  - increasing share without adding capacity
  - achieving a leadership position
  - synergy
- It is difficult to establish an accurate financial value on a potential acquisition candidate and even more difficult to establish its strategic value.

Further reading

Goold, M. and Campbell, A., *Strategies and Styles: the role of the centre in managing diversified corporations*, Blackwell, 1987.
Goold, M., Campbell, A. and Alexander, M., *Corporate Level Strategy: Creating value in the multibusiness company,* Wiley, 1994.

part 2

Strategy frameworks

Strategy management has developed pragmatically. Models or frameworks have been developed and tested. Sometimes they have worked and sometimes they have not. If they worked they have been copied and sometimes gained wide acceptance. Then they have been applied in circumstances where they were quite inappropriate and, as a result, have been seen to fail. Although they may have a perfectly sound basis, in the end, all frameworks have failed.

Part Two looks at the different strategy frameworks that have been widely used in practice. They are described in the chronological order of their emergence and application, starting with the accounting-based frameworks, which appeared to be more-or-less common-sense extensions of normal accounting practice, and culminating in the definition of custom-built frameworks specially designed to meet the needs of the individual business in its particular situation.

The idea of strategy management generated considerable excitement when it first emerged and new computer programming languages were developed to assist the development of suitable models. However, the initial hopes and expectations were never realised and the early strategy models appeared to offer little of strategic significance other than treating it with a longer time horizon. As planning became more sophisticated it gradually drew in more and more analysis of issues which were of genuine strategic significance, but as sophistication increased, so did complexity. The dream of a computerised strategy management information system which modelled all the apparently significant variables of a business and its environments was never realised. The more comprehensive the system, the less easy it became to use.

Thus there grew up a need for simplified ways which focused on essential issues and provided clear results. A succession of such frameworks has emerged over the past forty years. Each has embodied quite severe limitations or flaws and none has been universally applicable. However, they all contain something of use to the strategy manager, offering some distinctive insight which can aid understanding of the business in its particular situation.

Chapter 5 reviews the first generation of strategy frameworks which focused on detailed accounts-based planning. These were most widely adopted in the 1960s, but even today many companies still follow this approach. A survey published in 1997 (Quest Worldwide, 1997) showed that over three-quarters of companies around the world prepared strategic plans but most seemed to lack any strategic vision, tending to be driven by the demands of shareholders with the focus clearly on financial targets. The survey found that too many strategic plans identified no direction but focused on too many priorities with unrealistic timescales. Perhaps not surprisingly, there was a lack of commitment to such 'strategies' among people at all levels and many firms admitted that they were bad at putting the plans into action.

Accounts-based plans are necessarily based on extrapolations of the past and present, rather than on genuinely informed forecasts of the future. Forecast-based planning added considerably to the value of the planning process but also increased its complexity. The focus on development planning, rather than managing the existing business, added further strategic value but again at the cost of complexity. All these approaches tended to result in a rather bureaucratic process which made only a limited strategic impact.

In consequence, more structured models were developed which in the main did not require such comprehensive input and it was intended that these would focus management's attention on the real strategic issues. Chapters 6–10 describe the main frameworks to emerge.

Strategy frameworks provide a simplified account of the real world so that managers are not paralysed by analysis, but instead have their attention drawn to genuinely strategic decisions. These frameworks offer varying degrees of abstraction, simplification or complexity and provide a choice for relevance to a variety of situations. Several generations of strategy frameworks have been developed, culminating in the rather imprecise but more realistic contingent composite frameworks of today.

During its span of less than fifty years, strategy management has been subject to many fashions. Perhaps now more than ever, managers are the focus of hype around the latest fad; using last year's model is sometimes portrayed as ill-informed or naive. But the search for the fashionable and new is futile; we know that the next Michael Porter will not have the final solution. Moreover, today's authors will be unlikely to provide anything wholly new, perhaps only some new examples and some new language. The real need is for in-depth understanding and this will come, at least in part, from using different frameworks to get an appreciation of the business and its situation.

Understanding is helped by the fact that the frameworks themselves are, without exception, simple and straightforward. They have been widely abused, misunderstood and misapplied, and are sometimes so grossly oversimplified that they result in disaster, but it is not difficult to avoid these traps. For example, the Boston Consulting Group (BCG) and the PIMS database are both often quoted in support of the strategy of increasing market share because high market share is the key to profitability. However, the quest for high market share should not be pursued irrespective of the costs involved. According to the BCG's original model, high relative market share was attractive because it resulted in lower costs arising from 'experience' and increasing relative share of a growing market was generally a worthwhile strategy. But if market share was acquired so expensively that the additional costs (for example interest payments on the cost of acquiring the additional share) exceeded the savings from 'experience', then the increase in relative market share could

Boston Consulting Group's valuation of market share

The net present value, W, of an increment in market share is calculated as follows:

$$W = \int_0^{tf} \{P(t) - C_{11}(t)\} \cdot V_{11}(t) - \{P(t) - C_1(t)\} \cdot V_1(t) e^{-bt} dt$$

where, among other things,

$$C_{11}(t) = \frac{C_0}{n^{\lambda}} \left[n_0 + \frac{sM}{r_a} (e^{r_a t_0 - 1}) + \frac{sMe^{r_a t_0}}{r_m} (e^{r_m (t-t_0)} - 1) \right]^{\lambda}$$

only reduce profitability. The BCG itself provided a formula (see box) for valuing market share and emphasised that if it cost more than the formula then it should not be acquired. While the formula itself is not to be taken too seriously, the point should be recognised that, even for the BCG, the value of increments to market share was limited.

Such concepts are forgotten in the popular interpretation of the model which simply holds that high market share produces high profitability and is therefore a good strategy. This is a half understood half-truth which leads to fundamentally flawed strategy. Understanding is vital, both of the framework and of the organisation's situation.

The limitations and shortcomings of each framework are examined so that situations can be recognised where particular frameworks simply do not apply and can shed no light. Similarly, there are other situations where a particular framework, no matter how out of date it might generally be regarded, may be exactly relevant and provide management with a simple and valid means of taking strategic decisions.

Understanding the frameworks is easy; understanding the situation of a business so that the appropriate framework can be used to derive a practical strategy is rather more difficult; but the really hard part is taking strategic decisions on the basis of these understandings. How, for example, does a manager refuse profitable business simply in the interests of maintaining a strategic focus? Such decisions will never be easy, but they are made credible if the whole situation is understood and all its uncertainties acknowledged. This is why the contingency approach is adopted: the contingency approach recognises that there is no one best way – all depends on the particular situation – and that the framework that is most appropriate to the particular situation should be used. To do this it is essential to understand both the frameworks and the situations. The two together make it possible to define a strategy which just might be successful.

Chapter 5

Planning frameworks

Management's first explicit attempts to deal with strategy adopted a logical, linear mode of thinking manifested in the development of formal plans and were generally expressed in purely financial language.

The impact of these early methods in terms of corporate performance were disappointing. However, although strategic plans often tended not to work out, value was sometimes achieved through the *process* of planning which typically involved many members of the organisation and became a form of strategy communication.

Experience with these planning frameworks highlighted the need for ways of strategic thinking and strategy management which were both practical and focused on key strategic issues.

5.1 Introduction

This chapter describes the earliest explicit approaches to strategy management realised in the form of formal strategic planning. Entrepreneurs and managers have been implicitly concerned with strategic issues ever since large-scale business started. The actions, writings and sayings of the great entrepreneurs such as Ford, Sloan of General Motors, Watson of IBM, and others, show how sensitive they were to strategic issues. Even before them, their counterparts in other large-scale organisations, such as the state, the Church and the military, had also been similarly concerned going right back to Sun Tzu (Griffith, 1963) and Machiavelli (Wood, 1990).

Organisations which remain successful over the long term have always had to adapt to the ever-changing world. To do this they have needed some foresight and an ability to plan action. Often this concern with planning for the future has led organisations to diversify their activities. They do this firstly to reduce the perceived risk inherent in reliance on a single product line and, secondly, to seek out the more favourable environment they imagine to be available from doing something different. Thus they lose sight of their original business purpose and build hugely complex

Table 5.1 Evolution of strategic planning

Phase	Description
1 Basic financial	Based on annual budget, gave operational control, but slight strategic impact, largely resource based
2 Forecast-based planning	Environmental analysis, multi-year forecasts, static allocation of resources, some planning for growth
3 Externally oriented planning	Strategic thinking, situation analysis, competitive assessment, evaluation of strategic alternatives, dynamic allocation of resources, increasing response to customers
4 Strategy management	Creating the future, creative, flexible planning processes, strategically chosen planning framework, supportive value system and culture, orchestration of all resources to create competitive advantage

organisations. It is this complexity which leads managers to feel the need for a suitable planning system which will help to simplify the business and bring back the feeling of coherence and sense of direction and focus it once had. Thus deliberate and formal concern with business strategy as a systematic management discipline developed out of the conglomerate and multibusiness companies that emerged after the Second World War.

The main strands in the developing methods of business strategy are described below. The strategic impact of most of them fell short of expectations. However, much was learned and today's strategists can benefit from understanding these early approaches to strategy and the reasons why they largely failed to deliver. This is a significant thread in the contemporary fabric of strategic thinking.

The progression in strategic planning and management has been reviewed from time to time (for example Glueck, 1985). The categories shown in Table 5.1 are typical of this sort of analysis. In its simplification the progression is a rather idealised picture, especially in its portrayal of continuously increasing knowledge and understanding. It is certainly true that the flaws and limitations of successive approaches take time to be recognised and understood, but the theory of strategy management remains limited.

5.2 Accounts-based budget planning

Less than forty years ago most company accounts were prepared without the help of computers. Producing accounts was a labour-intensive task of considerable proportions, employing large numbers of white-collar workers, clerks and accounting technicians engaged almost wholly in producing accounts of the current year's operations.

Consolidation of subsidiary company accounts into the corporate whole provided the only formal measure of the whole organisation. So it was perhaps natural that the first forays into formal strategic planning were accounting based.

Typical early practice in multibusiness companies was to make projections of the company's consolidated financial accounts. The aim would be to make a projection that would be satisfactory from the shareholder's viewpoint, and the result of this projection might be the espousal of objectives of the sort indicated in the Cooper Soft Drinks case in Chapter 2. Thus, 17 per cent return on capital employed and 9 per cent growth per annum in earnings per share might have been calculated as beating the sector average and thus giving the company a strong defence against a hostile bid.

Having thus projected the consolidated position the task was then to deconsolidate the projections back to separate subsidiary businesses which were given the resultant figures as targets. For even a relatively small single-business company such as Cooper, the annual budget might well extend to twenty or so full-page schedules including such items as:

Profit and loss account
Balance sheet
Cash flow statement
Capital expenditure schedule
Overhead costs schedule
Sales budget for:
  each product line
  each 'territory'
Production budget:
  volumes for each factory section/unit
  costs for each factory section/unit
  factory overhead schedule

With the complications added by diversification, the number of budgeting schedules would grow geometrically. Prior to computers this complexity reduced the usefulness of such plans because asking quite simple 'what if?' questions was extremely troublesome and the cost of making changes to the budget was extremely high.

These simple but laborious accounting processes gave birth to formal long-range planning. They were not in themselves of any strategic significance but they provided the first moves to strategic planning. It was achieved by recalculating the main accounting schedules included in the annual budget to cover, typically, although for no particular reason, a five-year period. A five-year plan or budget comprised five times the data. The plan for a company comprising ten businesses would therefore comprise fifty times the data of a single-business annual budget, without considering the additional data generated through consolidation for the company as a whole or its divisions. The time and cost of manual calculation meant the focus became process, rather than outcomes, oriented.

The advent of computers, and particularly of powerful microcomputers, changed all this. Initially, mainframe computer systems and specialised languages such as

APL (A Planning Language) were made available to take over the clerical task. As systems improved and became cheaper, simpler and more available, they eliminated the labour required to produce such budget-based 'plans' and increased their flexibility by making sensitivity and 'what if?' analyses quick and cheap.

Today, many companies, particularly small and medium-sized firms, still adopt this basic, linear process for strategy planning. A single planner armed with a microcomputer can now produce 'instant' answers to any 'what if?' questions and simultaneously generate the resultant planning schedules. The five-year budget has become capable of almost infinite flexing. Today a typical plan document will comprise a set of arithmetically accurate and consistent accounting schedules, backed up with a wide variety of key statistics such as returns on investment, profit margins, net cash flow, and so on, showing the impact of alternative assumptions about, for example, sales volumes, prices and costs.

Most often these systems do not help strategy management in terms of direction, concentration and consistency. On such issues accounts-based plans are more-or-less silent. A return on capital employed of 17 per cent is a financial objective which says nothing about how that objective might best be achieved. Nevertheless, accounts-based plans represented a step forward for many businesses because for the first time they were encouraged to think beyond the current year. Moreover, accounts-based plans necessarily included the allocation of capital expenditure to specific and relatively large items. Although the financial justification for committing funds may be made on an individual basis as and when a project has been appraised in detail, the broad strategic decision as to whether the item is appropriate in principle may be taken at the time that the capital plan is put together. Thus capital budgeting, or planning, is a key strategic item in the accounts-based budget planning approach. It forced management to consider strategic issues, and the way capital decisions were taken had a strategic impact in terms of direction, concentration and consistency.

Many companies, particularly diversified MBCs and AFCs, still define their long-range plans in accounting terms and use financial models to make their projections. It may help to define the subsidiary/parent relationship but would offer little help in defining the strategic direction of the business, or in achieving concentration or consistency. Nor would accounts-based plans be in any sense transformational; the motivational impact of aiming for 17 per cent return on capital employed would be minimal.

These problems with the process of budgeting are widely recognised.

An obsession with budgets is holding back innovation . . . budgets are a wasteful business activity, no longer the way to plan and control managerial behaviour in an age when innovation, service quality and knowledge sharing are the defining attributes of competitive success. In many firms, the strategic direction and the budgeting system are contradictory. Few managers understand the damaging effect that operating within annual budgets has on their response to threats and opportunities that arise when you least expect them. It is easy to ignore technological breakthroughs or new market entrants if your attention is on achieving budgetary targets. . . . Numbers do not run businesses; people do, and with the information age closing around us these people are likely to be knowledge workers such as researchers, designers, engineers and marketing people. Such people are not driven by financial targets and incentives. The time spent preparing and managing budgets is anathema to them: they simply want to get on with their specialist work without their energies being drained by budget meetings. . . . the traditional budgeting process is too rigid, too internally focused, adds too little value, takes too much management time and encourages the wrong management behaviour. (Hope, 1997)

Similar views have been expressed by practitioners. In 1995, General Electric announced that 'the budget is the bane of corporate America and should never have existed' and a year later Ikea reported the downsizing of its budgeting: 'our business planning system was getting too heavy and we can use the time for doing other things better' (Kavanagh, 1997).

5.3 Forecast-based budget planning

The main concern with accounts-based planning was with the accuracy of accounting figures, but it was realised that the data, even if accurate, were based on the past. What was needed was strategically relevant information about the future. Thus attention was turned initially on the generation of forecasts of relevant data.

Relevance was required to be assessed clinically and objectively so that strategy could be formulated on a wholly rational analysis of the business and its markets. Many firms approached the analysis using a SWOT (strengths, weaknesses, opportunities and threats) checklist approach. This involved a detailed and exhaustive assessment of the strengths and weaknesses of the business and the opportunities and threats presented by its product markets and other environments such as suppliers and technology developers suppliers.

An audit of the company's strengths and weaknesses would include the items listed in Table 5.2 plus others that might be particularly relevant to the individual situation. It would involve a review, product by product, function by function, department by department, of the strengths and weaknesses of each area both in absolute terms and also in terms relative to competitors.

Similarly, the environmental analysis, identifying threats and opportunities facing the business, looks at each environment with which the business interacts, for example the product market, the suppliers' markets, technological environment comprising the political worlds and the financial environment including the stock market and banking community, as indicated in Table 5.3. The intention is to be comprehensive, to identify every threat and every opportunity in each environment.

Strengths and weaknesses, opportunities and threats form the basis of many forecast-based budget planning systems. Where a company's strength coincides with a market opportunity there is the potential for successful exploitation. Where a weakness coincides with a threat there is potential for disaster. In the two intermediate positions, further analysis of the problem is needed.

SWOT analysis is superficially appealing, but in practice is inimical to the definition of strategic direction and concentrating consistently on it. A thorough SWOT analysis will reveal innumerable strengths and weaknesses and threats and oppor-

Table 5.2 Strengths and weaknesses checklist

1. Market structure	**4. Investment**
Products and product lines	Cost of entry to industry
Product attributes	Cost of exiting from industry
Market segments	Rate of obsolescence of plant
Customers and customer needs	Importance of capital investment
2. Growth and profitability	**5. Marketing**
History	Importance of service and field support
Shape, scale and phase of life cycle	Importance and method of promotion
Forecasts and discontinuities	Method of promotion and selling
Margins and trends	Distribution channels
Liquidity patterns	Basic determinants of demand
3. Technology	**6. Competition**
Basic technologies and innovation history	Market shares by segment
Rate of development	Degree of concentration in industry
Physical potential for further development	Strength of leading competitor
Alternative/replacement technologies	
Importance of technology	
	7. Trends
	Demand and consumer tastes
	Market structure
	Technology

Table 5.3 Environmental audit checklist

1. Product market	**3. Financial**
Size, shares, segments, trends	Sector price/earnings ratios and trends
Distribution channel structures	Earnings per share and trends
Changes in usage and expectations	Takeover threats and opportunities
Price/cost/volume relationships	
Competitive positions	
Potential substitute products	
2. Technology	**4. Social, economic and political**
Developments and applications	Trade cycles, inflation, interest rates
Obsolescence	Balance of payments and exchange rates
Research and discoveries	Employment levels, trade union activity
Potential substitute technologies	Government policy, political stability
	Demographic changes
	Wealth and income distribution
	Education, attitudes and lifestyles
	Environmental regulation and trends

tunities; this is especially the case in strategic applications where the SWOTs being analysed are not only those which already exist but also those which might emerge in the relevant future. If the attempt is made to address them all, as is often the case in practice, the inevitable result will be that resources are spread extremely thinly across a very broad front. Thus concentration will be destroyed and, as a consequence, little of substance achieved. SWOT analysis rarely contributes coherence or focus and the decision on strategic direction is often frustrated. With no espoused direction, there is no criterion for recognising which factors are important and which trivial.

In the early days of strategic planning, when SWOT was widely used, it was common practice to establish the role of a professional specialist as a strategic planner who would develop alternative scenarios of the future for management to choose from. Alternative possible futures were considered and the planner would select a small number of different resource allocations for each and present the simulated results of these to managers who simply selected the preferred outcome. This process made management's task easier, but it was the planner, rather than management, who was making the important strategic decisions.

The dangers of staff specialists taking over the strategy management role were sometimes exacerbated by the establishment of strategic planning departments with responsibilities for many different aspects of the strategy process. First, they set out the economic assumptions on which a five-year plan might be based. In budget planning frameworks it is essential that these assumptions are made explicit so that the inevitable variations of performance against plan can be interpreted sensibly. For example, if a plan is framed on the assumption that inflation will run at 3 per cent per annum but the actual outcome is 6 per cent, interpretation of the reported results will need to take this variation into account.

A second major function fulfilled by many strategic planning departments was the provision of long-range forecasts and budget schedules covering items such as those listed in section 5.2 above. These would include many industry-specific items. Understanding how these might be critical to the success of the business concerned was expertise acquired by strategic planning department rather than among line management of the business. Consequently the planning departments increased their power and influence in many major companies.

Turner and Newall Ltd, one of the FT 30 Index blue chip companies in the early 1970s, employed at that time more than fifty highly qualified staff specialists in the annual production of its corporate plan, but the result of their efforts was hardly strategic. The corporate plan which resulted was distributed to the parent board under a 'strictly private and confidential' heading and, subtitled 'a document for discussion', was discussed for around ten minutes at one board meeting each year and was then filed without further reference (Pearson, 1985).

Nevertheless, forecast-based budget planning was a step forward in the development of the strategy management process. Firms taking that step undoubtedly understood more, both about their own business and about their situation, than they did before. But it should be regarded as a stage in the evolution of the strategy process rather than an approach to strategy in its own right.

5.4 Development-based budget planning

The appropriate allocation of resources was recognised early on as one of the key benefits that could be achieved from an effective strategy planning process. Although the purpose of strategy management was not explicitly recognised from the outset as the definition of strategic direction, concentration of resources and maintaining consistency, the need for a strategic perspective on the allocation of resources, particularly major capital outlays, was always apparent. The capital budget was often embedded in the strategic plan and sought to take account of the various corporate and environmental analyses referred to in the previous section. A broad picture of strategic priorities was established against which individual projects could be appraised using orthodox criteria.

However, capital expenditure is only part of the resource allocation problem. It is easy to control since it represents new resources and the individual decisions included all the major expenditures. But even with new activities, the capital resource would be only a small part of the overall story. A new product, for example, might require capital to produce, but it would also require many non-capital expenditures, some of which might be included in the financial appraisal (such as R&D and marketing costs), but many of which were often excluded. Most of these resources would not be new increments but reallocations of existing resource from existing products and business to the new. Cumulatively, these reallocations of resource resulted in loss of concentration and consequently had a crucial effect on the long-term prosperity of the business.

Various systems of budget planning were developed which sought to account for all resources engaged in business developments, not simply capital resources. The following paragraphs outline one such system, sometimes referred to as programme budget planning, which gained widespread adoption.

The aim of development-based budget planning is to identify all the resources available for business development, i.e. not required for maintaining the existing business, and then to allocate these resources, mainly people, skills, equipment and money, to various programmes within the development plan. Each programme aims to achieve certain broad thrusts, for example market penetration, new product development, production cost reduction, diversification or even acquisition.

There are a number of variations on development budgeting, but the essence of the system is to involve all line and staff management in the process of developing the business. Each functional manager is invited to propose development projects for inclusion in the development plan. To do this they specify each proposed projects in both qualitative and quantitative terms as well as estimating the amount of development resource of each kind the project would require. In the main, the development resource of greatest concern is time: person-weeks of research, development engineering, production engineering, marketing research, management accounting and so on. The managers of each of these resources would specify the total amount of time that could be made available for development projects, as opposed to the day-to-day business. Additionally, during the course of preparing the plan, all resource managers would prepare their estimates of the amount of time each proposed project would take by their department.

The planner's role in the above process is typically administrative. The planner ensures that proposals of projects and bids for resources are submitted and co-ordinated at the appropriate time and in the prescribed formats. Thus a list of fully resourced development project proposals is available together with a list of available resources. When this is completed, the planner is likely to take a more proactive role in the process. The ultimate strategy management decision is to choose the preferred allocation of resources to development projects. The planner facilitates this decision by offering a number of alternative allocations for consideration. Typically each alternative allocation is described by the planner in qualitative and quantitative terms in order to make the implications, risks and possibilities of each allocation quite clear.

This approach to development planning combines a number of virtues. First it involves the whole of the management team in the process, both in terms of being able to propose development projects and in working on them. Secondly, it provides top management with explicit alternatives from which to choose. Thirdly, it is so organised as to eliminate much of the clerical effort from line management and give it to the specialist staff planner. Such a system is described in the case of Inca Construction Materials (see Box 5.1) which raises some discussion points which should be considered at this stage.

BOX 5.1

Inca Construction Materials Ltd

Inca Construction Materials was established at the start of this century as a manufacturer of mineral-fibre reinforced corrugated building board, for which it held various patents and enjoyed a virtual monopoly until the early 1930s. Even after the patent protection had lapsed, the high costs of setting up production limited entry to the industry, and up to 1950 there were still only two producers in the UK, Inca having over 80 per cent of the market which was almost entirely concerned with the external cladding of industrial and agricultural buildings. INCLAD, Inca's proprietary name, was generic for what had become more-or-less a commodity, lacking any significant differentiation from one manufacturer to another. During the 1950s and 1960s there was substantial excess demand and sales director, Wilf Penney, well recalls customers calling him `sir' and pleading for an increase in their allocation. At this time two overseas producers established plants in the UK, but Inca continued to work at full capacity and enjoyed high profitability.

Exceptional cash generation during this period encouraged Inca to broaden its product range. The first substantial new product was a highly successful range of thermal insulation boards, called INSHEET, which became the market leader in internal cladding of industrial buildings. The technology used in producing INSHEET was quite different from that of INCLAD, being more like paper manufacture. This led to further diversification into electrical insulation papers and subsequently into phenolic and polyester resin impregnated papers for a wide variety of technical applications. These developments were expensive, but during Inca's years of plenty, such investments presented no problem.

INCLAD's loss of market share was at first regarded almost with relief by the top management – being too dominant was regarded as unsustainable and the company's reliance on a single product line for profit and cash was regarded as having a high risk.

New competitors therefore came into the market without any active discouragement from Inca. Transporting INCLAD long distances was regarded as uneconomical, so new competitors were allowed to pick off geographically specialised areas. The first of these was in Scotland where Inca did not have a manufacturing plant. As a result of this one change, Inca lost 10 per cent of its sales volume.

By 1970 the excess demand for cladding materials had ceased and Inca recognised that future growth for the main products would be slight. This realisation put more emphasis on the various diversifications that had been made and were being considered. Inca was already peripherally involved in plastics through impregnated papers and further commitment to plastics appeared tempting.

Inca therefore set up a well funded development programme, the aims of which were to reduce the company's reliance on fibreboard and buy its way into new growth markets. A corporate planning department was set up comprising eleven high calibre, graduate professional specialists. A thorough SWOT appraisal was carried out and presented to the Inca board of directors with an exhaustive study of the company's strategic options, including no less than twelve different ten-year scenarios. This work produced a development plan which included an extensive programme of new product development and diversification. The plan was seen as a race against time as the existing markets waned and then collapsed in the oil price crisis of 1973. By 1976 Inca had completed two greenfield developments to manufacture lightweight aggregate blocks, had acquired three high-quality facing brick manufacturers and taken its first tentative steps into thermoplastic resins.

By then INCLAD had lost further market share to around 40 per cent and the company as a whole was starting to record losses. Profit analysis showed the INCLAD and INSHEET ranges still generated 90 per cent of Inca's profit and 150 per cent of cash.

The development plan comprised the following four programmes:

1. Profit improvement
2. New product development
3. Diversification
4. Acquisitions

In total there were over 250 individual projects in the plan and apparently being worked on. However, only 20 projects were 'completed' in a year, 'completion' including projects taken out of the development plan because of failure of some sort, either technical or economic. Failure was itself a controversial issue and the elimination of a project that had not reached successful completion was never agreed unanimously. Always there would be one manager who felt that, in view of the efforts made and costs already sunk in the project, success would be relatively quick and cheap to achieve.

DISCUSSION POINTS

1. What do you think Inca's main mistakes have been so far?
2. What can Inca do to improve the results from the development plan?
3. Consider how the development plan has contributed to Inca achieving the purpose of strategy (see Figure 2.4 in Chapter 2)?

There is a danger that a proactive planner will in fact play the most influential role in deciding the resource allocation; more influential, for example, than the top management of the business who might be regarded as ultimately responsible for strategy.

Moreover, the system does not contain within itself any guidance as to direction and thus, despite the benefits of the process, it is likely to provide only a limited contribution to concentration and consistency. More likely, the aspects of development planning which inhibit concentration will have greater effect.

Formal decision-making of this sort is prone to what Cyert and March (1963) referred to as satisficing. When decisions are taken by groups, they tend to be taken by compromise, that is in such a way as to satisfy the minimum requirements of every member of the group, rather than in a way which might be in the group's overall best interests but possibly detrimental to the interests of one or more members. In this way, no member will achieve his or her target, but all will have grounds for some minimum level of satisfaction.

Development planning formalises this process. Each senior manager proposes a number of projects and each manager's lowest level of development involvement is likely to be discussed quite explicitly. An acceptable allocation may be one which includes at least all the projects which meet this lowest level of involvement for each department. Additionally there will be other projects for which there is a clear corporate or business need. Thus the process is likely to result in a large number of development projects in the plan. This means in most circumstances that there will be a relatively small amount of resource devoted to each project and consequently only limited development progress achieved in any time period. In other words, without direction there can be no concentration and consistency and the result will be that resources are allocated across a wide front and little achieved.

5.5 The bureaucratic tendency

As management attention was drawn to a new focus on strategy so the 'Where are we now?', 'Where do we want to get to?', 'How do we get there?' planning systems were developed. Figure 5.1 depicts a simple flowchart for one such planning process.

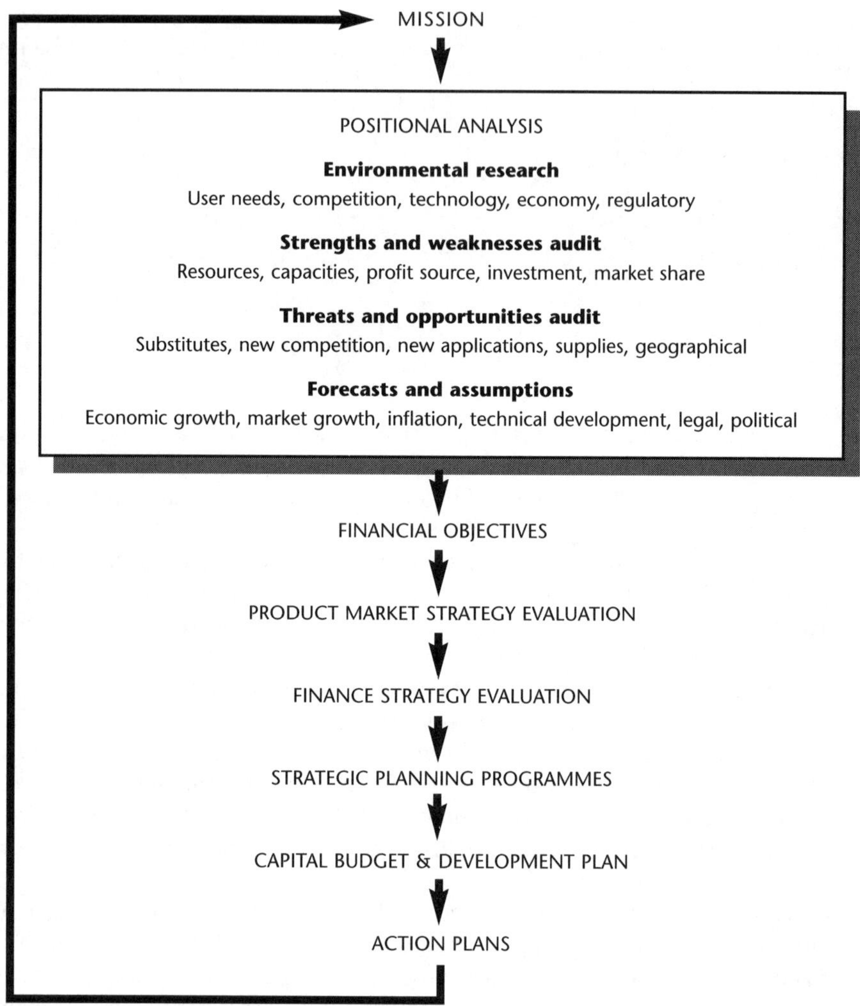

Figure 5.1 Typical bureaucratic planning system

This shows a rational cyclical process, each stage of which represents a substantial degree of analysis or evaluation. The positional analysis alone is a significant challenge. A thorough analysis of, for example, user needs may alone stretch the resources of many businesses. Ansoff was the pioneer of this approach to strategy and his depiction of a strategic planning model, which he refers to as 'tree of strategic management', is a bewildering elaboration (Ansoff, 1990, p. 478).

However, as indicated in section 2.1, the correlation between strategic planning and long-term business success is uncertain – strategic planning has not been shown to work. Some of the reasons have already been examined above. Of all the approaches to strategy, the planning approach is probably the least likely to be successful simply because planning systems are routinised, bound by rules and regulation and by the completion of proformae, rather than being open, flexible and attuned to seeking out and creating change. Strategic planning is a mechanistic approach to an organic problem.

Planning systems are nevertheless still widely used, despite their apparent ineffectiveness, and many writers have advocated such systems from Ansoff onwards, typified by, for example, Jones (1974) and Shaw (1981) who advocated a system based on the completion of large numbers of mainly quantitative detailed proformae for each business unit. Although strategy may find quantitative expression in some ways, its essence – the direction, position and culture of an organisation – is qualitative and can only be expressed in words. Thus Jones' approach produces a document which not only misses the strategic point, but even for the simple one-business company would be a lengthy document. A company plan involving six or seven businesses would become a severe problem to managers expected to read it, understand it and take decisions based on it.

Even today, the planning approach is advocated by the high street banks in their recommendations to small business clients and in courses leading to professional accounting qualifications. The bureaucratic tendency still persists (Freemantle, 1994; Bangs, 1995). It is a plausible, common-sense response to the strategy problem, but it has largely failed to provide strategic solutions.

Summary

- Whilst the leaders of large-scale organisations have probably always demonstrated a concern for key strategic issues, it is only over the past forty or so years that business managements have made these concerns explicit in the form of long-range plans.
- The first approaches to formal long-range planning were generally accounting-based and amounted to the projection of annual budgets, usually over five-year periods.
- These systems sometimes highlighted particular issues, but generally failed to achieve any substantial strategic benefit. They also failed to provide any significant understanding of the business.
- Accounts-based budget plans were based on extrapolations from the past and present, rather than being founded on forecasts of future corporate and environmental data.
- Forecast-based planning focused on the perceived threats and opportunities presented by the environment and the strengths and weaknesses relevant to the business.
- Such systems tended to frustrate the definition of strategic direction and as a consequence often led to a broad and thin spread of resources in order to address all SWOTs. Thus such systems actively discouraged concentration of effort.
- Development budgeting sought to focus attention on the allocation of resources aimed specifically at developing the business, as opposed to its day-to-day run-

ning. Again, the systems most widely used did not contribute to the identification of strategic direction and also tended to result in widespread and thin allocation of resources.

- These budget planning systems tended to become organisational processes in their own right and a recognised part of the corporate bureaucracy, having an apparent but unjustified importance. They were generally not justifiable by their contribution to strategy formation, i.e. to direction, concentration, consistency and flexibility. Nevertheless, they represented a stage in the learning process along the way to strategic thinking.

Further reading

Mintzberg, H., 'The fall and rise of strategic planning', *Harvard Business Review*, January/February 1994.

Mintzberg, H., *The Rise and Fall of Strategic Planning*, Prentice Hall International, 1994.

Chapter

6

Evolutionary frameworks

The search for a simplifying yet meaningful strategy framework started with the systems approach which focused on the evolution of products, businesses and industries.

The life cycle framework provides a perspective on strategic situations and, where applicable, can assist with the prescription of an appropriate strategy.

The experience curve framework, developed by the Boston Consulting Group, offers a parallel approach, which may be applicable in different circumstances and may suggest alternative strategic prescriptions.

These are the first two simplifying strategy frameworks.

6.1 Introduction

In the 1950s and 1960s, management scientists commenced the search for a simplified framework for thinking about the strategy of business. Although the strategy frameworks might be less comprehensive than planning models, they were intended to provide genuinely new ways of understanding. Chapters 6–9 examine various of these simplified strategy frameworks which have been widely adopted in practice.

The earliest framework viewed the business organisation as a biological system evolving through possibly predictable stages of birth, adolescence and growth to maturity and ultimately decline and death. This not only looked simpler to use than the bureaucratic planning systems, but it also promised genuine insights on which management could base its crucial strategic decisions. This chapter examines the origins of this evolutionary framework and the insights and understandings it provides and reviews its application to life cycles, industry evolution and the phenomenon of experience.

6.2 Basic systems model

Systems theory developed as a general approach to the analysis of living phenomena. It focused on the overall system properties and characteristics which appeared to apply generally to all living systems from a simple biological cell to a complex social organisation. The critical system properties and characteristics appeared capable of providing an overall explanation of the system from an analysis of the particular biological systems. Figure 6.1 shows the fundamental components of such a model with the basic open system inputs taken from the environment, converted in some kind of process and then delivered back as outputs to the environment. A common enhancement of this model, as shown in Figure 6.1, is a feedback loop with some measuring and correction mechanism which allows the system to maintain a steady state.

The human body replicates these system components in many different planes. We get hungry, we eat, our hunger is satisfied, we stop eating; we get hot, we sweat, the evaporation cools us down.

This simple model could also depict several different aspects of a business. The inputs that could be modelled include knowledge, raw materials, people and money; the processes might include R&D, production, marketing and selling, and training; the outputs might include new products, finished goods, trained/skilled employees and profits.

Modelling these various characteristics seems unlikely to generate any strategic insights since the element of time is excluded from the model. However, time is an essential ingredient in the systems model and the various life cycle phases are really the defining characteristics of any system. Biological systems such as a simple cell or a human being, physical systems such as an electronic component or, say, a lighted candle, and social systems such as a business or an industry, all share the well known stages of a life cycle.

The lighted candle was the model described by Koehler (1938) which usefully

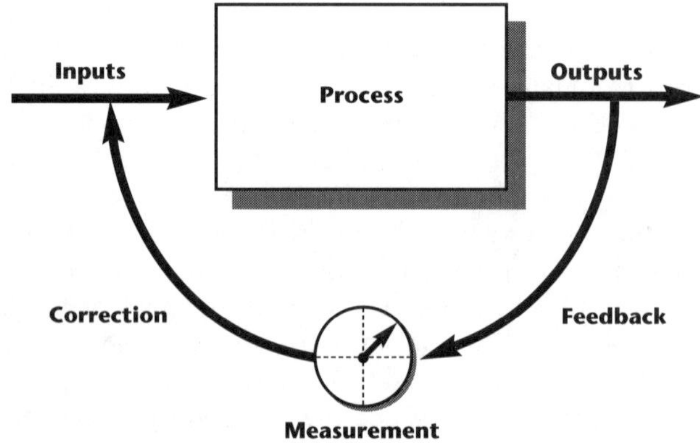

Figure 6.1 Simple open system

highlights many of the overall system properties and characteristics which change critically at the different stages of system evolution. At first when a flame is put to its wick the candle may spit and sputter and possibly go out several times before the wick achieves the temperature for ignition and is successfully lit. This birth, introduction or infancy stage is characterised in many systems by volatility and high rates of infant mortality, whether we are considering lighted candles, human babies, electronic components, business start-ups or new products.

If the candle successfully lights then the flame quickly burns up to its full size. This adolescent or growth stage is again typical of many systems in the speed and continuity of its growth up to a certain ceiling which marks the level of its mature phase.

As the candle reaches this ceiling it again exhibits a generally applicable characteristic of volatility before settling down to a mature phase steady state. The candle's volatility is manifested in a short period of flickering; adolescent human beings exhibit extraordinary volatility as any parent will vouch; the volatility of businesses and products as they move from growth to maturity is also remarkable and discussed in more detail below.

In its mature phase steady state, the candle exhibits the general systems characteristic of maximum strength and efficiency. In the case of the candle this is the phase when it burns the maximum wax and gives off the greatest light. It will maintain this maximum energy conversion steady state as determined by its inputs of wick, wax and oxygen and its system characteristics of size and composition of wick and diameter and length of candle. Human beings exhibit similar characteristics in their maturity, being then at their strongest and physically most efficient stage. Businesses also appear to be at their most efficient and intrinsically most profitable stage.

The steady state will end only when one of the determining factors changes. For example, the wax is used up to the extent that there is no longer a full quantity available for burning. At this stage the system goes into a decline, but again the change from the mature phase to decline is marked by further volatility as the candle flickers and putters and frequently goes out prematurely, i.e. before it has used up all its wax.

One of the intriguing characteristics of this general model is the apparent breadth of its applicability. All manner of systems appear to share these general characteristics and be subject to parallel pressures and influences at the different stages. This systems model not only seems applicable to a business organisation, but also offers insights which might not be available otherwise. These possibly unique insights are considered further below.

6.3 Evolution and system goals

All systems appear to evolve through the familiar stages of birth, growth, maturity, decline and death, and at each stage appear to behave as though driven by certain common goals, as summarised in Table 6.1.

In infancy, most successful systems are dominated by the need to survive. This is entirely natural and appropriate because of inherently high infant mortality rates. High infant mortality among humans has been reduced primarily by state provision

Table 6.1 System goal cycle

System phase	Dominant factor	System goal
Birth	Infant mortality	Survival
Adolescence, growth	Building strength	Achieve autonomy and maturity
	Phase change volatility	
Maturity	Competition	Longevity, control of environment, self-actualisation
	Phase change volatility	
Decline	Death	Stability, peace and quiet, seeking to delay the return to focus on survival
Death		Survival

in such areas as public hygiene and health. Moreover, infant humans are usually nurtured by loving parents in a generally benign adult population.

The infant business has few of these benefits. State support, despite the rhetoric, has in the past been disastrous, with interest rate policy taking money away from the fledgling business and redistributing it to the old, cash-rich leviathans. Only the founding entrepreneur will have any interest in the survival of the new business and he or she may lack the competence to ensure its success. The wider population is by no means benign. And if the infant business looks too successful its larger competitors will perceive the threat and try to bring it down.

Under such circumstances, an obsession with survival seems entirely appropriate for the infant business.

If it survives this first phase, the adolescent will be able to turn its attention to growth and the development of competitive strength. It progresses through adolescence by being quick, flexible, opportunistic and focused on satisfying customers' needs. It carries no spare weight, no passengers. It is lean and fit, quick on its feet and builds its strength through constant striving and exercise.

This phase sees the business change from being the creature of the founding entrepreneur with a simple structure, to employing an increasing number of professional specialists concerned with either the firm's technological development or the professionalisation of its various management functions.

In a growing market the adolescent business has to run fast in order simply to maintain its market share. If it fails to do this then in all probability it will not survive the first shake-out when market growth starts to falter. In a static market there is not the same necessity to grow. Many businesses stay small, providing relatively stable employment for small numbers of people. Nevertheless, other businesses are more ambitious and grow rapidly in order to achieve the critical mass at which the new specialists can be profitably supported. Growth in static markets can only be achieved by increasing market share or by moving into new markets, both of which may be problematic in highly competitive situations.

To achieve maturity is the goal of all systems. Maturity is the phase when a successful system achieves maximum entropy, the most efficient process of energy conversion, the closest to self-actualisation or fulfilment. In the case of a business, maturity is the phase when wealth creation is maximised, when the most surplus cash is generated and when the business achieves its position of greatest power and influence and when the business should be able to focus, with the least inhibition and interruption, on the achievement of its strategic objective or mission.

This general model of the overall system properties and characteristics explains why a business should be focused on achieving and maintaining the state of maturity. It is curious therefore that business maturity should be so widely regarded as an undesirable state. This may be partly because maturity is regarded as an early warning of decline. It may also be because mature organisations often exhibit the less desirable characteristics for which they are famed in the popular imagination. Whatever the reason, it is clear that many mature business opportunities are not exploited despite the lessons of the systems model.

Maturity is the result of successful infancy and adolescence. The success is usually based on doing the right things right and the business progressively becoming more expert. It learns successful ways of doing things. It finds out what its customers like and gets good at delivering those things. It develops its technological expertise. It uses recipes which work and it becomes efficient – and it becomes effective. All this either happens as a result of deliberate intent or by a process of trial and error, or by some combination of the two.

However, it is difficult for a successful business to make a fundamental change in what has established its leading position. This is especially the case with technology when a successful mature business is likely to have major investments sunk in the old technology. Getting into something new may mean writing off huge capital assets which will weaken the balance sheet and in the short term wreak havoc with profitability. Also there are psychological investments in the old technology. One of the fruits of maturity is the ability to pay top salaries and thus attract top calibre people. Many of these highly qualified professionals, managerial and technical, may have built their entire careers on the old technology and their very natural response to such a change is likely to be defensive and reactive. Nor is it at all certain that leadership in the new technology will necessarily follow; giving up a leading position should certainly not be done lightly.

A successful mature business, as the systems model suggests, is likely to generate substantial surplus funds which are not required in order to maintain the status quo. How these funds get invested depends very much on the circumstances of the individual business. Very few such businesses give the funds back to the shareholders, unless they are wholly owned and tightly controlled subsidiaries of financially oriented parents.

More typically, as indicated in section 4.3 in Chapter 4, surpluses are likely to be spent either on diversification or on various forms of organisational slack, either of which add substantial problems to maturity.

Diversification not only adds complexity and confuses strategic direction, but also creates an alternative focus for future development and an ongoing demand for investment which will in the end result in the starvation of the once successful mature business. Thus diversification leads naturally to the widely recognisable picture of a mature business which has lost its direction and failed to keep up investment in its key technologies.

Investment in organisational slack can be just as stultifying. It is a way of storing fat, which should be reversible. But the most frequently invested items are higher salaries, payments in lieu of salary and perks, as well as the employment of surplus people such as indirect professional specialists – accountants, planners, IT specialists, human resource managers and so forth. Although such investments are theoretically reversible, in practice they tend to develop a self-sustaining momentum of secondary recruitments, so that whole new departments and functions can grow up which only contribute peripherally, if at all, to the purpose of the business. Other investments in organisational slack include inessential investment in items such as luxurious office buildings, irrelevant research facilities, unnecessary production plant, even whole new factories may, in reality, only be items of slack, built because the firm could afford it.

In terms of goal orientation, the mature business, like many other systems, seeks to control its environment in order to ensure its own future well-being. The one thing the mature business, with all its heavy investments sunk in the status quo, seeks to avoid is change and the consequent instability. It will find it advantageous to invest heavily in preserving the current state of affairs. First of all it will seek to control its own industry, if possible through the achievement of a monopoly position, or as near monopoly power as it is possible to achieve. In this way it can hope to control prices at a level which ensures its own profitability and can control the level of business in order to set limits on the level of competitive activity at which it would be profitable for another business to enter the market.

For similar reasons it may well seek to achieve control over its sources of raw material supply if they are in any way insecure. It may seek to achieve this through the exercise of its purchasing muscle in tying up long-term supply arrangements. Or it may have to go as far as acquiring its key suppliers – such vertical integration is a common feature of many mature industries.

Other examples of mature businesses seeking to control their environment can be seen in the activities of organisations such as trade associations or industry research associations. Some such arrangements may be used purely for the interchange of technical information; others may reach covert agreements on what industry members will agree to pay for key raw materials; others still may agree precisely what prices will be charged and what price increases will be effected and when; others may even agree in what proportion particular markets will be divided among industry members. With varying degrees of legality, such practices remain common in the United States and EU as well as in the Pacific Rim economies. They may give the industry members concerned a feeling of security, but they are not to be relied on. At best, such arrangements will serve only as *temporary* insulation against harsher competitive forces further afield.

Cartels and explicit agreements to restrict competition, once the custom and practice among mature industries, are now clearly illegal in most advanced economies, but 'strategic global alliances', whose justification may be couched in terms of technology, may still result in the limitation of competition and the increase of stability and control over the environment.

Mature businesses tend to exhibit the tendencies outlined above. They do not appear to be the most effective stratagems. Diversification, unless done with great care, can have disastrous effects in reducing concentration and providing employees with confusing messages about the strategic direction of the business. Investments in organisational slack are almost invariably counterproductive in the messages they give to members of the organisation. Similarly with the various attempts to manipulate and control the environment. A mature business that successfully creates a protective barrier between itself and its competitors will inevitably become complacent and inefficient. Thus even if the product market does not go into terminal decline there are still pressures and tendencies working on the mature business which lead to decline and which will be reversed only by assertive management action.

In most systems, a biological cell or a candle, for example, ultimate decline and extinction are certain. For a business, this is not necessarily the case because a business can renew itself in ways that other systems cannot. Levitt (1960, and Reading Review 2) suggested that businesses become extinct only because of the myopic way they define themselves. Some tightly defined markets decline while others open up. The shape of the life cycle can be influenced by management. Product life cycles, business life cycles and even industry life cycles can all be manipulated. Although all biological systems die in the end, this is not necessarily so for social systems where maturity can be followed by renewal.

6.4 Life cycles

Understanding the systems origin of life cycles adds considerable depth and meaning to the usual simplistic depiction of an idealised graph, as shown in Figure 6.2.

The idealised shape shown in the figure is associated with an orthodox wisdom which has little connection with the model's system characteristics and has only uncertain empirical support. For example, it is commonly asserted that in the early stages of development of an industry, growth is slow. This sounds plausible because basic feasibilities and economic viability have to be investigated and demonstrated, the development resources must be built up and commitments to longer-term support made. The development of semiconductors and integrated circuits are examples from the recent past, while molecular engineering and biotechnology are examples where a body of knowledge and expertise is currently being built up. However, if the model were to be applied to a particular situation its characteristics would have to be considered carefully to see if slow initial growth was applicable.

In the idealised model, once commitment has reached a certain critical mass then growth takes off. During this phase, innovation efforts tend to centre around the product. New technology is applied to produce genuinely new products and radically improved products with more features and better performance. Participants in the industry focus all their development efforts on producing the latest technology. The past two decades have seen this phase in the development, for example, of the per-

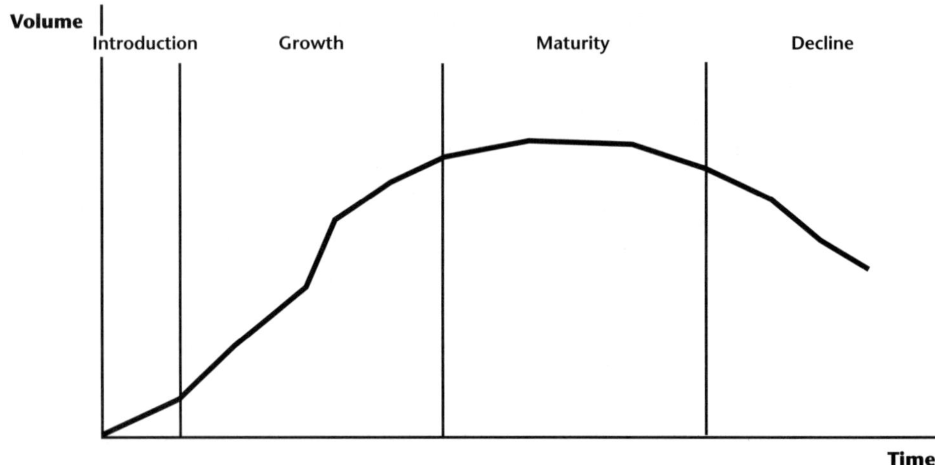

Figure 6.2 The idealised life cycle curve

sonal computer market. Growth took off with 8-bit machines such as the Apple II, Tandy TRS80 and Commodore Pet, followed by hundreds of others, all different and more-or-less incompatible with each other. New products were introduced almost daily and innovation was clearly focused on the product.

In due course, generally accepted standards of performance for the product emerge as the industry moves into the slower growth mature phase. During this transition there will be a radical reassessment of growth projections and several participants will realise that the volumes required in order to be profitable will not be available. Consequently there may be a period of fierce competition, during which a number of the weaker participants will decide, or be forced, to withdraw. The emergence of 16-bit technology and the introduction of IBM's PC operating system was such a phase in the microcomputer market. Most names associated with 8-bit technology are now distant memories, only Apple having survived the initial shake-out .

During the ensuing, relatively stable mature phase, the emphasis of innovation tends to move from product to production process, where innovations are aimed largely at reducing costs and improving efficiency. In the case of microcomputers the improvements in process fed back immediately into the product itself, especially in the form of ever more powerful chips enabling ever more sophisticated software. For some industries the mature phase may last a long time: several decades, even centuries, or more as in the case of clay bricks.

The mature phase comes to an end when either a completely new technology takes over (see many examples provided in Chapter 11) or some other structural change eliminates the existing business. Again the reduction in expectations of future business will be accompanied by increased price competition which forces the marginal businesses to be quickly eliminated through either closure or amalgamation.

These periods of shake-out and fall-out at the phase changes from growth to maturity and maturity to decline are the business equivalents of Koehler's flickering candle. Perhaps an even better analogy can be made with the theory of chaos. The changes from one more-or-less steady state to the next being signalled by intervening periods of chaos which have unpredictable outcomes. Fall-out will see the demise of the many, but the dawn of a new period of prosperity for the few who survive. For example, the British iron foundry industry appeared to go through a phase of terminal chaos in the early 1980s. For around three years foundries were closing at the rate of almost one a week. For the few businesses which survived, however, the late 1980s were extremely prosperous. Clearly there is considerable value in surviving to fight another day.

Figure 6.3 highlights these periods of phase change volatility and also explains part of the reasons for businesses being forced out. A major problem is the inability to predict accurately the timing of structural change. Extrapolating the existing state of affairs is much simpler, and most forecasting models are extremely accomplished at this. This universal phenomenon earned the schoolboy verse:

A trend is a trend is a trend,
  But the question is will it bend?
Will it alter its course
  Through some unforeseen force
And come to a premature end?

On the life cycle in Figure 6.3, at the point in time when the curve crosses the line from growth to maturity, participants in that industry will typically still be forecasting a continuation of the trend, i.e. growth. Consequently, anxious not to lose market share, businesses will seek to continue to supply increasing products to fulfil that growth expectation, building additional production capacity as necessary. When that growth is not actually realised the forecasters' typical response is to explain the short-

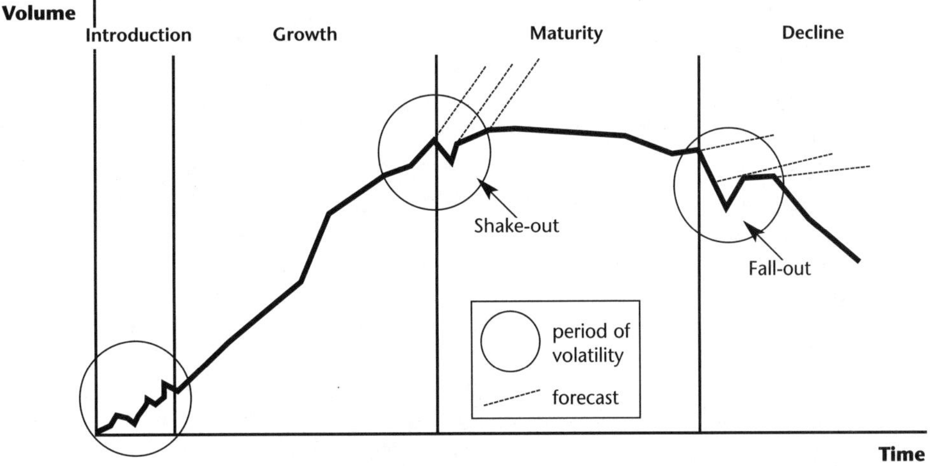

Figure 6.3 The life cycle phase changes

fall as a 'blip' and to forecast a return to the former growth in the near future. In fact it may take three or four time periods before the fact is acknowledged that the industry has ceased to grow and that the mature phase is now being confronted. During all that time additional capacity will have continued to be brought on stream, plant utilisation will have consequently declined and with it profitability in the industry. Profitability will usually be further destroyed by the competitive battle for shares of the diminished market which will often take the form of price wars. Under these conditions some firms will pull out, some will sell out, others will be forced out. This is the period of shake-out which will result in a smaller number of competitors left to enjoy the period of steady state maturity. A similar process typically occurs during the fall-out phase change from maturity to decline.

The characteristics of the four phases and management's typical responses are summarised in Table 6.2.

From the analysis in Table 6.2 it is possible to prescribe certain strategies as being appropriate for different participants at different phases. The strategic aim must be to achieve a dominant position during maturity when the greatest benefit can be obtained. Thus during the growth phase the strategy should be to build position so that the firm is well placed when the phase change occurs. In this position it is likely to benefit from the shake-out rather than be its victim and will thus be able to take full advantage of the mature phase. The aim then is to prolong the mature phase as long as possible and to maintain dominance, for example by judicious marketing action. In the decline phase the option is open to revive the product or to simply harvest from it. If a product's life cycle has apparently moved through its four phases

Table 6.2 Life cycle characteristics and responses

	Life cycle phase			
	Development	**Growth**	**Maturity**	**Decline**
Characteristics				
Sales	Low	Fast	Slow growth	Decline
Profits	Negligible	Peak levels	Moderating	Low
Cash flows	Negative	Moderate	Very positive	Moderating
Customers	Innovative	Mass market	Mass market	Laggards
Competitors	Few	Increasing	Many rivals	Fewer
Responses				
Strategic focus	Expand market	Market penetration	Defend share	Productivity
Marketing expense	High	High/reducing	Falling	Low
Marketing focus	Product aware	Brand preference	Brand loyalty	Selective
Distribution	Patchy	Intensive	Intensive	Selective
Price	High	Reducing	Lowest	Rising
Product	Basic	Improved	Differentiated	Rationalised

Table 6.3 Strategies and life cycle phases

	Phase of life cycle		
Competitive position:	**Growth**	**Maturity**	**Decline**
LEADER High market share	Build share by price cuts to discourage new competing capacity. Add capacity to anticipate future requirements	Hold share and prolong phase by improving quality and increased sales effort and advertising	Revive by new technology or marketing/harvest, i.e. maximise cash flow by cutting investment in advertising and R&D
FOLLOWER Low market share	Invest to increase share. Concentrate on particular market segments	Withdraw or hold share by lower prices and costs than leaders	Withdraw

and is clearly now in decline, management has to decide whether and when to cut its losses, or alternatively whether and how much to invest in the product's renewal.

The broad strategic prescriptions for the life cycle model are fairly limited. They focus largely on the action that can be taken with regard to market share because that is the main measure of success of a product or business when the market and its development are treated as given. The framework highlights the need to forecast phase changes and to position the business or product advantageously ahead of the transition from growth to maturity and maturity to decline. The strategic prescriptions are summarised in Table 6.3.

Life cycles, however, provide little detailed guidance as to how the various strategies might be achieved. The framework provides insights and understanding and sets the broad parameters. Management uses the broad guidelines against the background insights and understanding of its particular situation in order to make the strategy specific.

6.5 Using life cycles

Life cycles appear to have a wide validity and they seem, at an intuitive level, to offer interesting explanations of system behaviour whether it is a product, a business or an industry. The shape, size and stage of various life cycles could be used to illustrate, for example, that companies are now spending more money on computers and communications equipment than the combined expenditure on mining, agriculture and construction. Also there are now more people employed in the UK in Indian restaurants than in coal, steel and shipbuilding combined. Thinking of these various industries in terms of their life cycles offers some insights and understanding of the processes involved and the possible moves that participants might make. Life cycles seem both plausible and meaningful.

Life cycles raise a number of interesting issues, regarding positioning ahead of phase changes and about the attractions and characteristics of the different phases. In particular, they offer some insight into the potential attractions of mature business. Where previously it was easy to regard mature business as having limited value, life cycles are a reminder that every successful business matures and in its maturity it generates the greatest wealth.

For life cycles to be practically useful, it must be possible to identify the shape, size and current position of the particular industry or product curve. In some industries, for some products, this is not too difficult. For example, marketers have made extensive use of life cycle analysis for short-lived fashion goods where market potential is known, the speed of penetration is a key statistic and the only unknown is whether the customer will buy the product.

For some products there may be substantial evidence of the likely shape of its curve because of the shape of similar products' curves in the past. For example, successions of generic domestic white goods have had fairly predictable life cycle curves. From washing machines through refrigerators, freezers, microwaves and dishwashers, there has been a clearly identifiable total market and a predictable rate of penetration given both by previous product experience and by experience in other, earlier markets. Similarly, successive generations of computers, motor cars, container ships and aeroengines, to name but a few, have all exhibited fairly predictable life cycles, though predicting market shares, despite the small number of producers, may be more problematic. All these products share a predictability of total demand and an inevitability about the technological progression from one generation to another. But most life cycles lack this degree of predictability. Figure 6.4 highlights the problem. Which of the various projections best fits product C at time *t*? With knowledge of previous product generations it might be possible to predict the shape and position. However, if previous generations developed curves like products A and B, then the life cycle concept may be of little assistance.

For many other products, particularly ones enjoying a protracted mature phase with more ups and downs resulting from the general economy than from life cycle effects, it becomes impractical to use life cycle analysis.

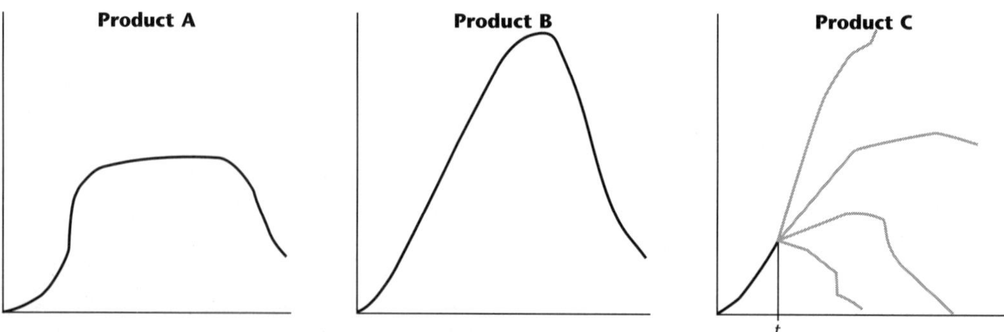

Figure 6.4 Different shaped life cycle curves

There is no real solution to this problem. Clay building bricks have been around now for upwards of three thousand years and might therefore be thought of as mature. The IBM PC, on the other hand, is a relatively new product using relatively (to the clay brick) new technology. But which of the two is furthest along its life cycle? Which is the more mature product? Which will last longer? Which will generate more wealth from this point on? Which represents the greatest opportunity for innovative development?

The important thing about mature business is not its maturity but its potential. Individual firms, whole industries and even entire economies depend, and will continue to depend, on products which have been around for a long time. They will change in detail, be developed and enhanced to achieve higher quality, improved performance, lower costs and greater acceptability, but they will remain, as they have for long past, fundamentally the same products satisfying fundamentally the same customer needs. In so doing, such products may appear to refute life cycle theory entirely.

A further problem which can arise from the over-simple application of life cycle curves is that they can become self-fulfilling prophecies. This is not peculiar to life cycles, but is a particular problem if the diagnosis of position is inaccurate. For example, if a business is diagnosed as being in the decline phase, it may well be starved of new investment and consequently decline. An alternative diagnosis, suggesting a continuity of the mature, maximum energy conversion (cash generation) phase, might suggest the level of investment needed to maintain the business.

Life cycles, although intuitively valid, may be fraught with difficulty in particular circumstances. Even after a clearly defined cycle has reached well into what appears to be its decline phase, there may still be potential for major new business. There is no reason why a curve should follow the smooth idealised shape of Figure 6.2. However, in situations where the shape and size of the life cycle can be clearly identified, the framework can provide the most useful insights and additions to understanding, thereby substantially enhancing the quality of strategic thinking. Consider the situation of Intel described in Box 6.1.

BOX 6.1

Intel in memory chips

Intel was formed in 1968 to develop and sell INTegrated ELectronic components. It was the first to focus on semiconductor memory and its breakthrough development was the silicon gate approach to memory chips. Previously, aluminium electrode gates built into semiconductors had meant production yields of less than 5 per cent, but Intel's use of polysilicon drastically reduced production bugs and radically improved yields. The technology smashed the cost of transistors.

In 1970, Intel introduced the 1103 memory chip, a brand new circuit design concept with more than 1,000 bits and over 4,000 transistors which quickly became the industry standard. Thereafter, Intel lived at the edge. As soon as it could make a device with a high yield, it turned its attack on costs by achieving ever more complex circuit design, which inevitably reduced yields. By 1973, the 1103 had reached its peak and already the 4K-bit chip had arrived. Of the several competing producers, Intel gained dominance through a reputation for reliability and delivery. Then a succession of new developments established the rule that the number of components that could be put on a chip doubled every year.

The 8080 processor was introduced in 1974 and was quickly established as the 8-bit standard. This was followed by the 8086 16-bit standard in 1978 and a continuing succession of revolutionary new products. In 1979, the USA had two-thirds of the world's semiconductor market; Japan had only 22 per cent, but the big Japanese producers moved quickly to reverse that ratio. They focused their attack on memory chips and, aided by MITI (Japanese Ministry for International Trade and Industry) and following the Intel technology, they gradually closed the volume gap and then managed to undercut Intel's prices.

While the development costs escalated with each new memory product Intel introduced, so Intel's technological lead over the Japanese became shorter, and the Japanese manufacturers' determination to achieve volume ultimately deprived Intel of any lasting cost advantage. In the end, after mounting various anti-dumping lawsuits against its Japanese competitors, Intel was driven to consider withdrawal from memory chips.

DISCUSSION POINTS

1. Is the life cycle framework applicable to Intel's situation? Propose one such application.
2. Would it be possible to define the shape and size of such a life cycle?
3. What strategy does the framework suggest Intel should consider?

6.6 Experience curves

During the 1960s the Boston Consulting Group (BCG) investigated the costs involved in the production and sale of various commodity products and found a surprisingly consistent relationship between those costs and the total amount produced and sold (Boston Consulting Group, 1968a, and Reading Review 4). This relationship was the foundation of one of the most influential of all strategy frameworks. Whilst in its origins the experience curve is quite unrelated to the life cycle, the parallels between the two frameworks are striking, each offering confirmation of the other.

The mature phase of the life cycle is distinguished by maximum efficiency: for a candle the maximum energy conversion and greatest amount of light; for a business the most efficient processes, lowest costs and greatest generation of surplus cash. This is intrinsic to the general systems model.

The BCG found that costs fell as experience increased, thus offering confirmation of the life cycle model. In the life cycle framework it was noted that the price of a product would be at its lowest in the mature phase (see Table 6.2). This is partly because in maturity attention is focused on efficiency owing to increased competition, and partly because of the effects of the familiar learning curve. Both these factors offer plausible explanations for the experience phenomenon.

The BCG found the relationship applied across a wide range of products and industries. They investigated twenty-four products and derived the total costs involved in their production. These were plotted against total volumes produced, as shown in Figure 6.5.

The smoothness of this cost/volume curve suggests an apparently stable relationship between the two. Based on the BCG's analyses, it appeared that unit costs reduced by between 20 per cent and 30 per cent every time total production (i.e. experience) doubled. This finding has been frequently replicated and confirmed by other researchers, for example Abell and Hammond (1979).

The products that the BCG investigated were all essentially commodity products such as transistors, diodes, crude oil, ethylene and polypropylene. It is important when interpreting experience curves to recognise that the curves are based on empirical studies of commodities, not highly differentiated branded products. The same is true of the various corroborative researches. For example, Abell and Hammond reported similar results in relation to integrated circuits, broiler chickens and steam turbine generators (Abell and Hammond, 1979).

A reduction in costs of 20–30 per cent is potentially a very significant factor. Accepting the experience relationship and making some fairly straightforward assumptions, it would be a simple matter of arithmetic to calculate the cost reduc-

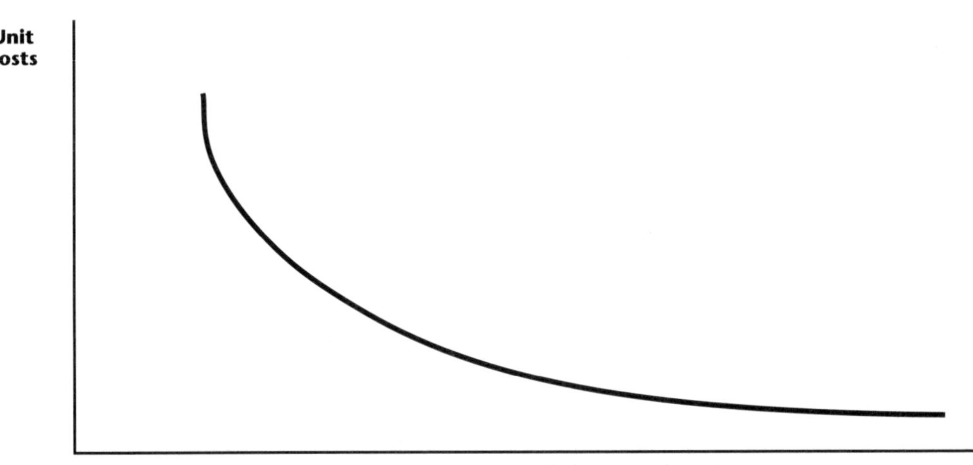

Figure 6.5 The experience curve

tions arising from experience in different industry situations. Assume that it might take an industry at least fifteen years to double its experience if it had reached its mature, low growth stage, say, some ten years previously. Such an industry would enjoy cost reductions from experience of substantially less than 2 per cent per annum. For a longer established industry it would clearly take a great many years before total production experience is doubled and the benefits therefrom would be completely insignificant. For a young industry, on the other hand, still experiencing its initial growth phase, production experience could be doubled within a matter of months and the cost reductions could be the dominant competitive factor in that industry. Cost reductions from experience in the first few years of an industry could clearly be decisive. Thus the impact of experience depends critically on the growth rate of that industry: unless growth is still high, experience will be unimportant.

The BCG suggested that experience effects apply equally to individual producers and to industries as a whole. An individual producer can achieve reduced costs by increasing cumulative experience more rapidly than its competitors. This can be done by increasing market share. The bigger the increase in market share the more quickly a firm would increase its experience relative to its competitors and thus enjoy the reduction in costs. The BCG took this line of analysis further, showing how to calculate the net present value of such an increase in market share (see page 83). However, the distinction between industry costs and the costs of the individual producer needs to be treated with care. It may well be that a new entrant to a mature industry joins with the latest technology and thus enjoys a cost advantage which completely belies the position in relation to experience.

For simplicity the cost/experience relationship is usually presented with both axes having logarithmic scales so that the smooth curve becomes a straight line as in Figure 6.6. This presentation is made so that the effects of competition can be more easily presented.

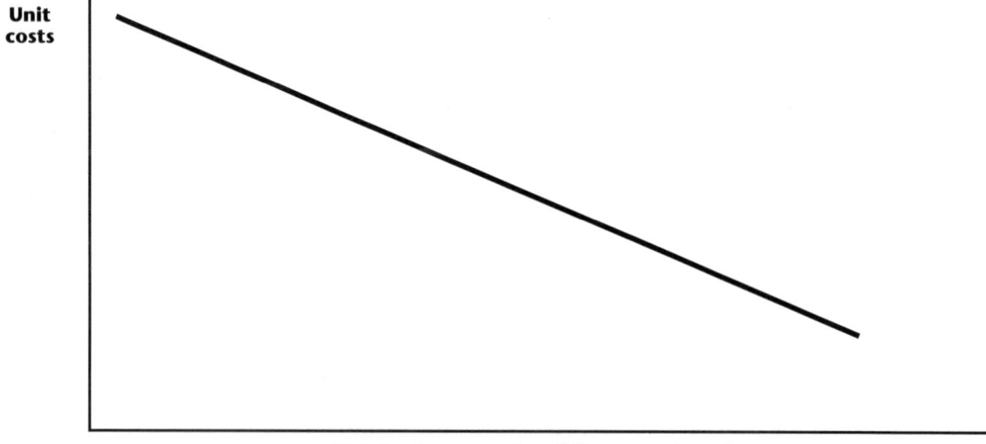

Figure 6.6 The experience relationship (log:log scaled)

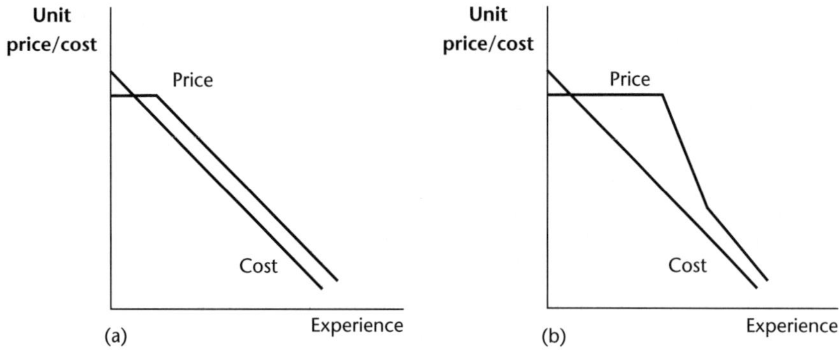

Figure 6.7 Costs and prices. (a) stable relationship; (b) unstable relationship

A second finding of the BCG's empirical study was that prices follow the same pattern as costs so long as the competitive scene remains stable (see Figure 6.7). This might seem almost to be tautological, since the BCG's concern is with commodity products where the only competitive weapon is price. The BCG suggested that a common situation would be for new products to be introduced at prices initially set below costs in order to create a market. Once established, unit costs would start to fall as a result of experience and in due course drop to a level which provides producers with an economic margin. Subsequently, costs and prices would fall more-or-less together. Producers might attempt to hold prices up and so earn higher margins, but this would be unlikely to prove sustainable for long. If super-margins were made then new competitors would be encouraged to enter the market. Consequently, existing producers would be encouraged to reduce prices to levels which would discourage new competition from entering. Thus, either way, a stable relationship between cost and price would ultimately prevail. Implicit in this model is the economists' assumption that price is the only competitive weapon.

If cost is a function of accumulated experience then it follows that the competitor with the most accumulated experience, i.e. the biggest cumulative market share, will have the lowest costs. The scale of this cost advantage will depend on how far the leading competitor's cumulative experience exceeds that of his nearest competitor. A good approximation to this would be to measure market share in relative terms, i.e. market share relative to the share of the leading competitor. This is the theoretical basis for the assertion that high relative market share will produce high profitability.

The connection between profitability and market share is not at first surprising, especially in these markets where there is a market price for undifferentiated commodity products. The idea of economies of scale implies nothing else. Furthermore, the theory was supported by empirical evidence from the influential and longstanding PIMS (Profit Impact of Market Strategy) databank of the Strategic Planning Institute:

> *a business's share of its served market (both absolute and relative to its three largest competitors) has a positive impact on its profit and net cash flow.* (Schoeffler, 1977)

If the market is growing rapidly then experience is doubled in a short period of time and consequently costs fall quickly. Under these circumstances the value of increased market share would be considerable because it would result in increasing cost advantage over competitors. On the other hand, if the market is mature and not growing significantly, increases in market share would not be worth a great deal, and, moreover, would only be available at great cost. Thus Bostonian analysis suggests that during the growth phase of a product or an industry, the returns from increasing market share are high. But for all other phases of product or industry life cycles, market share appears not to be particularly relevant.

However, the connection between market share and profitability is controversial, despite the PIMS evidence. The existence of a reliable correlation between market share and profitability is widely disputed. Even if it is accepted that there is a positive connection, the causal direction remains uncertain. It is at least as likely that dominant market share and high profitability are both the result of exceptional performance in some other aspect of the business, rather than profit resulting directly from share.

Even before the BCG analysis had emerged, Drucker wrote,

> *in many industries the largest company is by no means the most profitable one . . . the second spot, or even the third spot is often preferable, for it may make possible that concentration on one segment of the market, on one class of customer, on one application of the technology, in which genuine leadership often lies.*
>
> (Drucker, 1964, and Reading Review 3)

Prescott *et al.*'s survey into the connection between market share and profitability found that the connection depended on the particular situation. Eight environmental contexts were investigated and in five of these there was no positive relationship between market share and profitability (Prescott *et al.*, 1986).

Most analyses of the connection, and including the PIMS data, are in essence statistical and can only be very tentative when it comes to interpreting causes. Nevertheless, the idea that profitability stems from market share, for the plausible reasons explained, remains one of the foundations of the BCG analysis.

6.7 Using experience curves

The experience model is extremely simple. It assumes away all extraneous non-experience effects, largely by explicitly assuming that competition remains stable and is based solely on price; in the experience framework there is no non-price competition. Moreover, the strength to conduct price competition stems solely from relative costs. Thus the experience framework is not relevant to situations involving the marketing of branded differentiated products where price is not the only source of competitive advantage.

Even for commodity products the experience framework has little to offer unless the market is new and still growing fast. In mature situations the savings as a result of experience are insignificant. Moreover it is in just these situations that discretionary investments of surplus funds are typically made, but the experience frame-

BOX 6.2

Intel in memory chips (2)

Intel developed each successive memory product and exploited its cost advantage for as long as it could, but its more cost-oriented Japanese competitors bought market share and exploited their cost advantage to foreshorten Intel's involvement with each successive product.

DISCUSSION POINTS

1. What insights does the experience curve framework provide for Intel's strategic situation?
2. Why should Intel not achieve lower costs than its Japanese competitors?
3. What strategy does the experience curve framework suggest Intel might consider?
4. Do the life cycle and experience curve frameworks suggest different strategies for Intel?

work assumes that costs decline only as a result of experience; they do not increase as a result of maturity.

Thus the experience framework is precisely limited and simply not relevant to the vast bulk of industry. In particular, marketers who apply experience curve concepts in their marketing planning of mature branded products, as many do, are committing a basic error.

The strategic relevance of the experience curve framework is restricted to young, high-growth commodity products. In these precise situations, however, the concept is potent indeed. An example of this was highlighted by the early Intel experience in the memory chip industry described in Box 6.1. Now consider Intel's position from the experience curve framework as suggested in Box 6.2.

Summary

- Evolutionary frameworks were the first simplifying models used to develop the strategy of a business. They were derived from general systems theory which defined a life cycle which although based originally on biological systems, was applied to other phenomena such as a product, business or industry.
- Products, businesses and industries appear likely to progress through a four stage cycle: development, growth, maturity and decline.
- During the development phase, systems focus on survival. During growth they focus on achieving autonomy and maturity. During maturity they focus on con-

trol of the environment and on 'self-actualisation'. During decline they focus on stability and, in the end, once more on survival.

- For each phase of the cycle there appears to be a rational set of strategy management decisions which would optimise the economic results from the business.
- Each phase change is accompanied by periods of volatility which in business terms can result in a shake-out of industry participants.
- The analysis appears full of insights but it is beset by two major problems: how to identify the shape and size of a life cycle curve, and how to locate a product or business accurately on its life cycle curve.
- Consequently it is often unclear what the optimal decisions should be and there is a strong probability that such decisions become self-fulfilling.
- Experience curves are based on the Boston Consulting Group's empirical studies of twenty-four high-growth commodity products.
- Boston found that in these products, costs reduced by between 20 per cent and 30 per cent every time total experience (i.e. manufacture and sales) was doubled.
- During the early stages of an industry, where experience is doubling rapidly, this cost reduction can be crucial.
- Where price is the main competitive weapon, i.e. where products are not significantly differentiated, experience may be the key to competitive advantage.
- Experience is not of such strategic relevance to businesses which are growing only slowly, or for products for which competition is not based primarily on price.
- The experience that a competitor has, relative to other participants in the industry, can be proxied by relative market share, which is easier to measure.
- Experience curves suggest a model where the likely long-term profitability of a business is determined largely by just two characteristics:
  - the rate of market growth (which is an indicator of how long it will take for experience to be doubled), and
  - market share relative to the largest competitor's share (which is an indicator of competitive strength).

Further reading

Boston Consulting Group, *Perspectives on Experience*, BCG, 1968.
Emery, F.E., *Systems Thinking*, Penguin, 1969.

Chapter 7

Portfolio frameworks

Evolutionary frameworks suggest that a business should try to seek a balance among its subparts, whether those parts are product groups or whole businesses, so that they do not all peak together and decline together. Thus, the idea of a balanced portfolio developed naturally out of the evolutionary frameworks.

The Boston Consulting Group introduced the first business portfolio which originated in their work on experience. It was the only portfolio with any significant empirical foundation. It was also the simplest. Subsequently, more sophisticated frameworks were introduced, but they had most of the limitations of the BCG's and few substantive advantages.

This chapter reviews the portfolio frameworks and identifies situations where they may be applied.

7.1 Introduction

The BCG's empirical work on experience (Boston Consulting Group, 1968a, 1968b, and Reading Reviews 4 and 5) formed the basis of their original business portfolio. The portfolio is therefore applicable in the same situations as those in which the experience curve is relevant, i.e. high-growth markets where competition is between undifferentiated products conducted largely on the basis of price.

The BCG's portfolio is important, not simply because it was the first and achieved such widespread use, but because, of all the portfolios, it was the only one with any empirical underpinnings. It was also elegantly simple. A limited analysis of just two variables appeared to provide the keys to a strategic rationale for a whole multi-business company. There had not previously been any such framework available to strategy managers and it was adopted with enthusiasm.

The framework was applied in all manner of situations, some apt, others not. Where it was used out of the appropriate context it was not effective and in due course, as was probably inevitable, it fell into disrepute. The framework's limitations and shortcomings were recognised but its strengths in particular situations were never fully acknowledged.

More sophisticated portfolio models were subsequently developed by the BCG and others, two of which – the directional policy matrix and the business strength/market attractiveness matrix – are briefly described in this chapter. These combined the simple two-dimensional matrix with a more comprehensive economics-based analysis of the business and its environments. They answered some of the criticisms made against the original portfolio, but still suffered most of its shortcomings.

Portfolios are still used today, and misused. They have been discredited largely as a result of misapplication, but they survive and in the right situation still offer a simple, elegant solution to a real strategic problem.

The following sections focus mainly on the original portfolio model because it was the simplest, the only one with an empirical basis and because it embodies all the main strengths and weaknesses of the portfolio species.

Boston's original portfolio

The portfolio model is usually portrayed as a simple two-dimensional matrix (see Figure 7.1), the two dimensions being the rate of growth of the market and the share of the market that the business has relative to its largest competitor. The importance of these two factors was identified in the BCG's study of experience as described in the previous chapter.

Relative market share was assessed as the number of times the business' market share is that of its largest competitor. The break between the high and low sides of

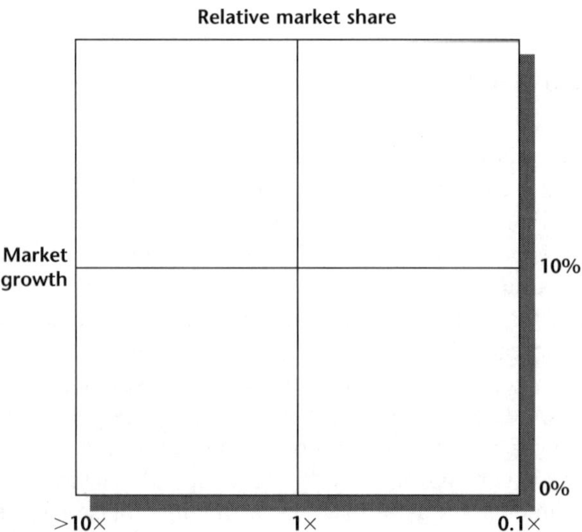

Figure 7.1 The original Boston matrix

the matrix was originally set at equality with the leading competitor (as shown in Figure 7.1). Thus, in any market there could only ever be one business on the high relative market share side of the matrix.

The concern with relative market share arises straight out of the BCG's empirical studies of experience. The measure is a proxy for relative experience, i.e. the experience that the firm in question has relative to its competitors'. This is important because this is measuring what its costs should be relative to its competitors', assuming always that the business is engaged in commodity markets which all take the market defined price, and not dealing with branded, differentiated products. Thus the Boston matrix relies on the experience-defined relationship between relative market share and profitability.

Market growth is important because it was only in rapidly growing markets that the experience-based cost reductions were likely to be significant. The low-growth half of the matrix should really be disregarded for this reason, i.e. in the low-growth half of the matrix the experience-based market share/profitability relationship no longer holds. The BCG originally set the break between the high and low market growth rates at 10 per cent per annum which was a reasonable marker as to the significance of experience – much above 10 per cent and the experience effects would be important; much below 10 per cent and they would most probably be insignificant.

As the framework gained widespread application, however, it became apparent that the vast majority of businesses for which the framework was used theoretically lay beyond its scope. This was because they operated in mature economies which were growing much less than 10 per cent per annum with only few industries realistically expected to exceed the growth barrier. Moreover, since only one competitor per industry could claim a high relative market share, it meant that most businesses would be accurately defined as in the bottom-right quadrant of the matrix. This had even more unfortunate consequences.

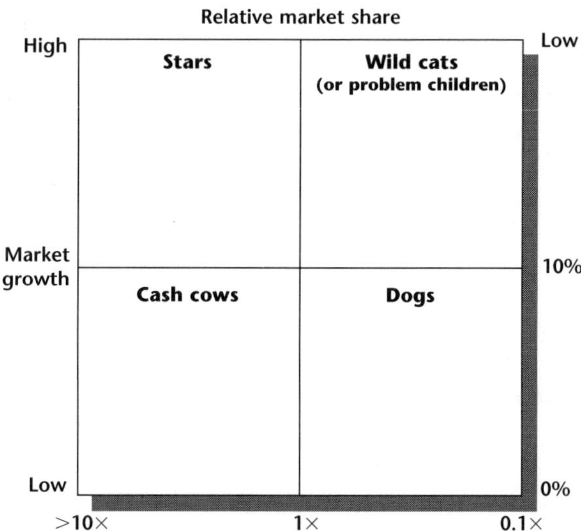

Figure 7.2 Amended Boston matrix

In the event, the BCG relaxed the definitions of relative market share and market growth, showing them simply as in Figure 7.2, where the dividing line between high and low was deliberately fudged. Subsequently, many applications of the matrix appeared to assume that the divide between high and low market growth was actually drawn at zero, so low growth was in fact a euphemism for decline.

This fudging of the definitions, which should have been quite clear since the definitions were based on empirical findings, led to many errors in the application of the framework. Nevertheless we will here follow the Boston route of relaxing the definitions, although not overlooking the problems it causes.

Businesses falling into the high growth, high market share quadrant were designated *stars*. Since they have high relative market share these businesses have the benefit of the greatest experience and therefore the lowest costs. In a commodity market where there is no price variation this means that they earn the highest profits and therefore are positive cash generators. However, since they are also enjoying high growth they also consume substantial cash, investing in new productive capacity as well as in working capital (i.e. trade debtors and stocks). It would depend on the particular circumstances whether a star generates sufficient cash to cover the necessary investment in growth. Thus, although profitable, stars might have either positive or negative net cash flow.

Businesses falling into the low growth, high market share quadrant were designated *cash cows*. These are profitable as a result of their high relative market share and so generate a substantial cash surplus. Moreover, they do not require to consume much cash since they are not growing. They therefore clearly generate surplus cash which can be invested elsewhere in the business.

Businesses falling into the low growth, low relative market share quadrant were designated *dogs*. These businesses are inherently unprofitable because of their low relative market share. However, since they do not need to invest in growth they might, overall, be cash neutral or even net generators.

Businesses falling into the high growth, low market share quadrant were clearly a source of some confusion. They have been referred to as *wild cats*, *problem children* and question marks. They are unprofitable as a result of their low market share, but they consume a lot of cash merely to maintain their market position because of the high growth rate. Thus, overall, these businesses consume cash. However, when markets are growing fast, the BCG analysis suggests that the value of increased market share is extremely high. Therefore it may be worth a very large investment in order to convert these businesses into stars.

From this simple analysis, the BCG developed equally straightforward strategic prescriptions as follows:

- *Stars*: Invest to maintain market share. Keep prices up, reducing them only in order to maintain market share.
- *Cash cows*: Strictly ration new investments. Keep prices up but ensure no new entrants to the market.
- *Wild cats*: Invest to convert into stars or withdraw on most advantageous terms by progressively pricing out of the market.
- *Dogs*: Manage tightly for cash and withdraw.

As was noted previously, all but one business in most mature economy industries would be defined as a dog, and the BCG's prescription for a dog was 'withdraw'. This would imply withdrawal from perhaps around 80 per cent of UK businesses. Although progress was undoubtedly made in this direction, strategy managers clearly did not apply the Boston matrix too literally.

The strategic value of a business is thus defined simply by having regard to two factors: market growth and relative market share. This simple idea with its familiar menagerie implies the anticipated direction of cash flows and the summary strategic prescriptions for the management of cash flows in order to achieve a balanced portfolio over time. Cash is invested as necessary in stars to maintain their relative market share so that when market growth slows down they become cash cows. Surplus cash from cash cows is used to fund stars and, where feasible, to convert wild cats into stars. Dogs are managed for cash and divested.

These are the 'strategies' shown in Figure 7.3. The direction of these various moves is the result of explicit management initiatives about strategy, and this represents the main contribution of the portfolio framework. For a relatively limited analysis it is possible to develop some simple and useful-looking strategic decisions.

With no strategic management intervention the more likely set of movements would be as shown by the thin arrows on Figure 7.3. The point has often been made that these anti-strategic moves are what frequently occur in businesses which are dominated by a cost-cutting culture. The thin arrows identify how the 'disinvestment spiral' really works: stars and cash cows are allowed to lose their leading positions and the rest follows with a simple inevitability.

By following the prescribed strategic moves, it is intended to achieve a balanced

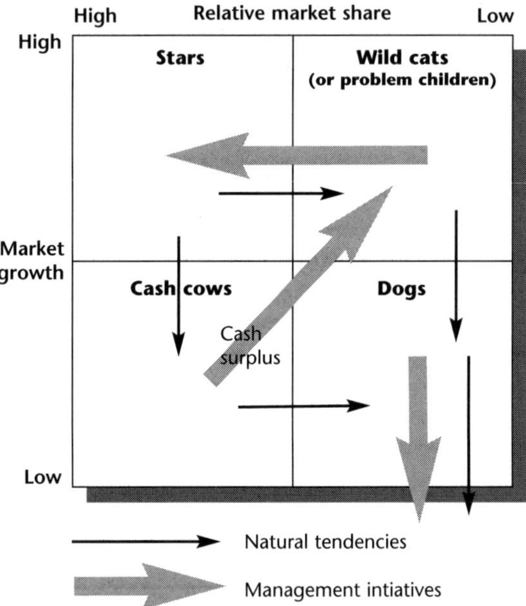

Figure 7.3 Moves on the Boston matrix

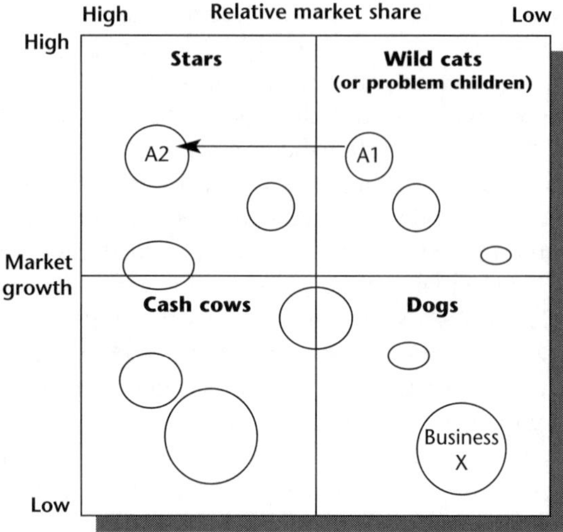

Figure 7.4 A balanced portfolio

portfolio of businesses with a selection of problem children (wild cats) to groom into stars, an adequate succession of stars ready to take over from today's cash cows and a sufficient level of cash cow business to fund the future. A typical portfolio is shown in Figure 7.4 where each circle represents a business, the size of the circle being proportionate to annual sales revenue. This diagram shows the position at a point in time but it can also be used to show intended strategic moves over time, as with the development and growth of business A from position A1 to A2.

The framework was very attractive for the corporate headquarters of many multi-business companies. They could eliminate much of the detailed planning and bureaucracy involved in the approaches described in Chapter 5 and, working with the portfolio framework, allow subsidiary businesses a 'maximum' autonomy, simply steering them by means of cash controls informed by the Boston prescriptions applying to their position on the matrix. This represented a substantial step forward in the strategy process, the opportunity to combine reduced bureaucracy and increased autonomy at business level with a realistic level of strategic control. However, there were some practical problems in implementing the system. Now consider the case of business X in Box 7.1.

7.3 Derivative portfolios

The strategic prescriptions derived from portfolio analysis, limited as they are to variations of buy, sell or hold, may nevertheless be extremely important. No decision to close or milk a business should ever be taken lightly. Yet the factual basis for the prescriptions in the BCG's model was restricted to knowledge about the market growth rate and relative market share. On the face of it this is an extremely superficial analysis for such important decisions. Interest focused on a more comprehensive analysis

BOX 7.1

The case of business X

Head office staff at ABC Plc have drawn up a portfolio of the group's businesses based on information submitted as part of the annual plan. The portfolio is as shown in Figure 7.4. The plan submission received from business X included an application for approval to a major capital project to double the size of its existing business.

DISCUSSION POINTS

1. As chief executive of ABC Plc, how do you view business X's strategy?
2. As general manager of business X, how can you persuade ABC to support your proposal?
3. What is the effect within business X of being categorised as a dog?

of markets than simply measuring their annual growth. Similarly, it was recognised that relative market share was in reality an inadequate measure of the competitive strength of a business.

Thus a number of variations on the original Boston matrix were devised. Two of the most widely used models are summarised in the following sections.

7.3.1 Directional policy matrix

A variation on the Boston matrix, the directional policy matrix (DPM) depicted in Figure 7.5, was published by the Royal Dutch Shell Group. The DPM retains the simple two-dimensional structure, but the definition of each dimension is considerably more complex. The more detailed inputs to the model make it possible to incorporate more of the data specific to an organisation's actual position and thus, in some sense, to make it a more realistic model. The DPM is also focused explicitly on the future.

The DPM replaces market growth by 'sector prospects', which comprise the following:

1. Market growth rates
2. Market quality (i.e. stability and consistency)
3. Raw material situation (i.e. reliability and ownership of supplies)
4. Environmental aspects (extent of restrictions, sensitivity of operations, and so on)

This more detailed analysis (than the simple Bostonian measure of market growth) still includes market growth as an important constituent of the attractiveness of the sector's prospects.

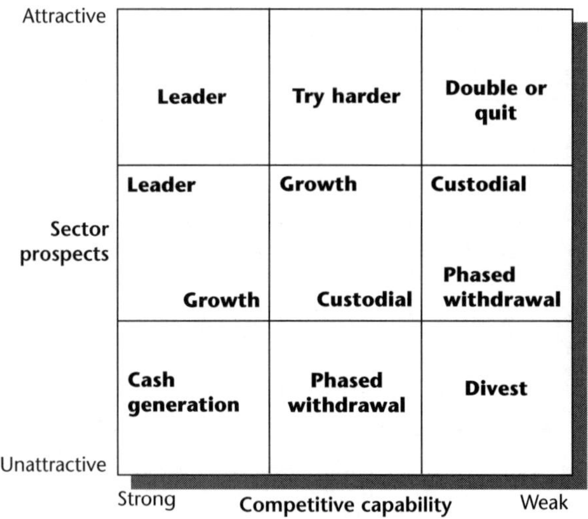

Figure 7.5 The directional policy matrix

On the other dimension, relative market share is replaced by the organisation's 'competitive capabilities'. These also require a more detailed analysis which could be shaped to reflect the factors which appear to be most significant in any particular organisation's own situation. The components of competitive capabilities are usually held to include the following:

1. Market position
2. Production capability
3. Product research and development

The market position measure could clearly include consideration of the BCG's relative market share measure, but goes beyond it in requiring a more qualitative assessment of position. The debt to Boston is apparent in these categories, as well as in the resultant matrix.

To some extent the DPM was a response to the over-simplification which was both Boston's main strength and, in the end, its greatest weakness. The analysis of sector prospects and competitive capabilities was a step forward in terms of a real assessment of what appeared likely to be important, but in being more complex also risked losing clarity in the resulting prescriptions.

The DPM is divided into nine boxes, and consequently the prescriptions appear to be rather more detailed than the BCG's and therefore sensitive to the more detailed analysis input to the model. This may, however, be more apparent than real.

The prescriptions are as follows:

- *Leader*: Allocate major resources
- *Try harder*: May be vulnerable over the long term
- *Double or quit*: Collect major business units for the future from this zone

- *Growth*: Allocate sufficient resources to grow with the market
- *Custodial*: Maximise cash generation without further commitment of resources
- *Cash generation*: Little further need for finance or expansion
- *Phased withdrawal*: Redeploy resources to more attractive businesses as withdraw from this area
- *Divest*: Get out quickly and redeploy resources

It is open to debate how much of an enhancement these prescriptions are compared with the BCG's. All portfolio models are stuck with variations on the three simple portfolio decisions: buy, sell or hold, and it is not at all certain that it is worthwhile subdividing these into nine rather than four. The added precision is probably an illusion.

Interest in portfolios persisted and several further enhancements were devised and used widely for a period. Perhaps the best known of these was the General Electric/McKinsey matrix described in the following section.

7.3.2 Business strength/market attractiveness matrix

The business strength/market attractiveness matrix emerged from the work of various contributors: McKinsey, General Electric and others. The particular version summarised here also incorporates aspects of the Shell approach.

The model goes into considerably more detail than the DPM, including no fewer than eleven factors as making up 'market attractiveness'. Prominent among these is the critical measure of market growth. Market attractiveness is measured through:

1. Market growth and product life cycle position
2. Growth cyclicality
3. Market size
4. Industry profitability
5. Ease of entry
6. Business environment
7. Raw material availability
8. Competitor concentration
9. Marketing intensity
10. Margin elasticity relative to quality
11. Customer concentration

Similarly with the business strength dimension, the model considers no fewer than thirteen factors. Not surprisingly these include the BCG's original, experience-based measure of relative market share as well as many of the factors which classical micro-economists would also recognise:

1. Relative market share
2. Change in relative market share

3. Profitability
4. Distribution
5. Product differentiation
6. Vertical integration
7. Management calibre and depth
8. Company reputation and image
9. Process economics, plant age, obsolescence, etc.
10. Plant capacity
11. Raw material availability and price
12. Investment intensity
13. Product R&D and technical competence

This approach gains considerably in realism by going into far greater detail in the business assessment than previous matrices. A similar analysis to that required to establish a position on the two dimensions of this matrix was later adopted by Porter in his competitive strategy model discussed in the next chapter.

The business strength/market attractiveness analysis would undoubtedly assist an understanding of both the business and its situation. However, for the analysis to be fruitful it must result in a business being located on the matrix, and the detailed analysis has therefore to be converted in some way into quantities which can be translated into matrix positions. The means of achieving this is heavily dependent on many subjective judgements. For example, it is first necessary to weight the various components of business strength according to their importance to the particular case. There is no objective way of doing this, it is a matter of judgement. Each of the thirteen factors must be given a weighting. For some of them it may be simple, they may be quite unimportant. But the overall weightings cannot be avoided and they will necessarily be made on subjective grounds. Likewise the eleven factors making up market attractiveness: having allocated weights to each of the factors which reflect their importance to the particular business situation, it is then necessary to give the actual scores for market attractiveness and business strength. It may well be that this weighting and scoring process itself enhances understanding and provides fresh insights, but the fact remains that the matrix result will depend crucially on these subjective judgements. In these circumstances it is difficult to assess the validity of any particular application of the enhanced portfolio frameworks.

The prescriptions output by this matrix are not greatly different from those already described. Whilst the number of prescriptions implied is greater they remain simple variations on buy, sell or hold. A low share of a low-growth market should still be divested, a high share of a low-growth market should be milked, and a high share of a high-growth market should be exploited. If the four Boston quadrants were overlaid on the matrix shown in Figure 7.6, it would be apparent that the prescriptions from the two models were quite similar. 'Invest and maintain dominance' on Figure 7.6 is not much different from 'invest to maintain market share; keep prices up, reducing them only in order to maintain market share', which the BCG prescribed for their similarly positioned star. Nor are the prescriptions much different from the

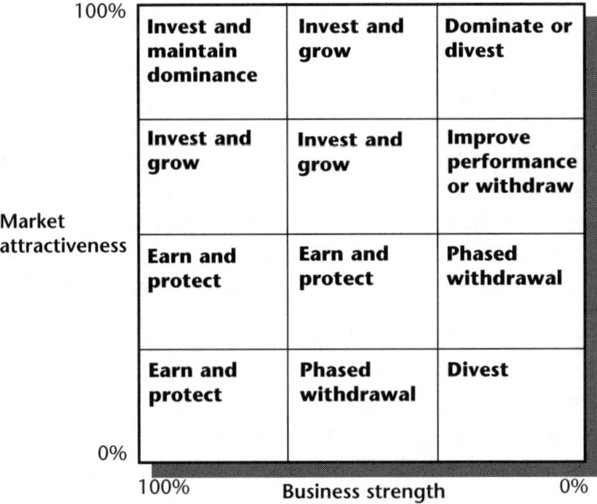

Figure 7.6 Business strengths/market attractiveness matrix

'allocate major resources' prescribed for that position on the directional policy matrix.

The business strength/market attractiveness matrix is a flexible model. Although it is necessarily shaped by subjectively scoring and weighting the various factors, this does mean it can easily be made to reflect whatever factors are most important in any particular business situation. Such an adaptation would not be based on any empirical foundation and so would amount to little more than a simple checklist, but checklists have their uses. If the particular factors which really make up market attractiveness and business strength are valid and yield insight then the analysis can be worthwhile.

If the purpose of using a portfolio framework is simply to fix a position on the matrix and then read off the appropriate prescription, the Boston method is clearly the most efficient and the variously enhanced models offer little. The only justification for using the later versions would be that they offer a deeper understanding of the business situation. If strategy management had not progressed beyond portfolios this would be a persuasive argument in their favour. However, strategic thinking took a great leap forward on Porter's introduction of his approach to competitive strategy and as a consequence the potential benefits of using the enhanced portfolios have been supplanted.

7.4 Using portfolios

By Boston's own bald definition, more than three-quarters of the UK economy would be categorised as dogs and should be closed down. Yet a lot of dogs in UK do good business. The same applies in the United States. Drucker listed a few of the most innovative, fastest-growing American companies which were all classic dog businesses:

> *a chain of barbershops . . . a chain of dentistry offices, followed by a manufacturer of hand tools and a finance company that leases machinery to small businesses. . . . One of the best performers is a company making and selling living room furniture; another one is making and marketing doughnuts; a third, high quality chinaware; a fourth, writing instruments; a fifth, household paints; a sixth has expanded from printing and publishing local newspapers into consumer marketing services; a seventh produces yarns for the textile industry; and so forth.* (Drucker, 1985. pp. 8–9)

Something must be wrong with the BCG's prescription. Not only were these successful dogs, they were all highly innovative businesses and their innovations were aimed not simply at cutting process costs, but at delivering something new to the customer. Yet the BCG would have closed the lot down.

Clearly Boston's portfolio has limitations. A business cannot be described by just two measures: market growth and relative market share. It would clearly be wrong to imagine that a business was adequately understood on the basis of that information alone. In practice, managers recognise the limitations of Boston's inputs and therefore also the limited nature of the outputs. No strategy can be adequately described in terms of simple portfolio decisions of buy, sell or hold.

Portfolio prescriptions may seem to contain rather more substance than this, but no matter how the prescriptions are elaborated, in truth the very notion of a portfolio restricts outputs to those simple decisions. For the investment manager of a unit trust that is clearly all that is needed. For the manager of an acquisitive financial conglomerate that may be all that is required. The Boston framework should serve to remind those at corporate headquarters that their role is in essence remote and hands-off; they do not have the detailed business knowledge to define business strategy beyond portfolio decisions. Consider the Pearson portfolio outlined in Box 7.2 and the questions raised therein. For the manager of a business, however, the concern is much more to do with customers, competitors and technologies, and buy, sell or hold is totally inadequate.

BOX 7.2

The Pearson portfolio

After around £1bn worth of disposals and £4bn of acquisitions, Pearson Plc was divided into the following four divisions:

- **Financial Times Group** comprising: Financial Times Newspaper, Financial Times Information, Les Echos Group, Recoletos, Pearson Professional, FT electronic publishing and on line services (eg FT Profile aand FT Quicken).
- **Pearson Education** comprising: Addison Wesley Longman (including HarperCollins Educational), Simon and Schuster, Financial Times Pitman Publishing, AWL & Headland Distance Learning on the WWW.

- **Pearson Television** comprising: Thames TV, Grundy, All American, Alomo, ACI.
- **Penguin Group:** Penguin Books, Penguin Putnam, Penguin classical music label.

Pearson are also still involved with various businesses (eg theme parks, wine production and investment banking) which are not seen as forming part of its strategic portfolio.

DISCUSSION POINTS

1. Although Pearson is an acquisitive group it does not indulge in transactions which are driven by financial criteria alone, but attempts to develop within a coherent unifying strategy. Do you think a group such as this could have a single coherent (non-financial) strategy?
2. Could Pearson's divisions be treated as coherent units and usefully positioned on a portfolio matrix?
3. Could the subsidiary business units listed above be similarly treated?
4. Could the business portfolio framework be useful in managing Pearson's strategy?

In situations where portfolio decisions are all that is required, the simplicity of Boston's inputs would be a benefit, so long as the inputs resulted in good portfolio decisions being made. Good decisions might be expected if the framework were used in circumstances where its empirical base suggests it would be valid. This means commodity products in high-growth markets. There appears to be no justification for using the Boston model for branded, differentiated products where price is not the only source of competitive advantage, or in low-growth markets where experience is of minimal value. But most business situations fall into one or both of these latter two categories.

Apart from this limitations to high-growth commodity situations and their restricted output of 'buy, sell or hold', there are a number of practical problems with the portfolio frameworks which have limited their usefulness.

First there is the problem of defining the served market. This is not so much a problem of identifying empirical truth as making a management decision. A subsidiary business management may be tempted to redefine its served market so as to avoid being categorised as a dog. If the served market could be defined more precisely, to exclude areas of the market where the business does not compete strongly, it may be possible to invent a market definition in which the business is a leading player. The revised definition of the served market would then change the Boston prescription to 'strictly ration new investments; keep prices up but ensure no new entrants to the market'. From the subsidiary's perspective this would be a more comfortable basis for the parent/subsidiary relationship than 'manage for cash and withdraw' and it might be expected to put considerable effort into achieving agreement to the revised market definition. Nor is this just politics. The framework is open to many and various served market definitions which are loaded with all manner of political and strategic overtones; there is no definitive right answer. If a management wants its business to succeed then it will strive for the most beneficial definition of its served market.

A similar problem exists in relation to the definition of the business unit. Typically, a business will comprise a number of products or product lines each of which is likely to enjoy different relative market shares in markets growing at different rates. Should every individual product, and every individual market it is sold into, be regarded as a separate business unit and be given a separate matrix position. If so, it is difficult to see how the strategic prescriptions could be applied sensibly. It might be impossible, for instance, to divest one such business and expand another if they represented the same physical assets such as plant and buildings. One way around this problem is to aggregate products and markets into strategic business units (SBUs) in order to make the prescriptions feasible. However, if this is done, the whole system appears to become incoherent. What is meant, for example, by a low growth, low market share aggregated SBU? Such a dog might in fact comprise a dozen or more separate products with very different share and growth characteristics. If so, it is unclear what the strategic prescriptions should be. A decision to close down or dispose of a dog business is often difficult to implement because the business may be closely linked with other businesses and the decision would also affect them. The dog might share a factory and office space with other categories of business – stars or cash cows – and closing the dog will only add cost to the remaining businesses. Such a decision, which may be justifiable on other strategic grounds, becomes extremely difficult if the Bostonian justification is not valid. And if there is no valid strategic prescription then there appears to be no point in the whole exercise.

These are very real problems in practice. Both the nature and the feasibility of the prescriptions for an SBU will be fundamentally dependent on how that SBU is defined, i.e. what it comprises: but there are any number of different ways to define SBUs. Roberts (1986) suggested the following criteria:

- Product groups
- End user groups
- Distribution channels
- Geography
- Technology
- Original equipment/replacement parts
- Custom/standard parts
- Manufacturing/marketing dominant
- Established business/development business

Not only are there many ways of defining SBUs but there is also no clear guideline as to which is best for any particular business. In many situations the use of portfolios is completely invalidated because there is no coherent way of defining meaningful, aggregated SBUs. Even where this is not the case the definition usually depends on highly subjective managerial judgements.

The portfolio framework has also been criticised for apparently excluding the possibility that management can make a difference. The framework defines a business according to the two dimensions of the matrix and then prescribes investment strategies based on the cash flows that, according to their analysis, should result from a business in that position. But managements do make a difference. It is management that makes Drucker's dogs so exciting, by differentiating their businesses from the competition.

Thus although portfolios may provide insights for the portfolio manager at corporate headquarters they offer little help to the business manager at SBU level. They do not identify ways in which managements can improve their businesses; they offer no help in what to build into the product that will make it better than competitors' and for which the customer is prepared to pay. Portfolios deny the possibility of managers affecting the position, for example through motivating people, effective marketing, efficient production and, most of all, through innovation. If an SBU management makes the difference, then it does not really matter whether the market is growing only slowly or that the SBU has only a small share of the overall market, the SBU will still be a superior performer.

The prescriptions arising from portfolio positions are little help in themselves to the business management process. They are of no assistance in choosing between two or more potential investments *within the individual business*. They provide no feel for the appropriateness of a particular competitive strategy. From the business, as opposed to the corporate, viewpoint, they provide little of strategic relevance.

Finally, and most importantly, portfolios make no contribution to the definition of strategic direction at the business level. Consequently they can offer no assistance in the achievement of concentration and maintenance of consistency.

Despite all these problems and limitations the portfolio approach is still used. This is not done blindly in ignorance of the limitations, but cautiously in full knowledge that the prescriptions may be wrong and need to be considered carefully before implementation.

Used by corporate headquarters dealing with SBUs of commodity products in fast-growing markets, the validity and usefulness of the original Boston model is undeniable. In this context the portfolio framework appears to have three main applications.

1. It provides strategic criteria for making or influencing business investment/divestment decisions. This is certainly one of the main benefits claimed by those who use the approach. However, caution is necessary since, if the application is flawed then it is likely to suggest wrong decisions. It should also be noted that portfolios tend to encourage the adoption of diversification and acquisition strategies in order to 'balance' the portfolio, there being no explicit, or implicit, commitment to any business: all are open to buy, hold or sell decisions.
2. Many corporate managers have indicated that they obtain considerable benefit from portfolios because portfolios simplify highly complex corporate situations. Portfolios help corporate headquarters to 'get a handle' on many subsidiary businesses in a way that other approaches would not permit. Using portfolios, corporate managers feel they know what makes the subsidiary businesses tick. However, caution is counselled since if portfolios themselves are problematic then the 'handle' may be illusory and the understanding mistaken and superficial.
3. Managers have indicated that portfolios are effective as an aid to strategic thinking (Hamermesh, 1986), and this is why they have been dealt with at some length in this text. They represent a way of looking at business which, despite its limitations, has probably had more impact than any other strategy framework

and is still widely used today. Being aware of the portfolio prescription for a particular business, whether or not it is accepted, serves to promote thinking along strategic lines.

Summary

- The Boston Consulting Group introduced the first business portfolio model in the 1960s based on their empirical work on experience.
- The portfolio was a simple two-dimensional matrix measuring relative market share (as a proxy for experience) and market growth.
- Being based on experience, the Boston matrix is relevant to high growth situations and to commodity, price-competitive products. For low-growth or differentiated products the relevance is limited.
- The Boston matrix clearly identified the cash flows in a business resulting from cash-hungry market growth and cash-generating relative market share.
- The BCG defined simple strategic prescriptions for each of the four quadrants of the matrix.
- The portfolio provides an illusion of understanding, but its simplicity, which could be a great virtue, results from its superficiality and it should only ever be used with great care.
- Use of the Boston matrix is problematic in terms of its effect on people in organisations and it can become a self-fulfilling prophecy.
- In practice, the BCG's prescriptions are often difficult to implement because of the interrelated nature of products and business units which, although inseparable, may not share the same quadrant on the matrix.
- The Boston model is susceptible to abuse by deliberate redefinition of markets and competitors.
- Subsequent portfolios such as the directional policy matrix and the business strength/market attractiveness matrix used much more detailed analysis than Boston's original and therefore provided a less simplistic picture of reality and a greater understanding of the real situation.
- However, these subsequent portfolios did not provide any significantly different strategy prescriptions.
- In general, portfolios do not provide guidance as to strategy direction and are not in any way transformational, i.e. they do not help the process of concentration.

Further reading

Hamermesh, R.G., *Making Strategy Work: How senior managers produce results*, Wiley, 1986.

Henderson, B.D., *The Logic of Business Strategy*, Ballinger, 1984.

Chapter 8

Competitive strategy

Porter's introduction to competitive strategy appeared at first to be a completely new approach to strategy, but is more accurately regarded as an incremental development to an organically developing strategy model.

Competitive strategy was different in being oriented more to the management of a business rather than to the investment decisions of the portfolio frameworks. In addition it did enable strategy to be both analytically sound and also transformational.

The competitive strategy model was introduced at a time when mature economies were experiencing low, or even negative growth. As a consequence it was focused on how the competitive process divided up the cake, rather than being concerned with how the cake could be enlarged.

Competitive strategy is the most generally applicable of all frameworks, with no explicit exclusions or limitations.

8.1 Introduction

Porter's first major contribution to the development of strategic thinking dealt with industry analysis (Porter, 1979, and Reading Review 6). His focus was on industry profitability and the simple idea that competition eliminates profit. An industry operating where competition is limited is likely to be highly profitable; an industry with fierce competition would be unprofitable. Porter therefore sought to identify those factors which determine the level of competitive rivalry in an industry. To do this he went to classical economics to identify the relevant factors. They were much the same as had been identified in the various enhanced portfolio models, for example the General Electric/McKinsey matrix discussed in the previous chapter. In effect, Porter's industry analysis redefined one dimension of an orthodox portfolio matrix.

In his subsequent contribution, Porter (1980, and Reading Review 7) addressed the other dimension which had previously been identified by terms such as 'business strength'. Porter used 'competitive advantage' to convey an equivalent idea to do

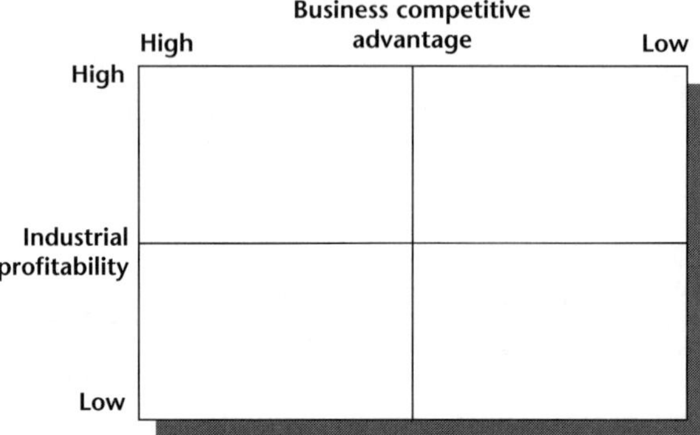

Figure 8.1 Porter's implied matrix

with the positioning of the individual business within the industry. Although he did not overtly define a portfolio matrix, one is nevertheless implicit in his analysis, as indicated in Figure 8.1.

The idea of assessing the attractiveness of an industry and the strength of the business within that industry is basic to the competitive strategy framework, just as it is to the portfolio framework. But Porter's approach made no use of a matrix because his orientation was not the 'buy, sell or hold' of portfolio decisions but the strategy of business fighting competitive battles.

Porter structured his industry analysis in a distinctive way, enumerating five competitive forces. This is a memorable device but probably has little other significance, especially since, as Porter himself suggested, a sixth force, government regulation, can often be *the* most important factor in determining the profitability of an industry. He cites the pharmaceuticals and airline industries as examples (Porter, 1988).

The competitive strategy framework seemed, when it was first introduced, to be a clean break from previous frameworks, but it can now be seen more as an incremental development in strategic thinking. The main change was the new focus on competitive advantage rather than the previous focus on portfolio decisions. At first sight it may appear that the detailed industry analysis is not exploited because no explicit matrix decisions are made. Porter suggests that the 'five forces' analysis can be used to improve industry profitability or at least to avoid inadvertently destroying it by ill-advised price competition. However, detailed Porterian industry analysis is hardly necessary to avoid such mistakes. Perhaps the best argument for the five forces analysis is the insights and increased understanding it provides. This was the argument raised in defence of the bureaucratic methods of the 1960s.

8.2 Industry analysis

Competition is seen as the crux of an industry's profitability which is determined by the competitive forces identified in Figure 8.2.

Each of the competitive forces is investigated in depth, firstly to ascertain the

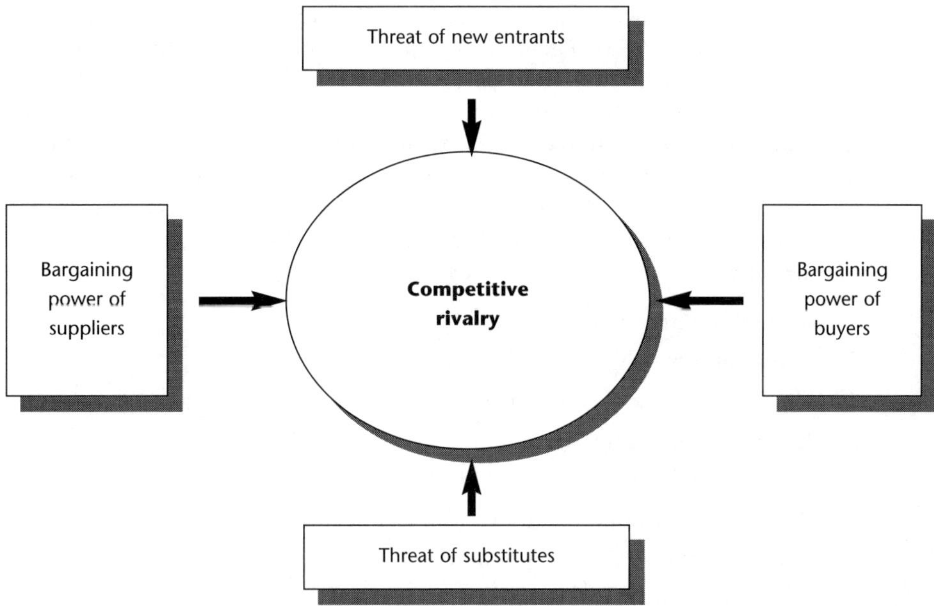

Figure 8.2 Competitive forces shaping industry profitability (Source: Porter, 1979)

extent to which it is relevant to the particular industry, and secondly to ascertain its strength in the particular situation. Porter's analysis is exhaustive and has been criticised as beyond the scope of most businesses. It is therefore crucial to establish the importance of each force and then to focus attention on those which are particularly pertinent, not wasting analytical effort on irrelevances. For the forces which appear relevant it is then important to assess their strength to the particular situation. The notes below explain these force by force.

Competitive rivalry depends on:

1. Market growth rate
2. Level of fixed costs
3. Frequency of overcapacity
4. Extent of product differences
5. Strength of brand identities
6. Cost of moving out of the industry
7. Comparability of competitive rivals

Broadly, these determining factors resolve into three main groups:

1. The rate and shape of market growth
2. The degree to which products and firms are differentiated
3. The extent to which firms are committed, financially, physically and strategically, to the industry

All three of these factors, growth, differentiation and commitment, affect crucially the degree of industry rivalry. For example, with no growth, little differentiation and a high degree of commitment, there is likely to be intense competition over market share, inevitably breaking out into intermittent price wars reducing industry profitability. If it is possible to reduce this rivalry, for example by differentiating the product from its competitors or by avoiding head-on conflict with a competitor who is locked in, then it should be possible to reduce the level of price competition and consequently achieve higher profitability.

The *threat of new entrants* depends on:

1. Capital requirements
2. Economies of scale enjoyed by existing competitors
3. Cost advantages enjoyed by existing competitors, e.g. learning curve benefits
4. Existing product differences
5. Strength of existing product brand loyalty
6. Access to distribution channels
7. Access to appropriate technology
8. Access to long-term supplies of raw materials

If these barriers to entry are low then new entrants will be attracted by any rise in industry profitability. Hence prices and profitability are clearly vulnerable to competition from new entrants. The threat of new entrants depends on the cost of entering the industry, the degree to which a new entrant would suffer running cost disadvantages, and the degree to which existing products are differentiated and consequently enjoy a high degree of brand loyalty from their customers.

Entry costs include the scale of investment required for specialised plant, or for advertising or R&D to achieve competitive economies of scale, or to counter the high switching costs of existing customers.

Running cost disadvantages include the degree to which existing firms have tied up economic raw material supplies, or might have achieved cost reductions through 'Bostonian' experience.

The *bargaining power of suppliers* depends on:

1. Monopoly power in the supplier industry
2. Degree of differentiation of suppliers' product
3. Costs of switching from one supplier to another:
   (a) for the supplier
   (b) for the firm in question
4. Importance of volume to the supplier
5. Importance of the supplier's product to the industry

The *bargaining power of buyers* depends on:

1. Buyer volume
2. Availability of substitute products

3. Costs of switching
4. Concentration of buyer's industry
5. Price sensitivity
6. Product differences
7. Buyer information

The *threat of substitutes* depends on:

1. Relative price of substitutes
2. Technical comparability of substitutes
3. Costs of switching
4. Speed of technological development in 'substitute' industries

Appraisals are made of all five forces having special regard to the level of commitment to the industry of each competing business, the existence of substitute products, the degree to which alternative products are differentiated and so forth. This multidimensional analysis of competition is intended to indicate the likely level of competition and thus the long-run profitability of the industry. This is the approach's unique contribution to thinking about strategy and it contrasts vividly with the proposition that market growth is the sole factor of any significance in determining industry attractiveness.

8.3 Competitor analysis

Just as an industry's profitability is determined by its level of competition, so the profitability of an individual business is determined by the amount of competition in which it has to engage. To some extent, this can be controlled by the business differentiating its product from those of its competitors, or, where it cannot reduce direct competition in this way, by establishing a sustainable advantage over competitors. The analysis of competitors is therefore crucial to the individual business and seeks to answer such questions as,

> *Who should we pick a fight with in the industry, and with what sequence of moves? What is the meaning of that competitor's strategic move and how seriously should we take it? What areas should we avoid because the competitor's response will be emotional or desperate?* (Porter, 1980)

The systematic analysis of competitors involves detailed reviews of their future goals and assumptions, their current strategies and capabilities. This is an extremely comprehensive analysis and if it were not done selectively would be beyond the scope of most businesses.

Just looking at competitor capabilities, the analysis should, according to Porter, include detailed appraisals of the following:

- Competitor's products

- Dealer/distribution
- Marketing and selling
- Operations
- Research and engineering
- Overall costs
- Financial strength
- Organisation
- General manager ability
- Corporate portfolio
- Personnel turnover
- Relationships with government bodies etc.

The analysis in each of these areas is quite detailed. For example, just looking at operations, Porter (1980) suggests that information is required on the following items:

- Manufacturing cost position – economies of scale, learning curve, newness of equipment, etc.
- Technological sophistication of facilities and equipment
- Flexibility of facilities and equipment
- Proprietary know-how and unique patent or cost advantages
- Skills in capacity addition, quality control, tooling, etc.
- Location, including labour and transportation cost
- Labour force climate, unionisation situation
- Access to and cost of raw materials
- The degree of vertical integration

Additionally, a detailed assessment of the competitor's abilities to grow, to respond quickly, to adapt to change, its staying power as indicated by such things as cash reserves, unanimity among management, long-term horizon in its financial goals and lack of stock market pressure.

The above relates only to the analysis of the *capabilities* of a competitor. In addition it is suggested that, with an adequate analysis of a competitor's future goals, assumptions, current strategies and capabilities, 'we can begin to ask the critical questions that will lead to a profile of how a competitor is likely to respond' (Porter, 1980). As the ancient Chinese sage put it: 'know your enemy' (Griffith, 1963).

Porter's analysis seems to aim at obtaining what economists refer to as perfect information, or as near to it as is feasible. The firm may have several substantial competitors that it needs to consider. Additionally, the business needs to analyse its customers, its technology suppliers, and its suppliers of raw materials in similar fashion. It needs to carry out the analyses individually and it needs to consider the strategic groups which may lead to quite different responses. Moreover, in this rapidly changing world, there is a need to continually update substantial elements of the information base.

The information requirements defined by Porter (1980) are extremely pertinent to strategy, but they pose a severe problem in terms of the time and cost involved in obtaining, processing and continually updating such colossal amounts of data. A comprehensive analysis would be impractical for most businesses and it is therefore crucial for management to be selective and to focus its attention on the few competitors who really matter and on the few factors which are really crucial in the particular situation. Selectivity, which is one of management's perennial problems in many situations, is the key to implementing a Porterian industry and competitor analysis. The critical skill is deciding what information is crucial and what would be merely nice to have.

8.4 Generic strategies

Industry analysis provides the information on which competitive strategies may be based. Competitive strategies specify the means by which a business will achieve the most advantageous position it can in the industry in which it operates. This is based on the simple model shown in Figure 8.3 which results from the basic assertion that

Profit = Revenue − Costs

This may not look too promising as the foundation of a strategic model, yet that is exactly what it is.

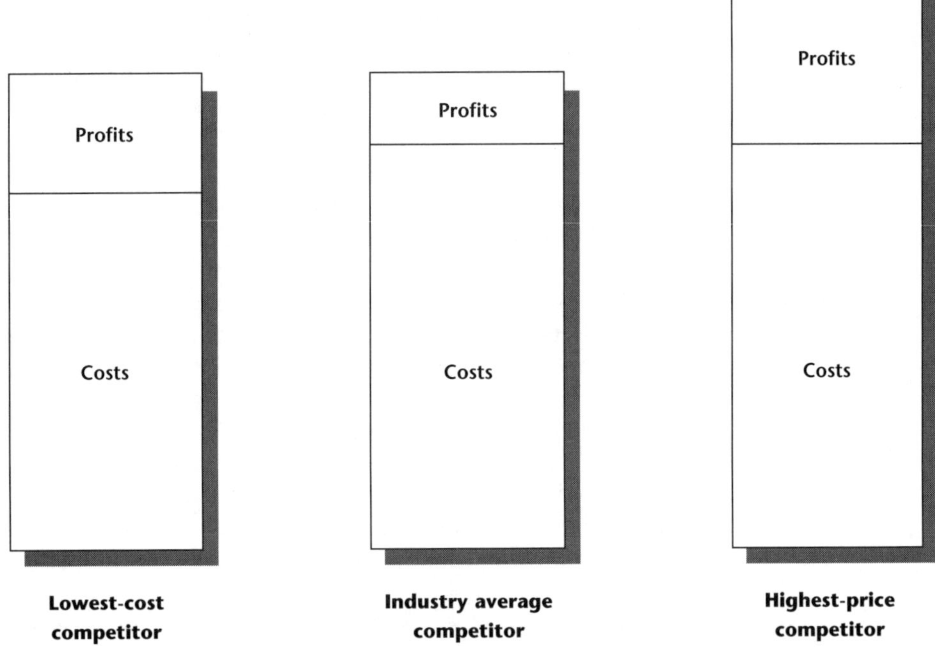

Figure 8.3 Profitability and competitive strategies

The question is asked of classical economics, 'How can a business maximise its profitability?' But Porter is freed from the constraints of perfect competition assumptions – as indeed he needs to be if competitive strategy is to be controllable by managers rather than just market forces. Thus, instead of having a single form of competitive enterprise in any industry, it is possible for Porter to envisage various different forms. Figure 8.3 illustrates the industry average performer and the two different approaches to achieving superior profitability.

From this analysis it seems that high profitability can, in principle, only be achieved in one of two ways: either by achieving the lowest costs or the highest prices. Thus any effective business strategy must aim to pursue one or other of these aims: to be the lowest-cost producer or the highest-price seller. It would be convenient to refer to these two strategies as cost leadership and price leadership except that 'price leadership' is used by economists to mean something rather different. Consequently the terms initially used by Porter were 'cost leadership' and 'differentiation', the latter referring to the means by which a premium price is earned. These two were referred to as 'generic' strategies because they are the only two ways, in this model, in which profitability can be achieved, that is, they are the only two sources of competitive advantage.

This derivation of the model sheds some light on two issues which have attracted considerable critical attention: 'focus' and 'stuck in the middle'. Porter initially presented focus as one of three 'generic' strategies alongside differentiation and cost leadership, but as is clear from the above, focus is different in kind from the other two. Subsequently Porter identified focus as a moderator of the two generic strategies limiting their scope. This issue is discussed in further detail below.

Regarding 'stuck in the middle', Porter was emphatic that failure to make the choice between cost leadership and differentiation means that a company is stuck in the middle, with no advantage. The result is poor performance. This is undoubtedly a great danger as has been highlighted by many other writers since Drucker's assertion that 'concentration is the key to real economic results' (Drucker, 1964, and Reading Review 3).

Moreover, the basic concept of strategic direction seems to imply much the same thing. Many companies which have a clear direction and a distinct position are also demonstrably *either* cost leaders or differentiators, but not both. Names like Porsche, Bic, Yves St Laurent and Kwik Save immediately classify themselves in one camp or the other. However, there is nothing *in the model* which suggests that a firm could not successfully combine aspects of both cost leadership and differentiation. Many cases have been reported of firms which appear successfully to combine low-cost strategies with differentiation, for example Philip Morris cigarettes combining lowest cost production with a differentiated brand position (Hall, 1980).

The key to success in combining elements of both is to understand and be explicit about the strategy and not merely combining elements of each by default. The most profitable firm in an industry could well combine elements of both a cost leader and a differentiator. Gilbert and Strebel (1988) even suggest that,

> *successful strategy rarely relies on the repeated implementation of the same move to maintain a static position . . . [but] generally consists of a planned sequence of moves from one position to another.*

This suggests building a market position with a low cost strategy and then trading up through differentiation. An example of this is the Komatsu attack on Caterpillar (see Box 9.9 in Chapter 9).

Nevertheless, 'stuck in the middle' is not an intrinsic rule of the model, but a pragmatic enhancement to warn of the dangers, a rule of thumb which may be broken with advantage, as long as it is done in full knowledge of the strategic aims being addressed. In practice, Porter is more often than not right and the rule is constantly broken unwittingly by businesses lacking a clear strategic direction and therefore failing completely to achieve the benefits of concentration.

Using slightly different language, it is clear that competitive advantage can be gained by beating competitors or avoiding them. Beating competitors means achieving lower costs than they so that they can be confronted head-on. In this way, with an undifferentiated (i.e. a commodity) product, commanding a standard market price, a firm is able to achieve the highest rates of profit in its industry, very possibly as a result of having the greatest experience. Avoiding competitors is achieved by differentiating the product from that of competitors and achieving both a premium price and customer loyalty as a result. The premium price enables higher margins to be earned that will lead to long-term prosperity.

Both of these strategies can be applied either across a broad front of the whole market or by focusing on a more limited segment of the market. Thus cost leadership, differentiation and focus were, for Porter, the only competitive strategy options available. They identify clearly the strategic direction of a business in a way that many other approaches do not. They therefore have the possibility of achieving concentration and consistency and can thus achieve the purpose of strategy.

The following sections look in rather more detail at Porter's three generic strategies.

8.4.1 Focus

Focus is different in kind from the other two generic strategies. It does not derive from the basic cost/price relationship, but is an additional dimension that should also be taken into account, as any marketeer would insist and as is implied in Figure 8.4.

The emphasis on cost *leadership*, arising from the maximisation aspects of the source model, has been relaxed in this revised version and reference is now made to 'low-cost strategies'. Clearly, in any industry there can only be one cost leader – all other would-be cost leaders would necessarily fail and their fate, according to the model, would necessarily be the same as if they were *stuck in the middle,* i.e. unclear as to their strategy and therefore achieving very little.

Competition erodes profits by the various means indicated in Porter's analysis of industries (i.e. substitutes, new entrants and so on) and perfect competition erodes profitability perfectly. A way of minimising this erosion would be to minimise competition. This can be done by focusing on areas of the market where there is the least competition. Hence the *focus* strategy.

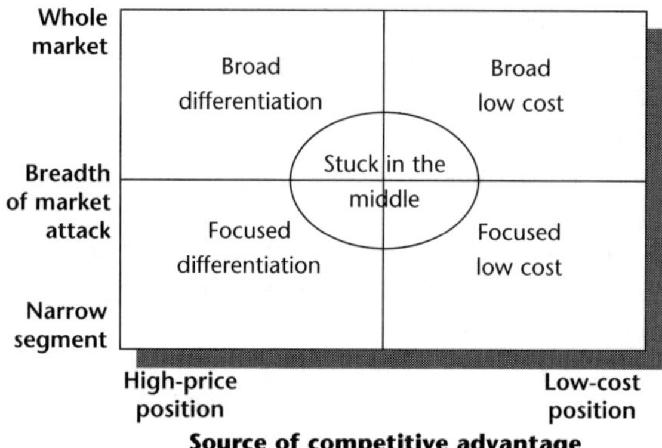

Figure 8.4 Four competitive strategies (Source: based on Porter, 1988)

8.4.2 Cost leadership

'Cost leadership' is an expression that has come to mean many different things. A firm which constantly emphasises efficiency is frequently referred to as having adopted a cost leadership strategy. This is not necessarily correct. One of management's jobs, no matter what the business strategy, is to try to operate efficiently, but this does not necessarily imply it is seeking to be cost leader and to exploit that position as the main foundation of its strategy.

The strategy of cost leadership applies to businesses which attempt to become the lowest-cost producer in an industry. If competing products are more-or-less undifferentiated and therefore sell at a standard market price, the competitor with the lowest costs will earn the highest profits. This will put that competitor in the strongest competitive position, able to win any price war should one occur.

However, in any industry there can only be one cost leader, and others following a cost leadership strategy cannot by definition succeed. The degree to which their costs exceed those of the cost leader is some measure of their vulnerability. In the event of direct price competition the would-be cost leaders who came second best will almost inevitably be forced to reduce market share or stand making losses, and in the extreme may be driven out of the industry altogether. Following a cost leadership strategy without success frequently leads managements to redouble its efforts to reduce costs. Its focus on cost reduction and efficiency, at the expense of all other factors, may become totally dominant and an end in itself.

Cost leadership strategies have been widely followed by firms in the UK and the United States in the interests of short-term profits, often with disastrous results. Skinner (1986, and Reading Review 12) referred to what he called the productivity paradox,

> *the efforts to improve productivity actually drive competitive success further out of reach. This is because cost leadership is a syndrome, a mind set, which stunts strategic vision and inhibits innovation. Breaking loose from . . . the mind-set is not easy. It requires a change in culture, in habits, instincts and ways of thinking and reasoning.*

This phenomenon had been previously identified in Hayes and Abernathy (1980, and Reading Review 8) and Hayes and Garvin (1982, and Reading Review 10). It was noted that American industry was starting to lose ground to Japanese and European competitors:

> *In the past, American managers earned world-wide respect for their carefully planned yet highly aggressive action across three different time frames:*
> *Short term – using existing assets as efficiently as possible.*
> *Medium term – replacing labour and other scarce resources with capital equipment.*
> *Long term – developing new products and processes that open new markets or restructure old ones.* (Hayes and Abernathy, 1980)

Whilst American managers were credited with continuing to achieve with the short-term actions, they were no longer effective in the medium- and long-term requirements. Hayes and Abernathy illustrated the point with a number of quotations from American managers:

> *'To undertake such [medium- and long-term] commitments is hardly in the interests of a manager who is concerned with his or her next quarterly earnings reports.'*
> *'We understand how to market, we know the technology, and production problems are not extreme. Why risk money on new businesses when good profitable low risk opportunities are on every side?'*

The short-term cost focus inhibits investment in new plant and new technology which in due course results in firms losing the ability to compete effectively. In the face of price competition such firms inevitably lose both in terms of profit and market share. Consequently,

> *morale sags, performance suffers, and employees – generally the best ones – begin to leave. Faced with these circumstances, top management often concludes that a division or product line is unsalvageable and purposely continues the process of dis-investment.* (Hayes and Garvin, 1982)

Once started, this disinvestment spiral is difficult to reverse, and at the very least, a strategy of cost leadership may therefore be regarded as dangerous. In practice, the actions taken by would-be cost leaders often prove counterproductive.

Moreover, cost leadership is in essence an inward-looking strategy that has no immediate implications for the customer. At best, cost leadership can only facilitate a customer-oriented strategy of old-fashioned price leadership. Some writers see cost leadership as an inconsistency in the model, having little *per se* to do with competitive advantage unless accompanied by price leadership (Coyne, 1986).

8.4.3 Differentiation

Whilst there is limited empirical evidence of successful implementations of cost leadership strategies, there is a great deal of support for the strategy of differentiation, that is, providing a product or service that is in some way differentiated from competitive products. For example, Hall (1980) investigated sixty-four American companies and found that businesses that followed differentiation strategies performed much better than the rest. All the high performers in Hall's sample,

> *used careful strategic analysis to guide their investments, avoiding simplistic adherence to doctrinaire approaches towards strategy formulation which come from naive application of tools like: share/growth matrices . . . experience curves and PIMS.*

The basis of the differentiation does not appear to matter. It may be to do with the product, its quality or with customer service. It may also, as previously noted, be combined with aspects of cost leadership, as with Philip Morris already quoted.

To be strategically valid the point of differentiation must be one for which there is a need, i.e. customers perceive it as being worth a premium price. Differentiation for its own sake has no strategic value whatsoever. If it is not worth a premium then the product will only command a basic, general market price and the business, unless it is the cost leader, will be unable to earn an economic return.

This point is worth emphasising since there have been some misconceptions about the nature of differentiation in the context of competitive strategy. Some have suggested that the idea is simply to maximise the differentiation from competitors. Thus, the product might be differentiated by virtue of the degree of automation involved in its production. The leader in such a form of differentiation may consider therefore that further investment in automation will serve to reinforce and strengthen the differentiation strategy. However, the critical point is whether the customer perceives, values and is prepared to pay for the differentiation, not whether the degree of differentiation from competitors is maximised.

The most successful differentiation strategies are those where the point of differentiation perceived and valued by customers coincides with the organisation's distinctive competence. This may be some skill or knowledge, often embodied in some unique or patented plant or process. It could also be in some organisational characteristic which, for example, enables the organisation to deliver product of uniquely high quality. Distinctive competence is the key to effective competition in specific market areas or niches.

8.5 The value chain and competitive strategy

Competitive strategy is focused firmly on the top-level strategic objective of beating competitors, or, as Porter puts it, achieving long-term competitive advantage. More than any other of the frameworks considered so far, competitive strategy can also be transformational. It can impact directly on how people in the business behave. Knowing that the 'direction' is 'customer service' or 'product quality' can help people in the organisation to know how they should allocate their efforts and enthusiasm, in a way that '20 per cent return on capital employed' or '30 per cent market share' do not. Such a directional strategy could readily form the basis of concentration and consistency.

For concentration and consistency to be achieved the strategy must pervade every aspect of the business so that every member knows what the strategy is and every decision and action is consistent with it and serves to reinforce it. Porter uses the

Value is the margin between cost and price that each business activity adds to the product. Activities in the chain are identified as follows:

Direct activities	**Indirect activities**
1. Purchasing and stock control	6. General management
2. Operations or production	7. Technological development
3. Order processing and distribution	8. Administration
4. Marketing and selling	
5. Aftersales support	

Figure 8.5 The value chain (Source: based on Porter, 1985)

value chain to mobilise these various strategic impacts (Porter, 1984). The value chain is simply a logical way of looking at the totality of business activities.

In a manufacturing business the value chain follows the route of the entry of raw materials through the production process and on to the despatch of finished product or service and beyond. The value chain includes the linkages which the business has with its various external direct stakeholders, so that, for example, the raw material suppliers are seen as an essential part of the chain, as is aftersales service.

Variations on this approach to business analysis have been widely used in the past. Cash delay centre analysis and cost chains, for example, have been used in cost and management accounting, while the inclusion of external linkages is an idea straight from systems theory. Usually such approaches divide the business into direct and indirect activities which are analysed separately.

Analysis for competitive strategy looks at each activity in the value chain (i.e. each of the functions shown in Figure 8.5) in order to assess the value that each activity adds and the cost incurred in its addition.

The direct activities are simply those activities involved in the business processing relating directly to the customer. The cost of such activities is usually not difficult to assess and even to allocate to the individual product unit. The proportion of price premium that each such direct activity contributes is, however, likely to be less easy to calculate. The indirect or infrastructural activities are potentially of equal importance in terms of external relationships, even though they may not be major unit costs. However, their contributions may be difficult to allocate to individual product units.

In theory, each activity can be assessed as to the net margin it contributes in the final product or service. Theory is simple, but in practice it is extremely difficult to apply the value chain convincingly. It may be difficult to identify with any precision the value that, say, order processing and distribution add to a product. It would be simple to identify the cost, but if the added value cannot be calculated then the margin that results from the activity cannot be assessed. The value chain therefore does not appear to achieve its prime purpose of assessing the contribution each activity makes. The model is therefore mainly of use as a checklist in competitive strategy.

As such, it can contribute to achieving concentration by requiring all activities to consider how they contribute to the strategy. If the strategy is cost leadership then activities which do not contribute to achieving cost leadership should be scrutinised to see if they could be reduced or eliminated. Similarly, with a differentiation strategy, the value chain could be used as a vehicle for achieving concentration. The concept is particularly useful in the context of making any new investment, as the following example of information technology illustrates.

The value chain is used to establish the extent to which IT could impact on each activity of the business, and in particular on how each activity of the business could improve its contribution to strategy, be it differentiation or cost leadership.

The analysis starts with consideration of the impacts on purchasing and stock control. These might be considerable. For example, the harmonisation and compatibility of both computer hardware and software are making it increasingly more feasible and efficient to be directly connected with major suppliers' computer systems. This could be beneficial in terms of reducing essential inventory levels and providing instant supplies information. Moreover, the benefits to the supplier are likely to be realisable in some form of price reduction and quality of service assurance.

Similarly, automated warehousing might produce easily realisable and critical reductions in costs and increases in performance. Or it might be worthwhile in some cases to link up directly with raw materials/commodities database systems giving instant information on availability and price movements.

The applicability and economic worth of these different facilities will vary from situation to situation. In some cases they might be an unnecessary and expensive sophistication, while in others they might represent the key to the achievement of an additional price premium, or to unlocking the competitive situation and taking a major additional share of the market.

The value chain is used as a simple checklist to analyse each business activity in some depth. For brevity, some potential IT applications in each value chain activity are simply listed below:

- *Production*
  Computer-aided manufacturing
  Flexible manufacturing systems
  Microprocessor control, robotisation, etc.
- *Order processing and distribution*
  Automated order processing
  Direct computer connection with customers
  Software harmonisation with customers
- *Marketing and selling*
  Use of videotext for instant information transfer
  New selling media: teletext, fax, etc.
- *Aftersales support*
  Computer scheduling/routing of maintenance vehicles
  Remote/local access to service advice/facilities
  Computerised aftersales follow-up of customers

- *General management*
  Internal information systems for fast feedback
  Access to strategic information databases, indices, etc.
- *Technology development*
  Computer-aided design
  Electronic market/technology research
- *Administration*
  Financial and planning models
  Computerised personnel records

The above is not intended to be comprehensive as to the ways in which IT might contribute to competitive advantage. There are, of course, many others. Moreover, there are many other potential applications and innovations outside the field of IT.

The value chain concept serves to make the implementation of competitive strategies more systematic. In pursuit of a cost leadership strategy, the approach leads to a more-or-less traditional cost accounting analysis of the business in terms of cost chains or delay centres. In pursuit of a strategy of differentiation the approach is more interesting and may provide useful insights. For example, take a business which differentiates its product from that of competitors by a high quality of customer service. Using value chain analysis, the possible contributions to that strategy could be identified for each business activity. Clearly, many of the IT items listed above might be relevant to the improvement of customer service. By comparison with competitors it would be relatively straightforward to identify the competitive performance on 'quality of customer service' in each activity and thus decide which applications would be candidates for investment. However, valuing the contribution made to improving customer service in a way which permits comparison with the cost of that contribution is not at all straightforward.

The value chain highlights that the framework, which appears *prima facie* so black and white and so simple, is in practice far less clear cut. Porter's own illustrations of competitive strategy (Porter, 1988) show how infinitely more subtle the real world is than the theoretical abstraction of the framework. The difference between a low-cost strategy and differentiation is one of many shades of grey rather than the simple black and white projected in theory. For example:

- *American Airways*, which is said to be a 'broad differentiator', is clearly very much concerned with costs and overtly makes trade-offs between the two positions.
- *Emerson Electric*, broad cost leader, has quality as its primary strategic concern in achieving 'best costs'.
- *La Quinta*, focused cost leader, is also very much concerned to deliver what its particular customers perceive as a top-quality product, and takes the utmost care to ensure that included in that product are whatever attributes its customers require but none at all that they do not value.
- *Ivory Soap*, broad differentiator turned broad cost leader, is also concerned with quality and with promoting and delivering a consistently high value product.

- *Cray Electronics*, focused differentiator, is the only example where there appears to be a complete attention to the one strategy with little regard for the other. In Cray's case, cost is of little significance, quality and performance everything. However, Cray's position was peculiar, if not unique, and few businesses would be able to emulate its strategy effectively.

What all these companies appeared to have in common was a thorough understanding of their own especial capabilities, their customers and their needs, and their competitors and their products. Furthermore, they all took great pains to communicate this knowledge both inside their organisation and also to the outside world. Finally, they were all fully aware of, and prepared to invest in or obtain through collaboration, the most appropriate technologies and systems available for producing and delivering these 'products' to their customers. The Fletton Brick Co. described in Box 8.1 is typical of many businesses experiencing problems exploiting their specialism and maintaining their strategic position. They may have to consider making some trade-offs which might be controversial or at least challenging.

Clearly, a business's understanding of both its own capabilities and the needs and desires of its customers, is crucial to the effectiveness of the competitive strategy framework. Porter focuses on the analysis that might produce this understanding, with the intention of achieving a leadership position either in terms of costs or in terms of some other differentiated aspect of the product or service.

BOX 8.1

Fletton Brick Co. Plc

Fletton Brick was a major producer of clay building bricks, the cost leader in its industry by a considerable margin. Its leadership arose from two main factors. First, the fletton brick was made from clay which came from a unique deposit north of London which contained a considerable amount of carbon material distributed as small particles throughout the clay. These carbon particles ignited during the kiln firing process thus significantly reducing the energy costs involved. Over the years, Fletton Brick had acquired all the other brickmakers with access to the carbon clay deposit and was now the largest brickmaker in UK and thus able to exploit the latest and most automated manufacturing, handling and distribution equipment.

The carbon deposits, however, also had some disadvantages. During firing, fletton bricks developed mottles and discolouration which meant that they could only be sold as 'commons' i.e. for applications where their appearance was not regarded as important. They were unsuitable for sale as decorative facing bricks. The price of facing bricks was at least double the price of commons and for any non-fletton producer the key to profitability was to maximise the sales of facing bricks and minimise sales of commons. Moreover, the market for common bricks was in decline in the face of ever-increasing competition from concrete blocks and in particular from foamed concrete which had substantial benefits in terms of thermal insulation properties.

A working party comprising heads of marketing, R&D and finance was formed to consider the strategic options open to Fletton Brick Co. This group quickly agreed that it was essential to reduce reliance on the traditional main product, the clay common brick. The R&D director proposed that this be done by putting a decorative face on the fletton brick – they had developed a way of doing this – thereby permitting flettons to be sold as facing bricks. It was recognised that pricing of Fletton's facing bricks was crucial: too high a price would limit and slow down market penetration; too low a price would reduce profitability and also risk giving the new brick a cheap image.

The R&D director agreed that there were likely to be quality problems with the new product as the process was unproven. In the light of this risk, the finance director proposed the acquisition of an existing high-quality clay facing brick manufacturer. Acquisition candidates were all very much smaller than Fletton – the largest had less then 10 per cent of Fletton's production capacity – but they would give Fletton the benefit of an existing premium 'name' in the facing brick market.

DISCUSSION POINT

Put yourself in the position of the marketing director. Bearing in mind Fletton's existing strategic position, which of the two proposals (internal development or acquisition) would you prefer and why?

The generic strategies of cost leadership and differentiation were derived from the simple equation 'profit = revenue − costs' as depicted in Figure 8.3, but the practical application of those strategies seems to focus on the customer rather more than Porter's original exposition. From the customer's perspective, cost leadership is irrelevant unless it is accompanied by the lowest prices or by some other quality at no extra cost. Thus, from this point of view, cost leadership is not an end in itself but a means to some other end which the customer values. This is not an issue which is addressed by Porter, but it is well covered in the literature of strategic marketing.

Strategic marketing

The inclusion of a section on strategic marketing is not intended to suggest a separate strategy framework but rather a means of making Porter's competitive framework operational – a front end to competitive strategy.

Many writers have advocated being close to the customer (Peters and Waterman, 1982) or even 'an almost blind, passionate commitment to taking care of customers' (Kotler and Armstrong, 1997). This may be an appropriate stance for marketers, but not for managing strategy. Strategy has to be calculating, not passionate. Customer orientation must not be blind or passionate, but focused and strategy driven. One company's customer orientation may be focused on providing service because that is the cornerstone of its strategy. Service is not the cornerstone of every business. Some thoroughly successful firms have prospered through the simple and valid strategy of 'pile it high and sell it cheap', or 'any color so long as it's black'. Such cornerstones are intrinsically no less customer oriented than 'service'. It all depends on what customer need the product is satisfying.

For customer orientation to have real effect in a business – for the strategy to be transformational – it must be all-pervasive; everyone in the firm must be customer oriented. It only takes one who cares nothing for the customer to undo months, even years, of painstaking reputation building. This is what concentration and consistency require. Peters and Waterman's 'excellent' businesses developed this orientation into their greatest strength. Excellent outcomes appear to result from the coincidence of a firm's greatest strength, or distinctive competence, with the satisfaction of the customers' perceived need. This coincidence is not accidental.

In section 3.7 it was noted that every viable business has some distinctive competence, something at which it is peculiarly effective. Otherwise it would not survive. This distinctive competence must accord with some customer need and be embodied in the product or service to create a leadership position, i.e. leading in 'something of value to the customer'. This may be customer service, or distribution, or some quite narrow aspect of the product. A leadership position attaching to anything which the customer values provides the business with economic results. With no leadership position, even if the firm has the major share of the market, the business will at best be 'marginal' (Drucker, 1964).

The difference between customer orientation and leadership is the difference between pleasing customers and beating competitors. Leadership, i.e. beating competitors, is the strategic objective; customer orientation, i.e. pleasing customers, is a means to that strategic end.

Strategic marketing focuses on the multifaceted product or service a version of which was described in section 3.6 and depicted again here in Figure 8.6. What matters about this complex product is the customer's perceptions of its various charac-

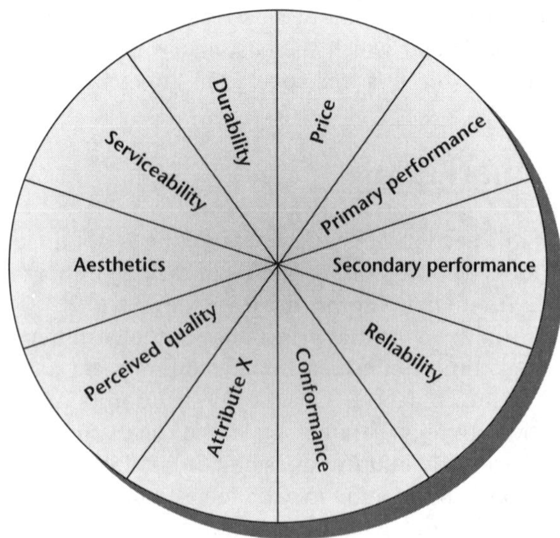

Figure 8.6 The ten-characteristic product

teristics or attributes. Producing the best mouse trap is of no avail if it is not perceived as such by potential customers. The customer's perception of the product is an amalgam of his or her perception of the various product attributes, *any* of which may be critical. He or she may buy it because the price is right – it satisfies an economic need; or its performance may be what is attractive; or its quality; or it might be some more deep seated psychological need which is satisfied by the product's design or image.

The customer's perception of products is not necessarily compatible with a common-sense notion of reality. Too great a divide between perception and reality is likely to be only short-lived, but there will nevertheless be differences, and some of them may be important. Even an attribute as apparently unambiguous as price may be affected by this dichotomy between customer perception and reality. A product which is cheap relative to its competitors may in fact be perceived as being relatively expensive. If customers regard price as the critical attribute, then it is their perception of the product's price which will dictate the buying decision. If they perceive brand A as cheaper than brand B, they will buy it even if the reality is that brand B has the lower price.

Customers may have perceptions about every product attribute, although many of them may not be sufficiently strong to affect the buying decision. An attribute as potentially woolly and complicated as brand image can be a powerful determinant of customer behaviour. This has frequently been shown with 'blind' product tests, a standard way of assessing brand image (King, 1967). In such tests, a panel of consumers is typically given two or more brands to test and compare, the brands being presented in plain packs so that their identity is unknown. The consumers may prefer brand A to brand B when they are anonymous, but when the real brand names are attached the results may be reversed. This suggests the existence of a brand image consisting of a set of associations capable of being set off by the brand name. This image can be sufficiently strong to overwhelm the previous experience and perceptions of the product tests and impacts directly on the buying decision. Image leads to the purchase of items which would not otherwise have been chosen. It applies to all product types, industrial as well as consumer, the main difference being that advertising, which is the prime image-building tool, is a higher proportion of the promotion expense in consumer products than it is in industrial products. Thus image may be more easily adjusted for consumer products.

The process of identifying what need the customer satisfies when he or she buys the product can be approached quite systematically. First it is necessary to know which product attributes the customer perceives as important. Secondly, it is important to know what the customer perceives as being ideal performance on these important attributes. Thirdly, it is important to establish how the customer perceives the firm's product as performing on the same attributes. Finally it is important to know if the customer perceives competing products in the same way.

Customer and potential customer perceptions are a crucial ingredient of strategic marketing and their identification is a key step in defining an effective competitive strategy. A differentiation strategy can be avowed simply by managerial decision without any recourse to customer perceptions. Such differentiation may fail because it is quite irrelevant to the customer who is not particularly concerned with the attribute being differentiated. Effective differentiation must therefore be based on a sound knowledge of customer perceptions.

Such precise information is unlikely to be achieved simply by being 'close to the customer'. Obsessions with service and quality, effective nichemanship and listening to the customer are what Peters and Waterman identify as 'close to the customer' (Peters and Waterman, 1982), but understanding customers' real needs and perceptions implies a more systematic form of customer orientation which has to include a technically reliable form of enquiry. Such methods are fairly straightforward. One such approach described below, preference mapping, enables customers' perceptions about the product and its competitors to be identified.

Preference mapping is an operational marketing technique and it may seem inappropriate to discuss it in any detail in a text on strategic thinking. However, the idea of overtly discovering how potential and existing customers perceive and value the various attributes of the product and its competitors is fundamental. This is the key to defining direction which is the basis of strategy, and a means of achieving this is required to make competitive strategy operational.

Preference mapping and product positioning are techniques of marketing research which embody the marketing philosophy so fundamentally that they capture the essence of strategic marketing itself. Preference mapping is a technique for identifying and presenting consumer preferences for the product attributes which they perceive as important in satisfying their needs. The technique has been described in operational detail in many texts (for example Green *et al.*, 1988), so a simplified explanation here is sufficient for the present purpose. A common consumer product such as instant coffee is ideal for illustrating the process.

First, orthodox qualitative methods such as unstructured and semi-structured interviews and consumer panel tests are used to establish a list of potentially significant attributes of instant coffee. As far as possible these attributes are generated, without prompting or leading in any way by the researcher. Possible attributes of instant coffee might include, price, strength, flavour, aroma, country of origin and brand image.

Secondly, the list of potentially significant product attributes are tested with selected samples of consumers to establish which attributes appear to be regarded as important. The apparently unimportant attributes can then be disregarded. In our instant coffee example we will assume just two attributes are found to be perceived as important: price and strength. Thus a 'map' could be constructed as in Figure 8.7. In practice, the number of important attributes is unlikely to be restricted to just two – this example is limited simply for ease of illustration. The process of graphical presentation of the map, which may have any number of independent dimensions has been computerised and presents no difficulty.

Thirdly, a selected sample of consumers are tested or questioned as to the nature of their 'ideal' instant coffee in terms of the important attributes of strength and price. This is done using methods which result in some sort of scaled response, for example placing responses along a seven-point scale from 'very strong' to 'very mild'. In this way the response can be scored and the respondent's position plotted on the map if similarly scaled (for example from +3 to –3). In this way the aggregate 'ideal' instant coffee can be positioned on the map, being simply the aggregate of all responses.

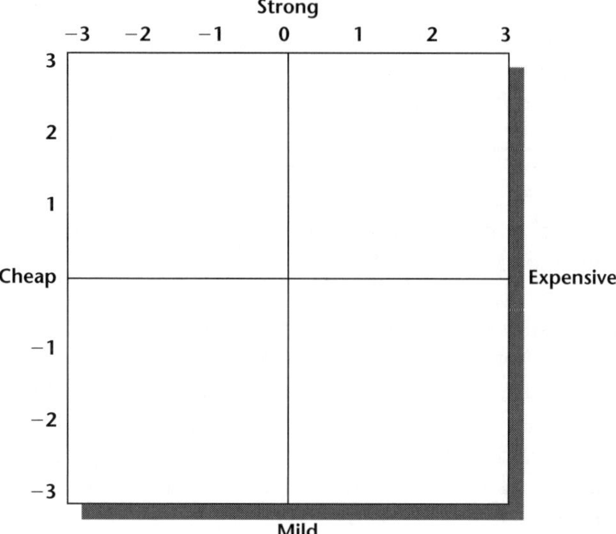

Figure 8.7 A preference map for instant coffee

Similarly, other 'ideal' instant coffees can be positioned relating to various subsets of the sample of respondents. The 'ideal' coffee of people living in Greater London may differ substantially from that of people in, say, Scotland or Wales. The samples used for testing may be selected on any basis (geographical, demographic, psychographic and so on) so long as the market segments they represent are actually measurable, accessible (i.e. capable of being focused on) and of sufficient volume to be economically worthwhile.

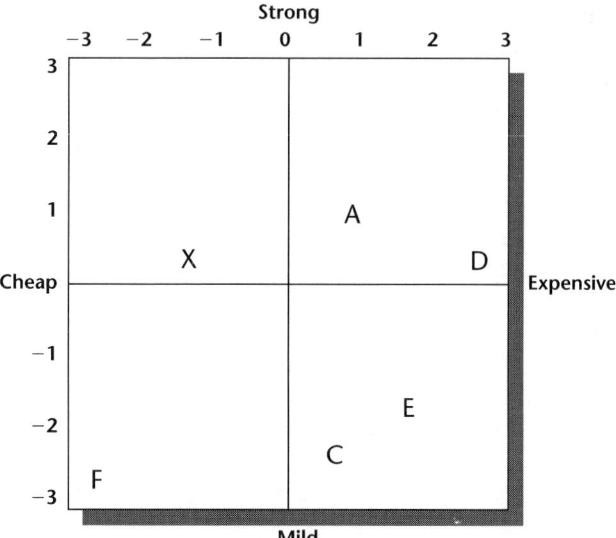

Figure 8.8 Brand positions on the instant coffee preference map

Having established 'ideal' positions, research is then conducted to establish the position of actual brands of instant coffee. Again this can be done either by testing or by direct questioning, or a combination of the two. Thus positions on the map may be identified as in Figure 8.8.

Position X marks the 'ideal' position of the relevant sample of respondents, while positions A to F represent the various competing brands. Brands C and E appear to be perceived as in close competition, whilst brands A, D and F are perceived as distinctive in terms of the two attributes perceived as important.

The implications for the manufacturer of brand F, for example, are that the product is perceived as being cheaper and milder than the ideal. Blind testing could be carried out to see if consumers' perceptions of its attributes differ significantly from its reality. For example, the test might show that the brand actually tastes stronger than its image suggests. In this case, the promotion of the product might be designed to emphasise strength, perhaps by suggesting some new ingredient. In this way the product could be repositioned closer to the 'ideal'. Similarly the 'new' product could be moved slightly up-market in terms of price in order to be positioned as close to the 'ideal' as possible.

This example is highly simplified, but the principles can be widely applied. For any product or service, a picture of customer preferences can be built up which shows what key leadership position, if any, the product enjoys, as perceived by its actual and potential customers. It is possible to identify how this strength could be improved, i.e. moved closer to the customer's perceived ideal, in order to position, or reposition, the product on the customer's preference map.

Preference mapping gives real focus both to pleasing customers and to beating competitors. Regular use makes it possible to detect changes in customer perceptions and needs, and in the position of competing products before they make themselves apparent in reduced product sales. The concept of leadership is thus made more specific and identifiable as the firm's competitive specialism or point of differentiation on which its competitive advantage rests.

This positioning is one way of achieving a coherent strategic direction, prerequisite to achieving concentration and consistency across the whole business, no matter how wide its products and product lines.

The complexity of product lines that few businesses avoid presents a real problem that strategy management must confront. Each product may have different attributes which are perceived as being the reason why customers buy. Thus a firm with, say, three product lines could find that customers value different attributes of each product. They might value one for its price, one for its quality and one for its brand image. Using the methods proposed here the firm will at least be aware of this problem. Many businesses are not and lose direction as a result. Would a firm such as Porsche sell a product on price? If Porsche were to move into writing instruments, would it be more successful selling a cheap, throwaway ballpoint pen or an expensive piece of designer jewellery with a writing head? There is a need for the firm to adopt a consistent approach, exploiting the same or compatible specialisms on every product. If this is not achieved then customer perceptions will tend to be confused, the confusion being at least as apparent within the firm as among its customers so that there is no clear direction.

Minor incompatibilities in the competitive specialisms of different products can be corrected by repositioning the product or business in question. However, a complete lack of consistency, as is likely to arise from repeated diversification, defeats any coherent business strategy. Such diverse specialisms are supportable only as the more-or-less random result of an investment portfolio put together on the basis of short-term financial criteria.

Acquisitions too require position consistency if they are to be successful in strategic terms. The acquisition of businesses with different specialisms is frequently the cause of failure to integrate satisfactorily. A firm whose specialism centres around its competitive pricing might acquire a competitor whose business is based on technological leadership. Not only would both sets of customers obtain conflicting messages, but both sets of employees can suffer similar confusion. The answer is to make the new position clear both internally and externally. If the strategy is to integrate the two businesses, the value of one specialism will be eliminated and this may well offset the value of any apparently more tangible synergy which may have justified the acquisition in the first place. Some of these issues are being confronted by the Fletton Brick Co. in Box 8.2.

BOX 8.2

Fletton Brick Co. Plc (2)

Fletton's board of directors discussed their strategy for reducing reliance on common bricks. They considered three alternatives:

1. Sticking a decorative 'face' onto the existing fletton bricks and selling them as 'facing' bricks at a substantially increased price.
2. Acquiring a high-quality facing brick manufacturer.
3. Non-brick acquisitions within the 'construction materials' industry.

In consideration of the facing brick proposal, one of the non-executive directors argued strongly that 'the only way any benefit from the brick acquisition would accrue to Fletton Brick Co. would be if fletton "facing" bricks were sold under the name of the acquired company and to do that would be deceitful.'

DISCUSSION POINTS

1. As chief executive of Fletton Brick would you agree with the non-executive?
2. Do the ethical issues, raising questions about corporate integrity, have any implications for strategy?
3. What are the pros and cons of diversification? What more information would you require in order to decide on the relative attractions of diversification?
4. Which of the three options would you favour? Why?

8.7 Competitive strategy revisited

Previous frameworks have clearly been applicable to certain situations and taken out of those particular circumstances have ceased to hold good. For example, experience is of little relevance in mature industries and its prescriptions are simply not valid to branded differentiated products. Competitive strategy has fewer of these limitations. To all intents and purposes this is a framework which has general validity, although it may lack the specific insights offered by more focused frameworks. Like the earlier frameworks, it has been frequently applied, sometimes failed and consequently come in for some criticism. Porter himself revisited the framework and considered its various components (Porter, 1996, and Reading Review 29). He sought few substantive alterations, apart from some relaxation of terminology and minor changes in emphasis. He highlighted five issues, each of which was intrinsic to the competitive strategy framework as originally propounded:

1. Strategy is not simply being efficient – efficiency is necessary but not sufficient for a successful strategic position.
2. Successful strategic positioning rests on being unique in some way rather than following competitors' strategies.
3. Incremental additions to a strategic position will weaken it; it will be strengthened only by concentration on its deeper exploitation.
4. A sustainable strategic position will necessarily require trade-offs, i.e. not doing some things simply in order to remain concentrated.
5. The whole organisation (i.e. all the activities in the value chain) must work together to ensure the competitive advantage is not only sustainable but also sustained.

The framework is generally applicable, but in its generality may be applied effectively or not. It is certainly analytical and identifies a quantity of analysis which is approaching the exhaustive. Its applications should therefore be analytically sound. The danger is that it will create Mintzberg's 'paralysis by analysis'. There is a clear need for strategy managers to be highly selective in their analysis but there is no guidance, intrinsic to the framework, as to what issues should be selected.

The term 'competitive advantage', used by Porter to define the focus of a competitive strategy, might at first sight appear rather cerebral and limited, but its translation into the more active phrase 'beating competitors' – which is what it really means – suggests that applications of the framework could also be made transformational.

Competitive strategy provides an opportunity for the clear definition of direction, the achievement of concentration, maintenance of consistency and at the same time could highlight the issues which should be the focus of flexibility. Nevertheless, there have been many inadequate applications of competitive strategy which have achieved none of these things.

Summary

- The competitive strategy framework was developed in a period of low growth when efforts were concentrated on how markets were divided between competitors rather than on how to make them grow faster.
- The approach focuses on the factors which determine the long-term profitability of an industry and the factors that determine a firm's competitive position in the industry.
- The approach, based on classical economic theory, is information intensive – information is the essential foundation of competitive strategy. The information requirements identified as necessary by Porter are so extensive as to be impractical for most businesses and it is therefore essential to be selective, collecting data which are crucial to the strategy concerned, ignoring data which are not relevant.
- Competitive strategy is concerned with how to beat competitors, or to avoid them. Unless victory is assured, head-on competition is futile.
- The strategy of beating competitors is achieved through cost leadership. In any industry there can only be one cost leader. Thus, all but one of the firms attempting to be cost leaders are doomed to mediocrity or failure.
- In practice it has often been found that the strategy of cost leadership is counterproductive and results in the business progressively cutting away its ability to compete – the disinvestment spiral.
- The strategy of avoiding competitors can be achieved by differentiating the product from the others on the market or by focusing on a small niche of the market away from the competition. Differentiation and focus appear to be more widely successful strategies than cost leadership.
- To be successful, differentiation must provide a product which is differentiated in a way that buyers perceive as worth a premium price. Without this premium the strategy of differentiation will not be rewarded by economic success.
- To be effective, competitive strategies must pervade and shape all activities of the business, including its relationships with its various stakeholders both internal and external.
- Implementation is therefore achieved through a methodical analysis of all business activities, both direct and indirect, possibly using the value chain.
- Financial and psychological investment decisions are then taken in accordance with the need to achieve a sustainable competitive advantage.
- The methods of strategic marketing can help the business to make its competitive strategy operational by identifying ways to please the customer and to beat competitors by exploiting its competitive specialism, involving every member of the business so that concentration and consistency are achieved.

- The first stage in this process is to analyse the product and its various attributes, physical, implied and psychological.
- It is then necessary to research customer perceptions of product attributes, as to their ideal product, the actual product and its competitors.
- This analysis is the basis of a preference map which can show the positions of the various competitive products and identify the action required to reposition the product to give it a greater competitive advantage.
- The product's position identifies the way that customers perceive the product in terms of its most critical attributes. The competitive strengths the customers thus identify represent the results of the firm's distinctive competence.
- Every viable business has some distinctive competence which sets it apart from other businesses. This may be limited and focused or it might be quite broad and general.
- For the distinctive competence to provide the basis of a leadership position, i.e. the way of beating competitors, it must be embodied in the product or service that the customer buys, and it must be perceived and valued by the customer. It thus becomes the firm's competitive specialism.
- This leadership position and its exploitation is the basis of an effective competitive strategy and the key to defining strategic direction.
- For a multiproduct business the satisfaction of customer needs implies that there should be a consistency and compatibility across all product lines. Otherwise the distinctive competence will be lost and the business will tend to drift. For a diversified business where strategy is controlled from the centre, this is a highly probable outcome.

Further reading

Porter, M.E., *Competitive Strategy: Techniques for analyzing industries and competitors*, Free Press, 1980.

Porter, M.E., *Competitive Advantage: Creating and sustaining superior performance*, Free Press, 1984.

Chapter

9

Transformational frameworks

This chapter introduces the last two frameworks which share a particular focus on the behaviour of people in the business. Both are transformational, and the focus of this motivational impact starts with a statement of strategic intent or mission.

The core competence framework of Hamel and Prahalad has been the most widely applied new framework of the 1990s. It was developed from studies of companies which achieved global technological leadership in one or more key technologies. The spirit of the framework is expressed by breaking down barriers and mind-sets, whereas the spirit of the earliest models was one of fit and feasibility.

The entrepreneurial framework was developed from studies of small firms at their start-up or entrepreneurial phase of development. This focuses on the few key ideas that successful founder entrepreneurs appear to embody. The theoretical base for this framework goes back to the earliest contributors on strategy management.

9.1 Introduction

The strategy idea involves both analytical and transformational components. If the purpose of strategy management is to concentrate consistently on a clear strategic direction, the necessity for both analytical and transformational components is clear. The definition of an appropriate strategic objective (i.e. direction) must be based on an objective understanding of relevant realities, i.e. on analysis. The achievement of concentration, not only of investment but also of the efforts and enthusiasms of the organisation's people, requires that they understand and are motivated to achieve the strategic objective, i.e. the strategy must also be transformational.

Understanding the real strategic position of a business is perhaps the most important part of strategy formation. The frameworks considered so far have been predominantly analytical. The aim has been, first, to gain a sufficient understanding of the business and its environments and then to manage the relationship between the two so that the business achieves a long-term strategic gain. These analytical approaches have each contributed some valuable insights and provided useful aids to decision making, but they are not in themselves transformational.

Mintzberg (1992) stresses both elements, although he uses the terms 'cerebral' and 'intuitive'. Most frameworks are theoretical constructions and therefore tend to be analytical; but analysis which does not lead to some transformation is simply expense. Attempts to achieve strategic transformation without soundly based understanding, i.e. without analysis, is even worse since it does not just lead nowhere, it may lead to disaster. Blindly following a charismatic leader can be extremely dangerous. As Drucker is wont to point out, this century's three greatest charismatic leaders were Hitler, Stalin and Mao. It is not the charisma that does the damage, but the lack of sound analysis and real understanding which the charisma blinds us to. An effective strategy system must contain both analytical and transformational elements.

The two frameworks outlined in this chapter are both explicitly transformational. They also include analytical components, but their predominant flavour is on the achievement of mould-breaking change.

The core competence framework defined by Hamel and Prahalad is based on their four *Harvard Business Review* articles (Hamel and Prahalad, 1989, 1991, 1993, and Prahalad and Hamel, 1990, brought together in Hamel and Prahalad, 1994; see also Reading Reviews 15, 17, 18 and 21). Their concern is mainly with major international competitors at the leading edge of global technologies. This rarefied world may be thought of as beyond the scope of many organisations whose managers might intuitively regard the possibility of their 'beating Xerox' as naively unrealistic. But this is the crux of the Hamel and Prahalad framework. They are concerned not with 'strategic fit' but with breaking out; they are not limited by existing strengths, but focus on leveraging up resources to achieve undreamed of capabilities; they are not so much concerned with understanding customer needs as creating whole new markets for hitherto unimagined products.

However, many businesses, although operating in markets with global competitors and using global technologies, succeed on a purely regional or even local basis without seeking global domination. For them, the Hamel and Prahalad framework may perhaps seem provocative and stimulating, but ultimately impractical. Such businesses may find the entrepreneurial framework more pertinent. This draws on lessons from the entrepreneurial start up, focusing on the distinctive strengths that such businesses enjoy. Like the Hamel and Prahalad framework, entrepreneurial strategy is concerned with the exploitation of competences in order to beat competitors, but the language of this framework is less particular and its application perhaps more general.

Both these transformational frameworks are concerned with the achievement of bold, even missionary, strategic objectives. Transformational frameworks focus on the behavioural, even inspirational, impacts of strategic objectives within the hierarchical system. The chapter, therefore, starts with an examination of mission statements as the most widely adopted transformational form of strategic objective.

9.2 Statements of mission

The strategic level of business objectives was identified in Chapter 3, as shown in Figure 9.1. The terms used to describe this top-level objective which defines the direction of the business may vary. Hamel and Prahalad use the term 'strategic intent'. But terminology is unimportant; the concern is for the strategic level of objective. This is what is meant here by mission.

Perhaps one of the best known such statements was President Kennedy's declaration that the United States would put a man on the moon by the end of the decade (the 1960s). This statement of mission was a classic of its kind for it contained all the essential characteristics of effective mission statements. It was short, easily understandable, unambiguous and memorable. Moreover, given the situation in which it was made, it was highly motivational. The Soviet Union had stolen a march on the Americans in the cold war space race, with the first spaceship and the first man in space, and Kennedy's statement was a defiant commitment for the United States to reassert its international position as *the* leading superpower. Relating Kennedy's statement to Figure 9.1, it was clearly a statement of how the United States was going to beat the Soviet Union in that particular sphere and, given the context, it incorporates a leadership position, something unique and a superlative. The American people were Kennedy's customer and it may be presumed that the vast majority perceived and valued the stated mission.

Kennedy's mission statement was undoubtedly all about beating competitors, but the way to beat them, i.e. the strategic direction, in this case putting a man on the moon, had to be based on sound analysis. Kennedy would not have declared the aim of putting a man on the moon by 1970 if analysis had shown that it was not within the bounds of feasibility. Had Roosevelt made the same pledge a quarter of a century earlier it would have been simply foolish, and recognised as such. Behind Kennedy's statement there was an appreciation of the possibilities of the technological and organisational requirements for success, and some knowledge and understanding, albeit incomplete, of the capabilities of the various space agencies involved. It was not simply an inspirational commitment, made without regard for the realities; nor was it simply a statement of the expected outcome from a plan that had been wholly

BEATING COMPETITORS through:
a LEADERSHIP position, or,
a UNIQUE characteristic, or,
a SUPERLATIVE in some aspect of performance that is PERCEIVED and VALUED by the customer.

Figure 9.1 Strategic objective, or mission

worked through in operational detail. It was somewhere between: a brave commitment made on the basis of incomplete knowledge which itself contributed substantially to its own fulfilment.

How can a simple statement like Kennedy's have this impact? The direct answer is by providing a focus for concentration: concentration of investment, of expertise, of effort and enthusiasm. With concentration almost nothing is impossible. With clear direction and effective concentration the most amazing strategies are realised. A mission statement that does not achieve concentration will have little effect.

It is not the mission statement that is important, but the mission itself. Campbell and Nash showed that if mission statements do not genuinely reflect how people in the business feel and behave then they are likely to be counterproductive. They will not only have no directional impact but they will merely demonstrate that management is out of touch (Campbell and Nash, 1993). Ideally the mission grows up with the company's founders out of the original purpose for which the business was set up and is embedded in the company's culture. The codification of mission in the form of a written statement only happens later, often when that original focus is in danger of being lost. A change of mission, like a change of culture, is difficult to achieve. Publishing a mission statement is, on its own, unlikely to have any positive effect. Campbell and Nash suggest that action should precede words if the mission change is to succeed. They quote the example of British Airways where CEO Marshall first got operations to land the planes on time and to pay attention to customers before this was reflected in a formal statement almost four years later.

Campbell *et al.* (1990) suggested that an effective mission statement should satisfy the following conditions:

1. Describe an inspiring purpose for the business.
2. Define a strategy, i.e. a business domain and a strategic position (e.g. the source of its competitive advantage) within that domain.
3. Identify values employees can be proud of and which reinforce the strategy.
4. Describe behaviour standards that serve as beacons of the strategy and which enable employees to know what is expected of them.
5. Capture the culture of the organisation and be easy to read.

An effective strategic mission statement will have the following characteristics:

- Short and simple
- Identifies a clear direction, e.g. competitors to be beaten, leadership position to be achieved
- Memorable
- Unambiguous
- Measurable
- Based on sound analysis
- Inspirational
- Top management commitment

Figure 9.2 Characteristics of strategic mission

Other writers focusing on the imperatives of effective communication (for example Carnall, 1990) have proposed other features. Figure 9.2 summarises these essential characteristics of effective mission statements. In the following paragraphs some famous (and infamous) examples of mission statements are considered and compared against the criteria of Figure 9.2.

In some mission statements, values and cultural issues, which have little to do with strategy, predominate. An example of this brand of mission statement was published by the American retail jeweller Zale Corporation some time before it filed for protection from its creditor (see Box 9.1).

BOX 9.1

Extract from Zale Corporation's statement of company mission

Our business is specialty retailing. Retailing is a people oriented business. We recognize that our business existence and continued success are dependent upon how well we meet our responsibilities to several critically important groups of people.

Our first responsibility is to our customers. Without them we would have no reason for being. We strive to appeal to a broad spectrum of consumers, catering in a professional manner to their needs. Our concept of value to the customer includes a wide selection of quality merchandise, competitively priced and delivered with courtesy and professionalism.

Our ultimate responsibility is to our shareholders. Our goal is to earn an optimum return on invested capital through steady profit growth and prudent aggressive asset management. The attainment of this financial goal, coupled with a record of sound management, represents our approach towards influencing the value placed upon our common stock in the market.

We feel a deep, personal responsibility to our employees. As an equal opportunity employer, we seek to create and maintain an environment where every employee is provided the opportunity to develop to his or her maximum potential. We expect to reward employees commensurate with their contribution to the success of the company.

We are committed to honesty and integrity in all relationships with suppliers of goods and services. We are demanding but fair. We evaluate our suppliers on the basis of quality, price, and service.

We recognize community involvement as an important obligation and as a viable business objective. Support of worthwhile community projects in areas where we operate generally accrues to the health and well-being of the community. This makes the community a better place for our employees to live and a better place for us to operate.

We believe in the Free Enterprise System and in the American Democratic form of government under which this superior economic system has been permitted to

flourish. We feel an incumbent responsibility to insure that our business operates at a reasonable profit. Profit provides opportunity for growth and job security. . . .
This mission statement spells out the creed by which we live.

Zale's document actually provides little guidance in the way of strategic direction. It identifies its business as being 'specialty retailing', but gives no further clues, referring simply to 'quality merchandise' without saying what it is; referring to 'a broad spectrum of customers' without identifying them at all; referring to their customer needs without identifying them; declaring that these unidentified needs would be catered for 'in a professional manner' without making it at all clear what that means. This vagueness could well be the studied avoidance behaviour of the typical committee, each member having different desires for the mission statement, each wishing his or her own particular interests to be accommodated, or at least not inhibited, by the statement. As a result, the statement fails to deliver direction, but instead indulges in double talk such as 'quality merchandise' but 'competitively priced'. Moreover, it is fogged by the other phrases of doubtful meaning such as, 'a wide selection' and 'delivered with courtesy and professionalism'.

From a strategy perspective, Zale's mission statement is largely without meaning. How, for example, would it help answer Drucker's three questions ('What business are you in?, 'Who is your customer?', 'What do they value?')?

Perhaps the purpose is not strategic, but simply a cultural game that is being played. The reification of the company and the revelation of its feelings about its employees and beliefs about free enterprise and the American Constitution are profoundly irrelevant to the company's strategy. The mission statement fails to fulfil any of the criteria identified in Figure 9.2 and, not surprisingly, the company failed to fulfil its stated 'ultimate responsibility'.

Zale's failure was probably not a direct result of its inept mission statement. Nor was Falcon Computer's. In this latter case, top management attempted to create a corporate culture based on highly laudable ideals relating to the quality of product, level of customer service and so on. But the reality, as enacted by top managers themselves, differed so far from the official version that all management's attempts to impose a quality and service culture were wholly counterproductive and resulted only in increased cynicism and alienation among employees:

> *Everyone knew the operative values at Falcon Computer were hierarchy, secrecy and expediency – regardless of what the official culture said.* (Reynolds, 1986)

Mission statements can backfire. If they embody all the criteria listed in Figure 9.2 except top management commitment, the statements will almost certainly be counterproductive, as they were at Falcon. If top management is seen to ignore the mission statement then an unofficial mission will become operative. Top management clearly has a key role to play in making mission statements transformational.

For a demonstration of the power of top management in making mission statements operative, consider the case of Ratner. Gerald Ratner, chairman and leading shareholder of the high street jewellers, addressed a high profile CBI conference. In an entertaining speech about the Ratner business he explained that some of Ratner's customers wanted inexpensive jewellery, priced no higher than the cost of a Marks & Spencer sandwich, although in fact they probably did not last as long. In the heat of the moment and an excess of good humour, he uttered the words that were immediately translated into the simple slogan '*we sell crap*'.

This statement fulfils all the Figure 9.2 mission statement criteria. It is extremely short and simple and makes the highly directional statement that the company is not concerned with quality in any way, but simply selling rubbish. It was certainly memorable, unambiguous, based on credible analysis, highly inspirational and, being delivered by the chairman himself, demonstrated a degree of top management commitment. The impact and damage to the business was profound, culminating in a £122m loss, 330 store closures and 2,500 job losses. There was an immediate and long-term devastation of the share price and the business only narrowly avoided liquidation. A proper recovery was only achieved when Gerald Ratner was finally sacked and the Ratner name removed from the high street.

The potential power of mission statements, as revealed by the Ratner experience, can be harnessed for more positive ends, as Kennedy's statement showed. For a less heroic enterprise the impact is more difficult to achieve.

Box 9.2 shows the stated mission of Alcan, the global aluminium company. Each phrase seems to represent a corporate response to some aspect of underperformance. The word 'innovative' may have been included in order to combat the possibility that Alcan in its maturity was losing its innovative fire. 'Environmentally responsible' seems a direct response to the environmental health problems potentially associated with aluminium. Reference to Standard and Poors is a typical corporate response to substantial underperformance. The inclusion of 'aluminium' may well have been in order to avoid any repeat of the unsuccessful diversifications away from aluminium. Thus, although the statement may have been framed largely in response to essentially negative situations, as is fairly typical, the resultant mission goes some way to defining direction, although there is the difficult-to-resist desire to be both the lowest cost and yet most excellent – such a confusion being likely to lead to Porter's 'stuck in the middle'. Although the net effect of Alcan's mission statement was probably not very strong, it may have had public relations value for shareholders, existing and poten-

BOX 9.2

Alcan's mission statement

Alcan will be the most innovative aluminium company in the world.

Through its people, Alcan will be a global, customer oriented and environmentally responsible enterprise committed to excellence and lowest cost in its chosen aluminium and related businesses. In the 1990s, Alcan's return on equity target is to outperform the Standard & Poor's Industrials.

BOX 9.3
Data-Med's mission statement

We aim to be the best known and lowest cost suppliers of quality software and hardware to the UK NHS regions and wider healthcare market.

tial. It probably short-circuited some internally generated proposals for diversification, but otherwise is not a strategically strong statement.

Box 9.3 shows the mission statement of Data-Med Ltd, a small computer software development company specialising in computerised healthcare management systems, selling products of its own development as well as Anglicised versions of existing US systems. In addition, and only as a service to its software customers, it also sold relevant hardware.

The statement is admirably succinct, if not memorable, but its precision is more apparent than real. It is clearly selling into the healthcare market, both National Health Service and the private sector. The mission statement adds no further focus to this – no regions or sectors are identified as being its special focus and it must be supposed that it is therefore attacking the whole market, of which it then had less than a 2 per cent share, with four competitors having more than 10 per cent share each and the leader with over 20 per cent. As with Alcan, it is not clear whether their main thrust is on lowest costs or highest quality, but with such a small market share and no focus it is unlikely to be realistic for Data-Med to strive for lowest costs and, unlike Alcan, it is not concerned with the supply of a basic commodity. The Data-Med focus on quality must therefore be more specific. Finally, it is not clear from the mission statement that Data-Med's core business is in the provision of software systems, rather than hardware, which in reality is incidental.

So there are three sorts of mission statement: cultural, non-directional and missionary. The cultural statements, such as those of Zale and Falcon, still have their adherents. Many of the recently privatised utilities and public sector organisations newly opened to the business management model seem to adopt the cultural version. Their mission statements appear to address all and any stakeholder, with no special purpose in mind other than to make some statement of values. Whether or not these are worthwhile is irrelevant to the current discussion – they are clearly not strategic.

The non-directional statements are perhaps the most common among established businesses. The Alcan and Data-Med statements are examples of this type. They reflect the strategic realities without having much effect on them. They might be useful in making minor incremental change and in defining constraints, but their effect is unlikely to be decisive.

The genuinely missionary statements include Kennedy's and, in a negative sense, Ratner's, plus the four examples of strategic intent quoted by Hamel and Prahalad shown in Box 9.4. These are expressed in simple unambiguous terms. They are capable of initiating and galvanising action and being converted into competitive challenges which are staging posts along the way. They tell everyone which way the

BOX 9.4

Examples of strategic intent

President Kennedy: Put man on the moon by 1970
Ratner: Sell crap
Canon: Beat Xerox
Komatsu: Encircle Caterpillar
Coca-Cola: Put a Coke within 'arm's reach' of every consumer in the world.
NEC: Exploit competence in computing and communications.

business is headed over the long term and can have a profound effect on the firm's stakeholders, both internal and external. Employees know what they are trying to achieve and therefore how they should make their greatest efforts; customers know what the firm's products and services embody; suppliers understand what the key elements are when dealing with the firm.

Hamel and Prahalad (1989) emphasise the motivational aspects of strategic intent. The intent should express some demanding, even crazy, ambition which embodies an obsession with winning at all levels in the organisation. People are motivated by the overall intent and the milestone targets which deserve personal effort and which remain consistent over time. These missionary statements need to be defined in such a way that they can be readily deconstructed so that the milestones along the route can be identified and progress at each stage monitored and the people involved rewarded according to progress. Try your hand at devising a mission statement for some of the companies that have been introduced in the text (see Box 9.5).

'Become the leading world producer of photocopiers' is a statement of strategic direction which could be a powerful organising and motivating concept. The strategic intent of 'beat Xerox' is nevertheless still more powerful, focusing as it does on

BOX 9.5

A statement of mission

DISCUSSION POINT

Cooper Soft Drinks Ltd (Boxes 2.3, 2.4 and 3.1)

Fletton Brick Co. Plc (Boxes 8.1 and 8.2)

Inca Construction Materials Ltd (Box 5.1)

Justify each statement both in fundamentals (see Figure 9.2) and in terms of a strategy derived from strategy basics and a relevant framework.

the major competitor and identifying the standards to be met. 'Beat Xerox' meets all the criteria asked of a mission statement in a particularly memorable way and, as Hamel and Prahalad explained (1989), it also formed the basis of a thorough analysis of Canon's business and the direction along which all the milestones were set, some of which were indicated in Box 3.3.

9.3 Core competence framework

The core competence framework embodies rather more than the idea of core competences, but is given that label for convenience. The framework starts with the idea of strategic intent expressed in terms of a competitive challenge and identifies the existing competences and those required to meet the challenge. The framework then devises a plan for acquiring those competences that need to be added.

Canon's strategic intent appears at the outset to be well beyond its capability. 'Beat Xerox' was clearly an impossible dream when it was first enunciated before Canon entered the photocopying business, but it was achieved.

The achievement was miraculous but it was not inspired by some charismatic leader, and it did not depend to any substantial extent on good fortune. It was achieved by the development of core competences. The use of the word 'competence', within the context of this transformational framework, is interesting. Competence is within the grasp of every business. The possession of a particular technological or managerial capability would be unlikely to differentiate a firm from its competitor possessing a similar capability. A core competence is a combination of such capabilities which provide the firm with a leadership position in the development of certain generic or core products. This is what gives the business a sustainable competitive advantage.

A firm's existing core competences can be identified by analysing its product or service. What are the fundamental skills and knowledge on which successful products are based? They may relate to straightforward world leadership in specific technologies or they may be related to particular organisational or managerial skills. Some examples are stated in Box 9.6. Companies that successfully build global leadership in more than one core competence are few and far between; those that have done so in several are extremely rare. Global leadership in two or more complementary fundamental competences provides the ability to create a stream of new products, some of them (for example personal hi-fi, electronic personal organisers) unimaginable with no known demand.

BOX 9.6

Examples of core competences

Benetton

Fast cycle times through computer-aided, just-in-time manufacturing, rapid customer response, distinctive product aesthetic design.

Toyota
Fast cycle times

Honda
Engines, power trains

Coca-Cola
Brand strength, geographic spread

Fletton Brick
Energy-efficient clay

Although most of Hamel and Prahalad's examples are global players, their cases are instructive for lesser businesses whether or not their intentions have a global dimension. Most of these global businesses started out as obscure firms and became global only through decades of persistently following an explicit and well understood strategic intent. Moreover, every business, whether in services or manufacturing, is affected by the new technologies which are themselves global. Even for those businesses which have no global ambitions and appear not to be vulnerable to global competition, the concept of core competences, although writ small, may well be relevant. Every management needs to know what competences form the foundation of its most successful products, so that it can develop those competences and nurture the people on whom they depend.

For many businesses, the acquisition and development of core competences is somewhat haphazard. As Mintzberg (1987a) noted, even the clearest strategic positions may emerge from a process of repeated trial and error, or even as a result of simple good luck. The extent to which strategic positions emerge, as opposed to being deliberately planned, can never be known – many emergent strategies are post-rationalised to give the impression of careful and sophisticated strategic thought.

For example, whilst Honda's development is apparently based on the overt exploitation of its position in engines and transmissions (four-wheel steering notwithstanding), its ultimately successful entry into the American motorcycle market was a saga of learning from trial and error, if not straightforward misunderstanding. Honda had originally intended to sell large bikes in Harley Davidson dominated America, not the 50cc Cub which it had taken over for the use of its own staff. Honda was surprised when American buyers showed interest in the lightweight Super-Cub bike (Pascale, 1994). In 1957, Soichiro Honda thought he had agreed to sell 7,500 bikes a month while his American agent had thought they were talking about an *annual* sale – 'Seventy-five hundred a month!' the agent exclaimed when he realised the misunderstanding, 'That's out of the question. Preposterous!' (Gilder, 1986, p. 187). A few years later Honda was selling around 20,000 bikes a month in America.

The breakthrough idea, or product, is by definition 'preposterous'. If it were not so then it would already have happened. Such breakthroughs themselves can lead to the development of new core competences which provide the basis of sustainable leadership positions.

The idea that Canon should set out, as a leading camera manufacturer, to beat Xerox in the photocopier market was preposterous, but it did it. Such successes do not arise solely as a result of trial and error or good luck. Even Honda's experience was not just lucky: its success was based on a technological position realised in a unique product. Such positions can be achieved through a clearly articulated strategic intent which is painstakingly implemented over many years, as the examples outlined in Boxes 3.3 and 9.7.

Core competences are the basis of competitive advantage in achieving strategic intent. Acquiring and nurturing competences which are not core is simply a waste of resources and effort and serves only to dissipate concentration. It has been suggested that it is much better to buy in non-core competences (for example Quinn *et al.*, 1990; Venkatesan, 1992) and focus all internal efforts on the acquisition and development of what really matters.

A firm's capacity for competitive innovation is based on its ability to acquire relevant core competences and to apply them effectively in the development of core products. Capability is infinite. It is not constrained by the competences or resources already owned, but can be extended by the careful definition of the competences required and the means of their acquisition and development.

Missing competences can be painstakingly developed internally through focused investment in R&D or acquired externally through various collaborative arrangements. Success by internal development may provide a sustainable leadership position where the acquisition of new technology is a continuous process with each advance laying the foundation for the next. However, internal development is

BOX 9.7

Milestones to Komatsu encircling Caterpillar

The milestones are an example of an outpacing strategy moving from quality to cost orientation to quality over a twenty-year period:

Acquire technology by licensing (early 1960s).

Raise quality above Caterpillar's (1961).

Company-wide quality programme (1962).

Cost reduction/quality maintenance programmes (mid-1960s).

Develop Eastern bloc markets.

Durability/reliability improvement programmes (early 1970s).

Establish sales and service departments in developing countries (mid-1970s).

Alternating planned cost reduction, quality improvement and product development programmes (late 1970s on).

(Based on Prahalad and Hamel 1990)

extremely expensive and beyond the means of all but the largest organisations. Moreover, in an era when the diffusion of technology is rapid, the resultant competitive advantage may be short lived. Also, a lot of new technology is not protectable and there is little commercial benefit in being the holder of patents the essence of which are immediately copied by competitors. As Ouchi and Bolton (1988) suggest, internal development is not the best way to progress in areas where the intellectual property may be 'leaky'.

So for a variety of reasons, the acquisition of core competences through collaboration has become an attractive proposition. It is a way of reducing costs and eliminating wasteful competition especially in R&D (Telser, 1987). It is also likely to be quicker to buy in technology rather than develop it in-house, and doing so opens up the potential of a business to the establishment of core competences far beyond what it could develop with its own resources, as the example of Canon shows. Canon used primarily a combination of external licensing and internal R&D in order to build the competences to compete with Xerox.

It is a way forward which accords very well with the business environment of the 1990s. Communications with suppliers, customers, competitors, shareholders, technological suppliers and independent sources of knowledge and expertise such as research associations, universities and commercial technology consultants have never been more important to the success of a business. Diffusion of innovations has never been more rapid, so the need to know what is happening in new technology through Europe, America, Japan and elsewhere has never been greater. Consequently, we are operating in an era of increasingly open communications.

Buyer/seller relationships have moved from the adversarial to collaborative (Spekman, 1990) so that transactions are not seen as one-off profit maximising deals, but as part of longer-term mutual dependencies where close collaboration can work to the mutual benefit of both parties.

It used to be thought that in order to compete globally a company had to be big (Chandler, 1990), but it is no longer true. The logic behind the trend to alliances and collaborations is based partly on the need to globalise when to do so is beyond the scope of the businesses if it operated alone, and partly on the need to survive in the face of rampant technology.

Collaboration, even between competitors, has thus become one of the key business issues, and examples of successful and disastrous collaborations abound. Businesses are having to adjust to this more open world of technology exchange, alliance and research (Ramo, 1989). The tremendous cost of maintaining a leading position in a globalised market or technology is beyond the capacity of all but the very largest corporations. Collaboration rather than cut-throat competition is becoming an imperative for smaller businesses if they are not to be left hopelessly behind.

Nowhere is industry technological co-operation growing more rapidly than in Europe. In the early 1980s, European companies were being outgunned by superior technology in the United States and Japan. Having recognised that in a unified market it is imperative to leverage technology continent-wide, they raced into technology partnerships to exploit both the single market and subsequently monetary union. In addition there is an increasing public investment in technological collaboration. Europe has become 'the world's hot spot for industrial co-operation and the growth of coalitions' (Madia, 1990).

Many of these collaborative ventures involve large firms which are already multinational, but this is by no means the whole truth. There are many opportunities for smaller businesses to be involved in publicly sponsored collaborative projects or directly with other firms.

The potential benefits from collaboration are tremendous, but the risks are also considerable. Many firms seem to enter such arrangements for reasons which are not very apparent, possibly even because they are fashionable, and as a result they lose out to their collaborative partner, sometimes disastrously. The overriding principle in engaging in any collaboration is to *make sure* you know exactly what you are trying to achieve when you enter a collaborative arrangement and then to make sure you achieve it. Some firms have adopted forms of alliance and mutual collaboration in order to close the competence gap, while others have simply opted out and bought in technology from elsewhere as a cost-saving device. More often than not this form of cost-reduction is the first step down the disinvestment spiral. Alliances must be strategy driven (Devlin and Blackley, 1988).

An interesting analogy is provided by Hamel (1987) which highlights two different attitudes to collaboration. Typically, the Japanese adopt the role of students or learners in their approach to collaboration. They seek to learn and understand as much as they possibly can from the arrangement. Western countries, on the other hand, typically adopt the role of teacher. The result is that the Japanese firms learn and the western company's give up their special expertise. The Japanese may learn a technology, but more often nowadays it is market understanding which they gain from collaborations. The western participants may gain today's technology (or even yesterday's) relatively cheaply, but in so doing stand out of the technology race and miss the long-term development, making it difficult for them to climb aboard at some later stage.

Therefore 'collaborate with your competitors, but be careful' (Hamel *et al.*, 1989). To make collaborations work it is crucial to fully understand the purpose of the partnership, to keep it simple, to trust each other and to be wholly committed to the success of the partnership (Turpin, 1993).

The framework differs from others in that the strength of a business is not seen in terms of a particular product, sector of the market or distribution channel, but in the underlying capability to generate a range of rapidly evolving products or markets. The traditional rationale for structuring an organisation as a collection of business units, each with maximum autonomy, becomes questionable. Instead, the overriding requirement is for the development and acquisition of common strands of expertise which cut across products, markets and business units.

This may lead to some apparently strange combinations of business activities. For example, 3M's products include 'Post It' notes, magnetic tape, photographic film, pressure-sensitive tapes and coated abrasives. These all have quite different production technologies, end consumers and channels of distribution. The rationale is based on the core competences in substrates, coatings and adhesives. Or again, what would be the justification for a product range including, lawnmowers, generators, motorcycles and cars? These are all quite different markets with unconnected distribution channels. Honda's success with this diverse range – 200 per cent growth between 1980 and 1988 – was based on the deliberate exploitation of its core competences in engines and power trains.

Prahalad and Hamel (1990) quote several such examples of the use of core competences. The success of NEC resulted directly from this approach (see Box 9.8). In similar vein, over the 1980s Canon grew by nearly 300 per cent to beat Xerox with a range of core products including image scanners, laser printers, photocopiers and cameras, based on core competences in precision mechanics, fine optics and microelectronics.

Honda's application of its core competences resulted in the introduction of four-wheel steering and multivalve engines among others. These developments can be introduced to give the competence-owner enhanced competitive advantage. For example, one of Canon's core products, developed straight out of its core competences, is the desktop laser printer engine of which it makes around 80 per cent even though sales under its own name are relatively small. Hewlett Packard, with a prior position in the marketplace, led the personal laser market using a Canon engine, but was faced with a competing Canon product with the same engine but with added features for the same price. Hewlett Packard was forced to respond at considerable cost to the company.

Core competences are not the sole preserve of manufacturing industry. The same concepts apply equally in services, although the competences may be related to technology imported from manufacturing. For example, fast cycle times are a critical factor in providing customer service in many industries. Sportswear producer and retailer, Benetton, owes its success and explosive growth almost entirely to fast cycle times made possible by the use of information technology (Bower and Hout, 1988).

BOX 9.8

NEC's core competences

NEC adopted the core competences approach by systematically exploiting the convergence of its competences in computing and communications (C&C). A C&C committee oversaw the development of these capabilities and the resulting core products. This was supported by other co-ordination groups and teams which cut across the traditional organisation structure and ensured that each member of the organisation knew and understood NEC's strategic intent. NEC developed competences internally and also through over one hundred purposive collaborations and alliances with other organisations.

Between 1980 and 1988 NEC's sales grew from \$3.8bn to \$21.9bn and the company became the world number one in semiconductors and a leading player in telecommunications and computers. Over the same period, its American competitor GTE, enjoyed sales growth from \$10bn to \$16.5bn and had to withdraw from several of its major business areas.

(Source: based on Pralahad and Hamel, 1990)

It starts in new product development with a computer-aided design system which automatically explodes a new design into a full range of sizes, transmits the patterns to computerised cutting machines to await customer orders. Undyed fabric is stored at demand scheduled just-in-time (JIT) factories and cut and dyed strictly to order. Retail outlets are also run on a minimum stock JIT basis. Cycle time, from placing the order at the retail store to receiving the specially made product, takes fifteen days, which both satisfies customers and avoids over- and under-production.

Most firms, whether in manufacturing or service sectors, are not competing on a global front and do not seek to be global leaders. Nevertheless, every firm is operating in a global context: the technologies used are available globally and every customer is conditioned by standards of quality and service which apply globally. Thus every firm must both ensure that it is aware of all the available technological capabilities and also decide which are the core competences which are needed to implement its particular strategic intent.

Core competences represent a distinctive definition and analysis of business strength, but what makes the framework unique is its transformational emphasis. It is focused on changing the rules of engagement, rather than accepting them and seeking an advantageous position within them. It is concerned with developing new core competences and generic products for new markets rather than allocating existing resources to satisfy existing customer needs. In short, it is concerned with 'breaking the mould' rather than simply adapting to it more efficiently. And it does this by having a transformational effect on the organisation's people.

Strategic intent embodies ambition out of all proportion to the organisation's existing resources or capabilities. The strategic intent should be 'preposterous'. The process deliberately defines a misfit between existing resources and strategic aspirations. A strategic intent is calculated to stretch the organisation.

Creating this resources/aspirations misfit is the starting point of the process. Rather than starting off with a passive analysis of the organisation's strengths and weaknesses, management seeks to identify a desirable, preposterous, competitor-focused goal and then to define ways in which it might be achieved. The goal must be out of reach of the firm's existing strengths, so that its resources must be leveraged in some way so that their effect is magnified. This is done in five ways:

1. Not surprisingly, Hamel and Prahalad identify concentration as the key to the more effective use of resources.
2. Resources can be accumulated more effectively.
3. One kind of resource can be complemented more effectively by another so as to create higher-order value.
4. Resources can be conserved wherever possible.
5. Resources can be recovered from the marketplace as fast as possible.

The core competence approach focuses on breaking away from existing marketing definitions and developing whole new generic products. The served market concept, embedded in the more analytical frameworks, inhibits the development of revolutionary strategies, seeking out innovative new products by adding new functional-

BOX 9.9
Fletton Brick's strategic intent and milestones

DISCUSSION POINT

Review the position of Fletton Brick and assume that it proceeds on the basis of both the internally developed 'facing' brick and the proposed facing brick acquisition. Develop a suitably transformational statement of its strategic intent and suggest three possible milestones to its achievement.

ity, by giving new forms for existing functionality, or providing new functionality in a new form.

The framework also seeks to break the mould in terms of prior price performance assumptions, for example Canon developing a $500 photocopier when the existing cheapest model was around $5,000.

The framework's focus on beating competitors applies at all levels of the organisation. This is achieved by widespread use of competitor intelligence and competitor products. For example, shopfloor units might have relevant components of competing products on display in their work sections as examples of quality they have to beat.

Everyone in the organisation needs to feel the sense of urgency to achieve the next milestone on the way to the declared strategic intent. Attention is focused on communicating the value of the target and making use of both individual and team contributions to its achievement (see Box 9.9).

The framework also requires emphasis on developing people so that they have the skills needed to work effectively and so that they are fully committed to achieving the strategic intent. The framework is more attentive to people and their behaviour than the more analytical frameworks. No strategy framework will be effective if people issues are ignored, but whereas the analytical frameworks deal with people separately as a part of strategy implementation, concern with people is embedded in the core competence approach.

The core competence framework uses its own language and is illustrated with many contemporary examples, but many of its base concepts have roots which stretch back to the early writers on general management such as Barnard, Chandler, Drucker and Selznick. Perhaps strategy management has come full circle. The entrepreneurial framework is based more directly on these early sources and can be seen to draw a some striking parallels with the work of Hamel and Prahalad.

9.4 Entrepreneurial framework

The entrepreneur came first; large-scale business followed and in its maturity often devoted a great deal of effort to trying to recapture the essence of its entrepreneurial beginnings: the original purpose of the business, its sense of direction, concentration of effort, consistency and flexibility inevitably lost during years of growth, bureaucratisation and diversification.

The entrepreneur's decision to set up a new business, the first strategic decision, is the bravest of them all. The new business can only be founded on an extensive personal financial commitment, a high degree of uncertainty and a reliance on superhuman personal efforts. Most established businesses would be unable to tolerate any manager who recommended such a reckless course of action – they have lost the capacity to deal with that level of risk, unless the alternative is terminal collapse.

The entrepreneurial approach to strategy is direct and simple. The purposes of strategy – direction, concentration, consistency and flexibility – are achieved, it appears, almost instinctively in the entrepreneurial start-up of the business. There are four critical parts to the start-up:

1. Understanding the purpose of the business.
2. Developing a distinctive competence to fulfil that purpose.
3. Communicating the competitive specialism to all stakeholders.
4. Exploiting the competitive specialism of the business.

For a start-up business these are relatively simple concepts to apply. Moreover, flexibility that causes large-scale businesses so much difficulty is a natural attribute of the single-product entrepreneur. The critical question is whether, by following this entrepreneurial example, larger businesses can recapture the essentially entrepreneurial characteristics.

The purpose of the business in a set-up decision is usually quite straightforward and has to do with satisfying a customer need that has been identified as not already satisfied in the same way. Not every new business is founded on this simple principle, but not every new business survives. Those that do survive do so because they have a valid purpose, not one based simply on providing the owner with a good living. That may be the entrepreneur's reason for setting up the business, but the purpose of the business itself is separate from this and prescribes the means of earning that return. If the business satisfies a customer need, customers will pay an economic price for the product. If an economic price is not paid then the business is not satisfying a customer need. This ability to spot the opportunity, the unsatisfied customer need, is the archetypal entrepreneurial skill.

Some infant businesses fail because they run out of cash as a result of trying to grow too quickly; but more frequently failure arises because there is no unsatisfied customer need, or because the business does not provide a competitive means of its satisfaction because the product is too expensive, too poor quality, too late, too slow, too heavy or lacking in some critical area.

The original business purpose, which was the basis of the set-up decision, seems to remain permanently valid in some businesses – Sainsbury, Rolls Royce Motors, Hewlett Packard, Marks & Spencer and many others have been well documented – but for most firms this is not the case. The original purpose may become completely irrelevant, or it may remain valid for only a small part of the business. After years of faltering progression down various paths, with endless product diversifications, the purpose of the business can become completely obscure, the only unifying elements being common ownership and use of the financial language.

Many companies focus attention on developing a mission statement in an attempt to recapture the previous coherence and rationale that everyone in the company can aspire to support. But, as we have seen, mission statements may or may not be effective. If they are simply statements of culture they will have little strategic impact. An entrepreneurial mission is a simple, direct, unambiguous and, above all, operational statement. For example, 'Our mission is to sell the fastest (or cheapest, or best) widgets on the (defined) market' tells a great deal about the business. People inside and out will know what it is about and everyone should understand where they should best concentrate all efforts. However, most mission statements fail to achieve this directness and simplicity.

Some companies have written up their company histories (Smith and Steadman, 1981) for use in management training to give useful insights both to the firm's current role and to likely future directions. Company histories are also used increasingly to create or reinforce aspects of corporate culture by explaining in symbolic terms some watershed event of the past or by giving exposure to some important role model, very often through stories about the original founder of the business. However, corporate history is an inadequate substitute for *knowing* the business purpose. This is the key to direction, but it is not in itself sufficient for high performance. The entrepreneurial business must develop a distinctive competence to fulfil its purpose.

The idea of distinctive competence was used by Selznick in 1957 to describe what a particular firm is uniquely good at by comparison with its close competitors. Selznick suggested how distinctive competence and what he called 'organisational character' – what we would call 'culture' – could be combined to fulfil an organisation's basic mission. Selznick pre-dates Hamel and Prahalad by more than thirty years but his ideas have many parallels with theirs. In highlighting the distinctive nature of his idea of competence he was focusing on competitors, just as core competences are used explicitly for beating competitors. Neither approach is satisfied to be 'me too' followers. Both demand distinction and leadership. Perhaps this is the prerequisite of a transformational framework – following is simply not a transformational concept.

The entrepreneurial framework is based on the idea of developing a distinctive competence into a competitive specialism in order to fulfil the business purpose as shown in Figure 9.3. For the start-up business this is straightforward; if the start-up proposal is not based on an understanding of customer needs and competing products and technologies, although perhaps not expressed in this language, it would be unlikely to attract any external funding and support. As the business grows it will be necessary to communicate the competitive specialism to the various stakeholders and the statement of mission forms a powerful means of that communication. Finally, as with all strategy frameworks, the process is repeated to ensure that the business is aware of relevant changes and responds to them appropriately.

There are many published examples of firms that ignore the competitive specialism. The decline in strategic and subsequently financial performance leads almost inevitably to the imposition of an accounting culture with the search for quick reme-

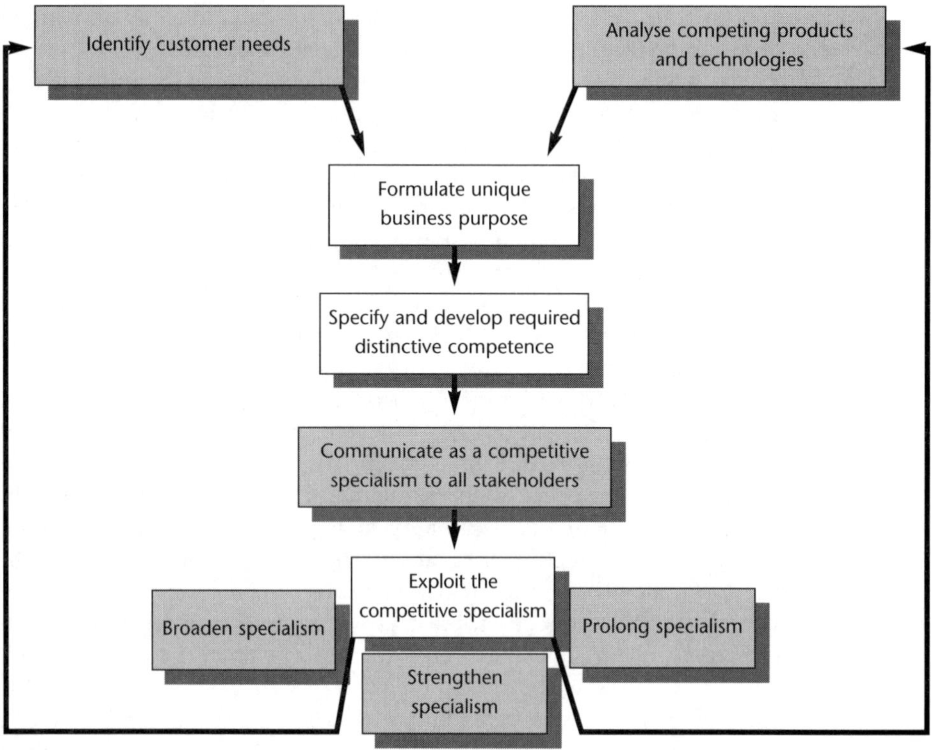

Figure 9.3 The entrepreneurial process

dies, firstly through cost-cutting and subsequently very often through diversification and acquisition, leading ever further from the competitive specialism and its potential for further exploitation.

A widely quoted example which typified this tendency was the car firm, Jaguar. Jaguar's original specialism was clearly related to the production and sale of fast, stylish but competitively priced saloon cars. Being a relatively small company, in due course Jaguar joined up with the rest of the then British-owned car industry and became part of British Leyland. It barely survived the experience. The state-owned parent forced Jaguar's attention down the objectives hierarchy onto financial targets. It lost quality and reputation and ceased to produce a product that fulfilled the Jaguar mission. Sales fell, productivity collapsed and the product became almost unsaleable. The vicious cycle was reversed only by a return to the firm's competitive specialism and a new concentration on quality and reliability which led logically to its separation from the state-owned company. During its low spell in 1972, Jaguar employed 160 engineers and many more accountants. By 1985 it employed over 600 engineers and was urgently seeking more. Whatever Jaguar's future under Ford ownership, it is clear that exploiting its competitive specialism, which was subverted during the Leyland years, provides its only credible prospect of success. The Jaguar example is still pertinent; a 1997 world survey found that a majority of firms' 'strategies' are still driven by financial objectives, largely to satisfy shareholders, and as a consequence lack vision and focus (Quest Worldwide, 1997).

Exploiting the competitive specialism is really the core of the entrepreneurial framework, but it is not always easy to achieve. There are three ways in which it can be exploited. First, it can be strengthened or intensified so that it is more readily perceived by customers or so that customers accord it a higher value and are therefore prepared to pay a higher premium. Thus, for example, a specialism related to product quality could be strengthened by increasing the quality of the product further or by promoting the quality of the product more effectively. The result will be to increase the actual and perceived level of quality and to reduce the price sensitivity of the product. A sharply focused specialism is perhaps the easiest to manage. However, it would be easy to increase quality beyond customer perceptions, i.e. build in unrecognised quality. Similarly it would be easy to provide quality at a price that the customer is unwilling to pay. Intensifying the specialism must be done only on the basis of hard information about customer needs and perceptions.

Secondly, the specialism can be broadened so that it satisfies the needs of more customers. The most obvious and least risky way that this can be done is by geographic broadening. However, any product which is focused on a narrow segment of the market can potentially have its focus broadened to appeal to other segments. Porter warns of the danger of this strategy. Businesses often feel themselves to be trapped in a perennial search for growth. For them broadening the specialism is tempting, but the risk is that in broadening, the specialism it will lose the uniqueness on which competitive advantage is based (Porter, 1996, and Reading Review 29). There will almost always be a trade-off between broadening the specialism and its intensity. Broadening the focus to encompass a wider market clearly risks reducing the perceived value to existing customers. Such strategic decisions must be based on solid information.

Finally, the specialism can be prolonged so that it survives through developing technology and changing consumer tastes. The automobile industry shows how the competitive specialism can be prolonged through all manner of fundamental changes and yet various products or brands continue, their competitive positions maintained. Some specialisms are related to single products, or to single, clearly defined markets, which have finite lives. In the face of inevitable decline it may well be necessary to accept the death of the business and to invest in something different while funds are still available. This happens occasionally. However, many products and product lines have been diagnosed as 'yesterday's breadwinners' or 'dogs' and as a direct consequence have been liquidated unnecessarily. The orthodox wisdom prescribes starving such businesses of investment and pricing them out of the market, while in many such cases it might have been perfectly feasible to revive the businesses concerned by identifying their specialisms and taking action to prolong their life cycles. Even generic products can be revived from maturity/decline to a phase of renewal with quite different prospects.

Barnard asserted top management's responsibility for communication to 'link the common mission with those willing to cooperate in it'. Communication was the means of turning mission into action. For Barnard (1948) executive work was the job of 'maintaining' the organisation and involved three prime tasks:

1. Formulation of mission and objectives.
2. Maintenance of organisational communication.
3. Securing essential services from individuals.

The entrepreneurial framework fits Barnard's proposition well. 'Formulation of mission and objectives' is adjacent to 'formulate unique business purpose' and 'specify and develop required distinctive competence'. These are the first tasks of strategy management.

Barnard's 'maintenance of organisational communication' and 'securing essential services from individuals' cover similar issues as the entrepreneurial framework's 'communicate as a competitive specialism to all stakeholders'. These activities are crucial to the implementation of strategy and focus on how people may be motivated to put their enthusiasm and effort behind achieving the mission and objectives of the business.

The importance of communication is widely recognised. Kanter (1990) identified open communications as prerequisite to creating an organisation where the individual member is both free to use his or her own initiative and be well disposed to doing so in a way which serves corporate needs. However, it is not sufficient merely for organisational communication to be open. Communication itself has a specific mission. It is not just 'management by walking about' (Peters and Austin, 1985). The message is a vital ingredient, not merely the process of communication. The aim in strategy is to convert objectives into action. The entrepreneurial framework requires everyone in the organisation to be aware of the specialism of the business so that all efforts can be concentrated on its exploitation.

Effective communication requires the message to be unambiguous. Strategic thinking aims to make trade-offs explicit and to overcome the natural tendency to fudge issues. It is easier to deliver conflicting messages full of ambiguity, such as the widely quoted example, 'Be innovative and take risks. But be careful.' Ambiguity of this sort is often compounded by the sender totally ignoring the inconsistencies and making them undiscussable. Such ambiguity destroys the message. Effective communication also depends on messages being short and simple. The competitive specialism must be capable of communication in brief, unambiguous statements, such as 'beat Xerox'.

The entrepreneurial framework requires that the competitive specialism message should be communicated to all stakeholders, therefore using every possible medium: in formal strategy statements, in newsletters, noticeboards, employee accounts, in house journals, product literature, advertising, public relations, bonus payment schemes, product training seminars, induction programmes, briefing sessions, consultation meetings, social gatherings and any other medium available. This widespread communication of strategy is sometimes treated with suspicion. There are those who suggest that strategy, being the preserve of top management, should be treated as confidential, despite all the clear benefits from open communication. On rare occasions there may be an element of strategy which has to remain secret for a time, but this must be the exception. The entrepreneurial framework requires strategy to be communicated openly and as widely as possible so as to give all members the sense of direction of the business. Only then are the decisions they all take, and the efforts they all make, made in a consistent manner so that the business continues to fulfil the customers' perceived need by continuing to exploit its specialism. Every member of the business, from boardroom to shopfloor, takes such decisions and therefore should know what the strategy is and where the business is headed.

The entrepreneurial framework is perhaps the most simple of all the frameworks. Analysis is based on systematic data collection and decision-taking is calculated and clinical. Business is customer oriented because it pays, not because there is a passion for the customer. The analysis of customer needs and perceptions is systematic and the aims are accuracy and precision. Communication is thorough and focused to ensure both that the efforts of all the firm's members are similarly focused and that there is no strategically irrelevant expenditure, i.e. to achieve concentration.

The competitive specialism is exploited in order to maximise competitive advantage, to deliver value to the customer as efficiently as possible and to avoid all waste. Create the customer, but do not give value away. The aim in the supplier/customer relationship must be to achieve the larger long-term slice of the negotiable surplus. This means measuring precisely what the customer values and providing it in measured terms. Business exists to serve the customer, but it also competes directly with the customer for the economic surplus arising from their mutual transactions. This is a calculated relationship, with little room for excess or altruism, but it is one which will need to provide mutual benefit over the long term.

Summary

- Analytical frameworks provide understanding of the business and its environments and help to identify strategic direction and ways of achieving strategic fit.
- Transformational frameworks engage people in the strategy process to achieve concentration consistently over time.
- For strategy to be implemented effectively it needs both analytical and transformational elements.
- Transformational strategies are all based on a strong directional idea, often expressed in the form of a mission statement.
- Culturally defined mission statements describing the way we do things or encapsulating some notion of values contribute little to transformational strategy.
- Non-directional mission statements only identify constraints and limitations on strategy.
- Other mission statements are truly missionary and express the strategic objective in clear, directional terms.
- To be effective, mission statements must be short and simple, memorable, unambiguous, measurable, based on sound analysis, embody top management commitment and be capable of inspiring action.
- Hamel and Prahalad's framework used the strategic intent version of mission to define direction (for example 'beat Xerox') and derive operational milestones.

- Strategic intent requires an organisation to leverage its resources and stretch its capabilities (core competences) for its achievement.
- Technological collaborations and strategic alliances of all kinds can help an organisation to achieve far more than it ever could on its own.
- The entrepreneurial framework encompasses much of the other frameworks and is both analytical and transformational.
- The entrepreneurial framework is based on four fundamental issues:
  - Understanding the purpose of the business.
  - Developing a distinctive competence to fulfil that purpose.
  - Communicating the competitive specialism to all stakeholders.
  - Exploiting the competitive specialism of the business.

Further reading

Hamel, G. and Prahalad, C.K., *Competing for the future*, Harvard Business School Press, 1994.
Ghoshal, S. and Bartlett, C.A., 'Changing the role of management: beyond structure to processes', *Harvard Business Review*, January/February 1995.
Ghoshal, S. and Bartlett, C.A., 'Changing the role of management: beyond systems to people', *Harvard Business Review*, May/June 1995.

Chapter 10

The contingency approach

This chapter compares and contrasts the frameworks that have been considered so far and traces their increasing sophistication as well as their common components. It is suggested that the different frameworks, rather than being regarded as separate models, are more usefully seen as evolutionary stages in the emergence of a single generic strategy framework.

The contingency approach assumes that there is no one best version of the framework which can serve all situations equally well.

The strategist's job is to identify the version which is most useful for the particular organisation and situation. It may conform to one of the frameworks already described or it may be necessary to shape a framework specially to fit a particular circumstance. Either way, the utility of the framework used will depend on the level of understanding not only of the framework but also of the organisation and its situation.

10.1 Introduction

There are many similarities among the frameworks. Even from the crudest SWOT model, frameworks have been concerned largely with the nature of the organisation and its environments and how the two might be advantageously related to each other. This overall shape of the organisation and its environment has persisted throughout the evolution of frameworks. The early models were concerned with such cerebral notions as strategic fit, the balance of objectives and resources and the 'satisfaction' of various stakeholders. Latterly, the models have focused on developing relationships with customers and competitors.

The many parallels and similarities between these various frameworks suggests that it may be more useful to regard them as stages in the evolution of a single generic model which places the organisation in relation to its various environments. This singular framework has developed various guises during its evolution and at each stage has provided new insights of particular relevance to the imperatives of the day.

In the 1960s, growth was the problem which excited strategy management and the model derived by the Boston Consulting Group addressed this issue. In the 1970s and 1980s, competing in zero-growth markets was answered by Porter. Currently, the dominance of technological innovation has produced the model described by Hamel and Prahalad. In due course some new model will emerge which will be of particular relevance to the problems of its day – there is no reason to suppose the process will stop. Equally, there is no reason to expect a fundamentally different framework, any more than Porter's competitive strategy was fundamentally different from the preceding portfolio models. The next framework to be hyped and adopted as the ultimate strategy panacea is likely to be just as flawed as all its predecessors have been, but will nonetheless almost certainly provide some new insight of value to managers of the early twenty-first century.

This perspective leads to a consideration of the essential characteristics of the generic framework. Does it contain some ultimate truth about strategy? Are there some enduring principles which might be applied, with confidence, to as yet unknown future situations? This is the subject matter of this final chapter on frameworks.

10.2 Framework characteristics

Table 10.1 summarises the characteristics of the main strategy frameworks. They are presented in the order in which they have been treated in the preceding chapters which more-or-less corresponds to their chronological development and adoption. The presentation also suggests that the earlier frameworks tended to be more limited than later ones and in particular were more passive, especially regarding their external orientation and focus on action to achieve change. The following paragraphs provide a brief explanation of Table 10.1.

The column headed 'strategic objective' indicates to what extent an objective system is an embedded part of the framework. Strategic objectives were not an essential part of the early planning frameworks. Although there would be nothing to prevent a strategic objective being combined with a planning framework, the language of the accounts-based framework is rather anti-strategic. It is not possible to express strategic objectives in accounting terms. A rate of return on investment is not a strategic objective, as was shown in Chapter 3, nor are any of the other frequently used financially expressed objectives. A SWOT-based framework also tends to be anti-strategic in its effect. It might be argued that there is an implicit set of objectives embedded in SWOT which requires strengths to be exploited, weaknesses to be strengthened, threats to be avoided and opportunities to be taken. The result of such a system would be to spread resources very thinly thereby failing to achieve concentration, which is one of the purposes of strategy.

The basic systems model provides explicit objectives for each stage of the systems evolution from 'survival' in the face of high rates of infant mortality to 'control of the environment' in maturity (see Table 6.1). The life cycle framework also provides explicit objectives (see Table 6.3). By explicit is meant these objectives are an integral part of the framework. If the framework is adopted, the objectives must necessarily be adopted too as part and parcel of the strategy system.

With experience curves the objectives are implicit. The effects of experience are powerful for commodity products, whose strategy is necessarily driven by considerations of cost, during the high growth phase of their development and it is fairly clear how a business might take advantage of these experience effects and what it must do to gain more experience benefits than its competitors. Nevertheless the strategic prescriptions are not made explicit in the experience model as they are in the various portfolio models. These frameworks can be, and often are, used quite mechanically for the simple purpose of developing strategic prescriptions: 'invest and grow', 'manage for cash and withdraw' and so on. The prescriptions are the main output of the frameworks and are completely explicit.

Porter's framework is less mechanistic and less prescriptive than the portfolios. With the later portfolios there was an increasing emphasis on detailed analysis of a particular kind which was aimed at increasing understanding. Unfortunately, the portfolio models then largely ignored the understanding by delivering their simplistic prescriptions. Porter uses the understanding in the development of a strategy which is based on one of his generics: focusing on least costs or highest prices either for the broad market or a clearly defined segment. The competitive strategy objective arises from the understanding provided by the analysis, not simply from the competitive framework itself. Porter's highlighting of the problem of 'stuck in the middle' makes it clear that the framework must result in a clearly defined direction and that the direction will be stated in terms of cost leadership, differentiation and focus. But the strategic objective is not an explicit part of the framework.

The strategic marketing framework may be best viewed as parallel to Porter's framework, or even as a front end to Porter's model. It provides a means of analysis to get answers where Porter's own analysis is silent. Where Porter refers simply to 'differentiation', product positioning defines the form of differentiation; it is a means of relating competitive strategy explicitly to the customers and their needs and perceptions. Strategic marketing provides the means of analysis that could be used in conjunction with other frameworks such as entrepreneurial strategy.

The final two frameworks are those which have a strong transformational element and, not surprisingly, they are driven by the enunciation of an effective strategic objective, whether it is in terms of beating customers or achieving a leadership position. These frameworks do not develop the objective in the same way as the portfolio models do, but they explicitly require the strategic objective to be developed as a foundation of the strategy formation process.

All but the most primitive planning frameworks require both internal and external analysis and mostly they relate the two in some way. However, most frameworks took a rather timid view of what management might actually achieve. Accounts-based planning comprises internal analysis alone and is entirely passive with respect to strategy. There is no external analysis and therefore no means of achieving growth or new activities. The only action arising out of an accounting framework is cost reduction: the disinvestment spiral and the cost cutting syndrome, which reinforces the macho/cynical accounting approach to things non-financial.

Table 10.1 Characteristics of strategy frameworks

Strategy framework	Strategic objective	Internal analysis: Content	Internal analysis: Active/ passive	External analysis: Content	External analysis: Active/ passive	Relates internal to external	Action to change internal	Action to change external
Accounts-based	No	5-year budget inc. P&L, balance sheet, cash flow	P	–	–	–	–	–
Forecast-based	No	As above + strengths, weaknesses	P	Threats and opportunities	P	?	–	–
Development-based	No	As above	A	Threats and opportunities	P	Yes	Yes	–
Basic systems	Explicit	Inputs and outputs	P	Outputs and inputs	P	Yes	–	–
Life cycles	Explicit	As above + evolution	A	As above + evolution	P	Yes	Possible	–
Experience curves	Implicit	Volumes and costs	P	Volumes and costs	P	Possible	–	–
BCG portfolio	Explicit	Relative market share	A	Market growth	P	Yes	Yes	–
Directional policy matrix	Explicit	Competitive capacity	A	Sector prospects	P	Yes	Yes	–

Business strength/ market attractive. matrix	Explicit	Many business strength factors	A	Many market attractiveness factors	P	Yes	Yes	–
Porter's competitive strategy	Implicit	Business positioning re. costs, focus and differentiation	A	Five forces shaping industry profitability	A	Yes	Yes	Yes
Strategic marketing	Implicit	Product attributes	A	Customer perceptions and needs	A	Yes	Yes	Yes
Core competence strategy	Explicit: strategic intent	Core competences	A Leveraging resources	Competitors, expeditionary marketing	A	Yes	Yes	Yes
Entrepreneurial strategy	Explicit: leadership position	Distinctive competence	A Concentration	Competitive specialism	A	Yes	Yes	Yes

Forecast-based planning is concerned with both internal and external analyses but takes the strengths, weaknesses, threats and opportunities, or other units of analysis, as given and seeks only to react to them, rather than to change them. The same is true of the evolutionary frameworks except that the life cycle model highlights some more proactive issues such as how to change the cycle by prolonging phases. The remaining frameworks (portfolios, competitive strategy and the transformational frameworks) all involve an active response to internal analysis, but the portfolio models take a passive view of external analysis: management can do nothing about market growth rates or more widely defined market attractiveness. In reality, many managers have inadvertently taken action which has reduced the attractiveness of the markets they serve, not uncommonly by initiating fierce price competition. This reality is built into the competitive strategy model which recognises that managements can take positive action to affect the attractiveness of their industry. The remaining models also recognise this reality.

The final three columns of Table 10.1 show a further advance with the chronological development of the generic model. All but the simplest planning frameworks highlight the relation between the internal resources, whether referred to as strengths, positioning, capabilities or competences, and the external factors described as growth, attractiveness, competitive pressures, and customer needs and perceptions. Each of the models makes this connection in its own language. Most of the models include the possibility of managements taking action to increase their internal strengths, and the later models also include the possibility of managements taking specific action to improve the external environments.

10.3 Generic strategy framework

The above brief overview of framework characteristics suggests the common components which form the foundation of the generic strategy framework. There are two main phases of analysis. First, there is the question answered by the portfolio frameworks: 'Is this a market, or an industry, which is worth buying into? Or, if we are already in, is it a market or industry which is attractive enough for us to retain or increase our involvement? Or should we seek to get out?' Having decided to participate in the industry there is then the second and much more interesting question about the strategy of the participating business. How do the strategy frameworks achieve the purpose of strategy? The general case process is illustrated in Figure 10.1 It is an iterative process of continuous refinement and improvement. It seeks to exploit the organisation's internal strength, whatever it is, in order to satisfy the customer's needs better than any competitor does, and in so doing to achieve the strategic objective.

At first sight this generic model of the strategy process may appear reductionist, but the aim is not to reduce strategy management to a simple five-stage cycle, rather it is to identify the common ground among all the different approaches to strategy. The language of the various models is very different but the general meaning is similar and most of them are not incompatible with Figure 10.1. Some do not encompass all five phases, but there are few elements of individual frameworks which would

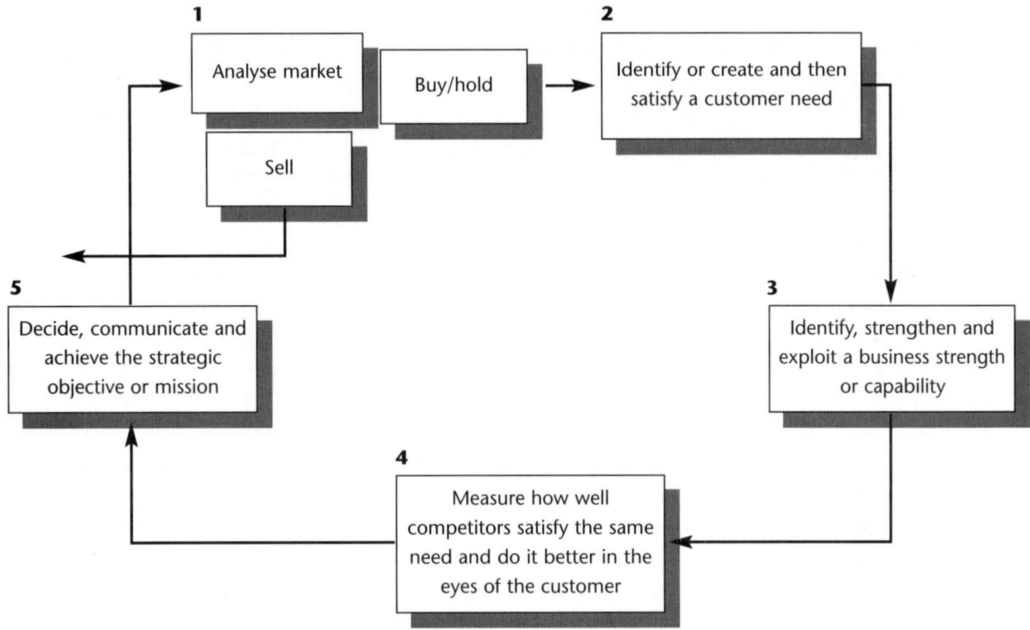

Figure 10.1 Phases of the generic strategy process

necessarily be excluded by the general descriptions on the diagram. In general, all the strategy frameworks share this generic structure.

All but the most primitive frameworks include phase 1, the market analysis. Accounts-based frameworks largely ignore this element in the strategy management process, focusing instead on the internal, and particularly financial, strengths of the business. Other frameworks start with this analysis, focusing on particular aspects, whether it is the evolutionary phase, the growth rate, some multivariate measure of its attractiveness or even simply the profitability of the industry. At the very least, this analysis is used to reach the 'buy, sell or hold' portfolio decision.

The majority of strategic frameworks take this market analysis into phase 2 to identify or even create customer needs that the business can satisfy. Creating a need can be a problematic idea. On the one hand, it may be a rather limited promotional concept where consumers are addressed with superficially different products in order to generate wants for the 'latest model' such as a detergent with a new ingredient. On the other hand, it may be the development of a previously unconceived generic product which arises from the conjunction of two or more new technologies, for example the personal stereo, the compact disk or e-mail systems. The creation of such customer needs lies close to the core of technological innovation on which man's social and economic progress depends and is an important aspect of strategy management. Phase 2 of the process, whether it is based on the creation or simply the identification of customer needs, involves pleasing the customer by the satisfaction of that need.

Most frameworks also include some variation of phase 3 of the process, the internal analysis. Even the crudest accounts-based planning models involve cash flow and balance sheet projections which give some view of the financial resources of the business. In forecast-based planning these may be elaborated by a wider-ranging review of the organisation's strengths and weaknesses. Evolutionary models and portfolios take more particular views of the organisation's strategic capacities, ranging from an analysis of the component products' life cycle position, their relative market share or aggregate strength in terms of orthodox microeconomic factors. The transformational frameworks take a more selective view, focusing on the organisation's core competences or competitive specialism, i.e. those particular capabilities on which the competitive strength of the business is based. Only Porter's model of competitive strategy gives little explicit prominence to this phase of the strategy process. In this framework an exhaustive analysis of industry attractiveness is followed by definition of generic competitive strategy. In practice, of course, competitive strategy is necessarily based on the deployment of organisational capability to achieve the lowest costs or highest prices.

Phase 4 of the generic strategy process focuses on the competitive position. Planning frameworks tended not to give much focus to competitive issues even though competition has always been one of the most fundamental concerns of business management in free enterprise economies. The fact that such considerations are not part of these planning frameworks does not mean that strategic management ignored competition, simply that the frameworks then used were inadequate in this respect. Evolutionary frameworks and portfolios included competition as a primary factor determining strategy, but the way competition was defined was limited and one-dimensional: life cycle models using a leader/follower dichotomy and the early portfolios using a relative measure of the relevant internal capability factors such as market share. In Porter's model, on the other hand, competition is the prime focus. The analysis required is such that the future actions of competitors can be predicted with confidence and appropriate decisions taken in pursuit of an effective competitive strategy. This level of analysis is exhaustive and often criticised as being too detailed to be carried out in practice by any but the largest organisation with a great deal of managerial slack. Nevertheless, the aim to understand the competition remains entirely valid. The means of its achievement may not lie through Porter's exhaustive analysis, but more on the ability to identify which few factors explain competitor behaviour in the particular situation. Thus competitor analysis, like strategy itself, needs to be focused rather than exhaustive.

Phase 4 of the process is also an integral part of the transformational frameworks. The definition of core competences requires definition in relative competitive terms just as much as the competitive specialism of entrepreneurial strategy. Both frameworks are firmly competitor oriented and define their strategic direction in terms of competitive positioning.

All strategy frameworks address phase 5 of the process, the definition of strategic objectives. The earliest accounts-based planning frameworks included the definition of objectives which were intended to be long term and therefore strategic. Such financial objectives, often defined in terms of stock market rating, or returns on investment or asset growth, were thought of as strategic because of their intended

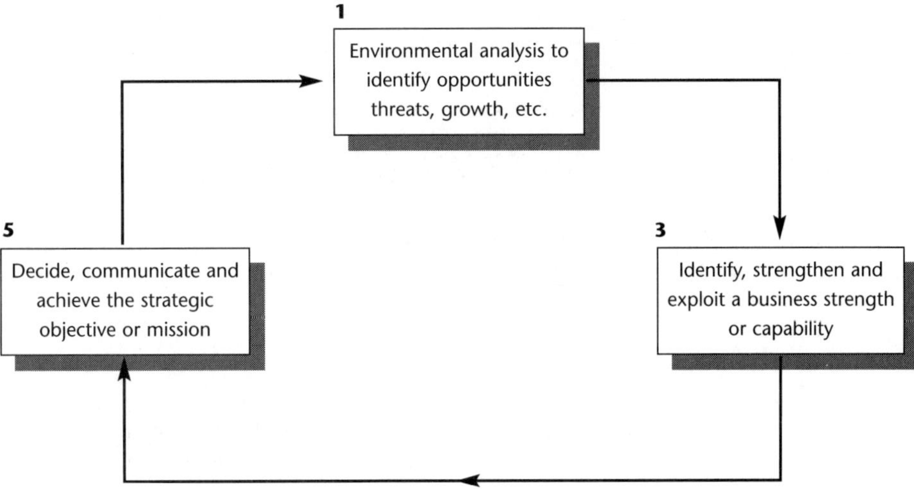

Figure 10.2 Phases of the simple generic strategy process

longevity and organisation-wide relevance. However, their lack of directional content or capacity for assisting concentration and consistency of thrust, means that, in the meaning of the terms used here, such objectives were non-strategic. Subsequent frameworks facilitated the definition of strategic objectives and could be used, in conjunction with a system such as that described in Chapter 3, to define the strategic direction of the organisation. The forecast-based planning, evolutionary and portfolio frameworks all accommodate the definition of genuinely strategic objectives. Porter's model leads to the definition of strategic objectives, while the transformational frameworks require it.

Figure 10.2 shows the very simplest version of the strategy process which all the frameworks appear to go through. This is how even these most basic frameworks achieve the directional idea underlying strategy as defined in Chapter 2:

- Where are we now?
- Where do we want to get to?
- How do we get there?
- How are we doing?

The fit is not precise, but clearly over several iterations the purpose of strategy will start to be achieved through this process. The purpose will, of course, be more fully achieved by the more sophisticated frameworks which go through all five phases of the process as shown in Figure 10.1.

The various frameworks presented in this text therefore share a general structure but differ in detail, in the emphasis of their analysis. This difference of focus results from the development of the different frameworks at different times, in different circumstances and in response to different imperatives. They are all special cases of the general strategy model. None serves adequately as a general solution to the strategy problem, but they all generate particular insights and have particular strengths and uses. Moreover, as with any model, they are simplifications of reality and therefore each also has particular weaknesses and shortcomings. With time and extensive use, most frameworks have also developed popular fallacies and particular potentials for misapplication. It is therefore crucial to understand the frameworks and to recognise the situations where they may be applicable and inapplicable. The selection and application of the must appropriate strategy framework, or even the development of a custom-designed framework, can then be achieved on an informed basis.

10.4 Contingency principles

The history of management is punctuated by the sudden emergence and adoption of panaceas which promise all. Techniques such as management by objectives, total quality management (TQM) and business process re-engineering (BPR), all promised general validity and applicability, and inevitably they all disappoint. Strategy management too has been subject to the same naiveté as has already been noted. There are no panaceas; there is no one best way.

Contingency theory, which simply holds that the best way depends on the particular situation and circumstances, is therefore especially pertinent to management and, in particular, strategy management.

The key to the effective use of the strategy frameworks lies in understanding both the frameworks and the situation in which they are to be used. Such understanding can then prevent many of the problems which frequently arise in strategy management. The flaws and limitations of frameworks will not be ignored, nor will they be applied in inappropriate situations. Frameworks will be selected which depend on inputs that can be made available and which can generate the outputs required. In short, the contingency approach requires selection or development of a framework which works for the particular situation.

The use of frameworks clearly depends critically on understanding the framework itself. Many applications of strategy frameworks simply reduce them to common-sense checklists. All the frameworks can be and are applied in this reductionist way, but the results are then limited to common-sense outputs which inhibit any fresh understandings or insights.

It is unnecessary to repeat material from earlier chapters here, but the point can be illustrated by reference to the Boston portfolio. BCG's perspective on business strength/capability/competence was relative market share. This was because of their empirical findings on experience in commodity products, for which cost was obviously the prime competitive driver. The BCG model emphasises relative market share as a proxy for cost-based competitive advantage. On the other dimension, BCG's perspective on environmental analysis was restricted to market growth. This was because the cost reductions achieved through experience, amounting to around 20–30 per cent each time that experience doubled, would be very significant in young, high-growth markets but less relevant in mature, low-growth markets. The Boston portfolio is therefore directly relevant to young, high-growth commodity markets. Examples of these might include many service industry situations such as banking where competition may be conducted through the development of financial products which differ only marginally from bank to bank. Moreover, it may be relatively easy to apply the Bostonian prescriptions of buy, sell or hold.

There may be many other applications where the BCG model has relevance. For example, petrol sales, supermarkets, fast-food and, ironically for such an apparently outdated framework, situations for which it appears to be well suited also include memory chip and microprocessor markets, where rapid growth has resulted in equally rapid commoditisation. It is tempting and it may be possible to justify premium prices by differentiating what is in essence a commodity product, and where this is attempted the Boston model contributes little. But where cost is accepted as the competitive driver the Boston portfolio may well be useful. In the particular situations referred to above, many of the inherent problems of portfolios are avoided. For example, defining the served market is not a major problem, nor is there the common difficulty of aggregating products because of shared facilities. So Boston's original portfolio still has its uses, and where it is valid its elegant simplicity can be fully exploited. However, there is little validity in applying the Boston portfolio in mature, low-growth markets for branded differentiated products where cost is not the competitive driver, or where the business unit or served market cannot be clearly identified, or where the portfolio decisions are not of interest.

The same applies to all frameworks. Each has its own particular uses as described in the previous chapters. For example, the life cycle model is not very helpful if it is not possible to identify the shape or size of the appropriate curve, or where positioning on the curve is not possible with any confidence. However, if it is possible to identify the potential maximum mature market size, for example, and to identify the shape and time likely to be taken to achieving that mature state, for example by reference to comparable earlier curves, then it may be an extremely useful model. The main use of life cycle decision-making is to ensure most advantageous positioning prior to the life cycle going through a phase change, for example from growth to maturity. If the life cycle is a long, slow-changing process then the relevant decisions will only be very occasional. However, if the shape develops rapidly then strategic decisions may be frequent and the life cycle model may be particularly useful.

Another example is the notion of core competence. As described by Hamel and Prahalad, the model relates specifically to leading-edge technological competence in global industries. But does this framework have any validity at a less rarefied level? If applied to local businesses and core competences were defined as less than leading edge, though nonetheless distinctive, does the application retain anything beyond the common-sense checklist validity? Alternatively, could the concepts of the entrepreneurial framework offer anything of value for global leadership situations?

There are no 'one best way' answers to these questions. The answers depend on the application, the situation and the strategic thinking that combines the two. Does the application require information inputs which are not available or are prohibitively expensive to obtain? Such is sometimes the case with applications of Porter's model. Does the application produce the required outputs? If definition of a clear strategic direction, for example, is the most required outcome, it will be of little avail to use evolutionary or portfolio frameworks because that is the area of their greatest weakness.

All these questions will need to be thought through in choosing a suitable framework. The questions might then be reformulated in terms of whether the framework chosen has offered up any ways of completing the strategy process which were not otherwise apparent. Has it provided new insights? Has it enhanced understanding? Has it enabled the strategic thinker to develop a strategy process which is different from that of competitors? The W.H. Smith situation described in Box 10.1 provides an opportunity to consider these issues in a practical situation.

BOX 10.1

W.H. Smith and the Waterstone strategy

W.H. Smith Ltd appeared to have been in a state of gentle drift for many years. Despite a corporate identity makeover in the 1980s, drift seemed to continue accompanied by a lacklustre share performance. In 1997, chief executive Bill Cockburn quit unexpectedly after only eighteen months in the job. After four leaderless months, W.H. Smith appointed long-serving Richard Handover as chief executive, but the appointment was widely seen as symbolic of Smith's failure to attract a suitable external debate.

In October 1997, Tim Waterstone, former W.H. Smith's employee who created the Waterstone chain of bookshops which he subsequently sold to Smith's, announced a bid for the group. After brief discussions with some of the company's directors the bid was formally rejected. However, it was widely reported that the full board was not given the opportunity to discuss the proposal and some of the leading institutional shareholders subsequently pressed the Smith non-executive chairman, Jeremy Hardie, to reopen discussions with Waterstone.

Waterstone's original bid involved an injection of £600m debt which would raise gearing to around 80 per cent of shareholders' funds. This was widely regarded as too high for a low-growth situation like Smith's. However, Waterstone's strategic proposals for the group did attract considerable interest. He at least appeared to know the business and have clear ideas about what should be done with it, which was a refreshing change for Smith's.

Waterstone proposed to dispose of the holding in the Our Price record chain and Smith's American operations, in order to refocus the main business on three activities: books, newspapers and magazines, and stationery. He had very specific ideas for each.

Smith's published accounts did not provide any breakdown of figures between the various activities, but Waterstone's bid suggested that in 1996 Smith's book business earned gross margins of 13 per cent, stationery 9.5 per cent, newspapers and magazines 6 per cent, video and music 3 per cent and other (including sweets and drinks) 3 per cent. The Waterstone proposals suggested these could be improved as follows: books to 19 per cent, stationery 17.5 per cent and news to 7.5 per cent. The other activities would be dropped. These figures gained some credibility from the fact that the Waterstone book business earned 20 per cent and it was clear that Waterstone himself had considerable knowledge of the W.H. Smith business and claimed it had lost its lead in all three core activities, being outpaced by Rymans in stationery and Waterstones in books and no longer being regarded as the authoritative newsagent. Waterstone aimed to return Smith's to the lead in all three activities. His proposals included detail of how the new business would achieve this by, for example, the establishment of what were called metro stores – small, in-town, convenience shops with focused product ranges. Metro stores in London, for example, would sell foreign newspapers and magazines.

DISCUSSION POINTS

1. Under Waterstone's proposals would W.H. Smith be a single-business company or a multibusiness company? Justify your answer.
2. Which of the following frameworks would be most pertinent to W.H. Smith? Explain why. Life cycles / Boston portfolio / competitive strategy / core competence.
3. What justification is there for Waterstone's proposals as outlined above?

10.5 Customised frameworks

There is no one best framework for processing strategy and it may well be the case that there is no ready-made framework which is even adequate for a particular set of circumstances. Understanding the frameworks and understanding the particular situation may serve only to highlight the certain fact that none of the models is a useful explanation of reality, at least none that already exists. Each of the frameworks is, after all, a simplification of reality, but it may be that the particular compromises that have been made are unfortunate in a particular case. So long as the framework and the situation are properly understood it may be possible to develop a framework which is custom-designed to reflect particular realities?

By going back to the notion of the generic strategy process it would seem perfectly feasible to develop within that general framework, measures of the particular factors which are crucial to the individual case. Again, it is simplest to use the original Boston framework to demonstrate this process. Thus the phases outlined in Figure 10.3 can be drawn from the generic outline in Figure 10.2.

Are market growth rates and relative market shares the most potent variables in the situation being considered? If not, what are? A generalised two-dimensional matrix is shown in Figure 10.4 where different measures from those that the BCG prescribed can be used. The directional policy matrix and other enhanced portfolios are simply special cases of this customisation process. For example, depending on the situation being considered, market value might be assessed as a function of growth, stability, opportunities for innovation and the degree of concentration. Growth is always likely to be an attraction even though it consumes cash. Stability is also an attractive intrinsic market characteristic, especially in mature, relatively non-

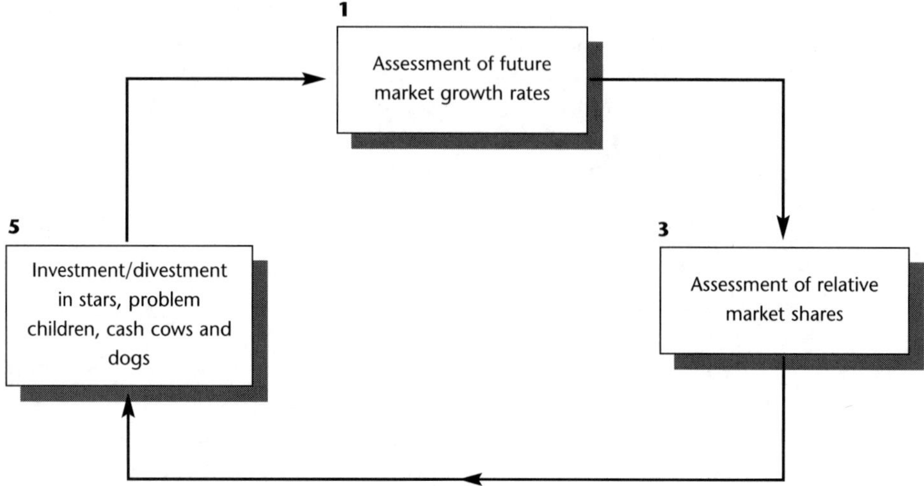

Figure 10.3 Phases of the Bostonian strategy process

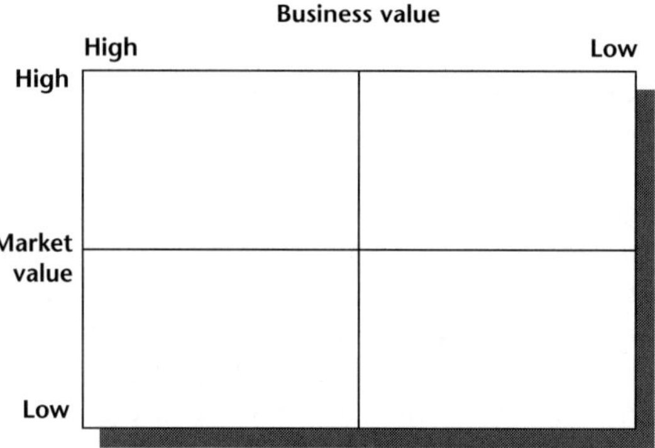

Figure 10.4 Generalised portfolio (derived from the original BCG model)

innovative markets. In innovative markets, intrinsic instability can be used positively to create structural change on the back of some specific technological innovations. The opportunity for technological innovation is also likely to be an attractive characteristic in most markets, although during a technological revolution this factor is unlikely to distinguish many markets since most industries abound with such opportunities. Finally, the degree of concentration can also be important to long-term profitability. Even among the followers in a concentrated industry there are profitable opportunities because of the structural faults and voids which are not worth the market leaders covering.

In other situations it might be feasible to assess the market value dimension in terms of attribute leadership, i.e. what the market considers as giving best value. Expressed in Porter's terms, this could focus on aspects of differentiation or cost leadership (although for many the idea of cost leadership is redundant since it is either non-strategic or it reduces into the pure Boston model based on experience). Using the strategic marketing framework it would be possible to assess the market value of differentiation on attributes such as price, quality, performance and conformance.

The second dimension, business value, might also be uniquely defined in any way that reflects the particular realities of the situation. To form a coherent matrix whose first dimension was defined in terms of attribute leadership, business value might be assessed as a function of the attribute strength of the various products of the business. Such a matrix might then be shaped specifically to meet the realities of the particular situation.

A limited example is shown in Figure 10.5 of an aluminium stockholder's product portfolio with a product development illustrated (A to B). In this case the diameter of the circles is proportionate to gross profit. The dimensions in this example are extremely simple because the industry and business concerned in many ways lend themselves to the pure BCG approach. The products are commodities and the prime attribute driving competition is cost. The dimensions of price (£/tonne) and volume (tonnes per annum) enabled a slightly different perspective to be taken on the stockholder's business and its competitive positioning.

These are simple examples of how the two-dimensional matrix might be customised, but a custom model need not be restricted to a portfolio of any kind, nor its prescriptions restricted to buy, sell or hold. A matrix focused on attribute strengths will define strategy in terms of achieving attribute leadership and may be specified in purely qualitative terms. Such a strategy would achieve its purpose (i.e. direction, concentration, consistency and so on) in a more direct and effective way than an orthodox portfolio model.

The various strategy frameworks are simply special cases of the generic model of the strategy process. Provided that there is real understanding of the situation and of the intrinsic characteristics of the frameworks, the generic model can be customised for application to particular and individual situations. However, in situations where the 'off-the-shelf' frameworks appear valid, there may be little benefit from customisation.

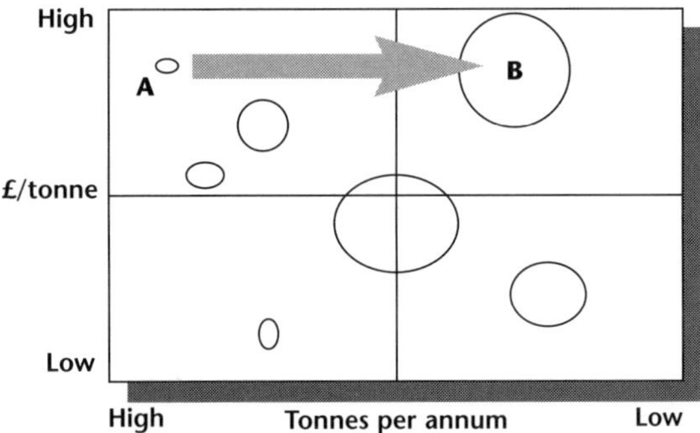

Figure 10.5 Aluminium stockholder's matrix

10.6 Change and dynamic strategy

Analytical model applications are frequently based on historical data. In the simplest case of analysing strengths and weaknesses, or of market shares and market growth rates, data are generally drawn from the immediate past. Yet the strategic action which results will be intended to impact the future five years or more ahead. This paradox was recognised early on and gave birth to forecast-based planning where strategy was related explicitly to forecasts of the future.

Even so, forecasts can be difficult to build in as the foundation for strategy. Particularly in businesses dominated by accounting mores of conservatism and prudence, it may be difficult to propose future market growth rates or market shares that are significantly different from the present or past experience. Such projections will be regarded as optimistic and imprudent.

Even where strategy is formulated explicitly on the basis of forecasts of the future there are still problems. Projections of continuity are easy to make and easy to accept. Forecasts of structural change or changes in direction are, on the other hand, difficult. Predicting the phase changes in life cycle curves has already been instanced (see Figure 6.3) where forecasting the structural change remains difficult even after it has occurred. Even if such a change has been forecast, few will accept it and be prepared to act on it.

The reality and shape of change are dealt with at greater length in Chapter 11. For the present purpose it is necessary only to recognise that although technological change is occurring rapidly and its effects are all pervasive, it is nevertheless difficult to accommodate such change in the strategy process. All too often, strategies tend to be based on static, historical data and assumptions about a continuation of the status quo.

Worse even than this, the strategies themselves tend to be static. If they are expressed in directional terms, which very often they are not, they tend to be expressed as a future intended state, which by definition is also static. Rarely is strategy defined as a dynamic repositioning, although the strategic objective might itself require such repositioning for it to be achieved. Strategy is not about continuity or the status quo but, as Hamel and Prahalad (1989) pointed out, it *is* about new directions, breaking out and the exploitation of change.

In winding up this discussion of strategy frameworks and the contingency approach it is necessary to emphasise two factors:

1. The strategy process looks forward and is based on forward-focused information, knowledge and understanding, not on projections from the past.
2. The strategy process is intended to achieve change. If it merely presides over a continuation of what is already being done then it is worthless: continuation will happen without strategy management.

Summary

- The previous chapters have described a variety of strategy frameworks, all of which have gained some, albeit temporary, prominence in terms of their adoption by businesses.
- Each framework represented a response to the realities of its time. They all have their particular strengths and weaknesses, uses and misuses.
- All the frameworks share a number of features, related mainly to the process of their application.
- Rather than treating them as separate frameworks they might be regarded as a single generic strategy framework comprising the following stages:
  1. Analyse the market.
  2. Identify or create and satisfy a customer need.
  3. Identify or create and exploit a distinctive business strength, competence or capability.
  4. Measure how well competitors satisfy the same need and do it differently in a way that the customer values.
  5. Decide, communicate and achieve the strategic objective or mission.
- Even the simplest strategy framework goes through stages 1, 3 and 5 above.
- Each framework accomplishes each stage in its own distinctive way. For example, the Boston portfolio restricts stage 1 to an assessment of market growth and stage 3 to estimating relative market shares.
- The contingency approach requires that the business and its environments and each framework be fully understood and that the most appropriate framework is selected to develop the appropriate strategy.
- If no framework fits the particular situation, then it may be possible to create an adaptation to fit the particular circumstance.
- The purpose of the strategy process is to look forward and create a different future from the one that would have emerged otherwise, i.e. to create change.

part 3

Strategic change and action

To make effective use of any strategy framework requires an understanding of the particular organisation's situation. There are no general rules for this – every organisation is different. However, a general contextual introduction was provided in the opening chapter which highlighted some of the background issues for business organisations as they developed during the industrial era. These issues were categorised as organisational, financial, technological, global and ethical. Currently the most influential of these is technological, the speed and extent of technology development. As Piatier described it, we are in the middle of the world's third industrial revolution and this will impact on every business, every organisation and every individual in some way or another. This is why strategic change and its management are currently receiving so much attention.

The long-term perspective offered by Piatier is intriguing and dramatic and provides a comprehensible context for the current spate of technology development. Chapter 11 takes a closer look. How do technological developments or innovations happen? What is their impact on the individual market or organisation? How can we cope with them? How can we exploit them? How can we create the changes that will be of greatest benefit to our particular organisation?

This more detailed analysis of innovation and change not only highlights many of the situational issues which need to be considered when choosing a framework for strategy analysis, but also provides some tools in its own right, based around a recognition of the continuities and discontinuities of technological progress, the advantages of competitive attack with a new technology and the problems of competitive defence with the old.

Every strategy is unique, responding individually to the particular organisation and situation. So the results of each strategy, i.e. the action taken as a result of that analysis, will also be unique. There are no universal truths, no generalisations which hold for all organisations. But as technological innovation is so dominant, its exploitation is probably the core strategy problem. Achieving a fast-moving, flexible organisation is therefore the dominant aim of strategy management. Thus the connection between strategy and structure is direct. As Chandler (1962) put it:

> *a company's strategy in time determined its structure and the common denominator of structure and strategy has been the application of the enterprise's resources to market demand. Structure has been the design for integrating the enterprise's existing resources to current demand; strategy has been the plan for the allocation of resources to anticipated demand.* (p. 383)

Chapter 12 looks at the question of organisation structure, from the classical writers to the current vogue for illustrative metaphor. Many contributors have played their part in the achievement of a flexible, innovative, learning organisation, designing the organisation best suited to carrying out strategy in an era of change. It has been widely held that choice of the most effective design will depend on the level of change envisaged in the strategy – little change requires a standardised, machine-like organisation with every cog and wheel designed to carry out a simple repetitive task in the most efficient and cost-effective way. But if substantial change is envisaged then the organisation has to be fast and flexible and the machine analogy becomes inappropriate. This requires a rather more dynamic form of analysis than structure. Burns and Stalker's mechanistic organisation is clearly defined by the language of structure, but when they grapple with organic organisations they embark on a study which takes them from structure to culture, from the skeleton of the organisation to its flesh and blood influences on how people behave.

Even the most traditional and mature industries are having to cope with unprecedented change and volatility. In this situation, the cultural perspective is likely to offer greater insight than the structural. Chapter 13 looks briefly at a model of the practical steps that can be taken to manage the cultural and strategic dimensions in order to achieve an innovative team-based organisation that will not only cope with change but also exploit it. This approach is based on a particular piece of empirical research that focused, conveniently for the present purpose, on the relationship between innovative effectiveness, strategy and culture.

Finally, Chapter 14 presents a brief outline of management initiatives that can be taken in order to implant the strategy process in an innovative team-based organisation.

Chapter

11

Innovation and change

This is a period of rapid technological development and business strategies are necessarily focused on exploiting strategic change. Changes occur discontinuously in lumps, not smoothly or in small increments. A technology is introduced and developed until the returns from further development are worth less than the cost of their achievement. Then the technology will either stabilise or be replaced. The replacement of a technology presents extraordinary strategic opportunities. Competitive structures which have been set firm for decades become fluid and market positions can be quickly changed. To benefit from these opportunities a business must become an effective innovator.

11.1 Introduction

The current technological revolution, as described in the opening chapter, is having a profound global, economic impact. Technological innovation creates economic growth as Schumpeter, Kondratiev and others demonstrated. Moreover, innovations tend to arrive in clusters, and clusters of fundamental innovations cause great waves of economic growth, whether it is every fifty years or less regularly, as Piatier suggested. They looked at the macro effects. This chapter looks rather more closely at how the individual business is affected by, and can manage, innovation to achieve its own strategic aims.

A business creates growth from innovation either by the direct development of new products or by the development of new and improved processes which enable the development of new products or reduced prices (see Figure 11.1).

This perspective on innovation examines how technology develops and how businesses can exploit this knowledge for their own strategic benefit by changing the way

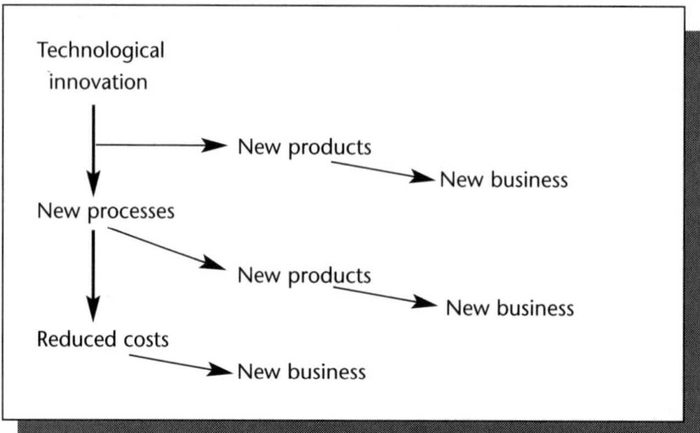

Figure 11.1 Innovation and economic growth

the strategy frameworks are used to understand industries and competitive structures. It not only provides a powerful means of concentrating on achieving strategic direction, but also suggests some of the crucial ingredients of flexibility.

11.2 The shape of technological progress

At the heart of any innovation is some creative idea or invention, which is increasingly knowledge- and information-intensive. The days of the fundamental breakthrough by the inspired amateur are long gone, if they ever existed. The story of James Watt visualising the steam engine prompted only by a boiling kettle is a useful memory aid but bears little relation to fact. Fleming's discovery of penicillin is similarly apocryphal if only because of what is left out. Watt and Fleming and all their illustrious soulmates shared this in common: they were all at or near the boundaries of knowledge in their particular fields, and already prepared to make the next small step forward into the unknown.

Innovation comprises both revolutionary and evolutionary developments. The vast bulk of innovations which make up the industrial revolutions are clearly evolutionary. On closer examination, even the fundamental breakthrough innovations appear really to comprise a multiplicity of lesser innovations. Watt did not invent the steam engine but merely improved it, in 1769 with the external condenser and in 1781 with rotational power. Newcomen's steam engines had been pumping water since 1712; even before that a primitive engine had been built by Savery in 1698, and there is evidence of ideas about steam power as early as the Renaissance. Just what exactly it was that prompted the explosion of growth which depended in great part on the improved steam engine remains illusive. It might even be argued that the steam engine was pulled into existence by demand for motive power where the driving force of water wheels was not available. The same indeterminacy applies to all the so-called revolutionary innovations. Almost without exception they appear to comprise a large number of incremental innovations.

The innovation process, although not always a strictly rational progression, does exhibit some identifiable, though lumpy, pattern. Initially it is a long and slow process. Typically, new technology emerges only gradually because in the stages of research and development only a few people are involved. Basic scientific knowledge must be won and engineering problems solved. It may take time to overcome the orthodox wisdom and to correct wrong assumptions. Moreover, funding may at first be limited and experimental equipment in scarce supply. All these factors may delay early progress.

However, a promising project that wins through this phase to commercial development will attract the needed support and start to grow fast. Efforts are typically then focused both on developing the key concept and on refining all facets of the technological execution by incorporating the best of existing practice. Competition during this rapid growth phase would also act as a spur to further rapid improvement.

Finally, progress slows, or ceases altogether, possibly because of diminishing returns from further development effort, or because of some natural block on further improvements in performance, or possibly because of some legal or societal limit.

This model of technological progress, graphed over time, would seem to imply an S-shaped curve as shown in Figure 11.2. The slow start, followed by rapid growth, which levels off against some limit imposed by nature or man, seems a plausible explanation of how technology might be expected to develop. Furthermore, it appears to line up with reality in many different situations.

The S curve has been used to model technological progress for many years, being one of the early tools of operational research developed during the Second World War. Even after so long it remains probably the most practical approach to forecasting technology development. The vertical axis can be measured in various terms without fundamentally altering the shape of the curve. For example, the following measures have been used: technical performance, cost per unit, return (i.e. perform-

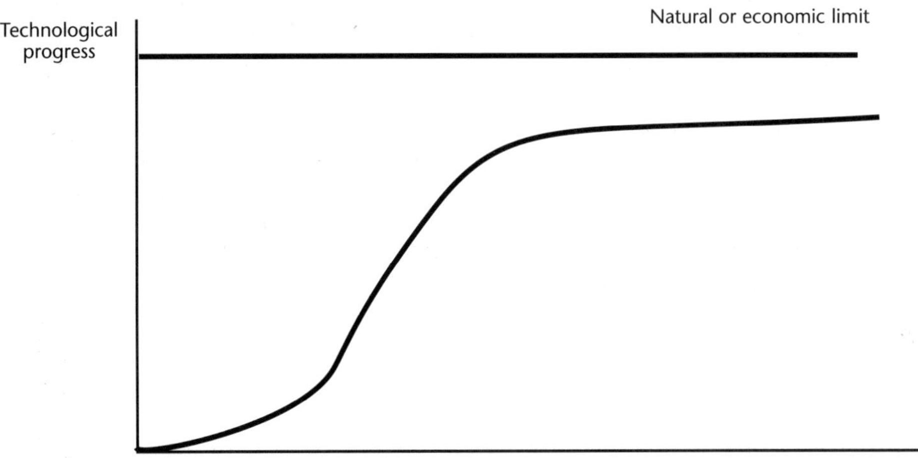

Figure 11.2 The shape of technological progress: the S curve

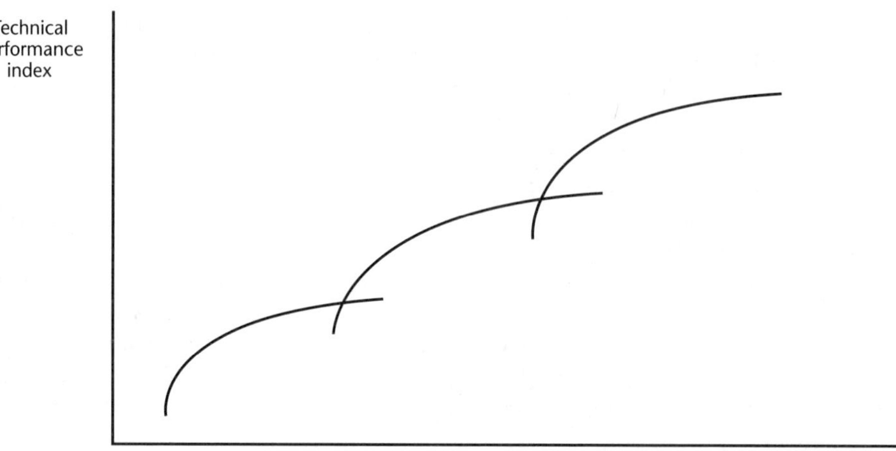

Figure 11.3 The development of successive technologies

ance increase) per unit of R&D (in £, or person-years, or calendar months) and many others. All appear to generate an S-shaped curve, or its inverse.

The most striking thing about the S curve is its apparent broad applicability. However, this can also be its biggest danger. The development of successive computer technologies has been instanced as a typical pattern of technological progress (Hall, 1969). Figure 11.3 shows the progression through three separate technologies (for example, in computers through valves, transistors and integrated circuits). Each of the three technologies is shown as having a rapid growth phase which in due course slows down and flattens out and is then overtaken by the succeeding technology. There appears to be a regularity about this pattern. When performance ceases to rise with one technology, in due course another technology takes over.

A similar progression has been recorded in tyre cord, with cotton replaced by rayon, then nylon and then polyester (Dewhurst, 1970), with each technology developing along an S-shaped curve, and the envelope curve also having a similar shape. Similarly with the envelope of different technologies in electric lighting (Lenz, 1983). In this case the theoretical limit to technological development is simply a matter of physics: white light is 289 lumens per watt. Such limits apply to all technologies although they are by no means always so simple to specify. Each individual technological solution has its own limits, which may in themselves be the spur to establishing the new technology which breaks through the particular constraints inherent in existing technology.

One last example of technological progress which has been of fundamental importance to both the growth of manufacturing and of further innovations is the accuracy of machining metal. Had accuracy not developed so quickly and so far, most of the fruits of mechanical engineering would have been unrealisable and the notion of mass production, of the internal combustion engine and a million other everyday items we now take for granted, would probably not even have entered our dreams.

The development of these technologies has been over centuries, from the earliest boring and screw-cutting machinery which enabled the eighteenth century Industrial Revolution to progress, through various milling machines and lathes, with micrometer and comparator measures, to today's laser technology. Each individual technology has been shown to exhibit a number of common features, typical of S curve progress (Bright, 1983). On introduction, the newly innovated technique or machine would show a significant improvement over the previous technology. Typically, the new technology will have been prompted by the previous one reaching the limits of its potential, the new technology not being subject to those same limits. After introduction there would be further rapid improvement as problems were eliminated and potential benefits realised. Then, after a period, the rate of improvement would progressively slow down as the new limits were approached. Thus the development of these individual technologies appears to follow the S-curve shape. Moreover, the envelope curve describing the overall technological progress may also approximate to the same shape: progress starting slowly, followed by rapid improvements, which gradually approach the limit of absolute accuracy.

The development of industrial revolutions, as described in section 1.4, also exhibit S-curve progression, with the revolution curve being the envelope resulting from the coincidence of many fundamental new technologies, each exhibiting S-shaped progression, the economic growth curve of the current technological revolution being the envelope of the individual curves of electronics, information technology, new forms of energy or energy substitutes, biotechnology, molecular engineering, genetic engineering, ocean development and new forms of transport or transport substitutes.

Many, but not all, technologies, progress along the lines of an S curve, as can be seen with hindsight. The problem with such analysis is that it is not always possible to tell where the current technology is on its S curve, where its limit lies and what alternative technologies might succeed and when.

11.3 Forecasting technological change

To make strategic use of S curves it is necessary to be able to forecast their development. The progressive substitution of new technologies for ones which have flattened out, however, may seem too simplistic to be true. If the real world happened like that then forecasting technological change would not really present much of a problem. Intelligent people involved with the technologies, the eminent industry experts, simply would not be capable of making wrong assessments of technological futures. But they do.

President Truman's chief military adviser, Admiral Leahy, said of the atom bomb, 'that damn thing will never go off'. Wilbur Wright's view of the helicopter was simply that 'it'll never work'. Professor Bickerton, a leading Canadian scientist in 1926 said,

> *this foolish idea of shooting at the moon is an example of the absurd length to which vicious specialisation will carry scientists working in thought time compartments. Let us critically examine the proposal. For a project entirely to escape the gravitation of*

> *the earth, it needs a velocity of 7 miles a second. The thermal energy of a gram at this speed is 15,180 calories. The energy of our most violent explosive, nitroglycerine, is less than 1500 calories per gram. Consequently, even had the explosive nothing to carry, it has only one tenth of the energy necessary to escape the earth. Hence the proposition appears to be basically impossible.* (Bright, 1983)

Clearly the possibilities presented by technological innovation can far outstrip the expectations of experts. Professor Bickerton was trapped in his own 'thought time compartment', having his own mind-set and being unable to open up to new possibilities. But he was a leading expert of his time. The vast majority of us continuously and substantially underestimate the technological possibilities and what innovations can achieve. We may be able to envisage the development of existing technologies, but we either wrongly assess their limits, or completely overlook the possibility of new replacement technologies or other extraneous events.

Detecting where a particular technology is on its S curve is one of the key issues in technological innovation. The limit itself may be a factor of some natural 'law' of physics, or it may be a matter of economics – further improvements using existing technology would cost more than the customer is prepared to pay. Or it may be a combination of the two: as natural limits are approached the law of diminishing returns applies to investment in R&D and the only option is to try alternative technologies or await their development. During the course of a technological revolution, many technologies which have been in this moribund state for years or even generations may suddenly be replaceable, thus providing once in a lifetime opportunities for new participants. Such a wholesale step change has occurred, for example, with the replacement of electromechanical controls by electronics.

Technological forecasting seeks to establish the position of a technology on its S curve and to assess the possibility of new substitute technologies taking over. Developing a picture of the S curve itself involves both factual analysis and experiential judgement. One without the other may be quite unreliable.

The historical development of the curve can normally be identified without too much difficulty. In the long-term the most important thing to understand is the envelope S curve, which represents the overall technological progress of the industry. Management should concentrate on three main questions:

1. How rapidly has technology evolved in the long-term past?
2. How rapidly is the technology advancing now?
3. What will the limit of the technology be and how will it be approached?

These questions provide a structure for investigating technological progress in a particular industry. They do not in themselves provide a technological forecast, but reliable answers to all three questions would provide a sound basis for forecasting.

Technological forecasting simply provides a structured way of looking at an industry and it can help management to detect the shape of innovations and the breaks and limits to technology. But it is a limited approach. It will not tell managements what business they should be in by the year 2010; nor will it forecast the profitability of great new innovations, nor predict scientific breakthroughs, nor the point at which chaos will take over. However, it can contribute to all these things and help give management some indications of when a technology is running out of steam and is ripe for replacement.

11.4 Innovation as a competitive weapon

No competitive advantage is sustainable for ever. Even when a new technology is emerging, defending the old, rather than grasping the new, is a natural, almost automatic response, but it is likely to fail. The replacement of vacuum tube manufacture by solid-state electronics was a good example. When transistors first came on the scene National Video, Rawland, Eimac and Lansdale Tube decided not to invest in the new technology. This effectively sealed their fate. Hughes, Transitron and Clevite decided to invest in the new, but chose the wrong technology, germanium, and consequently also lost. Of the successful vacuum tube manufacturers of the 1950s, only RCA and Philips successfully made the switch to semiconductors. However, deciding to invest in the right new technology is not the most difficult part.

As a technology approaches the flat part of its S curve and the returns from R&D start to diminish, it would seem sensible to concentrate on seeking out potential substitute technologies which might take over. Typically this would be done using the expert knowledge within the firm, by making full use of the rapidly growing external database of published technological information and perhaps by some form of Delphi-type enquiry among industry experts. Using any or all these approaches it should be possible to identify the new technologies which might take over. Once identified, it is relatively simple to monitor their progress and even to climb aboard and participate in the development.

What is much more difficult, especially for the industry leaders, is the decision to ditch the existing technology. This is where organisational conservatism really bites. The decision might mean simply writing off prematurely some plant which, although it has a one-off impact in the accounts, is not of any substantive importance. Or it might mean leaving an established leadership position and fighting on more-or-less equal terms with competitors to re-establish leadership in the new technology. This is a much more difficult decision. The leadership position may be long-standing; the existing technology may have lasted for a generation. The decision to change may confront all the existing industry recipes. It may render in-house expertise valueless; destroy the power base of the existing top management, overturn the implied meaning of major organisational symbols and break every cultural norm in the firm.

Transitions from one technology to another present great difficulties to firms with a heavy psychological investment in the existing technology. By psychological investment is meant not simply money and machinery, but also expertise, history, marketing strength and the strategic position and culture of the business. Such firms almost inevitably find themselves defending this investment when the time comes for a technological transfer. If the existing technology has run out of steam and the replacement technology is not constrained by the same limits, then the old technology will prove ultimately indefensible. But the existing leaders will almost always defend it nevertheless. This is what provides the attacking firms with great opportunities to change competitive structures and achieve once and for all competitive advantages (Foster, 1986).

At a time when technological change is beginning to gain momentum, the most and greatest opportunities are being presented. But for industry leaders who are bogged down in the existing ways of doing things, the new technologies may only spell disaster. Too many firms, across a very broad front, are casting themselves in this role. In the field of semiconductors, for instance, although there are only two of the original vacuum tube manufacturers still involved, the Japanese have attacked and the present list of participants includes NEC, Fujitsu, Toshiba and Hitachi. The defender faces a dilemma; the attacker has the advantage.

As technological innovations mature and industries settle down, so companies become accustomed to continually growing markets and establish steady-state systems of coping with the world as it then is. For a limited period, perhaps even a few decades, technology is on the back burner and marketing is likely to become the leading business discipline. This pattern can be seen in the second industrial revolution. During the 1950s and 1960s, purely cosmetic change ('bigger fins on cars, and stripes in toothpaste') to disguise maximum standardisation of product was all that was needed in the way of innovation in order to maintain a buoyant market.

However, in the early 1970s the oil price crisis brought that period of stable growth to a halt. Since then, technology has emerged once again as the trigger for future prosperity. Standardisation is no longer sufficient, except in some service sectors. Some distinctive feature which provides a competitive advantage is now required and it is primarily through innovation that such competitive differentiation is created.

Simply cutting costs was the orthodox wisdom in the 1980s, especially for mature businesses, but it is not enough to maintain competitive position. New technologies are creating completely new rules even in the oldest industries where the application of computers to machinery frequently results in the development of completely new products.

11.5 The innovation process

The process of innovation has been identified as comprising the following stages (Rogers, 1983):

1. Recognition of a problem or need
2. Preliminary evaluation
3. Invention
4. Research and development
5. Evaluation
6. Commercial development
7. Adoption
8. Post-adoption consequences

The point has often been made that this apparently logical sequence of events does not apply in every case. Nevertheless the model does serve to highlight some of the key issues.

There has long been a debate as to whether successful innovation results from the push of technology or the pull of market need. This could be an important issue when deciding how to organise for innovation in any particular business. Should the marketing function have the most influential role, or engineering and R&D? The point has been made that 'we have got to stop marketing makeable products and learn to make marketable products' (Hayes and Abernathy, 1980). Utterback (1976) found that that around 70–80 per cent of innovations result from demand pull and 20–30 per cent from 'technology push'. However, R&D engineers argue that demand pull provides plenty of 'slight product modifications' (for example, annual model changeovers and 'new improved' formulations) but few truly innovative products and major breakthroughs which have to come from technology push (Shanklin, 1983). This is an old debate and is difficult to prove or disprove. The most important question is whether the two, demand pull and technology push, are actually mutually exclusive. Chapter 13 suggests that an effective innovating business combines both the power of technology push with the direction and vision provided by a market oriented strategy. Thus the two can be mutually supportive.

Stages 1–4 of the innovation process comprise what is often termed *initiation* which is discussed in the following sections. Stage 5, *evaluation*, almost invariably involves a form of financial appraisal and much less frequently some form of qualitative assessment of the innovation's contribution to the strategy of the business. Stages 6–8 cover *implementation*, and include the management of change resulting from the innovation as well as the innovation itself.

The simple, initiation–evaluation–implementation model is sometimes accompanied by equally simple prescriptions such as 'creative freedom' being the essential prerequisite for initiating innovations, while management control is essential for effective implementation. This dichotomy between freedom and control is one of the fundamental dilemmas implicit in all management situations, but especially so in innovation. The difference is both philosophical and practical.

The initiation phase comprises the generation of ideas, the screening out of unsuitable ones, and some form of preliminary testing and development of the suitable ideas in concept prior to their financial evaluation. *Prima facie*, idea generation seems to be the really innovative part of the whole process, the part that demands some spark of creativity, the essence of innovation.

The whole process of innovation, including evaluation and implementation, is fraught with difficulty, but it is often thought that firms which fail to be innovative, fail because they lack the ability to be creative. They are too set in their ways, too committed to existing ways of doing things and too inflexible to be able to adopt new ideas, much less generate them.

There has been a lot of research into how innovative firms differ from the less innovative. To a great extent the differences centre around the way firms approach the processes involved in innovation. This chapter therefore looks into these processes in some detail and identifies the conditions that appear to be necessary for the creative generation of ideas.

11.5.1 Initiating innovations

The BCG's experience curve demonstrated the increasing efficiency with which operations are carried out the more often they are done. Repetitive routine was a crucial determinant of economic success, and consequently firms were encouraged to achieve high market share of growing markets in order to increase their experience and efficiency as rapidly as possible. For the BCG, market share was both the source and the result of success.

Successful firms established, possibly unwritten, industry recipes: ways of doing things which were regarded as good practice and which became widely adopted routine. Businesses were organised in order to perform these routines efficiently. The more successful the business and the more proscribed its routines, the less able it was to cope with change. The most successful, thus blinded by their success, might not even recognise change when it occurred.

As individuals, we all develop a perceptual bias based on our values and experience which results in a routine selection of perceived factors. We reject those which appear not to fit our value and experience set, and we accept those that do fit, as confirmation of the continuing validity of our perceptions. Charles Darwin apparently disciplined himself to write down every observation which did not fit his theories because, like the rest of us, he always forgot them otherwise and disregarded their consequences.

Businesses do the same. The American tyre manufacturers disregarded the benefits of the radial ply tyre because it did not fit the industry's accepted norms for cost, wear and performance characteristics. Instead they stuck to the old cross-ply technology for too long and let Michelin into the market with the radial which proved to be the next technology. The new idea did not fit the old recipe so it tended to be disregarded. This is not simply because of the huge capital investment sunk in the existing technology, but the even greater psychological investment of all the key individuals in the existing recipe.

There is therefore within any successful business the seeds of a mind-set which represses creativity and blocks off openness to new ideas. Mind-set is the antithesis of creativity, a fixed point of view which derives from experience and is reinforced every time that experience is successfully repeated and forces thinking along tightly proscribed lines.

Some advocate lateral thinking as an adequate response to the mind-set problem (De Bono, 1978). We all have the facility to think along straight lines or to think laterally. Lateral thinking, as a creativity technique, is a generic term covering a number of approaches which try to open up new ways of looking at problems. It seeks to change the way that individuals are able to perceive problems and potential solutions. However, innovation is today essentially a group problem. The knowledge and skills necessary to initiate innovation generally lie beyond the scope of the single individual no matter how gifted. Thus lateral thinking, although stimulating, does not address the problem of corporate mind-set which shows itself in the form of 'yes but' thinking (Rickards, 1985) which signals a closed, unreceptive outlook which can kill creativity.

Creativity is not dependent on 'sparks of genius' and is not a random process.

Newton and Leibniz invented calculus separately but simultaneously, not by chance or inspiration, but on the back of ten years' relevant experience and 50,000 bits of pertinent information (Simon, 1986). With the relevant experience and information absorbed it becomes possible to respond with speed, as though intuitively, and successfully. However, if the conditions are repressive and ways of thinking proscribed, innate creativity is frustrated.

Most approaches to creativity are therefore deliberate attempts to set up circumstances and processes which break out of this repressive regime, break down mind-set and eliminate barriers to imaginative ways of thinking. Probably the best known such technique is brainstorming. The essential idea of brainstorming is to break down mind-set simply by postponing judgement among the brainstorming group for the duration of the session. The intention is to generate a large quantity of potential 'solutions' which are sifted only later.

The 'freedom to be creative' is far from total even in brainstorming. As with all creativity techniques, there is first and foremost a need to be goal oriented. If there is no goal orientation the techniques cannot achieve results. Generally, the goal is the solution to some stated problem. Goal orientation is itself one limit on freedom. But freedom is further constrained because the normal barriers to creativity still have influence. For example, the belief that there is one right answer inhibits the examination of possibilities which clearly do not relate to that single track. Similarly, every member of the brainstorming group will have his or her own set of self-imposed barriers which arise out of the individual's own experience and values.

Moreover, the nuances of rank and status among different members of the group which attach in the ordinary working situation are not completely divested for the duration of a brainstorming session. Consequently the fear of looking stupid or of challenging the obvious will remain potent, and the desire to conform, or the equally inhibiting desire not to conform, will still affect creative performance. Thus even in brainstorming, where the rules of the game are reasonably well understood, and the reason behind those rules generally supported, the inhibitions to creativity are rarely dropped completely.

Initiating innovations involves both the generation of ideas and the screening out of unsuitable ones. The process of screening is deliberately separated from idea generation in brainstorming because it is so inhibiting to creativity. In other approaches the creative process itself is given rather more structure so that idea generation and screening go almost hand in hand.

Synectics, a more structured development of brainstorming, is one such technique which has achieved success in creative problem solving (Gordon, 1961). The technique involves a multistage process, using a brainstorming-style forum, first to agree appropriate definitions of the problem and then to identify potential solutions. The barriers to creativity in many cases are implicit in the way the problem is defined. Its redefinition by a synectics group may itself suggest new potential solutions.

Synectics sessions can be run in a variety of ways, with varying degrees of formality (Rickards, 1985). However a typical group might operate as follows:

1. Problem owner states his problem to the group.
2. Group in brainstorming mode identify potential alternative statements.

3. Problem owner selects a small number of problem definitions for further examination.
4. Group, again in brainstorming mode, identify potential solutions to one or more of the defined problems.
5. Problem owner selects from potential solutions for either further development by the group or for technical analysis, and so on.

The above is not intended as an operational explanation of synectics, but serves to highlight again the compromise that has to be made between the 'freedom to be creative' and the necessity to ensure that the work done is relevant. In brainstorming the relevance is intended to be established at the outset, after which the group works in as open and unproscribed a way as possible. In synectics the intervention of the problem owner and his continued participation in the group, either actively or passively, helps to maintain some form of relevance throughout the process. Other aspects of synectics act to reinforce the creative aspect of the process and to counteract the imposition of structure, for example the advocated use of metaphor in problem definition and solution proposal.

Initiation of innovation requires a positive breaking down of barriers to creative thinking. On the other hand, the common-sense requirement to make innovation relevant to the individual business inevitably results in the re-erection of barriers and the restriction of thinking.

These same considerations are the determinants not only of behaviour in specific circumstances such as brainstorming or synectics sessions, but also of behaviour in the wider organisation. They appear to have implications for how those organisations should be managed in order to be creative in their application of technology for strategic ends. The 'cultural' characteristics which are artificially and temporarily created for a brainstorming or synectics session may be just those which would help to create a truly innovative business.

11.5.2 Evaluating innovations

It is at the evaluation stage that a challenging, clinical business assessment can be made without inhibition. The delicate process of preliminary evaluation, invention and research have been completed. An apparently feasible and potentially viable proposal is available for evaluation. The questions raised at this stage are, 'Would it make an acceptable return?', 'Would it contribute to the long-term development of the business?', and 'Is it in line with strategy?'

Evaluation results in the rejection of a high proportion of innovation proposals and the most active hurdle is the financial one. This is because strategic hurdles are likely to be active only in companies which have a clearly stated strategy, and in those situations a proposal which did not meet the strategic criteria are unlikely even to reach the evaluation stage of the process.

Financial evaluation is an important filter in the innovation process and can be decisive in the way technologically based strategies are implemented. As a filter, its most significant role is the rejection of otherwise desirable innovations. The process by which these essentially negative decisions are made has been well documented, drawing particular attention to the differing practices in the United States and the UK on the one hand and Japan and Asian economies on the other (see Reading Reviews 8–12, and particularly Reading Review 11). Although the Japanese use different methods of financial appraisal, the main cause of difference was simply that they used less demanding discount or hurdle rates. In the United States rates typically fall in the range 15–25 per cent, with high-risk projects commonly being assessed at 30 per cent and more. These figures are fairly typical of the UK also. In Japan, the typical hurdle rate has normally been around 10 per cent or below.

Clearly, as a result of this fact alone, Japanese firms will accept many more innovations than their American and British rivals and thereby start to open up a technology gap. Put another way, the American and British firms have rejected many projects which the Japanese have accepted; as a consequence they have lost competitive position and turned increasingly to defensive cost-cutting investments and thus have been forced into a short-term focus.

The difference in hurdle rates clearly contributes to this difference in performance, which in turn justifies the different hurdle rates. But what causes the different hurdle rates to be used in the first place? There appears to be two prime reasons. First, the cost of capital. Asian bankers have been prepared to accept far lower returns in the short term in order to achieve greater success over the long term. This has been a successful policy over many decades. There are, however, clearly dangers in being insufficiently demanding, as recent experience in Korea in particular has demonstrated. The level of low interest indebtedness must be restricted if the lending institutions themselves are not to be threatened.

The second major reason for the Asian economies, and Japan in particular, charging a lower hurdle rate is their treatment of risk. It is British and American practice to increase the hurdle rate of a risky project by means of a risk premium of between 5 and 10 per cent, and not infrequently 15 per cent. In contrast, the Japanese do not use a risk premium at all. Since all but the simplest of cost reduction investments contain risk, a premium is almost invariably applied. The use of a risk premium alone largely explains the difference between the returns required in Japan and those required in the United States and the UK.

Furthermore, the longer term the project, the greater the penalty, because the perceived risk will inevitably be greater. Thus innovation is a prime victim of this practice and the more exciting the innovation, the longer term its effects, the more risky it is likely to be assessed and the higher the premium it will be set.

The use of a risk premium is based on statistical decision theory which asserts that if a firm has two courses of action, one with a pay-off of £100 and a probability of 0.8 and the other with a pay-off of £800 and a probability of 0.1, the 'expected' outcomes are the same despite the fact that the riskiness of the two projects is very different. The 'expected' outcome is simply the value of the outcome times the probability of its occurring. Thus a project with a probability of less than unity needs to earn a higher return than a risk-free project if its 'expected' outcome is to be the same. This extra return is a risk premium and the higher the risk the greater the premium will have to be to equate the expected outcome with that of the risk-free project.

However, the application of this approach to investment appraisal is problematic.

In theory, the expected returns from a project can be compared with those from a bunch of competing projects, and subject to achieving some preconceived risk profile, expected returns can be maximised by the choice of project. In practice, however, a firm appraises projects singly and compares the outcome if the investment is made with that if it is not made. Thus the risky element of the project will either occur or not occur. If it does occur, it will either damage the outcome or it will not.

In this context a risk premium is hardly relevant. It can serve only to reduce investment. It can have no other effect. The application of a premium in no way increases the return from a project, it merely reduces the probability of its going ahead. Since almost by definition all innovations are risky, the risk premium in particular serves to restrict investment in innovation.

By contrast, the Japanese rarely use this mechanical application of a risk premium. Instead they follow through the details of a project analysis and identify precisely what it is that makes it risky. For example, in the case of a new product innovation, it may be the probability of a punitive competitive reaction. If so, they consider what can be done to limit or avoid that reaction. What marketing or production tactics might make the short-term competitive advantage achieved by the innovation, sustainable in the long term? What will each of the main competitors do? What will the effect of their action be? What could be done about it?

This detailed analysis of what might inhibit the achievement of the innovation's potential return involves all members of the management team. The project is discussed in detail at all levels of the organisation, risk is investigated in every aspect and programmes devised to circumvent it. If a credible programme for the circumvention of risk can be devised, then the project is likely to go ahead because its appraisal will not be clouded by the application of an arbitrary risk premium.

The Japanese approach increases understanding of the risk involved and identifies how it could best be handled. Moreover, the detailed analysis itself has a number of side-benefits apart from avoiding the basic problem of investment appraisal. The process involves many members of the organisation and thus itself becomes a means of communication among members. It provides a genuine way for members to participate in organisational decisions. Both communication and participation are important aspects of organisational style, and Japanese practice endeavours to establish, during the course of project evaluation, a consensus among organisational members. The decision process itself is therefore relatively slow, but once taken, decisions tend to be rapidly and effectively implemented because the decision and its consequences have already been widely discussed throughout the organisation. If consensus is difficult to achieve, then the appraisal process takes longer. Achievement of consensus, after widespread communication and participation, means that organisational members all know and understand what the business is trying to achieve and which way it is headed.

The above paragraphs have focused on financial evaluation because this is the process by which so many new, strategically desirable, even necessary projects, are rejected. The consequence is not merely that the business falls short of its strategic aims, but also that it takes a step down the 'disinvestment spiral'. The unsurprising consequence is that the criteria for financial evaluation have become subject to widespread manipulation; a financial appraisal can easily be fixed to show an acceptable internal rate of return (IRR). Thus, for all the analytical effort involved, in many organisations financial appraisal has become an unreliable and untrusted filter.

Strategic evaluation is much more difficult to fiddle. Showing how a project takes the organisation forward in the prescribed direction to achieving its strategic aims is the acid test on any innovation. It may be specifically related to the achievement of some strategic milestone, or it may be more generally supportive of the espoused strategy of the business. But this evaluation should have overriding importance. If the project exceeds its financial hurdle but plays no strategic role then it should be rejected. If it is important strategically but fails to clear the financial hurdles then it should be reviewed in detail to see where the financial case is at fault.

Croxden Horticultural Products (see Box 11.1) is a company locked into a low-technology, mature market, but threatened by a weaker competitor that appears committed to an aggressive competitive push. Consider the questions raised in Box 11.1, giving special thought to the possible role of innovation.

BOX 11.1

Croxden Horticultural Products Ltd

Croxden is a producer of bagged horticultural products, composts, fertilisers, etc. One of its main product lines is a John Innes compost made in four formulations for seedlings, potting on, etc., the major difference being the strength of nutrients included. John Innes is the registered name of an insititute which prescribes formulations of soil-based composts.

The production process is one of simply mixing soil, sand and gravel and nutrients together and then putting measured quantities into polythene bags. Bulk raw materials are sterilised where necessary, moisture content corrected, mixed with nutrients and bagged. Strict control of the product mix, particularly the strength of nutrient additions, is crucial because of the risk of consequential damage to customers' plants. Basic formulations are generally controlled satisfactorily and so competition is based largely on price and delivery, but any lapses in quality control would be severely punished as Croxden found to its cost in the distant past.

Production costs are related predominantly to the bagging process. Croxden had three bagging lines, each handling different bag size ranges. The machines on all three lines are new and incorporate the latest technology. Utilisation of this plant is the key to profitability. At present it works on a two-shift basis for about nine months of the year and single-shift the other three months. Demand for product is highly seasonal and it is necessary to build substantial stocks for the spring and autumn sales seasons. Croxden has not attempted to run a three-shift, 24 hour a day operation.

Croxden has around 30 per cent of its served markets. These are divided into three sectors. First, Croxden make substantial sales of bulk (i.e. unbagged) product to the nursery/garden centre trade for their own use. Secondly, it also makes substantial sales of bagged product to garden centres and other specialist horticultural outlets for sale to the general public. Thirdly, it also makes substantial sales to five national supermarket chains.

Bulk sales to the trade are slowly declining. Garden centre sales are stable. Supermarket sales have been increasing rapidly and Croxden has succeeded in adding a new national supermarket chain each season for the previous four years and hopes to continue this growth.

Supermarkets and garden centres make extensive use of EFTPOS systems to facilitate collection and analysis of sales data which is input automatically to a sales order processing and stock control system to replenish stocks at each location and reorder on suppliers as necessary. It is rumoured that one of the biggest supermarket chains, SafeSave, is going a step further and may in future require all suppliers to adopt a computer system capable of running SafeSave's software linked to SafeSave's own system, communicating orders and instructions directly over the Internet.

One of Croxden's competitors is a small family business called ABC which has generally held around 3 per cent of the market supplying from old, obsolete plant. The proprietor of ABC has recently handed over management of the business to his son and ABC have subsequently bought two new high-output bagging machines of similar type to Croxden's. It is also known that ABC has been actively involved during the close season with all the retail chains, presumably trying to get new business in order to utilise the new plant. ABC has previously sold only to garden centres and a small amount of direct mail.

DISCUSSION POINTS

1. As marketing director of Croxden, what is your attitude to ABC's activities?
2. How seriously do you regard them as a threat?
3. How can Croxden best combat the threat from ABC?

11.5.3 Implementing innovations

For an innovation to be ultimately successful it needs not only to be the right project, but also to be implemented efficiently. These are terms with which management is likely to be familiar; it is the normal basis of assessing managers' performance – do they perform efficiently and effectively, 'efficiently' meaning are they doing the job right; 'effectively' meaning are they doing the right job.

As far as innovation is concerned, the initiation and evaluation of a project have already been considered – the innovation has been identified as the 'right job'. Its implementation needs to be completed efficiently.

The orthodox wisdom suggests that while initiation needs freedom and flexibility as created in brainstorming/synectics sessions, efficient implementation requires tight management control. This dichotomy has led many organisations to recognise the need to separate part of the organisation that is required to be innovative and creative from the rest of the organisation that is required simply to be cost efficient and profitable. Thus many businesses have set up separate new ventures departments or divisions, or even created separate subsidiary companies where different cultural rules can be applied to encourage innovation without losing strict control of costs in the main existing business.

This approach seems to assume that existing business can still be most efficiently managed through traditional systems of control. However, Burns and Stalker first pointed out that this is probably not true during a period of rapid technological change such as is now confronting almost all organisations, existing and new. Under these conditions, the form of organisation needed for initiating innovations may not be much different from the organisational form best suited to implementing innovations. At this time perhaps all organisations need to be 'organic'. The next two chapters look in greater depth at these issues.

Summary

- Innovation, the process of invention and its commercial exploitation, is a competitive tool available to all businesses.
- Being early with the new technology provides a substantial competitive advantage which can be used to make rapid and dramatic changes in long-standing competitive relationships.
- The technological strategic thinking framework seeks to increase understanding of how technology develops and can be used effectively as a strategic competitive weapon.
- The shape of innovation is surprisingly consistent and conveniently modelled by an S curve which tends to a limit of performance which may be either natural or man-made.
- Technological forecasting is a knowledge- and information-intensive activity and involves identifying the S curve and, as far as possible, the current position on it, the nature of the operational limits, the potential new replacement technologies and the likely timing of the transfer from the old technology to the new.
- The decision to ditch an existing technology is extremely difficult. It involves changes in the psychological investment of the business as well as its financial commitments. These will be particularly hard decisions for the leader businesses in the old technology.
- The process of innovation comprises three main stages: initiation, evaluation and implementation.
- Initiation comprises the generation, screening and developing of ideas. The fundamental prerequisite of successful initiation is the freedom to be creative.
- Creativity is the essence of innovation and is marked by an openness to new

thinking and an absence of mind-sets and linear thinking which is the natural result of a successful business operation.

- Nevertheless the freedom to be creative appears to need some structure and bounds to ensure that the creativity is harnessed to relevant business needs.
- Financial evaluation eliminates many strategically valid innovations and the different approaches of Japan, on the one hand, and the UK and United States on the other, have resulted in a technological gap.
- The differences between Japanese and American practice relate primarily to the investment hurdle rates, the treatment of risk and the calculation of returns.
- The treatment of risk is particularly significant; while the Japanese analyse all aspects and slowly build a consensus which can be implemented fast, the US/UK approach is to add a risk premium on the required return.
- Strategic evaluation is often not given the same importance as financial appraisal, but it is less easy to fudge and it should override the financial case.
- The implementation of innovation is often held simply to require efficient management control, i.e. the same organisational form as the existing business. However, in an era of rapid change, it is uncertain which organisational form is most effective.

Further reading

Drucker, P., *Innovation and Entrepreneurship*, Heinemann, 1985.
Scarborough, H. and Corbett, J.M., *Technology and Organisation*, Routledge, 1992.
Wilson, D.C., *A Strategy of Change*, Routledge, 1992.

Chapter 12

Structure, culture and symbolism

The aim of this chapter is to examine forms of organisation which are best suited to managing innovations in this era of change.

There is a long history of research and concern with organisational behaviour and the chapter looks at various approaches to structure, culture and organisational symbolism and the ways these can be managed for the better pursuit of strategic objectives.

Structure has long been recognised as an important aspect of the strategy agenda, but structure is no longer the simple classical concept – instead of hierarchies we are now looking at jazz combos and termite heaps.

Clearly, the right culture can help to achieve concentration so that the mission is achieved most effectively.

12.1 Introduction

It is people who turn strategic thinking into strategic action and that is why the transformational frameworks described in Chapter 9, despite their apparent shortcomings, are of such interest. Strategic thinking is worthless if people are not free, able and motivated to use their initiative and creativity in turning strategy into action. The transformational frameworks address this in part, but freedom and motivation are characteristics embedded in the structure and culture of the organisation itself, not just in the approach to strategy.

This chapter looks at the different ways of structuring organisations in order to give effect to strategy through its people, i.e. to help them achieve concentration and consistency, as well as flexibility, in pursuing strategic direction.

Understanding and motivating people is part of the strategic thinking agenda. This has always been obvious in service industries where the 'product' is embodied in the interaction between people in the organisation and the customer. However, all industries share this orientation now that technology has replaced large-scale production with small-scale, knowledge-intensive activity where quality is so dependent on individual personal behaviour (Hogg, 1986).

Concern for how various organisational characteristics impact on the behaviour and performance of people in organisations has long been a recurrent topic of management research. Initially the focus of attention was on structural characteristics. The most effective structure was found to be influenced by production technology, whether process, mass production, or large or small batch production (Woodward, 1958) and a dominant characteristic of structure was thought to be the number of layers in the hierarchy of an organisation from top to bottom. A tall, narrow organisation (as depicted on a traditional organisation chart) appeared to have a different impact on the behaviour of organisation members from that of a wide, flat organisation. Later researchers suggested that structure was influenced by the environment (Lawrence and Lorsch, 1967) and by market forces (Chandler, 1977).

In common-sense terms it seems quite predictable that an organisation with a lot of layers in it will tend to be bureaucratic and consequently either frustrate or facilitate certain behaviours. In addition, there are various other structural characteristics, as well as configuration, which appear to have similar effects and there has been a lot of research into quite how these impact on organisation member behaviour, organisation effectiveness and organisation strategy.

However, the concept of structure may not encapsulate the most potent determinants of behaviour. Other less tangible influences, such as implied by the term climate, may be more powerful. But then structure and 'climate' may even be different aspects of the same phenomenon. 'The relationship between structure and climate is totally interdependent. Together, they relate the structure of the organisation, its environment and behaviour and objectives of the individual member' (Kennedy, 1983).

Closely allied to the concept of climate is that of organisational culture. Culture is more long-lasting than climate and perhaps more influential, but, like climate, is difficult to measure in any reliable way.

Structure and culture are each aspects of organisation, and at the same time, ways of looking at organisation. Whereas structure may be defined in what appear at first sight to be precise and unambiguous terms in relation to such concepts as formalisation and specialisation (Pugh *et al.*, 1969), the extent to which such factual analysis explains how people in organisations behave remains uncertain. The cultural perspective, on the other hand, is not so amenable to unambiguous examination, but promises a fuller explanation of behaviour. Because of the difficulties in identifying and measuring culture, symbolic measures are sometimes adopted as proxies that can be measured. However, the compromise between measurability and richness of behavioural explanation remains.

The following sections trace how understanding of organisation forms has developed. This should provide some insight and understanding as to how organisations might be shaped and managed to fulfil strategies in this period of change.

12.2 Organisational structure

Businesses almost always start out with what might be called a simple structure, where each member reports direct to the founding entrepreneur. As they grow, firms progress through various evolutionary phases. Typically, when the firm has outgrown the simple structure, it adopts a functional organisation, based on the primary tasks such as production, marketing and finance. This enables the firm to accommodate functional professional specialists at senior levels of management and it also enables relatively short lines of communication to operate.

However, functional structures are not best suited to managing diversified activities. As firms grow and diversify into new product market areas there is an explosion of complexity which is generally contained by setting up an organisation of more-or-less separate businesses, either as divisions or as separate subsidiaries under a holding company organisation.

In the years after the Second World War there was a move towards divisional structure. Rumelt (1974) studied this evolutionary process in large American firms between 1949 and 1969 and identified a continuous trend to increased complexity from the single-business firm to the diversified conglomerate. In the UK, Channon (1973) found that between 1960 and 1970 the proportion of major British manufacturers using a divisional structure had increased from less than one-third to more than two-thirds. In the 1970s and 1980s this trend appears to have continued with an increasing emphasis on global businesses which in many cases operate divisional structures within an overall holding company organisation. More recently there has been some evidence of this process going into reverse, with many diversified groups demerging subsidiary businesses, but the preponderance of large companies are still organised divisionally.

A firm's organisation structure results from specific management decisions based on certain structural concepts. The organisation as described on an organisation chart is only one view of the structural picture and gives only a limited idea of how it actually works in practice.

Pugh and colleagues (1968) developed a model of structure which others have since replicated. The research was originally based on a diverse sample of 46 organisations whose formal structures were analysed in the following terms:

1. *Specialisation of functions and roles.* Specialisation refers to the extent to which different functions in an organisation are carried out by specialist individuals or departments and the degree to which those individuals are required to have specialist knowledge as denoted by formal qualifications.
2. *Standardisation of procedures.* Standardisation refers specifically to employment practices such as recruitment and selection, disciplinary and grievance procedures and the degree to which jobs are defined and governed by standard policies, rules and procedures.
3. *Formalisation of documentation.* Formalisation refers to the degree to which instructions etc. are written down, for example job descriptions, employee handbooks or rulebooks, agendas and minutes of management meetings.

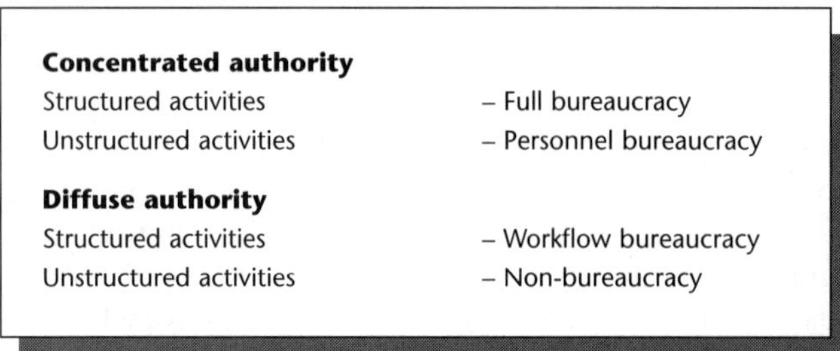

Concentrated authority	
Structured activities	– Full bureaucracy
Unstructured activities	– Personnel bureaucracy
Diffuse authority	
Structured activities	– Workflow bureaucracy
Unstructured activities	– Non-bureaucracy

Figure 12.1 Categorisation of bureaucratic structures (Source: based on Pugh *et al.*, 1968)

4. *Centralisation of authority.* Centralisation refers to the extent to which the taking of decisions is centralised and is measured by instancing specific decisions (for example the pricing of output, the allocation of specific resources) and establishing at what level in the organisation they are taken.
5. *Configuration of role structure.* Configuration refers to the shape of the organisation in terms of hierarchical layers and spans of control and is assessed by establishing the spans of control of specific jobholders, and the proportions of employees in the various functional specialisms.

The attraction of these factors is that they appear to be fairly straightforward to measure. They focus on two broad issues: the degree of concentration of authority and the degree of structuring of activities. These are measures of bureaucratic tendency which produce a categorisation of structures as outlined in Figure 12.1.

Typically, big businesses fell into the category of workflow bureaucracies, being highly structured but not as centralised as some organisations. Public service organisations were the personnel bureaucracies, having highly concentrated authority with procedures focused on hiring, promoting and firing of personnel, but relatively unstructured activities. Smaller units within large private or public groups were the full bureaucracies, and smaller firms in personal ownership the non-bureaucracies. The significance of these measures of structure and concentration of authority lies in the fact that they are proxies for factors that directly affect the way people are motivated, developed and led in the organisation.

Mintzberg (1983) added a number of other structural characteristics including, among other factors:

- Formalisation of behaviour
- Training and indoctrination
- Planning and control systems

Such measures relate more closely to the factors which actually determine how people in organisations behave and perform and thus promise to be of more practical use. The factors involved, however, are even more difficult to measure. Mintzberg identified five basic components of an organisation (see Figure 12.2) This analysis contains less precision, but more meaning than a traditional hierarchy structure. The shape of organisations might differ according to the relative importance of

- Traditional line of command:
  - Strategic apex
  - Middle line
  - Operating core
- Professional specialists/technostructure
- Administration/support staff

Figure 12.2 Components of organisation (Source: based on Mintzberg, 1981)

the different components. From this analysis Mintzberg originally derived the following taxonomy of organisational forms:

- Simple structure
- Machine bureaucracy
- Professional bureaucracy
- Divisionalised form
- Adhocracy

This model was subsequently elaborated by the inclusion of a sixth 'basic part', a cultural element which Mintzberg called 'ideology' (Mintzberg, 1996). From this Mintzberg identified what he referred to as the missionary organisation, one which is structured largely by its ideology rather than the orthodox hierarchies and other formal devices. Mintzberg also added an organisational form where none of the basic parts was dominant and the organisation is identified by a tendency for the basic parts to pull away from each other. He called this the political organisation. Mintzberg's 1996 taxonomy used somewhat simplified terminology as follows:

- Entrepreneurial organisation (simple structure)
- Machine organisation (machine bureaucracy)
- Professional organisation (professional bureaucracy)
- Diversified organisation (divisionalised form)
- Innovative organisation (adhocracy)
- Missionary organisation
- Political organisation

The entrepreneurial organisation, or simple structure has little standardised or formalised behaviour, minimal use is made of planning or training, there are few staff analysts and few middle managers because the business is run, more-or-less autocratically, by direct supervision from the top. The organisation is flexible and able to outmanoeuvre the bureaucracies. It is effective in simple but dynamic environments and, given the right chief executive, is ideal for rapid, flexible innovation. Most firms start out as simple structures, but few retain simplicity as large organisations.

The machine, professional and diversified organisations have already been briefly described in section 1.2. Machine organisation is typical of a mature business in a mature industry where mass production of standard product is still viable and the management problem is focused on large numbers of specialised, low-skill jobs with staff analysts to maintain the systems of standardisation and departmentalisation with a large-scale middle management hierarchy.

The professional organisation relies on standardisation of skills rather than organisational processes or products, ceding much of its power to trained professionals, but with an autocratic, non-participative structure for the substantial supporting administrative staff.

The diversified organisation is a means of setting up market, or product-based subunits with a considerable degree of autonomy, but nevertheless subject to central control which in effect imposes a structure of machine organisation at divisional level.

The innovative organisation (or adhocracy) is the ill-defined structure that has no standard form but which may, in whatever form it takes, facilitate flexibility, independence, innovation, risk taking and the ability to cope in environments which are both complex and dynamic. Mintzberg distinguished two types of adhocracy: the operating adhocracy, such as a creative advertising agency, which carries out innovative projects directly for its clients; and the administrative adhocracy, such as a producer of electronic components, which carries out innovative projects for itself and consequently has both an administrative and an operating structure.

Mintzberg's missionary organisation is referred to in other contexts as 'strong culture' organisations. Pascale (1985) included firms such as IBM, ITT and Procter & Gamble in this category (see section 12.4), although Mintzberg implies that his missionary organisations are fairly small because they rely on personal contacts among members in order for the ideology to become dominant. It is open to question whether larger organisations can successfully mimic this process by the deliberate development of a strong culture.

Mintzberg identified the natural tendency to bureaucratise, which is becoming increasingly inappropriate in a period of rapid technological change. The operating manager needs to innovate to achieve strategic objectives but is inhibited by the bureaucratic organisation and therefore feels the need to break down the existing structures to achieve change. Innovative organisation forms are therefore clearly of considerable interest. Other writers and practitioners have identified many approaches to creating an innovative organisation and these go beyond Mintzberg's categorisation.

Change can be adjusted to by more limited approaches to structural adjustment, either by concentrating on a subset of the whole structure (for example work design), or by setting up a separate structure within a structure which adopts different organisational rules and norms.

Work design has attracted much attention since the turn of the century with figures like Taylor and the Gilbreths who concentrated on the simplification, specialisation and standardisation of work so that the then new mass production technologies could be exploited. Much of the subsequent work on organisation development has aimed to reverse these tendencies to standardise and bureaucratise. However, as Leitko and Szczerbacki put it,

> *Organisational development (OD) has yet to escape from its past – from its origins within humanistic psychology, in part as a reaction to the restrictive and authoritarian conditions characteristic of the machine bureaucracies found in many manufacturing organisations. However, the limitations that this past has created for OD are becoming more apparent as . . . machine bureaucracies give way to more open systems within the manufacturing sector, and as OD experts study organisations outside the manufacturing sector.* (Leitko and Szczerbacki, 1987)

Work design has thus tended to move organisations away from bureaucratic structures through such processes as job enlargement, job rotation, job enrichment, various exercises in group technology, notably in the Swedish motor industry, and the Quality of Working Life movement which from time to time experiences revivals of interest (Heller, 1988).

Whilst these approaches address the problem of mechanistic structures which are difficult to change, they do so by changing the nature of only some jobs in the organisation, rather than all jobs. Moreover, these movements have tended to focus attention on non-managerial work. There has also been increasing interest in setting up an organisation within the organisation, specifically charged with the task of 'entrepreneuring'. The main organisation continues to be managed on a more-or-less bureaucratic basis because this is believed to be the most efficient mode for the stable conditions assumed to exist, while separate structures are deliberately created to handle innovation and are shaped with a behaviourally sensitive 'management of change' design. The management of change has almost become another cliché to rank alongside BPR, TQM, JIT and the other acronyms of management consultancy and its behaviouralist perspective appears only to provide short-term answers. The structure, culture and power perspective may be less easy to work within but seems more likely to provide lasting solutions (Cummings and Huse, 1989). The basic assumption that increasing participation and autonomy leads to more satisfied and productive people is only poorly supported by empirical evidence and Wilson (1992, and Reading Review 20) suggests a wider perspective is required which includes an understanding of the context.

These various approaches focus on the formal organisation, but the distinction between formal and informal structure is critical to considerations of organisation change. An organisation chart, representing the formal structure, may exist which clearly delineates the chains of command, the spans of control and the hierarchical strata of the organisation, but may have little to do with reality. It may be continually updated, but never used. The chart is a graphic representation of the formal organisation, but it may shed little light on how the organisation actually functions and how it affects the way people behave and the decisions they take. Structure alone cannot encompass all these aspects of organisation.

The idea of organisational structure seems to imply that the organisation has an independent existence, but because of the rate of technological change and increasingly global competition this is no longer true. The isolated, autonomous business unit is no longer viable. Venture finance is typical of many multibusiness companies and conglomerates where the structural demands are ambiguous. Consider the issues raised in the discussion points of Box 12.1.

BOX 12.1

Venture Finance International Ltd

Venture Finance is a successful and growing banking subsidiary of Apex Holdings Plc, an acquisitive, financially oriented conglomerate. As its name implies, the bank's main mission is to provide venture capital facilities to the corporate sector, and it focuses on small, fast growth, high-tech businesses. The bank has grown rapidly, but as a result of acquisitions has become involved in high street retail activity with personal, rather than corporate, customers.

Apex regards its own role as being to decide the broad strategy of its subsidiary companies and to hold the purse strings. The basis of the parent/subsidiary relationship is a monthly financial report which covers the main financial performance ratios, a precise three-month cash flow forecast with six- and twelve-month projections and a mandatory statement of any items in the annual rolling budget which are now expected to be inaccurate by a factor of 10 per cent or more. These monthly reports form the basis of the parent company's assessment of the business as a prospect for future investment, and of its top management as prospects for future advancement. The key to providing satisfactory returns was never to give surprises, even nice ones. An unexpectedly high positive cash flow, for example, would be treated by Apex as an instance of incompetence by subsidiary company management. The nature of venture finance made it much more 'lumpy' and prone to surprises than the more predictable personal retail business. The Venture Finance shopfront has recently become a well known, non-traditional 'bank shop', which contributes significantly to the overall success of the business.

DISCUSSION POINTS

1. Which of Mintzberg's organisational forms would you expect would best describe the Venture Finance structure? Do you think the structure is appropriate?
2. Which of Mintzberg's forms would be best for Venture Finance and for Apex?
3. Which is the more important in this situation, strategy or structure?

12.3 Alliances, networks and teams

Business partnerships, collaborations and alliances are made in order to 'gain additional access to new competences, to markets, to technology or to specific resources in order to sustain competitive advantage' (Lorange *et al.*, 1992) which sets the business apart and makes it distinctive in some way.

The current rapid rate of technological development and its equally rapid rate of adoption across the globe are affecting all businesses, large and small. Even a localised business, with no global pretensions itself, must take account of global developments in markets and technologies potentially relevant to its products and customers. This global awareness is essential to the maintenance of technological position (Clark, 1989). Awareness is essential but it is also desirable for any business to be at or around the leading edge of at least one of its technologies. Few individual firms can be at the forefront of all the technological developments impacting a particular sector. The technologies are too diverse and their rapid development too costly. The costs and risks are therefore spread by the formation of partnerships and collaborations among organisations with a common, often competing, interest. Being involved in such partnerships is the only way a business can maintain and extend its own distinctive competence.

The ever-increasing scale of investment required by advancing technology means that there must be a rapid exploitation of that technology in order for it to be exploited profitably. The required speed of exploitation means that the fruits of technology must be sold to ever larger markets, ultimately to the whole world. The assiduous pursuit of a global market results inevitably in convergence of consumer tastes (Ohmae, 1989); and changes in the global environment arise directly from global technology development (Miller, 1990). Just a few decades ago, the cultural differences between, say, Japan and Britain meant that it would be difficult to envisage the same consumer product succeeding equally in both markets. Now, tastes for many technically advanced consumer durables clearly coincide and the same product can be marketed in London and in Tokyo with only the most superficial differences.

The globalisation process appears irrevocable, globalisation of technology both facilitating and requiring globalisation of markets at an ever-increasing rate. Thus firms are tending to become ever more expert in ever more tightly defined technologies. In order to maintain this rapidly developing expertise, they need to focus all their efforts on the core technologies. They therefore find it both necessary and profitable to buy in those technologies which they have not defined as core to their own business. The notion of focusing on core competences and outsourcing all others has become one of the strategic orthodoxies for the 1990s, essential to survival in this era of rapid innovation. The approach is based on simple principles:

- *Focus on those components that are critical to the product and that the company is distinctively good at making.*
- *Outsource components where suppliers have a distinct comparative advantage – greater scale, fundamentally lower cost structure, or stronger performance incentives.* (Venkatesan, 1992)

This is a way of increasing concentration. The original theory behind the approach can be traced back to the economic theory of international trade, used by Porter in his approach to international business (Porter, 1990) and the ideas behind concentration. Unless there is the determination to outsource non-core components or technology there will be little chance of concentrating effectively on the core and achieving leading-edge competence. Reliance on external organisations for non-core, though essential, elements in the business process results in the establishment of various forms of strategic alliance.

Evidence of these global alliances is not restricted to the professional/academic literature. Hitachi took full page advertisements in the *Financial Times* to explain its approach under the title 'Localising the multinational: globalisation holds the key':

> *In our efforts to source more components and raw materials outside of Japan, Hitachi recently established an 'Asia Procurement Programme Centre' whose task is to locate suppliers of parts in countries such as Singapore and Hong Kong that can provide our manufacturing operations – both inside and outside Japan – with components ... [earlier] this year we reached an (OEM) agreement with IBM to market three types of personal computers in Japan ... we are also supplying mainframe computers to Germany's Compalex and Italy's Olivetti on an OEM basis and have licensed our 1-megabit and 4-megabit DRAM technology to Goldstar Electron of Korea ... Hitachi has established seven overseas R&D bases including Dublin, Düsseldorf and Milan ... development of a single electron memory device (in the order of 64Gb) which we developed jointly with Cambridge University ... working with Hewlett Packard (UK) to develop an artificial intelligence software program ... working with Trinity College, Dublin, we have developed an artificial retina ...* (Hitachi, 1993)

Hitachi is an archetype of the modern multinational. Collaborations are not restricted to friendly supplier/customer relationships or the essentially unthreatening industry/academe transactions. Fierce competitors are increasingly forced to collaborate for their future survival and prosperity. Hamel and Prahalad (1989) documented the ways in which Canon acquired technology from Xerox while establishing itself in photocopiers, and how Komatsu acquired and improved on the technology of its main competitor Caterpillar. Both of these were examples of collaborations motivated by the need to learn, to acquire key technological competence. This is perhaps the most powerful motivation of all.

Lei (1989) reviews several multinational-based strategic alliance systems. Eight American firms in the semiconductor industry having twenty-five such alliances with mainly Pacific Rim firms to achieve a variety of aims. Lei's examination of AT&T reveals alliances with seventeen autonomous, mainly foreign firms, some aimed at learning new core technologies, some at penetrating new markets, some at a combination of both. A similar examination of IBM's alliance strategy revealed no less than forty such strategic alliances.

It is worth re-emphasising that these are all genuine strategic alliances planned to last for a considerable time and in many cases regarded as indefinitely ongoing. All parties to these strategic alliances must necessarily be perceived as trustworthy or they would have been excluded from such mutually advantageous collaborations, left only to participate in those where the gains were strictly short term.

New and ever more surprising collaborations are continually being reported. Renault, Saab and Fiat, fierce competitors in the European executive car market, joined forces to develop and tool a new car body. Kodak and Xerox, erstwhile sworn enemies in photocopying technology, agreed to pool resources and work together on new products. Ford and Volkswagen, world competitors in people carrying, united to produce a new generation 'people carrier' to beat Renault's Espace. The list of such strategic alliances is surprisingly long and growing with great speed. British Aerospace, Aerospaciale of France and Deutsche Aerospace, part of Daimler Benz, have come together to form the European Supersonic Research Programme with the aim of developing technology to offer potential American and Japanese partners in the project to develop a successor to Concorde (itself the product of such a technological alliance). Amersham International, Hitachi and Molecular Dynamics of California formed an alliance to exploit the growing demand for instruments with which to sequence genes – all three companies already having products and expertise in the market.

A contrast between the traditional, vertically integrated monolithic organisation and the newer, more fragmented organisation of alliances and collaborations is shown in the aggregate comparison of Toyota and General Motors in Table 12.1.

Just as globalisation impacts all businesses great and small, so does the need to establish long-lasting alliances. It is advantageous for the major multinational firms to collaborate, but it is crucial for the minnows to do likewise and forge relationships which help them to leverage up their meagre resources. Only in this way can they hope to maintain any element of even localised leadership in their core technologies.

Globalisation and rapid technological change are the dual pressures forcing firms to establish long-lasting relationships in order to achieve two objectives. The first is to concentrate all their resources, efforts and enthusiasm on their core competences. Only by such concentration will they achieve leadership and superior economic results. This is done by deliberately buying-in the non-core competences – in practice one of the most difficult of strategic decisions to implement. The second is to replicate the speed and flexibility of small organisations so that they can be innovative and ensure that their leadership positions are maintained despite a rapidly changing environment. This is done by managing through networks and teams rather than through hierarchies and functions.

The deconstruction of the old, machine-like bureaucracies and the creation of new team-based, fragmented forms of organisation is currently a focus for consultants and academics alike.

For more than a decade, pundit after pundit, from Tom Peters to Harvard economist Michael Jensen, has sounded the death knell for large companies. The real world has appeared to bear them out: action by governments, shareholders and managements themselves has broken up all sorts of established dynasties, both sensible but unwieldy business monoliths such as AT&T, and illogical conglomerates such as ITT.

Table 12.1 A comparison of network and traditonal organisations

	Network organisation (Toyota)	Traditional organisation (General Motors)
Vehicles produced	4,000,000	8,000,000
Number of employees	37,000	850,000
Vehicles per employee	108	9
Costs incurred 'in-house'	27%	70%
Bought-in costs	73%	30%

(Source: Womack *et al.*, 1990)

> *Other big companies have reacted by stripping themselves 'back to basics': concentrating on their core businesses, and divesting or 'outsourcing' the remainder. A fashion has even developed for voluntary de-merger.*
>
> *In the marketplace, lumbering giants, from IBM, Sears Roebuck and General Motors to the American TV networks, have been overtaken by more sprightly upstarts – Microsoft, WalMart, Toyota, CNN – and been attacked by hordes of smaller innovators.*
>
> *Small is now beautiful it seems – at least until, like Microsoft, you become big enough to join the ranks of the bad and ugly. In his new book,* Global Paradox, *John Naisbitt, the futurologist who made his name with Megatrends, declares that 'the bigger the world economy, the more powerful its smallest players'. He claims that 'we have moved . . . from bigger is better to bigger is inefficient, costly, wastefully bureaucratic, inflexible and, now, disastrous'.* (Lorenz, 1994)

This is the orthodox wisdom and Lorenz highlights its dangers. But being big is not all bad news – there are benefits as well as costs. Being big does not necessarily mean being inefficient. ABB, Hewlett Packard and 3M, for example, are all big in their chosen markets but exceedingly lean in the way they are managed. The same applies to a growing number of large multinationals which, stripped back to their core businesses and focusing on their key technologies, are managed increasingly like a collection of small businesses, but with the difference that they also share various degrees of management skills, research, design, development and purchasing, as well as aspects of distribution and service. Bigness can certainly bring benefits, but achieving these benefits while avoiding all the dysfunctions of large-scale bureaucracy is one of the perennial issues of management.

Child and Faulkner (1998) highlight a possible solution: the development of federations among multinationals. They example IBM which transformed itself from a single 'strong culture' monolith into a federation of fourteen potentially competitive companies whose success will depend on their ability to co-operate as partners rather than being co-ordinated by hierarchy.

ABB of Zurich is a widely quoted exemplar of the modern network organisation form. ABB is a big company in any terms. It employs around 225,000 people (including 25,000 managers) in more than 1,200 subsidiary companies and 5,000 profit centres. This is the key to its organisational form: a multiplicity of semi-autonomous subsidiary units, connected to their parent by a computerised umbilical cord. Potentially this organisational form could achieve an ideal balance between the benefits of scale and the advantages of being small. The force of ABB's anti-bureaucratic style can be seen by the no doubt far from painless reductions in numbers employed in their various subsidiary head offices. For example, Stromberg's head office staff was reduced from 880 to 25, Mannheim from 1,600 to 100, Combustion Engineering of Stamford from 600 to 100. ABB's group headquarters comprises no more than 100 people.

The modern business is in essence a processor of knowledge. Drucker suggests that the key economic resource is no longer labour, capital or land, but knowledge; the central wealth-creating activity is no longer the allocation of capital and labour to production processes but the allocation of knowledge to productivity and innovation;

the key groups in this new post-capitalist society are the knowledge workers who know how to allocate their knowledge to this productive use and who will own both the means of production (through their pension funds) and the tools of production (i.e. knowledge) (Drucker, 1993, and Reading Review 22).

Hogg (1986) provided an early illustration of how this process occurs in practice. Former large-scale employers automate away unskilled and semi-skilled work, but create new, highly specialised and skilled work to develop and maintain the new technology. Increasingly, the robots which replaced shopfloor workers are not maintained by full-time employees of the firm but by small specialist firms on maintenance contract to ensure the robots achieve agreed levels of performance in terms of downtime, availability and so on. This process, clearly under way a decade ago, has continued apace, increasingly involving the operation of new technology as well as its development and maintenance.

> *The new organisation consists of bits and pieces of various firms, plus an array of independent contractors, which the partners gather like members of a movie company for a limited time to perform a discrete task.* (Peters, 1994)

Various models of this new 'organic' organisational form have been proposed. Drucker suggests the symphony orchestra as the prototype of the new knowledge-processing organisation whose function is to make the best use of specialists. The best specialists are effective as specialists not generalists – neurosurgeons get better the more they practise neurosurgery, not by being promoted into general administrative work as often happens in hierarchically-based organisations. In order for them to practise their specialism and to produce results, organisation is needed. In the symphony orchestra, each of the players is a specialist. While each is playing a part towards the overall mission, each subordinates his or her speciality to the overall task, and they all play only one piece of music at a given time (Drucker, 1993, and Reading Review 22).

A 'team of associates' is widely held to be the most effective organisational form for today's knowledge-processing, learning organisation. This is a stage further than organic organisation. The replacement of hierarchy with teams and of mechanistic structures with networks has been widely reported (for example McGill *et al.*, 1992, and Reading Review 19). The ABB example quoted earlier shows how effective a very large organisation can be in minimising hierarchy, using a team-based structure with strong networks throughout the firm to exploit the advantages of large scale.

Team-based organisation facilitates the individual knowledge workers contribution in a form of 'collaborative individualism' (Chorn, 1992) focused on the task in hand. This implies a fluidity of organisation where individuals' contributions to different teams will vary over time as the relevance of their particular knowledge specialism varies. The permanent organisation form is an arrangement of networks of teams of associates for which various metaphors have been used:

> *Quinn called them 'spider's web organisations' ... Weick, a researcher at the University of Michigan, likes the improvisational theatre metaphor. Charles Savage, management guru from Digital Equipment, cottons to jazz combos.* (Peters, 1994)

> *Gavaghan (founder of First Direct, Midland Bank's electronic telephone banking*

> *service) looks outside the business world to find models for the virtual company. A surgeon's team . . . a film production unit . . . the Desert Storm force in the Gulf War.*
> (Bowen, 1994)

Even within a traditional monolithic organisation there is an increasing reliance on networks. A network is not simply a group of communicators. Such a group may be connected at random to exchange information of an undefined nature. They may well lack the essential purposive element. 'Have a nice day' is a communication – or at least it meets most of the requirements of an orthodox definition of a communication. Its purpose is, however, limited.

> *The term network is the communications analogue of the sociological concept of 'group', but 'network' is distinct from 'group' in that it refers to a number of individuals (or other units) who persistently interact with one another in accordance with established patterns.* (Mueller, 1986)

Corporate networks take many different forms. The informal grapevine is a communications network, in most organisations fulfilling the very clear purpose of communicating corporate information which has not (yet) been communicated by official channels. Mueller describes a semi-formal network which he used to great effect, a networking system comprising various subnetworks which might serve particular purposes. For example, within the main file there would be specialists on the market, on technology, on government and so on. The network system was set up carefully and very deliberately by Mueller to help him fulfil his managerial purpose more effectively.

Networks may be internal, connecting individuals and departments which have no other formal organisational links. They may have a physical form, as with electronic networks, operating as important aids to communications. Or they may be external, connecting the organisation with its existing and potential customers, competitors, and technology suppliers, or other external systems such as financial markets. The science park concept derives its strength from networking. Silicon Valley is not just a geographical area, but a network too.

Networks are systems of communications links which overlay the formal organisation and are increasingly replacing it. They may be informal and activated only irregularly, but they are persistent and, most important of all, they are clearly purposive.

External communications, i.e. networks involving customers and technology suppliers, both existing and potential, as well as other networks concerned with competitors though not necessarily involving them directly, are crucial to the achievement of an effective business. Without such networks, the firm's strategy will be based on an inadequate understanding of customer needs, a lack of knowledge about technological developments and an ill-formed view about competitive strengths and weaknesses.

Communications networks are set up directly with the sources of primary information such as customers, suppliers, technology suppliers or less directly related experts who may be useful in providing strategically relevant information in one field or another. As the speed of technological development increases and markets become more global, so the inadequacies of the individual organisation are exposed and the networks become more important, to the extent that they may take over parts of the organisation where their expertise gives them an advantage. Jönnson showed how communications inside problem-solving groups generates commitments to the group which are more binding as the group is seen as more competent, trustworthy and deserving to have its knowledge and opinion taken into account (Jönnson, 1996, and Reading Review 28). Thus there is a self-reinforcing cycle at work, both within and between groups, where norms and practices develop which co-ordinate the groups' activities without the need for external hierarchical control.

Morgan (1993) illustrated the six stages in organisational evolution from mechanistic bureaucracy to loosely coupled networks of autonomous teams, and finally used the spider plant as his favoured metaphor for the modern organisational form.

Networks and teams and collaborations and alliances are all part of the same process: the deconstruction of the purpose-built modern organisation of the mass production era to the fragmented organisational form of today and tomorrow. This organisation is or will be difficult to define in structural terms. Rather it will be more appropriately defined in terms of its culture – 'the way we do things around here' (Bower, 1966).

Continuing the organisational metaphor, Morgan (1993, and Reading Review 23) describes 'the way we do things around here' in terms of the activities of 'strategic termites', nudging, pushing, catalysing, facilitating, initiating, encouraging and supporting activities consistent with the strategic direction. McGill *et al.* (1992, and Reading Review 19) outline the management practices in learning organisations, and Garvin (1993, and Reading Review 24) gives a more operational example of much the same sort of strategy and culture-building activity.

12.4 Organisational culture

As the study of organisational structure has developed to include these many concepts beyond the imagination of classical theorists, it still provides only a limited explanation of behaviour in organisations. The study of organisational culture seems to offer the prospect of a more comprehensive explanation and over the past decade or so has attracted considerable research interest. Bower's 'the way we do things around here' gives the flavour of culture but little hint as to how it can be made operational. Other definitions include:

> *A family of concepts like symbol, language, social drama and ritual.*
>
> (Pettigrew, 1979)

> *The behaviour patterns and standards which bind a social group together and which are built up over many years and is a unifying philosophy, ethic and spirit.*
>
> (White, 1984)

> *A set of basic tacit assumptions about how the world is and ought to be that a group of people share and that determines their perceptions, thoughts, feelings and, to some degree, their overt behaviour.* (Schein, 1996)

These definitions imply a richer description of organisation which could include both the openness and flexibility needed to convert strategic thinking into strategic action, and at the same time, contribute to the sense of direction and 'climate of success', beyond what could be achieved through structure. The meaning that these phrases convey is subjective. To some they may seem to get to the core of what a business is all about; to others they may be meaningless. The concept of culture seems still to be riddled with ambiguities.

To some, the distinction between structure and culture has been purely semantic; to others, culture is shorthand for every conceivable aspect of the organisational scene. It comprises both formal and informal structure: the structure that is overtly decided and the structure which develops apparently of its own accord and comprises social organisation, shared or unshared beliefs and values, informal communication systems, stories, language, a hundred or more factors which become invested with symbolic meaning and which together determine to a large extent the effectiveness of an organisation.

Whatever it is, culture has been widely recognised as hugely important. For example, Brown suggested that 'an organisation's culture has a direct and significant impact on performance ... strategies and structures and their implementation are shaped by ... culture' (Brown, 1995, p. 198). Kanter (1983) identified factors which she described as relating to organisational climate and which can be broadly grouped under the two headings communication and participation. Non-innovative 'segmentalist' firms were characterised by closed communications, hierarchical information flows up and down the line, and by a lack of horizontal interdepartmental communication. Segmentalist firms are also characterised by non-participative systems. By participation Kanter meant persuading (rather than ordering), team building, seeking input from others, showing political sensitivity, willingness to share rewards and recognition.

There is surprisingly little agreement as to what corporate culture actually is and still less about whether it can be managed. Clearly, if it is not a manageable commodity then it is of lesser interest to managers, although even as a metaphor it is a concept which can increase understanding. Alternatively, if it provides the means of changing mechanistic organisations into flexible, innovative, organic ones, it would be an important management tool.

There are two diametrically opposed views as to the nature of culture (Smircich, 1983). One school of thought holds that culture is one of the many variables which make up organisation; this is the 'way we do things around here' brand of culture. It can be changed by management almost as simply as changing the pay system. The other school of thought holds that culture is not an organisational variable, but a way of looking at organisations; a metaphor for the organisation itself; a perspective which provides new insights and fuller understanding as to how the organisation might be managed, but which is not itself manageable.

The term 'culture' originates from anthropology, which according to Webster's Dictionary is 'the study of mankind, especially its societies and customs'. The classic picture is of the nineteenth century researcher, in bush hat and khaki drill shorts, going off to some remote and primitive part of the world to study the customs and practices of some previously unknown native society. The anthropologist sought to identify the customs, rituals, hidden meanings, taken-for-granted assumptions and shared values of the community being studied in such a way that the society could be understood as it really was.

The achievement frequently fell far short of this ideal. Early anthropologists were criticised for their inaccurate descriptions and lack of true understanding. Quite clearly their presence in a small community disturbed the setting – the community studied was not the same as it would have been had the researcher not been present. Also they were not able to avoid their own ideas and perceptions colouring the way they saw things. Even if their description was coldly factual, their selection of what things were important enough to describe, and subsequently their selection of what was important enough to report, was inevitably subjective. They would be unduly influenced by things which they found surprising and thus would give a biased account. To overcome these problems, anthropologists tried to avoid taking anything for granted. They tried to avoid interpretation, concentrating on recording and explaining, as far as possible, in the native's own terms.

Modern researchers still take this same approach: they try above all else to prevent their own experience and personality from biasing their portrayal of the social group being studied, whether it is a tribe in Borneo or a modern public corporation. Organisational anthropology has a further particular cause of bias arising from the fact that, almost without exception, it is in reality undertaken from the standpoint of management, what Burrell and Morgan (1979) refer to as the functionalist paradigm. The traditional researcher might claim a straightforward desire to record the various components of a culture simply in the interest of expanding the store of knowledge. With such an open position it might be possible to approach the native's point of view. The organisational culture researcher is not usually operating in such an open-handed way. He is usually carrying out research for the express benefit, either directly or indirectly, of one group of participants in the organisation: management. A few studies have been undertaken on behalf of other groups such as shopfloor operatives and trade unions, but the overwhelming majority of research has been done for the benefit of management. So far as is known, no modern organisational anthropology has been carried out with the sort of disinterest that, say, a village elder from Borneo might bring to the task.

Consequently there tend to be two fundamentally opposed views as to the nature of organisational culture. The one accepts that it is simply seeking out what there is in the concept that can be manipulated for management's benefit; the other tries, however imperfectly, to use the cultural perspective to increase understanding of organisations for any purpose, including that of management. The former approach appears on the face of it to be the more practical and effective, while the latter approach seeks to achieve a more objective analysis.

The early anthropologists sought out their primitive and isolated societies because they represented in some sense virgin territory. They were small, enclosed groups, as yet unpolluted by contact with other cultures. This not only heightened their potential value as objects of study, but also made that study very much simpler. Every member of the tribe shared much the same experience. All were born in the tribal village, grew up in it, lived in it and eventually died in it. Consequently they shared the same experience, beliefs and understandings, made the same assumptions about their lives, and understood the same symbolic meanings which they attached to their various sayings, rituals and artefacts. In their isolation from other societies they uniquely represented what might be called a monolithic culture.

No group of people in the modern world could achieve a comparable separation, no matter how hard they tried. Modern society is highly cosmopolite and complex in its intercultural relations and a business is possibly more multicultural than most contemporary social organisations. People at work originate from different geographical locations, have different racial backgrounds, differentiated educational experiences and differing economic and social standings. For two-thirds of their lives these factors are dominant. For the other one-third, they form into groups at work which are themselves further differentiated according to which side of the management/worker divide they occupy, the industry they work in, the function they fulfil, the product divisions to which they owe allegiance and in some cases the geographical location of their particular unit. Moreover, they are further subdivided by the professional allegiances they owe outside the business, for example their accounting association, engineering institute or trade union. All these various pressures affect the individual's values and understandings, the symbolic meanings attached to actions, objects and words, even the language which is used.

Language is sometimes made deliberately obscure to exclude members of other subgroupings with the deliberate intention of creating a mystique or a closed shop. Newly emergent specialisms typically use this approach as a means of establishing their professional status, as for example computer specialists did in the 1950s and 1960s. Even without the explicit use of such competitive measures, language frequently acts as a barrier between subcultures. For example, accounting has increasingly become the language of management and some of the jargon has spilled over into the everyday language. The term 'bottom line', for example, is widely used and it has a nuance of tough, unflinching realism. But the real 'bottom line' actually comprises tough, unflinching realities plus value judgements plus guesses. Accounting jargon, like all specialist language, is a barrier to communication across the organisation, even though it may be an efficient shorthand within its specialism.

In such complexity it is clear that organisational culture is not simply homogeneous, but the sum of many subcultures, each of which contributes its own nuances of meaning and its own rituals and images. Although there is a popular view that culture is 'the glue that binds organisation together' (Deal and Kennedy, 1982), it is clear that culture can in fact be divisive just as easily as cohesive. In the absence of any dominant superculture, the various subcultures may well be in conflict with each other. On occasion this conflict may become overt and sometimes highly dysfunctional, but more usually the conflict will be bubbling below the surface. The culture of an organisation is this mixture of cross-cutting subcultures which continually react against each other in some more-or-less cohesive, or divisive, not necessarily stable, equilibrium (Gregory, 1983). In short, culture is a mess which is not necessarily amenable to efficient analysis.

Nevertheless, Peters and Waterman recounted how 'stories, myths and legends appear to be very important, because they convey the organisation's shared values, or culture. Without exception, the dominance and coherence of culture proved to be an essential quality of the excellent companies' (Peters and Waterman, 1982). The implication is that culture can in some way be controlled to make management's desired culture both coherent in itself and dominant over other subcultures.

The idea of culture management seems to imply the sort of approach taken by the great and famous originators of such organisations as IBM, Hewlett Packard, NCR, ITT, Mcdonald's. These businesses all share 'strong', deliberately established and maintained, coherent, dominant 'cultures'. Put another way, each of these organisations appears to have gained the active participation of all their members in fully exploiting their organisation's distinctive competence, whatever it happens to be.

Selznick argued that it is vitally important for an organisation to define its distinctive competence which then becomes the focal point of the organisation's culture (Selznick, 1957). Pascale looked at the way some big firms, (including IBM, ITT, Procter & Gamble, Morgan Guaranty), achieved their 'strong' cultures (Pascale, 1985). He found that these companies all used a systematic process of socialisation for their management recruits, based on the following seven steps:

1. *Careful selection of entry level candidates, based on apparent ability and compatibility with the corporate culture. This implies that right from selection, potential maverick's are filtered out of the system. Relative youth is also a key factor, recruitment straight from university or after a relatively short period, ensures that recruits are still highly suggestible.*
2. *After selection recruits are exposed in their first months to a period of 'humility inducing' experience in order to precipitate self questioning of their prior behaviour, beliefs and values. This is essentially a period of breaking down any potential resistance to accepting corporate values and beliefs. IBM typically put their new recruits through training which puts them under fairly extreme pressure, working through the early hours of the morning on their own material and then going on to help others. Procter and Gamble involved their potentially high flying recruits in colouring in maps of sales territories.*
3. *The third phase involved 'in the trenches' training in one of the core disciplines of the business such as customer support.*
4. *Meticulous attention was given to systems for measuring operational results and rewarding individuals according to their performance.*
5. *Careful adherence was required to the firm's transcendant values, such as the ideals of the firm serving mankind, or providing a first class product for the benefit of society etc. This enables employees to reconcile personal sacrifices necessitated by membership of the organisation.*
6. *A system of reinforcing folklore is provided through legends and interpretations of watershed events in the firm's history that validates its culture and its aims.*
7. *Consistent role models and consistent traits are associated with those recognised as being on the fast track. Firms needed to create high flyers in order to fulfil these role models – the characteristics of high flyers being their visible consistency with corporate values etc., rather than any inherent super ability.*

The success of this seven-step process was apparent in the way employees performed and in particular how they fulfilled the firm's expectations in exploiting its distinctive competence. However, such approaches have been widely criticised because they seem to have elements of 'brainwashing', and their use of culture and symbol possibly has parallels in populist political movements. There is potentially a moral problem in deciding how far it is proper for a firm to go in socialising its employees. But there are other problems with the approach which may be even more pressing.

First, it is important to note that the seven stages provide a systematic, integrated programme: there is no suggestion that any one of the steps can be effective on its own. Attempts have been made to implement 'culture programmes' on a more limited front without success. Attempts to create artificial cultures, by rewriting the company history, creating artificial company stories, circulating overzealous statements of corporate mission, all seem doomed to fail. Reynolds description of the Falcon Computer case has already been referred to. At Falcon, a Silicon Valley computer firm, top management went through the motions of creating a corporate culture. Because the reality differed from the official version it was trying to elaborate, all its attempts were counterproductive and resulted only in increased cynicism and alienation among employees (Reynolds, 1986).

The IBM mainframe engineer of old was persuaded to perform beyond what one might regard as the normal call of duty because of a basic belief that the business was in some way working for the greater good of society. This belief, or value, was deliberately instilled and reinforced during the new employees' induction programme and was centred around the company's distinctive competence, which was the focus of its differentiation strategy, in IBM's case, according to Pascale, customer service. Whether the methods of socialisation are acceptable or not, it is clear that the desired result would not be achieved if employees were unable to believe in the basic integrity of the organisation's strategy.

At a crude level, corrupt and dishonest management destroys the possibility of corporate integrity. Some may believe that getting caught is what matters, and since they are not caught their dishonesty is not known and therefore no harm is done. However, this is a delusion. A dishonest senior manager may never be brought to book for his or her dishonesty despite the fact that almost every member of the organisation knows perfectly well that he or she is regularly abusing their position of trust. It would be most unusual for dishonesty among senior managers not to be known. At the same time it is still unusual for it to be openly acknowledged and punished. Lack of corporate integrity produces only cynicism and alienation among members. With integrity, the strategy of the business becomes the means of achieving consensus among members and concentration of their efforts.

Even if the seven steps identified by Pascale are all carefully implemented and the strong culture successfully created and maintained, the result may be far from ideal. For example, this may explain why IBM, with all its resources, was never in its mainframe heyday known as a technological leader. Strong culture may be merely the contemporary way of achieving the sort of conformity and obedience that was formerly achieved through more overtly autocratic methods of management.

> *The value driven organisation is capable of tight control . . . because the shared values provide a common perspective. . . . Linkage through a shared strategic vision can replace bureaucratic mechanisms of command and control.*
>
> (Leitko and Szczerbacki, 1987)

Conformity appears to be the end result of this process of socialisation, but conformity is only a feature of bureaucracy in another guise and is inappropriate in times of rapid change because it stifles flexibility and innovation.

A more sensitive approach to culture management might involve influencing the cross-cutting of the various subcultures so that they tend to support the culture desired by management. To achieve this, management would define some minimum set of cultural characteristics to which all subcultures should be encouraged to subscribe. A minimum set might consist simply of an understanding of the purpose of the business and its strategic objectives. With this as common ground among all employees, management's cultural role would be firstly to eliminate cultural elements which confuse, or subvert, the understanding and achievement of the purpose and strategic intent of the business and replace them by cultural elements which clarify and expound. By cultural elements is meant the aspects of culture which are made manifest in symbolic form. Now consider the issues raised in Box 12.2.

There have been few thorough surveys of culture management, presumably because of the complexity of the subject. One researcher identified general managers who had been successful over a five-year period and found that only a few undertook activities which they themselves felt could be characterised as 'culture management'. However, those that did were among the top performers (Kotter, 1982). The actions they took, which they regarded as culture management, fell into two categories. First, actions related to items such as leadership and motivation, which would have been

BOX 12.2

Venture Finance International Ltd (2)

So far as strategy was concerned, Apex was anxious that Venture Finance appeared to be drifting away from its original role in providing venture capital in return for equity. This role is attractive to Apex because each investment presents a low risk but in-depth way of assessing future acquisition opportunities. A number of such investments have eventually become full-scale acquisitions and two were subsequently floated with full stock exchange quotations. This was very good business for Apex; however, for Venture Finance management, it is much easier to achieve Apex's no-surprises financial targets by expanding the retail business.

DISCUSSION POINTS

1. As a senior Apex executive how would you propose to encourage Venture Finance to fulfil the strategic role required of it?
2. Should Apex seek to define that strategic role, or is it a matter solely for Venture Finance management? Is it important to Apex what strategic role Venture Finance fulfils, or is it just important whether the business is successful?
3. What inducements or controls can be put in place to lead Venture Finance to give its business the emphasis required by Apex?

taken anyway, without any knowledge or understanding of the culture concept. Secondly, actions which could be much better understood as symbolic rather than cultural. The power of organisational symbols is substantial and, unlike culture, they can often be managed effectively.

12.5 Organisational symbolism

When Michael Edwardes took over the running of the insolvent British Leyland motor company it was in effect being run by the communist-led shop stewards, headed by Derek Robinson, the senior convenor at the Longbridge factory in Birmingham. According to Edwardes, Robinson's thirty-month stewardship had resulted in 523 industrial disputes and cost the company 62,000 cars and 113,000 engines. The climax of these industrial relations was reached when Robinson opposed Edwardes' recovery plan for the company. Although radical and painful, the plan had already been approved by the workforce. Edwardes response to Robinson's opposition was to dismiss him with immediate effect, seeing this as the 'last chance of gaining manageability at Longbridge' (Edwardes, 1982). The dismissal of Robinson was, above everything else, a symbolic act. In all the subsequent discussions with unions over this dismissal, management never wavered from its original decision because of the symbolic importance that any fudging might have had. It was a watershed event in the history of the company, marking the point when management started to manage and the politically motivated local stewards lost control. Robinson had become a symbol of communist-driven worker control challenging management's 'right to manage'. Edwardes recognised that Robinson therefore had to be removed. The story of Robinson's removal itself became a symbol of the firm's step 'back from the brink'.

Symbols are the more-or-less tangible manifestations of culture. Robinson was a symbol of the numerically insignificant militant communist subculture at Longbridge. Within his own subculture he was a hero; to other Leyland subcultures he was a villain; to all subcultures he had come to embody symbolic meaning.

Symbols can be anything: people, words, events, stories, actions or physical objects. What makes them symbolic is the fact that they convey meaning beyond their face value. Many businesses make use of specific events to reinforce culture through symbolic means. The making of long-service awards and the official marking of an employee's retirement can be used to highlight the value the company places on loyalty, its respect for employees and appreciation of their work. Similarly, the making of awards for performance is now widespread. Though 'star employee' recognition by a framed photograph in a public place may not seem very imaginative, award symbols appear to be more powerful in their effect than direct and formal statements of what the company stands for and values. In this instance, actions can certainly speak louder than words.

Culture is manifested through stories or myths, many of which identify the roles of heroes or villains at watershed events in the company history. A common story is about the intimidating old president coming into the workplace and being accosted by an innocent new employee who insists on the proper exercise of company rules no matter if his assailant does claim to be president. In a benign culture the story goes that the president rewards the employee; in a malign one the result is instant dismissal. Stories about the young employee being rewarded for initiative, or the old employee getting his reward for dogged devotion to duty, are repeated in many different organisations (Martin *et al.*, 1987). Some of the stories are created deliberately in order to communicate a particular symbolic meaning. Others seem to originate from some factual basis and are then amended and embroidered over time, so that they communicate some meaningful point about the culture in question.

Management has no monopoly on the creation of potent symbolic stories. For example, the story was told in the 1970s of how a shopfloor operative at a Ford assembly plant collapsed and died and his workmates were forced to carry on working without going to their colleague's assistance for a full ten minutes before the supervisor took any action to see if there was anything wrong with the man (Beynon, 1975). A similar incident had also been reported at another car assembly plant, the only difference being that the length of delay in this latter case was fourteen minutes. The same story has also been repeated in the British steel industry and in iron foundries. The story, in its various versions, may or may not be based on some incident that actually happened, but it is extremely unlikely to be wholly true. Few managements would wish to behave in such a way, and even if they did, very few would have established such iron discipline that would keep people working in such circumstances. The point of the story is clearly symbolic, intended to illustrate the vicious, exploitative nature of management. Where its source has been identified, the story has emanated from 'organised labour' in the form of local union representatives who have clearly seen themselves as in conflict with management.

Symbols do not have to be created by conflicting subcultures to be dysfunctional to management's desired dominant culture; they can arise directly from management either accidentally or gratuitously. Ratner's 'we sell crap' statement referred to in section 9.2 was an inadvertant but powerful symbol for that business. Other accidental symbols may be remnants of a historical position which have become inappropriate over time.

Even symbols which are deliberately created by management may not convey the intended meaning. For example, an incompetently or insincerely performed long-service ceremony is likely to be counterproductive in that the symbolic meaning it communicates is the exact opposite of that intended. In such cases the whole institution of long-service awards could become symbolic of the cynical disregard management has for its employees.

Old established businesses have been notorious for the labyrinthine status symbols they deploy, such as keys to the executive toilets, carpets in offices, size of company car and convenience of allocated parking space, different eating arrangements from the directors' dining room to the works canteen, and so on. All such symbols convey the simple meaning that hierarchy is what matters, not serving the customer.

An understanding of the dynamic equilibrium of culture in an organisation can be used to reinforce the desired or consciously created subculture. Cultural inconsistencies in an organisation can arise both from the head-on conflict of different subcultures and from the unconscious or unintentional 'dropping' of conflicting symbols. By ensuring that symbols of the desired culture convey meanings which are both consistent and dominant they can be made to contribute positively to the concentration on the intended strategic direction.

Moreover, this link between the strategy pursued by an organisation and its culture can be reinforced by the planned use of the more tangible images of the firm's material symbols, such as its products, its logo, its architecture. The elimination of inconsistent images and the reinforcement of consistent ones inevitably contributes to the dominance of the desired culture over other subcultures, so that a positive strategic equilibrium position is achieved.

Even so, organisational culture is hard to change. Once it has matured into a readily recognisable form it develops a robustness which seems impervious to orthodox approaches to organisation development. Deliberate attempts to change the culture have often been unsuccessful. Those successes that have been documented (for example Tunstall, 1983) have been slow and painstaking, and have generally involved a good many mistakes along the way. Not only is culture itself difficult to change, but the stronger the culture the more it tends to inhibit other organisational change.

The most effective means of changing the culture of a business is through symbolic change, from the obvious and crude but effective firing of top management, to the less dramatic, more subtle detailed changes involving the elimination of conflicting symbols and the creation of new, reinforcing symbols.

12.6 Manageable characteristics

Auditing culture is extremely difficult. The 'tacit assumptions about how the world is' are rarely made explicit. People rather infer them through diverse concrete symbols. Moreover, some of these tacit assumptions may contradict overtly stated norms, so people may be reluctant to admit them. Even if these difficulties are overcome, 'the diversity and size of many organisations require us to consider how representative a culture audit's findings really are' (Wilkins, 1983). They may only be representative of one or more subculture in the organisation.

Kanter (1983) identified an aspect of organisational culture that she called 'empowerment' as being a prerequisite of effective innovation in the large US corporations she studied. The word has since been widely used and abused. Her research compared successful and less successful innovators and found that the successful ones had found a way round their own structures and bureaucratic tendencies through empowerment.

Empowerment comprised three ingredients:

1. Resources – funds, materials, space, time, etc.
2. Information – technical and market data, expertise, etc.
3. Support – endorsement, backing, approval and legitimacy.

For empowerment to operate effectively, firms had to have open communications and what Kanter called 'network' forming arrangements which cut across the usual organisational structures.

Communications in an organisation are generally described in terms of being open or closed. When an organisation enjoys open communications it means that communications, both formal and informal, take place across the organisation as well as up and down chains of command. It means that they take place freely between all members of the organisation without restraint and protocol. A chief financial officer may talk to a junior sales clerk without risk of causing any emotional disturbance among other organisation members. Moreover, the junior sales clerk may speak to the president without restraint or inhibition of any kind. Not only may these communications take place, but if communications are open, they actually do.

Closed communications, on the other hand, mean that communications occur only formally up and down direct lines of command, and mainly down. Communication across the organisation would be psychologically loaded and widely perceived as even damaging to career prospects and, consequently, do not occur.

Clearly these descriptions are of extreme cases – in reality organisations steer between the two, but tend in one direction or the other.

The other characteristic associated with empowerment is participation, i.e. the degree to which members of the organisation are involved in the decision-making process. To some extent, consideration of participation overlaps the structural idea of centralisation, but participation goes further into the organisation than structure, being a characteristic of the whole organisation including parts which may be relatively untouched by the decision-taking style adopted by central management.

Problem-solving groups, taskforces, quality circles, or any form of shared responsibility team are all vehicles for increasing the degree of participation which appears prerequisite if organisation members are to contribute to strategic action. Despite these various widely used approaches to establishing effective participation, there are problems and paradoxes in introducing participative systems: participation is something the top orders the middle to do for the bottom.

Kanter found that participation on job-specific issues worked effectively, i.e. improved a firm's effectiveness as an innovator, whereas attempts to provide participation on company-wide issues tended to create alienation and cynicism. Thus the sort of participation which has long been provided through statute in continental Europe, providing for employee representatives on the board of directors, would be likely only to be counterproductive in an American (or most probably British) firm's attempt to innovate.

Kanter found that the participative operation of effective teams was difficult to achieve. Differences in rank, personal calibre, skills, expertise and knowledge could all upset teamwork – the tendency to form a hierarchy applied to problem-solving teams just as it did to the mainstream organisation. Moreover, the fruits of the participatory process were long term. They were realised in terms of a more adaptive, innovative organisation that could respond to, and stay ahead of, the change in its various environments.

Kanter's approach to empowerment and participation tackles the issue of culture management head-on, while the manipulation and control of organisational symbols suggests various practical ways in which the process can be achieved. For a company situation like that of Apex subsidiary Venture Finance, the issues may remain problematic (see Box 12.3).

BOX 12.3

Venture Finance International Ltd (3)

Venture Finance has been approached by a well known computer software firm promoting a new expert loan decision system which has a number of advantages over previous computerised systems. This software eliminates the need to use any judgement or discretion in around 80 per cent of Venture Finance's loan decisions. The software has been used with great success in Germany where counter staff have been trained to use it, thus freeing branch management to do other things. The literature on the system shows a Frankfurt manager doing business on the golf course.

DISCUSSION POINTS

1. As chief executive of Venture Finance, what is your attitude to this new computer software? Is it important or simply a matter for branch managers?
2. Does it have any strategic implications?
3. Could it help your prospects for promotion within Apex?

Summary

- Structure, culture and symbolism provide a perspective on organisations which emphasises the paramount importance of people in turning strategy into action thereby achieving concentration, consistency and flexibility.
- The original structural concepts of standardisation, specialisation, formalisation, configuration and centralisation offer an incomplete description of structure and are not as unambiguous as they are sometimes portrayed.
- Mintzberg's extension of the structural concept, although even less readily measured, produces a potentially usable taxonomy of structural forms. Even allowing the extreme difficulties in accurately measuring structure, some pragmatic prescriptions for management action are apparent.
- The need for organisations to be flexible and innovative has increased the importance of technological collaborations and strategic alliances of all kinds. At the same time, technological specialists have become the key people in the new organisations, rather than the bureaucrats and administrators at the top of the organisational pyramid.
- Organisations can therefore be represented increasingly as sets of relationships between autonomous and semi-autonomous units and individuals. A symphony

orchestra, a termite colony or a spider's web might be a more appropriate metaphor for the contemporary organisation than a machine or a pyramid.

- A valid form of cultural analysis remains problematic. The anthropological approach to analysing culture is not practicable and the validity of less time-consuming approaches to 'culture auditing' is difficult to justify.
- The culture of an organisation is made manifest in the meanings attached to organisational symbols and this seems to provide the key to understanding organisational culture.
- The creation, shaping and elimination of organisational symbols is a feasible enterprise. To some extent managers may do this intuitively, without understanding or overt regard for the symbolic aspect of their actions.
- Overtly adopting the symbolic perspective could provide management with powerful new insights, helping them to influence the behaviour of the organisation.
- Symbol management, including communications, actions and physical objects, including structural characteristics, can ensure that symbolic meanings reinforce strategy rather than undermine it.

Further reading

Burns, T. and Stalker, G.M., *The Management of Innovation*, 3rd edition, Oxford University Press, 1994.

Child, J. and Faulkner, D., *Strategies of Co-operation: Managing alliances, networks and joint ventures*, Oxford University Press, 1998.

Deal, T.E. and Kennedy, A.A., *Corporate Cultures*, Addison-Wesley, 1982.

Chapter 13

Creating innovative teams

The connection between strategy, culture and innovativeness modelled in this chapter is based on an empirical study, in the mainstream of innovation research, of the UK textiles industry.

The model suggests that to be an effective innovator a business must have a focused strategy. In addition, it is highly advantageous to have a progressive culture.

A focused strategy requires that a business has a clear strategic direction, good external communications, a long-term orientation, expertise in its core technologies and a focus on the needs of customers.

A progressive culture requires that a business enjoys an empowering management philosophy, high corporate integrity, encourages involvement in leadership decisions and motivates commitment to achievement of the aims of the business.

These are not factors which are espoused simply by top management, rather they are felt by everyone in the business.

The model indicates ways of improving innovativeness.

13.1 Introduction

In considering strategic change and action we have looked in some detail at the way technological change occurs inside organisations and its impact on those organisations. Pursuit of a strategic direction during a period of rapid change imposes different pressures on management than in more stable conditions. The need to be concentrated on a singular strategic direction remains but it is made more

BOX 13.1
Innovation research

Since the Second World War there has been an increasing interest in the problems of industrial innovation. In 1956 a British government sponsored report was published (Carter and Williams, 1956) based on investigations in 269 firms and 4 separate industries. By 1962, Everett Rogers was able to refer to 405 innovation studies in his book *Diffusion of Innovations*. In the second edition published in 1971 this number had quadrupled to 1500. The third edition in 1983 referred to over 3,000 and the fourth edition in 1995 to approaching 4,000. Some of these studies were obscure and of little practical use, but there were also 2,297 empirical studies and these, plus many more since, have generated a much deeper understanding of the processes of innovation and the prerequisites for success.

Source: Rogers, 1983

difficult by the new imperative to be flexible and innovative. These can be achieved only through quite different structures and cultural arrangements.

Aspects of structure and culture management have been suggested in the previous chapter. This chapter focuses on a simple 'competitive model' which combines specifically defined versions of 'strategy' and 'culture' which can be managed in order to improve the innovativeness of organisations. The 'competitive model' is described in operational detail elsewhere (Pearson, 1992), but it is introduced here because it encapsulates many of the ideas which are fundamental to this current text. The model is based on a very large number of studies of how businesses have succeeded or failed to be competitive, innovative and flexible (see Box 13.1).

Not surprisingly, these studies do not all agree as to the critical components, but there is an emerging consensus on which the 'competitive model' is based. It is concerned largely with two clusters of organisational characteristics which can, to some degree, be managed and controlled. The two clusters have been given labels of convenience as follows:

- *Strategy*, which is about people in the organisation knowing what the organisation is intended to achieve and how it aims to achieve it.
- *Culture*, which is about engaging the intelligence, expertise and commitment of people in achieving the strategy.

These are not intended to be general definitions of the two terms, but are commonsense descriptions of the two clusters of organisational characteristics which were identified in this particular piece of research.

Before they can be of practical use these characteristics must be capable of measurement so that a firm can see how it appears to perform; this is the purpose of the 'competitive model'.

The assessment of strategy is achieved in terms of being focused or dispersed. A focused strategy is where a business is clear about its intent and all the members of the business know and understand what that strategy is and how it is to be achieved.

The measurement of culture is made in terms of being progressive or traditional. A progressive culture is one where the people have the freedom to take initiatives and are personally involved in, and committed to, the achievement of organisational aims.

Both culture and strategy are composite characteristics which comprise a number of factors. A focused strategy comprises a clear strategic direction and position, an openness to external communications, an orientation to long-term development, awareness of customer needs and desires, knowledge and use of appropriate technology, acquisition and development of core organisational competences, understanding of competitive products and competences and the ability to put all these together in order to deliver real value in the business product or service.

Similarly, a progressive culture is defined for this model as comprising a particular philosophy about people in business organisations, a consistently upheld corporate integrity, the participation of people in decision-making and their involvement in leading the organisation, and their proactive commitment to the strategic aims of the business.

The model can be drawn as a two-dimensional matrix as shown in Figure 13.1. The four quadrants of the matrix contain quite distinct but readily recognisable types of organisation. Intuitively it might be expected that the most advantageous position would lie within quadrant 2, the progressive, focused quadrant, and that the model should indicate ways of positioning an organisation in that quadrant.

Although the competitive model was drawn directly from a single, obscure research, its real provenance is broad based and its findings not only compatible with the general thrust of innovation research but also, as should become clear, echoed by much of the organisational and strategy literature which has been the basis of the rest of this text.

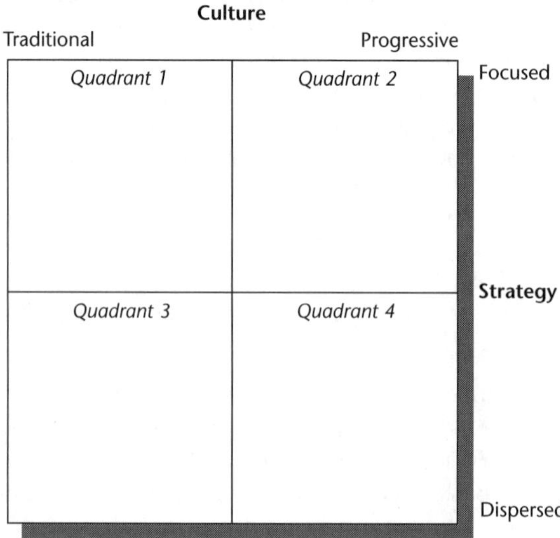

Figure 13.1 The competitive matrix

Before looking at the matrix overall it will be useful to describe the two dimensions in some detail so that the model and its use can be better understood.

13.2 The strategy dimension

The five main components of strategy were identified as:

1. Strategic direction
2. External communications
3. Long-term orientation
4. Core competence
5. Customer focus

Each of these components itself comprises various subsidiary elements. The importance of strategic direction has been repeatedly identified in many innovation studies (for example, Holloman, 1967; Robertson, 1973; Hopkins, 1981; Cooper, 1982). If strategic direction is stated clearly and is well understood by people in the organisation it can achieve a real concentration of resources, efforts and enthusiasm on progressing in that direction. Moreover, if it is maintained consistently over time it can in due course serve to define a known strategic position which will itself work to sustain the strategic direction. Thus within this one factor there is a virtuous cycle which will tend to reinforce itself once established.

The importance of external communications has been consistently identified from Carter and Williams (1956) on. Nevertheless, it is often overlooked by firms who may give merely lip service to the concept without making any real attempt to exploit the opportunities which are available to them. Some of these opportunities arise from routine transactions of the business. The firm's direct relations with suppliers, customers and technology suppliers proceed whether or not the firm makes any deliberate efforts to maximise its learning from the process. In many cases, relations with competitors are also an essential part of normal business operations, whether they are in the form of fairly routine collaboration, or through the auspices of a trade association or industry research body. Again, few businesses manage these relations with the intention of maximising corporate learning. Every firm also has interactions in a broader context, the political, social, economic and most importantly the technological environments which may critically determine the future of the business. A firm may adopt a variety of approaches to external communications ranging from straightforward avoidance to a proactive programme of networking and systematic analysis of secondary sources.

Long-term orientation has also often been identified as a key factor in innovativeness (for example, Carter and Williams, 1956; Myers and Marquis, 1969; Project SAPPHO, 1972). It is simple to describe but apparently difficult to achieve. It is not easy, in the face of short-term external pressures, notably from institutional shareholders, to espouse and focus all attention on long-term objectives which by their nature are not expressed in financial terms such as earnings per share or return on investment. The average quoted British business pays out around twice as much dividend as its German counterpart and three times as much as its Japanese competitor. Long-term orientation is therefore not easy to achieve consistently, but consistency is exactly what is required if firms are to maintain their position in the technology race.

The achievement and nurturing of valuable core competences is also widely identified in empirical research as a crucial component of innovativeness. Although the terminology used was slightly different the early studies (for example, Carter and Williams, 1956; Centre for Study of Industrial Innovation, 1971; Project SAPPHO, 1972) all highlighted the importance of technological sophistication, pre-dating Prahalad and Hamel (1990) by several decades. Core competences can be acquired through long-term investment in technology, either directly through R&D or, increasingly, indirectly through collaboration. The first stage in achieving core competences is awareness of global technological and market developments. The second stage may be through direct investment in technology development or through the spreading of these costs by way of collaborative arrangements or some form of strategic alliance. However they are achieved, it is clear that the establishment of core competences rather than the pursuit of some quantified financial target, is the driving force of strategic development.

The last key component of strategy is customer focus which again has been widely identified in the innovation research literature including all those referred to above as well as Peters and Waterman (1982), Chisnall (1997) and many others. Development of core competences which are not related to delivering value to the customer is futile (Hamel and Prahalad, 1989). Long-term orientation which is independent of the long-term development of customers and their needs is unlikely to provide any benefit. External communications which are unrelated to providing the customer's needs are unlikely to be particularly useful. And strategic direction which is not aimed at beating competitors in serving the customer will not provide an adequate focus for concentration and consistency.

If all these elements are present then the organisation is likely to have a focused strategy, i.e. members know what the organisation is trying to achieve and how they can contribute to its achievement.

13.3 The culture dimension

The four components of culture have been identified as:

1. Empowerment
2. Corporate integrity
3. Involvement in leadership
4. Motivation to commitment

These different elements of culture intertwine and overlap to form a more-or-less seamless web. The empowerment of people, integrity, involvement and commitment to the organisation cannot be separated in the work situation, but are just different aspects of the organisation's character or culture. The North East General Hospital is a running illustration of the issues of structure and culture which are discussed in this and the preceding chapter and it will be helpful to consider the issues raised in Box 13.2 at this point.

BOX 13.2

North East General Hospital

At the North East General Hospital the routine system for carrying out blood and urine tests on ward patients was as follows:

1. Consultant's morning visit to patient results in request for blood or urine tests.
2. Ward nursing staff take sample from patient.
3. Sample bottle is despatched to laboratory.
4. Laboratory staff carry out tests and complete analysis report.
5. Laboratory report is returned to patient's ward and added to patient's notes.
6. Consultant looks at report on next ward visit.

In more than 60 per cent of cases the report was returned to the ward on the day *after* the consultant's morning visit, there thus being a 48-hour delay from the time the consultant requested the analysis and it being read by the consultant. The remaining 40 per cent of cases, including all identified as urgent, were processed within 24 hours.

A recent technological innovation could provide instantaneous results from blood and urine tests. The new equipment carried out a full analysis completing all routine tests in a matter of seconds. Moreover, it could be operated by non-specialist staff after a brief period of training. Thus, using the new technology it would be possible for ward nursing staff to provide the blood analyses while the consultant was still with the patient on the ward.

This new instantaneous method had a number of advantages:

1. It was quicker, thus speeding up the process of returning the patient to full health.
2. It was cheaper to operate.
3. It freed the laboratory staff from a significant amount of routine work and allowed them to concentrate on more important jobs.

DISCUSSION POINTS

From the point of view of the patient and the consultant the new system appears to be wholly beneficial with no apparent disadvantages.

1. Are there any disadvantages or problems with the new system from the points of view of other parties involved?
2. Which group is the most important in this situation?
3. What, from a strategic point of view, would be the most satisfactory outcome?

The foundation of culture is the management philosophy which may be oriented, on the one hand, to empowerment or, on the other, to authoritarian control. Many researchers have identified this dichotomy, for example McGregor's Theory X and Theory Y (McGregor, 1960) and in the field of education Carl Roger's progressive and traditional approaches to learning (Rogers, 1969). It is not simply a style of management which can be put on or discarded as the situation demands, but is bone deep and constant. An empowering philosophy is one of the fundamental beliefs on which the organisation is managed.

Also permeating every aspect of the organisation's activities, and particularly its various relations with the outside world, is the level of corporate integrity. There is rich support for this in the ethics literature which has already been referred to in sections 1.6 and 3.3 and by Hosmer (1994, and Reading Review 27). This too is bone deep, not simply a tool which can be used when needed and disposed of when inconvenient. These two, empowerment and integrity, influence every aspect of organisational life and activity.

There is a similarly rich supporting research for the other two characteristics of culture. Involvement in leadership has been thoroughly studied and the competitive model's dichotomy is supported in the leadership literature (for example, Lewin *et al.*, 1939; Blake and Mouton, 1964; Evans, 1970, 1974; House and Dessler, 1974; Kotter, 1990; Ferguson, 1990). The supporting literature on motivation is probably the richest of all (for example, Maslow, 1943; McLelland *et al.*, 1953; Atkinson, 1964; Vroom, 1964; Alderfer, 1972; Lawler, 1973; Mitchell, 1974; Campbell and Pritchard, 1976; Hackman and Oldham, 1980).

Each of these four characteristics making up the 'culture' dimension can be measured along the same axis from progressive to traditional (using Roger's terminology). A progressive organisational culture could achieve a profile which is fairly even across all four characteristics.

In these two sections describing the culture and strategy dimensions of the matrix, some attention has been given to providing corroborative references. These have been given without any substantial account being provided here: that is available elsewhere (see Pearson, 1992). The purpose here is simply to indicate that the competitive model, though apparently obscure in its immediate origins, is actually in line with the mainstream of empirical work in these areas.

13.4 The matrix

The interpretation of the two dimensions of the matrix have now been summarised. The components of strategy are measured along a continuum from focused to dispersed. A focused strategy is where everyone in the organisation knows what the organisation is trying to achieve and how to achieve it. Similarly, the components of the culture dimension are measured along a continuum from traditional to progressive. A progressive culture is one based on a philosophy of empowerment and integrity where people are involved in leadership according to their skills and capabilities and where they are motivated to a commitment to the organisation's strategic aims. The various locations on the matrix (which can be identified using the questionnaires in Pearson (1992)) indicate the necessity for specific management action which is discussed later.

Strategy is knowledge intensive. To have a focused strategy suggests having knowledge about customers, suppliers, competitors and technology, about the economy, government regulation, demographic and social trends and about what is going to happen to all these in the medium and long term. It requires detailed understanding of the customers' needs and perceptions and of what is required to satisfy these needs. It requires the identification and acquisition of the requisite core competences and their application in the pursuit of a strategic intent which everyone in the organisation can understand and identify with. A competitive organisation will have this knowledge and achieve this focus in its strategy. Many organisations may be strong in some areas, few achieve consistency over all five aspects of strategy.

In many organisations, top management is clear about the organisation's strategic direction, but few of the other members of the organisation share that clarity. As a consequence, the few big one-off investments are made in a consistent way which reinforces top management's avowed direction, but other decisions are made randomly. All the daily, mini-resource allocation decisions, the efforts and enthusiasms of people throughout the organisation are pragmatic, with no coherent strategic focus. As a consequence resources tend to get misallocated.

A firm aiming to be a leader in quality nevertheless operates its whole management ethos on the basis of strict budgetary control. The reward systems within the organisation serve to reinforce low costs as the organisational paradigm, rather than the stated aim of high quality. As a result when an employee is confronted with a minor decision which trades cost against quality, he or she decides wrongly in favour of reducing costs.

Thus it is important that the organisation's strategy is focused so that *everyone* knows and agrees what it is trying to achieve. Similarly the strategy profile also has to be consistent, i.e. a focused direction has to be supported by focused knowledge, competence and customer orientation.

Similar considerations apply with the culture dimension. The profile has to be held by all members of the organisation and held consistently across all four factors. Inconsistency in one factor leads to dissonance with the other factors and the loss of a progressive culture. This is most easily exampled by considering the impact of low integrity on the other aspects of culture and particularly its potentially corrosive effects on the involvement and commitment of organisation members. A management which is seen not to practise what it preaches in terms of integrity is not only likely to lose the commitment of its members, but also to actively encourage their disillusion.

The best innovators were found in the original research to be located in quadrant 2 of the matrix, the focused/progressive quadrant. In Figure 13.2 this has been annotated *innovative teams* which, like the other labels shown, were applied by respondents in the original research to their own organisation. This is the quadrant that accommodates those organisations which are best adapted to today's environment of rapid technological development, change and global competition.

The management actions which are implied by the model are those which would achieve a repositioning of the organisation into the innovative teams quadrant of the matrix.

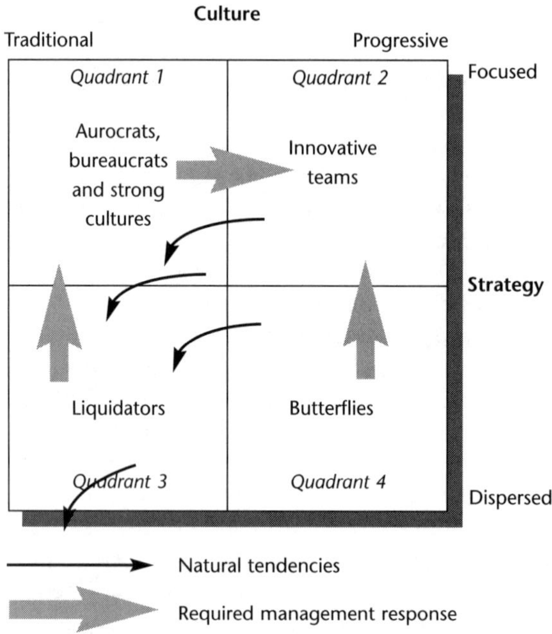

Figure 13.2 The competitive matrix: natural tendencies and management responses

The matrix positions are important, but the individual factors which make up an organisation's strategy and culture profiles are, in terms of management action, even more important. Two companies with identical overall culture scores may well have quite different scores at the level of the individual components and therefore require different management initiatives in order to change the overall position in regard to culture.

The innovative team concept seems to encapsulate the essence of the progressive/focused quadrant 2, the teamwork being facilitated by the progressive culture and the target for innovation by the focused strategy. Typically, the management of such an organisation takes deliberate steps to achieve its progressive culture. For example, such firms will generally take explicit initiatives in their corporate communications strategy, involving both regular consultation meetings with employees and formal briefings involving every member of the organisation. In addition, every member of the organisation who has responsibility for the work of a group or team, no matter how small, is likely to receive communications training. In all quadrant 2 organisations there is strong evidence of effective open communications, across the organisation as well as two-way communication up and down the management line.

A high-scoring quadrant 2 organisation may well not have a recognisable management line or chain of command which extends from the top of the organisation to the bottom, or at least not one which matters very much to organisation members. Many such firms are adopting a project team approach to management of all but the most routine problems. Even firms in the motor industry – the spiritual home of stan-

BOX 13.3

North East General Hospital (2)

The new technology would require a change in working practices, and hospital staff, like the rest of us, prefer not to have to change the way they do things unless they see it as in their own interests, or, in some circumstances, as being for the greater good.

DISCUSSION POINTS

Consider the implied changes in working practices firstly for the nursing staff and, secondly, for the laboratory staff. Which are likely to create the greatest problems? Why?

dardisation, mass production, scientific management and the machine bureaucracy – have achieved some success by organisation through work teams. A hospital is a very different form of organisation but still has many of the problems of the machine bureaucracy with its different groups of internal stakeholders not necessarily working as co-operating teams. Box 13.3 provides an opportunity to consider this issue further.

Nevertheless, progressive management practices are becoming more widely used, not merely in terms of the organisation of routine work but also, as has been noted, more particularly in the improvement and development of business organisation, with a direct and consequential result in terms of member involvement and commitment to strategic aims.

Firms in the traditional/quadrant (quadrant 1) appear to fall into three broad categories: autocrats, bureaucrats and strong cultures. A firm which tends towards the autocratic form of traditional culture, dominated by a single top manager, was found in the original research to be an effective innovator and competitor. A bureaucracy, on the other hand, is the antithesis of innovative. Being competitive through the exercise of bureaucratic rules is a contradiction in terms, even if the rules have been drawn up in a way which is designed to ensure a high degree of strategic focus. In contrast, the autocracy does not necessarily contain this fundamental contradiction of innovativeness. It may be extremely inhibiting to members of the organisation and make it very difficult for them to be innovative and competitive in the face of change. However, the autocrat him or herself has maximum freedom. He or she can make the rules, take instant and personal decisions, pass instructions to his subordinates and anticipate rapid and total compliance.

The effectiveness of an autocracy as a competitor and innovator depends very much on the effectiveness of the autocrat. It is possible, in certain circumstances, that the autocrat can provide the organisation with the strategic focus required to be innovative. However, such circumstances are specific and limited, first, to small organisations (which are frequently the creation of a single person who presides over every aspect during the early phase of growth), and secondly, to organisations in crisis, where quick, decisive action is the key to survival. Either situation is unstable and cannot be counted on to last for long.

Autocracy may be an unattractive position even for the autocrat. In the original research one such described his business ruefully as, 'in terms of senior management it's a bit of a one man band.' He was clearly aware of the potential difficulties that the organisation was vulnerable to as a consequence. If he was successful, the company would rapidly become too big for the present structure and management arrangements to cope with. Moreover, he was also aware of his own mortality.

Not only was the chief executive aware of these problems but he was also endeavouring to address them as best he could. He had become very interested in the subject of organisational culture and saw the possibility of creating a 'strong culture' as the best solution. The precise meaning of strong culture in this context was not completely clear, although it appeared to be a deliberate attempt to create the effect of infrastructure and order without the problems associated with the traditional bureaucratic approach. Strong culture was certainly seen in some way as inducing a high degree of control if not motivation among organisation members to become involved in decision-making and committed to the aims identified by the chief executive.

In the traditional/focused quadrant it seems apparent that the autocracy could be competitive and innovative, depending on the nature of the autocrat. Bureaucracies would be largely incapable of the flexibility to compete and innovate. Strong cultures, although not fully defined, would seem to accumulate essentially the same characteristics as bureaucracies and thus to be ill equipped for competing in a fast-changing environment.

Organisations positioned in the dispersed half of the matrix appear unlikely to be effective innovators whatever their culture profile. This is because either they have espoused strategic aims which are incapable of concentrating resources and efforts, or they appear to have no consistent set of strategic aims at all. In the former category were firms driven by purely financial targets such as return on capital employed, asset growth, profit margins. These firms invariably fall into the traditional/dispersed quadrant (quadrant 3). Dominated by financial considerations, they are likely to have a rigid, though not necessarily autocratic, culture. Hayes and Garvin (1982) showed that a company driven by financially stated aims tended to be a liquidator, going down what they identified as 'the disinvestment spiral'. They might espouse a strategy of cost leadership, which becomes a mind-set and as a consequence leads down the liquidator's path.

Quadrant 3 may also include relatively new start-ups still struggling to get past the stage of vulnerability to infant mortality. The concepts of liquidation and disinvestment are all too pressing to such firms if they experience any adverse movements in their environment (economic slump, high interest rates and so on) and it is vital that these young businesses make full use of such financial criteria if they are to survive. At this early stage of their evolution, however, entrepreneur's are still very clear about their business purpose and have a personal commitment to the strategic direction on which they were set when the business was created. Thus, although such firms are in the liquidator quadrant of the competitive matrix, a more focused strategy is on 'hold', pending successful negotiation of the minefield of infancy. Some of these firms will therefore progress to the traditional/focused quadrant (quadrant 1) in due course. Others will be forced to follow the liquidator route.

Other types of organisation falling into the dispersed half of the matrix, may have progressive cultures but less clear and consistent strategies. Organisations in the progressive/dispersed quadrant (quadrant 4) might sometimes appear to have clearly stated aims, but still change 'from day to day', with the consequence that members would be unaware of the strategic aims, or at least the current ones, and the organisation would be unable to concentrate action and resources consistently in order to achieve the strategic aims.

A respondent from one such organisation in the original research described the company's management as 'nice guys, but . . .' and went on to suggest that in his view they were insufficiently decisive and unprepared to be ruthless. A stereotypical example of this quadrant was described as a 'butterfly – always flitting from one project to another with no consistency over time.' In this company it seemed clear that innovativeness was enabled through a progressive culture, but in the absence of focused strategy, the company failed to be innovative. Not only that, but over time, members of the organisation became progressively more disillusioned and even alienated, and an increasingly high management turnover rate resulted.

Whilst it is again emphasised that the matrix is an aggregate device, the annotations serve as shorthand for certain intuitively recognisable organisational types representative of the four quadrants. In the original research there was no evidence of competitive innovative organisations being positioned in the dispersed strategy half of the matrix. It seems that a focused strategy is a prerequisite of the competitive organisation. For an organisation positioned in the dispersed area, the required management action would be to achieve a focused strategy.

A progressive culture, on the other hand, was not necessarily a prerequisite of innovativeness, but the autocratic innovator is less robust and reliable, for the reasons already identified, than the innovating team. The traditional/focused quadrant (quadrant 1) is thus less desirable than the progressive/focused quadrant (quadrant 2). Management action for any traditional/focused company should therefore focus on achieving a progressive style in order to achieve a more reliable and robust performance as a competitor and innovator.

Organisations are subject to a number of apparently natural tendencies as they mature. They are not inevitable, and most of them certainly not desirable, but sufficient firms appear to succumb to them that they have given rise to an orthodox wisdom about the likely characteristics of a mature organisation.

A young organisation, in a rapidly developing industry, is likely to be entrepreneurial, flexible and highly innovative. In terms of the competitive matrix, such a firm would seem likely to fall either into quadrant 1 if run by a single individual, or into quadrant 2 – an innovative team. As it grows up and its innovation slows down, it typically starts to surround itself with various institutional practices, rules and regulations, pecking orders and so on, i.e. to become bureaucratic. There is thus an apparently natural tendency to migrate from the innovating team of quadrant 2 to the bureaucrats of quadrant 1. Moreover, as the organisation becomes even more mature, it becomes less and less flexible; it starts to ration investment strictly to cost-cutting items in order to remain competitive. Thus there is a natural tendency for the quadrant 1 firm to migrate to quadrant 3 where the focus is strictly on short-term financial performance. In due course, management of a quadrant 3 firm almost inevitably becomes the responsibility of financial specialists who, when results decline, may feel they can make better use of the assets elsewhere. The business therefore starts down the disinvestment spiral which leads ultimately off the matrix altogether. Thus there is a natural tendency, as businesses mature, to migrate from quadrant 2 to quadrant 1 to quadrant 3 and, finally, to extinction.

It also seems clear that firms in quadrant 4 cannot stay there for long – their waste of corporate assets is too prolific. They are likely to run out of funds in due course and at that stage are likely to be forced into a financial strait-jacket in order simply to survive. Thus there is a natural tendency for quadrant 4 firms, if they survive long enough, to migrate to quadrant 3.

The direction of these natural tendencies is indicated in Figure 13.2, together with the directions of management thrusts required to counteract these tendencies and to achieve the most advantageous positioning for effective competition and innovation. The direction of these natural tendencies is widely accepted and understood, but the appropriate management responses may be less clear. Box 13.4 presents the problem within the North East General Hospital and the question of how its working culture can be modified so that the different internal stakeholders co-operate for the overall benefit of the hospital and the fulfilment of its strategy.

BOX 13.4

North East General Hospital (3)

The purchase of such test equipment is in practice controlled by laboratory management. It initiates and evaluates all such equipment and makes recommendations as to purchase. Its recommendations are invariably accepted, limitations on funding being the only reason why investment is sometimes delayed.

DISCUSSION POINTS

1. As a senior member of the laboratory staff you have been asked to make a recommendation as to whether the new equipment should be purchased. What additional information do you require before making a recommendation?
2. What new working practices will be necessary if the new equipment is to be fully exploited and the patient to be given the full benefits?
3. Assuming that the cost of the equipment is not prohibitive, what recommendation would you be likely to make?
4. What problems do you foresee in using the new equipment?

13.5 Repositioning

In terms of the competitive matrix, the position to be aimed for is high up in the progressive/focused quadrant which is labelled innovative teams. The competitive model suggests how organisations falling outside that quadrant may take action to reposition themselves. Some of these actions are straightforward. However, the sort of management action required to modify structural and cultural characteristics may be problematic. It is these factors which appear to impact directly on the way that people in organisations behave. In general, the required action is intended to create new, fluid structures to replace older, more rigid systems.

For firms which appear relatively stable it may be sufficient to adopt ways round the existing organisation. There are a number of permanent and temporary structures which can be adopted to achieve an innovative subpart of the organisation while not interfering with the control orientation of the main business. For most firms, however, these partial approaches will not be enough. What is required is to make the whole organisation entrepreneurial. The following sections discuss the main repositioning moves to create a focused progressive organisation suited to the conditions of the 1990s.

13.5.1 Repositioning butterflies

Butterflies are quadrant 4 organisations. They enjoy a progressive culture but lack a focused strategy. Top management in these organisations is often extremely intelligent and well educated, but sometimes too idealistic. Its basic philosophy is based on the seemingly enlightened ideas of recruiting the right people and giving them both the freedom and resources to do the job. The assumption is that satisfactory results will automatically follow. It seems rarely to work out like that. The difficulty is that the organisation needs to know what it is trying to achieve and the strategic intent needs to be understood and supported by the people in the organisation. Obvious though this may seem, there are many butterfly organisations where skilled, intelligent, motivated people are progressively reduced to alienation by a lack of coherent direction.

The difficulty is that people will be unlikely, spontaneously, to agree and work to a focused strategy. The establishment of a strategic focus can be a long and painstaking process. It may involve the development of some formality in planning in order to establish strategic direction, together with some formal monitoring system to maintain a measure of how effectively resources, efforts and enthusiasm are being concentrated and how consistently over time. It may involve the setting up of external communications, as well as a formal means of identifying and acquiring core competences, all focused on the satisfaction of customer needs which again require formally identifying and linking with the other initiatives.

Setting up these explicitly formal systems is the main task in repositioning a butterfly into the innovative teams quadrant (see Figure 13.3). The systems have to be formal. Otherwise, in a 'butterfly' they simply will not happen. Formality is a characteristic of bureaucracy, not of progressive cultures. The sort of creative, intelligent

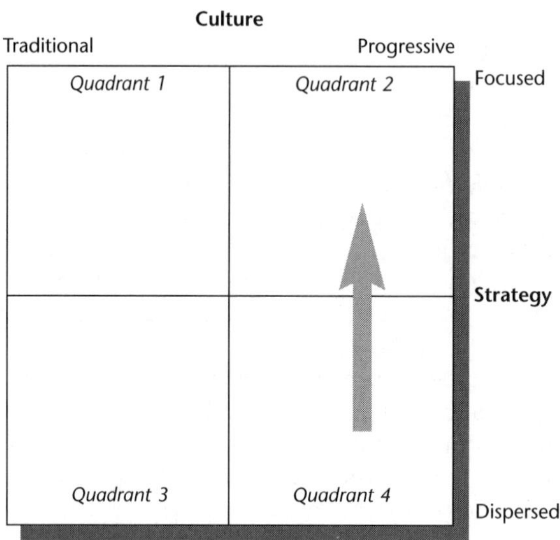

Figure 13.3 Repositioning butterflies

people who are likely to be found in butterfly organisations may well be temperamentally unsuited to formal systems, or anything that smells of bureaucracy. This is the main difficulty in effecting any repositioning moves: the imposition of any systems which might be construed as bureaucratic is likely to be met with strong resistance.

The alternative, retaining a dispersed strategy is, however, not a long-term option. The inevitable lack of financial performance is bound in due course to force a change on the organisation. More often than not, this will be the imposition of strict financial controls. Thus, rather than frittering resources away in a random scatter, the organisation will cease to invest except where essential to survival. This natural tendency to migrate towards quadrant 3, does nothing to solve the underlying problem of the butterfly organisation, but may disguise the fact that lack of a focused strategy is the basic problem, caused by whatever the survey responses suggest need to be rectified before a coherent strategic direction can be concentrated on with any consistency.

Formal systems are necessary for the move from quadrant 4, but without bureaucratic excess. The aim is solely to focus the strategy without stifling initiative and creativity. But the approach has to be formal and timetabled because if it is not then it will not happen. Recognition of the butterfly before it becomes a liquidator may provide a sufficient opportunity for management to reposition the organisation in quadrant 2.

13.5.2 Repositioning liquidators

In the case of liquidators, it is clear that both culture and strategy need to be changed in order to achieve a position in quadrant 2. There are few successful examples of firms which have achieved this double change simultaneously.

Within quadrant 3 are organisations which are managed entirely through the imposition of short-term financial controls. There are organisations which may be unwitting liquidators, which in order to reduce costs to remain competitive relinquish the possibility of ever regaining real competitive capability. They are the firms which have developed a cost leadership mind-set; which are sliding down the disinvestment spiral; which have not foreseen the logical conclusion of their short-term decisions.

In addition, there are those organisations which are clearly in crisis and for which either turnaround or closure is the obvious choice. With these firms there is nothing unwitting about the imposition of short-term financial controls: the intended outcome is simply survival. Without that there is no long term and so long-term considerations are deliberately put on the back burner. Some of these organisations do not survive. Those that do either struggle on under continuous threat of extinction or are enabled to raise their sights above survival and embark on a programme which could ultimately reposition them in the innovating teams quadrant.

The difficulty of achieving a double change in both strategy and culture is usually overcome by approaching them sequentially. For example, for a firm which is struggling back from extinction with a position in quadrant 3, the first change that is made is to identify an appropriate strategic focus, thus making the move from quadrant 3 to quadrant 1 (see Figure 13.4). Only subsequently would the management turn its attention to the cultural issue to move from quadrant 1 to quadrant 2. These moves have been identified in many cases of recovery. They may be the only responses that can be made in that situation, all other responses being likely to lead to termination of the business either directly or after a painful period of liquidation. Slatter (1984) identified the four phases in corporate recovery:

1. *The analysis phase* – problem identification and initial decision as to immediate actions.

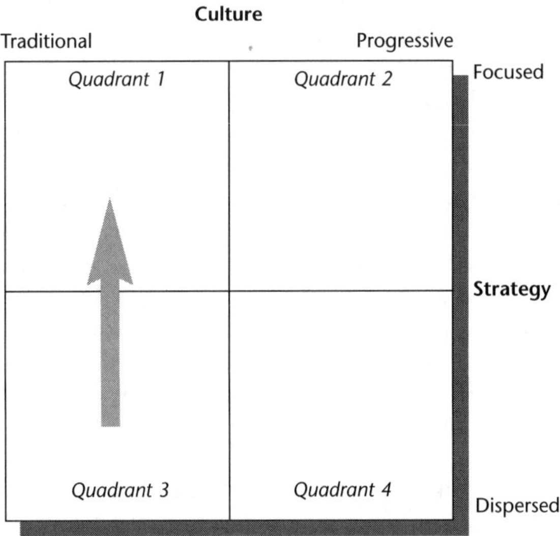

Figure 13.4 Repositioning liquidators

2. *The emergency phase* – actions necessary to ensure survival, e.g. emphasis on cashflow and tight central financial control.
3. *The strategic change phase* – focus on product market segments where the organisation has greatest competitive advantage, study of long-term viability of business.
4. *The growth phase* – growth organically, by new product development or by acquisition, on the back of a recovered balance sheet.

This progression is probably fairly representative of successful turnarounds. Not surprisingly it focuses on the first phase of change which takes the organisation from liquidator (quadrant 3) to quadrant 1. The cultural change which has to follow if the organisation is to become truly entrepreneurial goes beyond the turnaround situation.

13.5.3 Repositioning autocrats, bureaucrats and strong cultures

Both of the repositioning moves described above are relatively simple. In both cases the organisations concerned are in crisis. The butterfly organisation will typically find itself unable to retain good people, and if it does then it will be uncomfortably aware that those people are demotivated. This is the best butterfly position. Most probably they will also perceive the lack of financial results and recognise the inevitable consequences. The liquidator, on the other hand, is an organisation already on the brink of disaster. In both cases, the necessity for action is apparent to all. And in both cases the aim of the action should be to take the organisation away from the brink, so that it can stop liquidating and start to invest in its long-term future.

Repositioning a quadrant 1 organisation is much more difficult. The necessity for action is not immediately apparent, especially to the top management or autocrat. The organisation may be extremely successful. It may have achieved good financial results and see a good future for its core business. Nevertheless it should be clear that such organisations are not best able to engage the talents and enthusiasms of their highly skilled knowledge workers. Moreover, the autocrat category remains vulnerable to the limitations or even mortality of the individual autocrat.

In order to move from quadrant 1 to the innovative teams quadrant (see Figure 13.5), structure has therefore to be circumvented by one means or another and its inhibiting pressures avoided. This can be done by setting up a separate structure within the main organisation where the normal control-oriented rules can be relaxed and different organisational rules and norms apply to the unit specifically charged with the task of innovating or 'entrepreneuring'. The main organisation can continue to be managed on a traditional basis in order to maintain tight financial and management control without inhibiting the entrepreneurial unit. Such arrangements might be temporary or permanent.

This approach was popularised by Peters and Waterman (1982) who suggested that company performance could be aided by simultaneously 'loose–tight' organisational structures. It was repeated by Kanter (1983) who suggested parallel structures, a 'mechanistic' organisation for maintaining the existing business and an organic organisation, in parallel, for initiating change. Such organisation structures

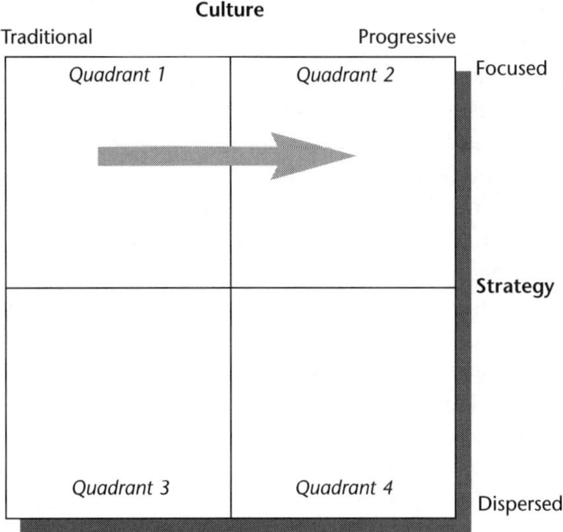

Figure 13.5 Repositioning autocrats, bureaucrats and strong cultures

are widely held to be important determinants of the company's innovative role and performance.

The idea of parallel, or matrix, structures can take many different forms. The critical variations relate to the degree of centralisation or decentralisation of control and the degree of permanence of organisational arrangements. For example, in a multidivision company with centralised control, responsibility for product innovation might be held within the central corporate planning function. By contrast, responsibility might be decentralised so that each division controls its own product innovation with no involvement from the centre. Alternatively it would be feasible to have dual control, with involvement both by the divisions and central planning. The potential advantages and disadvantages of these different arrangements are not hard to envisage.

As well as these rather rigid approaches, there are writers who advocate setting up unofficial *skunkworks*, which work on time and resources hijacked, or bootlegged, from the company, in the knowledge that if they go through official channels they will get nothing done (Peters and Austin, 1985). Dixon (1990) described a German study of 73 industrial innovations, most of which had been progressed in this way:

> *The originators kept their idea to themselves until their feasibility could no longer be questioned, often working on refinements secretly . . .*

The idea of project champions has also gained some favour for similar reasons. Champions help the innovative project to circumvent the rigid structure of the existing organisation.

These approaches are all symptoms of a malaise at the heart of the organisation. The fact that they may be beneficial to an innovative project merely highlights the fact that the existing organisation is incapable of handling innovation and change. In an era of rapid change this is the problem that needs to be overcome by a root and branch change in the way the whole organisation works. Rigid structures deliberately need to be broken down and replaced by more fluid organic matrices.

The problem presented by an autocratic chief executive is even more difficult to *melt down* than bureaucratic structures. The only solution to repositioning of most autocratic organisations may rest simply on a palace revolution or other mode of getting rid of the autocrat. Reluctant autocrats are rare, although they do exist and may themselves seek to reposition their own organisation.

Strong culture organisations are, to all intents and purposes, similar to bureaucracies in the problems they present for repositioning. The difficulties are, however, likely to be even greater since not only will the strong culture have been built up deliberately and painstakingly, it will also be based on the invisible, but robust and long-lasting foundation of the naturally evolving culture. Moreover, the strong culture may well not be recognised as a flexibility problem and the will to change it may therefore be distinctly absent.

There are two approaches to melting down rigid structures. In some circumstances it may be possible to create a major change with an almost immediate effect. For example, the removal of an autocratic chief executive would present such an opportunity. The fact of his or her removal will have major symbolic impact. It announces to every member in the organisation that the world has changed; everything may be different from now on. Immediately, every member is sensitised to look for clues as to the new state of affairs. They are receptive to change and eager to seek improvements.

In these special circumstances it is possible to make the change from the autocrat quadrant to the innovative teams quickly and efficiently. However, it does not happen automatically. If the old autocrat is simply replaced by a new appointee with no planning of how the change to innovative team will be made, then the organisational customs and practices which reinforced the previous incumbent as autocrat will quickly envelop the replacement and merely create a new autocracy. The change has to be planned, with the various components of a progressive culture being designed and implemented at the time of the change so that the new incumbent is associated with the new culture.

Other than in these special circumstances the move from traditional to progressive cultures is a long, slow process. There are no quick fixes or magic formulae. A programme of initiatives will need to be carefully designed to establish the four main components of culture: empowerment, integrity, involvement and commitment.

Detailed analysis of the culture profile and of responses to individual statements will identify the sort of management action that may be required. Formation of project teams for various initiatives is a useful means of breaking down rigid structures, not merely because they offer a sound operational means of achieving change, but more importantly because they provide an alternative means of organisation to the traditional structure. The need is for task-oriented teams which progressively take on more and more responsibility for organisation operations. The teams themselves need to involve everyone in the organisation, be non-hierarchical and led on the basis of expertise. For example, the chief executive of the organisation should participate as a member of one or more of the project teams, and should not necessarily lead any team of which he or she is a member. In some organisations this may seem perfectly natural; in others, less well fitted for survival, it might represent an utterly incredible arrangement.

The tasks for which team operations take responsibility are specifically related to the improvement and development of the business, for dealing with specific initiatives which may be temporary or permanent. But the role of teams should progressively be increased. Although line management in a modern organisation is a relatively routine task, even in this there are some opportunities for the use of group-working to improve the quality of working life. However, team operations strength lies in their organisational development possibilities. Solving new problems that arise from the work situation is work for problem-solving teams, some of which will be short-lived and simple, while others will be almost permanent and capable of fulfilling tasks of extreme complexity.

Team membership and participation in leadership can provide inexperienced people with direct learning opportunities in a way that orthodox line management structures would take a lifetime to provide. Management by project teams is a rapidly growing part of the literature on new forms of organisation which replace the old monolithic hierarchies.

There are various approaches to the establishment of management by teams. Hierarchy cannot be eliminated but it can be limited and to some extent, as suggested by Jönsson (1996), replaced as a 'controlling mechanism', by trust and reputation. Team-based organisations appear to depend on communications that are open in all directions.

Belbin (1981) found that effectiveness also depended on the team comprising the right combination of individuals, with complementary personalities and abilities. Under normal circumstances the team leader should attend to the setting of team objectives whilst encouraging all team members to engage their intelligence, talents and efforts in the pursuit of team goals.

The essential message is effectiveness: not just empowerment, but empowerment for a purpose; not just involvement, but involvement in leadership to a strategic end; not just communications, but communication of a particular message about the strategic direction; not just motivation, but motivation to a commitment to the organisation's strategic aims.

These ideas are to a considerable extent reflected in the learning organisation idea described by Senge (1990) and Garvin (1993 and see Reading Review 24). Goh (1998) identified five building blocks of the learning organisation as: shared leadership and involvement, a culture that encourages experimentation, the ability to transfer knowledge across organisational boundaries, teamwork and co-operation, clarity and support for mission and vision. Thus, there appears to be a coming together of ideas about structure, culture, leadership, strategy and mission which are more suited than old ideas about bureaucracy to the current excitingly changing times.

Summary

- This chapter is based largely on a specific piece of research which studied organisational factors which distinguished innovative organisations from less innovative ones.

- Whilst this is a single piece of research its methods and findings are in line with the mainstream of empirical work on innovation, strategy and organisation.
- The study found that there were two clusters of organisational factors which appeared to be important.
- One cluster, subsequently labelled 'strategy', included the following:
  Strategic direction
  External communications
  Long-term orientation
  Core competence
  Customer focus
- The other cluster, subsequently labelled 'culture' included the following:
  Empowerment
  Corporate integrity
  Involvement in leadership
  Motivation to commitment
- The factors included in strategy were assessed along a continuum between focused and dispersed. A focused strategy broadly meant that the organisation members knew what the organisation was trying to achieve and how they could contribute to its achievement.
- The factors included in culture were assessed along a continuum between progressive and traditional. A progressive culture was one where organisation members enjoyed the freedom to use their own initiative and were engaged in using it to progress the organisation's strategic direction.
- A focused strategy is a prerequisite for an organisation to be an effective innovator.
- A progressive culture, while not being prerequisite for an effective innovator, was nevertheless important, especially for organisations which were not led by a dominant and innovative individual.
- A two-dimensional matrix was used to present the culture and strategy dimensions.
- On this matrix an organisation which fell into the progressive culture/focused strategy quadrant was placed most advantageously to be innovative. These were called innovative teams.
- Courses of action could be identified to move organisations across the matrix to the innovative teams quadrant.
- Similarly, courses of action are identified for getting round the existing organisation or for melting it down.

Further reading

Pearson, G., *The Competitive Organization*, McGraw-Hill, 1992.

Chapter 14

Implanting strategy

This chapter is addressed primarily to practitioners and is based more on practice than on theory. The aim is to examine what a strategy manager actually does to implant strategy in an organisation.

All organisations are different so there is no one best way. However, there are some general guidelines that may be useful. Despite all the warnings that have been given in this text about the dangers of bureaucratisation, it has to be acknowledged that for strategy to work it has to have some minimum element of formality.

The first task of the strategist in a multibusiness company is to identify the strategic portfolio of core businesses. Business in the strategic portfolio become the focus of attention for strategy.

In most situations, implanting is likely to mean replacing, i.e. there is likely to be some form of strategy process already operating which may inhibit strategic progress.

The means of implanting strategy depend on individual circumstances but invariably involve a programme of consultation and communication: consultation to reach decisions, and communication to achieve concentration.

Implanting strategy demands some craft skills, persistence and some courage.

14.1 Introduction

The chapters so far have covered the ground that might reasonably be expected for a student of strategy management and might well form a basis for student assessment. This last brief chapter is intended to be of more particular interest to those with some executive responsibility for the practice of strategy management. Today, at last, the practice of strategy is recognised as a fundamental perspective – see Whittington (1996, and Reading Review 30), but there is still very little of any weight written on such issues.

Imagine the first day of a job as director with responsibility for a company's strategic development. Having previously taken delivery of a rather nice company car you have arrived in suitable style. You then have an hour or so with your new boss, the chief executive, and then go to meet your three managers in their offices, the chief accountant, personnel manager and IT manager. Finally, you arrive in your own office, which has been newly decorated and furnished for your use. You close the door and slump down in a big, plush 'executive' chair behind a rather pretentious looking desk. For a few minutes everything is very quiet and you cannot help thinking to yourself 'What the hell do I do now?' That is what this chapter is really all about.

The title 'implanting strategy' might seem to imply that no prior strategy process exists, but this is rarely the case. Most companies engage in some form of strategy process, but even today most such processes do not engage with anything which might be regarded as truly strategic in the way that this book has described. A 1997 survey (Quest Worldwide, 1997) indicates that most strategy systems are still focused on financial criteria with much less concern with the ideas of direction, concentration, consistency and flexibility. Implanting strategy, therefore, will most often also involve the modification, if not purging, of existing systems.

Strategy management is not like other jobs. In most executive positions, like marketing or operations, or even finance or IT, things start to hit the desk pretty quickly and in no time there is a backlog and the problem is how to keep up with the pace. Strategy management is not like that. The job is supposedly about thinking and about the long term. The strategy manager will be expected to be one move ahead of the game and able to guide the business into green pastures and clear of trouble. If he or she does not, then they will quickly be seen by their peers as an expensive and non-contributing overhead. Consequently, there is a strong temptation to be drawn into the nuts and bolts of delivering some quick, short-term benefits. Here we are concerned solely with the 'what do I do now?' question in terms of strategy. There have been a number of clues in the preceding chapters, some of which will be referred to again here, but there is a role that the strategy manager has to play in implanting strategy which has not so far been made quite apparent.

14.2 Planning and formality

A concern of all strategy managers is the degree of formality in the process and the sheer quantity of planning that should be required. A theme which has run throughout this text is that too much emphasis on planning often frustrates strategic achievement. It has been said in many different ways. The paradox of using bureaucratic means (i.e. planning) to achieve entrepreneurial ends (i.e. strategy) has been pointed out. Mintzberg's 'paralysis by analysis' has been warmly quoted. Reference has been made to the many researches which have indicated that little strategic good appears to come from formal planning systems. The planning-based approaches to strategy have been reviewed and the implausibility of their contributing to direction and concentration has been noted. In short, planning has been rejected; and yet, it is not possible to avoid planning altogether.

Strategy management requires some minimum level of formality in its process and documentation for it even to exist beyond the strategist and gain the involvement of people throughout the organisation. The process needs to involve all the people in the organisation, in either consultation or communication, or both, if the organisation is to achieve a 'focused strategy' and 'progressive culture'.

The formality should be such that the importance of strategy and its process is symbolically recognised, but detailed planning is not an important part of that process. Detailed plans will be essential at an operational level to ensure the strategic milestones are practical and measurable, but even at this level it is important to ensure the bureaucratic processes do not get in the way of real achievement. The minimum requirement is for a formal strategy document which provides:

1. A statement of the strategic objective either as a mission or strategic intent.
2. A brief qualitative statement describing the strategy in terms that should make it comprehensible and relevant to people in the organisation.
3. A short listing of the main critical milestones described in concise and measurable terms.
4. If appropriate, a statement or code of business practice defining the ethical standards to be achieved.

The first three items are probably an irreducible minimum. The statement of business practice may be less critical although, for some companies, ethical issues may be an essential part of their strategy (for example, Body Shop, Co-op Bank). For most businesses, codes of practice are quite separate from mission and should not be confused as was done, for example, at Zale Corporation (see Box 9.1 in Chapter 9). No business exists purely to make 'sweet music', though it may well be a desirable by-product.

14.3 The strategic portfolio

The first question, and perhaps the most important that a strategy manager will have to address, is the strategic portfolio; the selection of businesses that the MBC (multi-business company) will seek to maintain and develop. This question does not arise for the SBC (single-business company) and is of little interest to the AFC (acquisitive financial conglomerate), but for the MBC it is perhaps *the* crucial decision.

In Chapter 7, various portfolio methods were considered. Under certain circumstances the original Boston portfolio in particular was found to be useful, but it was noted that that approach contributed little to the achievement of direction, concentration and consistency which is the purpose of strategy. The strategic portfolio comprises businesses which share the same strategic direction, however defined, and cannot therefore be identified using orthodox portfolio methods.

The idea of a shared direction, possibly leading to a single recognised position and culture, has been widely recognised as the essential glue which holds business units together and gives them coherence. Ansoff suggested there were economic benefits if diversification was constrained and some 'common thread' was maintained among businesses (Ansoff, 1965). Goold *et al.*, (1994) also found that some commonality was likely to be beneficial in that it would facilitate what they called 'corporate parenting' to create value rather than, as is done by most corporate parents, destroy it.

This commonality of direction was considered from a marketing perspective in Chapter 8, where perceptions of product attributes were recognised as the key measure. It was noted, for example, that if Porsche were to move into writing instruments, it would offer a top quality fashion item rather than a cheap ballpoint pen. To do otherwise would only confuse customers and employees alike and lead the business towards what Porter referred to as 'stuck in the middle'.

From Chapter 2 onwards the ideas of direction, concentration and consistency have recurred at various stages in the text. They are basic to the idea of strategy. Exploiting a competitive specialism which is based on a distinctive competence is one way of expressing it. Using different language, Porter (1996, and Reading Review 29) asserts that strategy rests on unique activities: 'the essence of strategy is choosing to perform activities differently than rivals do'. He suggests that a sustainable competitive position requires what he refers to as 'trade-offs', meaning not doing things which do not fit the strategic direction.

Peters and Waterman (1982) advocated 'sticking to the knitting'; other writers have advocated focusing on core competences and outsourcing the rest (for example, Prahalad and Hamel, 1990; Venkatesan, 1992). The popularity of management buy-outs during the 1980s and 1990s was based largely on diversified companies focusing their attention on core activities and being prepared to divest non-core. The idea of a strategic portfolio is therefore not new, although its definition has perhaps previously been rather vague. For our purposes, the strategic portfolio includes the subsidiary business in an MBC which is in line with the strategic direction of the company, which derives its strength from the company's distinctive competence and which exploits its competitive specialism.

Identifying the strategic portfolio is the first task of an MBC strategy manager. Business which lies outside the strategic portfolio may be identified as non-core. The widespread use of this common-sense terminology has some advantages, but also some dangers. Non-core activities are widely assumed to refer to business units which can be clearly identified, separated from the core and divested. This is only rarely the case. When it is so, then focusing on the strategic portfolio is not difficult because the non-core is readily separable and disposable. But activity which lies outside the strategic portfolio may not be a business unit at all. It may be an apparently intrinsic part of an activity which is very much part of the strategic portfolio. Focusing on the strategic portfolio means, by definition, not doing other things. But if these 'other things' are not readily separable then they are difficult to stop doing. This is the crux of strategy management. This is why, although the theory is easy, the practice is difficult. This is why so few MBCs have a clear strategy.

Porter (1988) gave several examples of firms focusing on their strategic portfolios: Cray Research refusing to go into mini supercomputers, La Quinta focusing exclusively on the travelling business representative market and, most difficult of all, Skil Corporation pulling out of major distribution channels, cutting a large proportion of its product range and deliberately losing around 40 per cent of its sales revenue in order simply to focus on its strategic portfolio.

The strategic case for doing this is simple to make. However, it will almost invariably be counter to the orthodox financial case which inhibits any course of action that produces a short-term disadvantage. The fact that finance and strategy tend to provide diametrically opposed solutions has been noted several times, but the difficulties that this can create for strategy as practice cannot be overstated.

14.4 Strategy processes

There are a number of strategy processes which, although carried out independently of each other, are all connected by the people they involve and by their cumulative effect in terms of direction, concentration, consistency and flexibility. These processes all involve at least two stages: a decision stage and an implementation stage. For example, the strategic portfolio process involves deciding which business is in the portfolio, while the implementation stage involves divesting the business which is excluded.

Of course, this is an over-simple view of process. Figure 10.1 in Chapter 10, which depicts one version of a generic strategy process, clearly includes various forms of analysis before each decision and each implementation. Moreover, the processes are necessarily iterative. It is not possible to decide which business is in the strategic portfolio without knowing the purpose and distinctive competence of the business, or knowing something about the markets it serves. Figure 14.1 shows one such iteration. It is similar to the process shown in Figure 10.1 but uses different language. The terminology is unimportant. It hardly matters that Hamel and Prahalad define and use core competence slightly differently from the time-honoured definition of distinctive competence. What really matters is understanding how the broad concept can be applied to the particular situation, which may be 'Chandleresque' or 'Hamelite'. To emphasise this point, alternative terminologies are offered in Figure 14.1. 'What is our focus?' is Porter's approach to Drucker's question 'Who is our customer?' 'What does the customer value?' is Drucker's simple form of asking the question about the importance of different product attributes. The different nuances suggest that in reality there is a considerable consensus over the component parts of the strategy process. The order in which they are approached may be in doubt, but that is less important since the cycle is repeated. With each iteration the process can be further refined. The initial broad analysis can become more focused in subsequent iterations on the items which are recognised as being of greatest significance to the particular case. Analysis for the business which falls outside the strategic portfolio can be minimised until it is divested. The choice of an appropriate framework, whether it is 'off the shelf' or custom designed, will itself streamline the process further so that analysis becomes more focused and less exhaustive.

The aim of the process is to influence the items in the box headed 'action' (Figure 14.1). These are all shaped by the strategy process. The trade-offs are made directly in order to achieve the desired strategic direction. Technology and marketing are developed in order to beat competitors. The structure and culture are shaped to achieve concentration and consistency. As noted in Figure 2.4 in Chapter 2, as a successful strategy becomes embedded in the organisation's culture it tends to become

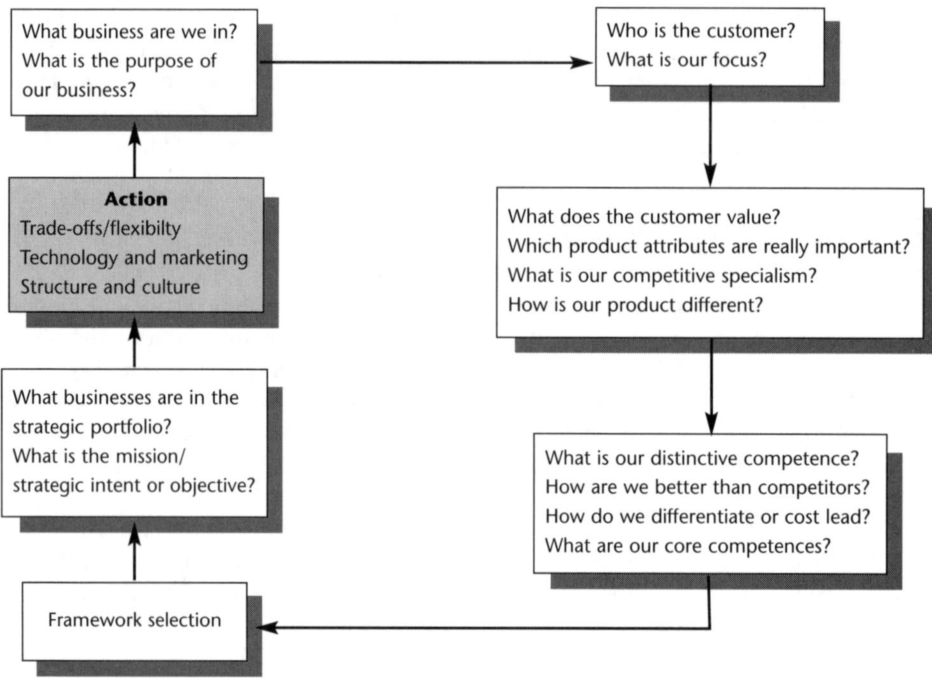

Figure 14.1 A strategy process

set and increasingly resistant to change. Each time a new trade-off is made, i.e. the commitment to a strictly defined direction becomes more concentrated, so this risk of myopia and inflexibility is increased. Thus with each trade-off flexibility needs to be reviewed. Most trade-offs will make the business more closely dependent on some area of business, some group of customers, or perhaps some technology. So with each trade-off the organisation's vulnerability is potentially increased. It is therefore vital for the organisation to be aware of each ratcheting up of its vulnerability and to maintain a very close monitor on the critical issues. For example, when the Skil Corporation focused all its efforts on just two distribution channels it improved its performance beyond recognition, but if anything had happened to threaten its chosen channels, Skil would have been in trouble; it therefore kept a very close eye on what was happening in its channel markets.

The strategy manager's major challenge is to establish strategic thinking among his or her peers. This is often difficult because the dominant norms in which those peers are likely to operate are financial, and the immaculate logic of finance gives the greatest weight to the short term. Even those who are educated to think strategically may find it difficult, or too intimidating, to support a strategic case which is not also justified by orthodox financial criteria.

This very real difficulty is confronted by every strategy manager at some time or another. The most thorough strategic analysis may have resulted in sound, clear-cut strategic conclusions for presentation to an executive meeting. Let us assume, as is mostly the case, that the strategic conclusions are not supported by orthodox financial analysis. If the case is presented without prior preparation of the members of the meeting, it is most unlikely to be accepted. If any one member of the meeting is taken by surprise, he or she is almost certain to make use of orthodox criteria and therefore argue against the strategic case. For other members of the meeting, to support the strategic case in the face of orthodox financial criteria may be a personally hazardous enterprise. One forcefully made logical case against is likely to destroy the strategy. It is important therefore to ensure that every member of the meeting has had the benefit of full consultation and is fully aware of the strategic arguments involved prior to the meeting.

In many situations it may be necessary to go further back than this. Even today only a minority of senior managers have benefited from strategic management education or training and it would be futile to mount a strategic case among members who lack strategic awareness. So a strategy awareness programme may be a necessary precursor to making any strategic case. Even then a systematic programme of briefing and consultation may still be essential prior to making any strategic case to an executive meeting. If this due process is ignored, strategically justified cases are likely to be rejected and the credibility of the strategy manager among his or her peers will be reduced. Such rejection is unlikely to be motivated by any personal animosity, or by ignorance, but simply because the orthodox criteria by which such decisions are normally taken are unlikely to support the vast majority of strategically justified decisions.

This aspect of the strategy process is being given heavy emphasis here because it is often in this almost hidden part of the process that strategies fail and sound strategic decisions are rejected. The strategist's job is to ensure that if such decisions are rejected then they are rejected for valid reasons. By emphasising the 'off-line' role of briefing and consultation it is not suggested the strategist should embark on a programme of political 'wheeling and dealing'. It is simply intended that those involved in taking strategic decisions should have a strategic perspective and awareness when they are so involved. It is not a matter of getting a decision through an executive meeting, but of gaining an informed consensus among those involved in the decision. It is the consensus which sees decisions, once taken, implemented quickly and successfully (as noted in section 11.5.2 with respect to Japanese practice).

The strategy manager must be the catalyst of consensus around any strategic position. Such a role demands a considerable effort being put into consultation and communication. Consultation is the means of achieving consensus among decision-makers during the process of forming strategy. Communication is the means of disseminating the fully formed strategy to the firm's stakeholders, both internally and externally. Both consultation and communication are vital skills of the strategy manager.

Each of the questions raised in Figure 14.1 is likely to involve a process of consultation as well as analysis. Once the answers to the questions have been agreed, the strategy document can be prepared and the strategy communicated. The purpose of the analysis and consultation is to form a consensus over the actions to be taken. The purpose of communication is to broaden that consensus so that all people, not just those contributing to the decision process, can make their own contributions to strategy through their daily allocations of time, effort and enthusiasm. The process is therefore not simply one of decision and action, nor even of analysis, decision and action, but of analysis, consultation, decision, communication and action.

Communication has received a considerable amount of attention, especially among management trainers, with the emphasis being very much on the communication process itself. Communications skills, interpersonal skills, listening skills, presentation skills and so forth are not topics of much importance here. What matters much more is the message that is communicated, not the skill with which it is done. Regular communication of interesting messages quickly improves the effectiveness of the communicator – practice makes perfect. The message is what matters. The required content of communications should be quite clear, but communicating matters of strategy is still often regarded with suspicion. Some managers still appear to feel that strategy should be confidential. The simple rule is that strategy is never secret. The more people who know the strategy the better. Only in rare circumstances, and then only for short periods of time (for example prior to introducing a new product, or negotiating a strategic alliance), should strategic issues be treated as confidential.

The way this process is completed depends on the individual situation, the strategy and culture of the organisation and the people involved. There can be no generally applicable rules. Two examples are quoted below which outline the process in two different organisations, one apparently lacking any strategic focus, the other where the problem was more to do with a traditional culture which inhibited the efforts of people in the organisation.

14.5 Repositioning actions

The two examples below list actions taken in two organisations trying to implant an effective strategy process. In both cases the actions taken were largely concerned with consultation and communication. In the first case this was not a new process as the company was very open and progressive. What it lacked was a clear strategic direction. In the terminology of Chapter 13, this organisation was a butterfly.

The second organisation was very different. The problem there was not that it lacked direction but that the organisational culture was repressive and inhibited employees from contributing to strategy as they were well capable of doing. In the terms of Chapter 13, this organisation was an autocrat and a strong culture.

14.5.1 Achieving strategic direction

Actions taken included the following:

1. Formation of small teams (three or four members each) to identify and prepare concise written reports on the items listed below. These reports to be circulated prior to an awayday workshop.
   (a) Customer needs
   (b) Core competences
   (c) Competitor product strengths

   (d) New technology
   (e) Long-term industry trends and changes
2. An awayday workshop to:
   (a) Receive reports from the above teams – 30 minutes presentation + maximum 30 minutes discussion on each. Discussion to include renewed briefs for each team
   (b) Discuss options for strategic direction
   (c) Consider options for a challenging strategic intent in terms of competitors to beat
   (d) Consume a high-class dinner
3. Formation of a 'strategic direction' team to propose a one-sentence statement of strategic objectives, supported by operational detail not to exceed a single side of A4 in total.
4. Formation of a 'strategic planning' team to create a planning timetable and minimum planning standards including paperwork requirements and monitoring arrangements.
5. Agreed rotation of members (from all the above teams) to report on strategic issues to the board or executive committee each month.
6. Agreed rotation of members of board or executive committee (excluding chairman or chief executive) to have responsibility for strategic issues.
7. A second awayday workshop to agree the following items:
   (a) Statement of strategic direction
   (b) Statement of competitive strategic intent
   (c) Milestones along the route to the strategic intent
   (d) Annual strategy planning timetable and process
   (e) Regular monitoring and reporting arrangements

The above actions started the strategy process off in a way which involved a large number of organisation members. Team memberships and other roles were rotated from time to time so that the expertise of individuals was fully exploited, but at the same time their experience and knowledge was broadened.

The programme gives a number of ideas but still leaves a lot of room for shaping to the needs of the individual organisation. Care should be taken to introduce an element of formality and time commitment without introducing the sort of fruitless paperchase which many large, mature, bureaucratic organisations have succumbed to. In this particular case it was felt important that the 'butterfly' be encouraged to give some emphasis to planning – not an initiative that is usually required.

14.5.2 Achieving a more progressive culture

The programme included the following initiatives:

1. A programme to improve internal corporate communications, both formal and informal. Opening up informal communications, i.e. between departments and individuals across the organisation, was attacked through communications and interpersonal skills training programmes. Formal communications were

improved by written media including a house journal, news-sheet, employee financial report, and *ad hoc* noticeboard statements as well as verbal communications using communications and consultation committees formed across the organisation, regular team briefings and occasional business-wide short 'conferences' where top management spoke directly to all members. The creation of project teams for a wide variety of purposes also played a key role in opening internal communications. Open communications were only part of the story; the other part was concerned with the message being communicated. This needed to be concerned with strategic issues which were previously regarded as confidential and included the strategic direction and intent, milestones towards a competitive challenge, issues arising from external communications and long-term orientation, competitor analysis, technological developments and targets, core competences and customer information.

2. A programme of people development including training and education, job enrichment and job rotation, involvement in project teams designed to broaden individual experience and responsibility.
3. Corporate integrity initiatives were taken explicitly by, for example, the setting up of an ethics committee and the development of a code of practice appended to a mission statement. The establishment of a high level of corporate integrity was a slow process. Lip service needed to be confirmed by continuous and painstaking practice which had to be seen to be done.
4. A programme of recognition of individual contributions was started by making valued awards for individual performance.
5. A programme to involve groups normally excluded from the processes of strategic development and improvement of the business. It was a strongly unionised business and employee representatives, not in all cases union representatives, were set up to meet customers, technology suppliers, shareholders and competitors. Employee representatives also joined key project teams with roles beyond their normal scope.
6. A programme was instituted by human resource management to encourage members to grow and develop, not only by training and promotion but also by ensuring as far as possible that jobs were meaningful, that people enjoyed a maximum practical degree of autonomy and that all jobholders received feedback on their performance.
7. A consultation process was commenced to investigate the possible means of involving members in ownership of the business, either directly through a share scheme or indirectly through participation in the benefits of ownership in the form of profits or growth.

Conclusions

Strategy management, let alone strategic management, is time-consuming and expensive and its short-term returns are most often extremely limited if not negative.

Its long-term returns must therefore be substantial for the process to be worthwhile. For many organisations, in many situations, this is demonstrably the case. With no focus on strategy they would not have got to the top of the heap; indeed they may well not have survived at all. For other organisations, it may seem that they can survive perfectly well just by managing the day-to-day professionally and efficiently, making continuous incremental improvements. Surely, for them, it might be argued, their performance is good enough without wasting time and money on implanting a strategy process.

This may be so. But it is impossible to say how long the situation will last. Tomorrow may be the day when logical increments in performance cease to be sufficient. Then implanting a strategy will become an urgent necessity.

For those privileged to be engaged in the process there are challenges aplenty. The theoretical challenge is moderate, but there are heroic difficulties in practice. Partly this is because the strategic perspective and the perspective of finance are incompatible and incommensurable, and it is the financial perspective which embodies the orthodox wisdom of management. The strategic case has usually therefore to be argued in the face of overwhelming odds. The strategy manager has to have the courage to put his or her career (not to mention personal credibility and pension) on the line in pursuit of strategic ends, or, alternatively chicken out, hit budget and accept strategic failure.

That is part of the reason why the practical difficulties are so 'heroic'. But there is more to it than that. Porter advocates daring to make trade-offs, giving up business which contributes positively to financial results. He advocates being different from competitors, not following a 'me too' strategy. Pursuing a copycat strategy invariably produces only moderate results; being unique will be much more exciting – likely to produce dazzling success or cataclysmic failure. This is the risk. It may be calculated, but risks must be taken. 'Who dares wins' is not quite right. 'Who wins has dared' may be wholly true, but 'who dares either wins or loses' is also true. The strategy manager must push to take risks, in the face of a risk-averse peer group and without the orthodox means of justifying that risk.

If hitting budget sounds more attractive, keep out of strategy.

part 4

Reading reviews

This section provides in concise form an uncritical review of some significant contributions either to specific topics or to the mainstream of strategic management literature. Presentation as reading reviews is intended to provide a memory aid of these important inputs. By providing them separately in this form it is hoped to avoid confusion between the original contribution and any critical assessment which might appear in the main text.

Each review seeks only to capture the main points and spirit of the original. The review process has necessarily meant the exclusion of some of the points made in the original which those more illustrious authors clearly felt were important. Almost invariably they have excluded, or at any rate ruthlessly limited, reference to many examples originally quoted. Whilst they are not intended to include any interpretations of, or value judgements about, the original text, they inevitably remain personal selections and interpretations, and for this reason, if for no other, readers are strongly recommended to the original publication.

The selection of what will be most useful to students of strategy management is inevitably subjective. Some of the readings are classics of general significance (for example the Levitt, Hayes and Porter inclusions), while others are included because they highlight some particular issue which has sometimes not appeared to be well supported (for example Hall, Wilson and Whittington); still others because they provide interesting interpretations in their own right (for example the Mintzberg, late Drucker, Morgan and Jönnson inclusions).

The readings are arranged in chronological order starting forty years ago with the Levitt articles which really highlight how perennial some issues remain. Levitt's plea for managers not to get sidetracked away from the main thrust of business into making 'sweet music' remains as relevant today as it was in 1958. Similarly, his plea for managers to take a non-myopic view of their business and its customers still remains a widely quoted source. Some of the examples that Levitt quotes may now seem incongruous but the general thrust remains vibrant. The early Drucker inclusion, over thirty years old, is also still relevant and yields insight today.

From these early contributions to strategic thinking several strands develop. There is a strand which includes the three apparently very different strategy frameworks: Boston Consulting Group's simple model for price competition in commodity markets, Porter's more general business economics-based model, and Hamel and Prahalad's less rigorously analytical but rather more transformational framework for exploiting technological advance.

There is a group of contributions from the 1980s which relates to the strategy versus finance debate. Firms in the United States and UK have tended to be dominated by the finance and accounting axis, and as a consequence appear to have paid a fearful strategic price. Hayes, Abernathy, Garvin, and Skinner describe the situation, what caused it and what should be done about it. Their message has been heeded to some degree, and the Anglo-Saxon decline, which at one time seemed so inexorable, has been reversed in many industries in the United States and to a lesser extent in the UK. Nevertheless, the finance/strategy dichotomy remains despite attempts, typified here by Grundy, to link the two.

The Mintzberg contributions set out some fundamental strategy categories on which others, including the current text, have built. These contributions provide an extremely useful analysis of the basics of strategy which are, in outline, almost universally valid.

The contributions of the past decade are focused almost entirely on the problems that strategy has to confront arising from the rapid rate of technological development. Clearly the old stable bureaucratic organisations cannot cope with the new circumstances. Their incremental strategies, focused on becoming ever more efficient, are inadequate. Their rigid structures and hierarchies inhibit their mobility and development. This is what drives Hamel and Prahalad, who describe a mould-breaking, inspirational process for exploiting technology to beat competitors. Porter's look at the competitive advantage of nations is also concerned with the capability to innovate rather than consideration of a nation's natural resources.

There is an increasing interest in the practicalities of implementation. Strategic management texts have previously restricted interest in implementation to issues mainly to do with the structuring of organisation. Clearly these are hugely important in the way that strategy is accomplished. Everywhere structures are breaking down and being replaced by more fluid organic systems which replace hierarchy with lateral communications and control. The McGill *et al.*, Wilson, Morgan, Garvin and Jönnson contributions all focus on such issues, the Jönnson article reinforcing the importance of ethical considerations as a co-ordinating ingredient in the flexible learning organisation, which aspect is also developed by Hosmer. Drucker too, in his general picture of the state we are in, post-capitalism and communism, focuses on our need to form non-hierarchical organisations to develop and exploit knowledge. He uses the symphony orchestra as a metaphor for the new organisation form, while Morgan proposes a termite colony as an elegant metaphor for the new organisation and the new mode of forming strategy in times of flux. McGill *et al.* and Garvin are drawn into the consensus with a practical view of 'how to' build a 'learning organisation'.

The penultimate contribution from Porter goes back to the basics of strategy theory, making valuable use, as ever, of practical illustrative examples. The terminology has been changed somewhat since the earlier Porter contributions, but the principles remain almost wholly intact. There is less of an emphasis on 'stuck in the middle', but more stress on the practicalities of making trade-offs. The original three generic strategies are relabelled but remain otherwise almost as enunciated in 1984. The strategy framework remains valid.

The final contribution from Whittington is not a definitive break with the past, but a rather tentative pointer to a new direction for strategy management. It is included here because it accords with the general thrust of this text. Strategy as practice is hugely important. Ignoring the problems it raises is likely to limit the effectiveness of strategy management. It has been largely ignored and the empirical evidence on the effectiveness of strategy management remains extremely uncertain.

Reading review

1

'The dangers of social responsibility'

T. Levitt, *Harvard Business Review*, September/October 1958

In response to the widespread populist attacks on big business, some managers started to think about the social responsibilities of their business, the needs of its employees in terms of education, health and social welfare. Such concerns are now widespread. Top managements now seem to share a genuine concern for these social responsibilities. The claim that business exists 'to serve the public' is today far more acceptable than the capitalist notion of making profits. The profit motive is no longer fashionable.

The social responsibility concept might be explained away as all talk. When it comes down to it, would a company be prepared to pay more for its supplies to help maintain employment in a depressed area, or would it buy from the best cost supplier irrespective? If the latter, and social responsibility is then clearly only talk, it is perhaps not so important. The problem is that if people talk enough about such things in the end they start to believe them. Concern with social responsibility is now starting to move into the believing stage and is therefore becoming dangerous.

The free enterprise system of capitalism is dependent on a pluralistic society of variety, diversity and freedom for the individual. It cannot prosper in a monolithic welfare state, but there is a high risk that big businesses will take on all-pervasive responsibilities and consequently powers which in the end will lead to them operating themselves as mini-welfare states, though still ultimately driven by materialistic self-interest.

There have already been examples of American organisations seeking to dominate whole lives and not just religious cults. Some trade unions broadened their focus

This reading review aims to capture the main points and the spirit of the original in readable form. It may not cover all the points raised in the original text or quote the examples referenced. It is not intended to contain any value judgements about the original text but inevitably it remains a personal interpretation. For a comprehensive appreciation readers are strongly recommended to the original article. Copies of the full article are available from HBS Publishing, *www.hbsp.harvard.edu*

beyond the economic and social welfare of their members and adopted far wider responsibilities. Several examples are given including a Toledo union which started a drive for 'respectability' in dress and hairstyles for teenagers because it found leather jackets, 'DA' hairstyles and rock'n'roll unacceptable.

Big businesses will adopt this sort of influence if they continue to extend their social responsibilities and we will end up with a form of fascism. It may sound far-fetched, but already the propounders of corporate social responsibility are making the speeches and writing the books which propound the virtuous ideology. 'There is nothing more corrupting than self-righteousness.' Business may not intend to go down this route but it has the power to and that is the direction in which it is headed.

Pluralism is the key to capitalism's future. The responsibility of business is making money not providing social welfare. The responsibility of trade unions is their members' wages and work conditions, not their clothing and hairstyles. Welfare is the responsibility of governments. These groups and their responsibilities must be kept separate for a pluralist society to prosper.

The state takes care of social welfare out of the successes of business, so the best way for business to respond to its critics is not to preach and practise social responsibility, but to do its business well and to proclaim its successes so that its critics are silenced.

Business could and should be more forthright in pressuring the state to accept its responsibilities for social issues which affect business, whether it is urban renewal, health insurance, pensions, school construction or most particularly civil rights. Too often business managements have remained silent on these matters. But for itself, the only social responsibilities which business should exercise itself are those for which there is a sufficient economic return. There is no room for altruism in business. Employee welfare programmes, share option schemes and the like should only be supported where they can be seen to pay. If people want more than this then they must turn to their unions or to government itself.

Business will survive better if its aims are unconfused – long-run profit maximisation must remain the dominant aim in practice as well as in theory. This aim must be pursued within the law and in a spirit of integrity, but material gain must remain the unambiguous aim of business.

Reading review

2

'Marketing myopia'

T. Levitt, *Harvard Business Review*, July/August 1960

Industries stop growing only because they become focused on their product rather than their customer. The decline of railways was not caused by a decline in demand for transportation, but because the railways themselves allowed competing forms of transportation to take their customers. Hollywood barely survived its self-definition as the film industry instead of entertainment. Other examples given include dry cleaning, electric utilities and grocery stores.

Every industry appears to go through an unnecessary cycle of growth and decline because top management believes in continuous growth because of demography, is focused on its own products and not alive to potential substitutes and believes it can maintain growth simply by product improvement and cost reduction. The example is given of the oil industry which remains myopic and is consequently vulnerable.

Mass production industries have achieved unimaginable reductions in cost and an imperative to sell huge volumes. Consequently the focus has been on selling rather than marketing with its focus on satisfying customer needs. Detroit's failure to provide compact cars until after the successful arrival of foreign producers is a good example. Mass production is a dangerous cause of myopia, but Ford himself is often misunderstood. He was a supreme marketer who set the product's low price in order to appeal to millions of customers. Mass production was the result, not the cause, of low prices.

Product improvement and cost reduction lead ultimately to decline. No amount of improvement and cost reduction could have saved the horse whip industry from the automobile. But the horse whip industry might have survived if it had defined its business as transportation. It would have done so by changing to produce car components. The oil industry is currently looking on while substitutes for petrol-driven car engines are the focus of much attention by others. The ultimate demise

This reading review aims to capture the main points and the spirit of the original in readable form. It may not cover all the points raised in the original text or quote the examples referenced. It is not intended to contain any value judgements about the original text, but inevitably it remains a personal interpretation. For a comprehensive appreciation readers are strongly recommended to the original article. Copies of the full article are available from HBS Publishing, *www.hbsp.harvard.edu*

of petrol is inevitable because customers do not want it for itself and because it pollutes.

Another cause of myopia is the belief that growth will continue as a result of technological product innovation. The electronics industry currently appears to share this belief. The complexity of the technology leads to industry domination by electronics technologists and consequently an increased concentration on the technology and the product instead of the customer. The same applies in the oil industry which focuses on exploration, extraction, refining and distribution, but hardly at all on marketing and the customer.

Business is about satisfying customers, not producing goods and still less about technology. But marketing is widely ignored in high-technology industries.

Seventy-five years ago American railway companies were the toast of Wall Street and the idea they would be challenged by transportation through the air would have been thought insane. But many insane ideas become commonplace realities.

A customer-creating and satisfying business requires a clear definition of 'the company's style, its direction and its goals' and this requires both organisation and leadership.

Reading review

3

'Business realities'

P.F. Drucker, *Managing for Results*, Harper & Row, 1964

Executives simply do not spend enough time on the future – today takes all their time. All their time is spent fire-fighting, reacting to short-term pressures, mounting often unsuccessful crash programmes to solve recurrent problems. They need a systematic approach to break out of this situation.

There are three aspects to the task of business management:

1. Making the existing business effective
2. Identifying and exploiting its potential
3. Changing the business to exploit a changed future

Individually these three are hard enough to achieve, but they have to be addressed together as integral parts of the management task. To do this successfully requires a practical understanding of business as an economic system. Without this understanding, the job of management inevitably degenerates into fire-fighting.

Though all businesses are different, using different technologies, serving different customers, with different products, and being different in size, structure and culture, nevertheless there are some assumptions which appear common to all business. These 'realities' are widely experienced and recognised, but few managers make practical use of them in managing their own business.

The assumptions or 'realities' are:

1. *Profits and resources are only obtained from outside the business.* It is the customer who decides whether or not the activities of the business are worth an economic price, i.e. a price which produces economic results. Similarly, the only distinctive resource that a business has is knowledge and that too exists outside the busi-

ness. The job of business is to convert outside resources (knowledge) into outside results.

2. *Profits come from exploiting opportunities, not solving problems.* Problems cannot be ignored, but should be minimised. Solving problems only eliminates restrictions – results must come from exploiting opportunities.
3. *Resources need to be allocated to opportunities.* The entrepreneur's task is to maximise opportunities, being effective is more important than being efficient, doing the right thing than doing the thing right.
4. *Profits are only achieved through leadership.* Profits are achieve by being distinctive in some aspect that the customer values. This does not mean being the biggest, or the market leader, but it does mean being the leader in *something* the customer values.
5. *Leadership positions do not last long.* The profitability of leadership attracts imitators who inevitably erode profitability. Management's job is give new direction and energy to achieve new leadership positions and so maintain profitability.
6. *Today's business is already half obsolete.* The business of today, its assets, people, technologies, products, markets and successful recipes, are all the result of past decisions and they are unlikely to be appropriate for the business of tomorrow.
7. *Resources tend naturally to be allocated thinly across a wide front.* This is a universal truth in the social world. Ten per cent of products generate 90 per cent of profit. 10 per cent of sales staff generate 90 per cent of new business. But, although 10 per cent of customers generate 90 per cent of sales, resources (e.g. time, money, energy etc.) will usually be spread equally across all customers, rather than being focused on the productive few.
8. *Concentration is the source of profitability.* To be profitable a business must concentrate all its resources, efforts and enthusiasms on the few really productive opportunities (i.e. the 10 per cent). This is the most violated of all business realities.

These assumptions should form the basis for understanding the particular business situation. They may not all be true for every business, but they are the starting-point for making the existing business effective, identifying and exploiting its potential and changing it to exploit the future.

Reading review

4

Perspectives on Experience

Boston Consulting Group, 1968

Cost data show that total costs consistently decline by between 20 and 30 per cent each time accumulated production (i.e. experience) is doubled. The cost decline is not automomatic, but depends critically on competent management driving costs down as volume increases.

This relationship of costs to experience is graphed as a curve representing a similar meaning to the learning curve but representing all costs (including for example, R&D, selling, promotion, overheads etc.) rather than simply production. The curve itself is best represented on log:log scales as a straight line.

In an industry that is growing fast then experience will be quickly doubled and the consequent cost reductions very significant. In an industry which is not growing at all the significance of experience cost reductions will rapidly diminish. An industry which has existed for many years and which has stopped growing will gain no significant benefit from experience.

The performance of competitors within the industry will also be bound by this cost: experience relationship. So long as their market shares remain the same relative to each other and have done so from the beginning then their costs relative to each other will also remain constant.

Data on prices and experience show that prices tend to decline by the same characteristic rate as costs, so long as competition remains stable. If prices do not fall as rapidly as costs then in due course new competitors will be attracted by the high margins being achieved and the increased competition will eventually force prices down. This may result in some shaking out of competitors before prices resume their close relationship with costs. A common example of this is where prices for a new product are set initially below cost in order to create a market and then maintained at that level even after the requisite cost reductions.

This reading review aims to capture the main points and the spirit of the original in readable form. It may not cover all the points raised in the original text or quote the examples referenced. It is not intended to contain any value judgements about the original text, but inevitably it remains a personal interpretation. For a comprehensive appreciation readers are strongly recommended to the original text.

If costs depend on experience and prices follow costs then, so long as there are no non-price barriers to competition, profit will depend on cumulative market share. The competitor with fastest reducing costs will take market from those with slower reducing costs and this instability will continue until one competitor dominates the market (i.e. has over 50 per cent or double the largest competitor). Then the smaller competitor will either have to increase market share or accept lower profit margins. In the end, the smaller competitor is likely to be eliminated.

There is a great deal of evidence of these relationships in situations of direct price competition.

There has been phenomenal technological advance yet cost reduction (e.g. $3 transcontinental phone call, £100 TV set etc.) has had far greater impact than new product introductions. The implications are profound: a producer that does not reduce costs at the industry rate will become uncompetitive; the producer with the largest cumulative market share should have the lowest costs; new products must usually be introduced at prices below costs to create a market; competition will ultimately force prices down as fast as costs; market share in fast-growth markets is extremely valuable; market shares are unstable until one producer dominates.

It is possible to calculate the value of changes in market share so long as there is a direct relationship between market share and accumulated experience which may not always be apparent.

If products are growing fast, and particularly if they are new, having little accumulated experience, then the impact of experience-based cost reductions will be dramatic. If growth is slow the impact of such cost reductions may be minimal.

The return from increasing market share in a rapidly growing market can be very high. In a low-growth market, the returns would be much reduced and the likely costs of disturbing settled market structures extremely high.

New products should be priced at a level, almost invariably below cost, which will not only create a market but also deter other competitors entering the market. The lower the initial price, the quicker experience and cost advantage is built up.

The aim of experience-based strategy is to achieve market dominance so that they become the most profitable producer. This is usually achieved by price leadership, but once achieved the lowest-cost producer will tend to allow the high-cost producer to make market prices. This will increase profits, so long as prices do not become so high as to encourage new entrants or to make it feasible for the high cost producer to consider re-engaging in battles for market share.

The strategic implications of experience curves apply to all growth businesses, but for low-growth situations experience curves are of 'little strategic importance'. Even for high growth businesses it is essential to understand the competitive context before adopting an experience-based strategy. Misunderstandings about competition can occur when competitors have differing financial resources, different time horizons, differing abilities to plan and execute pricing strategies, conflicting market information and when they started out at different times.

One of the unknowns of any strategy is how the competition will respond. Experience curves provide a rationale for understanding likely responses to attempts to change market shares, so long as all competitors understand the implications.

Experience curves should in practice not be used mechanically to measure situations, but as a means of understanding competitive relationships. There are a number of practical problems in their use. For example, defining the product is problematic. The empirical base of experience curves is all related to basic products such as plastics, gasoline, semiconductors etc. As the product definition narrows into sectors the basic relation holds but the products themselves are either joint productions or partial by-products and a clear-cut precise product definition is rarely possible. And costs depend very much on product definition. Similarly, costs are often difficult to identify with precision because of allocations and variations in accounting treatment. Similarly, inflation can be a complicating factor.

Appendix A provides experience curve data and graphs of the 24 selected products which were the basis for the 20–30 per cent reduction in costs every time accumulated production doubles. They are all generic products, i.e. commodities where the focus of competition is likely to be price. They are: germanium transistors, silicon transistors, germanium diodes, silicon diodes, integrated circuits, crude oil, motor gasoline, ethylene, benzene, paraxylene, low density polyethylene, polypropylene, polystyrene, pvc, primary aluminium, primary magnesium, titanium sponge, monochrome tv sets, total free standing gas ranges, total free standing electric ranges, facial tissue, Japanese beer, electric power, refined cane sugar.

Reading review

5

The Product Portfolio

Boston Consulting Group, 1968

To be successful a company needs a portfolio of products which is in balance in terms of cash flows, i.e. some products will generate surplus cash while others need cash to be invested if they are to maintain their position.

Empirical work on experience curves showed that the competitor which had gained the most experience in producing a product would enjoy the greatest cost reductions and therefore should enjoy the lowest costs. In an industry where products are largely undifferentiated (i.e. commodity products) and therefore take a simple market price, the lowest costs will translate directly into highest profit margins. Relative market share is taken as a proxy for accumulated experience. Thus the competitor with the highest relative market share should achieve the highest profitability and therefore generate the largest cash surpluses. In short, high relative market share implies high cash generation.

Products that are growing rapidly need cash to be invested both in building their physical assets and in increasing their working capital (i.e. stocks and work in progress and trade debtors). The higher the growth, the more cash is required. Products which are growing only slowly if at all should generate cash surpluses.

High market shares are either earned through the achievement of some competitive advantage in terms of product attributes, or can be purchased. The value of increases in market share can be extremely high, especially in a rapidly growing market.

No market grows indefinitely. The aim must be to achieve an advantageous position when the market growth slows down and the benefits in terms of cash surpluses can be realised.

High relative market share/low growth products are referred to as 'cash cows'. They generate a large surplus cash because of their market share and require little to

This reading review aims to capture the main points and the spirit of the original in readable form. It may not cover all the points raised in the original text or quote the examples referenced. It is not intended to contain any value judgements about the original text, but inevitably it remains a personal interpretation. For a comprehensive appreciation readers are strongly recommended to the original text.

be reinvested because of their low growth. So typically they will generate more cash than is required to maintain their position, i.e. cash that can be reinvested elsewhere.

Low relative market share/low growth products are referred to as 'dogs'. They generate little profit because of their low relative market share though they may show an accounting profit. They do not require much to be invested, but nevertheless may require all cash generated to be reinvested to maintain their position. Their only value is what can be extracted from them in liquidation.

Low relative market share/high growth products are referred to as 'problem children'. They generate little cash because of their low relative market share and require substantial investment to maintain their position in the high growth market. So they consume cash. When growth slows down they will naturally become dogs and this can only be prevented either by acquiring more market share to become a star during the high growth phase, or by liquidating.

The high relative market share/high growth product is referred to as a 'star'. These generate cash because of their high profitability derived from high market share, but also consume a lot of cash to build capacity etc. in order to maintain its position. Overall they may well be cash consumers. It is crucial to maintain their star position until growth slows and they become cash cows.

The benefits from achieving high relative market share are very high and the returns from leading a growth market could ultimately be enormous.

The successful company needs a portfolio which is balanced between cash generators and cash consumers, i.e. cash cows to invest in problem children to turn them into stars which will eventually become cash cows. Dogs are not wanted – they are simply symbols of failure.

Reading review

6

'How competitive forces shape strategy'

M.E. Porter, *Harvard Business Review*, March/April 1979

Strategy is all about coping with competition, the state of which is embedded in the underlying economics of an industry. There are five competitive forces which determine an industry's underlying profitability. Analysis of these forces does not merely define the level of competition and therefore profitability, but also suggests how a business might best position itself within the industry and how it might influence the forces.

The five forces behave differently and have differing importance to each industry. It is vital to know which is, or are, the most important for your industry.

If the *threat of new entrants* coming into the industry is low then the existing participants may enjoy high profits. Barriers to entry depend on six factors: economies of scale achieved by existing participants; differentiated products with their existing brand loyalties; scale of required investment; cost advantages of existing participants, e.g. through experience, patents, strategic material supplies, etc.; distribution problems; government regulation, e.g. licensing. Apart from these factual barriers, the industry may have a behavioural track record (e.g. how previous potential entrants were treated) which raises or lowers the barriers to entry. All of these factors are subject to change, either because of changing conditions or as a result of explicit strategic decisions within the industry.

Each industry buys in from its suppliers and sells to its customers and the amount of surplus from these transactions that remains within the industry depends on the *bargaining power of suppliers* and *bargaining power of customers*. Suppliers will take most of the surplus if they are few in number, they provide a differentiated product,

This reading review aims to capture the main points and the spirit of the original in readable form. It may not cover all the points raised in the original text or quote the examples referenced. It is not intended to contain any value judgements about the original text, but inevitably it remains a personal interpretation. For a comprehensive appreciation readers are strongly recommended to the original text. Copies of the full article are available from HBS Publishing, *www.hbsp.harvard.edu*

they have little competition, they might integrate forward and/or the customer industry is relatively unimportant to them. Customers will take most of the surplus if they are big, if the product they buy is a standard or commodity product, if the product they buy is an important part of their overall costs, if their industry works on tight margins, if the product they buy does not save them money and if the customers might integrate backwards.

Choice of buyers and customers are important decisions which should take account of their relative bargaining power. This is particularly important if the product is neither the lowest cost nor adequately differentiated from its competitors.

The existence of *substitute products* clearly limits the price at which products can be sold unless they can be adequately differentiated from the substitutes. The most dangerous substitutes are those that promise most price performance improvements and those that are supplied by a highly profitable industry.

The fifth competitive force is the *competitive rivalry* among existing participants. In the economist's perfectly competitive industry, rivalry is unconstrained and profitability is bid away. This happens when there are many competitors, when they are of a similar scale, products are similar, growth is slow, fixed costs are high and increments in capacity are large scale and exit barriers are high.

Having assessed the industry's five forces the strategist must identify the relationship between the particular business and the individual factors underlying each of the forces. This is the basis for making strategic decisions about positioning the company, influencing the competitive forces and repositioning in anticipation of changes in the underlying factors.

Positioning the company assumes the forces are fixed and identifies the positions where competition is least. Generally this means differentiating the product from the industry norm and doing it somehow differently in terms of production, distribution or service.

Influencing the competitive forces can be done again by differentiating the product, or by capital investment in new facilities or by forward or backward integration. Change is not easy to achieve because the forces are mainly dependent on external factors, but influencing them is feasible in many cases.

Repositioning to take advantage of change requires the change to be forecast first. It may be possible, for example, to identify approximately when an industry is going to mature and growth come to an end, when different rules of competition might apply, and to reposition to take advantage of the new phase of the life cycle.

The key to strategy is to position in a way which avoids head on competition whether from existing rivals, new entrants or substitutes and to recognise the dangers of the position being eroded by the growing power of suppliers and customers. This positioning may involve any number of new initiatives, e.g. new ways of differentiating the product, developing strategic alliances with customers or suppliers, developing technology leadership, etc.

Reading review

7

Porter's generic competitive strategies

There are just three ways of outperforming the competition in the context of the five forces which shape industry profitability. They are *overall cost leadership*, *differentiation* and *focus*.

Overall cost leadership requires a management concentration on cost control and cost reduction in all areas of the business. Achieving the lowest costs needs more than just competent management and the benefits of high relative market share (i.e. most experience). It requires a cost-focused culture which affects the way everything in the company is done. At the same time, since the cost leader's product achieves the market price it must also achieve competitive quality and service – it is not a strategy of 'cheap and nasty'.

The cost leader is in a relatively strong position with respect to each of (Porter's) five competitive forces, especially head-to-head competition among rivals.

Differentiation is the strategy of making the product or service recognisably different across the whole industry in order to achieve a premium price. The source of difference can be anything: technology, design, brand image, features, service, distribution and so on. Differentiation is more sustainable, i.e. less easy to copy, if it covers several product attributes. Differentiation, like cost leadership, is a means of positioning advantageously with respect to the five forces. The essence of differentiation is that customers are prepared to pay a higher price for the difference. This may mean that the differentiator has to accept a smaller market share.

Focus is the strategy of attacking only a particular niche of the market defined by buyer group, geography or product segment. The strategy involves delivering either the lowest cost or best product or service to the chosen market niche.

Each of the strategies requires consistent pursuit over time if it is to be successful.

This reading review is based on multiple sources including the original description by Porter in chapter 2 of *Competitive Strategy* (Porter, 1980), and also Mintzberg's treatment of the topic in Mintzberg and Quinn, (1996, p. 87). It aims to avoid any value judgements about the content of those texts. For a comprehensive appreciation readers are strongly recommended to the original material.

This usually involves the building of different organisational capabilities and skills. Cost leadership requires sustained investment in process technology, low-cost product design and low-cost distribution, tight labour supervision, incentives based on quantitative targets. Differentiation requires strong marketing and product development skills, focus on quality and technology with ability to exploit creativity and attract and motivate highly skilled labour and technical people.

The strategies are different ways of coping with the competitive forces. But a firm that does not adopt one of these strategies gets *stuck in the middle*, unable to be the lowest-cost producer, nor able to maintain high-margin customers in the face of effective differentiating competitors. Such firms will also have an ill-defined corporate culture which delivers confusing messages to its people. Firms that are stuck in the middle must decide which strategy to adopt. Cost leadership usually involves large-scale investment in new technology and possibly the acquisition of market share, while the differentiation or focus strategies are likely to involve significant reductions in market share. In many industries the viability of these decisions is confirmed by the fact that both the largest market share and the smallest (differentiators and focusers) achieve high profitability while the medium-sized firms achieve low margins.

There are two risks involved in adopting any of the strategies. First, the strategy may not be achieved, and secondly, the competitive position may be eroded.

Risks of cost leadership are that new technology may eliminate the benefits of previous investments; newcomers may start with new technology; product demand may change; and costs may rise narrowing the cost leader's advantage.

Risks of differentiation are that the cost leader may open up such a price advantage that the differentiation is no longer regarded as worthwhile. Alternatively, points of differentiation may be effectively copied and the difference eroded.

Risks of focus are that the cost advantage of the focuser against the broad market cost leader may be eroded, the point of differentiation between the focuser and broad market differentiator may be eroded, or the focuser may be outfocused by even narrower market segmentation.

Reading review

8

'Managing our way to economic decline'

R.H. Hayes and W.J. Abernathy, *Harvard Business Review*, July/August 1980

For two decades after the Second World War American managers were highly successful, but times have changed. America has given up its leadership of industry after industry. Germany's productivity growth is now four times America's, even France's is three times. There are many popular explanations, but the truth is that American managers focus on short term costs rather than long term technology and use analytical detachment rather than hands-on experience.

American managers used to be efficient, invest heavily in labour saving capital and be creative in new product development. They are still good at short term efficiency, but they have lost their way in making long term risk decisions. Productivity growth, investment in R&D and the ratio of capital investment to labour all peaked in the mid 1960s in America and American performance in these areas now lags many other countries. It is a failure of American management.

We believe this failure has arisen not because managers have suddenly en masse become risk averse, but because they have been educated to prize detached analysis over experience and insight. An important part of the new orthodoxy is that large organisations be broken into profit centres which are 'controlled' by essentially short term measures such as return on investment. Typically the profit centres are controlled from the centre through some form of portfolio management system which inhibits long term investment and offers a way for managers to detach themselves personally from making risk decisions.

Over the past 20 years also American managers have been taught to make what the customers want, rather than sell what they can make. Perhaps this has gone too

This reading review aims to capture the main points and the spirit of the original in readable form. It may not cover all the points raised in the original text or quote the examples referenced. It is not intended to contain any value judgements about the original text, but inevitably it remains a personal interpretation. For a comprehensive appreciation readers are strongly recommended to the original text. Copies of the full article are available from HBS Publishing, *www.hbsp.harvard.edu*

far: technology has given us the laser, xerography and the transistor, while marketers have given us new shaped potato crisps and feminine hygiene deodorant. Market driven strategy has its limitations. This new orthodoxy based on financial control, portfolio management and market driven behaviour has a profound impact on management behaviour. For instance, market driven behaviour will always favour investment in imitative product design over innovative. Innovative investment undermines existing skills and resources and in return offers the possibility of a high return later. Imitative investment offers quicker, surer returns even though they may not be as substantial.

Similarly, the new orthodoxy with its focus on short term cost reduction and aversion to taking risk naturally favours backward integration acquisitions. But these decisions tend to lock the business ever more firmly into its existing technologies and inhibit future strategic moves.

Decisions to invest in process development are similarly restricted to the quick payback cost reducing incremental investments and for large scale investment in new processes to be inhibited.

The reasons why American managers have bought into this new orthodoxy are several. Firstly, it is clear that since the mid 1950s there has been a dramatic increase in financial and legal executives getting to the top of American companies. Secondly, companies have increasingly filled their top vacancies with executives from outside, very often with people from outside their industry. There has consequently developed a preoccupation with the pseudo-professional manager, someone with no knowledge of the industry or its technology, who can run a company simply on the basis of financial information and control its development without technical knowledge on the basis of oversimplified decisions.

The consequent focus on mergers and acquisitions is therefore not surprising, since the top managers' expertise is largely financial or legal. However, it has been damaging in leading companies to neglect their core technologies and to render them vulnerable to attack by more focused competitors.

German, French and Japanese managers are different. They accord a much higher priority to the technology and invest much more heavily in creating new product opportunities ahead of customer demand. Their focus is on long term survival much more than short term measures such as ROI. To prosper in the long term it is necessary, as it always was, 'to invest, to innovate, to lead and to create value.' We will not achieve this simply through control, market analysis and portfolio management.

Reading review

9

'Survival strategies in a hostile environment'

W.K. Hall, *Harvard Business Review*, September/October 1980

This article identifies strategies that appear to be successful in dealing with an increasingly hostile business environment typified by low growth, high inflation, increased regulation and rising competition particularly from overseas where profit expectations are low. It is based on a study of 64 companies in 8 basic and mature industries where exposure to these adverse environmental pressures is greatest.

The study showed that even in this situation companies can be highly successful, by achieving and maintaining a leadership position in their basic industry and that diversification is unlikely to prove successful. The leaders of such industries might be referred to as 'dinosaurs' or 'dogs', but in terms of return on equity or capital they outperform leading international, high tec and conglomerate glamour stocks. A study of the top two leaders in each industry reveals some interesting common strategic factors which appear to lead to their success. All 16 companies share a dedication to achieving either the lowest costs, or the most strongly differentiated position (i.e. best product, service or quality), or both, in their industry.

In most cases they focused on either costs or differentiation, but three companies combined the two: Caterpillar combined lowest-cost manufacture with differentiation through outstanding distribution and aftersales support; Philip Morris combined lowest-cost manufacture with differentiated branding and promotion; Daimler Benz combined lowest-cost heavy trucks with high-cost differentiated cars.

Cost leaders grew more slowly than differentiators and operated on lower margins in order to achieve volume gains and reduced fixed costs. Differentiators grew more rapidly with higher gross margins and higher promotional and R&D costs and a more flexible asset base.

This reading review aims to capture the main points and the spirit of the original in readable form. It may not cover all the points raised in the original text or quote the examples referenced. It is not intended to contain any value judgements about the original text, but inevitably it remains a personal interpretation. For a comprehensive appreciation readers are strongly recommended to the original text. Copies of the full article are available from HBS Publishing, *www.hbsp.harvard.edu*

The success of these companies was not achieved by naively adopting the prescriptions of PIMS, experience curves or business portfolios. It was achieved through the pursuit of their strategic direction, cost leadership or differentiation, often making investments clearly against the prescription of the strategy models. Leaders in mature markets were not 'milked', but aggressively invested. Low costs were by no means the only source of success in mature markets – differentiation was equally effective. Vertical integration was not the source of lowest costs; a focus on achieving lowest costs in at least one stage of the vertical chain was more important.

Unsuccessful companies in the sample had achieved neither low costs nor a differentiated product, or if they had originally they had not defended their leadership position. For them the hostile environment was merely the last straw – their lack of appropriate strategy had made them vulnerable. Diversification is rarely the answer; though the sample included two successful diversifiers, but the others lacked the financial strength and management capacity to succeed.

Reading review

10

'Managing as if tomorrow mattered'

R.H. Hayes and D. Garvin, *Harvard Business Review*, May/June 1982

The use of discounting methods (DCF) in the capital budgeting process has become more-or-less universal among large manufacturing businesses in the United States over the past two decades. Over the same period American business' investment in capital and R&D has declined. The authors believe this is not coincidental. DCF inhibits investment because it uses a false picture of the economy and because it is usually wrongly applied.

There are various theories to explain why US business investment in capital, R&D and human resource development has declined so substantially. One view is that managers focus on short term performance because their promotion depends on quick results. Another suggests that a multibusiness company (now the dominant form) has to control its subsidiaries through financial measures which are essentially short term because Wall Street demands it. Others suggest various environmental factors are the cause: inflation, high rates of tax, government regulation, etc. Alternatively it is said the risks of takeover force managers to minimise long term investment. None of these explanations is entirely satisfactory.

US business has the funds to maintain investment levels, but chooses not to. It is therefore putting its future at risk. Yet US managers firmly believe in the investment appraisal techniques they are using and ignore their weaknesses which result in short term decision making.

DCF theory is simple. A dollar now is worth more than a dollar in a year's time and the difference in value is the amount of risk-free interest that it could earn in the interim. This is the basis of discounting. All cash flows can be discounted back to a

This reading review aims to capture the main points and the spirit of the original in readable form. It may not cover all the points raised in the original text or quote the examples referenced. It is not intended to contain any value judgements about the original text, but inevitably it remains a personal interpretation. For a comprehensive appreciation readers are strongly recommended to the original text. Copies of the full article are available from HBS Publishing, *www.hbsp.harvard.edu*

present value so that sums can be aggregated and compared taking full account of when they arise. So the cost of an investment now can be compared with the present value of the cash flows it will generate in future time periods and so enable a decision as to whether the investment is worthwhile, i.e. better than the best alternative investment. Alternative investments do not all arise at the same time, so they are proxied by using a hurdle rate which any investment must clear if it is to proceed.

Thus, using DCF it is perfectly rational to disinvest – i.e. not to replace wearing assets if the expected return does not exceed the hurdle rate. However, the DCF calculations themselves require assumptions about future profitability, asset deterioration and future interest rates and US managers, to a great extent dominated by accounting norms, have tended to assume these variables are all making investment less and less viable.

For example, most managers believe their company's earnings are far below former levels, but in real terms (i.e. removing inflation) this is a fallacy. There was a blip in the 1960s when net profit margins rose to around 10 per cent, but the historical norm has generally been around today's norm of 5 per cent.

Also the cost of many capital goods has risen faster than the price of the products they make. Thus it has become relatively less attractive than previously to replace plant and equipment, especially when the energy costs of operating the equipment have also multiplied. Thus, as technology advances and existing plant and equipment becomes obsolete, it seems to become increasingly attractive to delay its replacement.

These various factors contribute to US managers using an extremely high hurdle rate – from 25 to 40 per cent in appraising capital investments. Moreover they also often require projects to pay back in as little as three years.

Hurdle rates bear little relation to the (weighted average) cost of a company's capital. Hurdles of 30 per cent will often be used by firms which return less than 20 per cent pre-tax on investment. Why do they do this?

A major reason is that they seek to cover for the riskiness of the investment. For example, the investment itself might provoke some unforeseen competitive response which would reduce future cash surpluses. Similarly, the hurdle rate may be loaded to counteract the tendency of managers to fudge the projected cash flows simply to clear the hurdle! Whatever the source of the risk, increasing the hurdle rate to accommodate for it is simply not logical.

Thus it appears, according to discounting procedures, reinvestment in existing business is becoming less and less attractive, especially when compared with the apparently more attractive business that can be obtained through mergers and acquisitions. Consequently US managers have allowed their core businesses to decline.

DCF is biased against strategic capital expenditure in various other ways too. For example, it favours shorter payback periods. It also invariably favours incremental expansion of existing facilities over greenfield development. Each incremental decision may appear valid in its own right, but the stream of such decisions can lead to the development of hugely complex, impossible to manage, unprofitable operations. Moreover, DCF invariably favours delaying expenditure because it can take no account of the many benefits of investing early, such as the early development of new skills, the acquisition of crucial knowledge and understanding and the development of new expertise, new products and different cost profiles.

Thus, DCF, as applied in America, leads ultimately to disinvestment. Consider two evenly matched companies competing in the same technology. A new technology becomes available which will increase quality and reduce costs. Company A uses a high hurdle rate, for the reasons explained above, and as a consequence rejects investment in the new technology. In contrast Company B, with a lower hurdle rate (or possibly, as with most Japanese competitors, no hurdle rate at all since they do not make extensive use of discounting), proceeds to invest in the new technology and achieves the lower costs and subsequently takes business from Company A. Thus Company A's ability to invest in future technologies is further reduced. And so on down the *disinvestment spiral.* This process leads to reduction in performance, collapse in morale, the loss of key individuals and ultimately to bankruptcy.

The question is how can the spiral of disinvestment be reversed? Clearly it cannot be done using the same techniques and logic that produced the situation in the first place. The only possible way is to invest, without delay, in the factories and technologies for tomorrow.

Reading review

11

'Impacts of investment appraisal methods: a comparison of US and Japanese practices'

G.J. Pearson, The Strategic Discount: Ways to an entrepreneurial strategy, Wiley, 1985

DCF methods of financial appraisal (such as net present value and internal rate of return) have recently come in for widespread criticism and have been blamed for the lack of capital investment in US manufacturing industry. Comparisons have been made with Japan where there appears to be a greater readiness to make long-term risky investments and where DCF is little used. Comparisons have been made between practices in the two countries and it is concluded that it is not so much the DCF methods themselves which are at fault but the way they are misused in America which leads to a focus on apparently non-risky short-term investments.

Although few Japanese firms make explicit use of DCF, most take some account of the time value of money, for example by charging a project's residual investment each year with an imputed interest charge. Projects are assessed on the basis of either their projected cash flows (including the imputed interest), or on the basis of a simple return (e.g. in an average year) calculated as a percentage of the original investment, again calculations would include the imputed interest. It should be noted, however, that the interest rate charged is typically low so the adjustment for the time value of money is considerably diminished. Moreover, many Japanese firms make these calculations without taking account of taxation.

This reading review aims to capture the main points and the spirit of the original in readable form. It may not cover all the points raised in the original text or quote the examples referenced. It is not intended to contain any value judgements about the original text, but inevitably it remains a personal interpretation. For a comprehensive appreciation readers are strongly recommended to the original text.

These appraisal methods are rather crude and simplistic by comparison with DCF. This may be because of the relative lack of sophistication among Japanese managers, but it may also result from the Japanese focus on achieving a consensus over major decisions. This process, involving a large number of managers from different areas of the organisation considering a wide array of 'what if' questions relating to the proposed project, requires a simple and widely understood appraisal method. The consensus-building approach may depend on crude calculations, but it has several benefits. The structure of a project and the assumptions underlying it will be scrutinised, modified and agreed by all the relevant functional managers, with the result that they all understand the whole of the project (i.e. marketers understand the production aspects and vice versa) before it has even been approved. The process also appears to eliminate the need for making allowances for riskiness, particular risk aspects being discussed in detail and contingent action agreed. The decision-making process may appear ponderous, but once taken, the decision can be implemented fast because everyone knows all about the project.

In America, on the other hand, appraisal practice is now dominated by DCF methods. They frequently use discount or hurdle rates which include a premium for expected inflation. In addition, most firms also add a further premium to take account of the riskiness of a project. Moreover, many firms add a further premium to take account of an assumed capital rationing situation so that the less profitable projects are screened out. Consequently, in US, hurdle rates of around 30 per cent are common.

The premium for inflation is only valid if future cash flows are also inflated, which is often still not the case. The premium for risk is extremely problematic. The calculation of risk is itself very difficult. The riskiness of an individual project might be assessed but its spreading role in the risk profile of a portfolio of projects ignored. Risk also tends to be overestimated because the ability of management to respond positively to changed situations is not accommodated in the calculation. More than this, the notion of a risk premium is itself problematic, since it results in compounding the annual charge for risk, while the actual riskiness will diminish each year as management learn and act appropriately.

The appraisal process in US firms is also different from that in Japan. Typically, projects will be put forward by individual functions or departments with no consensus being sought. This may be efficient in terms of management time at the appraisal stage, but results in projects being based on assumptions and forecasts for which there may be little support.

In summary, financial appraisal in Japanese firms appear to be less numbers driven than in America and much more dependent on face-to-face discussion of project details. The treatment of risk is a particularly crucial difference. By talking through the elements of risk Japanese managers are prepared for it. By raising their hurdle rates to around 30 per cent to take account of it, American managers simply reject risky projects.

Reading review

12

'The productivity paradox'

W. Skinner, *Harvard Business Review*, July/August 1986

America's response to the success of foreign competitors in its own domestic markets has been to redouble the focus on labour productivity improvement. Truly heroic efforts have been made and some productivity gains achieved, but little or no progress achieved in regaining competitive edge. Twenty-five manufacturing companies were investigated to find out why.

The source of failure is certainly not energy – everywhere productivity initiatives are being pursued with typically 'American hustle and determination'. But not only are they ineffective in competitive terms, they can be directly counterproductive. The point is that manufacturing-based competitive advantage is only dependent on labour productivity to a very limited extent. Questions of quality, delivery, service, innovation and flexibility can be far more important weapons than manufacturing cost. Though much competitive ground was lost to foreign manufacturers by their cost advantage, the ground will not be regained simply by chasing those costs down. Productivity programmes are focused on the wrong targets and, more than this, are diverting management attention away from innovation in the areas that really matter.

An exclusive focus on productivity alienates the workforce, inhibits investment in new technology and reinforces a short-term cost mind-set, which repels the best people from coming into manufacturing. Focus on productivity improvement thus effectively prevents competitive progress.

Some companies have broken out of the mind-set, but it is not easy. They have first to recognise that their focus on productivity is not working and that they need a different manufacturing strategy which focuses attention on the elements of competitive advantage which are dependent on manufacturing. In particular, this will

This reading review aims to capture the main points and the spirit of the original in readable form. It may not cover all the points raised in the original text or quote the examples referenced. It is not intended to contain any value judgements about the original text, but inevitably it remains a personal interpretation. For a comprehensive appreciation readers are strongly recommended to the original text. Copies of the full article are available from HBS Publishing, *www.hbsp.harvard.edu*

focus on the adoption of new process technologies which will require widespread change in all the support systems of the organisation. Inevitably it will also focus on the development and motivation of new manufacturing people with a wider vision than simply labour productivity.

Reading review

13

'The strategy concept I: five Ps for strategy'

H. Mintzberg, *California Management Review*, Fall 1987

There are many definitions of strategy and this article considers five.

Strategy as plan
This is the standard dictionary definition, a deliberate, intentional way of dealing with a situation to achieve specified results. A strategic plan defines the overall approach to achieving the long term results.

Strategy as ploy
Like a plan this also is a deliberate, intentional way of achieving results, but is much more limited and specific and describes actions that are intended to achieve more-or-less immediate results. Ploys are competitive moves or manoeuvres (e.g. threats to increase capacity or cut prices etc.) aimed at reducing the probability of competitor retaliation or in some way changing competitive bargaining power.

Strategy as pattern
Not all strategies are deliberate and intentional but may nevertheless be achieved. Strategy can be inferred by considering the end resulting behaviour. If the behaviour becomes consistent, i.e. develops a pattern, it may be just as much a realised strategy even though it is not intended. A journalist, for example, might infer a pattern in corporate behaviour and label it strategy. A manager may do the same about a competitor. They may go further and impute intentionality but this is unnecessary. Plans and patterns may be independent: plans may be unrealised and patterns be unpreconceived, but nevertheless emerge.

This reading review aims to capture the main points and the spirit of the original in readable form. It may not cover all the points raised in the original text or quote the examples referenced. It is not intended to contain any value judgements about the original text, but inevitably it remains a personal interpretation. For a comprehensive appreciation readers are strongly recommended to the original text.

Strategy as position

Strategy can be defined as a position i.e. how the organisation positions itself in its various environments, particularly its market and competitive environment. It might describe the position in a broad market focusing on head-on competition, or a position in a niche market occupied in order to avoid competition. Strategy as position describes the competitive posture either for an independent indvidual business or in relation to its interlocking competitive relationships (strategic alliances, joint ventures etc.) aimed at competition avoidance.

Strategy as perspective

Organisations are perceived, both internally and by the outside world, as having distinctive characteristics which both result from, and have a strong influence on, the way those organisations behave. For example, some organisations are perceived as innovative, flexible and fast moving, while others may be recognised as mature, stable and protected. This perspective definition of strategy refers to the corporate personality, culture, ideology or driving force and is a shared view of the organisation and is key to how it behaves in given circumstances and how it may be expected to behave.

Interrelating the Ps

Clearly, strategy as position may be compatible with strategy as perspective. Moreover, position and perspective can be either planned or simply emerge as a pattern. But the interrelationships of the five Ps may be more complex than simple compatibility. They may be causal – a perspective may result in specific plans and ploys, an emergent pattern may be recognised and become an intended plan and perspective.

Plans, ploys, position and perhaps patterns also, may be readily changed, but a perspective (or culture) can only be changed slowly and with difficulty. If perspective is permanent then changes in the other strategies are limited to those compatible with the perspective. McDonald's introduction of the Egg McMuffin was a change of position within the same perspective. Candlelit McDuckling à l'Orange with waiter service would be a change of perspective.

The five definitions each add to understanding of strategy. They may complement each other or substitute for each other in any organisation. Plans deal with how businesses want to achieve their strategic objectives; ploys focus on competitive moves in the strategy process; patterns focus on the essential action outcomes of strategy and highlight the importance of consistency; position focuses on an outward view of the strategic context; perspective focuses on a more internal definition of the organisation's culture. All five provide useful insights, but it is essential to be clear which of the five definitions we are using when we refer to strategy.

Reading review

14

'The strategy concept II: another look at why organisations need strategy'

H. Mintzberg, California Management Review, Fall 1987

This article looks at the orthodox justifications for strategy – setting direction, focusing effort, defining the organisation and providing consistency – and reconsiders why organisations might or might not need strategy.

Setting direction is the first benefit of a planned strategy and it is widely held to give a huge benefit over those competitors with no direction. Examples abound. But it is worth remembering that a wrong direction can be disastrous and that when everything is in a state of flux, total flexibility, i.e. no direction may be beneficial.

Focusing effort is the second benefit widely claimed for a clear strategy. With no strategy there is no concentration and only marginal results.

Defining the organisation in terms of perspective or culture means that people inside and out of the organisation can readily understand it and what it is trying to achieve. A clear perspective is necessarily a simplified model which represents a highly complex reality and there may be dangers in oversimplification. Lack of clear perspective does not prevent patterns emerging and highly effective actions being taken, but a clear perspective can serve to enthuse suppliers and customers as well as employees.

Providing consistency answers a need that becomes particularly strong in an unstable and fast changing world. In a stable environment, consistency enables an organisation to fully exploit its existing competences in the efficient pursuit of its strategic goals. But when that environment changes, consistency can be dangerous.

This reading review aims to capture the main points and the spirit of the original in readable form. It may not cover all the points raised in the original text or quote the examples referenced. It is not intended to contain any value judgements about the original text, but inevitably it remains a personal interpretation. For a comprehensive appreciation readers are strongly recommended to the original text. Reviewed by permission of the Regents of the University of California.

Clear strategic direction aids the focus of effort and definition of the organisation's culture and also provides consistency which, though it may be wanted by the people, can be wholly dysfunctional for the organisation. Successful ways of doing things are difficult to change not simply because of the capital sunk in relevant assets, but more importantly because of the experience and expertise invested in its people.

In fast-changing circumstances strategies may be vital for their absence.

Reading review

15

'Strategic intent'

G. Hamel and C.K. Prahalad, *Harvard Business Review*, May/June 1989

Many western managers are moving heaven and earth to remain competitive with eastern, particularly Japanese companies, through imitation. They try such initiatives as product line rationalising, downsizing, de-layering, quality circles, just-in-time production, business process re-engineering, benchmarking, continuous improvement, Japanese human resource management practices and the rest, and when these all fail they form strategic alliances with their tormentors. But imitation is not good enough. By imitating they will never catch up. They need to rethink strategy from the bottom up.

Western orthodoxies such as strategic fit, the strategy hierarchy, logical incrementalism, generic strategies etc. tend to lead to strategic decline while eastern firms, working without these constraints, break out of existing structures, leverage their resources and achieve the wildest sounding ambitions.

Few western firms successfully anticipate new global competitors because their competitor analysis focuses on the existing resources (human, technical and financial) of present competitors – a 'snapshot of a moving car' – the pace at which new competitive advantages are being built is rarely recognised. It is vital to understand the resolution, stamina and inventiveness of potential competitors.

Successful competitors begin with crazy ambitions – an obsession with winning at all levels of the organisation and a 10–20 year quest for global leadership. This is referred to as *strategic intent*. For example, Komatsu's 'Encircle Caterpillar' and Canon's 'Beat Xerox'.

Strategic intent focuses the organisation's attention on winning, motivating people by communicating the value of the target, leaving room for individual and team initiatives, sustaining enthusiasm by providing new operational definitions as

This reading review aims to capture the main points and the spirit of the original in readable form. It may not cover all the points raised in the original text or quote the examples referenced. It is not intended to contain any value judgements about the original text, but inevitably it remains a personal interpretation. For a comprehensive appreciation readers are strongly recommended to the original text. Copies of the full article are available from HBS Publishing, *www.hbsp.harvard.edu*

circumstances change, and using intent consistently to guide resource allocations. It states a target that deserves personal effort and which remains consistent over time.

Strategic intent is different from, perhaps incompatible with, strategic planning. A strategic plan acts as a *feasibility sieve* which filters out unrealistic goals such as global leadership for a relatively minor player. But strategic intent deliberately sets a goal which is dramatically beyond the reach of existing resources. It then focuses the organisation on closing the gap by passing a series of discrete milestones. For example, Canon first had to understand Xerox patents, then license Xerox technology to make a product to gain market experience. It had to gear up internal R&D, then license out its own technology to pay for further R&D. Then it entered market segments initially where Xerox was weak, then in its main markets by an innovative means (e.g. selling rather than leasing) etc. This is a long haul achieved by a series of challenges that stretch the organisation. A similar picture is given of how Komatsu encircled Caterpillar.

For a challenge to be effective individuals and teams throughout the organisation must understand it and its implications for their own jobs. Top management must therefore:

1. Create a sense of urgency or quasi-crisis.
2. Create a competitor focus at every level through widespread use of competitive intelligence.
3. Provide employees with the skills they need to work effectively.
4. Give the organisation time to digest one challenge before launching the next.
5. Establish clear milestones and review mechanisms.

Success will only be achieved if employees are engaged intellectually and emotionally and top and bottom of the organisation share the pain and gain in a reciprocal responsibility for competitiveness.

All competitive advantages are short-lived and an organisation's most robust competitive advantage is its capacity to improve existing skills and learn new ones.

To achieve a strategic intent a company must usually take on and beat a larger, better financed competitor. Imitation results in failure; competitive innovation is required for success. Hamel and Prahalad note the following four approaches to competitive innovation:

1. Building layers of advantage
2. Searching for loose bricks
3. Changing the terms of engagement
4. Competing through collaboration

Building layers of advantage is instanced by the Japanese TV industry. It started on the basis of cheap '*bowl of rice*' labour. This was vulnerable so they built channels and brands to achieve a global franchise, global marketing and now regional manufacturing and design, to tailor products to national markets.

Searching for loose bricks: for example, many Japanese industries have entered markets at the low-cost end through the supply of commodity components and progressively fought upmarket with finished products.

Changing the terms of engagement: e.g. Canon taking on Xerox by selling rather than leasing.

Collaboration (e.g. licensing, outsourcing, joint ventures etc.): the Japanese attacked TV manufacture with low costs and, once established, offered to produce the next generation products (e.g. VCRs, CD players etc.). American firms succumbed, saving on R&D etc., but in many cases found it impossibly expensive to climb back on board the new technology and thus forfeited their future.

Competitive innovation is likened to judo – the game is to upset rivals by using their weight against them; recognise and upset their existing success recipes.

Nearly all the examples of strategic intent illustrate Japanese firms beating, encircling or upsetting American and/or European firms, but it is the American and European firms which have the 'sophisticated' strategy models. Playing the strategy orthodoxies is competitive suicide. BCG, Porter, SBU orientation, professional general management (i.e. not industry specific or expert), leadership myths and the rest, in the end, all fail. They only lead to top management caution and organisational conservatism which, even if based on successful recipes, ultimately only fulfils investors' short-term orientation, leaving strategic success to the ambitious, unorthodox achievers of strategic intent.

Reading review

16

'The competitive advantage of nations'

M.E. Porter, *Harvard Business Review*, March/April 1990

Competitiveness in international trade does not result from a nation's natural resources, labour costs or exchange rates, but is created through innovation and product improvement stimulated by fierce domestic competition. The ability to innovate bred through competition in home markets is the foundation of international success; protection and regulation only smother international competitiveness.

Innovation can be broadly defined. It can be incremental or revolutionary and can involve new products and new processes, new markets, new marketing, new design or even new ways of training. The new can come from anywhere and be applied to anything, but it is entirely dependent on toil and sweat both for its achievement and its sustenance. Once a new product or process has been successfully introduced it will quickly be copied and the more successful it is the more quickly will it be imitated. The new therefore needs to be supported by continuous upgrading and improvement to keep ahead of imitators.

In addition, studies suggest two other prerequisites for sustaining competitive advantage. First, it requires a truly global strategy which is therefore open to competition from all quarters. Secondly, it requires a willingness to render its existing competitive advantages obsolete by the establishment of the new.

National competitive advantage is dependent on four sets of conditions:

1. National resources and infrastructure
2. Domestic customer market factors
3. State of supplier and related industries
4. State and structure of domestic competition

This reading review aims to capture the main points and the spirit of the original in readable form. It may not cover all the points raised in the original text or quote the examples referenced. It is not intended to contain any value judgements about the original text, but inevitably it remains a personal interpretation. For a comprehensive appreciation readers are strongly recommended to the original text. Copies of the full article are available from HBS Publishing, *www.hbsp.harvard.edu*

National resources and infrastructure are not simply the factors of production of classical economics. Much more important are the knowledge-based factors, particularly those which are specialised to the particular industry and which require large scale investment to create. An abundance of traditional factors may lead nations to rest on these natural advantages, while a lack of traditional factors may well be a spur to the creation and development of specialist bodies of knowledge. Thus national competitive disadvantage can lead to the development of advantage especially where the disadvantage is likely to spread to other nations and where the other three conditions are basically favourable to the development of competitive advantage.

Domestic customer market is a training ground for global competition. If consumers are sophisticated and ahead of world trends, if the domestic market is well developed and competitive rivalry is high and if the nation itself tends to lead world tastes, then competitors from that nation will tend to be well equipped for success in the global market.

The state of supplier industries goes far beyond questions of availability of strategic raw materials and is largely concerned with the global competitiveness of supplier industries realised particularly in terms of their ability to supply innovative leading-edge products. Where this is the case an industry will also benefit from a rapid interchange of technical knowledge and innovation.

The state and structure of domestic competition is crucially important as a determinant of national competitive advantage. Many different influences are relevant. Managerial norms may make some industries more effective than others. For example, the Germanic hierarchy system with a technical manager at the top appears to be highly successful in engineering oriented industries; while the Italian system of privately owned, small or medium-sized enterprises appears successful in customised products for niche markets where flexibility and rapid response are the keys to success. Investment practices can also be crucial. For example, German and Swiss firms are owned largely by banks who hold shares for long-term returns and where, as a consequence, mature industry firms can afford to invest in R&D etc. By contrast, shares in US firms are traded for short-term gains, managers rewarded on the basis of annual performance and consequently mature, low-growth situations are ill supported. Finally, strong domestic competition is a powerful spur to the creation of national advantage through continuous innovation and improvement which is further multiplied by geographical concentration.

These four sets of conditions which determine national competitive advantage are interdependent. They may be self-reinforcing or they may be self-destructive, with one weak force undermining the others. Domestic rivalry is the key to how they work together, strong domestic rivalry serving to reinforce and stimulate the others. National competitive advantage will not exist in single, isolated industries, but tend to develop in clusters of associated industries.

The old theory of international trade based on comparative advantage in traditional factors of production no longer works. The competitive advantage of nations based on the four sets of conditions provides a better explanation of the current international trading position.

Government has a role to play in creating national competitive advantage but it is not the protective regulatory role suggested by the orthodox wisdom and does not involve intervention in factor and currency markets. Government's job is to create the required infrastructure, especially for knowledge-based industries this means education and specialised apprenticeship schemes to focus support on particular sectors; it means establishing high health, safety and environmental standards; it means ensuring active competition rather than collaboration within an industry by deregulation and vigorous antitrust enforcement; and it means encouraging investment through tax incentives.

The company role in achieving national competitive advantage is through innovation. They can achieve this by buying from the most advanced suppliers, selling to the most demanding customers and by outperforming the most competent competitors. In doing this they should focus on strengthening the conditions on which national competitive advantage rests. Above all they should seek out competition and use the advantages so gained to build further advantage, using strengths from elsewhere in order to achieve global leadership.

Reading review

17

'The core competence of the corporation'

C.K. Prahalad and G. Hamel, *Harvard Business Review*, May/June 1990

In the 1980s managers were assessed on their ability to restructure and de-layer their organisations. In the 1990s it will be their ability to identify and exploit the core competences that make growth possible.

Compare GTE and NEC. From 1980 to 1988 GTE sales went from $9.98bn to $16.46bn while NEC's went from $3.8bn to $21.89bn. In 1980 GTE looked much better placed than NEC, but NEC outperformed it because it thought of itself in terms of core competences.

NEC articulated a strategic intent to exploit the convergence of computing and communications – 'C&C'. This was communicated to everyone inside the firm and outside in the mid 1970s. A 'C&C Committee' oversaw the development of core products and core competences. This was supported by co-ordination groups and committees cutting across SBUs. They also multiplied internal resources through collaboration (over 100 alliances as of 1987) and accumulated a broad array of core competences, quickly and cheaply (following Japanese tradition). The strategic intent behind these alliances was well known and understood by all NEC managers.

GTE sees itself as a portfolio of businesses whereas NEC sees itself as a portfolio of competences – the comparison is repeated with Honda vs Chrysler, Canon vs Xerox, and others.

In the short run, competitiveness depends on product price/performance attributes, but fairly shortly demanding standards of price and quality are established as the prerequisite of survival. In the long run, competitiveness comes from the ability to build core competences (corporate-wide technologies and production skills that

This reading review aims to capture the main points and the spirit of the original in readable form. It may not cover all the points raised in the original text or quote the examples referenced. It is not intended to contain any value judgements about the original text, but inevitably it remains a personal interpretation. For a comprehensive appreciation readers are strongly recommended to the original text. Copies of the full article are available from HBS Publishing, *www.hbsp.harvard.edu*

empower individual businesses to adapt quickly to changing opportunities) quicker and cheaper than competitors in order to build features and sophistication into products and develop completely unanticipated products.

Core competence is about harmonising streams of technology, the organisation of work and the delivery of value. It requires communication, involvement and a deep commitment to working *across* organisational boundaries. For example, theoretical know-how is not enough for Casio to produce business card sized radios – it also needs to combine competences in miniaturisation, microprocessor design, material science and ultra-thin precision casing.

Core competences are not only about combining streams of technology, but also about organising work and delivering value. To bring Sony's competence in miniaturisation to fruition it also needs to ensure that technologists, engineers and marketers all understand customer needs as well as the technological possibilities.

3M's competences in substrates, coatings and adhesives have produced businesses as diverse as Post-It notes, magnetic tape, photographic film, pressure-sensitive tapes and coated abrasives. This is an example of the tree analogy: roots = competences, trunk = core (generic) products, branches = businesses, leaves/fruit = end products.

Examples of core competences are given: Honda's core competences in engines and power trains applied to cars, motorcycles, lawnmowers and generators. Canon's core competences in optics, imaging and microprocessor control applied to photocopiers, laser printers, cameras and image scanners.

Core competences have the following features:

1. They provide potential access to a wide variety of markets (e.g. display systems lead to calculators, miniature TVs, laptop monitors and car dashboards).
2. They should make a significant contribution to the perceived customer benefits of the end product.
3. They should be difficult for competitors to replicate.

Any firm is unlikely to achieve global leadership in more than five or six fundamental competences. Firms need to list their competences and those of their competitors rather than simply compare products in terms of price/quality attributes.

It is easy to throw away core competences – e.g. Chrysler outsourcing engines to Mitsubishi and Hyundai – Honda does not do this. Several US and EU companies have got out of TV manufacture and thus seem likely to miss out on high resolution TV in the 1990s. If you get off the train it is very unlikely that you will be able to walk to the next station and climb aboard again. For example, Motorola missed out the 256 K generation of DRAM chips. Sony lost out on Betamax, but retains its core competence through 8 mm camcorders. Managements stuck in the SBU mind-set miss out on these opportunities, for example, General Electric and TV.

Core products are based on core competences, e.g. Honda engines, Canon's laser printer engines, Matsushita's refrigerator compressors. Thus JVC established VCR supply relationships with leading national consumer electronics companies, thus gaining the cash and diversity of market experience which enabled it to outpace Philips and Sony.

Global leadership is fought at three levels: core competences, core products and, most superficially of all, end products. The SBU is thus an anachronism which results in underinvestment in developing both core competences and core products, in terms both of money and, more importantly, of skills and people. The result is therefore only in incremental end product development, i.e. 'bounded innovation', rather than radical innovation in fundamental new developments.

Strategic management's task is therefore to establish a corporate architecture which guides competence building through collaborative partnerships externally and the rotation of key people through different areas of the business internally; e.g. at Canon people are moved from cameras to photocopiers to precision optics and later to cross-divisional project teams. Prahalad and Hamel emphasise there is no one best way of organising the corporate architecture.

SBUs should bid for core competences (i.e. people) just as it does for funds. The people critical to core competences are corporate assets to be deployed by corporate management. Competence carriers should be regularly brought together to trade notes and ideas in order to build a strong feeling of community among these people. Their loyalty should be to the integrity of the core competence they represent (not to their SBU).

Core competences are the wellspring of new business development. An obsession with competence building will characterise the global winners of the 1990s.

Reading review

18

'Corporate imagination and expeditionary marketing'

G. Hamel and C.K. Prahalad, *Harvard Business Review,* July-August 1991

In the 1980s, global competition was waged over price and quality, but in the 1990s the battle will be about creating new markets with new, previously unimaginable products. Differences in cost, quality and cycle time will become insignificant among the survivors. They will need not only to invest in maintaining and developing their core competences. They will also need corporate imagination and expeditionary marketing to envision new opportunities and create new competitive space before their competitors.

To achieve this a firm must be able to liberate itself from the fixation with ROI and other short-term measures and instead be able to accept extremely long delays before opportunities come to fruition. This requires an almost instinctive belief in the ultimate benefits of the new opportunities identified. In Japan, corporate imagination has produced many new markets and despite the orthodox wisdom that large firms are not innovative, firms such as Sharp, Sony, Yamaha and others have succeeded.

Corporate imagination

Most companies get big because they are good at what they do and so it is almost inevitable that they develop a concern for defending their existing business. This inhibits their focusing on new opportunities, but they can still develop a corporate imagination through the following four initiatives:

1. *Breaking out of the existing market.* By thinking of the company in terms of core competences rather than products or business units, it is possible to envision new

This reading review aims to capture the main points and the spirit of the original in readable form. It may not cover all the points raised in the original text or quote the examples referenced. It is not intended to contain any value judgements about the original text, but inevitably it remains a personal interpretation. For a comprehensive appreciation readers are strongly recommended to the original text. Copies of the full article are available from HBS Publishing, *www.hbsp.harvard.edu*

core products by exploiting two or more competences which have previously not been combined.

2. *Discovering mould-breaking new product ideas.* This can be achieved by adding new functionality to existing products (e.g. Yamaha's electronic recording piano – many such possibilities are being currently exploited through newly computerised product controls), by offering existing functionality in new forms (e.g. pocket calculators), or by offering new functionality in new forms (e.g. home fax machines).
3. *Smashing the existing price/performance norms.* New technology presents opportunities to offer previously inconceivable levels of performance at substantially reduced cost.
4. *Leading customers rather than following them.* Customers very often cannot conceive the possibilities offered by new technologies so asking them what they want can be futile in exploiting corporate imagination. Companies that lead or educate their customers as to the possibilities develop marketers with technical imagination and technologists with marketing imagination. Neither technology nor marketing alone can create new competitive space, but multidisciplinary teams and individuals can.

Expeditionary marketing

This is the potentially risky process of creating new markets (where orthodox market research is likely to be inaccurate) ahead of the competition. Letting others take the lead reduces the risk but also the prospects of ultimate success. Learning about the market by introducing new products as a learning exercise and with controlled amounts of risk progressively accumulates information about the mix of functionality, price and performance which will ultimately lead to success. It requires a willingness to make mistakes – like shooting arrows, a miss is used to learn and adjust the aim rather than being rejected as a failure. Expeditionary marketing raises the number of hits by increasing the number of product offerings, market niches and opportunities, thereby rapidly increasing managerial knowledge and understanding.

The development of core competences and core products can increase the number of potential hits. Many examples are given of successful expeditionary marketing. Further support for the approach is provided by instancing General Electric's attack on CAD/CAM and CIM. GE did not adopt the expeditionary marketing approach but attacked the opportunity on an all-or-nothing basis. It found the market took longer than hoped to develop and eventually GE pulled out, only to come back to the market at a much reduced level and with partners to share the risk. An expeditionary marketing approach would have been much safer and more successful from the outset.

Financial criteria are inadequate for measuring managerial performance in expeditionary marketing and corporate imagination. The time and risk adjustments of financial theory mean that this orientation is too short term and inhibits managerial risk-taking.

The old mind-set focuses on served markets, defending today's business, conceiving the company as a portfolio of businesses, following customers, focusing on product markets, maximising the hit rate and a measuring commitment in purely financial terms. In contrast, the expeditionary marketing approach focuses on opportunity horizons, creating new competitive space, conceiving the company as a portfolio of core competences, leading customers, focusing on functionalities, maximising learning and measuring commitment in terms of persistence.

Reading review

19

'Management practices in learning organizations'

M.E. McGill, J.W. Slocum Jr. and D. Lei, *Organizational Dynamics*, Summer 1992

There are two categories of learning: adaptive and generative. Most organisations are adaptive learners, i.e. they seek to cope with the new by making small gradual, incremental changes when absolutely necessary. They deliberately limit the degree of change and are unlikely to envision entirely new situations, products or processes that do not already exist. They are predictable and therefore vulnerable to 'smart' competitors.

Organisations which have achieved leadership in their industry often find it difficult to change – the trappings of their former success inhibit their adaption to the new. General Electric, for example, focused on labour and materials cost reduction, outsourcing even core technologies where ever it could reduce costs and went from near global dominance in consumer electronics to withdrawal over a 20 year period. Sears Roebuck exhibits a similar experience.

A 'learning organisation', on the other hand, is one that emphasises generative learning and fundamentally transforms its basic processes in response to new situations. Generative learning is a process of continuous experimentation and feedback. Management practices in learning organisations rest on the following five characteristics: openness, systemic thinking, creativity, a sense of personal efficacy and empathy.

Several examples of generative learning organisations are provided: Arthur Anderson who transformed itself from an arm's length auditor to an information and technology consultant, from an outsider to an insider that might provide a client's CFO or even the whole finance department; Eastman Kodak moving from silver-

This reading review aims to capture the main points and the spirit of the original in readable form. It may not cover all the points raised in the original text or quote the examples referenced. It is not intended to contain any value judgements about the original text, but inevitably it remains a personal interpretation. For a comprehensive appreciation readers are strongly recommended to the original text. Reviewed by permission of the American Management Association International, New York, NY. *http://www.amanet.org*

based film to electronic photography and thence into multimedia; IBM's transformation to the 'open systems' philosophy and its multiple collaborations motivated by the desire to create new knowledge.

Generative learning can only be implemented by new internal processes and management practices. Adaptive learning organisations in fast-changing environments are bound by the limits of their existing knowledge and continually driven by the need to catch up. Generative learning organisations, on the other hand, are not bound by what they know, but driven by the actual process of learning which depends on the five characteristics already mentioned: openness etc.

- *Openness* requires that managers give up their reliance on control and adopt 'cultural/functional humility', i.e. accept that contributions from other cultures or functions can have equal value. The required management practices include:
  - cultural–functional diversity of people
  - functional diversity of workgroups
  - absence of 'expert' jargon
  - conflict identification and resolution skills
  - open access for all to all information
- *Systemic thinking* requires that managers have a holistic view of the organisation, not just individual aspects and that organisational learning is the foundation of its competitive advantage. Required management practices include:
  - sharing of real (as opposed to invented) organisational histories
  - recognition of relationships based on real interactions rather than hierarchy
  - eradication of line/staff distinctions
  - focus on interactions across the whole organisation and its external interactions
- *Creativity* widely recognised as essential but difficult to achieve. It depends on managers' personal flexibility (i.e. the ability to change behaviour in light of current realities) and willingness to take risks (i.e. preparedness to fail, not just take carefully calculated risk). These are both personal as well as organisational factors, managers as well as the whole organisation must be capable of ditching old recipes and routine ways of working. Required management practices include:
  - reward practices that focus on the long term, not just short term
  - people mobility across the organisation
  - positive personal development policies and practices
  - development of team culture
- *Personal efficacy* refers to the view that one can and should improve the world in some small way. It depends on a manager's accurate knowledge of their own values and goals and their focus on solving problems. By accurate is meant that their own view reflects the views of others. In most organisations, managers do not have the benefit of feedback from others, but in learning organisations this is actively sought. Required management practices include:
  - clarifying strategic direction
  - recognising individual efforts to progress that direction
  - linking learning with action

- *Empathy* requires that managers are socially responsible, sensitive to personal interests and individual dignity and motivated to repair personal relationships. Required management practices include:
  - integrity in all personal dealings
  - active corporate citizenship
  - recognition of people's out of work contributions
  - preparedness to be responsible for relationships

Given the continuing rapid pace of technological change, organisations must be willing to experiment and fail. A generative learning organisation will gain new insights from these experiences and use them to develop further.

Reading review

20

'A strategy of change: some conclusions'

D.C. Wilson, *A Strategy of Change*, Routledge, 1992

Theories of organisational change have to a considerable extent been obscured by the fashionable practice of change management which is driven by recipes and checklists of best practice. This is worrying for both the theoretician and the practitioner because the management of change cannot be reduced to a single universally applicable formulae. There is a gap between theory and practice which appears to be widening. The theory is drawn from many different disciplines, is complex, situation dependent and not necessarily definitive, but aims to increase understanding. The practice is largely skill based, is attractively packaged and fashionable but may be superficial and ineffective.

Management of change is not simply a behavioural issue. It consists of behavioural, economic, historical, decision making, political and social aspects. However, as with much of management, these have been simplified into a skills versus context dichotomy which affects the practitioner very fundamentally. For example, a common problem of multibusiness companies is that they articulate a focused strategy but have a range of products or businesses which is actually quite diffuse. The problem is how to bring the strategy and the actuality into agreement. Most often this will be approached by trying to focus the product range to make it agree with the strategy. How can this be done? The process is often held to be one of communication, negotiation, team building, resistance reduction, persuasion, internal selling, by attention to management style and influencing skills.

Alternatively, the outcome might be achieved as a result of political, rather than behavioural analysis, the key to achieving change being to understand the context and therefore the likely outcomes of action.

This reading review aims to capture the main points and the spirit of the original in readable form. It may not cover all the points raised in the original text or quote the examples referenced. It is not intended to contain any value judgements about the original text, but inevitably it remains a personal interpretation. For a comprehensive appreciation readers are strongly recommended to the original text. Reviewed by permission of Routledge.

The situation may be more complex than simply to bring actual activities into line with the desired focus. It may also be necessary to achieve a degree of innovativeness and creativity through the development of open communications and an absence of formal structures. Such a process may then generate new products which do not lie within the desired focus.

The current vogue for addressing these problems from a behaviouralist perspective appears, according to the empirical research, only to provide short-term answers, perhaps because they depend on a single individual. The structure, culture and power perspective may be less easy to work within but appears to provide longer-term solutions (Cummings and Huse, 1989).

This is not to suggest that the behavioural organisational development (OD) techniques are worthless. But the basic assumption that increasing participation and autonomy leads to more satisfied *and* productive people is only poorly supported by empirical evidence. A wider perspective is required. Innovation can be encouraged through the formal planning systems of an organisation and managed by various well worn paths, e.g. decentralisation, de-layering etc., but we know that structural concepts are only part of the answer to organisational change and learning.

Argyris and Schon (1978) made the distinction between 'inner-loop learning' (learning by increments appropriate in stable environments) and 'outer-loop learning' (learning by deep ideological changes necessary in highly uncertain environments). For them, therefore, management of change was not simply a behavioural matter, but one which required inclusion of the rate and level of uncertainty in the organisation's operating context. In the late 1980s the operating context included not only rapid technological change, but also a high rate of business failure in manufacturing and relative growth of the service sector as well as an increase in the level of acquisitions and joint ventures, globalisation of markets, improved quality, new technology and marketing plus an increased focus on corporate culture and R&D.

This degree of change and uncertainty in the operating context inevitably limits the effectiveness of change management initiatives which are restricted to the traditional behavioural OD strategies. The 'excellence tradition' suggests the creation of a strong culture, but there is little empirical evidence to support direct explicit attempts to manage culture.

Globalisation and an increased emphasis on R&D raises the role of some stakeholders in strategic decisions, but other stakeholders are likely to resist any pressures to change the power balance unless something out of the ordinary occurs, such as a technological breakthrough, a new source of information or ideas, a new conflict between powerful stakeholders, a new topic for strategic decision, or threatened extinction.

There can never be a universal model of change management because change is itself variable in terms of amount, breadth, speed and immediacy. Adoption of new technology can be regarded simply as an economically determined option, or as a means to further social and political change. Change is therefore a complex quantity, not simply a subset of organisational behaviour manageable through a bag of simplistic behavioural tools. The effectiveness of any such tools or programmes will be dependent on the operating context in which they are applied. A thorough understanding of the macro context is crucial to any effective 'strategy of change'.

Reading review

21

'Strategy as stretch and leverage'

G. Hamel and C.K. Prahalad, *Harvard Business Review*, March/April 1993

There are some unexpected winners of (global) competitive battles. The biggest and best resourced do not necessarily win in the long term. Why is this? Where does competitiveness come from?

Situations are analysed in detail, but analysis tends to focus on the existing orthodoxies such as measures of efficiency, quality and customer orientation. Inevitably the result is that Company X is shown to have inadequate quality or too high costs etc. These are the 'whats' of competitiveness, but we need to identify the 'whys'. Why are some firms first with new forms of competitiveness? Why do some firms break the mould while others take it as fixed?

National cultures and systems (e.g. fiscal and industrial policy) may have some impact, but this is often overstated as many examples show. There are more powerful explanations.

Breaking the mould

The orthodox wisdom, the ways of doing things that have been successful in the past, the agreed industrial recipes, determine both the success and failure of a business. Managers are taught these norms both in their formal education and in their work experience. In the days when national markets were insulated this worked reasonably well because all competitors played to the same set of rules. But now markets have been opened up to international/global competitors who provide a wide variety of different norms and recipes. Thus the existing managerial orthodoxies are being continually challenged by new competitors coming from different national backgrounds.

This reading review aims to capture the main points and the spirit of the original in readable form. It may not cover all the points raised in the original text or quote the examples referenced. It is not intended to contain any value judgements about the original text, but inevitably it remains a personal interpretation. For a comprehensive appreciation readers are strongly recommended to the original text. Copies of the full article are available from HBS Publishing, *www.hbsp.harvard.edu*

Thus global competition is not so much competition of products as competition of managerial mind-sets.

From fit to stretch

The western mind-set about strategy is that it is concerned with:

- investing long term
- allocating resources
- fitting the business most effectively to its environments

This is not necessarily wrong but it is not the only view. An alternative focuses on:

- consistency of direction over the long term
- leveraging resources
- stretching the business beyond its apparent capability

For example, Company A is a market leader that accepts or even defines the orthodox wisdom and recipes of the industry. Typically Company A will seek to maintain market share and achieve a reasonable return on investment. In contrast, Company B is an ambitious new entrant which boldly seeks to challenge Company A's leadership position. In any direct competitive war Company A seems certain to win and Company A therefore plays according to the orthodox rule book. Company B also recognises these realities and is therefore forced to adopt other, less direct tactics. For example, it focuses on undefended market niches, rather than attacking the broad market as a whole. It will concentrate on achieving leadership in a small number of competences and outsourcing the rest, rather than trying to achieve leading edge competence across all activities.

The difference between Company A and Company B is not just that B has the speed and flexibility of small scale, but that it has a bigger misfit between its resources and its aspirations. Company A on the other hand has no need to change, or 'stretch', in order to achieve its objectives. Creating 'stretch' is the most crucial task of strategic management.

From allocation to leverage

Sheer weight of resources is no guarantee of competitive success as many examples demonstrate. The productivity of resources is more important than their scale. Productivity can be raised either by cutting the input or increasing the output. Cutting the input (e.g. by re-engineering, downsizing, de-layering etc.) has been widely adopted, but leads to a cost-cutting mind-set and, ultimately, to failure. Raising the output, i.e. leveraging, is a more challenging and fruitful process.

Resources can be leveraged in five main ways: *concentration*, *accumulation*, *complementary use*, *conservation* and *recovery*.

Concentration of resources requires that all the resources of the business, people, plant and equipment, money, functions and systems are focused consistently on achieving the strategic objectives of the business consistently over time.

Accumulation of resources means making full use of expertise and knowledge within the organisation, particularly if it challenges existing orthodoxies. It also requires obtaining knowledge and expertise from external sources, e.g. customers, suppliers, competitors etc. and defines the learning relationship within any alliances and joint ventures.

Complementary use of resources requires the combination of technological resources in order to multiply their impact, for example, combining two or more core competences to identify new core products. It also requires the business to balance its resources to achieve competitiveness in product development, production and marketing and distribution – a weakness in one area will devalue strengths in others.

Conserving resources requires skills and competences to be exploited by all the company's relevant business units, thus multiplying the impact. This doesn't only refer to technologies, but to production processes through flexible manufacturing and to brands. Resources can also be conserved by combining with other organisations to achieve a common goal such as the defeat of a common competitor. Finally resources should be conserved by not fighting head-on with the focus competitor, but seeking out under-defended niches and doing things in ways which are counter to their managerial mind-set.

Recovering resources: the speed of resource utilisation is crucial – doing it twice as fast requires half the resource – there are many examples of this phenomenon in product development cycle times.

Stretch without risk

Resources should not be committed without adequate knowledge and understanding of the business and its customers and competitors. Strategic management's job is to accelerate the acquisition of this understanding and thus minimise risk of failure – more haste less speed.

Thus strategy by stretch is not achieved through the development and implementation of a massively detailed plan, but by the identification of a consistently held long-term strategic intent and its achievement by many incremental steps along the way.

Reading review

22

Post-capitalist Society

P.F Drucker, Butterworth/Heinemann, 1993

Introduction

History is made up of long periods of stability interspersed with short periods of rapid change when within a few decades the world is suddenly different. For example:

- 13th century – the European world became centred on the city with City Guilds etc.
- 15th century – invention of printing, Luther's Reformation, the Renaissance (1470–1500), rediscovery of anatomy, adoption of Arabic numerals.
- 18th century – Industrial Revolution, birth of capitalism and communism.
- Present – technological revolution, electronic computer and microprocessor, mass education, post-capitalist society a society of organisations with the market as the integrator of economic activity.

Capitalist society was dominated by two social classes: capitalists and blue-collar workers (Marx's alienated, exploited, dependent proletarians). Because of the *productivity revolution* the blue-collar workers became an affluent middle class. Because of the *management revolution* the blue-collar workers began to decline in numbers, power and status. By 2000 there will be no advanced economy where blue-collar workers account for much more than 10 per cent of the workforce.

Ownership of the means of production is now held by financial institutions, pension funds etc., i.e. by employees. Thus capitalist societies are, in Marx's terms, socialist – ownership of the means of production etc. by the proletariat!

The destruction of Marxism as an ideology and communism as a social system brought to a close 250 years dominated by secular religion – salvation by society

This reading review aims to capture the main points and the spirit of the original in readable form. It may not cover all the points raised in the original text or quote the examples referenced. It is not intended to contain any value judgements about the original text, but inevitably it remains a personal interpretation. For a comprehensive appreciation readers are strongly recommended to the original text. Reviewed by permission of Butterworth Heinemann and the author.

(from Rousseau to Marx). The same forces are also making capitalism obsolescent. In post-capitalist society the basic economic resource – the means of production – is no longer capital, nor natural resources, nor labour, but *knowledge*. The central wealth-creating activity will be neither the allocation of capital to productive uses, nor labour; it is the allocation of knowledge to productivity and innovation. The leading social groups in this society will be the knowledge workers who know how to allocate knowledge to this productive use.

Knowledge workers will predominantly be employed in organisations. Unlike employees under capitalism they own both the means of production (through their pensions funds) and the tools of production (knowledge). The economic challenge of the post-capitalist society will be the productivity of knowledge work. The social challenge will be the dignity of the less educated service workers who will still form the majority.

Simultaneous with the collapse of communism has been the rise of transnational political organisation (e.g. European Union, Gulf War etc.) with more organisation between states and less emphasis on the sovereignty of the individual nation state. Internally, developed countries are fast becoming pluralist societies of organisations; externally, some governmental functions are becoming transnational, others regional and others more local.

The post-capitalist period is one of transition; a time to make the future; a time for action.

From capitalism to knowledge society

From 1750 to 1900, capitalism and technology conquered the globe. This process was driven by a radical change in the meaning of knowledge. Previously knowledge had been seen as applying to *being*, suddenly it was applied to *doing* – it became a resource and a utility.

In the first phase of this change, knowledge was applied to tools, processes and products; it created the Industrial Revolution, economic growth and great wealth, but it also caused alienation, class war and communism. In the second phase of the change, knowledge was applied to productivity and the productivity revolution converted the proletarian into a middle class bourgeois with a near upper class income. In the last phase, starting after World War II, knowledge was applied to knowledge itself – the managerial revolution.

From the earliest times, innovations have been able to diffuse fast. For example, Roger Bacon, English Franciscan friar, invented reading glasses around 1270; by 1290 they were used at the papal court in Avignon; by 1300 at the Sultan's court in Cairo; by 1310 at the court of the Mongol Emperor of China. Only the sewing machine and telephone, fastest of 19th century inventions, diffused as fast. But such technological inventions remained confined to one craft or application. For example, it took 200 years for Bacon's glasses to be applied to near sightedness; the potter's wheel was in full use in 1500 BC, but it took 2500 years to apply the same principles to women's work of spinning; the windmill was redesigned around 800 AD to become a real machine, but it took 300 years to apply the same principles to sailing ships. In the 18th century industrial revolution, however, inventions were applied immediately across the board. Watt's improvement of the steam engine (1765–76) made it a cost-effective provider of power. Watt used it for pumping water out of mines, as Newcomen had, but it was quickly applied to blowing air into blast furnaces, then driving all sorts of industrial machinery, driving steam-ships and then railway engines. By 1840 it had transformed every single manufacturing process, domestic and naval transport and was starting to transform agriculture; it had penetrated every part of the globe except Tibet, Nepal and the interior of tropical Africa, and it had changed social structure and created new social classes.

Since Plato (400 BC) there have been just two theories as to the meaning and function of knowledge. It is either for the intellectual, moral and spiritual growth of the individual (e.g. Plato, Socrates, Taoist and Zen), or it is to make the holder of knowledge effective. Both views are agreed that knowledge does not mean ability to do or utility. Utility is skill – the Greek *téchne* – not knowledge. *Téchne* was specific rather than generally applicable – knowledge of how to navigate from Greece to Sicily could not be applied to anything else. A skill could not be explained in words, written or spoken, but only demonstrated. As late as 1700 the English did not speak of 'crafts', but only 'mysteries' and the holder was sworn to secrecy from anyone who had not been apprenticed to a master. From 1700 to 1750 technology was invented, technology being a combination of *téchne* (i.e. the mystery of a craft skill) and *logy* (i.e. organised, systematic, purposeful knowledge).

Technology brought the first schools of engineering and technical universities (France and Germany) which codified, systematised and published existing knowledge of the craft mysteries; it also brought the use of technical patents (in England) to reward invention, i.e. the development of new knowledge.

This change in the meaning of knowledge enabled the development of technology and the subsequent social and political change stemming from the Industrial Revolution. Whilst the generation of unprecedented wealth could be seen to benefit mankind, the speed of change was so breathtaking as to be deeply traumatic and to create the problems described by Marx – exploitation and alienation of the proletariat etc.

When knowledge changed its meaning it began to be applied to tools, processes and products. Taylor then applied knowledge to the study of work. The only way a worker could produce more was by working harder or longer hours. Taylor challenged this and started a *productivity revolution.* His intention from the outset was that the prime beneficiary should be the worker, not the owner/employer, so that owners and workers, capitalists and proletarians, shared a common interest in productivity. His axiom, that all work could be analysed and organised by the application of knowledge, challenged the old craft skill mystery still clung to by many trade unions. At the start of American involvement in World War II America had little military capability, but by applying Taylor's 'task study' they trained unskilled farm-workers in 60–90 days into first-rate welders and shipbuilders and within a few months to producing precision optics (of higher quality than the Germans) on production lines. All the post WWII economic powers – Japan, South Korea, Taiwan, Hong Kong and Singapore, owe their rise to Taylor's training.

For hundreds of years there had been no increase in the ability of workers to make and move goods – machines created greater capacity but workers themselves remained no more productive than they had ever been. After Taylor productivity began to rise by $3\frac{1}{2}$–4 per cent per annum, i.e. doubling every 18 years. As late as 1910, workers in advanced economies worked as long as they always had – 3000 hours a year. Today they work around 1800 hours a year and produce 50 times as much output. And most of the increase in productivity has gone, as Taylor predicted, to the worker.

When Taylor started out, 90 per cent of workers in advanced economies were involved manually making or moving things. Today only 20 per cent are so engaged, and by 2010 it will be less than 10 per cent. The productivity of those so engaged still rises at the historical rate ($3\frac{1}{2}$–4 per cent pa) but the productivity revolution is over. From now on what matters is the productivity of non-manual, knowledge workers. This is concerned not with the application of knowledge to work but knowledge to knowledge – the *management revolution.* The definition of management has changed – it used to be related to responsibility for the performance of people, now it is related to the responsibility for the application and performance of knowledge. Thus knowledge is now seen as the essential economic resource – where there is effective management (i.e. application of knowledge to knowledge) the other resources can always be obtained.

Underlying these three phases (the industrial, productivity and management revolutions) of the shift to knowledge there has been a fundamental change in the meaning of knowledge. Traditional knowledge was general; now it is highly specialised. Educated persons were generalists – they knew enough to understand, talk and write about a good many things, but they did not know enough to *do* any one thing. The knowledge we now consider knowledge proves itself in action. Results are outside the person, in society or economy or in the advancement of knowledge itself. We have moved from knowledge (liberal education) to knowledges (specialised disciplines).

The society of organisations

An organisation is a human group, composed of specialists, working together on a common task. It is purposefully designed and intended to endure. It is always specialised, defined by its task and is effective only if it concentrates on the one task for which it was designed. A symphony orchestra is a good prototype of the modern organisation. Each of the players is a specialist; they are each playing a part towards the overall mission; each subordinates his speciality to the overall task; and they play only one piece of music at a given time.

The function of organisation is to make knowledges productive. This is done by making best use of specialists. The best specialists are effective as specialists not generalists – neurosurgeons get better the more they practise neurosurgery, not by playing French horns. In order for them to practise their specialism and to produce results, organisation is needed. The results of organisation are always external. The results of an orchestra is the music heard by the audience, results of a hospital are cured patients returned home, results of an army are wars deterred or won. Thus results may be a long way away from the individual specialist organisation member. An absolute prerequisite of an organisation's performance is therefore that the task or mission must be absolutely clear and results must also be clear and unambiguous and if possible measurable.

Membership of an organisation is optional. Thus organisations need to market membership – they have to attract people, hold people, recognise and reward people, motivate, serve and satisfy people. Because organisation is organisation of knowledge specialists it has to be an organisation of equals, of colleagues, a team of associates, rather than an organisation of ranks and hierarchies.

Managing a post-capitalist organisation involves the application of knowledge to tools, processes and products, to work and to knowledge itself. Management is therefore continually creating change. 'It must therefore be organised for constant change. It must be organised for innovation . . . for the systematic abandonment of the established, the customary, the familiar, the comfortable whether products, services and processes, human and social relationships, skills or organisations themselves.'

As well as being organised for this creative destruction, organisations also need to be organised for the creation of the new, firstly by continuous improvement (kaizen), secondly, by exploitation of knowledges (i.e. by developing applications), and finally, by innovation. Unless the knowledge-based organisation achieves this continually it will soon find itself obsolescent, losing the capacity to perform and to attract suitable specialists.

Post-capitalist society comprises of individuals who are dependent on access to an organisation to make their contribution (or living). There are two sorts of such individuals – the low skilled service workers and knowledge workers. The dignity and welfare of service workers is a central social problem for governments; the productivity of knowledge workers is the crucial managerial problem. And since knowledge workers have the means of production in their heads, are highly mobile and cannot be supervised, the old managerial methods are no longer appropriate.

Labour, capital and their future

During the years of manufacturing decline, production in USA remained more-or-less proportionate to GNP – 22 per cent in 1975, 23 per cent in 1990, both increased $2\frac{1}{2}$ times over the period. But between 1960 and 1990 employment in manufacturing fell from 25 per cent of the total workforce to 16 per cent. The size of the workforce doubled over the period though with few of the new jobs being in manufacturing. These trends seem set to continue with manufacturing remaining at around 23 per cent for the next 10 or 15 years during which time it will double again and with employment in manufacturing falling further to around 10–12 per cent of total.

The same trends are apparent in Japan. But whereas in USA there is gloom over the decline of manufacturing industry, in Japan there is delight in the increase in manufacturing production. In US manufacturing, jobs are seen as a priceless asset and billions of dollars are devoted to attracting them; in Japan they are seen as a liability. In Japan practically all young people get a high school degree and are therefore seen as overqualified for manual work; in America this is less true, especially of the Black population. Americans think that the industrial base, and that means manufacturing, is vital to the economy; in Japan they argue that there are more than enough potential blue-collar workers (i.e. with no schooling but well able to be quickly trained for manufacturing work) in the developing world and that encouraging blue-collar work in Japan would actually weaken the economy. Money should be invested in education of future knowledge workers rather than in creating blue-collar jobs.

The Japanese view seems to be right. The USA has the world's strongest agricultural base though less than 3 per cent of its workforce are involved. It could still be the world's greatest manufacturer with only 10 per cent of its workforce involved in manufacturing. It is not sufficient for an advanced economy to have a manufacturing base, it needs to be a knowledge worker based, rather than labour based, manufacturing, if it is to survive and prosper. Creating blue-collar jobs in developed economies is a short-term expedient, and is unlikely to be viable in competition with Third World low labour cost manufacturers.

Capital too has changed out of all recognition. Pension funds and mutual funds are now the dominant sources of capital. In the USA, by 1992 these institutions owned over half the share capital of large companies and an almost equal proportion of the fixed debt of large and medium sized companies. This concentration of capital is unprecedented. Legally, pension funds are owners, but in reality they are trustees for the ultimate owners the future pensioners. As such the funds are essentially deferred wages – as Marx suggested capital is accumulated through the expropriation of wages, but in this case it is done by the wage earner, for the wage earner! The pensions funds are not owners in the accepted sense – they cannot manage their business and they cannot sell their investment – their holdings are simply too big, no one could purchase them except other pension funds. Therefore they have to make sure that the business is being managed effectively through some sort of evolving business audit.

The productivity of the new workforces

Forty years ago people doing knowledge work and service work accounted for less than one-third of the total workforce whereas today they account for four-fifths in all developed countries and their productivity is *the* productivity of a developed economy. And it is abysmally low. One-third of the capital investment in developed countries in the last 30 years has gone into information handling kit – computers, faxes, cctv, electronic mail etc., yet the number of people whose work benefits from this investment has risen faster than GDP – i.e. they appear to be getting less, rather than more, productive. The lowest productivity is in government employment, yet governments everywhere are the largest employers of service workers. In the USA, government employs 20 per cent of the entire workforce and most of them in routine clerical work.

Taylor's productivity methods are more difficult to apply to service work than to making and moving things because in the latter the worker serves the machine and is machine paced whereas in service work the machine serves the worker. It is even more difficult to apply to knowledge work.

Another difficulty in applying productivity to service and knowledge work is the question of how it should be organised. Service and knowledge work depends on teamworking. There are three sorts of team – cricket (where everyone has a different role to play to the best of their individual ability), soccer (where though everyone is a specialist, they have to support each other and play to each other and develop skills under their coach), and doubles tennis (where each knows the other's strengths and weaknesses and covers for the other). Each is distinctive and cannot be mixed. In the cricket team, information comes from the situation, in soccer information comes from the coach, in doubles tennis it comes from each other.

Traditionally, most making and moving things work has been organised along cricket team lines with a CEO supported by strong functional executives. Traditionally, work on new products was done by cricket type teamwork, each specialist function doing its particular task and then handing it on to the next function. Around 1970, Japanese car firms started to switch to soccer team type organisation to speed up development of new models and improve flexibility. More recently, TQM, flexible manufacturing has forced Detroit to switch from cricket to doubles tennis team organisation.

Concentration on the job is the last prerequisite for productivity in service and knowledge work. In machine paced work the machine concentrates the worker, but in service and knowledge work this is not the case so great efforts have to be made to eliminate whatever does not contribute to the performance of the worker. The task of nurses in hospital is patient care, but every study shows they spend around three-quarters of their time on tasks unrelated to patient care, two-thirds of it filling up forms. This destroys productivity, motivation and pride.

In service and knowledge work it is essential for service and knowledge workers themselves to contribute to defining the job so as to ensure its continuously improving productivity. This will result in radical restructuring, very often eliminating layers of management and command hierarchy. Outsourcing of service work from specialist service organisations will also raise productivity and provide a means of enhancing the dignity and income of service workers.

The responsibility-based organisation

The post-capitalist organisation must be based on responsibility rather than command and control. The old organisation was based on the assumption that the man at the top knew all the jobs in the organisation; the knowledge-based organisation has to assume that superiors do not know the job of their subordinates. Knowledge workers are specialists who know their own jobs better than anyone else in the organisation. The knowledge-based organisation therefore requires that everyone takes responsibility for their objectives, their contribution and for their behaviour.

The task of management in the knowledge-based organisation is not to empower everyone so that everyone is a boss, but to make everyone a contributor.

Knowledge: its economics; its productivity

While the world economy will remain a market economy and retain the market institutions, its substance has been radically changed. The industries that have become central over the past 40 years are involved with the production and distribution of information rather than things. The new industries are telecommunications, computers, semiconductors, software etc. Even the pharmaceutical industry product is knowledge – the pill or ointment merely packaging. The non-businesses which produce and apply knowledge – health and education – have grown even faster than the knowledge-based businesses. The old businesses which have been most successful are those that have reorganised themselves around information and knowledge.

We do not yet fully understand how knowledge works as an economic resource. The perfect competition model does not work; nor is knowledge responsive to changes in levels of consumption or investment as traditional models suggest; moreover, knowledge is not homogeneous – there are three distinct kinds: continuous improvement, exploitation and innovation and all three are necessary for economic growth.

Knowledge is expensive. Developed countries spend around 20 per cent of GNP on education, employing organisations spend another 5 per cent of GNP on continuing education of their employees and a further 3-5 per cent of GNP is spent on R&D. This is far in excess of the rates of capital formation. The return on this investment, i.e. the productivity of knowledge, is the key factor in economic success. For example, Britain has a notoriously poor productivity rate – since WWII she developed antibiotics, the jet engine, the computer, body scanner etc., but failed to turn these into successful products and services, jobs, exports and market standing. The UK's low productivity of knowledge has been the root of its economic failure. Similar experience is now being enjoyed in America. Germany's knowledge productivity has been high in terms of applying, improving and exploiting old knowledge, but it has not been so successful exploiting new knowledge. Japan's knowledge productivity has been supreme.

Productivity of the knowledge resource is crucial. Interest in the productivity of capital is a largely post-war concern, and 30 years or so ago was the focus of many planning attempts. In the West these were not pursued because of their apparent failure. In communist countries planning was continued with ultimately disastrous results in terms of the productivity of capital investment. Government planning does not work, what is required to increase the productivity of knowledge is decentralisation and diversity plus, at the level of the business unit, systematic effort and organisation.

Making knowledge productive is a management responsibility; it cannot be done by government or by market forces. The first rule is that knowledge has to aim high if it is to produce results. It may get there by a series of small steps but each must be clearly focused on the ultimate aim which must be to make a difference. High knowledge productivity – whether in improvement, exploitation or innovation – comes at the end of a long gestation period, so management must manage the balance between the short and the long term. In addition, since knowledge is becoming so specialised into knowledges, management must try to ensure that connections are made across knowledges so that opportunities to improve, exploit or innovate are always recognised.

Reading review

23

'Strategic termites'

G. Morgan, *Imaginization: the art of creative management*, Sage, 1993

Termites may be small, blind, ugly little insects and they may appear to work randomly as individual earth shifters, but as a colony of many thousands they design and build cities of staggering efficiency and majestic proportions. They start their building operations by moving earth in several randomly positioned but closely adjacent sites and commence building upwards. When their vertical columns have reached the appropriate height the termites then join them up with the characteristic curved arch formation. The resulting structure comprises thousands of well ventilated, humidity controlled corridors and chambers which can accommodate millions of individuals and a typical termite heap is the equivalent of a mile high in human terms.

These masterpieces seem to result from a self-organising process. Each one is unique in detail, but the finished nest is immediately recognisable for what it is. The apparently chaotic and certainly unplanned activities of the individual termites results in the achievement of a grand purpose towards which individual activities must be guided by some overall sense of direction.

The termite is a good model for strategic management to follow in times of rapid change. A formal detailed plan imposed from above would be both unnecessary and restrictive. Strategic management following the termite example would let strategy evolve. They know what they would like to achieve but they do it in an open-ended way, encouraging desirable initiatives, taking relevant opportunities as they arise and building piece by piece and in many diverse ways towards the ultimate aim.

The chapter provides three examples of successful strategic termites: a training and development manager in a large decentralised company, a finance and administration manager in a government department, and a business unit manager in a large conglomerate. Each example, in very different ways, shows how successful strategic termites can be. They might have appeared opportunistic and disjointed, but their

This reading review aims to capture the main points and the spirit of the original in readable form. It may not cover all the points raised in the original text or quote the examples referenced. It is not intended to contain any value judgements about the original text, but inevitably it remains a personal interpretation. For a comprehensive appreciation readers are strongly recommended to the original text. Reviewed by permission of Sage Publications.

results were strategic. They shared a clear view of what they wanted to achieve and they did it by nudging and pushing the system in the appropriate direction.

If the problem is the introduction of a new product, or the opening of a new factory, there will clearly be a need for detailed plans the timing and sequencing of which will be crucial to success. The traditional linear view of management as 'planning, co-ordination and control' is still apt for such circumstances. But such detailed planning will be no good for managing in most of today's fast changing chaotic conditions. They would simply be strait-jackets. Moreover, they would tend to fizzle out because all the energy and talent goes into the planning rather than the doing.

There are not many linear situations today, though some may appear linear with hindsight. We tend still to rely on linear explanations of non-linear events. For example, Honda's attack on the US motor cycle market in 1959. They planned to sell big bikes but experienced some quality problems. By accident they started selling the lightweight Cub moped, but were flexible and smart enough to take the opportunity presented. Over the next seven years they took over 60 per cent of the market. Honda knew they wanted to capture the US motor cycle market – they had the vision and the strategy to achieve it emerged.

Strategic termites nudge, push, catalyse, facilitate, initiate, encourage and support activities consistent with the aspiration. They are opportunistic and open to learning and innovation and look for opportunities to create consistent 'mounds' of activity which gradually gather critical mass for the achievement of the overall purpose.

Reading review

24

'Building a learning organization'

D. Garvin, *Harvard Business Review*, July/August 1993

Continuous improvement programmes are everywhere but most fail because they require a commitment to learning not just cosmetic change. But the concept of a learning organisation remains confused, partly because academics have *utopianised* the term and rendered it impractical.

A learning organisation is simply one that changes its behaviour in response to new ideas that it might have either created itself or acquired from outside. It sounds simple and some organisations have succeeded, but it is surprisingly tough. Many business schools and consultancies fail to achieve it: they preach it but can't do it themselves.

Yet those organisations that succeed, achieve their success as a result of deliberate attention to five main activities:

1. *Systematic problem solving*: Using scientific methods to process hard data (rather than soft assumptions); training people to challenge the whole process, the quality of data, the aptness of analytical methods and the accuracy of results; refusing ever to accept 'gut feel'.
2. *Experimentation with new approaches*: Systematic acquisition and testing of new knowledge either on a continuous basis or as one-off demonstration projects. Continuous programmes acquire data regularly by monitoring technology, customers or competitors and feeding them into systematic problem-solving models. For example, Corning continually experiments with new raw materials; Allegheny Ludlum regularly tries out new ways of steel rolling. Such pro-

This reading review aims to capture the main points and the spirit of the original in readable form. It may not cover all the points raised in the original text or quote the examples referenced. It is not intended to contain any value judgements about the original text, but inevitably it remains a personal interpretation. For a comprehensive appreciation readers are strongly recommended to the original text. Copies of the full article are available from HBS Publishing, *www.hbsp.harvard.edu*

grammes need a culture that rewards risk-taking and does not punish failure on such experiments.

Demonstration projects are usually higher-profile exercises having a more profound structural impact on the organisation. Again they are based on scientifically processed knowledge acquired specifically for the experiment. They may be limited *learning by doing* trials which if successful may be applied across the whole organisation. They may involve sensitive precedents and will usually be developed by a multifunctional team reporting to a top manager. For example, Copeland transformed itself from a single all purpose plant to multiple focused manufacturing facilities.

3. *Learning from past experience*: For example IBM's 360 success was built on the failed Stretch computer; Boeing set up a team to learn from the problems experienced with 737 and 747 launches and explicitly built that learning into the 757 and 767, its most successful launches ever.
4. *Learning from others*: Benchmarking, identifying best practice organisations, systematic analysis of those practices and comparison with one's own, and development of action recommendations and implementation.
5. *Transferring knowledge*: To ensure that learning gained is not restricted but is made immediately available organisation-wide and supported by relevant education and training programmes.

If organisational learning is real it must be measurable. Various techniques have been used in the past: learning curves, progress in manufacturing costs, experience curves etc., but they are not enough, because they relate only to cost and ignore quality, delivery, new product development etc. The 'half-life curve' is one better way of measuring – the time it takes to achieve a 50 per cent improvement in any measure of performance. But even this is not the full story since it focuses only on results.

Organisational learning is a three-stage process: cognitive change, behavioural change, performance change. A proper measure of organisational learning would assess all three stages and this has been done through specific surveys involving questionnaires and interview programmes.

The first step to building a learning organisation is to create a culture of learning where people are trained in relevant skills (e.g. brainstorming, problem solving etc.), functional boundaries are broken down (e.g. cross-functional meetings, project teams etc.). Then learning forums can be designed focusing on issues of strategic importance confronting the organisation with the aim not only of achieving solutions, but more importantly of learning from the process itself.

Reading review

25

'Putting value on strategy'

T. Grundy, *Long Range Planning*, Vol. 26, No. 3, 1993

The article explores how managers from four major UK organisations co-ordinate financial and strategic methods of evaluating capital investment decisions.

Financial theory suggests that the procedures for reaching investment decisions can be self-contained, should focus on cash flows rather than profits, the cash flows should be discounted and the decision should be based on a comparison of proceeding versus not proceeding with the investment. A number of problems have been identified with this approach such as risk assessment and the inclusion of intangibles.

Strategic theory treats investment decisions as part of the overall allocation of corporate resources and uses various models such as portfolios or Porter's competitive model to assist this process. However, the linkage between strategic position and financial return is not explicitly made. Other attempts to link strategic and financial appraisal, such as the PIMS database, Porter's value chain and shareholder value analysis, are hardly more successful.

Empirical work on organisational decision processes highlights the messiness of decisions which are not made solely on the basis of financial logic, but also incorporate political considerations and are made in the context of 'cognitive overload'.

This research investigated whether managers understood how to link strategic and financial appraisal. It reports the implementation of 'value-based management' at British Petroleum from 1989 to 1991. BP's traditional measure of corporate performance, on which senior managers were themselves appraised, had been return on capital employed. This was regarded as problematic because it did not address the creation of shareholder value, was backward looking and was not congruent with the discounted cash flow (DCF) investment criteria BP used.

Phase 1 of BP's value-based management (VBM) project involved the assessment of the net present value of all the group's businesses. This produced some 'surprises'

This reading review aims to capture the main points and the spirit of the original in readable form. It may not cover all the points raised in the original text or quote the examples referenced. It is not intended to contain any value judgements about the original text, but inevitably it remains a personal interpretation. For a comprehensive appreciation readers are strongly recommended to the original text. Reviewed by permission of Elsevier Science.

with some of the newer businesses, with no competitive advantage in unrelated (to core) markets, being worth less than expected. During subsequent phases VBM was found to be a useful learning tool that permitted wider issues than simply financial data to be considered, but it did not produce definitive answers. Nevertheless, the results were fed back into the group's control and reward systems.

It was found that managers found the greatest difficulty dealing with uncertainty, whether it was to do with structural changes in an industry, valuing 'new' markets or quantifying intangible items. There were also some more mechanical problems related to DCF procedures such as defining the 'base case' i.e. what happens if the investment is not made. Managers tried to make linkages between the strategic appraisal and financial appraisal at various stages of the process, but were not altogether successful. The differences between financial and economic measures were exacerbated by behavioural factors and made more problematic because strategy was only vaguely expressed, imperfectly communicated and there appeared to be no connection between statements of mission and operating plans.

The study concluded that it was not possible to create a simple prescriptive framework which would combine both strategic and financial forms of appraisal. This was not only because the measurements used in each perspective are so different but because there were also behavioural tensions which made such a combination even more unlikely to succeed. Nevertheless the problem might be soluble. Rather than a definitive framework it might be more appropriate to incorporate the 'soft logic' of managers' individual intuitive judgement on investment decisions.

Reading review

26

Corporate level strategy: creating value in the multi-business company

M. Goold, A. Campbell and M. Alexander, Wiley, 1994

Some multibusiness companies manage to create value in their subsidiary businesses, but the vast majority destroy value. The difference between the value creators and destroyers is one of corporate level strategy relating to two main decisions: what businesses should the company invest in, and how should the parent 'manage' (i.e. influence and relate to) its subsidiary businesses.

The first question has received some attention over the years since Ansoff first suggested the idea of a 'common thread', but simply having subsidiaries which share technologies or markets does not ensure the parent will create additional value.

Porter (1987) found that most acquisitions failed – more than half his sample of acquisitions among large American companies being resold, usually within 5 or 6 years of being acquired. He suggested that a test for the suitability of an acquisition would be that the acquired business should gain some competitive advantage from the link with its new parent.

Acquisitions can be justified only if the parents avoid value destruction (e.g. by imposing bureaucratic structures or unnecessary strategic constraints) and aim to create substantial value by their influence on the subsidiary business.

Creation of value will be achieved only if the subsidiary business needs and can exploit the resources, technologies, skills etc. that the parent can provide. This is a continuously changing relationship and the parent needs to ensure that the fit remains valid over time.

The parent needs to ensure not only that it is creating value for its subsidiary businesses but also that it is creating more value than any other parent could. This requires a thorough search for opportunities to create value and an understanding of how to bring these opportunities to fruition and how to avoid falling into the various value destruction traps which ensnare so many parent companies.

Value can be created through the parent company's fit with its subsidiary. This can be achieved on a one-to-one supportive basis, through linkages between fellow subsidiaries, by the provision of central functions and services and through corporate development, for example by acquiring new businesses which offer further linkages.

A company can assess how well it is likely to fit a potential acquisition by a comparative assessment of its own characteristics such as culture, structure, processes, central functions and resources and decentralising capabilities, with the needs of the subsidiary business.

Multibusiness companies must focus on this parent subsidiary relationship if they are to avoid destroying value and create it instead.

Reading review

27

'Strategic planning as if ethics mattered'

L.T. Hosmer, *Strategic Management Journal*, Vol. 15, 17–34, 1994

Ethical considerations were seen by Barnard (1938) and many other early contributors to strategic management as an intrinsic part of what he referred to as the executive process. However, business ethics is today given little exposure in the strategic management literature and this article questions whether it is possible and worthwhile to build contemporary strategy on a 'foundation of ethical reasoning'.

The focus of managerial ethics is on moral problems which are here defined as the harms that are done to others in ways that they cannot control. These are problematic because harms to some are usually associated with benefits to others. Ethical analysis seeks to determine whether a particular mixture of harms and benefits is 'right' and 'just' and 'fair' or the converse. The article briefly discusses ten approaches to ethical analysis, emanating mostly from moral philosophy, which are held to be objective, consistent and timeless. This contention is justified by the distinction between morals, values and ethics. Our moral standards and value judgements are culturally determined, but ethical principles are not.

Strategic management determines the goals, policies, culture and competitive position of a firm using quite different modes of analysis. The question is whether these ethical principles should be applied to strategic management and the article argues, through four propositions, that it is essential for firms to be moral.

Proposition 1 – Companies depend on many stakeholders.

Proposition 2 – Companies depend on stakeholders for innovation as well as co-operation.

This reading review aims to capture the main points and the spirit of the original in readable form. It may not cover all the points raised in the original text or quote the examples referenced. It is not intended to contain any value judgements about the original text, but inevitably it remains a personal interpretation. For a comprehensive appreciation readers are strongly recommended to the original text. Reviewed by permission of John Wiley & Sons Ltd.

Proposition 3 – It is difficult to motivate co-operative and innovative behaviour among stakeholders; a prerequisite is the building of trust, commitment and effort among stakeholders.

Proposition 4 – This can only be done by basing strategic management on ethical principles.

There is limited empirical support for propositions 3 and 4, which suggest a sequence of ethics–trust–commitment–effort. However there is plenty of anecdotal evidence supporting the sequence and some theoretical justification can be drawn from the work of Etzioni (1988) and Sen (1991).

The article concludes that no large-scale enterprise can completely avoid causing harms as well as benefits and that it is senior management's responsibility to allocate the harms and benefits among stakeholders. This can be done 'thoughtfully' using ethical principles. If it is recognised among stakeholders that management is conducted on the basis of ethical principles, stakeholders will develop trust towards the firm and will in due course show commitment to its future. This commitment will be manifest in co-operative and innovative behaviour which will lead in the long term to competitive and economic success.

Reading review

28

'Decoupling hierarchy and accountability: an examination of trust and reputation'

S. Jönsson, in *Accountability: Power, ethos and the technologies of managing*, International Thomson Business Press, 1996

The American form of managerial capitalism has depended for its success on, among other things, a hierarchical managerial structure; without it any industrial nation, it is said, will tend to fall behind. Chandler (1990) cites British industry as failing to create adequate managerial structures. Goold and Campbell (1987) argued that the most profitable British companies operated with decentralised strategic control and central financial control, but Chandler (1991) pointed out that such conglomerates were typically unable to uphold technological complexity and capital intensity and so retreated to service and low-tech industries.

The multidivisional, hierarchical structural form is still the dominant form of organisation in the United States. For Chandler (1991), successful large corporations need large central staff that formulate strategies and control the divisions through strict monitoring of financial performance.

Channon (1973) looked at large British enterprises, structured mostly as holding companies with subsidiary operations in overseas markets capable of responding to local conditions. This followed the model of British colonial experience. Channon described this structure as representing 'extreme decentralisation', lacking clearly defined executive hierarchies and with the 'group executive function' which led so many successful American companies quite absent in the British firms which lacked

This reading review aims to capture the main points and the spirit of the original in readable form. It may not cover all the points raised in the original text or quote the examples referenced. It is not intended to contain any value judgements about the original text, but inevitably it remains a personal interpretation. For a comprehensive appreciation readers are strongly recommended to the original text. Reviewed by permission of S. Jönsson, Gothenberg Research Institute.

sufficient separation of centrally formed strategy from divisionally based implementation. Channon was able to report 'progress' as the multidivisional hierarchical form became dominant in Europe, and the UK in particular, during the 1960s and 1970s, the process being initiated by management schools of the 'Harvard persuasion' and by the highly successful American management consultancies such as McKinsey.

The American multidivisional form first emerged to exploit a single, huge domestic market, whereas the British model developed to exploit many smaller overseas markets each with quite different characteristics. In the current era of rapid, knowledge-based change and global markets it is open to conjecture which model would be most effective, although faith in the American model still survives. This article suggests an alternative structural form that could be described as 'neighbourly chats between teams in the organisational village'.

Work can be divided into three categories: routine labour, personal service and knowledge work and there is a widening gap between the value of knowledge work and the other categories. As knowledge work becomes more knowledge intensive so the competence of managerial hierarchies to take decisions over that knowledge work, and particularly its objectives, becomes less certain and less legitimate unless the decisions are taken in consultation with the relevant competent knowledge workers.

To be competent means to fulfil expectations, i.e. to be trusted and to be accountable for deviations from the expected performance. Trust involves leaving something of value in the hands of others and it therefore exposes the truster to risk, to the whim of those to whom they are entrusting. It therefore takes time to build trust. Creating trust involves keeping one's conduct in line with the expectations of others. This has a constraining effect on members of a social group, known as *bonding*. But it also has a productive effect: by conducting themselves visibly the competent person strengthens expectations over their future behaviour.

A trusted person is considered competent to apply judgements on behalf of others and to represent them in sensitive matters and be entrusted with things of value. Trusting a person not only means exposing oneself to risk, but also freeing oneself from worry to concentrate on other things. Trust therefore reduces complexity and could be a forceful organising factor. The extension of trust over time gives members of a group the energy to perform co-ordinated action without hierarchical control. This may explain why some groups outperform expectations and others fall short.

Orthodox financial control of the sort employed in multidivisional organisations is a general principle applied without regard to the individual circumstances or people involved. Trust results from applying a particular principle, i.e. taking explicit account of the circumstances and person involved. The person involved in a transaction is not just any person but a particular one that is trusted and for whom one is prepared to break the rules, thus demonstrating both friendship and competence. Such a rule breaking may be for the good of the company, e.g. solving a problem for the company and therefore known by the participants to be justified and which can be accounted for in its particular context.

'It is on this particularist orientation in interaction between trusted, competent, problem solving persons that lateral responsibility is built.'

There are different levels of skill at work and each requires different forms of communication. For example, low-skill work requires only that the worker goes by the book and the only communication required is to report when something goes wrong. At a higher level, the work is done according to the function and communications relate to the tuning and maintenance of the operation. At the highest level, work is largely a matter of judgement and communication is aimed at relating work to the needs of the customer. So skill relates to levels of communication, but communication also generates trust. A communication game has constituent rules to which players are expected to adhere.

At high levels of work, competent, responsible, communicating individuals can break the organisation's rules for the organisation's benefit and subsequently be open about having done so and thereby build trust both within and for the group among external groups.

The article reports a case study which illuminates many of the ideas discussed. It shows how inner dialogue in the team generated successful problem solving which gave the group recognition and prestige. Being recognised as competent led to an outer dialogue, still focused on problem solving, aimed at forming contracts with other groups. Contracts were implicit within the group, but explicit with other groups.

Norms and practices develop which co-ordinate the group's activities without the need for an external hierarchical control. This lateral responsibility emerges out of communication. Communication inside a problem-solving group generates commitments to the team that are more binding as the team is seen as more competent, trustworthy and deserving to have its knowledge and opinion taken into account.

This emphasis on ethos contrasts with the American multidivisional form and with the idea that strategy is formulated centrally and implemented and monitored through objective controls. In a differentiated and changing environment the communicative approach has greater promise, but it depends on trust, which can only be safeguarded through communication in conversational form between competent people.

The multidivisional form may still work for very moderately differentiated environments, but the lateral structures which develop in learning organisations are complementary to the formal structures. Moreover, they will grow in importance as knowledge intensification proceeds, and as they do so the organisation's capacity to deal with differentiated and volatile environments will be enhanced.

Reading review

29

'What is strategy?'

M.E. Porter, *Harvard Business Review*, November/December 1996

Strategy goes beyond questions of operating efficiency. All the currently prevalent management techniques such as total quality management, benchmarking, business process re-engineering and so on are aimed at achieving operating effectiveness. This may be necessary for a successful strategy, but it is not sufficient. It merely implies performing activities better than rivals; strategic positioning means performing different activities to produce a unique mix of value which it must be able to defend against copiers. This unique mix of value must be either different from competitors or comparable but at lower cost, or both.

There are three broad types of strategic positioning, i.e. of delivering the unique mix of value. Positioning can be based on the specialised or limited variety offered; it can be based on the needs of specific customers; or it can be based on access to specific customers.

For the positioning advantage to be sustainable it will require trade-offs to be made, i.e. decisions to be taken about what will not be done as well as what will be done. Examples are given of attempts to avoid these trade-offs. Continental Airways tried to straddle both a differentiated position and a cost-oriented position with the result that it was unable to sustain a competitive advantage. Many companies are operating quite inefficiently and for them it is feasible both to reduce costs and to increase differentiation, indeed it is probably essential. However, when costs are already competitive, i.e. the business is operating at the 'productivity frontier', the trade-off between further cost reduction and adding to the product quality, for example, is a very real problem that strategic management must confront.

To achieve a competitive advantage and to sustain it over time requires all activities of the business to complement each other and to concentrate on reinforcing the

This reading review aims to capture the main points and the spirit of the original in readable form. It may not cover all the points raised in the original text or quote the examples referenced. It is not intended to contain any value judgements about the original text, but inevitably it remains a personal interpretation. For a comprehensive appreciation readers are strongly recommended to the original text. Copies of the full article are available from HBS Publishing, *www.hbsp.harvard.edu*

strategic positioning. For example, a sophisticated salesforce will be required for a high-tech product. This integration of all activities in achieving the same end is referred to as 'fit'. Three types of fit are identified: simple consistency between activities and the overall strategy, reinforcing fit where activities complement and reinforce each other, and the optimisation of effort.

There are three major problems which often inhibit the establishment of effective strategy:

1. It is difficult for managements to choose a different and distinctive strategy from those already pursued in an industry. The pursuit of operating effectiveness leads almost inevitably to an imitational strategy.
2. Managements are also vulnerable to the growth trap and encouraged to make incremental additions to their business which blur strategy. Strategic positions should be strengthened and deepened rather than broadened or weakened.
3. Being different, making trade-offs and rejecting growth for its own sake takes courage. Making successful strategy in practice requires leadership.

Reading review

30

'Strategy as practice'

R. Whittington, *Long Range Planning*, Vol. 29, No. 5, 1996

Research into strategy has never been so diverse. Interest started in the 1960s with the development of tools and techniques to help practitioners plan direction. In the 1970s researchers focused on the results from pursuing different directions, initially focusing on diversification policies and more recently looking also at acquisition, joint ventures and international development policies. Since the 1980s researchers have studied the process by which organisations identify the need to change and then achieve it. These three approaches are labelled 'planning', 'policy' and 'process'. A fourth approach is then identified which focuses on what strategists actually do and how they achieve results. This is referred to as the 'practice' approach.

Research into strategy as practice focuses on what strategists say and do. It shifts attention from the core competence of the corporation to the personal ability of the strategy manager. Success depends not only on the exciting things like spotting opportunities and understanding and managing situations, but also on the ordinary mundane management activities like attending meetings, filling in forms and general communications. These craft skills and a real knowledge of the way the local situation works, including an understanding of the roles of the various people involved in the strategy process, enables strategy to be done within existing structures, which is likely to be more effective than the imposition of any textbook solution.

This new strategy as practice perspective has profound implications for academic researchers and teachers. Since the local craft skills are important it will not be sufficient for teachers simply to deliver classroom lectures. Teachers will need to be involved in counselling and coaching. They will need to experience and understand the local realities within which strategy is formed and managed. They should become a source of trusted practical advice. This greater focus on the role of individual managers should also be reflected in the way case studies are used in the learning process,

This reading review aims to capture the main points and the spirit of the original in readable form. It may not cover all the points raised in the original text or quote the examples referenced. It is not intended to contain any value judgements about the original text, but inevitably it remains a personal interpretation. For a comprehensive appreciation readers are strongly recommended to the original text. Reviewed by permission of Elsevier Science.

with less attention on what the organisation should do and more on what the individual should do within the overall process.

Research too needs to respond to the strategy as practice perspective. There has been a great deal of research into the process of decision making and 'achieving cognitive change' within an overall concern for the whole organisation, but there has been little attention given to the individual participant, apart from the research into leadership, which sheds little light on strategy.

Strategy as practice requires an understanding of the 'unheroic' routine of strategy management, the practical skills required and work actually done to complete the process and the learning that is needed for strategic competence. To be effective, strategists certainly need to understand the theory, but in addition they also need practical skills and local knowledge. The research agenda is to find out what mix of skills and understanding is needed to 'strategise' effectively. The teaching challenge is to engage with these practicalities so that strategy practice can be improved.

part 5

Case studies

Readers of this text may be unlikely, in the immediate future, to assume responsibility for the global strategy of a major international corporation. More likely they will be called on to help shape strategy in the more limited context of a relatively small company or part of a larger one. This is the context that most of these cases seek to emulate. Nevertheless the principles of strategy management have a wide applicability.

The theory is in essence quite simple, but most real organisations fail to apply it effectively in practice. This is not so much because real organisations are managed badly but because the simple lessons of strategy management are difficult to apply. Often the difficulty arises because action which is strategically justified appears to run counter to the organisation's short-term financial interests. It might be difficult, for example, to give up profitable sales amounting to a substantial proportion of total turnover in order simply to achieve a strategic focus. Managers steeped in accounting mores and beliefs would be most unlikely to support such a proposition, yet this text has given many examples of companies that have done just that and consequently achieved long-term success.

This is why case studies are so useful as a substitute for real organisations. In case studies we can practise a bold approach to analysis and decision-making, uninhibited by fear of what the accountants or the shareholders might say. So we can develop a facility for real strategy analysis and decision-making, aware of likely objections that would most probably be raised and therefore giving thorough consideration to how such strategy decisions would be justified. In this the simple logic of the strategy frameworks, if applied rigorously, can play a crucial role.

There is an abundance of general strategic case studies published elsewhere in strategic management textbooks. This part therefore introduces a number of situations which are used to highlight the use of particular frameworks or the exercise of particular decisions. The following notes provide some guidance in the analysis of case studies.

Case studies are simply proxies for the real situation. They vary in content and length but usually contain information on the development of the business, the external environment in which the firm operates and its internal situation. Strategy case studies tend to be multifaceted and provide information on a wide range of issues relating to the business. They deal with actual business situations and provide an opportunity to appreciate the nature of decisions which are of long-term importance to the organisation.

Case analysis can be quite demanding. One difficulty which is frequently experienced is the unstructured nature of the problems faced by strategy managers. This is reflected in the mass of information which cases often present and which needs to be analysed. An essential skill that will develop with practice is the ability to recognise what information is important and what less relevant.

Conversely, it sometimes appears that cases do not provide enough information to analyse the firm's position adequately or to make a recommendation for action. These problems apply in real situations – managers never have all the information they would like in order to make a decision. Nevertheless, managers are expected to come to reasoned conclusions and make decisions or recommendations based on less than complete information. Similarly, in case analysis it is necessary to work with the information provided and where necessary make reasonable assumptions.

The essential task in all case study work is a deep understanding of the organisation and situation presented. The total dimensions of the case will not be grasped if the case is read only once. Usually the significance of much of the information presented does not become clear until a detailed analysis is undertaken.

It is important to appreciate that the analysis of a case will not result in a 'right' answer being found or recommendation of the 'correct' course of action. These notes will only help to ensure that the relevant factors will have been considered thus leading to a better diagnosis of the situation with recommendations for action which can be adequately justified. The justification for recommendations is most important if the recommendations are to stand up to challenge, whether it is from fellow managers or from the student peer group. Justification has to be made on the basis of a thorough grasp of the fundamentals of strategy management as well as an understanding of the chosen strategy framework and its application.

In general, case analysis addresses three basic issues:

1. Analysis
2. Options
3. Recommendations

The *analysis question* may be framed in many different ways, but in essence asks for identification of the main problems facing the company and the priorities set for dealing with them. The *options question* asks for identification of three or four strategy options the organisation might consider. The options are not necessarily identified in great depth, but should give some indication of the breadth of choices open to the organisation, including some consideration of the unthinkable. The *recommendations question* requires a particular strategy to be recommended. The strategy will be identified in some detail and, most importantly, justified by reference to the strategy framework chosen. Justification of the recommended course of action lies in its coherent underpinning provided by selection and use of the most appropriate strategy framework. Use of the framework should demonstrate understanding of its shortcomings and limitations as well as its practical utility.

An important preliminary of the internal analysis of a company's strategic position is consideration of its financial status. It is no use identifying a good long-term strategy if the organisation is already insolvent – remember that the latest published information is likely to be at least 18 months out of date. The analysis must therefore include an assessment of the organisation's liquidity. If it is insolvent, or headed in that direction, the survival objective will take precedence over strategic development while the cash problems are solved. Similarly, there is no point in identifying a strategy which is financially out of reach – the analysis must recognise the problem and propose a credible way of overcoming it. The company's gearing will suggest its debt-raising capacity without the addition of new equity and so give an idea of the finance available for investment in its strategic development. Finally, a strategy based on the expansion of unprofitable business would be highly questionable – it is essential to know which activities produce a return and which do not. Thus, strategic analysis must at least include an assessment of the firm's liquidity and debt-raising capacity and the profitability of different activities whenever relevant information is provided.

Following these general guidelines is often the best way of coming to terms with the details of the case even when asked to consider specific questions. This general approach should also help with an appreciation of the integrated nature of most case studies in strategy management.

The practical steps in analysing a case effectively are as follows:

1. Read the case through once relatively quickly to get an overview of the case. After a second, more careful reading, you should consider the information provided and try to identify what really matters – focus on the relevant; discard the rest.
2. Check the financial information provided for liquidity, gearing and profitability.
3. Attempt to identify fundamental strategic issues (e.g. direction, concentration, consistency and flexibility, objectives and mission etc.). The case itself may not make these issues clear – an unclear strategy is often the major problem.
4. Read the case again. This time sift through the material carefully and identify the key strategic factors facing the organisation. Where appropriate, use relevant concepts and tools of analysis to investigate the organisation. Consider the resource capability of the firm and how it might leverage these up and use a stretch strategy. Analyse liquidity, gearing and profitability, current position and trends.
5. Select the strategy framework (e.g. life cycles, experience curves, Boston's portfolio, Porter's competitive strategy etc.) which is most appropriate to the case situation. Carry out the analysis required by the framework chosen (e.g. for the Boston portfolio, market growth rates and relative market shares). From this analysis identify three or four alternative strategies open to the firm and express them in terms appropriate to the framework used and represent the firm's development in terms of the chosen model (e.g. show repositioning on the Boston matrix).
6. Briefly consider the implications of using a different strategy framework – would it suggest a fundamentally different strategy?
7. After considering the pros and cons of each strategy make a choice on which one to recommend as the most fully justified course of action for the firm to take.
8. List a set of objectives appropriate for the firm to focus on the selected strategy and

make suggestions as to the action which must be taken to implement the strategy. Include consideration of organisation structure, corporate culture and human resource development as well as marketing, operations and financial strategies, ensuring they are internally consistent and compatible.

9. Suggest a suitable set of identifiable milestones that could be used to assess progress and identify when the recommended strategy needs amendment.

Most case studies introduce the company, giving a potted history which highlights the watershed events and introduces the key individuals, typically the founder, his or her successors and the current top management team. Some cases include thumbnail character sketches of key personnel and care must be taken not to allow these subjective signposts to divert the analysis.

Most cases provide information on objectives – these are rarely clear and frequently inconsistent and conflicting. It is therefore important to consider fundamental issues of direction, concentration, consistency and flexibility. It is at this stage that consideration can be given to the strategic portfolio – which business activities are core and which are not. If consideration is not given to this stage of analysis then future stages are unlikely to be well founded because it will be difficult to propose a coherent strategy for an incoherent set of activities.

Many case studies include 3–5 years of profit and loss accounts and balance sheets so that the basic financial analysis can be carried and any problems or opportunities highlighted. Remember that a single figure, even a ratio, is not as useful as a trend or a sector comparison.

Marketing research is a key source of data and some industry information is often available which highlights areas of growth and decline as well as any structural changes which are taking place. This may also include information on current and new technologies.

The current position is described in some depth giving realistic amounts of information. Realism suggests the information will be sufficient to highlight the key problems and issues, but not enough to remove all uncertainty. In many strategic management case studies, realism also means some information is included which is simply not relevant to the main issues – it is therefore vital to distinguish between what matters and what is unimportant.

The above guidance applies to most general strategic management cases from any source. The cases included here are rather more concise and specific than is typical. They are designed to provide opportunities to recognise situations where particular frameworks are relevant and to apply those frameworks to provide solutions.

Hesketh Design Partnership

Alan and Adèle Hesketh met at Chelsea Art School, fell in love and were married within six weeks, with two years of their degree programmes still to go. Alan was from Sheffield which, as well as being the centre of the UK steel industry, had an ancient tradition of fine cutlery and silverware marked by the 700 year old Sheffield assay office. On completion of their courses it was their intention to return to Sheffield and set up a business in artistic design specialising in silverware. This they did shortly after they both graduated with good degrees in fine arts in 1974. Their business was called the Hesketh Design Partnership (HDP).

During the first few years of operation they took whatever work they could get. Alan undertook several interior design jobs for a chain of upmarket Italian restaurants. The work involved painting huge Romanesque murals which he enjoyed, and a lot of more mundane interior design, specifying colour schemes, furniture designs, curtains and carpets, which he hated. Subsequently, he managed to obtain some industrial design contracts. Some of these were extremely boring, but two jobs did present interesting design problems which attracted his interest. One of these was for a series of outer casings for industrial lathes and the other was for a domestic lawnmower. On the back of these two contracts he employed two young specialist industrial designers and a craftsman model-maker.

Despite this success the work that Alan really loved to get involved in was to do with one-off jobs which were really more art than design. For example, he obtained various prestigious commissions in silverware design. He designed and produced a silver trophy for the ladies champion of one of the leading international tennis tournaments, also a huge silver bowl for presentation to the Queen Mother on her eightieth birthday and some specifically designed altarpieces for a Church of England cathedral. These were all exciting jobs to be involved with and they gave him full opportunity to exploit his artistic talents. However, even he recognised such work was unlikely to be the basis of a business of any substance and consequently felt it was important to drive HDP to become more involved in the run-of-the-mill industrial design work and they picked up contracts when and where they could designing anything.

During this early period Adèle specialised in designing and making silver jewellery. The jewellery was quite successful and she quickly developed a number of retail customers who, unlike the prestigious customers Alan had attracted, came back for more on a regular basis. The repetitive nature of the work gave Adèle an opportunity to develop a distinctive style of jewellery which was in due course immediately recognisable to her customers. This Hesketh design was a form of carving and embossing which provided a highly attractive surface pattern on jewellery items which were themselves rather chunky. The chunkiness was important since the price of most items in silver was determined largely by the weight of metal used. Adèle had concluded therefore that maximising the amount of silver per hour of her time was the most effective way of working with silver.

After ten years in business, HDP had developed three separate strands of business: the one-off high prestige jobs, silver jewellery and industrial design work. Of these, the industrial design work was the least interesting to both partners and yet they were forced to recognise, quite early on, that it was this that earned them their main income. On dark days Alan sometimes wondered whether his real talents were not as a salesman.

In 1989, they were approached by S.H. Boden, an internationally reputed retail jeweller, to provide a distinctive design for a new line of silver cutlery. Initially this commission did not appear particularly interesting, although they spent a considerable time looking at different possibilities. In the end it occurred to them that Adèle's established jewellery design might be suitable for adaption to cutlery handles. They therefore proposed just the one design. Boden enthusiastically accepted the design as submitted without any modifications and then asked HDP to tender for the manufacture of what would have been, for HDP at least, very substantial business of around £5m per annum.

Again HDP was not very interested in tendering for the manufacture, but Alan happened to attend a formal dinner at the Cutler's Hall and was placed next to John Smith, owner of one of the few remaining traditional silver cutlery manufacturers in Sheffield. Over dinner they discussed the Boden job and, in short, they ultimately agreed to tender for the job on the basis of subcontracting most of the work to Smith, with HDP merely finishing off the distinctively designed handles. The tender was successful and in due course the Boden business became a very substantial part of HDP's turnover. Subsequently HDP extended the design to cruet sets, serviette rings and a variety of small cream jugs, sugar bowls etc. all of which they made themselves. At around this time they ceased to be a partnership and became HDP Design Ltd.

HDP had originally set up business in a converted barn in the Peak District village where Alan and Adèle lived on the outskirts of Sheffield. It was not just an ordinary barn – the conversion had won its architect several awards for combining innovative design with a respect for the surroundings. The premises served as both office and workshop, and as the business had grown they had found it necessary to convert part of the building to a showroom where the jewellery, cutlery and prestige jobs could be displayed to great advantage.

In due course it was necessary to expand further and they had leased additional premises in the same village from COSIRA, a quango responsible for job creation in rural areas. These they converted to use as workshops and model production plus cutlery finishing, packing and despatch. The original premises were converted for use solely as offices and showroom.

By 1995, they employed 34 people and had sales revenue of almost £7.5m. The board of directors included Aldous Heron, non-executive chairman and partner of the local firm of accountants who acted as auditors, Alan Hesketh, chief executive, Adèle Hesketh, managing director, and John Williams, finance director and a full-time employee who acted as a general administrator/accountant. In addition, they employed three designers, two draughtsmen, a workshop manager, two model makers, one blacksmith, five workshop operatives/labourers, three cutlery finishers, two packers, a book-keeper and wages clerk, two general clerks, three drawing office/designer trainees, a sales representative, a sales office assistant, a telephonist/receptionist, a general handyman/cleaner/gardener and two part-time showroom staff.

The sales and net profit figures in 1996 are shown in Table 1.

The figures for the cutlery work are not comparable with the others because a substantial amount of the turnover was simply bought in, but since HDP acted as the principal to Boden the total value invoiced went through its books. In truth, HDP's added value on this business was relatively small. A substantial proportion of the accompanying silverware and the silver jewellery was also accounted for simply by the value of metal used, whereas the revenue for industrial design work was largely payment for their design skills and expertise.

The prestige jobs, shown as earning nothing in Table 1 were difficult to assess. The £94,000 in 1996 was for a single job, an original sculpture in silver and acrylic, being a sponsor's trophy for a motor rally competition. In some years the figure was less than this and in others substantially more. This was the work Alan really enjoyed doing and he spent a fair amount of time networking and making contacts which might lead to these jobs coming his way. Adèle, having found she had a natural talent for PR, also spent some time ensuring the prestige jobs gained maximum exposure on a national and sometimes international basis. However, their time was never charged against the jobs they achieved. Any surplus on these jobs, after charging direct material costs and any bought-in work, was generally factored off by charging 'spare' workshop time to them so that they showed no profit.

Table 1

Product	**Sales revenue £000**	**Net profit £000**
Cutlery	5,037	98
Associated silverware	105	19
Silver jewellery	146	24
Industrial design	2,010	229
Prestige work	94	0
Total	**7,392**	**370**

Both Alan and Adèle recognised that these jobs were probably not worth taking on from a strictly short-term profit perspective, but they did get HDP a lot of exposure and at least one of their major industrial design clients had come to them as a direct result. But their greatest importance to Alan was simply because he loved being involved with them, instead of the more mundane business of running the company, 'selling' etc.

They both felt that HDP was making demands they really resented. Alan really wanted nothing more than to be doing the prestige work and Adèle to be creating jewellery, but neither of them had the time to be doing what they really liked. The cutlery was not interesting to them and they felt it was not very profitable anyway. The only problem with cutting out that business would be that they would have to get rid of almost one quarter of their staff. As far as the industrial design work was concerned, Alan was rather ambivalent. Some of the jobs were quite exciting and challenging, but there was a lot of straightforward 'graft' which he was very glad to off-load to his staff.

After a board meeting in early 1997, chairman Aldous Heron and finance director John Williams had a private conversation about the company's general progress and, although neither of them was explicit, it was clear they were both concerned over the Hesketh's' personal aims and their commitment to the future development of HDP Design Ltd.

DISCUSSION POINTS

1. How well do you think HDP is achieving the purpose of strategy?
2. What do you think Alan and Adèle should do with the business?
3. Identify and compare Alan and Adèle's personal aims with HDP's business objectives.
4. Suggest a suitable strategic objective, or mission, for HDP Design Ltd.
5. Suggest a strategy framework which might be suitable to HDP's situation.
6. Recommend and justify a strategy for HDP Design Ltd.

Grand Prix racing

The days are gone when a great driver in an average car could beat an average driver in a great car. At least, that is in the dry. In the wet it is different. Michael Schumacher won the 1996 Spanish Grand Prix with, by common consent, one of the greatest wet weather drives of all time. 'He flew past me and I never saw him again,' admitted Jacques Villeneuve driver of probably the best car on the day. Damon Hill was nowhere, having chosen the wrong set-up on his car.

Schumacher is generally rated head and shoulders the best of today's Grand Prix drivers, bearing comparison with the brilliant Ayrton Senna whose dominance was also most evident in the wet. Senna was sixth on the grid for the 1993 European Grand Prix at Donington. But it was wet and before the first lap was complete he was in the lead. On that occasion his car benefited from computer-aided traction control, as did all the leading teams' cars. For sheer unassisted wet driving genius, look at Senna's first ever Grand Prix win. It was 1985 in Estoril and the weather was filthy. Driving a Lotus, Senna simply disappeared from the rest of the field right from the start and maintained his position to the end.

A better car should be better, wet or dry, but the car's limits are less clearly defined in the wet and results will then depend more on the driver's control, confidence, feel and sheer courage. But it is not just the driver and the car that win races. With the leading machinery all being highly competitive – to less than one second a lap on most circuits – several tracks offer only half chances of overtaking on the road and even a Schumacher may have to wait until the pitstops for tyre replacement and refuelling to get past a slightly less quick competitor.

Over most circuits, teams can plan to complete the race with either two or three pitstops, it being a matter of judgement whether the time lost through a stop can be made up by the increased adhesion of a fresh set of tyres and lighter weight from less fuel on board. Pitstop tactics can be crucial to success – a second or two gained at a pitstop can be translated into a couple of hundred yards on the track. Most of the 25 seconds or so that a stop takes is fixed. Speeds are restricted in the pit lane, so the time it takes to slow from race speed and to accelerate again is more-or-less the same for all competitors. The crucial difference can be made by the pit team servicing the car while at rest. A change of tyres can take around seven seconds. Refuelling as well can take anything from eleven to fourteen seconds or more. Any mistakes by any of the team can slow these times disastrously. Two or three seconds lost at a pitstop can easily lose a race.

DISCUSSION POINTS

1. Propose a suitable strategic objective for a Grand Prix team.
2. Suggest lower-level objectives.
3. Identify some relevant milestones.
4. How easy would it be for a Grand Prix team to achieve the purpose of its strategy?

Various metaphors have been suggested for teamworking in a knowledge- and service-based organisation. For example, Drucker [Reading Review 22] suggests:

1. *Cricket*, where the play is fairly well structured and everyone has a defined role to play which they do to the best of their ability.
2. *Football*, where play is less structured and substantially determined by the opposition, where everyone is a specialist and has to support each other and develop new skills under the coach.
3. *Doubles tennis*, where additionally each knows the other's strengths and weaknesses and covers for the other.

Perhaps a Grand Prix pitstop team is another metaphor where skill and precision are refined to a very high degree and where any lapses are punished disproportionately.

Winning races depends on the whole team: driver, car and race organisation. Running one of today's leading teams is hugely expensive – the annual wages bill alone is likely to be around £9m – and it probably costs more than £1m a race to have any real chance of winning. But what is left when the race is over and the winners have emptied champagne over each other in an excess of laddish exuberance? Who calculates the return on this colossal investment of money, effort, expertise, adrenaline and sometimes human life? How could it be calculated?

It is clearly a big business, but is it a business at all? Frank Williams, founder and boss of Williams Grand Prix Engineering Ltd, until recently manufacturers of the best Grand Prix racing car, was quoted as saying, 'It's still a sport between 2 and 4 on a Sunday afternoon [i.e. during the race itself], but all the rest of the time it's just commerce really.'

It is possible to see the commercial process in terms of attracting sponsors to fund the creation of a team capable of winning races to attract sponsors. But this is not what drives people like Williams and the hundreds of other dedicated engineers, designers, drivers and just simple enthusiasts who live and breathe Grand Prix racing. The normal accounting measures of business performance seem unlikely to be relevant to the core business of winning races. No one would go into Grand Prix racing to make 15 per cent return on investment or 10 per cent annual growth in net assets.

There has always been a dichotomy between racing as sport and racing as business. Before the Second World War, the dominant players, Alfa, Maserati, Auto Union and Mercedes, were all road car manufacturers and the cost of winning races might be justified in terms of publicity for their more bread-and-butter products. Racing for these manufacturers was a cost, never a business in its own right. After the war these teams re-emerged but were soon eclipsed by the new technology developed by a generation of racing enthusiasts and entrepreneurs.

Modern Grand Prix racing started with John Cooper, whose name still adorns the Mini-Cooper. He introduced a tiny racer made of steel from air raid shelters, using a single cylinder 500 cc motorbike engine driving from the rear of the car. It was cheap, quick and went round corners very well. Lots of young drivers had their first racing experience hurtling round makeshift tracks on the many disused RAF airfields littering the southern and eastern half of England. It was the next most exciting thing to flying Spitfires. Their motivation was having fun.

But it was more than just fun. Cooper himself added sports car production and sub-contract work for other racers. Others followed. The Vanwall racing car which took on the might of Ferrari and Mercedes Benz was designed by Colin Chapman (who started Lotus) and Frank Costin (the 'cos' of Cosworth and of Marcos). It was powered by four 500 cc Norton engines stuck together in line at the rear, Cooper fashion, and was driven by Stirling Moss. Eric Broadley started Lola (still a leading Indycar player in America and with plans to return to Grand Prix racing). These and many others attracted overseas drivers such as Brabham and McLaren who both started their own Grand Prix teams in England.

So a self-perpetuating critical mass of Grand Prix expertise was developed in England in much the same way as computer expertise developed in Silicon Valley, California. In both cases, technology was the spur that caused the excitement. In racing, Cooper's original innovation of putting the engine at the rear of the car to improve weight distribution, handling and aerodynamics was the start. As late as 1957, Enzo Ferrari still asserted that Ferrari would 'never put the cart before the horse', but by 1960 had been forced to follow suit. Chapman further streamlined the car by laying the driver on his back and later introduced the first monocoque body-chassis construction which was lighter and stiffer than the previous body and separate space tube chassis.

Engines and gearboxes were developed by separate companies. Coventry Climax set the engine benchmark through the 1960s, and Cosworth, badged and partially funded by Ford, through the 1970s. At that time a fairly standard Grand Prix car set-up became established among the leading race teams: a plastic/aluminium monocoque as the front half of the car, designed in-house but made by a third-party supplier, a Cosworth motor in the middle and Hewland gearbox at the back. Brabham, Lotus, McLaren, Williams, Tyrrell, March and Hesketh all adopted this formula and, whilst often accused of being mere assemblers (like so many micro-computer producers today), they won the races.

The costs of putting a winning team together were then still relatively small. A Cosworth motor, for example, cost only around £10,000 in 1970. The other side of the coin was that racing enjoyed little television exposure and lacked sponsorship. Pictures of Jim Clark in action, one of Grand Prix's all-time greats, are remarkable today for their lack of advertising, the clean uncluttered lines of the Lotus being emphasised by its unadorned racing green broken only by the restrained presentation of the small yellow Lotus badge. By today's standards there was limited money flowing into Grand Prix racing, but also relatively little flowing out. It was still fun.

Today, the same parts of England, defined roughly according to the distribution of wartime RAF airfields, is still the centre of the Grand Prix universe. Lotus may have stopped racing, but McLaren, Benetton, Ferrari (design), Williams, Arrows, Pacific, Tyrrell, Jordan, TWR, Stewart and Lola are all based in the 'airfield belt'.

The Grand Prix industry outsources most components. Engines attract some major manufacturers such as Honda, Renault, Ford and Mercedes, but several power units wearing familiar badges are really products of the airfield belt. Cosworth makes the Ford engine and Ilmor makes the Mercedes unit which now powers McLaren cars, while Judd services Yamaha engines and Mugen looks after Japanese Honda engines. Other components from suppliers in or around the airfield belt include air filters, brakes, castings, clutches, drive shafts, electronics, fuel cells, gearboxes and spark plugs. Such is the racing car expertise built up in this area that it also now dominates design and manufacture of Indycars for America.

The two most successful teams over the past 25 years have been McLaren and Williams. Over that period they have vied for leadership until 1993 when the McLaren challenge took a dive. Both have won seven drivers' championships, but Williams has won eight constructors' championships to McLaren's six. Frank Williams himself lays more emphasis on the constructors' championship, because this is the best measure of the car's success and the prime job of Williams Grand Prix Engineering Ltd is designing and building cars that win races. Williams drivers have been good but, perhaps Prost apart, their world champions – Jones, Rosberg, Piquet, Prost, Mansell and Hill – would not be included in a list of all-time greats. The greatest Williams driver of all, Ayrton Senna, sadly survived only three races with the team.

Williams has an ambivalent attitude to drivers and this is demonstrated by its handling of world champions. Mansell won the championship for Williams in 1992 and Williams replaced him with Prost for 1993. Prost won it in 1993 and was replaced by Senna for 1994. Neither Mansell nor Prost were sacked – in both cases they could have stayed but not as designated team leader. Damon Hill was promoted from test driver when Mansell left and took over as team leader when Senna was killed at Monza. He missed the championship by a single point in his first year, had a mediocre 1995, but won the championship in 1996. His contract was not renewed. Williams has been accused of ruthlessness in its treatment of drivers, but the evidence suggests that it regards drivers as secondary to cars. It aims to make its cars so good that they do not need the very best drivers. Until 1998 this approach worked well and no doubt the team will soon be back to winning regularly again.

How does Williams do it? Grand Prix teams are typically flat organisations although there is a tradition of charismatic, dominant or, some might say, overbearing leaders. A traditional organisation chart would not explain a race team's organisation. Perhaps Morgan's termite heap might be more appropriate (Reading Review 23). The thumbnail sketch of Williams (see box) outlines the main functions required by any Grand Prix team, but the scale of Williams' operation, with an annual wage bill approaching £10m, is beyond the scope of most. The barriers to entry have become extremely high.

Williams has deliberately made itself utterly dependent on Grand Prix success. If it does not win races it will not survive. Sun Tzu (Griffith, 1963), whom Frank Williams may or may not have read, advocated such a strategy, choose to fight in 'death ground' where there is no alternative but to fight to the death; make it plain to your men that there is no chance of survival so they fight with the courage of desperation to the death and follow commands implicitly.

Williams' premises reflect this concentration and focus. Although it has an impressive conference centre where past achievements are celebrated and displayed, it is considerably lower key than those of McLaren and Benetton, two of their most successful rivals for sponsorship. Williams' main sponsor is Rothman, but it also receives support from Elf, Renault and Goodyear. The tobacco industry has been a major sponsor ever since Grand Prix racing first stuck transfers on the cars. Imperial Tobacco led the way with its Gold Leaf and later John Player Special sponsorship of Lotus. Today, Williams, Benetton, McLaren, Ligier and Ferrari all get their main arm's-length sponsorship from tobacco companies.

A thumbnail sketch of Williams

The operation is design driven. Patrick Head who gained experience at Lola, is technical director and until 1997 he worked with chief designer Adrian Newey, now widely recognised as the best. They were aided by various top-flight specialists looking after aerodynamics, gearboxes, suspension etc. They have formidable resources at their disposal: a £4.5m wind tunnel, a state-of-the-art machining centre for pattern and model-making, electro-hydraulic and mechanical testing facilities to test electronic suspensions and gearboxes, and the functional and fatigue testing of components and composite materials. They also have a suite of over 20 CAD/CAM workstations.

Apart from the bought-in components, Williams makes everything in-house. This includes composite materials, machining, electronics and hydraulics. Over 100 people are employed in manufacturing. In addition, it has more than a dozen Renault engineers looking after the engines.

Williams, like most Grand Prix teams, takes a car for each driver plus a spare, to every race. Each car has its own team of mechanics who work closely with the car's driver. The annual wage bill for the whole race team including transporter drivers and caterers is approaching £10m.

On top of this the team needs to attract and maintain sponsorship. Its marketing and PR budget was said to be around £35m in 1995.

Finally, and inevitably, there is a small administrative and general management staff.

The position on sponsorship is always unsettled. The reliance on tobacco is insecure. Legislation to prohibit tobacco promotion in all its forms is EU policy and the current exclusion of Grand Prix from the ban is thought by many unlikely to last the ten years agreed so far. Television rights are also in flux. In the UK the Independent Television Network has taken the contract from the BBC after many years and this has led to some additional money flowing in. However, it may only be a stopgap arrangement. There seems little doubt that the satellite and cable media will in due course move in and outbid terrestrial TV. This will no doubt also produce a short-term increase in money flowing into Grand Prix racing, although the longer-term position remains very uncertain.

McLaren, as successful as Williams over the long haul, and now winning again, appears to have laid more emphasis on drivers. In its pomp it had the services of the two best drivers in the world, Alain Prost and Ayrton Senna, and in 1988 won 15 of the 16 Grand Prix. When Senna won his last race in 1993, McLaren overtook Ferrari as winners of most Grand Prix races ever, a position it has since lost back to Ferrari.

Ron Dennis took control of McLaren in 1982 and signed Lauda and Prost to drive the Porsche-engined cars designd by John Barnard. Barnard, not notoriously docile himself, said that working with Dennis was like 'being in a room with a hand grenade rolling around without its safety pin and about to go off making a horrible mess.' The Dennis/Barnard partnership may have been made in hell but it lasted till 1987 when Barnard joined Ferrari, and it produced the goods. Under their leadership, McLaren was easily the most innovative, professional and successful Grand Prix team. From 1987 it had the best engines (Honda), it still had the best monocoque chassis designs (Barnard's) and undoubtedly until 1993 it also had the best drivers.

Perhaps Dennis' biggest mistake was to be taken by surprise when Honda withdrew from racing in 1992, and through to 1997 McLaren had not yet recovered. By 1994, McLaren had finally exhausted the Barnard design influence, it no longer had Honda engines and it depended on two second-ranking drivers. The team won nothing, finishing the season behind, Benetton, Williams, Ferrari and even Jordan. There were flickers of hope in 1996 with the Ilmor Mercedes engine, but the team only started to win races again at the end of the 1997 season. They led the field in 1998 at last winning the championship again. They clearly have highly competitive engines, but some feel they still lack a designer of Barnard's stature and wonder how long they will stay on top. Moreover, its drivers, Hakkinen and Coulthard, although among the best of the current crop, are not quite in the same league as Prost and Senna.

Dennis, once described as 'Britain's best manager', still has ambitions for McLaren beyond racing. He seeks to emulate the entrepreneurial exploits of the Coopers, Lolas and Lotus's of the 1960s and 1970s. Why should success on the track not be converted into commercial success in adjacent activities? He is quoted as favouring the development of a series of satellite operations all serving specialised parts of motor racing, in much the same way the airfield belt itself started off. This way the organisation could start to generate some of its own income rather than depending entirely on 'here today, gone tomorrow' sponsorship. Moreover, if the worst happened, say, a ban on tobacco sponsorship, a more diversified McLaren group might still survive.

McLaren has mooted various other possible developments, from building a new Grand Prix circuit, a technology park, a land speed record breaking car and, the only one to come to fruition so far, the ultimate grand tourer road car. This last project, the £0.5m F1, won the 24 hour Le Mans road race in 1995, its debut year, but so far must be some way from serious commercial success. Nevertheless, McLaren has these several options to consider.

DISCUSSION POINTS

1. Identify the key external issues for a Grand Prix team to focus on.
2. How valid a model is the Grand Prix team for other sorts of business organisation to follow? For what sorts of situation would it be particularly relevant?
3. Suggest an organisational metaphor that might be appropriate for a Grand Prix team and suggest how Williams or McLaren might fit the metaphor.
4. Suggest which strategy framework might be appropriate for the Grand Prix situation.
5. What are the key factors suggested by the framework which might explain the performance of McLaren and Williams?
6. Suggest strategic objectives which McLaren appears to be aiming to achieve. Comment on their appropriateness and suggest a more appropriate mission. Do likewise for Williams.
7. What are the key variables in the Grand Prix industry that will determine its future attractiveness?

Bird's the Confectioners Ltd

The brothers, Frank, Reg and Tom Bird started the business in 1919, shortly after the end of the First World War. They bought premises in Upperdale Road, just off the centre of Derby in the East Midlands. Derby was a thriving industrial town, home to two world class manufacturers: aero engine and auto manufacturer Rolls Royce, and the Midland Railway Company which was one of the world's leading railway engine producers. Around these two major engineering firms there grew up a thousand or more small specialist suppliers all contributing to the town's growth and prosperity.

The business the brothers started was simply a small bakery and shop, on the face of it no different from many thousands of such businesses up and down the UK. It is estimated there were probably more than 40 such shops in the Derby area alone when the Bird's first opened their business. Some of them prospered and survived a long time, but more-or-less all now have closed or been taken over. Bird's alone survives with two sizable factories, over 40 retail outlets and around 800 employees.

Right from the beginning the brothers were both ambitious and successful. Within three years of opening their first small shop, they had moved into the centre of the city and opened large prestigious premises in St James's Street, still in 1996 the flagship of the business.

Every weekday morning, the St James's Street shop, like most other Bird's shops, still attracts queues of customers all keen to get the best bread, cakes, pork pies and pastries in town. Everyone in Derby knows that a Bird's pork pie is the best pork pie in England, which is the home of pork pies. The bread also is of the highest quality and the cakes, tarts and traditional fancies have a peerless reputation. There is an almost palpable sense of anticipation in a morning queue outside a Bird's shop and it climaxes with the delicious aromas of fresh baking and confectionery in the shop itself.

Bird's shops open at 8.30 in the morning with a full complement of staff who, through the best part of the morning, work at breakneck speed serving queues of customers. Gradually, the pace slackens and some of the part-time assistants leave at lunchtime. In the afternoon the remaining staff become progressively less busy till around 3.30 they start cleaning the shop and preparing it for opening again the following morning. By the time the shops close they have usually more-or-less sold out of produce. This is just as well because anything unsold is destroyed. The profitability of any shop is therefore highly dependent on receiving the right amount of stock each morning. Too little and sales, if not customers, will be lost; too much and waste will destroy profits.

Bird's cakes, many of them filled with fresh dairy cream – it uses 600 gallons a week – are packaged in stiff protective card boxes tied with a traditional paper string. Packing cakes in the boxes and tying them with an elaborate carrying loop takes time and slows down customer service. Also Bird's has not yet adopted computerised tills and, even in 1997, sales staff have to add up customers' bills manually. This also takes time and therefore further lengthens the queue of customers outside the shop, which over the years has become a Bird's trade mark and advertisement.

However, the real key to Bird's success is quality, top traditional quality. The shop windows are dressed in the traditional way with glass stands and swathes of richly coloured silk. And the products themselves are traditional with some of the best-selling lines exactly as they were fifty years ago. Even some of the old names remain: 'penny creams' with their apricot and black-currant fillings and 'tanner tarts' that used to sell for 6d. They are unique, the ultimate in flour confectionery.

Patrick Bird, the current boss and third generation of the family, joined his father Paul Bird in the business at age 16. He is dedicated to upholding the famous Bird's quality. He was recently quoted as saying,

> *there's a duty to carry it on in as good a way as it's been done – and I hope, do that little bit better. I'd like to see the business move forward as much during my lifetime as it did during my father's.*

Patrick started at the bottom and has done most jobs in the business. He is steeped in the Bird's way of doing things, but he has also spent three years at Salford School of Food Technology and is a member of the British Confectioners' Association. He has also worked in Switzerland and Belgium learning how they do the trade and, from time to time, he brings in continental ideas to add interest to the product range. But Bird's products, now extending to around 180 items, remain largely traditional. And it keeps to traditional seasons. For example, unlike their supermarket competitors, Hot Cross Buns are sold only in Bird's shops at Easter-tide. At Christmas, traditional items dominate the business: it consumes over 300 sides of pork and 350 legs of ham per week over the season, not to mention the ingredients for the inimitable Bird's Christmas cake.

The quality of the products is assured by using only top quality ingredients and by ensuring that products are sold completely fresh. The best ingredients are sought from all over the world: Australian sultanas, French cherries, Canadian wheat flour. They cost more and can sometimes be difficult to get hold of, but Bird's does not compromise. It uses the best English pork and ham for its pies, sausages, roast ham and ham on the bone. Its famous pork sausages are still made to the traditional recipe, despite the temptations to reduce costs. It even sticks to the traditional gelatine-free jelly for the pork pies, just to ensure that there is no compromise on quality.

Perhaps even more important than the very best ingredients is the question of freshness. Bird's uses no preservatives. Delivering fresh to all its shops every day is a key competence that distinguishes a Bird's product from the average shrinkwrapped, extended shelf-life supermarket product. Freshness is, above all else, what drives the Bird's system. It is ensured by two simple rules. First, any product not sold by 5pm at any Bird's shop is destroyed. The only exceptions to this are a number of naturally long-life items, such as chocolate and marzipan confections and decorated celebration cakes. So customers know that everything is freshly made on the day of sale. This rule, which enables preservatives to be avoided, is absolutely fundamental to Bird's quality.

The second key rule, set out by Paul Bird, Patrick's father, is that all shops must be within 20 miles of the factory. The reason for this is not simply economic, but also to make sure that there are no compromises on freshness as encapsulated in the first rule. A consequence of the 20 mile rule, however, is to limit the company's growth. In 1975, it decided to open a factory in Nottingham, 16 miles from Derby, in order to serve new markets. By 1995, it was again more-or-less up to the limit. With 40 shops it appears to cover the geographical area within 20 miles of Derby and Nottingham.

Within the context of these two simple rules, work is arranged so as to manufacture as late as possible for delivery to the shops by 8.30am. The renowned cream cakes, for example, are not made till after 6am and are chilled and transported using the latest temperature control systems. Similarly with bread, which is often still hot when delivered to the shops.

Adherence to these rules is difficult to sustain at Christmas. Pork pie production, for example, is continuous, 24 hours a day until the shops close on Christmas Eve. It would be much cheaper to manufacture earlier and hold stocks in deep freeze, thereby smoothing out production and reducing costs. But such compromises are resisted in favour of sticking to the freshly made product.

The main factory at Derby has a floor area of around 7,500 square metres, over 2,000 square metres having been added in 1995 to accommodate an expanded section producing the range of savoury products. The factories have a unique combination of the latest technology and some very traditional people and craft-intensive methods. Eccles cakes, for example, are filled and closed by hand, some small pies are cut out manually, and all the wedding and anniversary cakes are iced and decorated by hand. Machines cannot achieve the same quality as a skilled craft baker or confectioner.

People are therefore a crucial element in the Bird's formula. Staff turnover among the 800 employees is low and many people spend their whole working lives with the company, either in the shops or in the factories. They have a profit-sharing scheme, started back in the 1960s, which demonstrates the mutual respect and loyalty between the Bird family and its employees. This philosophy is reflected in one of the few general statements made in the 1996 director's report. Under the heading of 'employee involvement' Nicholas Bird, Patrick's brother, writes,

> *The Board believes that although successful involvement requires support and impetus from most senior level, the key to its effectiveness lies in giving it a local focus. Rather than relying wholly, however, on formal systems and structures, great import-*

ance is attached to managerial style and the quality of direct contact and relationship with employees.

In 1995, they celebrated the company's 75th birthday and, as Patrick Bird said at the time, 'We're all proud . . . and we're looking forward to it being 100 years.'

Nicholas Bird finally joined the company in 1991 as joint managing director responsible for finance and administration, having previously gained wider management experience both in the UK and America. The strategic position of the business was not then immediately apparent, but through the early 1990s gradually became clearer. Despite the magnificence of its product range the future was not without its problems.

First, the trend away from high streets to out of town super- and hypermarkets appeared relentless. Large retail businesses grew by 75 per cent between 1987 and 1995, while small retail businesses grew less than half as fast, losing considerable market share. This is seen more specifically in the loss of specialist retailing outlets in the high street. Between 1990 and 1995 the number of specialist butchers in the UK reduced by 1,894 (11 per cent), specialist greengrocers reduced by 1,939 (14 per cent), fishmongers by 924 (31 per cent) and bakers by 1,156 (17 per cent). The reduction in specialist bakers was wholly accounted for by the growth of in-store supermarket bakeries. Also, as can be seen from the Table 1, the actual volume of bread and flour confectionery sales peaked in 1993, since when there has been a slight, but perceptible decline.

Bird's shops are all high street or shopping precinct based. The only exception to this is a new in-store shop in a Co-op superstore at Derby. The success of this venture is being watched carefully because it might offer a way of reversing the slow but continuous reduction in sales volume per shop which was resulting from the high street decline.

The main reason for the decline in high street shopping for bakery products is convenience. It is clearly seen as more convenient to buy bakery products with the weekly shop at the supermarket than to go to the high street. Bird's quality appeared

Table 1 Bread and flour confectioners – Sales revenue (£m in 1990 prices)

Year	Index	Sales
1987	0.83	1,151
1988	0.85	1,179
1989	0.92	1,276
1990	1	1,387
1991	1.03	1,429
1992	1.06	1,470
1993	1.12	1,553
1994	1.11	1,540
1995	1.09	1,512
1996	1.05	1,456

to have insulated it to some extent from this competition, but a survey had shown that younger people were less concerned with quality and were prepared to trade it for convenience. The age profile of Bird's customers tended to be 40+, and this will clearly become an increasing problem over time.

Moreover, the new technology used in the supermarket in-store bakeries makes it possible for them to compete on freshness and, in some cases, to beat Bird's at its own game. With one or two exceptions, however, the supermarket products are not competitive with Bird's in terms of quality of ingredients and, of course, do not share the traditional Bird's recipes.

Other successful regional bakers, although less well protected by such a tradition of quality, have taken different routes. For example, Gregg's has developed its high street business by a concerted attack on the takeaway snack business which has enjoyed considerable growth even in the high street. This provides a way of getting more people into the shops. However, it is open to question whether such people would become loyal customers. It is also unclear whether selling takeaway snacks, particularly hot snacks with their heavy aroma, are compatible with the traditional Bird's product. Using a microwave to heat pasties and pies for the takeaway customer would certainly seem at odds with the Bird's culture.

Warburton is another example. Originally a regional baker based in Bolton, Lancashire, it decided many years ago to achieve growth as a baker, specialising in bread, supplying the supermarket chains on a national basis. For Warburton this has proved successful but the opportunities for repeating the strategy now appear limited. It could only be achieved at the expense of one of the existing competitors, who would not be expected to give up market share easily. In any case, such a strategy would not exploit Bird's distinctive competences in manufacturing and selling fresh products.

The location of shops is crucial to success and Bird's has not always got it right. With all retail business, the characteristics of the immediate area have a profound effect on the nature and extent of its custom. The area within the 20 mile rule has to be analysed carefully to ensure that all opportunities are exploited. There are, no doubt, some unexploited and potentially worthwhile locations, especially if the 20 mile rule is interpreted 'as the crow flies' rather than as roads go. On this basis, a 20 mile radius from Derby and Nottingham would also include Newark, Mansfield, Chesterfield, Matlock, Loughborough and Melton Mowbray. There might be some justification for revising the 20 miles definition in this way since roads and vehicles, including temperature control have improved substantially since the rule was first agreed. Slightly further afield, but now connected by the M1 motorway, lie the major conurbations of Sheffield and Leicester. It would be possible to extend the business and substantially increase factory utilisation by going into these additional locations, without the major capital investment of a third strategically sited factory. Alternatively, it would be possible to establish new outlets in one of these major cities and consolidate them subsequently with the establishment of a third factory.

However, the high street decline is a national phenomenon that cannot be ignored. There have been various initiatives, following successful American examples, for high street retailers to take direct responsibility for reviving their own town centres by refurbishing run-down areas and providing high quality public facilities such as seating, lighting, security and policing. With government support these initiatives can have a substantial impact making high street areas safe and friendly places for shoppers to come day and night. In the UK there are as yet only a few such initiatives and they are by no means guaranteed success. Continuing high street decline seems the only safe assumption to make when considering the Bird's business.

Bird's is clearly competing with the supermarkets, and the in-store shop in the new Co-op superstore is a vitally important experiment for the company. It may be possible to make arrangements for starting more in-store shops in major new supermarkets. Another option might be to extend distribution to non-Bird's outlets; it could even consider making special arrangements to supply top of the market outlets such as Fortnum & Mason in London.

Patrick Bird was recently quoted in an interview as saying,

> *We want to produce something that's had a lot of care and attention put into it, that our customers are able to afford and which they're going to enjoy and feel they've had value for money from.*

Nicholas Bird has said,

> *The business is all about **making, distributing** and **selling** top quality, fresh bakery and meat products. We do all three. That's where our key skills lie.*

Now look at Bird's financial schedules and consider the discussion points raised below.

DISCUSSION POINTS

1. What are the key strategic issues identified in this case?
2. Propose a top-level strategic objective for the Bird's business.
3. Would either the life cycle framework or Boston's portfolio be helpful in understanding Bird's situation?
4. Identify the framework which seems most relevant to Bird's. Justify your choice.
5. Identify the scale of investment that Bird's might be able to support without any capital restructuring.
6. Suggest why Bird's might have bought back their own shares in 1996.
7. Propose and justify a suitable strategy for Bird's using the strategy framework chosen above.
8. Identify some of the critical milestones on the way to achieving that strategy.

Bird's (Derby) Ltd profit and loss account (£000)

		1996		1995		1994		1993		1992
Sales revenue		13,439		13,003		13,610		13,287		12,774
Cost of sales		11,367		10,892		11,035		10,851		10,531
Gross profit		2,072		2,111		2,575		2,436		2,243
Distribution costs	544		561		544		528		482	
Administrative expense	554		553		541		516		561	
		1,098		1,114		1,085		1,044		1,043
Operating profit		974		997		1,490		1,392		1,200
Investment income		868		452		420		395		527
Less Profit sharing scheme		189		133		222		225		221
Net pre-tax profit		1,653		1,316		1,688		1,562		1,506
Taxation		456		469		630		503		567
Dividends		380		115		115		115		234
Extraordinary items (note 1)		6,674								
Retained profit		–5,857		732		943		944		705

1. The extraordinary figure in 1996 relates to purchase of own shares.

Bird's (Derby) Ltd balance sheet (£000)

		1996		1995		1994		1993		1992
Fixed assets										
Land and buildings		3,253		3,261		2,968		2,712		2,606
Plant and equipment		1,810		1,940		874		862		874
Fixtures and fittings		1,694		1,702		1,752		1,434		1,111
Motor vehicles		213		246		290		235		210
		6,970		7,149		5,884		5,243		4,801
Current assets										
Stocks	468		528		460		394		393	
Debtors (note 2)	2,202		382		403		483		518	
Investments (note 3)			1,488		1,390		1,084		1,031	
Cash	620		3,109		3,907		3,808		3,261	
	3,290		5,507		6,160		5,769		5,203	
Creditors (due in less than 1 year)	3,845		1,685		1,852		1,827		1,756	
Net current assets		–555		3,822		4,308		3,942		3,447
Total net assets		6,415		10,971		10,192		9,185		8,248
Long-term debt (note 4)		1,200		0		0		0		0
Provisions (deferred taxation)		689		566		521		457		399
Issued share capital		12		33		33		33		33
Freehold property reserve										78
Transfers from P&L		4,514		10,372		9,638		8,695		7,738
Total capital		6,415		10,971		10,192		9,185		8,248

2. The figure for debtors in 1996 includes £1,781,000 of recoverable advance corporation tax.
3. All investments in quoted securities were realised in 1996.
4. The figure of £1.2m in 1996 refers to a bank loan repayable within 5 years.

Bird's (Derby) Ltd cash flow statement (£000)

	1996	1995	1994	1993	1992
Cash inflow from operations	1,088	1,320	1,728	1,626	1,268
Cash inflow from investments	868	452	420	395	527
Dividends	–380	–115	–115	–179	–234
Tax paid	–313	–525	–470	–350	–417
Capital expenditure	–475	–1,890	–1,181	–924	–1,662
Investment expenditure	1,919	–40	–282	–22	–24
Purchase of own shares	–6,674				
Net cash flow	–3,967	–798	100	546	–542

Harry Ramsden's Plc

Harry Ramsden's fish and chip business has gone through three distinct phases since it started in 1928. The opening phase lasted 37 years and saw the original business start up in Guiseley, Yorkshire, first in a green-and-white painted hut measuring around 10 feet by 6 feet, followed in 1931 by a magnificent 94 seater restaurant where the Harry Ramsden reputation for high-quality food was really established. This palace of a dining room was furnished to the highest standards with the finest table linen, crockery and cutlery displayed to classical standards. One eminent food critic of the time said of Harry Ramsden's, 'There is probably no fish restaurant in Great Britain which surpasses the high standard of this Guiseley establishment. It provides fish dishes comparable with those enjoyed in London's exclusive West End, at prices within reach of the average person.'

Harry himself retired in 1954 and the business was taken on by his manager Eddie Stokes and his wife, but apart from a complete redecoration of the restaurant, business carried on much as before.

The second phase started in 1965 when major suppliers, Associated Fisheries, took the business over and in effect doubled the size of the restaurant. This was done with great sensitivity, preserving all the unique features of the original restaurant by building an exact replica alongside it. Even the beautiful arched leaded windows of the original restaurant's outside wall were removed and refitted in the new exterior wall. The business continued to prosper and enjoyed the fierce devotion of its huge clientele which included many of the great and good as well as the ordinary working people from Leeds, Bradford and beyond.

In 1989 phase three began. On 15 June of that year a company called Ableserve Plc was incorporated for the purpose of buying out the Harry Ramsden business from Associated Fisheries. On 17 October Ableserve changed its name to Harry Ramsden's Plc and before the end of the year obtained a quote on the Third Market. A year or so later it obtained a listing on the Unlisted Securities Market, and in March 1995 its shares were introduced to the Stock Exchange Official List. By the end of 1997 Harry Ramsden's had over 30 outlets worldwide, with many more to come, a healthy brand licensing and endorsement business with considerable growth potential and a whole new business concept based on replicating Harry's original fish and chip shop hut being tested with the intention of establishing a hundred or more such units in the UK.

The first two phases saw the Harry Ramsden name and reputation established while the third phase was, and is, one of brand building, extension and exploitation. The prospects for a successful third phase would have been quite remote had the company not established such a solid initial reputation. As it was, the directors had difficulty persuading the City to take them seriously when they set out to float on the stock market. It was a fish and chip shop and everyone knew that fish and chips were in decline. The number of outlets was dropping; share of the fast-food market had been lost continuously and over the long term to sandwiches, burgers, pizzas and pasta which, on the face of it offered a healthier diet than fried battered fish, greasy chips and mushy peas. Fish and chips, like warm beer and cricket on the village green, were surely just history.

But John Barnes, now the executive chairman, had done his homework whilst still heading up Kentucky Fried Chicken UK. Fish and chips were still immensely popular with the British public. The reason it was losing share was because it was not organised to compete. The market was fragmented, quality was variable and there were no brands. Barnes had spent a lifetime in the brand-building business, first with Procter & Gamble then with KFC. He recognised the fundamental strength of Harry Ramsden's. It was a Yorkshire institution, but Barnes' vision was to spread its Yorkshireness across the globe.

What finally convinced the City that there might be mileage in the Harry Ramsden's fish and chip business was the response to a ten second advertisement on Yorkshire TV. Would-be investors were invited to call a number for a copy of the company prospectus. The response was phenomenal. Obviously, people who knew the business were excited by its prospects and wanted to buy in. The offer was two and half times oversubscribed; phase three, Harry Ramsden's Plc, was launched.

The key to Harry Ramsden's is the brand and what it embodies. To understand this it is necessary to look at the company's beginnings in a little more detail.

Even before starting the business in Guiseley, Harry Ramsden ran an ordinary fish and chip shop in Bradford. It was ordinary in the sense that it looked ordinary; it was located in a typically working class district of Bradford; it operated in typical fish and chip shop premises; and it worked with all the standard fish and chip shop equipment. But, as every Britisher knows, no two fish and chip shops are the same. There are so many variables: the fish, the batter, the fat, the length of frying, the temperature, the mushy peas, the vinegar, the salt, even the demeanor of the fryer him or herself. It is possible to get all these ingredients exactly right, but most often a fish and chip shop will fall short of perfection on one or two items at least. Very occasionally, it gets everything exactly right. Even less frequently a particular fryer gets it exactly right all the time. When this happens their reputation is made. Word spreads abroad and, night after night, the ever lengthening queue outside the perfect fish and chip shop announces its achievement. It seems that Harry Ramsden ran such a fish and chip shop. It was by far the best in Bradford and for a long time the only one also to offer a sit-down meal. His was the place to go, not just for the local people but also for the visiting celebrities appearing at the variety clubs.

Then Harry's wife contracted TB. Their doctor said she must move out to the country and this was how he came to set up shop in Guiseley. Guiseley lies on the northern side of Leeds and Bradford, midway between the two at the edge of Wharfdale and really the gateway to the beautiful Yorkshire Dales. Moreover, when Harry first moved there, Guiseley was the terminus for both Leeds and Bradford trams. It was an ideal location and he had not been operating long before people were making a special journey from Leeds and Bradford to enjoy his delicious fish and chips. He also attracted all the hikers, ramblers and cyclists making their way to the Dales, as well as the local people from Guiseley and Yeadon.

His first premises, the small green-and-white painted wooden hut already mentiond, can still be seen alongside the main restaurant. There was certainly nothing special about the hut – it was the fish and chips that attracted the crowds. Harry himself was a big man. Dressed in the ribboned straw boater of a fishmonger, with a winged collar, dark tie and starched apron, he was an imposing character. He was apparently an exuberant character and no doubt added to the experience of a visit to his fish and chip shop, but it was the perfection of his food that drew the custom.

He was an ambitious man. He had borrowed £150 to set up the Guiseley business in the first place, but in no time he was dreaming of a far bigger business. He wanted to build the biggest fish and chip shop in the world and he borrowed another £6,000 to do it. So in 1931 the new, and now famous, restaurant was opened. It was a remarkable and audacious venture. The restaurant itself was an elegant and impressive room, with elegant chandeliers, a life-sized mural on the end wall and top quality furniture and furnishings. The customers loved it. It was not only the biggest fish and chip restaurant in the world it was also undoubtedly the best.

At one end of the new building there was a takeaway section, elegantly tiled from floor to ceiling, which for many years established world records for the fish and chip business; the biggest single order for fish and chips – 490 portions; the most portions of fish and chips served in a day – 10,000 (since beaten three times, each time by Harry Ramsden's); almost 1 million customers a year who consume 264,000 lb of haddock, 660,000 lb of potatoes, 6,500 bottles of vinegar and 20,000 bottles of sauce.

All this success stemmed from the excellence of the fish and chips and their extremely good value. This is what the Harry Ramsden's brand stands for. But it is a bit more than this. The directors of the current business are extremely concerned that, as the business grows, its brand strength also grows and is not diluted by substandard performance in operations which are no longer under personal and direct supervision. They therefore put a lot of effort into getting regular feedback from customers, and chairman John Barnes, a genuine Harry Ramsden's enthusiast, is not above getting personally involved. He once approached two burly male customers in the Guiseley restaurant and asked if their fish and chips were satisfactory:

'Ay,' came the muffled reply.
'Is the service good?'
'Ay . . .' again, followed by an awkward silence.
'Is there anything else we can do for you?'
'Ay, lad, you can booger off.'

BOX 1
Harry Ramsden's Guiseley menu

STARTERS

Chilled Orange or Tomato Juice	90p
Soup of the Day	£1.35
Yorkshire Pudding with onion gravy	£1.40

MAIN COURSES

Fried Haddock Fillet	£5.45
Fried Fillet or Plaice	£6.10
Fried Halibut Fillet	£8.25
Poached Haddock Fillet	£5.80
Fried Scampi	£8.25
Fried Fish Bites	£4.95
Parsley Fish Cake	£4.35
Yorkshire Fish Cake (Harry's original)	£4.35
Vegetarian Dish of the Day	£5.35

MAIN COURSE SPECIALITIES

Harry's Special (larger fillet of haddock fried in batter with chips, mushy or garden peas, or beans plus tea, coffee or soft drink)	£7.50
Harry's Challenge (Whole giant prime haddock fillet accompanied as above)	£10.25

Daily Specials
(Consult the blackboard)

SIDE ORDERS

Traditional Mushy Peas	65p
Garden Peas	65p
Baked Beans	65p
Pickled Onions	40p
Gherkin	65p

SWEETS

Steamed Ginger Pudding	£1.80
Bread & Butter Pudding	£1.70
Apple Pie	£1.90
Sticky Toffee Pudding	£1.99

Above all served with custard, cream or ice cream

Ice Cream (vanilla, strawberry or chocolate)	£1.35
Sherry Trifle	£1.80

PLEASE ASK FOR SEPARATE CHILDREN'S MENUS ... from £2.99

DRINKS & BEVERAGES

Soft Drinks: Coca-Cola, Diet Coke, Sprite or Fanta: Standard	75p
Large	95p
Coffee	75p
Decaffeinated Coffee	75p
Tea (per pot)	65p
Sparkling Spring Water	£1.05
Milk	65p
Harry's Ale (500 ml bottle)	£1.95
Yorkshire Bitter (per pint)	£1.90
Lager (per pint)	£1.99
Low Alcohol Lager (per bottle)	£1.25
House Red or White Wine (per bottle)	£6.25
House Red or White Wine (per 125ml glass)	£1.40
Liebfraumilch (per bottle)	£7.10
Muscadet (per bottle)	£7.75
Champagne	£19.95

Harry Ramsden's is the world's biggest and best fish and chip business, but it is not a sophisticated seafood restaurant. There is a basic 'Yorkshire' integrity embodied in the brand which remains to this day and its appeal to the working population rather than the more affluent middle class can be seen from a glance at the menu shown in Box 1 (1997 prices). The subtext to the Harry's Challenge item reads 'Go on, we dare you! . . . Harry Ramsden's challenge you to eat this gigantic meal. Meet the challenge and you will be given a signed certificate and a sweet of your choice *absolutely free*'.

The company's financial schedules for the years from 1992 to 1996 are summarised and shown at the end of the case. As an independent company there has been limited finance available to finance growth. Consequently, the business plan has made maximum use of franchising, brand licensing and endorsement as well as a limited expansion of company owned outlets which by the end of 1997 included Guiseley, Gateshead and Dudley in the Black Country. By then there were 31 outlets in total, as listed in Table 1. Some of these were proper restaurant facilities while others were restricted to over-the-counter takeaway units. The first overseas outlet was established in Hong Kong in 1992. This was a 200 seater restaurant and takeaway facility closely modelled on the original Guiseley restaurant. The menu also followed the Guiseley original with the majority of items, including the haddock, being imported from the UK. The Hong Kong restaurant and takeaway was franchised by Bluelane Ltd in which Harry Ramsden's took a 33 per cent stake.

The overseas experience gained in Hong Kong was repeated in Dublin, Melbourne, Singapore and Jeddah in Saudi Arabia, all places with sizeable expatriate or immigrant British populations. In each case the business has been established by a local franchisee with Harry Ramsden's taking a minority share where appropriate. For example, the Melbourne outlet is owned and run by Just Caught Pty Ltd in which Harry Ramsden's Plc initially took a 33 per cent share, since increased to a controlling interest. The Melbourne outlet currently holds the world record for the number of portions of fish and chips sold in a day – 12,105.

Table 1 Harry Ramsden's outlets as at 31 December 1997

Belfast	**Airports (Compass):**
Birmingham	Glasgow
Blackpool	Heathrow T1
Bournemouth	Manchester
Bristol	
Cardiff Bay	**Motorways (Granada):**
Merry Hill, Dudley	Hilton Park M6
East Kilbride	Exeter M5
Edinburgh	Thurrock M25
Gateshead	
Glasgow	**Overseas:**
Guiseley	Dublin Naars Road
Inverness	Dublin Jervis Street
Liverpool	Hong Kong
Manchester	Jeddah
Nottingham	Melbourne
Oxford	Singapore
Southampton	Tenerife
Swindon	

An over-the-counter restaurant has also been opened in Tenerife. Chairman Barnes has been quoted as saying, 'The plan is to go places where the British go on holiday. Majorca is a place we'd like to go to and Gran Canaria, and we would love to be in Marbella.'

UK growth has also been rapid and the pace is quickening year on year. Harry Ramsden's has minority (and often non-voting) shares of a dozen franchisees. In addition, the company has negotiated deals with Compass for the opening of quick-counter-service restaurants. The plan is to open facilities at major airports. A similar deal has been reached with Granada for the provision of facilities at motorway service areas.

In addition to the growth of these various fish and chip outlets, the company has established a number of brand licensing and endorsement agreements. For example, the company has established with Ross/Young an oven-bake range of Harry Ramsden's approved fish and chip products, including fish and chip combined packs and mushy peas. Harry Ramsden's fish cakes are planned to follow in due course. Harry Ramsden's tomato ketchup and brown sauce are also licensed, with further licence and endorsement arrangements in the pipeline. This is not simply an additional source of income, but as Mr Barnes says, 'it gets our name into 6 million households.'

With such rapid expansion, it is crucial to ensure that the brand is not diluted in any way. Attaching the Harry Ramsden's name to oven chips, for example, seemed to run a high risk of diluting what the brand stood for – Harry Ramsden's chips are definitely not the oven bake variety. However, customer research was carried out and it was found that such endorsement did no harm to the brand and the additional exposure given to the name from such endorsement was clearly worthwhile. The emphasis on brand-building and strengthening nevertheless means that quality control is of vital importance.

A recent exchange on the Foodcourt Kopi Tiam bulletin board based in Singapore (see Box 2) highlights the potential problem. Whilst these are clearly not definitive assessments of the Singapore outlet, they do provide an insight into how some customers might react if quality control is not strictly maintained. Even then there is a question as to which quality standards should be adopted: Guiseley or local Singapore seafood standards. It is clearly a big problem for any international operation, but especially difficult for largely franchised business where control is not necessarily direct.

The company's main thrusts on quality control are aimed first at its most important single commodity, fish. Ramsden's has a long-standing relationship with its principle supplier which operates a fleet of trawlers. Its purchasing power enables it to lay the strictest quality criteria. Moreover, fish are distributed centrally with all the overseas restaurants receiving the same fish distributed using containers.

In each part of the world the company hires a firm of 'mystery shoppers' to make monthly checks on its outlets. Every restaurant table carries a customer comment card addressed to head office and John Barnes takes a great personal interest in this feedback. One person who complained was so surprised to receive a call from the chairman he dropped his telephone and then, in typically English fashion, apologised for complaining.

BOX 2

Messages posted on the Foodcourt Kopi Tiam Bulletin Board

From: F&C Gourmet 8 July 1997

Harry Ramsden's

Ugh! Don't go to HR's for 'English' Fish and Chips – the food is revolting, too oily, and cooked in oil that is not hot enough so the batter and chips become soggy. If you want to experience the real thing I'm afraid you'll have to go to the UK: either to the original HR's of Geales Fish Restaurant (in London). Even the Honkies in the UK can cook better Fish and Chips than HR's at Kallang.

From: Jamez 14 July 1997

Harry Ramsden's Fish & Chips

It's true!!!! The Fish & Chips is revolting and really no value for money!! Had it once . . . I now get disgusted when I drive past the place!!!! Puke!!

From: meltdown (meltdown@pacnet) 25 July 1997

It's true

I've been to the ORIGINAL Harry's in Guiseley in Leeds, UK, and there they take much more care in preparing the fish. Here in Kallang, the fish is no different from any other fish and chips that is being sold in Singapore.

From: Lisa 13 August 1997

Not worth the money spent

We will never spend our money on those food again. Our comments: (1) too expensive, (2) too oily, (3) food is not fresh: left $\frac{3}{4}$ of grilled salmon on the plate, it smelled and tasted funny, (4) dessert is too sweet for human consumption though they said it's original UK recipe.
Better spend your money somewhere else.

From: Jo (jotpc@pacific.net.sg) 12 September 1997

Izzit???

Very surpised to have seen all ur comments. Cos heard from a UK guest (i used to work in hospitality industry) tt HR's a must-try for fish and chip lovers. He's been at Kallang's HR once and said it's really UK style. Intend to try it out for myself. Thanx for ur advice though.

The second major thrust on quality is through the recruitment and training of staff. A company statement indicates 'we continue to strive to create a uniquely customer friendly environment in our outlets. Key to this is the role of our human resources and training teams in recruiting, training and retaining the right people. We discriminate positively in favour of long-term unemployed in recruiting for new restaurants based on this policy's proven success in improving staff retention rates. We believe our training programmes and career opportunities are among the best in the industry and through the developments of our associates we are delighted to be creating hundreds of worthwhile jobs and new career paths.'

The company is clearly getting some of it right. BAA, the old British Airports Authority, which owns and operates UK's main airports, commissioned the internationally recognised independent food critic, Egon Ronay, to be its resident gadfly and improve the standard of food and drink at its seven airports. Ronay and his four full-time airport inspectors test all 130 outlets at least once a month and issue ratings and detailed reports every quarter. The Harry Ramsden's outlet at Heathrow's Terminal 1 gained the top award of three chef's hats. According to Ronay, Harry Ramsden's breakfast and fish and chips were at least as good as those served at Claridges or Langan's Brasserie. And Egon Ronay should know. If it can maintain those standards in every new outlet it will have little problem strengthening, as well as exploiting, the Harry Ramsden's brand and all it stands for.

As well as the further growth of restaurants and takeaways – it is actively seeking properties in London and hopes to sign deals for Aberdeen and St Andrews – plus licensing and endorsements, Harry Ramsden's was at the end of 1997 undertaking a new market test which might lead to the re-emergence of Harry's original green-and-white painted wooden hut. The idea was to introduce a small retail outlet, takeaways with a small seating area, modelled on Harry's original still to be seen on the Guiseley site. Known as 'Harry's Huts', four of these prototypes are being tested on retail parks in Scotland. The initial results are extremely encouraging. If they prove successful the plan is to open one hundred or more in the UK.

DISCUSSION POINTS

1. What is your assessment of Harry Ramsden's financial progress over the five years for which data are provided.
2. How fast can HR grow? Could it have grown faster? Would it have been prudent to have grown more slowly? Do you think it is more important, in Harry Ramsden's situation, to be prudent, or to be opportunistic?
3. Outline the pros and cons of franchising, having regard to both financial and operational issues.
4. Is Harry Ramsden's Plc a company which exhibits the characteristics of a single-business company, a multibusiness company or an acquisitive financially oriented company?
5. Identify Harry Ramsden's Plc's corporate strategy and suggest suitable corporate objectives.
6. Suggest a strategy framework which might be appropiate for analysing Harry Ramsden's situation.
7. Recommend a suitable strategic objective or mission for Harry Ramsden's and indicate some appropriate milestone objectives.

Harry Ramsden's Plc profit and loss account (£000)

		1996		1995		1994		1993		1992
Sale revenue		4,887		4,326		3,716		3,289		2,869
Cost of sales		607		596		610		809		785
Gross profit		4,280		3,730		3,106		2,480		2,084
Administrative expense	2,752		2,509		2,272		1,917		1,581	
Other operating income	12		4		1		154		74	
	2,740		2,505		2,271		1,763		1,507	
Operating profit		1,540		1,225		835		717		577
Equity account profit		−12		78		246		157		16
Net interest payable		192		149		130		59		−15
Net pre-tax profit		1,336		1,154		951		815		608
Taxation		402		358		258		243		178
Dividends		441		441		397		340		270
Retained profit		493		355		296		232		160

Harry Ramsden's Plc balance sheet (£000)

	1996		1995		1994		1993		1992
Fixed assets									
Intangible assets (note 1)		731		634		520		421	307
Tangible assets (note 2)		5,035		5,030		5,005		4,780	4,115
Financial assets (note 3)		3,198		3,239		2,657		1,709	955
		8,964		8,903		8,182		6,910	5,377
Current assets									
Stocks	113		125		110		104		105
Intra-group debtors	1,340		759		479		370		122
Other debtors									
(inc. prepayments)	1,048		590		405		235		324
Cash	75		154		122		124		87
	2,576		1,628		1,116		833		638
Short-term loans	2,301		1,960		1,383		1,774		324
Other creditors									
(due in less than 1 year)	1,572		1,445		1,238		1,152		1,120
	3,873		3,405		2,621		2,926		1,444
Net current assets		−1,297		−1,777		−1,505		−2,093	−806
Longer-term debt		65		65		0		0	0
Provisions		193		165		137		105	57
Total net assets		7,409		6,896		6,540		4,712	4,514
Issued share capital		882		881		881		800	800
Share premium		5,614		5,611		5,611		4,162	4,162
Goodwill reserve		−819		−819		−819		−819	−789
Retained earnings		1,732		1,223		867		569	341
Total capital		**7,409**		**6,896**		**6,540**		**4,712**	**4,514**

1 Intangible assets include brands and patents and costs of their development depreciated at a rate of 20 per cent per annum.
2 Tangible assets include all freehold and leasehold property and all other fixed assets owned by the company.
3 Financial assets include all equity and loan investments in associated companies.

Harry Ramsden's Plc cash flow statement (£000)

	1996	1995	1994	1993	1992
Operating profit + depreciation	1,883	1,420	971	833	665
Increases in working capital	909	435	238	114	-99
Dividends from associated cos.	46	15	0	0	0
Interest received	17	19	17	2	33
Interest paid	209	168	147	64	13
Dividends paid	441	397	368	330	210
Taxation paid	282	147	140	112	171
	105	307	95	215	403
Investments:					
Acquisitions	0	0	0	0	586
Investment in associated cos.	206	574	827	675	488
Capital expenditure	288	334	434	925	302
	−389	−601	−1,166	−1,385	−973
Financed by:					
Long-term debt raised	0	65	0	0	0
Share capital issued	0	0	1,530	0	0
Currency appreciation	−14	−10	25	−28	−5
Net increase in cash	**−403**	**−546**	**−389**	**−1,413**	**−978**

Mills Office Equipment Ltd

In 1994, Henshall Group Plc employed just over one thousand people in its five divisions, achieved group sales of £98m and pushed net pre-tax profits above £10m for the first time in the company's history. It was a diversified group. The divisional activities, which included hotels, entertainment, publishing, printing and office equipment, had only ownership and an East Anglian geographical base in common. Each of the divisions was also diversified within itself. Entertainment, for example, included three seaside funfairs and shares in a second division football club, while office equipment included wholesale and retail stationery, contract furniture and office machinery, mainly computer equipment. The group appeared to be anything but coherent and it performed as well as it did largely because of the effort and energy of its founder and chief executive Tom Henshall.

The office equipment division, which traded as Mills Office Equipment Ltd, had been expanded through a series of small acquisitions. Henshall thought there was an opportunity to carve out a sizeable business in East Anglia and the Midlands from Birmingham to North London. By 1994 it had branches in Norwich, Ipswich, Chelmsford, Northampton, Leicester, Nottingham, Leamington and Coventry. There were also clear opportunities to acquire further businesses in Birmingham, Luton and Cambridge. However, Mills' profitability had been disappointing and Henshall hesitated before expanding further. Growth had initially produced an increase in bargaining power which had improved margins, but latterly there seemed to have been some loss of efficiency and margins had reduced with increasing scale rather than increased.

The original Mills Office Equipment Ltd was acquired in 1979, the first company Henshall had acquired in office equipment. It was based in Ipswich with branches in Norwich and Chelmsford, and its managing director Roland Avery became the divisional chief executive. Avery enjoyed a close personal relationship with Tom Henshall and was jointly responsible with Tom for developing the division's acquisition strategy. In 1988, after several years successful growth, he was invited to join the board of Henshall Group Plc, the parent company. Avery was in effect both the architect of Mills Office Equipment Ltd and its chief executive.

It seemed to Avery that the fall-off in profitability was because Mills was not taking full advantage of the opportunities provided by the acquisitions. The businesses were added with very few changes being made apart from the odd redundancy of junior staff. Each of the Midland acquisitions, i.e. businesses with branches in Northampton and Leicester, Nottingham, Leamington and Coventry, had been incorporated but continued to work with very little change apart from their proprietors joining the Mills board along with Roland as MD, finance director Jason Avalon and John Rudd stationery director.

The original Mills business ran retail stationery shops in each town which also sold office machinery and furniture. They also had two furniture showrooms and a warehouse plus a three-man salesforce specialising in contract furniture. Avery's boast that Mills could kit out a newly built office block 'down to the last paper clip' had been demonstrated many times over. Each of the acquired businesses also had stationery shops, but they did not offer the same range of product. The Coventry and Leamington businesses did not offer the same furniture ranges; the Leicester and Northampton branches sold little retail stationery but had excellent furniture business supported by good town centre showrooms; the Nottingham business was completely individual, selling totally a different range of furniture, stationery and machines. Each branch organised its premises in a completely individual way, dividing between stationery shop, furniture showroom and warehouse. There had been only a limited effort to integrate the various businesses, partly for fear of losing customers, but largely because Avery was reluctant to upset the acquired management who had agreed to join the Mills group on the basis that they would still be in charge of their own business.

Avery had reluctantly come to the conclusion that he would have to intervene much more actively in the day-to-day running of the branches to make sure that every opportunity was taken to achieve cost reductions and exploit purchasing muscle. The problem was that he did not have the time to intervene, even if he had the aptitude to do it effectively. What he needed, he confided to Tom Henshall, was a good 'hatchet man'. That was Tom's kind of language, but Avery actually set about trying to recruit a bright young professional manager, not necessarily with office equipment experience, but highly educated and competent. He got Jill Simpson, a 32 year old management consultant with broad industrial experience.

For Roland Avery the recruitment exercise was traumatic. Mills attracted a large field of candidates, but it quickly resolved down to a shortlist of four. On all objective criteria there were no grounds for excluding Jill, and Roland was happy to have her on the shortlist. He even boasted to his wife that they had shortlisted a female. Nevertheless, he was unable to take her candidacy really seriously because he knew they would appoint a male in the end – a 'hatchet woman' wouldn't quite fit the bill. But as the interview and assessment process went on it became clear that she appeared to have the best experience, mainly in management consultancy, and qualifications (science first degree plus an MBA). The traumatic part was convincing himself and then Tom Henshall that a woman could do the job. But he did.

The appointment was originally intended to be as a PA to the chief executive and for a board appointment to follow a six-month probationary period. However, the PA title carried secretarial connotations which were quite inappropriate for this post

Table 1 Mills' gross margins, 1994

	Sales revenue (£000)	Gross profit (£000)	Gross profit as a % of sales revenue
Stationery	7,906	488	6.2%
Furniture	10,224	1,890	18.5%
Machines	1,901	60	3.2%

and Avery decided it would be a particularly unfortunate title for a female. After careful consideration he decided on an immediate board appointment as director of strategic development and this was agreed.

The brief given to Jill Simpson was to investigate the causes of declining profitability and recommend corrective action. She was to work as an internal consultant and was promised total backing by Avery.

Jill started work with certain predispositions. One of the selection interviews had taken place in the Ipswich showroom, seated round a beautiful Danish rosewood boardroom table which Avery had indicated was priced at over £4,000. He had stroked the table lovingly as he told her about the Danish workshops where it had been produced. 'This isn't just a showroom,' he had said with a huge smile, 'it's an Aladdin's cave where the customers come to wonder and be seduced.' He was obviously a great enthusiast for the products he was selling and it had made a big impression on Jill during her interview. She was suspicious that his enthusiasm may not be well founded from a business perspective.

Jill started work with a detailed analysis of the Mills business. She divided sales into the three main areas, stationery, furniture and machines. Her initial (see Table 1) analysis showed the gross margins.

Even on this crude basis the machines, mainly microcomputers and peripherals, did not look worth doing. They clearly made hardly any contribution, let alone a positive net profit. As part of her initial familiarisation Jill had interviews with all the branch managers and took the opportunity to find out their views. Three of them pointed out that they handled computer hardware simply as a customer service, part of the contract work. Moreover, they really only processed the administration of ordering etc. and rarely handled the equipment physically. For this service they made a charge that was intended to cover their costs plus a small margin. They said it was sometimes important to getting big contracts that they were able also to provide the hardware: 'without it the "down to the last paper clip" boast would be pretty empty.' The other branch managers were less concerned with the machines business. The Coventry manager simply said it was 'a waste of time'.

The profitability of the business clearly depended on furniture, but Jill still had a hunch that the contribution made by Danish exotica and similar was unlikely to be substantial. The next stage of her analysis therefore involved a detailed breakdown of sales, product by product over the previous four years. This was done for both furniture and for stationery.

Over that period Mills had sold almost 5,000 different items of furniture. She noted wryly that over that period only one Danish rosewood boardroom table had been sold and that appeared to have been sold at cost. Further investigation revealed her hunch to be absolutely correct: the upmarket designer furniture accounted for less than 3 per cent of sales. She mentioned this to Avery in one of her periodic meetings with him and was concerned to find he appeared quite tetchy on the subject. 'It's not really the point,' he explained. 'We're creating an ambience, an atmosphere where customers will understand we are in the quality end of the market, we know what quality is, and they will be prepared to pay that little bit extra as a result.' 'But do they?' she thought, but said nothing.

Around 80 per cent of sales revenue came from ranges of standard wooden office furniture, associated chairs and metal filing cabinets and cupboards. Although the different branches handled product from different manufacturers they were quite similar in design and finish as well as broadly comparable on price. Most manufacturers offered furniture in light, medium and dark oak, light, medium and dark mahogany and light and dark teak. Desks were offered in three sizes with single or double pedestals and five different drawer options in each pedestal. Thus the full range of desks of a single design was extensive and Mills appeared to have made sales of more-or-less every combination.

As she became more familiar with the furniture business Jill visited the branches and talked to the warehousemen. It was clear that the extent of the furniture ranges on offer caused huge problems. It generally took 6 to 8 weeks to obtain deliveries from the manufacturer, so it was essential to have stocks of frequently sold items available for immediate sale. Sod's law usually seemed to apply and the correct item was 'never' in stock. Or if it was it was never in the right place; if the customer was in Leamington the particular item they wanted would be in Ipswich. The growth of the company had made ex-stock deliveries more available but at a cost of many interbranch transfers. Jill traced one particular item which had made no fewer than five interbranch transfers – the best travelled desk in the country she imagined.

Stock control was computerised and nominally under central control in Ipswich, but branches had the ability to book stocks and to buy their own items where they had their own suppliers. There would obviously be considerable advantage in imposing much stricter control from the centre, and Jill anticipated that a central warehouse might also make good economic sense especially as three of the branches were continually short of warehouse space and wanted to move into more spacious premises.

Jill also looked at the stationery business. Sales were split almost half and half between wholesale and retail. Retail stationery achieved a much higher gross margin, but sales were made in small quantities and necessitated a town centre retail outlet. These shops were also used to display a few items of furniture and also served as mini warehouses and offices. If the cost of the shops was all charged against the retail stationery business then it would be shown to make a substantial loss. Jill made some enquiries that indicated that the wholesale stationery and furniture business could be accommodated in out-of-town premises at around half the cost of the town centre shop. But even if only half the shop costs were charged to retail stationery it would still not be viable.

Finally, Jill made a detailed analysis of furniture sales, customer by customer and location by location. Using an algorithm called the travelling salesman, which she had learned on her MBA, she calculated the most efficient route to achieve the actual pattern of sales. This was to find a suitable location for a central warehouse. This turned out to be a few miles east of Newport Pagnell in Buckinghamshire. She surveyed the possibilities in the area and costed suitable warehouse premises adjacent to exit 14 on the M1. She then established the practicalities of servicing all of Mills' areas from this single warehouse.

Around eight months after joining the company, Jill was pretty clear about the best way forward for Mills. Moreover, she had also got to know the people in the company and had a good idea of how they would respond to her proposals: mostly it was likely to be negative. As a consultant she could have devised the plan, incorporated a few sweeteners, made a presentation, offered continuing support as required and walked away from it. Her position was now a bit different.

Jill's plan involved the following:

1. Cease the machines business.
2. Cease retail stationery.
3. Close the town centre shops.
4. Develop a standard furniture range – she had identified a list of 145 items.
5. Feature the standard furniture range and wholesale stationery in a glossy catalogue.
6. Write off and dispose of all non-standard product.
7. Close the furniture showrooms and warehouses.
8. Locate central warehouse at Newport Pagnell to accommodate only standard product.
9. Impose strict purchasing and stock control at the centre.
10. Impose standard product on all branches.
11. No stocks of non-standard product to be kept anywhere.
12. All standard product to be offered ex-stock – 48 hour delivery guaranteed.
13. All standard product to be offered with a 10 per cent discount.
14. Non-standard product to be sold with no discount and subject to manufacturer's normal delivery (i.e. 6–8 weeks).
15. Sales representatives bonus not to be paid on sales of non-standard product.

It was clear that such a radical plan would upset everyone with the possible exception of Tom Henshall. The great strategic benefit would be that the Mills acquisition and growth strategy could be put back on the road. Acquiring the businesses in Birmingham, Luton and Cambridge would add substantial profitable turnover. But rather than taking on the costs of three new shops, showrooms and warehouses, these fixed assets could all be eliminated or substantially reduced and the expansion increase profitability, rather than, as at present, merely increase complexity and reduce profitability.

That aspect would appeal to both Henshall and Avery, but Jill knew that the means of achieving it would give Avery apoplexy. She could just imagine his face turning red with anger at her suggestion that they get rid of the 'Aladdin's caves' and his pet items of designer furniture. Nor would Avery be alone. The closure of the stationery shops would have a similar effect on John Rudd the stationery director. She also knew full well that the branch managers jealously valued their autonomy and right to buy items as they saw fit. In her discussions in the branches she had been careful not to divulge her plan but had discussed the possibilities in a way that allowed the branch managers to offer their views. 'All you would need are branch monkeys,' was one off-the-cuff remark, while another suggested 'we'd just be sales reps then.' A third said simply 'it wouldn't suit me' in response to the notion of a more limited range of furniture. Finally, three branch managers would be extremely upset at being told to stop offering to sell office machinery.

Whilst the logic of the plan seemed fine – it should provide an immediate upturn in profitability and the possibility of highly profitable expansion – even Jill acknowledged it was not free of risk. Part of the plan involved leasing the new warehouse and filling it with over £3m of standard product range in the hope that 75 per cent of customers would buy standard items. She could imagine Jason Avalon's measured response: 'I'm not sure that it would be very prudent . . .'. She knew there would be worries about how many customers would be persuaded to buy standard product and there would be genuine concerns about how many customers would be lost because of the 6–8 week delivery and no discount on non-standard items. Then there was the problem of the catalogue. There were a lot of cheap discounting catalogues around and they would clearly have to distance themselves from competing with that business. They would not be a national and courier distribution business; they would be regional with a more personal and customer service oriented business. They would certainly need to sharpen up the focus of their business.

As she thought through the different ways of proceeding it suddenly occurred to her that she had hit upon a plan, perhaps the only one in the world, that would unite everyone in the company against her. Yet from both her own extensive consulting experience and from the factual analysis within the company, she knew the plan was the only way to bring Mills back on stream.

She had recently been reading a biography of the American physicist Richard Feynman and remembered one of his early brushes with the establishment when the wife of an eminent professor had put him down with a devastatingly patronising, 'Surely, you're joking, Mr Feynman.' Jill could imagine Roland Avery reading her report and responding in similar fashion, 'Surely, you're joking, Miss Simpson.'

She was excited by the plan, but extremely concerned about how to persuade the company to adopt it. She could see various ways of softening it and making it more gradual. Closures could be phased. The Ipswich 'Aladdin's cave' could even be retained, at least for the time being until the validity of the basic plan became apparent to Roland who she was sure would then pursue it with enthusiasm. But the plan would be nothing without a commitment to the whole package.

She could picture presenting the plan to a board meeting. Roland Avery, Jason Avalon, John Rudd and the four branch manager directors. On such occasions she became extremely aware of gender, as though there was some magic ingredient that allowed male managers to get things through 'on the nod' that females were forced to struggle with and often to accept failure. Yet she knew it was not really a gender issue.

She thought of backing off. It would be perfectly possible to come up with some compromise project which would improve profitability and enable the growth strategy to be resumed with some success. But she knew that would be a failure of courage.

DISCUSSION POINTS

Assuming that Jill's plan is valid,

1. What problems do you see that Jill must overcome if she is to get the plan accepted?
2. Should Jill pay much attention to 'politics' in her implementation efforts?
3. Suggest how she should approach each of the key stakeholders.
4. Outline a suitable programme for getting the plan adopted, identifying key stages and issues.

Après Shower

On 1 January 1997, Mike Godwin decided that his New Year resolutions must include the determination of a clear strategy for Après Shower. The product had been on the market for five years and yet Mike still had no real feel for whether it was primarily for physically challenged users, or whether there was an untapped luxury segment or whether, even, this was a product with mass market potential as an everyday bathroom accessory. The 'grey' market might represent yet a further opportunity. Après Shower's sole product had been introduced by Mike in 1991. It was the equivalent of a warm air hand dryer for the whole body and was named 'Easydry'.

Easydry took two years to develop and was designed particularly for use within a shower cubicle, although it can be installed over a bath or on any wall. The dryer consists of an electric motor which blows jets of warm air over the body. The electric motor is encased in a tough plastic 'pod' which is installed just above the height of the shower cubicle away from the flow of water. The air, at a constant temperature of 70 degrees Fahrenheit, which cannot burn the skin, passes through a hollow 'leg', which runs vertically down the wall, and out through jets at an angle of 30 degrees downwards. The unique design of this leg ensures that the air is distributed evenly along the length of the body so ensuring even drying.

Easydry is also safe and efficient. The high technology motor and fan components are imported from Germany and have been rigorously tested to ensure both complete user safety and continuous product reliability in a wet environment. Easydry complies with European Electrical Safety Regulations (EN60 335-2-23 1990). Mike recommends that Easydry be used during showering for a 'hydrotherapy' effect and also suggests that it can double up as a room heater. Efficient operation means that the user is 'touch' dry (rather than 'towel' dry) in five minutes, costing only 5 pence in electricity.

Although Mike originally conceived Easydry as a way of catering for those who might want an added touch of luxury in their bathing routine, it soon emerged that there was a very real and present need for such a product amongst the physically

This case is by Ian Wilson, Staffordshire Business School, Staffordshire University, England.

challenged. A touch pad was thus designed which could be located anywhere within a shower cubicle (including the tray, for toe operation) and used air pressure to start the dryer. Other customers have the option of a starter button located flush in the underside of the pod.

Easydry works most efficiently when installed within a shower cubicle where the smaller volume of warm air is recycled. The pod is secured to a corner with two screws and the leg is simply positioned between the pod and the lip of the shower tray. The dryer cable is then routed outside the shower area and connected to a 13 amp fused spur switch. However, Easydry can also be mounted above a bath (the leg can easily be cut to size) and in a commercial bathing/changing area. According to Mike, any competent do-it-yourselfer would find fitting the dryer both quick and easy.

Easydry is sold with a twelve months parts and labour guarantee. Once installed, it requires no servicing. In the unlikely event of a leg being damaged (perhaps in collision with a wheelchair), spares can be provided.

Après Shower Dryers Ltd was established in 1991 by Mike Godwin to manufacture and market the dryer. Although Mike was a successful entrepreneur, being a fully qualified electrical engineer and having established one of the region's most successful electrical contracting businesses, he had no previous experience of marketing products on a national scale. After some early success, Mike made limited further headway and turned to Kevin Pritchard, an honours graduate with over twelve years' experience in blue chip companies, specialising in the sales and marketing of new products. Impressed by the concept, in April 1993 Kevin established Après Shower Distributors UK Ltd to market, sell and distribute the product.

In 1994, both Kevin and business manager Judith Russell left. They had failed to lift Easydry sales beyond a trickle. Mike attributed this largely to a lack of investment in marketing. Back in 1991, having invested significantly in the technical development of Easydry and the production of tooling, an advertising agency had told Mike that he would need to spend £200,000 on promotion to allow Easydry to take off. Mike was thus left to do the marketing and administration as well as the procurement, assembly, product development and submissions for patent registration/renewal and standards testing.

Some progress was made but this was mainly in terms of consolidation of Easydry's position in the physically challenged segment, which continued to account for over 95 per cent of sales. Some 70 per cent of sales was made through a network of eight countrywide distributors specialising in the sale of a range of equipment for the physically challenged. Although called distributors these outlets acted as non-exclusive retail outlets for Easydry and were not permitted to sell to sub-distributors or other retail outlets.

Excluding a limited amount of *ad hoc* exports, the remaining sales were made direct, to users, often following referral by an occupational therapist. A review of the physically challenged and grey markets underlined the overall potential in these areas (see Box 1).

By the end of 1996 Mike felt that Après Shower was well known amongst occupational therapists and distributors/retailers of equipment for the physically challenged. Advertising expenditure to this sector was thus cut to around £1,000 pa.

BOX 1
Environmental review

1. Greater freedom for occupational therapists to select from a wider range of providers of technical aids.
2. Increasing variety of channels for technical aids – specialist shops, dedicated mail order catalogues, kitchen and bathroom showrooms, builders' merchants, DIY and homecare outlets amongst others.
3. Increasing number of organisations which will display and distribute free of charge information about technical aids, e.g. disabled living centres.
4. On average, three homes modified each week by each social services department to meet the needs of the physically challenged.
5. Estimated current 10 per cent per annum growth rate in shower installations into the homes of the physically challenged.
6. Over 12 million people in the UK aged over 60.
7. According to the 1989 OPCS Survey of Disability there are 6.2 million adults in Britain with a disability above the threshold level. Of these, 5.8 million live in private residences and 7 out of 10 use some form of disability related equipment.
8. The Community Care Act 1994 will result in declining hospital beds and increased numbers of patients receiving care in their own homes.
9. Predictions in 1989 by Hay Management Consultants suggest that the number in the over-75 age group will be one-quarter higher by the year 2000.
10. Breakdown of the nuclear family implies more independent living.
11. Rising expectations regarding standard of living and maintenance of that standard into old age.
12. Only 31 per cent of persons with disabilities under pensionable age are in paid employment.
13. Seventy-five per cent of people with disabilities rely on state benefits as their main source of income.
14. Increasing numbers of elderly are benefiting from incomes from private pension schemes.
15. On average, for those aged over 75, the cost of the health service is six times higher, and the cost of social services twenty-six times higher.

Attempts to penetrate new segments, on the other hand, had been sporadic and unrewarding. Easydry appeared in Harrods for a few days where it sold in reasonable numbers, but in the small electrical appliance department. It had been shown to a national house builder who was interested but took it no further. Despite continued growth in the leisure industry no attempts had been made to sell Easydry to hotels, health farms or sports and fitness centres.

Mike tried a (necessarily) limited amount of direct response advertising. Two insertions in the Daily Mail's *You* magazine produced 100 replies and 30 unit sales. A similar exercise was tried using the *Bury Times*, playing on the local invention angle and tying in with displays in three leading Bury bathroom showrooms. Mike always felt that if Easydry could be seen (but perhaps not heard) running then it would be bought. It is too early yet to evaluate this attempt to create a local word of mouth campaign. An American film star bought three but the fee demanded by his agent for a testimonial exceeded total annual sales value.

Other potential options have opened up recently for Après Shower. Following publication of the first case study on the company, approaches have been made to Après Shower by a large distributor of plumbing equipment and by a manufacturer of bathroom sanitaryware. Mike found it intriguing that while he was currently supplying direct to a small number of individual retail customers, there remained the possibility of entering the bathroom market at several different levels within the marketing channel. Mike had decided that Après Shower did not have the funds to support research into Easydry specifically but perhaps the markets for shower controls and enclosures were sufficiently related to provide some sort of guide. Some work undertaken by AMA Research had revealed that the annual shower control market would be around 1.77 million units in 1997 and was growing at around 3–5 per cent annually. Household penetration of shower controls was believed to be around 55–60 per cent.

The shower enclosure and screens market had outperformed the shower control sector and it was surprising that few control manufacturers appeared to have taken advantage of their distribution strengths by entering the enclosures/screens market. The supply of an integrated shower package from one source did not yet seem to be an issue. Nor had many firms yet addressed the co-ordination of enclosures with sanitaryware.

Although the shower enclosure market had shown considerable growth, household penetration was estimated to be only 13 per cent by 1994. The number of homes with shower-only installations was thought to be minimal but expected to increase as the number of single-person households grows. Trade opinion suggested that saturation point for separate shower installations might be 30–35 per cent of all households. However, a shift to showering instead of bathing and the trend towards multiple shower ownership (main bathroom, en suite and downstairs toilet) could lift this figure much higher.

Hitherto the market has been concentrated on new installations in new build or new installations in existing households (retrofit). However, having been installed over ten years ago, some enclosures and screens would now need replacing. Replacements are also likely to be upgrades. About one-third (in volume) and one-half (in value) of enclosures and screens are estimated to be sold through builders merchants. Nearly 45 per cent of volume sales are through DIY outlets but these represent only some 30 per cent of value. Bathroom specialists account for about 5 per cent of volume and 12 per cent of value. Merchants and specialists tend to focus on higher quality, better featured branded products, often as part of total shower packages and usually professionally installed. DIY outlets tend to focus on general replacement and own brands with minimal presentation and screens.

Mike's belief in a 'luxury' market for Easydry was fuelled partly by the conspicuous growth in non-essential products for the bathroom. AMA estimated, for example, that by 1994 some 10,000 to 12,000 whirlpools and spas had been installed in consumers' homes. There was, of course, a wide range in terms of quality and features, reflected in price variations from under £500 to £3,000 plus. Some products now cater for two-person bathing and feature head and arm rests, underwater lighting and built-in radios and telephones. Latest developments include combined shower and steam enclosures. Veronica Hannon* summed it all up when she described 'the bathroom as a place in which consumers can relax after a long day at work. A sensual place to pamper themselves in. . .'.

Although being heavily constrained in terms of the time and money available for Après Shower, Mike had nevertheless turned his attention to the subsequent development of the Easydry product. A number of added value features were under consideration, although as yet only one had reached the marketplace. This had resulted in the product being included in the Toys for Handicapped mail order catalogue where it was branded Sirocco. Ribbons attached to the holes in the leg brushed against handicapped children thus providing pleasurable stimulation. The product was thus being installed in a playroom environment rather than in a shower.

There was also some price development in 1996. The initial price of £275 plus VAT and carriage was finally increased to £301.27 plus VAT. A volume-related discount was available to all retail outlets. Installation costs would vary according to each situation but an electrician might charge £50–£60 on average.

Mike's thoughts turned to the benefits which Easydry offered, many of which had not been envisaged until after years of usage experience:

- Touch dry in five minutes
- Kinder to sensitive skin
- More hygienic than towels
- No wet towels lying around
- Saves cost of laundering towels
- Relaxes aching joints and muscles
- Warms bathroom
- Dries shower curtains
- Reduces condensation in bathroom
- Permits privacy and dignity for persons with reduced mobility who previously needed the help of a carer
- Saves the expense of a carer in the above situation
- Provides a touch of luxury
- Twenty-first century lifestyle

DISCUSSION POINTS

1. What sort of mission statement should Après Shower have?
2. What should Après Shower's priority objectives be: short-term profitability or

long-term growth? If growth, should this be achieved by growing the market, by market development, by product development or by diversification?

3. Should Après Shower plan to stay independent or should it seek a partner of one form or another?
4. Do you see Après Shower's business as being in a niche market or in the early stages of a mass market?
5. What do you see as the main barrier to growth and the main threats to Après Shower's future?
6. Should Après Shower pursue a broad or narrow strategic target?

Apres Shower Dryers Ltd profit and loss account

	1996	1995	1994	1993
Turnover	54,183	27,135	22,176	35,449
Cost of sales	17,866	8,437	11,570	28,493
Gross Profit	36,317	18,698	10,606	6,956
Administration	29,734	24,794	17,472	23,790
Operating profit/(loss)	6,583	(6,096)	(6,066)	(16,034)
Less Interest payable	562	1,068	983	660
Net pre-tax profit/(loss)	6,021	(7,164)	(7,849)	(17,494)

Après Shower Dryers Ltd balance sheet

	1996		1995		1994		1993	
Fixed assets								
Property improvements		3,678		4,203		4,728		5,253
Plant and machinery		27,953		32,886		38,690		45,518
Fixtures and fittings		1,185		1,394		1,640		1,930
Motor vehicles		1,345		1,793		2,391		3,188
Computer equipment		1,340						
		35,501		40,276		47,449		55,889
Current assets								
Stocks	10,200		5,170		4,700		5,950	
Debtors	21,715		6,632		2,146		781	
	31,915		11,802		6,846		6,731	
Less Creditors (due in less than 1 yr)	145,822		136,505		131,558		132,034	
Net current assets		(113,907)		(124,703)		(124,712)		(125,303)
Total net assets		(78,406)		(84,427)		(77,263)		(69,414)
Called-up share capital		100		100		100		100
Profit and loss account		(78,506)		(84,527)		(77,363)		(69,514)
Shareholders' funds		(78,406)		(84,427)		(77,263)		(69,414)

Autoliv AB

Autoliv AB of Sweden is one of the world's leading groups for airbags, seat belts and other equipment for passenger safety in automobiles. It was for many years a wholly owned subsidiary of Electrolux. In 1994, Electrolux sold the company in a public offering and Autoliv's shares are today listed on the Stockholm stock exchange. Autoliv has more than 40 wholly owned subsidiaries and joint venture companies with 10,300 employees in 23 car-producing countries.

Although the legal entity Autoliv AB was incorporated in 1937, the car occupant restraint business of the Autoliv Group can be traced back to the activities of Gränges Weda AB, a subsidiary of the Swedish Gränges group, in the 1970s. During this decade, Gränges Weda AB, which was involved in a number of industrial activities including the manufacture of seat belt retractors, increased the focus of its business on the manufacture of seat belts through a number of strategic acquisitions. In 1980, the Gränges group was purchased by Electrolux group and in 1984 the name Gränges Weda AB was changed to Electrolux Autoliv AB.

Throughout the 1980s and early 1990s, the group expanded through a number of acquisitions of seat belt manufacturers, predominantly in Europe but also in Australia and New Zealand. In the late 1980s and early 1990s the group established a number of joint venture operations to expand into new markets outside Europe and into new areas of technology. In 1994, the name of the company was changed from Electrolux Autoliv AB to Autoliv AB.

Autoliv's goal, as expressed in its annual report, is to be a world leader within its area of operations. In short, the following cornerstones characterise the company's goals:

- *Technical leadership* in systems for frontal collision protection, and in new areas such as improved protection for side collisions, rear-end collisions and rollovers.
- *A global presence* allowing the company to serve the needs of its customers for

This case is by Dr Thomas Hartman, Department of Management, Keele University, England.

technical support in all countries where they have and intend to establish vehicle manufacturing operations.

- *Cost efficiency* through adequate vertical integration, continuous product simplifications, automation and utilisation of low-cost countries for labour-intensive production.
- *Reliability* through a high level of quality, dependable shipments and building long-term customer relationships.

Products

Autoliv designs, develops and manufactures car occupant restraint systems and markets them to the world's major automobile manufacturers. Car occupant restraint systems encompass a variety of safety devices, the most significant of which in the current market are seat belts and airbags designed primarily to protect the occupant from injuries in frontal impacts. New products to protect car occupants from side and rear impacts are in the early stages of introduction to the market or are under development.

Seat belts

Since their introduction in the 1950s, seat belts have undergone significant improvements in terms of safety and comfort. Autoliv's current seat belt restraint systems are based upon three-point seat belts and comprise a number of individual components which are used in combination, according to the specification agreed with the customer. The principal components of the seat belts developed and manufactured by Autoliv are the buckle, the retractor and the height adjuster. A recent development associated with the buckle or the retractor is the addition of a pre-tensioner. The major component sourced externally by Autoliv is the seat belt webbing.

Buckles

The buckle comprises a clip with a steel tongue attached to the webbing and a mounting which is secured either to the chassis of the car or to the seat structure. Of particular importance is the safe functioning of the buckle in conjunction with pre-tensioners.

Retractors

The retractor stores unutilised belt webbing on a spindle, releases the webbing when the belt is drawn out, and retracts after the belt has been fastened to eliminate slack. In a crash situation, the retractor is designed to lock and prevent release of the webbing, thereby restraining the car occupant. One of the most significant improvements is the use of a sophisticated web-lock within the retractor, which in a crash reduces the webbing available for stretching.

Pre-tensioners

Pre-tensioners are associated with either the buckle or the retractor and their function is to tighten the belt by up to 150 mm before the occupant's body has started to move forward in a collision. Autoliv designs and manufactures both mechanical and pyrotechnical pre-tensioners. The latter can be co-ordinated with the deployment of an airbag by using a common sensor.

Height adjusters

Height adjusters allow the height of the shoulder belt to be altered, increasing the effectiveness of the seat belt in a crash situation as well as the ease and comfort of use for car occupants of above or below average height. Recent developments which have been introduced to the market by Autoliv include a retractor with an integrated height adjuster.

Airbags

Differences in the legislative background requiring the use of restraint systems between Europe and the United States have resulted in different designs of airbags being developed for each market. In the US market, because seat belt use is not mandatory in all states, the airbag system is required by federal law to provide protection to unrestrained occupants. In the European market, where seat belt use is mandatory and compliance with the law is generally high, smaller Eurobags have been designed for use in combination with seat belts. Autoliv manufactures both larger-sized US airbags and Eurobags according to its own system designs, which are adapted to meet each customer's specification.

The complete airbag system produced by Autoliv comprises the airbag module, sensors and the electronic unit. Deployment is initiated electrically and in most models the electronic unit not only performs this initiation, it also checks the integrity of the electrical connections, wiring and back-up power supplies. Generally, a greater proportion of the value of the components used in the production of Autoliv's airbags is bought in either from joint venture companies or from external suppliers, compared with Autoliv's seat belt production.

Customers

Autoliv's customers are the world's major automobile manufacturers. In Europe, Autoliv is a supplier of seat belts to most of the European-based automobile manufacturers such as Audi, BMW, Ford, Mercedes Benz, Nissan, Opel/Vauxhall, Peugeot and Citroen, Renault, Rover, Saab, Volvo and Volkswagen. Significant customers outside Europe include Chrysler, General Motors, Isuzu, Mitsubishi, Nissan, Suzuki and Toyota.

In the airbag market, Autoliv currently supplies Eurobags to BMW, Ford, Peugeot, Renault and Rover for certain of their European models, and US airbags to Saab and Volvo for both their European and North American models.

Owing to the importance of each customer to its business, Autoliv has concentrated on developing long-term relationships founded on close collaboration between the engineering and design departments of Autoliv and its customers. During the period of a new car model development, Autoliv undertakes the design and testing of the occupant restraint system in accordance with the automobile manufacturer's specification. In so doing, Autoliv aims to become one of the principal suppliers of car occupant restraint systems for a particular model. Autoliv will then typically expect to supply between 25 and 75 per cent of the manufacturer's purchasing requirements for car occupant restraint systems over the life of the model.

Autoliv also operates a 'just-in-time' delivery system designed to accommodate the specific requirements of certain of its customers for low levels of inventory and a rapid stock delivery service.

In recent years, automobile manufacturers have increasingly sought competitive quotes from suppliers and demanded significant staged price reductions over a product's life cycle. In line with its customers' purchasing strategies, Autoliv has implemented cost-saving programmes which are reducing its own materials, production and administrative costs.

Approximately 70 per cent of Autoliv's sales are made to seven major automobile manufacturers. Autoliv has in many instances been a long-term supplier to these major customers and in certain circumstances worked closely with them in the development of products. Autoliv typically supplies occupant restraint systems for a number of models, and supply arrangements are usually negotiated on a model by model basis. However, there can be no assurance that Autoliv's major customers will continue to purchase similar volumes of products or that prices can be achieved.

As a consequence of the major automobile manufacturers' strong purchasing power, and the competitive pressures amongst the car occupant restraint system suppliers to maintain and increase market share, the company believes that the unit prices of seat belts and airbag systems will continue to decline over the next few years. In addition, similar to other automobile component manufacturers, the company expects that it will, under certain circumstances, quote fixed or maximum prices for long-term supply arrangements. The group's future profitability will therefore depend upon, among other things, its ability to continue to reduce its per unit costs and maintain a cost structure, internally and with its suppliers, that will enable it to offer competitive prices. The maintenance and growth of profits may also be influenced by the group's success in designing and marketing technological improvements in car occupant restraint systems which are able to command higher prices in the market and upon which higher profit margins can be achieved.

Autoliv supplies its products to automobile manufacturers whose volumes of production are cyclical, being dependent upon general economic conditions and the level of consumer spending. In recent years the volume of car production in the group's most important markets in Europe has fluctuated considerably, year on year. These fluctuations in production by the automobile manufacturers give rise to similar fluctuations in the demand for the company's products.

Despite stringent testing of the effectiveness of its products and the maintenance of quality controls in the manufacturing process, the sale of car occupant restraint systems entails an inherent risk of product liability claims, particularly within the US market. Furthermore, in the case of systems that have been introduced relatively recently such as airbags, the potential product liability claims are more difficult to assess. Although the group has obtained its own product liability insurance, there can be no assurance that the coverage limits of the group's insurance policies will be adequate, and in the future product liability insurance may not be available on acceptable terms. In addition, insurance against punitive damages is currently not available to Autoliv. A successful claim brought against the group resulting in a recovery in excess of its insurance coverage could have a material adverse effect on the group's financial condition and results of operations.

Autoliv aims to maintain at least two suppliers of components sourced externally for use in the assembly of its car occupant restraint systems and generally has achieved this aim within its seat belt assembly operations. It also manufactures a number of the most important components itself. However, because airbag system assembly operations have only started relatively recently, the Autoliv Group is dependent in certain instances on just one supplier for certain components which make up the complete airbag module. Delays or stoppages in the delivery of such components to Autoliv could result in it being unable to supply its customers with complete products. Such an event could result in Autoliv's customers having to halt their own production processes. A failure to supply would result not only in loss of income to the group on the reduced volume of supplies, but could also result in the customer seeking reparations for the consequential losses incurred due to its own lost production.

An important aspect of Autoliv's strategy has been to be actively involved in the original design and marketing of innovative car occupant restraint systems. In this regard, Autoliv has developed a considerable amount of proprietary technology and now relies on a number of patents to protect this technology, especially in its seat belt production activities. There can be no assurance that any patent now or hereafter owned by Autoliv will afford protection against competitors which develop similar technology.

An element of Autoliv's strategy for the supply of key components, technological advancements and long-term growth in the car occupant restraint market has been the establishment of joint ventures. In most instances, ownership of the joint venture companies and the composition of the board of directors of the joint venture companies are equally divided between Autoliv and its respective joint venture partners, with neither party being able to exercise overall voting control at either the shareholder or the board of directors level.

Competitors

Both the seat belt and airbag markets are characterised by strong competition between suppliers to secure supply contracts with the major automobile manufacturers. Through Autoliv's early involvement in the design and marketing of seat belts and a number of strategic acquisitions in the major automobile producing countries in Europe, Autoliv has become the largest seat belt manufacturer and supplier in the European market, with a market share estimated by Autoliv to be approximately 50 per cent.

From its strong position in Europe, Autoliv has achieved a leading position in Australia and New Zealand and has expanded into the North American and Japanese markets. In addition, Autoliv has recently entered other markets such as China, Hungary, India, Mexico, South Africa, Taiwan and Turkey through the establishment of joint venture operations. However, Autoliv's share of the seat belt market outside Europe is low and is estimated to be less than 5 per cent in North America and Japan. On a worldwide basis Autoliv estimates that, largely as a consequence of its high market share in Europe, its total share of the world seat belt market is approximately 20 per cent.

In the airbag market, Autoliv, as a European-based manufacturer, entered the market later than some of its competitors which had become involved in the earlier development of the US airbag market. Consequently, Autoliv's market share is concentrated in Europe where it estimates that it holds a market share of approximately 25 per cent (1993).

Autoliv's strongest competitors include major manufacturing groups such as TRW Inc. and Takata Corp. which have extensive operations in both seat belts and airbags and are able to market a wide range of car occupant restraint systems. In addition, there are specialist manufacturers of airbag components and systems, such as Morton International Inc. and Breed Technologies Inc., whose operations are currently concentrated in North America. In Europe, other leading airbag manufacturers include Petri AG and Magna International Inc.

Production

Excluding joint ventures, Autoliv has seventeen production facilities located in ten countries. The production facilities can be divided into component factories and assembly factories. The Autoliv component factories manufacture pressed steel parts, springs, moulded plastic parts, and over-moulded steel parts used in seat belt assembly. One-piece woven bags, gas generators and electronics are made at the production facilities within Autoliv's joint venture operations. The assembly factories source components from a number of parties, including Autoliv's own component factories, and assemble the completed restraint system for 'just-in-time' delivery to customers.

Autoliv's component factories are located at Caudebec-les-Elbeuf (France), Norderstedt (Germany), Turin (Italy), and Chichester and Milton Keynes (UK).

Autoliv's assembly factories are located at Melbourne (Australia), Gournay-en-Bray (France), Dachau, Döbeln, Elmshorn and Rellingen (Germany), Chichester (UK), Landgraaf (The Netherlands), Auckland (New Zealand), Barcelona and Valencia (Spain), Vårgårda (Sweden) and Indianapolis (United States).

Assuming that the supply of raw material and components is not disrupted, Autoliv's assembly operations are not generally constrained by capacity considerations. Adjustments to capacity in response to changes in demand can be made within a few weeks by the addition or removal of relatively standardised production and assembly lines. Most of Autoliv's assembly factories have sufficient space to accommodate additional production lines to satisfy foreseeable increases in capacity.

Quality management

In order to meet increasing customer quality and internal production efficiency requirements, Autoliv has operated for several years an advanced quality management system. This system is based upon preventive principles involving the measurement of a number of quality indicators and it embodies the objective of a zero defect rate. By reference to the best practice within industry segment, Autoliv has developed 'benchmarks' applied throughout the company and places great emphasis on continually improving the quality of its products, customer service and production processes. This system meets the strict quality requirements demanded by Autoliv's customers, all of whom have approved the system and many of whom have formally acknowledged the high standards attained by Autoliv.

As part of a company-wide cost-saving programme, purchasing, which was previously organised at a local level, has become increasingly centralised. This has involved the appointment of 'group lead buyers' and their assignment to each of Autoliv's major suppliers. These group lead buyers are now responsible for negotiating the purchase requirements of particular types of components for the whole company. In addition, product development projects have increasingly involved the selection of certain suppliers to participate in the engineering stages of product development in order to improve both processes and products. In order to aggregate purchase volumes, reduce purchasing costs and allow closer collaboration in product development, the total number of suppliers is gradually being reduced.

Research and development

Autoliv invests continuously in research and development. This investment can be divided into three categories: research into new restraint and protection systems, product development and engineering. Research is concentrated at one location, Vårgårda in Sweden, whilst product development takes palce at Autoliv's other technical centres located at Gournay-en-Bray in France and Dachau in Germany, as well as at Vårgårda. Engineering is undertaken at all of Autoliv's production sites and within its joint venture operations in close collaboration with each site's local customers and utilising the resources of the three technical centres when necessary.

Each of the three technical centres is equipped with an advanced crash laboratory which possesses crash sled tracks which can simulate crash environments in dynamic tests. In addition, mathematical simulations of collisions are also performed in parallel with the dynamic tests.

The cost to Autoliv of research, development and engineering activities amount to approximately 5 to 7 per cent of annual net sales.

DISCUSSION POINTS

1. Is Autoliv AB a single-business or a multibusiness company?
2. What are the major strategic issues facing Autoliv AB?
3. How well do you believe Autoliv has achieved the purpose of strategy?
4. Suggest a strategy framework which might be used to model Autoliv's situation.
5. Using that strategy framework suggest alternative outline strategies that Autoliv might adopt.
6. Recommend and justify a a future strategy for Autoliv.

Autoliv AB financial performance and key ratios (SKr m)

	1995	1994	1993	1992	1991
Sales and income					
Sales	10,201	8,947	5,333	3,534	2,691
Operating income after depreciation	916	664	310	211	157
Income before taxes	1,009	680	240	167	93
Net income	649	430	125	97	36
Financial position					
Current assets excluding liquid funds	2,666	2,661	1,826	1,304	873
Fixed assets	1,845	1,205	1,073	928	590
Non-interest bearing liabilities	(2,738)	(2,632)	(1,529)	(973)	(625)
Capital employed	1,773	1,234	1,370	1,259	838
Net liquid funds/(net debt)	754	806	(169)	(448)	(272)
Shareholders' equity	2,527	2,040	1,201	811	566
Total assets	5,585	4,911	3,058	2,380	1,516
Earnings per share (k)	23.60	16.30	5.90	4.10	2.30
Ratios					
Operating margin (per cent)	9.0	7.4	5.8	6.0	5.8
Pre-tax margin (per cent)	9.9	7.6	4.5	4.7	3.4
Return on capital employed (per cent)	68.5	52.7	22.6	19.7	17.8
Return on equity (per cent)	28.0	25.6	19.0	15.0	11.3
Return on total capital (per cent)	19.0	17.4	10.6	10.0	11.1
Equity ratio (per cent)	45.2	41.5	39.3	34.1	37.3
Debt/equity ratio (per cent)	12.7	11.7	27.3	73.4	57.5
Interest cover ratio (per cent)	54.0	16.2	3.9	3.4	2.2
Other data					
Seat belt sales	5,339	4,818	4,055	3,469	2,683
Airbag sales	4,862	4,129	1,278	65	8
Capital expenditure	749	588	388	518	156
Number of employees	6,670	5,740	4,392	4,531	3,566

Guy Tobin Plc

Guy Tobin Plc started out in the mid-nineteenth century as a traditional twist lace maker and quickly established a reputation for work of the highest quality, a reputation that proudly survives to this day. Quite early on the company also ventured, in a small way, into knitted 'lace' manufacture in order to extend its product range into nets and tattings as well. This led Tobin into the technology of warp knitting which today accounts for the bulk of its turnover.

Most knitted clothes and fashion items are produced by weft knitting where the machine simply replicates hand knitting of a single continuous thread. Warp knitting on the other hand uses many threads and many needles operating simultaneously. The process was devised over two hundred years ago. It is potentially the quickest way of converting yarn into fabric and so was used to produce cheap and simple materials for army uniforms and blankets. However, right from the start warp knitting machines were also adapted to produce fancy work such as 'laces' and net fabrics.

The viability of warp knitted fabrics rests largely on low cost which was determined to a great extent by the speed with which the machines could operate. By the late nineteenth century, machines were running at speeds of around 100 courses per minute (cpm), a course being the completion of a row of simultaneous stitches across the width of the machine. By the 1920s, as a result of continuous development, machines were running at 240 cpm. By 1939, again as a result of continuous development, speeds had almost doubled again to 450 cpm. The threads were knitted by moving a bank of needles up and down against a stationery bar which held the thread loop, the speed of the machine being determined largely by the distance of movement of the needles. In 1939, a compound needle was introduced which contained two parts which moved up and down against each other allowing the distance of travel of the knitting elements to be halved, thereby doubling the speed of the machine to almost 1,000 cpm. After the war, further incremental developments and improvements were made till today it is possible to run machines at over 2,500 cpm.

Another critical factor in achieving these advances in speed has been the development of artificial fibres. Variations in the thickness of the thread would have an immediate impact on the tension before and after stitching which would result in flaws in the finished fabric, so it was important to use thread of uniform thickness. In addition, uniformity of thread strength was also crucial. If a thread broke the fabric would 'ladder' and be unusable. Natural fibres, such as cotton, lacked this uniformity both of thickness and strength. The introduction of synthetic fibres such as nylon and polyester solved these problems at a stroke and caused a massive increase in warp knitting volumes for both household and apparel markets.

In the 1960s, warp knitted nylon fabrics quickly dominated the mass markets for men's shirts and bed linen. The attractions of the new fabrics were many and various. They were extremely hard wearing, did not crease and did not need ironing after washing. At its peak, more than 60 per cent of men's shirts were made of knitted nylon fabric and around 40 per cent of bed sheets and pillowcases. Tobin entered both mass markets with enthusiasm and with financial support from the synthetic yarn manufacturers, invested heavily in new plant to produce the fine gauge sheeting and shirting fabrics and quickly became one of the three leading producers.

These markets were particularly attractive to Tobin because their growth coincided with the long-term decline of their traditional lace market. In 1960, Tobin had over 100 Leaver's lace machines dating from the early years of the twentieth century, but removed 40 of these to make space for the new warp knitting equipment to produce the sheeting and shirting fabrics.

The factory was in effect split into two: the lace plant and warp knitting. The split was not simply of shopfloor areas; it was fundamental. In lace manufacture, quality was everything, margins were high and volumes low. In warp knitting, speed and efficiency were paramount, margins low and volumes extremely high. Lace making was a craft-intensive process dependent on highly skilled people. Warp knitting was dependent on efficient organisation and required people to perform fairly simple tasks fast.

The strength of warp knitting was such that Tobin was in due course able to open three new custom-built factories dedicated to sheeting and shirting fabric. The warp knitted products were, however, not without problems in the market. Nylon sheets had the unfortunate characteristic of being slippery and, aided by any small movement of the consumer, tended to slide off the bed during the night. Attempts were made to overcome this problem by providing various means of secure attachment, but none of these was very convincing. In shirts the problem was associated with the intrinsic non-absorbancy of nylon filament. Even when accompanied by the ventilation of a heavy string vest, the problem was not completely overcome. The string vest and nylon shirt, a very visible and popular combination at the start of the swinging decade became, within a very short space of time, a symbol of non-chic.

In the mid-1960s the weaving industry found a way of producing fine cotton sheeting and shirting which had some of the 'easycare' characteristics of nylon while being both absorbant and non-slip. Initially cotton fabric was chemically treated to achieve drip-dry non-iron characteristics. The reduction in wear durability was subsequently overcome by the inclusion of a proportion of man-made fibre in the cotton weave. So quite suddenly in the mid-1960s both knitted nylon sheeting and shirting lost consumer acceptance. In a matter of a few months both were largely eliminated from the market. The impact on the industry was catastrophic.

Tobin survived this crash only by closing three of its four factories and making 60 per cent of its employees redundant. Other producers were not so fortunate and closed altogether. Since that time the search has been on for another mass market application of knitted fabric, but none has emerged. Tobin itself has developed a diverse product range which, it believes, will insulate the company from any future cataclysmic changes in the industry.

Tobin's main bread-and-butter products are lining materials for clothing and curtains which use the machinery originally acquired to produce shirting and sheeting fabrics. These are high volume, low cost fabrics made on fast, simple machines which run more-or-less continuously producing the same standard product. The quality standard of fabric is important, but the main selling point is without any doubt price, and Tobin is able to produce at lower cost than any of its UK competitors.

Tobin also continues to produce traditional twist lace of a very high quality and price. It completely rebuilt twenty of its original Leaver's lace machines and by the mid-1990s had the best equipped traditional lace factory in the world. So long as the current level of prices are sustained this will remain a highly profitable business, but without any substantial growth potential.

The other strand of the warp knitting industry which had originally been the cause of Tobin becoming a warp knitter was focused on producing a form of lace fabric which copied the traditional twist lace. Knitted 'lace' was very much quicker and cheaper to produce but was limited in the patterning effects it could achieve. Over the years, warp knitters had successfully improved the quality of knitted lace and the complexity of patterning they were able to achieve. Today, around 80 per cent of traditional lace designs can be copied satisfactorily so that it is indistinguishable to all but the most knowledgeable eye from the traditional product, and is produced at a fraction of the cost. Because the prices of these new 'lace' fabrics were so much lower, whole new markets were opened up which had simply not existed before. However, the potential volumes were difficult to assess and would undoubtedly be subject to the vagaries of any fashion-based industry as was demonstrated by experience with knitted lace pantyhose (tights) which became extremely popular when first introduced in the early 1980s.

Tobin had not ventured into the knitted 'lace' market, regarding it more as a threat to its traditional lace business than as an opportunity. However, it looked at many other new markets for warp knitted products. Although it is a mature industry, many new products have been developed over the past decade or so and some completely new markets have been created. Most of the successful warp knitters are active in these new product areas rather than being restricted to the traditional markets where highly efficient production of cheap standard product is the key to survival.

These new products include:

- Weft insertion lining fabrics – weft insertion gives additional dimensional stability
- Multi-axial insertion fabrics – for similar reasons; these fabrics made from carbon fibre or Kevlar and impregnated with plastic resins are used for missile nose-cones and satellite communications antennae and other structures
- Terry towelling sheeting – single-sided loop fabric popular in Germany for bed linen

- Terry towelling gown fabric
- Sun and light protection nets
- Tile support and plaster nets
- Grass catcher bags
- Falling rock protection nets
- High tensile polyester (htp) protection padding
- Reflective warning garments
- Kermel heat protection fabric
- Waffle fabric
- Glass fibre and htp conveyor belting
- PVC coated htp tubing
- Polyester geo-membrane
- Water embankment reinforcement fabric
- New elastomeric fabrics primarily for foundation and support garments
- Weft insertion coated flat roof covering and tarpaulin fabrics
- Secondary carpet backing
- Fishing nets
- Floatable water protection nets
- Anti-dazzle nets
- Weft insertion tyre cord
- Kevlar and epoxy reinforced fabrics for artificial arteries and bone structures.

Many of these new products were developed as a result of the new knitting technology, stemming largely from the application of electronics and computer control systems. Tobin had implemented a number of such innovations. Most of its machines now had electronically controlled yarn tension regulators. It had also acquired two weft insertion machines to broaden its product range. Additionally it had spent some R&D time looking at the various Kevlar applications. None of these developments promised to grow into major new business and Tobin appeared to be stuck with its two main businesses in low margin standard knitted product and high quality traditional lace.

In a further attempt to break out of this strait-jacket, Tobin decided to attack the knitted lace market. It spent some considerable time and effort seeking out an acquisition of an existing lace warp knitter, but was unable to identify an acquisition candidate that was both available and had the desired high quality reputation. It therefore decided to set up a new knitted lace business from scratch.

On traditional equipment, lace patterns were developed using manually produced artwork and systems for converting artwork to machine patterning instructions. These were then converted into patterning chains of punched metal cards which controlled the way the fabric was knitted. For the more elaborate patterns these chains could weigh several tons and take up to three weeks to build, during which time the lace machine would be unable to produce. This amount of downtime was one of the main elements of cost and meant that the producer had to run the machine on any pattern for a lengthy run, whereas the customer probably only wanted a small amount of this very expensive lace. Consequently the producer also became a substantial stockist of finished product.

Using the new technology, patterns were developed at a computer terminal. Some famous old patterns could even be reproduced automatically by scanning items of old lace. The patterning instructions were then transferred to the machine by a computer tape rather than a pattern chain in a matter of seconds rather than weeks.

The new electronically controlled 'jacquardtronic' machines cost over £350,000, around ten times the cost of Tobin's ordinary warp knitting machines. Tobin considered establishing a unit of six machines which would immediately put it among the best equipped lace manufacturers in the industry. It would need to take a 25 per cent share of the UK market at current prices in order to make the unit viable.

The new equipment could provide some interesting possibilities. Not only would Tobin be able to develop patterns on computers and dump the patterning instructions direct to the machine in a matter of seconds, it would also have a system of production control which monitored each machine on a continuous basis and provided continuous status reports. This system enabled making instructions to be passed to the machine from the production control office. In fact, it would be technically possible for any customer with a modem to pass making instructions, including full patterning details, direct to the production control system. It would then be possible for a job to be dumped to a machine without the intervention of any person at Tobin. Such a system would be the ultimate in terms of responsiveness to customer requirements. In addition, it would also enable the unit to run on continuous three-shift continental working with only a skeleton staff to oversee operations. To achieve this Tobin would need to take over 40 per cent of the UK market, but its costs would then be so reduced that it could lower prices to achieve that penetration. The possibilities were exciting, though Tobin's management were concerned over the potential loss of control if it went too far down the systems automation route.

Before deciding the move into knitted lace, Tobin reviewed the prospects for all its various business activities. Despite the ups and downs of warp knitting over the years, the basic linings business seemed fairly secure. It was a mature business with little growth potential, but Tobin was well established, highly competitive, not vulnerable to imports. The margins were low, but the business made a good contribution.

The traditional twist lace business was also fairly stable. The patterns it was making were the most complex and high value of all laces and not vulnerable to further penetration from knitted lace. However, the business was not growing either and although the gross margins were extremely good, the net position was questionable largely because of the high value tied up in stocks of finished goods. There was probably some export potential if the company put the marketing effort behind it, but its twenty machines were already over 70 per cent fully occupied on a two-shift system and it was questionable whether it could recruit and train suitable people to operate a night shift.

The other warp knitted products that it had diversified into more recently (i.e.

weft insertion and Kevlar products) were interesting but seemed unlikely to develop into substantial turnover, and from time to time it was proposed the company pull out of these products because they seemed to cause a disproportionate amount of trouble.

The knitted lace business offered Tobin the prospect of considerable and profitable growth. The market was continuing to expand at around 7–10 per cent per annum and it was felt there were substantial export opportunities particularly in northern Europe and Scandinavia. The Tobin name in traditional lace would help the company to penetrate these markets. Though the competitive responses from existing producers was uncertain it was felt that Tobin was strong enough to achieve a profitable business with substantially higher margin than the linings business, though perhaps more volatile and subject to varying rates of plant utilisation.

DISCUSSION POINTS

1. What are the key strategic issues in this case?
2. Which strategy framework, or frameworks, would be must useful in analysing Tobin's situation?
3. Identify Tobin's main strategic options.
4. How much can Tobin afford to invest without a major capital restructuring?
5. Recommend and justify a future strategy for Tobin.
6. Suggest a suitable strategic objective.

Guy Tobin Plc profit and loss account for years ending 30 April (£000)

		1996		1995		1994		1993
Sales revenue								
Warp knitted linings	28,013		27,460		28,018		25,244	
Twist lace	9,546	10,434	8,948	10,666				
New warp knit products	2,452		1,987		1,300		0	
Total sale revenue		40,011		39,881		38,266		35,910
Less Cost of sales		23,869		24,899		23,666		21,877
Gross profit		16,142		14,982		14,600		14,033
Less								
Distribution costs	8,312		7,912		7,165		6,882	
Administrative expense	4,354		5,109		4,902		5,353	
		12,666		13,021		12,067		12,235
Operating profit		3,476		1,961		2,533		1,798
Add extraordinary income		452		122		302		34
Net pre-tax profit	3,928		2,083		2,835		1,832	
Taxation		538		438		318		324
Dividends		436		436		436		436
Retained profit		2,954		1,209		2,081		1,072

Guy Tobin Plc balance sheet at 30 April (£000)

		1996		1995		1994		1993
Fixed assets								
Land and buildings		4,002		4,341		4,505		4,598
Plant and equipment		8,978		8,004		7,443		6,422
Motor vehicles		1,522		1,400		1,286		1,090
		14,502		13,745		13,235		12,110
Current assets								
Stocks	8,007		6,014		5,812		4,508	
Debtors	6,324		5,801		5,834		5,600	
Cash	456		377		12		351	
	14,787		12,192		11,658		10,459	
Creditors								
(due in less than 1 year)	8,409		7,462		7,213		5,807	
Net Current assets		6,378		4,730		4,445		4,652
Total net assets		20,880		18,475		17,680		16,762
Non-convertible loan stock		5,800		5,800		6,800		6,800
Issued share capital		4,800		4,724		4,724		4,508
Share premium account		1,576		1,576		1,576		1,576
Revaluation reserve		1,124		1,124		1,346		1,346
Profit and loss account		14,766		11,822		10,613		8,532
Total capital		28,066		25,046		25,059		22,762

British Industrial Adhesives Ltd

In 1993, Sir Arthur Bateman, chairman of Industrial Components Plc (IC), was looking forward to a well earned retirement. He had devoted his entire life to the company and spent over twenty-five years on the parent board. He had started out as a management trainee on IC's first ever cohort of graduate management trainees. He had joined one of the leading subsidiary companies, British Industrial Adhesives Ltd, having graduated with a good Oxbridge degree in medieval French. He had grown up and matured with the company, being heavily involved in many of IC's acquisitions during the 1960s and early 1970s. His success had been crowned with a knighthood, a customary British reward for heading a large company.

However, his final years as chief executive of IC had not been a great success. The company had grown continuously and rapidly for around twenty-five years after the end of the Second World War and since the late 1960s had been regularly referred to in the press as blue chip. Inevitably its growth had slowed down, and after a period of some rationalisation during the 1970s it had stabilised into two main areas of activity focused largely on serving the automotive and construction industries.

While post-war Europe was rebuilding, IC had found business very easy to achieve and, like many large companies, it had tended to get rather fat and sloppy, not worrying too much as new competitors entered its markets and started to erode its dominant market shares. However, by the end of the 1960s the world was starting to change rapidly.

Competition had increased dramatically, particularly from overseas, and in its automotive markets and many of its construction markets too, IC had lost share very substantially, almost halved in some markets. Then, in 1973, the oil price crisis devastated the business. The company was forced to work a three-day week during a prolonged miners' strike and oil price hike. Energy costs increased threefold overnight and demand for all IC's products was decimated. The company moved into losses for the first time in its ninety-year history. This was when Sir Arthur took over as group chief executive.

He was fearless, some said ruthless, in slashing costs, closing loss-making operations and selling off surplus assets, particularly properties. Under his leadership, the losses were eliminated and the company resumed a period of quite rapid growth achieved mainly through opportunistic acquisitions. For a period in the late 1970s and early 1980s, IC earned a rather bad press as an asset stripper, and several of the acquisitions of this period appeared to make little industrial sense, but did result in IC's balance sheet being hugely strengthened. Bateman was a disciple of James Hanson, though he would never have admitted as much. On three occasions companies were acquired and the full costs of acquisition were repaid from the disposal of hardly more than peripheral assets of the acquired company.

During this time IC moved into several new industries including paints, aluminium extrusion and castings, and plastics and plastic coatings. Moreover, its existing operations were also diversified. The company progressed, gradually re-establishing its blue-chip credentials under Bateman's leadership through the Lawson boom to the recession of the early 1990s. Then troubles began again.

British Industrial Adhesives Ltd (BIA) had accommodated several of Bateman's acquisitions, manufacturing a variety of specialist adhesives, materials and fastening components, mainly for the automotive and construction industries, was also now supplying substantial turnover to the furniture industry. BIA was a very diverse business compared with the tightly focused adhesives business that had accommodated Bateman during his early years with the company.

By 1993, BIA employed around 4,000 people in nine different locations. All nine factories were under-utilised even before the 1991/92 slump in demand, and it seemed there was little prospect of volumes ever recovering sufficiently for the production facilities to become profitable again. With a turnover of over £200m in 1993, BIA made a net loss of over £1.5m with the promise of mounting losses in the future unless some decisive management action was taken to reverse the trend.

BIA's head office and original factory were at Smethwick near Birmingham. This factory produced the whole of BIA's product range. This included adhesives for wood, metals and construction materials, including a range of internally developed polymer-based adhesives, as well as the aluminium-based range of fastenings and components and furniture materials. The basic adhesives products had always been produced at Smethwick ever since the factory was first opened, but the additional ranges had accumulated largely from the various acquisitions. There was a fairly strong R&D department based at Smethwick, but its only real success had been the introduction of the highly profitable polymer adhesives which were produced only at the Smethwick and Greenock factories.

BIA operated two other large factories, one at Erith in Kent serving the London area, the other at Leigh, near Manchester, serving the North West. The Erith factory, like that at Greenock, had been opened from a greenfield site by BIA, while all the other factories, located at Rhoose in South Wales, Chelmsford, Avonmouth, Hartlepool and Banbury, had all resulted from acquiring other companies. In the main they were small and unprofitable.

The products made at each factory varied, again being determined largely by acquisition history rather than by any carefully planned programme of allocation. It had been recognised for some time that there would have to be some rationalisation of production facilities because the factories were substantially under-utilised. However, it was not a simple matter because the closure of any one factory would mean the capacity to make one or more product ranges would be permanently reduced. Moreover, the costs of closure, redundancy etc. were substantial, the concomitant loss of skills and expertise might be highly damaging and the costs of distribution from a more distant factory source would tend to reduce the improved profitability. Table 1 provides an overview of the situation as it was at the end of 1993. The figures have been rounded to an approximation of the position over the previous three years, but it should be noted that sales generally over that period were

Table 1 BIA's situation at the end of 1993

Factory	Products	Turnover £m	Factory £m
Smethwick	Building adhesives	42	
	Wood adhesives	19	
	Metal adhesives	6	
	Aluminium fastenings	6	
	Furniture materials	5	
	Polymer products	4	82
Erith	Building adhesives	19	
	Wood adhesives	11	
	Metal adhesives	7	
	Aluminium fastenings	6	43
Leigh	Wood adhesives	11	
	Metal adhesives	8	
	Aluminium fastenings	6	
	Furniture materials	4	29
Chelmsford	Wood adhesives	4	
	Metal adhesives	5	9
Banbury	Aluminium fastenings	2	
	Furniture materials	3	5
Rhoose	Metal adhesives	5	
	Furniture materials	2	7
Hartlepool	Metal adhesives	3	
	Aluminium fastenings	2	5
Avonmouth	Metal adhesives	2	
	Aluminium fastenings	3	
	Furniture materials	4	9
Greenock	Building adhesives	10	
	Polymer products	8	18
Total		**207**	**207**

declining. All products appeared to have reached a stage of advanced maturity with the possible exception of polymer products.

Table 1 suggests that BIA produced six ranges of products, but this is really an oversimplification. Where acquired businesses produced duplicate products these had been superseded by BIA's own brand and in some cases production moved to Smethwick. Where the duplication had been less clear-cut, production had continued without change, the differences being maintained by the continuation of old brand names. It was recognised in BIA that this was not a long-term solution, but some of the smaller products clearly attracted a loyal following among BIA's own management if not among the customers. The categorisation was also somewhat artificial in that not all products fitted in. In fact the furniture materials group was really more of a miscellaneous category and included several products that were unrelated to furniture or to anything else that BIA produced.

Rather than focus on detailed figures a rather macro view is taken of the position in Table 2. Each of the product groups achieved gross profits which were only slightly varied according to the producing factory.

It is a fairly simple matter to calculate the approximate gross profit earned by each factory. This gross profit, amounting almost to £50m, had to pay for various indirect and overhead costs, both at the factories and centrally. Factory indirect costs are shown in Table 3.

This left what was referred to as an operating profit of around £11.5m which was not quite sufficient to cover the head office and overhead costs of £13.4m. It was recognised within BIA that this position would be likely to deteriorate further unless decisive action were taken.

The problem was largely to do with plant utilisation. Although it varied from factory to factory, BIA's overall utilisation was running at little more than 50 per cent of full two-shift operation. This meant that some factories were running on overtime, notably the Greenock factory, while others were having to operate short-time work-

Table 2 Product group profitability, end 1993

Product group	Gross profit %
Building adhesives	30
Wood adhesives	25
Metal adhesives	20
Aluminium fastenings	15
Furniture materials	10
Polymer products	35

Table 3 Factory costs

Factory	Indirect costs £m pa
Smethwick	15.8
Erith	9.2
Leigh	4.3
Chelmsford	2.1
Banbury	1.1
Rhoose	0.9
Hartlepool	0.9
Avonmouth	1.1
Greenock	2.6
Total	38

ing from week to week because of poor sales of some products, notably furniture materials. In theory, each factory could have worked three shifts thereby increasing production output by a further 40 per cent or so, but it is doubtful if this would have been practicable in some areas.

In due course the edict came from Sir Arthur Bateman's office for BIA to submit a recovery plan to the IC's executive committee, such proposals being to bring BIA back into profit within three years and to identify a positive strategy for the company's long-term development.

BIA's original reputation had been made with products sold mainly to trade customers in bulk containers, typically 10 and 25 kilogram drums. Until the mid-1980s it more-or-less completely ignored the DIY and small tradesman markets. Then it introduced a line of silicone-based products in half kilo easy dispenser tubs. These were BIA's traditional high-quality products packaged for the DIY or occasional trade user and were highly competitive on price. These products, supported for the first time by some mass advertising, firmly established BIA's leading brand name, Biastick, in the consumer market. Biastick claimed to be the best quality through its established reputation.

The Smethwick head office was a glorious art nouveau anachronism. It had been built in 1922 and the entrance foyer was a large open space with a granite floor and black marble tiles and chromium walls with decorative 1920s style stained glass windows. There were four ways out of the foyer. The most impressive was up an elegant sweep of staircase rising to the first floor and a wide pair of light oak and glass doors which gave onto the director's suite of offices. In addition there were two lifts, one with brightly polished brasswork. There was also a doorway at the left-hand side which led to a long corridor and some backstairs. Use of these various entrances and exits used to be determined strictly according to seniority – only directors having use of the stairs and senior managers (i.e. those who reported directly to a director) of the polished lift – but these anachronisms of hierarchy had now been largely ridiculed into disuse. Nevertheless some symbols remained. For example, senior managers had carpets on their office floors and were delivered trays with glasses and fresh carafes of drinking water in their offices each morning.

The doors to the director's suite were facing south and thus often had the sun shining through them. They were popularly known as the 'golden gates'. On the other side of the golden gates the carpet was double thick and the walls were adorned with an impressive selection of original Impressionist oil paintings.

This was the office that Sir Arthur had himself first joined in the 1950s as a management trainee. He knew it well. Nevertheless, BIA's management thought they knew him well and reckoned that their plan would have to be extremely persuasive if it was to be given any central support.

BIA's management devised two alternative schemes, A and B, details of which are provided below.

Scheme A

- Almost half the Smethwick factory was to be closed and the plant and machinery stripped out and scrapped, and a business rate reduction negotiated. 380 employees redundant.

- Half the Erith factory to be closed and the plant and machinery stripped out and scrapped, and a business rate reduction negotiated. 180 employees redundant.
- Banbury factory to be closed and sold. Production moved to Smethwick. 160 employees redundant.
- Rhoose factory to be closed and sold. Production moved to Smethwick. 140 employees redundant.
- Hartlepool factory to be closed and sold. Production moved to Greenock. 160 employees redundant.
- Avonmouth factory to be closed and sold. Production moved to Smethwick. 195 employees redundant.
- It was believed the Banbury, Rhoose and Avonmouth factories would be easy to sell and approximate figures were included in the scheme's cash flows, as was a void of business rates on the relevant parts of the Smethwick and Erith factories. The half factories at Smethwick and Erith and the factory at Hartlepool would not be readily saleable and no benefits were included.
- The plan involved around 1,315 redundancies including 100 from head office.
- The scheme projected to return BIA to profitable operation within nine months.
- It was proposed to maintain all existing product lines, but with some rationalisation of brand names to ensure that BIA no longer competed with itself in mature markets.
- The projected internal rate of return for Scheme A was 22.3 per cent compared with a normal hurdle rate imposed by Industrial Components of 15 per cent.

Scheme B

- Closure of the Smethwick factory site in its entirety. Building adhesives and polymer products production and the polymer R&D activity moved to Greenock. Other R&D activities stopped. Wood adhesives and metal adhesives moved to Erith. Aluminium fastenings and furniture materials production stopped. 1,000 employees redundant.
- Closure of the Smethwick head office. 200 employees redundant, mainly from administrative offices of management accounting, central production control, purchasing and R&D administration and control.
- Offer for sale of the whole Smethwick site. This disposal would be an added bonus. However, because it would probably take some considerable time to achieve a satisfactory sale and because it was anyway a non-trading item, no figures for this 'bonus' were included in the Scheme B cash flows.
- Closure of Banbury factory. All production stopped. 190 employees redundant.
- Closure of Avonmouth factory. Metal adhesives production moved to Erith. 100 employees redundant.
- Closure of Rhoose factory. Metal adhesives production moved to Erith. Furniture materials production stopped. 170 employees redundant.
- Closure of Hartlepool factory. Metal adhesives production moved to Erith. Aluminium fastenings production stopped. 80 employees redundant.

- As with Scheme A, the Banbury, Rhoose and Avonmouth factories would be sold and the proceeds were included in the scheme's cash flows. No benefits were included from the sale of the factory at Hartlepool.
- To enable these changes to take place there would need to be substantial capital expenditure at both the Erith and Greenock factories to recommission transferred plant and to expand capacity as required.
- It would also be necessary to establish a new head office accommodating a maximum of 50 people and it was proposed to do this in refurbished and extended offices on the Leigh factory site.
- The scheme was based on considerable rationalisation of product ranges, eliminating duplications of brand names and the elimination of the aluminium fastenings and furniture materials product ranges. This would involve a reduction of around £70m of sales or some 35 per cent of total turnover.
- Production facilities would also be rationalised onto the four remaining factories:
  - Erith producing building, wood and metal adhesives and polymers
  - Greenock producing building adhesives and polymers
  - Leigh and Chelmsford both producing wood and metal adhesives
- The plan involved around 1,740 redundancies including 200 from the head office.
- Scheme B was expected to take over two years to complete implementation and the full benefits were not expected to be achieved until after four years.
- Scheme B would require a considerably higher capital commitment than Scheme A as new and enhanced production facilities were required as well as the substantially greater costs of transferring products to different factories.
- The cash flows in Scheme B were also substantially affected by the redundancy payments which were almost 50 per cent greater than Scheme A and these all occurred in the first months of the scheme.
- Scheme B cash flows were also adversely affected by the loss of 35 per cent of total business which made a substantial contribution.
- The internal rate of return for Scheme B was only 15.4 per cent, just above the IC imposed hurdle rate of 15 per cent. However, it was recognised that there should be longer-term benefits in Scheme B which would not apply to Scheme A but which were difficult to quantify. The sale of the Smethwick site was prime among these, but even without that a comparative projection of net returns on assets after ten years had been made and showed Scheme B to be the clear winner.

BIA's board considered which scheme it should recommend to the parent company. Scheme B was the more radical proposal, involving more upheaval, specially for head office staff, but promising the potentially greater long-term benefit. Whilst Scheme A was on paper quicker to implement, there was considerable feeling among BIA management that the savings were far from certain. For example, making substantial savings from closing half a factory would be much less certain than the elimination of costs if a site were vacated altogether. Nevertheless, it was recognised that Scheme A would be much less disruptive and, it was argued, possibly less damaging to morale.

BIA's management found it difficult to decide between the two schemes and at one stage in their deliberations attempts were made to compromise between the two. However, in the end it was decided to recommend Scheme B to Industrial Component's executive committee. They felt this was the more courageous route, offering a greater challenge to management but ultimately a better prospect of success.

In due course they were surprised and disappointed that their recommendation was rejected in favour of Scheme A. No reason for this was given formally, but it was rumoured that Sir Arthur had destroyed Scheme B simply by saying that 'closing BIA's head office would be like tearing the heart out of the business.'

DISCUSSION POINTS

1. Was the final decision right? Outline the key issues for each scheme.
2. Do you think it was a financially, culturally or strategically defined decision.
3. How would you describe BIA's strategic position, in terms of strategy basics and in terms of an appropriate framework.

Baxters of Speyside Ltd

The story of Baxters started in 1868 when George Baxter, then a gardener on the Duke of Richmond and Gordon's estate, borrowed the princely sum of £10 to set up a grocer's shop in the village of Fochabers on the banks of the River Spey. The great Spey here cloaks its riches of salmon in its broad meanders below the Wood of Ordiequish as it flows by Fochabers and out to the North Sea at Spey Bay around 70 miles due south of John O'Groats. The river, like this whole area of Scotland, is ever changing with the seasons, sometimes wild and angry, sometimes gentle, but in the end always civilised and with great beauty and character.

Fochabers lies north of the Cairngorms and east of the Great Glen which cuts northern Scotland in two from Moray Firth in the north east, through Loch Ness, Loch Lochy and Loch Linnhe to the Firth of Lorn which separates Oban from the Island of Mull. It is about 230 miles from Glasgow and well over 600 from London. It is no place to run a business.

George Baxter's shop was a modest success. Margaret, his wife, made jam from local produce and he sold it through the shop. The jam was good and soon earned a reputation far beyond the village. This was the start of a family tradition which involved generations of Baxter women contributing massively to the company's development.

George's son William extended the business further, both geographically, selling to other retailers from Wick to Aberdeen, and in terms of its product range. Baxter's opened its first jam-making factory in 1916. It was William's wife, Ethel, who in 1929 developed the now famous Royal Game Soup. William's son Gordon took over the business in 1946 by which time the company was making thirty different kinds of soup plus a range of high-quality preserves, chutneys and a continually widening range of other canned and bottled foods. It was under Gordon's leadership that the company became a nationally and internationally recognised name, synonymous with quality food products.

At the end of the Second World War there were only eleven employees and the main task was to get an increase in the company's can allocation. At that time there were more than twenty firms still making jam in Scotland; now there are only two.

Similarly, there were forty soup-makers; now there are only three and the other two are both American. Under the circumstances, survival was clearly a considerable achievement, but Baxters did far more than survive.

Gordon, now non-executive president of the company, fishes the Spey with his friends who include the bosses of the major supermarket chains as well as leading executives from the boards of Marks & Spencer, Sainsbury, Quaker Oats and SmithKline Beecham who have joined the firm as non-executive directors and he can feel justifiably proud of the firm he inherited and developed and has been able to pass on to the fourth generation of the Baxter family.

Gordon's wife Ena, following family tradition, has played a hugely important part in developing the company's ability to innovate new food varieties. She is a recognised authority on Scottish cuisine, has cooked on television both in the UK and America, published her own Scottish cookbook and received honorary degrees from both Aberdeen and Strathclyde universities for her services to the Scottish food industry.

In 1986, Baxter's success was celebrated by the opening of the visitors centre set overlooking the banks of the Spey. It now attracts over 200,000 visitors a year, coming to recapture the tradition that has made Baxters a household name. Highland cattle doze in the sunshine; the Spey sparkles blue in the distance; the sound of the bagpipes greets the visitors as they arrive at the Great Hall and choose their programme for the day which might include a cooking demonstration, a tour of the modern factory, a traditional Scottish meal in the Spey Restaurant or the rather grander Gordon Room, a wander along the row of shops which includes a restored nineteenth century replica of George's original establishment and, finally, a visit to the Best of Scotland shop which sells a range of Scottish gift items all chosen personally by Gordon and Ena.

The fourth generation of the family is now in control with Gordon's daughter Audrey as group managing director, Andrew Baxter as group deputy chairman and Michael Baxter as deputy managing director and product development director. Members of the fifth generation are already on the way and will no doubt be groomed to take up the challenge in due course. The maintenance of family control is fundamental to the Baxters philosophy. They believe their success has been based on the brand strength which embodies characteristics of family, quality and Scottishness, and a great deal of effort is put into building each of these brand characteristics. Whether this is because it makes good business sense or because it lines up nicely with the personal desires and characteristics of family members is not clear. But the picture of Gordon Baxter salmon fishing the Spey with Joe Barnes, former joint MD of Sainsbury's and now non-executive chairman of Baxters, symbolises this serendipitous combination of interests, as does their sponsorship of a major new book which celebrates the achievements of Scots whose inventions and influence helped change the way we live and work. It has nothing directly to do with managing a successful international business, but it does contribute to the projection of a consistent and coherent image.

Baxters' success is demonstrated by its continuous profitable growth. Turnover has expanded from £18m in 1987 to £35m in 1992 and £52m in 1996 and expected to reach more than £70m by 1998. It now employs more than 800 people and spends around £2m a year on advertising. It achieves a pre-tax profit of 9.5 per cent of sales, which is high for this extremely competitive industry. Heinz, for example, achieves much lower margins; although Heinz figures are rather difficult to assess because of non-trading items, disposals etc., it seems unlikely that it achieves much better than 3–4 per cent pre-tax profit. Baxters' financial results for the past four years are summarised at the end of this case.

In a recent article in *Business Age* magazine it was asserted that the real ambition of the fourth generation family was 'to make their company the *next* Heinz'. Heinz are the giants of the industry with over $9 billion sales in 1996 and some 43,000 employees worldwide. To become the next Heinz, even on a fairly modest scale, Baxters would need to float the company on the stock exchange in order to finance the necessary growth. This the family is not prepared to do because it would fundamentally undermine the company's paternalistic/family culture and this could have unpredictable consequences. In truth, emulating Heinz has never really been its aim, but Michael Baxter has identified the family's aim for the business as 'achieving continuous growth and aiming to be the leader at the premium end of all chosen markets'. It is not necessarily concerned to become a multinational company, because, again, this might undermine the existing family and Scottish aspects of its culture.

The formal company mission statement is as follows:

> *The purpose of the independent Baxter family business is to create and market processed food products of the highest quality under the Baxter brand at prices that represent good value to customers.*

This statement emphasises independence, family, quality and, interestingly, value. Baxters is not aiming for a product which appeals for its quality irrespective of price, or even *because* of its high price, but rather is aiming for the top end of the mainstream market.

The company's objective function might be described, in slightly more operational terms, as achieving continuous growth through leadership of the premium end of all chosen markets, subject to maintaining family control and initially to producing only at Fochabers. These two constraints are substantive though difficult to quantify. Moreover, they also appear to rule out the possibility of growth by acquisition.

At present the family controls around 98 per cent of the equity, so it is not difficult to estimate roughly how much finance could be raised through debt and by raising further equity without losing family control. However, it is not so easy to establish how feasible it would be to maintain its current trading regime under such revised financing arrangements. For example, it is suggested that the family's modest dividend take means that the company can allow its suppliers to make a reasonable profit so long as they continue to deliver the required quality. Moreover, it also permits its customers, the supermarkets, to take a higher than average margin, for which Baxters is able to command much greater shelfspace support. This all comes about because the family has supported the development of the brand rather than insisting on the level of payouts that would be required if the company was publicly quoted. It is not clear how refinancing to permit non-family shareholders would make it necessary to compromise these arrangements.

It is also difficult to assess the implications of limiting production to Fochabers.

There may be further increases in productivity through more advanced automation. It may also be possible to increase output by full 24-hour continuous working of the existing plant as well as by extending the present factory. However, both these would be subject to the availability of sufficient numbers of people in the surrounding area to work the extended facility. Moreover, there may be increasing logistics problems as turnover from Fochabers grew.

The supply side of achieving continuous growth therefore is not without problems. On the demand side the position is also not completely clear. The broad markets that Baxters serves are all fundamentally mature and achieving only low growth. They will therefore have to achieve either greater penetration or move into, or create, new markets. The creation of new markets may not be easy for Baxters with its advertising budget limited to £2m pa. Even after ten years or more of constraint, Heinz nevertheless spends over $90m pa which makes it much easier for it to create and penetrate new markets.

Another problem for the Baxters business is the customer profile which is mainly ABC1 with an age profile of 45–60. To combat this, Baxters has identified various segments which are growing and which focus on younger consumers. In soups, for example, Baxters has introduced a vegetarian range, a healthy choice range and a special occasion range to augment its traditional products. It has also looked at the fresh soup market which has a more youthful clientele and which has grown rapidly in recent years but the company has so far decided not to enter the market. Obviously the logistics for fresh product are not so easy from Fochabers as it would be from, say, Covent Garden. Nevertheless, Baxters has an enviable product development record and is continuously reassessing opportunities.

Baxters has established its range of premium foods including soups, jams and preserves and various other lines such as beetroot, fruit chutneys and cooking sauces in a ruthlessly competitive UK food retailing sector. The concentration of food retailing in the hands of the leading supermarket chains (Tesco, Sainsbury, Safeway, Marks & Spencer, Somerfield, Waitrose, Asda and Morrisons) has worked to the advantage of Baxters. These supermarkets now account for more than 75 per cent of the UK food retail market, and it is possible for a relatively small firm like Baxters to deal with these few powerful customers on a personal basis. Gordon Baxter still takes key customers fishing on the Spey and until recently even managed without a salesforce, though the company has now established a new fourteen-strong selling team.

Baxters has also recently taken a more focused approach to export markets. At one time it sold in very small volumes into no fewer than sixty overseas markets. But it has now decided to focus export efforts on the European Union (especially Germany and Ireland) plus America and Canada. Again it has targeted specialist segments after undertaking thorough marketing research. For example, a soup range has been specially developed and packaging custom designed for the specially health conscious American market emphasising '99 per cent fat free' and 'reduced sodium'. Export sales responded to this new approach with a 25 per cent increase in 1996. Nevertheless exports still account for less than 20 per cent of volume and the key to Baxters performance is what it achieves in the fiercely competitive UK market. Here it has recently overtaken Campbells as number two in soups in UK.

Baxters now claims to be the number one producer of:

- Quality soups in the UK
- Beetroot products in the UK
- Mini-jars of jams and preserves for hotel and airlines worldwide.

This is some measure of how it is achieving leadership of the premium end of all chosen markets. It has some way to go with its other product ranges, but the Baxters brand is sufficiently strong to make further progress certain. Thus, although the markets in which Baxters compete are not without problems, the brand is currently being hugely successful.

A further problem for producers selling to the supermarket chains is the rise of the supermarkets' own-label products. Kellogg's, for example, gives great prominence to its refusal to produce for sale under any other brand than its own. Eighty-five per cent of Baxter's production is sold under the Baxters brand name. Whilst Baxters provides no data on the other 15 per cent, it is estimated that most of it is sold to one customer, Marks & Spencer, who demands the highest quality and maintains prices which reflect the premium product.

Compare this record with that of Heinz. Over the past decade the value of the Heinz brand has clearly fallen. It has been a good middle-of-the-road brand but has been under attack from own-brand labels whose quality has been more-or-less equivalent. Under O'Reilly's leadership this erosion has been at least in part caused by Heinz itself making and canning own-label product of comparable quality to its own but which is sold at substantially lower prices. This may have provided some short-term profit but the strategic impact has been more-or-less wholly adverse. Moreover, Heinz further added to its difficulties by limiting brand-building advertising which is currently less than it was ten years ago (see an account of the Heinz position in Box 1.1 in Chapter 1).

Not surprisingly, Baxters is a perpetual acquisition target. Gordon Baxter claims to have received almost two hundred enquiries over the years from such companies as General Foods, General Mills, Distillers, Campbell's, Heinz, United Biscuits, Quaker Oats, Rowntree and so on. The answer is always no. 'I tell them I'll leave a note for my executors to contact them if there's a change of mind,' says Gordon ironically.

It would obviously be very attractive to a multinational company to have an upmarket brand such as Baxters in its stable that would justify a premium price. It could clearly exploit the Baxters name to a greater extent than the Baxter family does, simply by eliminating the constraints on growth imposed by the family's retention of control. The Baxters brand could be attached to products produced anywhere in the world and so long as the acquiring company was careful to ensure that the brand was not devalued, it could be the foundation of substantially more wealth creation than is currently the case. Nevertheless the risks of the brand being devalued would be considerable since it would clearly no longer embody the concepts of family and Scottishness. Nevertheless, the brand characteristics of quality and innovativeness could be maintained and even strengthened.

DISCUSSION POINTS

1. How would you envisage the Baxters business developing (a) under continued family control, and (b) as a subsidiary of a major multinational? Consider each scenario from the perspective of each major stakeholder and identify which scenario you feel would be preferable.
2. How much do you think it would be prudent for Baxters to invest in its long-term development (a) without introducing new equity, and (b) introducing new equity but without the loss of family control? (Assume all new equity is issued to non-family members.)
3. What is the importance of the visitors centre to the Baxters core business?
4. Does the Baxter family provenance matter? If so, to what and to whom?
5. Does the Scottishness matter? If so, to what and to whom?
6. 'If Baxters were competing in a fast-moving industry such as electronics, computers or biotechnology, it might not be possible for the family to retain control.' Why do you think this might be? Should it be any different merely because they are competing in a mature industry?
7. Which strategy framework would you select to analyse Baxters' strategic position. Why?
8. Using that framework, briefly outline three broad strategic options Baxters might consider.
9. Using the same framework, recommend a suitable strategy, identifying an appropriate strategic objective or mission and some suitable milestones to its achievement.

Baxters of Speyside Limited profit and loss account (£000)

		1996		1995		1994		1993
Sales revenue		44,718		38,439		36,546		31,557
Cost of sales		25,759		20,812		19,866		16,958
Gross profit		18,959		17,627		16,680		14,599
Distribution costs	8,007		7,254		7,212		6,470	
Administrative expense	6,895		6,607		5,937		5,272	
		14,902		13,861		13,149		11,742
Opening profit		4,057		3,766		3,531		2,857
Interest received		191		237		110		218
Net pre-tax profit		4,248		4,003		3,641		3,075
Taxation		1,417		1,335		1,224		1,031
Dividends		820		770		700		600
Retained profit		**2,011**		**1,898**		**1,717**		**1,444**

Baxters of Speyside balance sheet (£000)

		1996		1995		1994		1993
Fixed assets								
Land and buildings		7,539		4,842		4,207		3,690
Plant, equipment and vehicles		9,381		5,876		5,529		5,461
		16,920		10,718		9,736		9,151
Current assets								
Stocks	7,767		7,871		7,589		7,321	
Debtors	6,210		5,146		4,982		4,873	
Cash	624		3,398		2,426		950	
	14,601		16,415		1,4997		13,144	
Creditors								
(due in less than 1 year)	9,556		7,710		6,343		6,044	
			5,045		8,705		8,654	
7,100								
Total net assets		21,965		19,423		18,390		16,251
Long-term debt		2,058		1,959		2,906		2,649
Provisions (deferred taxation)		1,920		1,488		1,406		1,241
Issued share capital		100		100		100		100
Transfers from P&L		17,887		15,876		13,978		12,261
Total capital		**21,965**		**19,423**		**18,390**		**16,251**

H & R Johnson Tiles Ltd

Industry background

The ceramic tile industry could justly be described as mature. The earliest known examples are Egyptian, of around 4000 BC. Tiles were made by the Assyrians, Babylonians and the Islamic empire and early examples can be seen in Tunisia (9th century), Iran (11th century) and today many Middle Eastern mosques display Koranic scripts using highly coloured relief tiles dating from the 12th century onwards.

The earliest tiles in western Europe date back to the late 10th century. From the early 1500s Moorish tile-making slowly spread north through Spain and into France while around the same period tin-glazed tile-making spread from Holland to England with blue patterned Delft tiles imported into England in large numbers and providing the impetus to start the UK tile industry.

Tile-making in England expanded progressively during the Industrial Revolution and through the 1800s when many of the companies that were ultimately to become part of H & R Johnson Tile Ltd were started (for example Richards Tiles Ltd in 1837, T & R Boote Ltd in 1842, Minton Hollins Ltd in 1845 and Maw & Co. Ltd in 1850). The industry continued to grow, and by 1918 the UK was producing more than 1 million square metres a year and was exporting around one-third of its production.

During the Second World War many tile companies ceased and the UK industry was subsequently rationalised with the formation of the H & R Johnson business which then had around two-thirds of UK production of around 12 million square metres (msm).

The UK market has continued to grow and today stands at around 40 msm, but its share of the world market has nevertheless declined as production facilities have been established on a massive scale in many developing economies. Also, the UK's technological position has been lost to other European producers, particularly Italy which now produces more than 450 msm of tile and has a monopoly of tile manufacturing machinery.

Today, tiles are produced in more than forty countries, and although it is an extremely mature industry, technological developments in machinery, raw materials and glazes have radically changed the economic, technical and aesthetic possibilities of tile. Tile manufacture is currently undergoing something of a renaissance. Architects, builders and individuals are tending now to look on tile more as a fashion product than a commodity, and there is a new interest in how tile can be used to enhance both interiors and exteriors of homes, public buildings and places of work.

A global industry

Tile manufacture is a genuinely global industry with a world market of 3 billion square metres per annum. It is an industry which is inherently attractive to developing economies. Wherever there are deposits of suitable light-coloured iron-free clay containing sufficient kaolinite, production of basic white body earthenware tiles – about 60 per cent of the total market – is likely to be started because it does not depend on high technology and does not require massive capital investment. Moreover, it is labour intensive, and cheap labour is a prime source of competitive advantage for developing countries.

Almost inevitably there is chronic overcapacity worldwide and this has lead to fierce price competition for the basic product as producers struggle to achieve viable levels of plant utilisation which is particularly critical to this industry as kilns which are so energy intensive have to be run continuously.

Being flat and mainly rectangular, tiles are inherently easy and cheap to pack and transport. Tiles produced in China, for example, can be delivered in UK at a cost of around 40 pence per square metre compared with a selling price in the UK of around £8 per square metre. Thus a manufacturer who produces a standard basic product but is unable to compete with world prices will struggle to survive.

European producers

Italy claims the leading position not only in earthenware floor and wall tiles but also in the more specialised porcelain and terracotta floor tiles. Italy's lead was further consolidated in the late 1970s when its manufacturers produced the world's first ceramic tile by a single firing operation using clays containing iron oxides.

Traditional methods require the glazed tiles to be double fired, first the biscuit alone and second the biscuit complete with glaze. The single-fired process not only slashed energy costs but also greatly simplified production and production scheduling and reduced levels of work in progress.

At first, decorative finish options for once-fired tiles were limited, but refinements to the process and the glaze technology have produced a plethora of eye-catching designs and finishes combined with toughness and durability. In all of this Italy has established a formidable lead which is reflected in the commercial success of Italian manufacturers. Half of the 450 msm produced by Italy is exported, while a single company, Marazzi, has around 12 per cent of Italian production – substantially more than the whole of UK production.

Spain too is a progressive manufacturer and has refined the once-fired technology with the development of Monoporosa tiles which have a very high flexural strength allowing production of tiles in excess of 40 cm long. This, combined with a wealth of delicate patterns and reliefs, has been hugely successful in the premium price markets.

In both Italy and Spain, tile manufacture is concentrated in a fairly small geographical area located on the clay deposits which provide the raw material. The Spanish industry is concentrated within an area of around 10 square miles. As with Silicon Valley and the US computer industry, this provides considerable advantages to manufacturers who do not need to achieve substantial vertical integration, but need only buy in prepared raw material on a just-in-time basis; if material is not needed it is not accepted. This arrangement works also for the clay processor who has another 150 potential customers in the adjacent area.

The UK industry

H & R Johnson is the seventh largest tile manufacturer in the world, with plants in the UK, Australia, South Africa, India and Greece. In the UK, though, its share has dropped from the heady days of the late 1960s when it was responsible for around 70 per cent; it is still the market leader with 20 per cent of the market. The next largest producer is Pilkington with around 10 per cent. No other producer has more than 2 per cent and most have substantially less than 1 per cent.

The UK, with its mature markets and relatively high labour rates, is not an obvious place to start tile production. However, in this volatile industry there has been a continuous series of start-ups, expansions, acquisitions, rationalisations and closures. In the 1990s, Spring Ram started a UK operation producing 2 msm pa and Candy set up a more substantial business with the latest technology presumably hoping to break into a mature market where the leader, H & R Johnson Tiles Ltd, having lost share from 70 per cent to 20 per cent, might have appeared vulnerable to serious competition.

The cases of Spring Ram and Candy are instructive. Success in competitive markets is not achieved solely through massive capital investment in the latest technology. Production hardware is only part of the story. Process control has to be based in this industry on a real understanding of how clay behaves and how glazes work. The learning curve is steep. Moreover, market trends and fashions must also be understood and the sales and marketing costs of servicing the different segments are high. In the event, both Spring Ram and Candy were unable to break in successfully and went into receivership in 1994 and 1998 respectively.

The Norcros connection

In 1979, H & R Johnson was taken over by the one-time acquisitive financial conglomerate Norcros Plc. For several years subsequently, the financial performance of Norcros was only moderate and its management ultimately took the decision to rationalise the group structure, disposing of underperforming subsidiaries and seeking an industrial logic for the remaining operations. This has resulted in a substantial reduction in the size of the group.

By 1997 Norcros turnover had almost halved from its highpoint of around £450m. Summary figures for 1995–1997 are shown in Table 1. The group is now engaged in just three core activities: tiles, adhesives and showers, with tiles being the largest of these accounting for around 40 per cent of the group's core turnover (not

Table 1 Summary financial statistics of Norcros Plc for the year ending 31 March

	1997	1996	1995
Turnover (£m)	234.6	285.5	393.5
Operating profit (£m)	12.7	13.9	−14.1
Profit before tax[a] (£m)	52.6	10.0	−55.0
Funds employed (£m)	166.2	174.7	204.9
Net borrowings (£m)	16.6	47.0	89.7
Average no. of employees	3,646	4,673	6,759
Operating profit per employee (£)	3,375.0	2,574.0	−2,546.0

[a] Figures for profit before tax have been substantially affected by disposals and acquisitions.

including the Indian tile company which is only part-owned and is treated as an equity investment in the accounts).

Although these three activities are clearly adjacent to each other in the ceramics industry in terms of their markets, there is little genuine synergy between them. Norcross has redefined itself as an MCB but, as yet, improved financial performance has been limited largely to the impact of the various disposals. This has had a substantial impact on the balance sheet with borrowings substantially reduced to less than 10 per cent of total capital. The change in the group's strategic position may yet produce substantially improved operating results.

The 1997 Norcros directors' report included the following comments on the UK tile business of H & R Johnson:

> *H & R Johnson recorded a substantial increase in operating profits despite sales showing only a modest increase of 2% on the previous year. The UK housing and construction markets continued to suffer in the first half of the year with a lack of confidence in the trade sector resulting in heavy de-stocking and continuation of fierce competition in the contract sector. Towards the end of this period, the UK's largest tile distributor went into receivership both affecting sales demand and releasing significant amounts of excess stock onto the market.*
>
> *The second half of the year, however, saw a welcome upturn in the UK market. The company achieved major gains as a result of new product programmes in its retail and contract ranges, competitive pricing in the contract sector, where the company has benefited from its 'one stop shop' capability with global sourcing and its expertise in logistics, systems and product range management. Overall UK sales increased by nearly 4% compared with the previous year. Export markets were extremely difficult throughout the year, with European markets very depressed and European competitors massively overstocked. Given the strengthening pound the company's export performance was commendable.*
>
> *Internally the company has successfully managed the principal elements of a complex capital investment and restructuring programme which has progressively benefited the results.*
>
> *Further gains were also achieved in energy, raw material and packaging costs.*

Looking ahead, the cost base is expected to reduce further from the full year effects of the restructuring, ongoing capital investment projects and other programmes to improve production and business performance.

The company received national awards for energy management and internet developments during the year; and it has recently been honoured with the Queen's Award for Environmental Achievement.

H & R Johnson Tiles Ltd is the main repository of the group's knowledge and expertise in tile manufacture and marketing, and all Norcros tile companies use the Johnson brand name. However, the overseas companies are not subsidiaries or associates of H & R Johnson Tiles Ltd but report directly to the parent company; H & R Johnson therefore has to fit within the overall Norcros structure and its performance in terms of cash and profit must necessarily reflect Norcros realities.

H & R Johnson background

H & R Johnson has inherited many strengths and weaknesses from its illustrious past. As the leading producer with 70 per cent of the post Second World War market, the company sold a complete range of wall and floor tile products, and it manufactured everything that it sold. Perhaps it would be more accurate to say that it sold everything it manufactured and it manufactured everything. The product range extended from the cheapest to the most expensive and everything between from the lowest-quality earthenware wall tiles selling for a few pence each, up to hugely expensive hand-made encaustic floor tiles of original Victorian and art nouveau design sold into prestige locations such as the Palace of Westminster.

Such product variety proved difficult to manage profitably. Moreover, the company allowed its product design to stagnate and its production technology to become outdated. Inevitably, financial performance collapsed. H & R Johnson may look like a classic case of a company 'stuck in the middle' with no clear direction and a limited ability to buy its way out of trouble. As recently as 1993, manufacturing was located in five different factories with around 1,300 employees producing between 7 and 8 msm pa of tile extending to more than 8,000 different line items. The company was competing at the low-price end of its product range with new producers from the Third World and in the higher-quality products with design-conscious Italian, Spanish and other producers operating efficient plant to produce product ranges typically limited to around 700–800 line items.

Moreover, H & R Johnson does not share the 'Silicon Valley' advantage enjoyed by the Italians and Spanish. It is the only substantial tile manufacturer in the English Midlands region and it has to purchase raw clay, largely from the south west of England and abroad, mix it with appropriate additives and process, dry and deliver the material to production lines one kilometre distant. Consequently it has the added complication of having to keep raw material production and tile manufacturing carefully balanced. Not for them just-in-time deliveries by third-party suppliers.

Only in the ultra-expensive hand-made product has there been no competition, but the sales volume of these products is extremely small and of limited significance to the main business apart from its PR value. It is run as a separate unit so as not to obscure the core business issues.

Product variety is reflected in the different distribution channels. There are three main areas of business: contract sales, DIY multiples and independent retailers, and they each have quite distinct requirements from their suppliers. H & R Johnson being still the dominant UK producer, double the size of its largest competitor, must sell product through all three channels to achieve critical mass. This again might be a further cause of getting 'stuck in the middle'.

Progress so far

The current generation of top management under the leadership of managing director David Dry has made substantial strategic progress although this has not yet been fully reflected in financial results (see Tables 2 and 3).

Table 2 H & R Johnson Tiles Ltd summary P&L for the year ending 31 March (£000)

	1993	1994	1995	1996	1997
Turnover	57,240	59,420	57,689	51,453	52,484
Operating profit/(loss)	−1,833	1,135	1,357	1,511	2,081
Net profit before tax	−2,044	1,317	523	453	1,070
Taxation	342	280	333		
Retained profit	−2,386	413	10,256	9,198	214

Note: The figures above have been adjusted to remove some exceptional transfers between the company and its parent Norcros Plc which, whilst substantial, were not related to the company's normal trading.

Table 3 H & R Johnson Tiles Ltd summary balance sheet as at 31 March (£000)

	1993	1994	1995	1996	1997
Fixed assets	36,687	33,802	28,459	25,227	28,900
Current assets					
Stocks	14,753	15,812	14,639	13,826	16,152
Debtors	11,937	12,089	12,991	8,967	10,099
Cash	49	43	39	33	31
	26,739	27,944	27,669	22,826	26,282
Current liabilities					
Creditors	30,518	24,657	28,277	28,291	31,385
Net current assets	–3,779	3,287	–608	–5,465	–5,103
Total net assets	32,908	37,089	27,851	19,762	23,797
Financed by:					
Long-term debt	23,226	26,994	28,012	9,156	12,977
Shareholders' equity	9,682	10,095	–161	10,606	10,820
	32,908	37,089	27,851	19,762	23,797

Note: The figures above include some exceptional transfers between the company and its parent Norcros Plc relating to an interest-free long-term loan to the company to finance its substantial restructuring and development and subsequent part-repayments of the loan by transfers from the company's transferable reserves.

Three factories have been closed and the company now operates from the two remaining plants situated in Tunstall, Stoke on Trent – one of the original six pottery towns which is now a rather depressed area and something of a wasteland. These closures have seen a reduction in the workforce from 1,300 to 810. The product range has also been severely pruned and now comprises less than 3,500 line items. As has been pointed out elsewhere, 'anyone can cut – the clever bit is building': and this is the main thrust of the current management action. Large-scale investment has been made in new technology, including some once-fired production facilities. So despite the cuts in plant and people, volume has been maintained at 7–8 msm pa level. The company has also achieved substantial savings from recycling scrap production and from various energy conservation initiatives.

The achievement of such reductions has been achieved only with the support and involvement of the Johnson workforce, and top management has put a considerable effort into initiatives to promote communications with all members of the company. Examples of this include the implementation of total quality management, the publication of *Tile Times*, an uncensored employee-operated paper, and monthly briefings from top management in which transparency is maximised. More than this, the development of individuals and exploitation of their knowledge and experience has been focused through the Johnson Improvement Programme, a form of kaizen, which has incorporated, to date, around 130 continuous improvement teams.

Progress has been substantial. However, the company is still hindered by its heritage of a too diverse product range produced on old plant, inefficiently located. With too many products forced to sell at uneconomic prices and labour rates around £3,000 pa per person above their major competitors, H & R Johnson seems destined always to struggle to achieve even a 5 per cent margin on sales.

It has been concluded that, without massive further investment, being the lowest-cost producer in this global marketplace will never be a viable option for H & R Johnson, or for any other UK-based producer. In recognition of this, the company has developed a considerable expertise supplying bought-in product that it cannot produce economically in its own facilities. Tiles have been sourced from overseas H & R Johnson factories, particularly Greece and India, but also from non-Johnson manufacturers. Nor has outsourcing focused exclusively on tiles that the UK company cannot make cheaply enough. Purchases of quality product from Italy and Spain now amount to more than 2.5 msm pa. To do this efficiently the company has developed considerable expertise in logistics and computer systems and has in effect been able to present itself as a one-stop shop providing a huge range of product although its own production had been so substantially reduced. This expertise has developed to such an extent that some foreign competitors have given up attacking the UK market directly and have opted instead to supply exclusively through H & R Johnson.

Being the cost leader is therefore not an option for H & R Johnson. It can achieve a premium price for its own production through higher quality and better designs, but the problem is achieving a sufficient price premium to compensate its cost disadvantage compared with the main European competitors. The best strategy for H & R Johnson is thus not immediately obvious. It must continue to reduce its costs in order to remain in the market and it must differentiate its offering in some way that customers appreciate and are prepared to pay for. But it is not clear how best this can be done. The application of professional management to achieve continuous improvement in all the main value-adding activities will remain important to H & R Johnson's survival, but beyond this it needs a clear directional strategy.

Management initiatives to reduce costs have been outlined above. In addition to this the company has refocused its attention on tile design. This is not simply a matter of the application of aesthetic and artistic characteristics on a piecemeal basis. Design is recognised as having to take full account of market trends and developments in such factors as materials, glazes, tile sizes, applications and consumer tastes. New designs have to be soundly based on this appreciation of new developments and on H & R Johnson's position in relation to them. The company has acknowledged the importance of design by appointing a new design chief at board level, and as a consequence the success of new product introductions has radically improved. The rate of successful new design introductions has doubled and the volume of sales from the new introductions has been some 200–300 per cent above expectations even though prices have been raised at the same time by 20–30 per cent on average.

The impact of this design success should be cumulative. As more successful new products are introduced, the company will be encouraged to take bolder decisions regarding the culling of existing product lines. Its aim may be to get closer to the number of line items supplied by its Italian competitors, i.e. somewhere around 1,000 rather than the 4,500 currently offered. It is likely that designs will have a shorter life cycle but a higher and more profitable sale while they are offered.

H & R Johnson has also made changes to its sales and marketing operation, addressing the different needs of each main distribution channel by establishing three separate salesforces. Contract sales are handled by a team of technically qualified salespeople whose job it is to work with architects and other specifiers in order to establish Johnson as (the) approved supplier and identified as such in tender documents etc. Sales to the DIY multiples are handled by a team of five salespeople whose job it is to achieve close and mutually beneficial relationships with the small number of 'supersheds' such as B&Q and Do It All. An example of this co-operation is the in-store tile management being provided by H & R Johnson to the Wickes chain.

Sales to the multitude of independent retailers present quite a different problem. H & R Johnson distribute through some 23 distributors, but its most active selling is to the literally hundreds of smaller retailers. This selling effort requires a large, well supported salesforce. The company has provided elaborate tile display units to more than 400 retailers and this support, together with the extensive personal sales attention, encourages retailers to specify H & R Johnson product to their distributor suppliers.

Considerations for the future

All these actions have reversed H & R Johnson's decline, but the company still struggles to achieve even a 5 per cent operating margin on sales. Further changes will be required to capitalise on the company's undoubted strengths.

There is still development potential in UK tile markets, particularly in floor tiles where penetration has been much less than in other EU and Scandinavian countries. Although H & R Johnson no longer produces floor tiles it is active in the market with bought-in product. It would be possible, though expensive, to concentrate further onto a single factory. Such an investment could involve eliminating considerable expense in materials movement and handling. If such a radical step were taken it might also be possible to cease all the traditional twice-fired production, replacing it with once-fired technology. This would inevitably mean cutting some good profitable products, but once-fired technology has developed well so that the penalty might not be as great as it would have been even five years ago.

The cost reductions that could be achieved by these means would probably require a capital input approaching £20m. This could be funded partly by the disposal of the vacated site if a suitable purchaser could be found. The site is in a depressed urban area that planners might be keen to see developed in the context of urban regeneration.

Only with such a radical investment could H & R Johnson compete on cost and this would imply halving the size of the workforce again and substantially reducing rates of pay.

H & R Johnson might be able to compete in terms of quality and design across a large part of the wall tile product range, although global leadership in these terms would not seem to be a realistic aim.

The challenge facing the MD David Dry is to develop a strategy for H & R Johnson which lifts it out of its 'stuck in the middle' position. This is the trap that has probably entwined the business since it was formed in the 1960s. The strategy must go well beyond operating effectiveness and provide H & R Johnson with a recognisable and sustainable position which will promise to generate solid financial results in this most competitive of global markets.

DISCUSSION POINTS

1. Which strategy framework do you think would be most useful to analyse H & R Johnson's situation?
2. Which frameworks would you think inappropriate and why?
3. Within the terms of the chosen framework suggest a future strategy for H & R Johnson Tiles Ltd.
4. Using an alternative framework suggest an alternative strategic option.
5. What are the major trade-off decisions the company has to confront?
6. What do you understand H & R Johnson's core competences to be?
7. Would you propose any changes to H & R Johnson's organisational arrangement with Norcros Plc?

References

Abell, D.F. and Hammond, J.S. (1979). *Strategic Market Planning: Problems and analytical approaches*, Prentice Hall. (Chapter 3 'Cost dynamics: scale and experience effects' reproduced in Mintzberg and Quinn, *The Strategy Process* 3rd edn, Prentice Hall, 1996.)

Alderfer, C.P. (1972). *Existence, Relatedness and Growth*, Free Press.

Ansoff, H.I. (1965). *Corporate Strategy*, McGraw-Hill (rev. edn 1987).

Ansoff, H.I. (1990). *Implanting Strategic Management*, Prentice Hall.

Argyris, C. and Schon, A. (1978). *Organisational Learning: Theory of action perspective*, Addison-Wesley.

Atkinson, J.W. (1964). *An Introduction to Motivation*, Van Nostrand.

Axelrod, R. (1984). *The Evolution of Cooperation*, Basic Books.

Bangs, D.H. (1995). *The Business Planning Guide*, 7th edn, Upstart Publishing.

Barnard, C.I. (1938). *The Functioning of the Executive*, Harvard University Press.

Barnard, C.I. (1948). *Organisation and Management*, Harvard University Press.

Baumol, W.J. (1959). *Business Behaviour, Value and Growth*, Macmillan.

Baumol, W.J. (1986). 'Entrepreneurship and a century of economic growth', *Journal of Business Venturing*, No. 1.

Belbin, R.M. (1981). *Management Teams: Why They Succeed or Fail*, Heinemann.

Beynon, H. (1975). *Working for Ford*, EP Publishing.

Blake, R.R. and Mouton, J.S. (1964). *Managing Group Conflict in Industry*, Gulf Publishing.

Boston Consulting Group (1968a). *Perspectives on Experience*, BCG.

Boston Consulting Group (1968b). *Growth and Financial Strategies*, BCG.

Bowen, D. (1994). 'Virtual power to the people as companies fade away', *Independent on Sunday*, 27 March.

Bower, M. (1966). *The Will to Manage*, McGraw-Hill.

Bower, J.L. and Hout, M. (1988) 'Fast cycle capability for competitive power', *Harvard Business Review*, November/December.

Brech, E.F.L. (1957). *Organisation: The framework of management*, Longman.

Bright, J.R. (1983). *Practical Technology Forecasting*, Industrial Management Centre, Inc.

Brown, A. (1995). *Organisational Culture*, Pitman.

Burns, T. and Stalker, G.M. (1994). *The Management of Innovation*, 3rd edn, Oxford University Press.

Burrell, G. and Morgan, G. (1979). *Sociological Paradigms and Organisational Analysis*, Heinemann.

Cadbury, A. (1987). *Final Report of the Committee on the Financial Aspects of Corporate Governance.*

Campbell, A. and Nash, L. (1993). *A Sense of Mission: Defining direction for the large corporation*, Addison-Wesley.

Campbell, J.P. and Pritchard, R.D. (1976). 'Motivation theory in industrial and organizational psychology', in M.D. Dunnette (ed.), *Handbook of Industrial and Organizational Psychology*, Rand McNally.

Campbell, A., Devine, M. and Young, D. (1990). *A Sense of Mission*, Hutchinson.

Carnall, C.A. (1990). *Managing Change in Organisations*, Prentice Hall.

Carter, C.F. and Williams, B.R. (1956). *Industry and Technological Progress: Factors governing the speed of application of science*, Oxford University Press.

Centre for Study of Industrial Innovation (1971). *On the Shelf – A Study of Shelved R&D Projects.*

Chandler, A.D. (1962). *Strategy and Structure: Chapters in the history of industrial enterprise*, MIT Press.

Chandler, A.D. (1977). *The Visible Hand: The managerial revolution in American business*, Harvard University Press.

Chandler, A.D. (1990). 'The enduring logic of industrial success', *Harvard Business Review*, March/April.

Chandler, A.D. (1991). 'The functions of the HQ unit in the multibusiness firm', *Strategic Management Journal*, Winter.

Channon, D.F. (1973). *The Strategy and Structure of British Enterprise*, Macmillan.

Child, J. and Faulkner, D. (1998). *Strategies of Co-operation*, Oxford University Press.

Chisnall, P.M. (1997). *Marketing Research*, 5th edn, McGraw-Hill.

Chorn, N.H. (1992), 'Organisations: a new Paradigm', *Management Decision*, Vol. 29, No. 4.

Clark, K.B. (1989). 'What strategy can do for technology', *Harvard Business Review*, November/December.

Cooper, R.G. (1982). 'Now product success in industrial firms', *Industrial Marketing Management*, No. 3.

Coyne, K.P. (1986). 'Sustainable competitive advantage: what it is and what it isn't', *Business Horizons*, February.

Cummings, T.G. and Huse, E.F. (1989). *Organisational Development and Change*, 4th edn, West Publishing.

Cyert, R.M. and March, J.G. (1963). *A Behavioural Theory of the Firm*, Prentice Hall.

Deal, T.E. and Kennedy, A.A. (1982). *Corporate Cultures*, Addison-Wesley.

De Bono, E., (1978). *Lateral Thinking*, Penguin.

Demsetz, H. (1973). 'Industry structure, market rivalry and public policy', *Journal of Law and Economics*, Vol. 16, pp. 1–9.

Devlin, G. and Blackley, M. (1988). 'Strategic alliances – guidelines for success', *Long Range Planning*, Vol. 21/5, No. 111, October.

Dewhurst, H.A. (1970) 'The long range research which produced glass fibre reinforced tyres', *Research Management*, Vol. 13: 201–8.

De Wit, R. and Meyer, R. (1994). *Strategy: Process, content, context*, West Publishing.

Dixit, A. and Nalebuff, B. (1991). *Thinking Strategically: The competitive edge in business, politics and everyday life*, Norton.

Dixon, M. (1990). 'On the receiving end', *Business*, June, p. 153.

Drucker, P.F. (1955). *The Practice of Management*, Heinemann.

Drucker, P.F. (1964). *Managing for Results*, Harper & Row (rev. edn Heinemann, 1989).

Drucker, P.F. (1985). *Innovation and Entrepreneurship*, Heinemann.

Drucker, P.F. (1993). *Post-capitalist Society*, Butterworth/Heineman.

Edwardes, M. (1982). *Back from the Brink*, Collins.

Emery, F.E. and Trist, E.L. (1965). 'The causal texture of organisational environments', *Human Relations*, No. 18.

Etzioni, A. (1988). *The Moral Dimension: Towards a new economics*, Free Press.

Evans, M.G. (1970). 'The effects of supervisory behaviour on the path goal relationship', *Organisational Behaviour and Human Performance*, No. 5.

Evans, M.G. (1974). 'Extensions of a path goal theory of motivation', *Journal of Applied Psychology*, Vol. 59.

Fayol, H. (1916). *Administration industrielle et générale*, Pitman.

Ferguson, A. (1990). 'The myth of leadership dismantled', *Independent on Sunday*, 10 June.

Foss, N.J. (1997). *Resources, Firms and Strategies*, Oxford University Press.

Foster, R.N. (1986). 'Innovation: the attacker's advantage', *Summit.*

Frederickson, J.W. and Mitchell, T.R. (1984). 'Strategic decision processes: comprehensiveness and performance in an industry with an unstable environment', *Academy of Management Journal*, Vol. 27.

Freemantle, D. (1994). *The Successful Manager's Guide to Business Planning*, McGraw-Hill.

Garvin, D.A. (1987). 'Competing on the eight dimensions of quality', *Harvard Business Review*, November/December.

Garvin, D.A. (1993). 'Building a learning organisation', *Harvard Business Review*, July/August.

Gauthier, D. (1991). 'Morality and markets: the implications for business', in B. Harvey, H. van Luijk and G. Corbetto (eds), *Market Morality and Company Size*, Kluwer.

Gilbert, X. and Strebel, P. (1988). 'Developing competitive advantage' in J.B. Quinn, H. Mintzberg and R.M. James (eds), *The Strategic Process*, Prentice Hall.

Gilder, G. (1986). *The Spirit of Enterprise*, Penguin.

Glaser, B.G. and Strauss, A.L. (1967). *The Discovery of Grounded Theory*, Weidenfeld & Nicholson.

Glueck, F.W. (1985). 'A fresh look at strategic management', *Journal of Business Strategy*, Fall.

Goh, S.H. (1998). 'Towards a learning organisation: two strategic building blocks', *Sam Advanced Management Journal*, Spring, pp. 16–21.

Goldsmith, W. and Clutterbuck, D. (1985). *The Winning Streak*, Penguin.

Goold, M. and Campbell, A. (1987). *Strategies and Styles: The role of the centre in managing diversified corporations*, Blackwell.

Goold, M., Campbell, A. and Alexander, M. (1994). *Corporate Level Strategy: Creating value in the multibusiness company*, Wiley.

Gordon, W.J.J. (1961). *Synectics*, Harper & Row.

Green, P.E., Tull, D.S. and Albaum, G. (1988). *Research for Marketing Decisions*, 5th edn, Prentice Hall.

Greenley, G.E. (1986). 'Does strategic planning improve company performance?', *Long Range Planning*, April.

Gregory, K.L. (1983). 'Native-view paradigms: multiple cultures and culture conflicts in organisations', *Administrative Science Quarterly*, September.

Griffith, S.B. (1963). Introduction to and translation of Sun Tzu's *The Art of War* (originally written between 400 and 320 BC), Oxford University Press.

Grundy, T. (1993). 'Putting value on strategy', *Long Range Planning*, Vol. 26, No. 3.

Hackman, J.R. and Oldham, G.R. (1980). *Work Redesign*, Addison-Wesley.

Hall, P.D. (1969). 'Computer systems', in Wills, G., Ashton, D. and Taylor, B. (eds.), *Technological Forecasting and Corporate Strategy*, Bradford University Press.

Hall, W.K. (1980). 'Survival strategies in a hostile environment', *Harvard Business Review*, September/October.

Hamel, G. (1987). 'Corporate strategies and technological cooperation', paper presented to a

UACES Conference on European Technological Collaboration, Brunel University, 14 May.

Hamel, G. and Prahalad, C.K. (1989). 'Strategic intent', *Harvard Business Review*, May/June.

Hamel, G. and Prahalad, C.K. (1991). 'Corporate imagination and expeditionary marketing', *Harvard Business Review*, July/August.

Hamel, G. and Prahalad, C.K. (1993). 'Strategy as stretch and leverage', *Harvard Business Review*, March/April.

Hamel, G. and Prahalad, C.K. (1994). *Competing for the Future*, Harvard Business School Press.

Hamel, G., Doz, Y.L. and Pralahad, C.K. (1989). 'Collaborate with your competitors – and win', *Harvard Business Review*, January/February.

Hamermesh, R.G. (1986). *Making Strategy Work: How senior managers produce results*, Wiley.

Hayes, R.H. and Abernathy, W.J. (1980). 'Managing our way to economic decline', *Harvard Business Review*, May/June.

Hayes, R.H. and Garvin, D. (1982). 'Managing as if tomorrow mattered', *Harvard Business Review*, May/June.

Healy, P.M., Palepu, K.G. and Ruback, R.S. (1997). 'Which take-overs are profitable? strategic or financial?', *Sloan Management Review*, Summer.

Heller, F.A. (1988). 'Working models on the shop floor', *Times Higher Education Supplement*, 29 January.

Henderson, B.D. (1984). *The Logic of Business Strategy*, Ballinger.

Hitachi Ltd (1993). 'Localising the multinational: globalisation holds the key', *Financial Times*, 17 September.

Hogg, S. (1986). 'A dance to the music of economic time', *The Times*, 17 June.

Holloman, J.H. (1967). *Innovation and Profitability*, Science of Science Foundation.

Hope, T. (1997). Visiting Professor of Accounting at INSEAD, address to the Institute of Personnel Development Annual Conference.

Hopkins, D.S. (1981). 'New product winners and losers', *R&D Management*, May.

Hosmer, L.T. (1994). 'Strategic planning as if ethics mattered', *Strategic Management Journal*, Vol. 15: 17–34.

House, R.J. and Dessler, G. (1974a). 'The path goal theory of leadership: some *post hoc* and *a priori* tests', in J.G. Hunt and L.L. Larson (eds), *Contingency Approaches to Leadership*, Southern Illinois University Press.

House, R.J. and Mitchell, T.R. (1974b). 'Path goal theory of leadership', *Journal of Contemporary Business*, Autumn.

Jones, H. (1974). *Preparing Company Plans*, Gower.

Jönsson, S. (1996). 'Decoupling hierarchy and accountability: an examination of trust and reputation', in R. Munro and J. Mouritsen (eds), *Accountability: Power, ethos and the technologies of managing*, Thomson Business Press.

Kanter, R.M. (1983). *The Change Masters: Corporate entrepreneurs at work*, Unwin Hyman.

Kanter, R.M. (1990). *When Giants Learn to Dance*, Unwin Hyman.

Kavanagh, J. (1997). 'Money mad chiefs stifle technological innovation', *Computer Weekly*, 6 November.

Kennedy, A. (1983). 'The adoption and diffusion of new industrial products', *European Journal of Marketing*, No. 2.

Kim, W.C. and Henderson, B.D. (1997). 'Value innovation: the strategic logic of high growth', *Harvard Business Review*, January/February.

King, J. (1967). 'Can research evaluate the creative content of advertising?', *Proc. Market Research Society Annual Conference*, 1967.

Koehler, W. (1938). 'Closed and open systems', *The Place of Values in the World of Fact*, Liverwright.

Kotler, P. (1984). *Marketing Management: Analysis, Planning, Implementation and Control*, 5th edn, Prentice Hall.

Kotler, P. and Armstrong, G. (1997). *Marketing: An introduction*, 4th edn, Prentice Hall.

Kotter, J.P. (1982). *The General Managers*, Free Press.

Kotter, J.P. (1990). *A Force for Change: How leadership differs from management*, Macmillan.

Kudla, R.J. (1980). 'The effects of strategic planning on common stock returns', *Academy of Management Review*, No. 20.

Lawler, E.E., III (1973). *Motivation in Work Organizations*, Brooks/Cole.

Lawrence, P.R. and Lorsch, J.W. (1967). *Organisation and Environment*, Harvard Business School Press.

Lei, D. (1989). 'Strategies for global competition', *Long Range Planning*, Vol. 22 No. 1.

Leitko, T.A. and Szczerbacki, D. (1987). 'Why traditional OD strategies fail in professional bureaucracies', *Organisation Dynamics*, Winter.

Lenz, R.C. (1983). 'How to project technological development through trend extrapolation', *Technological Forecasting*, October.

Leontiades, M. and Tezel, A. (1980). 'Planning perceptions and planning results', *Strategic Management Journal*, No. 1.

Levitt, T. (1958). 'The dangers of social responsibility', *Harvard Business Review*, September/October.

Levitt, T. (1960). 'Marketing myopia', *Harvard Business Review*, July/August.

Lewin, K., Lippitt, R. and White, R.K. (1939). 'Patterns of aggressive behaviour in experimentally created "social climates" ', *Journal of Social Psychology*, No. 10.

Lorange, P., Roos, J. and Brønn, P.S. (1992). 'Building successful strategic alliances', *Long Range Planning*, Vol. 25, No. 6.

Lorenz, C. (1992). 'The good and the bad of bigness', *Financial Times*, 8 April.

Maddison, A. (1982). *Phases of Capitalist Development*, Oxford University Press.

Madia, W.J. (1990). 'EC technology partnerships', *Strategic Direction*, February.

Martin, J., Feldman, M.S., Hatch, M.J. and Sitkin, S.B. (1987), 'The uniqueness paradox in organisational stories', *Administrative Science Quarterly*, Vol. 28: 438vT–53.

Maslow, A. (1943). 'A theory of human motivation', *Psychological Review*, Vol. 50.

McClelland, D.C., Atkinson, J.W., Clark, R.A. and Lowell, E.L. (1953). *The Achievement Motive*, Van Nostrand.

McGill, M.E., Slocum, J.W., Jr and Lei, D. (1992). 'Management practices in learning organizations', *Organizational Dynamics*, Summer.

McGregor, D. (1960). *The Human Side of Enterprise*, McGraw-Hill.

Meyer, A. De., Nakane, J., Miller, J.G., and Ferdows, K. (1989). 'Flexibility: the next competitive battle – the manufacturing futures survey', *Strategic Management Journal*, No. 10.

Miller, W.F. (1990). 'Technology and global strategy', *Strategic Direction*, January.

Mintzberg, H. (1981). 'Organisation design: fashion or fit', *Harvard Business Review*, January/February.

Mintzberg, H. (1983). *Structure in Fives: Designing effective organisations*, Prentice Hall.

Mintzberg, H. (1987a). 'The strategy concept I: five Ps for strategy', *California Management Review*, Fall.

Mintzberg, H. (1987b). 'The strategy concept II: another look at why organisations need strategies', *California Management Review*, Fall.

Mintzberg, H. (1992). 'The Two Faces of Management', Melrose Masterclass Video, Melrose.

Mintzberg, H. (1994a). *The Rise and Fall of Strategic Planning*, Prentice Hall.

Mintzberg, H. (1994b). 'The fall and rise of strategic planning', *Harvard Business Review*, January/February.

Mintzberg, H. (1996). 'The structuring of organisations', in H. Mintzberg, and J.B. Quinn, *The Strategy Process*, 3rd edn, Prentice Hall.

Mintzberg, H. and Quinn, J.B. (1996). *The Strategy Process*, 3rd edn, Prentice Hall.

Mitchell, T.R. (1974). 'Expectancy models of job satisfaction, occupational preference, and effort: a theoretical, methodological and empirical appraisal', *Psychological Bulletin*, Vol. 81: 1096–1112.

Morgan, G. (1993). Strategic Termites? *Imaginization: The art of creative management*, Sage.

Mueller, R.K. (1986). *Corporate Networking: Building channels for information and influence*, Free Press.

Myers, S. and Marquis, D.G. (1969). *Successful Industrial Innovations: A study of factors underlying innovations in selected firms*, National Science Foundation.

Norburn, D. and Schurz, F.D. (1984). 'The British board-room: time for a revolution', *Long Range Planning*, October.

Norton, D. and Kaplan, R. (1997). *The Balanced Scoreboard*, Harvard Business School Press.

Ohmae, K. (1989). 'Managing in a borderless world', *Harvard Business Review*, May/June.

Ormerod, P. (1994). *The Death of Economics*, Faber.

Ouchi, W.G. and Bolton, M. (1988). 'The logic of joint research and development', *California Management Review*, Vol. 30, No. 3.

Pascale, R. (1985). 'The paradox of "corporate culture": reconciling ourselves to socialization', *California Management Review*, Vol. 27, No. 2.

Pascale, R. (1994). 'Perspectives on strategy: the real story behind Honda's success', *California Management Review*, Vol. 26, No. 3.

Pearson, G.J. (1985). *The Strategic Discount: Ways to an entrepreneurial strategy*, Wiley, 1985.

Pearson, G.J. (1990). *Strategic Thinking*, Prentice Hall.

Pearson, G.J. (1992). *The Competitive Organisation*, McGraw-Hill.

Penrose, E.T. (1959). *The Theory of the Growth of the Firm*, Wiley.

Peters, T. (1993). 'Crazy Ways for Crazy Days', BBC Training Video.

Peters, T. (1994). 'Which way is up in a web?', *The Independent*, 20 March.

Peters, T.J. and Austin, N. (1985). *A Passion for Excellence*, Random House.

Peters, T.J. and Waterman, R.H. (1982). *In Search of Excellence*, Harper & Row.

Pettigrew, A. (1979). 'On studying organisational culture', *Administrative Science Quarterly*, No. 1.

Piater, A. (1984). *Barriers to Innovation* (a study carried out for the Commission of the European Communities Directorate), Francis Pinter.

Pinchot, G. (1985). *Intrapreneuring*, Harper & Row.

Porter, M.E. (1979). 'How competitive forces shape strategy', *Harvard Business Review*, March/April.

Porter, M.E. (1980). *Competitive Strategy: Techniques for analyzing industries and competitors*, Free Press.

Porter, M.E. (1984). *Competitive Advantage: Creating and sustaining superior performance*, Free Press.

Porter, M.E. (1987). 'From competitive advantage to corporate strategy', *Harvard Business Review*, May/June.

Porter, M.E. (1988). Video film and pamphlet: 'Michael Porter on Competitive Strategy', Harvard Business School Video Series.

Porter, M.E. (1990). 'The competitive advantage of nations', *Harvard Business Review*, March/April.

Porter, M.E. (1996). 'What is strategy?', *Harvard Business Review*, November/December.

Prahalad, C.K. and Hamel, G. (1990). 'The core competence of the corporation', *Harvard Business Review*, May/June.

Prescott, J.E., Kohli, A.K. and Verbstramen, N. (1986). 'The market share – profitability relationship: an empirical assessment of major assertions and contradictions', *Strategic Management Journal*, Vol. 7: 377–394.

Project SAPPHO (1972). *Success and Failure in Industrial Innovation*, Science Policy Research Unit, University of Sussex.

Pugh, D.S., Hickson, D.J., Hinings, C.R. and Turner, C. (1968). 'Dimensions of organisation structure', *Administrative Science Quarterly*, Vol. 13: 65–105.

Pugh, D.S., Hickson, D.J., Hinings, C.R. and Turner, C. (1969). 'The context of organisation structure', *Administrative Science Quarterly*, Vol. 14: 91–114.

Quest Worldwide (1997). *Strategy into Action: Survey analysis*, Quest Worldwide Consulting Ltd.

Quinn, J.B. (1978). 'Strategic change: logical incrementalism,' *Sloan Management Review*, Fall.

Quinn, J.B., Doorley, T.L. and Paquette, P.C. (1990). 'Beyond products: services-based strategy', *Harvard Business Review*, March/April.

Ramo, S. (1989). 'National security and our technology edge', *Harvard Business Review*, November/December.

Reynolds, P.C. (1986). 'Corporate culture on the rocks', *Across the Board*, September.

Ridley, M. (1996). *The Origins of Virtue*, Viking.

Rickards, T. (1985). 'Creative Decision Making', programme at Manchester Business School, 1985, where Professor Rickards is Director of Creativity and Innovation Programmes.

Roberts, K.J. (1986). 'How to define your market segment', *Long Range Planning*, August.

Robertson, A. (1973). 'The marketing factor in successful industrial innovation', *Industrial Marketing Management*, Vol. 2.

Robinson, R.B. and Pearce, J.A. (1983). 'The impact of formalized planning on financial performance in small organisations, *Strategic Management Journal*, No. 4.

Rogers, C.R. (1969). *Freedom to Learn*, Charles Merrill.

Rogers, E.M. (1983). *Diffusion of Innovations*, 3rd edn, Free Press.

Rumelt, R.P. (1974). *Strategy, Structure and Economic Performance*, Harvard Business School Press.

Schein, E.H. (1996). 'Three cultures of management: the key to organisational learning', *Sloan Management Review*, Fall.

Schoeffler, S. (1977). *The PIMSletter on Business Strategy*, No. 2.

Schumpeter, J.A. (1939). *Business Cycles: A theoretical, historical and statistical analysis of the capitalist process*, McGraw-Hill.

Selznick, P. (1957). *Leadership in Administration*, Harper & Row.

Sen, A. (1991). *On Ethics and Economics*, Blackwell.

Senge, P.M. (1992). *The Fifth Discipline: the art and practice of the learning organisation*, Century Business.

Shanklin, W.L. (1983). 'Supply side marketing can restore "Yankee ingenuity"', *Research Management*, May/June.

Shaw, W.C. (1981). *How to do a Company Plan*, Business Books.

Simon, H.A. (1986). 'How managers express their creativity', *Across the Board*, No. 3.

Skinner, W. (1986). 'The productivity paradox', *Harvard Business Review*, July/August.

Slatter, S. (1984). *Corporate Recovery: Successful turnaround strategies and their implementation*, Penguin.

Smircich, L. (1987). 'Concepts of culture and organisational analysis', *Administrative Science Quarterly*, Vol. 28: 339–58.

Smith, G.D. and Steadman, L.E. (1981). 'The present value of corporate history', *Harvard Business Review*, November/December.

Taylor, F.W. (1947). *Scientific Management*, Harper & Row.

Telser, L.G. (1987). *A Theory of Efficient Cooperation and Competition*, Cambridge University Press.

Thompson, J.L. (1993). *Strategic Management Awareness and Change*, 2nd edn, Chapman & Hall.

Trapp, R. (1993). 'Competitors click in for a better profile', *Independent on Sunday*, 29 August.

Tunstall, W.B. (1983). 'Cultural transition at AT&T', *Sloan Management Review*, Fall.

Turpin, D. (1993). 'Strategic alliances with Japanese firms: myths and realities', *Long Range Planning*, Vol. 26, No. 4.

Urwick, L.F. (1947). *The Elements of Administration*, Pitman.

Utterback, J.M. (1976). 'Innovation in industry and the diffusion of technology', *Science*, 15 February.

Venkatesan, R. (1992). 'Strategic sourcing: to make or not to make,' *Harvard Business Review*, November/December.

Vroom, V.H. (1964). *Work and Motivation*, Wiley.

Warner, J. (1996). 'Hanson breakup leaves city cold', *The Independent*, 17 August.

Weber, M. (1947). *The Theory of Social and Economic Organisation*, Free Press.

Wernerfelt, B. (1984). 'A resource based view of the firm', *Strategic Management Journal*, No. 5.

White, J. (1984). 'Corporate culture and corporate success', *Management Decision*, No. 22.

Whittington, R. (1993). *What is Strategy – and does it matter?*, Routledge.

Whittington, R. (1996). 'Strategy as practice', *Long Range Planning*, Vol. 29, No. 5.

Wilkins, A.M. (1983). 'The culture audit: a tool for understanding organizations', *Organizational Dynamics*, Autumn.

Williamson, O. (1963). 'Managerial discretion and business behaviour', *American Economic Review*.

Wilson, D.C. (1992). *A Strategy of Change: Concepts and controversies in the management of change*, Routledge.

Womack, J.P., Jones, D.T. and Ross, D. (1990). *The Machine that Changed the World*, Macmillan.

Wood, N. (1990). Introduction to Nicolò Machiavelli's *The Art of War* (first published 1521), De Capo Press.

Woodward, J. (1958). 'Management and technology', *Problems of Progress in Industry*, No. 3, HMSO.

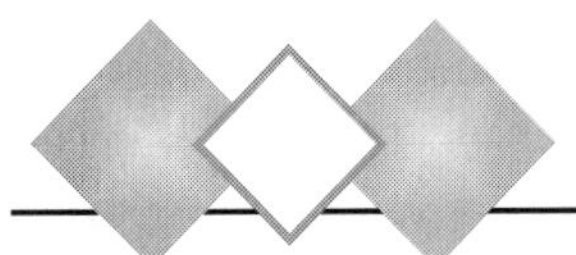

Index

ABB, 43, 234, 235
Abell, 113
Abernathy, 8, 43, 145, 213
accountancy, 51
Ackerman, 2
acquisition, 42, 71, 73, 77–9, 157
acquisitive financial conglomerate (AFC), 70–9, 88, 273
adhocracy, 227, 260
advertising, 58, 63, 109, 138, 153
Alcan, 167–8
Alderfer, 256
alliances, 21, 34, 54, 173, 174, 230–7
American Airways, 149
analytical perspective, 47–8, 161
Ansoff, xii, 25, 73, 96, 97, 273, 274
Armstrong, 151
asset disposal, 71
  stripping, 69
Atkinson, 256
attribute X, 61–2
Austin, 20, 182, 267
autocrats, 258, 259
  repositioning, 266–9
Axelrod, 55

balanced scorecard, 52–3
bargaining power of buyers, 137, 138–9
bargaining power of suppliers, 137, 138
Barnard, 177, 181–2
Bartlett, 184
Baumol, 11, 51
beating competitors, 57, 63, 64, 158, 162, 163
Belbin, 269
benchmarking, 20, 63
Benetton, 170
Beynon, 245
biological systems, 99, 100
Black & Decker, 66
Blackley, 174
Blake, 256
Blue Circle Aggregates, 37, 77
Bolton, 173
Boston Consulting Group (BCG) xii, 82, 83, 112, 114–16, 118, 119–24, 186, 188, 194, 195, 198, 199, 214
Bowen, 21, 236
Bower, 237
brainstorming, 215, 216, 220
Brech, 7
Bright, 209, 210
Brown, 238
BTR, 72,
bureaucracy, 8, 20, 124, 259, 260, 268
  divisionalised form, 227
  machine, 7, 46, 227
  professional, 227
  workflow, 226
bureaucratisation, 8
bureaucratic tendency, 95–7
bureaucrats, 258, 259, 261
  repositioning, 266–9
Burns, 6, 7, 9, 204, 221, 249
Burrell, 239
business
  adolescent, 102–3
  existence, 53
  infant, 102
  mature, 103, 104, 105, 110, 228
  portfolios, 48, 119–34, 186, 190, 193, 194, 195, 198
  process reengineering (BPR), 194, 229
  strategy, xi, 43–5, 46
    objectives 53
  strength, 127–9
  survival, 53
business strength/market attractiveness matrix, 120, 188
butterfly, 258, 261
  repositioning, 263–4

Cadbury, 17
Campbell, 80, 164
candle, lighted, 100
Canon, 34, 65, 169, 170, 172, 173, 175, 176
capital asset pricing model, 78
capital budgeting, 88
  budget, 92
Campbell, 256
Carnall, 165
cartels, 104
Carter, 253, 254
cash cows, 121–4
cash delay centre, 147, 149
Caterpillar, 143, 169, 172
centralisation, 226
cerebral approach, 162
Chandler, xii, 7, 73, 173, 177, 204, 224
Channon, 225
charisma, 162
Child, 234, 249
Chisnall, 254
Chorn, 235
clarity, 55
Clark, 231
classical management, 5, 237
Coca-Cola, 169, 171
collaboration, 173, 174, 230–7
commitment, 254
common thread, 73, 273
communications, 4, 258, 278
  external, 253
  open, 173, 247

competence, 162, 194
  core, 170–7, 189, 192, 253
  distinctive, 54, 63
competitive advantage, 131, 135, 146, 149, 156, 158, 173, 183, 194, 230
  capability, 126
  challenge, 170
  forces, *see* five forces
  model 250–69
  rivalry, 135, 137
  specialism, 157, 179–81, 183, 192, 274
  strategy, *see* strategy, competitive
competitor analysis, 139–41
competitors, beating, 63, 64, 143
complexity, 73, 76, 81, 103, 225, 240
concentration, 31, 38–9, 74, 88, 92, 105, 142, 143, 146, 148, 158, 161, 178, 198, 274, 275
configuration, 226
conglomerates, 69, 225
consistency, 39–40, 74, 88, 92, 143, 146, 158, 178, 274, 275
contingency principles, 194–7
Cooper, 253
core competence, *see* competence, core
core product, 170
corporate parenting, *see* parenting, corporate
cost chains, 147, 149
cost leadership, 142, 143, 144–5, 151, 265
Coyne, 145
Cray, 38, 150, 274
creative freedom, 213, 215
culture, 33, 35, 36, 179, 224, 273
  dimension of competitive model, 251, 252, 254–6
  progressive, 252, 256, 261, 273
    achieving, 279–80
  strong, 258, 259, 260,
    repositioning, 266–9
Cummings, 229
customer orientation or focus, 151, 152, 191, 253
customers, pleasing, 58–63, 70
customised frameworks, 197–9
Cyert, 51, 95

Data-Med, 168
De Bono, 214
De Wit, xii
Deal, 35, 240, 249
Demsetz, xii
design school, xi
Dessler, 256
Devlin, 174
Dewhurst, 208
differentiation, 142, 145–6, 151, 153, 154, 156
direction, 38, 50, 74, 88, 92, 103, 105, 142, 143, 146, 158, 161, 163, 178, 187, 250, 253, 260, 273, 274, 275, 278–9
directional policy matrix (DPM), 120, 125–7, 188
disinvestment spiral, 123, 145, 218, 260, 262, 265
distribution, 58, 62, 174
diversification, 30, 73–6, 103, 104, 157
distinctive competence, 54, 63
Dixit, 55, 68
Dixon, 267
dogs, 121–4
Drucker, 5, 9, 21, 23, 26–8, 31, 40, 51–2, 63, 64, 68, 116, 129–30, 132, 142, 152, 162, 165, 177, 222, 234, 235, 276

economics, classical, 51, 127, 135, 142
Eden, xii
Edwardes, 244
emergent strategy, xii, 25, 29
Emerson Electric, 66, 149
Emery, 52, 118
empowerment, 246–7, 254
entrepreneurial framework, 177–83, 189, 192
  process, 180
entrepreneurial start-up, 162
entrepreneuring, 20, 229
entropy, maximum, 103
environmental analysis, 89–91
Evans, 256
experience, 99, 120, 121,
  curves, 48, 112–17, 187, 188

factory, era, 7
  system, 5,
fall-out, 106, 107
Faulkner, 234, 249
Ferguson, 256
financial, evaluation, 216–19
  objectives, 56
  planning, 8, 48
  sector, 9
five forces analysis, 135, 136–9
flexibility, 40–1, 158, 178, 275
focus, 142, 143, 181, 263, 265
Ford, 3, 4, 5, 32, 85
forgivingness, 55
formalisation, 225
Foss, xii
Foster, 212
Fredirickson, 25
Freemantle, 97

Garvin, 8, 43, 59, 145, 237, 260, 269
GATT, 15
Gauthier, 54, 55
General Electric, 89, 127, 135
General Motors, 72, 233
generic strategies, *see* strategy, generic
geographical expansion, 73
Ghoshal, 184
Gilbert, 142
Gilbreth, 228
Gilder, 171
global competition, 14,
  market, 14,
globalisation, 34, 173, 231, 233
Glueck, 86
Goldsmith, 71
Goold, 43, 76, 80, 274
Gordon, 215
Green, 154
Greenley, 25
Gregory, 240
Griffith, 85, 140
Grundy, 57, 67

Hackman, 256
Hall, P.D., 208
Hall, W.K., 142, 145–6,
Hamel, xii, 64, 161, 162, 163, 168, 169, 170, 174, 177, 179, 184, 195, 200, 232, 254, 274, 276
Hamermesh, 133, 134
Hammond, 113
Hayes, 8, 43, 145, 213, 260
Healey, 76
Heinz, 10
Henderson, 63, 134
Hewlett Packard, 175, 178, 234, 241
hierarchy, 4
highest price competitor, 141, 142
Hitachi, 232
hitting budget, 281
Hogg, 224, 235
Holloman, 253
Honda, 171, 175
Hope, 89
Hopkins, 253
Hosmer, 19, 55
House, 256
human relations, 5
Huse, 229

IBM, 111, 234, 241, 242

industrial revolution, 5, 11–14, 209
industry analysis, *see* five forces analysis
  evolution, 99
infant mortality, 101, 186
innovation, 20, 205–21
  evolutionary, 206
  revolutionary, 206
integrity, 51, 54, 254
Intel, 111, 117
intuitive approach, 162
Ivory soap, 149

Jaguar, 180
job, enlargement and enrichment, 229
Jones, 97
Jönnson, 19, 55, 237, 269
just-in-time (JIT), 5, 62, 176, 229

kaizen, 62
Kanter, 182, 238, 246, 266
Kaplan, 52–3, 68
Kavanagh, 89
Kay, 23
Kennedy, 35, 224, 240, 249
Kennedy, President J.F., 163, 169
Kim, 63
King, 153
Kodak, 34
Koehler, 100, 107
Komatsu, 143, 169, 172
Kondratiev, 11, 205
Kotler, 58, 151
Kotter, 243, 256

La Quinta, 149, 274
Lawler, 256
Lawrence, 7, 224
leadership, 40, 63, 152, 156, 163, 170, 187, 198, 199, 211, 233, 254
Lei, 232
Leitko, 228–9, 242
Lenz 208
Leontiades, 25
Levitt, 17, 55, 105
life cycle, 48, 99–111, 186–7, 188, 192, 195, 200
  characteristics, 108
  product, 105
liquidators, 258, 260, 261
  repositioning, 264–6
logical incrementalism, 32,
  increments, 63
Lorange, 230
Lorenz, 234
Lorsch, 7, 224
lowest cost competitor, 141, 142

Machiavelli, 85
machine bureaucracy, 7, 46
Maddison, 11
Madia, 174
management problem, 51
  utility maximisation, 51
managerial problem, 3
March, 51, 95
market attractiveness, 127–9
marketing mix, 58
Marks & Spencer, 71–2, 178
Marquis, 253
Martin, 245
Maslow, 54, 256
McGill, 235, 237
McGregor, 256
McKinsey, 127, 135
McLelland, 256
mechanistic organisation, 5, 266
Meyer, xii
Miller, 25, 231
Mintzberg, xi, 7, 25, 26, 29, 36, 46, 49, 64, 98, 158, 162, 171, 226–8, 272
mission, 57, 70, 163–70, 179, 182
Mitchell, 25, 256
Morgan, 21, 237, 239
motivation, 254
Mouton, 256
Mueller, 236
multi-business company (MBC), 70–6, 88, 273, 274
Myers, 253

Nalebuff, 55, 68
Nash, 164
NEC, 169, 174, 175
networks, 230–7, 246
niceness, 55
Norburn, 31
Norton, 52–3, 68
not-for-profit, 4

objectives, 50–68, 69, 70
  and organisational types, 69–73
  business, 51
  hierarchy, 53–7, 70
Ohmae, 14, 231
Oldham, 256
organic organisation, 6, 7, 9, 235
organisation, diversified, 227–8
  entrepreneurial, 227, 228
  missionary 227, 228
  political, 227, 228
  professional, 227, 228
organisational characteristics, 251–3
organisational slack, 103, 105
organisational structure, *see* structure
Ormerod, xii

Ouchi, 173

Parenting, corporate, 77–9, 274
participation, 247
partnerships, technology, 173, 230–7
Pascale, 171, 228, 241, 242
Pearce, 25
Pearson, 4, 91, 251, 256, 257, 270
Pearson Plc, 78, 130–1
Penrose, xii
perfect competition, 51
personal selling, 58
Peters, 21, 39, 151, 152, 154, 182, 233, 235, 240, 254, 266, 267, 274
Pettigrew, 237
Philip Morris, 142, 146
Piatier, 11–14, 203
PIMS (Profit Impact of Marketing Strategies), 115
Pinchot, 8,
planning, accounts based, 82, 86–9, 186, 187, 188, 192
  and formality, 272–3
  bureaucratic systems, 99
  development based, 82, 92–5, 188
  financial, 8, 48
  forecast based, 82, 86, 188, 192, 193
  frameworks, 85–97
  process 95
  strategic 29–31, 91
pleasing customers, 57, 58–63
Porter, 38, 57, 62, 64, 66, 75, 76, 82, 128, 135–51, 158, 160, 181, 186, 187, 189, 192, 195, 198, 231, 274, 276, 281
portfolios, *see* business portfolios
post-capitalist society, 235
Prahalad, xii, 64, 161, 162, 163, 168, 169, 170, 177, 179, 184, 195, 200, 232, 254, 274, 276
preference mapping, 154–6
Prescott, 25, 116
prescriptions, *see* strategic prescriptions
prisoner's dilemma, 55
Pritchard, 256
problem children, *see* wild cats
Procter & Gamble, 241
product, 58–62, 152–7, 223
  attributes, 59–61, 153–6, 274
  positioning, 154
productivity, 144, 234
  paradox, 11
profit maximisation, 18, 19
  maximiser, 51,

promotion, 58
provocability, 55
psychological investment, 211
public relations, 58
Pugh, 224, 225–6
purpose of business, 178
purpose of strategy, 36–41

Quest Worldwide, 181, 272
question marks, *see* wild cats
Quinn, 31, 64, 172

Ramo, 173
Ratner, 15, 166–7, 168, 169, 245
relative market share, 121, 127
resource based school, xi, xii
Reynolds, 48, 166, 242
Rickards, 214, 215
Ridley, 23, 55
risk, 73, 74, 76, 178, 182, 217, 218
Roberts, 132
Robertson, 253
Robinson, 25,
Rogers, C, 256
Rogers, E.M., 212
Rolls Royce Motors, 178
Rumelt, 225

S-curves, 207–9
Sainsbury, 178
sales revenue maximisation, 51
SAPPHO, projecy, 253, 254
Schein, 237
Schoeffler, 115
Schumpeter, 11, 205
Schurz, 31,
scientific management, 5
sector prospects, 126
self-actualisation, 54, 103
Selznick, xii, 54, 177, 179
Senge, 269
served market, 131
shake-out, 106
shareholder wealth maximisation, 71
Shaw, 97
Shell, 125, 127
Simon, 215
single business company (SBC), 70–71, 273
Skil, 62, 66, 274
Skinner, 8, 11, 43, 144
Slatter, 265
Sloan, 85
SMEs, xii
Smircich, 238
Smith, 179
Smith, W.H., 196–7
specialisation, 4, 5, 225
Spekman, 173
spirit of capitalism, 18
stakeholders, 53, 75, 185
  satisfaction of, 53, 57, 70
Stalker, 6, 7, 9, 204, 221, 249
standardisation, 5, 225
stars, 121–4
Stedman, 179
strategic, alliances, 105
  business unit (SBU), 132–3
  control, 76, 124
  evaluation, 219
  health, measures of, 66–7
  intent, 70, 163, 176
  marketing, 151–7, 187
  milestones, 64–5
  objectives, 53, 57, 63–4, 161, 186, 228
  planning, 29–31, 91
    departments, 91
    evolution of, 86
  portfolio, 273–5
  position, 158, 162,
  prescriptions, 109, 122, 126, 128, 132, 133, 187
  repositioning, 278–80
strategy as pattern, 36
  as plan, 36,
  business, 43–4, 45, 46, 74
  competitive, 141–6, 146–51, 158, 186, 189, 190
  corporate, 42–3, 45
  dimension of competitive model, 251, 252, 253–4
  focused, 252, 254, 261, 273
  for business, xi, xii
  functional, marketing, 44–5
    operations, 45
  generic (Porter's), 141–6
  generic process (or model), 186, 190–9
  implanting, 271–81
  in business, xi, xii
  integration of, 45
  levels of, 41–2
  'me too', 63, 281
  process, 275–8
  purpose of, 36–41, 190
Strebel, 142
structure, 7, 20, 174, 223, 224, 225–9
  matrix, 267
  simple, 225, 227
stuck-in-the-middle, 75, 142, 144, 187, 274
Sun-Tzu, 85
survival, 53, 57, 186, 265
SWOT analysis, 89–91, 185, 186
symbolism, 244–6
synectics, 215, 216
synergy, 77, 157
systems, 100–1, 188
  goals, 101–5
Szczerbacki, 228–229, 242

Taylor, 3, 4, 228
teams, 230–7
  innovative, 257–8, 261, 268
technological forecasting, 209–11
Telser, 173
Tezel, 25
Thompson, 73
threat of new entrants, 137, 138
threat of substitutes, 137, 139
tit-for-tat, 55
total quality management (TQM), 20, 62, 194, 229
Toyota, 171, 233
trade-offs, 274, 276–7
Trafalgar House, 73
transformational (strategy), 47–8, 161–83, 187, 190
Trist, 52
trustworthiness, 54, 56, 58
Tunstall, 246
Turner & Newall Ltd, 91
Turpin, 174

unity of command, 4
Urwick, 7
Utterback, 213

value chain analysis, 146–51
Venkatesan, 172, 231, 274
vertical integration, 73, 103
Vroom, 256

Warner, 74
Waterman, 39, 151, 152, 154, 240, 254, 266, 274
Weber, 4, 18
Wernerfelt, xii
White, 237
Whittington, 25, 271
wild cats, 121–4
Wilkins, 246
Williams, 253, 254
Williams Holdings, 72
Wilson, 222, 229
Womack, 233
Wood, 85
Woodward, 7, 224
work design, 229

Xerox, 65, 162, 169, 172, 173, 182, 232

Zale Corporation, 165–6, 16